CAMBRIDGE GREEK AND LATIN CLASSICS

D0219821

LIVY

AB VRBE CONDITA

BOOK VI

EDITED BY

CHRISTINA SHUTTLEWORTH KRAUS

New York University

Published by the Press Syndicate of the University of Cambridge
The Pitt Building, Trumpington Street, Cambridge CB2 1RP
40 West 20th Street, New York, NY 10011-4211, USA
10 Stamford Road, Oakleigh, Melbourne 3166, Australia

First published 1994

Printed in Great Britain at the University Press, Cambridge

A catalogue record for this book is available from the British Library

Library of Congress cataloguing in publication data

Livy.
[Ab urbe condita. Liber 6]
Ab urbe condita. Book VI/Livy; edited by Christina Shuttleworth Kraus.
p.   cm. – (Cambridge Greek and Latin Classics)
Latin with introd. and commentary in English.
Includes bibliographical references and index.
ISBN 0 521 41002 9. – ISBN 0 521 42238 8 (paperback)
1. Rome – History – Republic, 510-265 B.C.   2. Patricians (Rome)
3. Plebs (Rome)   4. Manlius, Marcus, 4th cent. B.C.   5. Camillus,
Marcus Furius, d. 365 B.C.   1. Kraus, Christina Shuttleworth.
II. Title.   III. Series.
DG235.L58   1994
973'.02 – dc20   93-41170 CIP

ISBN 0 521 41002 9 hardback
ISBN 0 521 42238 8 paperback

AO

For my mother and brother

CONTENTS

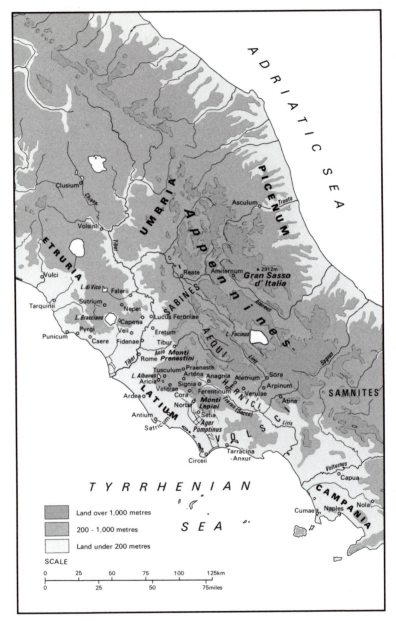

ADRIATIC SEA

TYRRHENIAN

SEA

	Land over 1,000 metres
	200 - 1,000 metres
	Land under 200 metres

SCALE

0   25   50   75   100   125km

0   25   50   75miles

UMBRIA

PICENUM

Clusium

Chiana

Asculum

Tronto

Volsinii

Tiber

ETRURIA

APPENNINES

Vulci

Reate

Amiternum

Gran Sasso
d' Italia

▲ 2912m

L. di Vico

Falerii

Sutrium

Nepet

SABINES

Tarquinii

L. Bracciano

Capena

Lucus Feroniae

Aternus

Pyrgi

Veii

Eretum

Tibur

L. Fucinus

Punicum

Caere

Fidenae

AEQUI

Liris

Anio

Monti
Prenestini

Segnus

Rome

Tusculum

Praeneste

Aletrium

Sora

L. Albanus

Aricia

Artena

Anagnia

Arpinum

Velitrae

Signia

Verulae

Ardea

Cora

Ferentinum

HERNICI HILLS

Atina

LATIUM

Norba

Monti
Lepini

Setia

Trerus (Sacco)

Liris

Antium

Ager
Pomptinus

SAMNITES

Satricum

Circeii

Tarracina
-Anxur

Volturnus

Capua

CAMPANIA

Cumae

Naples

Nola

PREFACE

Since the 1960s Livy has enjoyed a revival of serious interest. The second pentad is currently receiving particular attention: in addition to the present work, which is the first commentary in English on Book 6 in ninety years, a full commentary on Books 6–10 is in preparation by Stephen Oakley. He and I have agreed not to exchange our work, and I am grateful for his friendly willingness to coexist in an ever narrowing field.

In analysing Livy's language, I have had two chief aims: to show its place in the historiographical tradition (hence there is a great deal of both Sallust and Tacitus in the notes), and to bring out its innovative, often unique character. To that end, I have made much use of D. W. Packard's *Concordance to Livy* (1968) and of the PHI CD for Latin literature. But the reader is advised that these tools, as well as their user, are fallible, and that when I say a word or phrase 'never occurs elsewhere' I may sometimes mean 'hardly ever.' In keeping with the conventions of this series, I have restricted references to less accessible and foreign works, though it has not always been possible to exclude them. Where I cite German secondary sources, they are generally of the nature of lists in which the reader may find more examples of a given phenomenon.

This commentary began life as a doctoral dissertation at Harvard University, and for their guidance and encouragement I thank the members of my committee, Wendell Clausen, John Bodel, and Richard Thomas. Since then many people have generously lent their time and expertise. It is a pleasure to acknowledge and to thank the Department of Classics at New York University, especially Sean Redmond and Jim Mulkin, who in a graduate seminar on Livy contributed to my interpretations of the second Allia and of Appius Claudius' speech; the National Endowment for the Humanities, which funded an early stage of this project; and Jeff Wills, who has for years patiently answered countless questions about language and stylistics.

The last year has been spent in happy concentration in Durham, a leave made possible by the support of the Leverhulme Trust and the Department of Classics at Durham University; particular thanks

are due to John Moles, Peter Rhodes, Clemence Schultze, and the
Woodman family. Jane Chaplin, John Henderson, Jim Luce, and
Peter Morgan read and improved the Introduction; David Levene
and Peter Wiseman did the same for the Commentary, which has
profited immensely from their careful attention. Professor E. J.
Kenney gave the entire manuscript a characteristically gracious
and meticulous reading. But my greatest debt by far is to Tony
Woodman, whose library and learning have improved virtually
every page of this book, and whose friendship has made all the
difference.

August 1993   C. S. K.

INTRODUCTION

1. LIVY: LIFE AND WORKS

In the main hall of the Palazzo della Ragione in Padua, handsomely mounted in a sixteenth-century marble frame, is the sepulchral inscription of a *libertus* of Livia Quarta, daughter of one T. Livius (*CIL* v 2865). It is one of a number of inscriptions (including *CIL* v 2975, an epitaph which has been claimed for the historian's own) pertaining to Paduan Livii; if they refer to our L.'s family, they comprise the only non-literary information about him to have been preserved.[1] L. has inscribed his northern origin in the first paragraph of his history (1.1.2–3), where he narrates Antenor's settlement of Padua before turning to Aeneas' more illustrious foundation farther south; but this encoded information is recognizable only if one knows from other sources that he was born in Padua.[2] His allusive recording of his birthplace, in contrast to the declarations of the Greek historians (e.g. Hecat. *FGrH* I F I,

---

[1] The epitaph records a wife and two sons, one of whom may be the geographer cited by Plin. *NH* I *auct. lib.* 5, 6 (*RE* 'Livius' 10). Jerome synchronizes L.'s birth with that of M. Valerius Messalla Corvinus, Tibullus' patron, which he puts under the consuls of 59 B.C.; the date is wrong for Messalla, and both men are usually pushed back to 64 (Syme (3) 414, following Borghesi and Hirst). Also according to Jerome, L. died in A.D. 17 (followed by e.g. Luce (1) 231 n.61, M–W 179); this date, too, is moved back to A.D. 12 by some (so O. p. 1, Syme (3) 415, *LHA* 19). L. seems not to have held any public office (n.17); we do not know if he served in the military, though it is perhaps naive to argue, on the basis of his battle descriptions, that he did not (as *LHA* 4, O. p. 2; see R. T. Ridley, *SS* 133 n.53).

[2] E.g. Martial 1.61.3. Quintilian reports that Asinius Pollio accused L. of *Patauinitas* ('Paduosity'), which he mentions in discussions of local idioms (1.5.56, 8.1.3, cf. 1.7.24 on L.'s Paduan spellings and see K. Latte, *C.P.* 35 (1940) 56–60). Pollio may have meant more by it (he had a vicious tongue: G. L. Hendrickson, *A.J.P.* 36 (1915) 70–5); if so, rather than subscribing to Pollio's (supposed) views (as e.g. Syme (1) 486 'Pollio knew what history was like. It was not like L.', cf. McDonald 172, Walsh 31), better to understand their political rivalry as Roman *v.* Italian patriotism: L.'s subject was not just the governing class, but the growth of Rome to include Italy and after it the world – i.e. the whole *populus Romanus* (below, pp. 26–7).

Herod. 1.1,[3] Thuc. 1.1.1) or the personal history in the prefaces of
Sallust's monographs and Tacitus' *Histories*, sets a pattern that continues through the work. Though he often uses the first person
(9.3n.), even his programmatic statement in the Preface says nothing about the 'real' Livy. More than in the case of most ancient
historians, we have to deal with a *persona*.[4] To make matters worse,
the *persona* itself sends thoroughly mixed signals. At the start of a
monumental history of Rome from the beginnings to the present,
'Livy' adopts a position of nearly incredible modesty, a combination of magisterial assurance and polite uncertainty that will recur
throughout the work.[5]

Perhaps in consequence, the exiguous and sometimes confusing
collection of anecdotal *testimonia* has been taken very seriously indeed. Most of these anecdotes fall into three contexts. First, the historiographical canon, in which L. is usually paired with Sallust.[6]
Second, he is connected with the imperial family: he encouraged
the future emperor Claudius to write history (Suet. *Cl.* 41.1) and
was on friendly, perhaps joking, terms with Augustus (Tac. *A.*

---

[3] The MSS differ between Halicarnassus and Thurii, a nice example of
rivalry for an author's provenance; cf. Cic. *Arch.* 19, the fight among Greek
cities for the right to be Homer's birthplace.

[4] 'The work of a good historian is unlikely to embrace much autobio-
graphical detail' (*LHA* 1; though Walsh 10–11 finds the Preface 'a more personal statement than any of his predecessors' '); if any of L.'s contemporary
history had survived, there might have been more such detail. On L.'s
prefatory voice see Moles, and on the authorial *persona* see Booth (with extensive bibliography).

[5] *Praef.* 1, 3 *Facturusne operae pretium sim si a primordio urbis res populi Romani
perscripserim nec satis scio nec, si sciam, dicere ausim ... et si in tanta scriptorum turba
mea fama in obscuro sit, nobilitate ac magnitudine eorum me qui nomini officient meo
consoler.* M. J. Wheeldon in A. Cameron, ed., *History as text* (1989) 56 points
out the extraordinary density of first-person verbs in the first sentence. The
historian also says he wants to turn away from present ills – then claims that
his history is a cure for them (*Praef.* 5, 9–10); on his problematic authority
see further p. 13 and 12.2–6nn.

[6] E.g. Sen. *Contr.* 9.1.14, Quint. 10.1.102 *nam mihi egregie dixisse uidetur Seruilius Nonianus pares eos magis quam similes.* This ancient connection with Sallust
challenges Syme's pronouncement (at (3) 452) that '[i]n sentiment as in style,
L. does not fit into the development of Roman historiography that links Sallust to Tacitus'. Other refs. to L. in this context include Servius (quoted
n.16) and Tac. *Agr.* 10.3 (L. an *eloquentissimus auctor* among former historians).

4.34.3 with M–W).[7] Finally, though he is mentioned in connection with no triumviral or Augustan literary circle, <u>his name does appear several times in the Elder Seneca's anecdotal history of the fashionable declamation schools</u>, the only circle in which his active participation is securely attested. This literary movement was, perhaps more than any other, to give imperial literature its distinctive character; yet L.'s interest in it has been minimized.[8] But Seneca remembers him taking part in an argument about translating epigrams (*Contr.* 9.1.13–14), while audiences tolerated his son-in-law's mediocre declamations for L.'s sake, indicating personal acquaintance and respect (Sen. *Contr.* 10 *praef.* 2).[9] Other contemporary historians were similarly involved (e.g. Pollio, Labienus, and Seneca

[7] Claudius' wish to begin his history with Caesar's death (a project quickly quashed by his mother and grandmother: Suet. *Cl.* 41.2) indicates that L.'s independence was uncompromised (see further below, pp. 6–9). At least one piece of evidence for his closeness to Augustus is shaky: 4.20.7 *cum Augustum ... se ipsum ... legisse audissem* need not refer to a 'deliberate and probably direct' communication from the emperor, as argued by e.g. Luce (1) 213. Imperial interest in L. continued: Gaius found L. wordy and careless, but Virgil too was *nullius ingenii minimaeque doctrinae* (Suet. *Cal.* 34.2); Domitian had a *consularis* executed for, among other things, carrying around with him a map of the world and *contiones ... regum ac ducum ex Tito Liuio* (Suet. *Dom.* 10.3).

[8] Syme (3) 427 denies it: 'The oratorical style in vogue in that age is well known from the specimens of declamations preserved by the elder Seneca ... the tyranny of the Triumvirs, by banishing oratory from the Comitia and the Senate, drove it into the schools ... the growth of despotism confirmed its sway. Declamation and the new style are inextricably bound together. L. stood by Cicero'; but see Bonner (1) 133–4. No one has hesitated to credit L. with an interest in 'proper' oratory: Quintilian reports Livian rhetorical precepts *in epistula ad filium scripta* (10.1.39; E. Norden (*Hermes* 40 (1905) 525) conjectured that it was a treatise analogous to that of Horace to the Pisones), while Syme (3) 426 suggests that L. taught rhetoric. Some have gone further, e.g. H. V. Canter, *C.J.* 9 (1913) 26: 'the voice of public eloquence being stilled under the Empire, L. became a historian in order to remain an orator'.

[9] L.'s recitations of his history are said to have been attended by a small (but enthusiastic) audience (Suidas *s.v.* Κορνοῦτος; see Wiseman 255). Declamatory influence *has* been detected in the Alexander-digression (9.17–19), though it has there been ascribed to a combination of youth and poor judgment, later improved (against this view see Luce (1) 218–29).

himself),[10] and as a cultural practice declamation was associated with the writing of history.[11] Declamatory influence is above all visible in L.'s style, which like that of Ovid (another non-professional who frequented the halls, cf. Sen. *Contr.* 2.2.8–12) represents an early stage in the development of the pointed and paradoxical style of imperial Latin.

L. attained *gloria* in his own lifetime – Pliny recalls the story of a man travelling all the way from Spain just to see him – and became something of a local hero in Padua after his death.[12] It is likely, however, that he spent his working life in the capital,[13] where he must have devoted most of his time to his history of Rome.[14] Called *Ab urbe condita* (1.1–3n.), this began at the beginning (with the capture of Troy: 1.1.1) and continued in 142 books through the year 9 B.C. Of these, thirty-five are extant (1–10, 21–45), together with the late antique *periochae*, or summaries, of all but two of the original books.[15] When complete, the *AVC* included the three

[10] L. would have been *c.* 10 years older than Seneca and *c.* 13 years younger than Pollio (b. 76), who often declaimed (e.g. Sen. *Contr.* 4 *praef.* 2–6, 7.1.4, 4.3); other declaiming contemporaries included Arellius Fuscus and Porcius Latro.

[11] On the close relation between history and oratory see *RICH* 70–116 and R. Nicolai, *La storiografia nell' educazione antica* (1992). Declamatory exercise was, of course, part of advanced education (Bonner (1) 27–50).

[12] Plin. *Ep.* 2.3.8 *numquamne legisti, Gaditanum quendam Titi Liui nomine gloriaque commotum ad uisendum eum ab ultimo terrarum orbe uenisse, statimque ut uiderat abisse?*; for refs. to L. simply as *Patauinus (vel sim.)* cf. Stat. *Silu.* 4.7.55, Sidon. *Ep.* 9.14.7, *C.* 2.189, 23.146; for *Nachleben* see Walsh 32–3.

[13] *LHA* 18–19, confirmed by the many refs. to urban topography in the *AVC* (e.g. 4.12); they are discussed by R. von Haehling, *Zeitbezüge des T. Livius in der ersten Dekade seines Geschichtswerkes* (1989). *Contra*, Syme (3) 428 'Perhaps he was never long or frequently at the metropolis.'

[14] There is ancient testimony for other works: for the *epistula ad filium* see n.8; Sen. *Ep.* 100.9 mentions philosophical dialogues with a historical slant, generally assumed to be *juvenilia* (*LHA* 4).

[15] Missing are *per.* 136–7. That the *periochae* stop with Book 142 is our evidence for there having been 142 books in total, a patently uncomfortable argument made more so by the presence in some MSS of the last summary of an event from A.D. 9, which Syme (3) 448 thinks may have come from an epilogue. It used to be assumed that L. died pen in hand (the 'consecrated phrase': Syme (3) 412); for the suitability of 9 B.C. as a stopping-point see *RICH* 139 (after Syme). That the *AVC* was unfinished is a hypothesis to which this person inclines; see *LCH* 24 n.50 with the caveats of Henderson 71–2.

main types of historiography found at Rome,[16] i.e. history *a Remo et Romulo*, universal or world history (as Rome expanded to encompass and indeed to create the 'known' world), and contemporary history.[17]

This vast *opus* was structured and published in groups of five books (pentads).[18] The first pentad shows signs of a second edition; the unit as we have it can be dated between 27 and 25 B.C., while 6–10 were published before 23.[19] It is likely that L. started writing before Actium (31 B.C.), and that the Preface, in which he voices Sallustian pessimism about the state into which Rome has fallen

[16] On the types see Wiseman 246–8 and cf. Servius *ad* Virg. *A.* 1.373 *Liuius ex annalibus* [=past history] *et historia* [=recent] *constat.* Roman history is at bottom local history writ universal (Fornara 23–8).

[17] Evaluation of the *AVC*, crippled by the loss of all L.'s recent history, is further complicated by the figure of the 'senatorial historian', the man who writes history after learning 'how history is made' (Syme (3) 453, cf. 'The senator as historian' in *Ten studies in Tacitus* (1970) 1–10). Thucydides is the prototype, Tacitus the ideal of such a writer. According to the promoters of this model, since L. held no public office, he could understand neither the events happening around him nor the political, constitutional, or juridical issues of the Roman past (O. pp. 24–5 is representative). No one would maintain that L.'s work shows the same interest or expertise in Curial procedure as does Tacitus' (he had a different agenda: pp. 18, 26–7); on the other hand, detachment has always been claimed as a virtue for a historian, whether in the form of 'freedom from bias' (n.38) or a more modern ability to step back from one's subject. Moreover, the senatorial historian is likely to be a bad historian: 'the unfortunate tendentious maxim "it takes one to know one," ... if applied, would put an end to the historian's enterprise; historians, after all, are committed to entering the world of the other, no matter how distant in time, place, or cultural habits' (P. Gay, *Freud for Historians* (1985) 53–5); see also Badian 9 on Catonian history as 'polemic and apologia,' *LCH* 296, T. J. Cornell, *PP* 79–80.

[18] For analyses of the structure see Syme (3) 401–10 and Stadter; the extant books are treated in detail by *LCH*. Syme held that the pentadic structure broke down as early as Book 45, a collapse intensified by the revolutions of the last century B.C.; against this see Stadter, who correctly argues that the organization continues through 120. (His analysis is developed by Walsh 8–9, stressing the integral role of these divisions in L.'s historical interpretation.) L. may have exploited the tensions between his formal structure and his (often boisterous) content, providing a model for Tacitus' procedure (n.49).

[19] Arguments and bibliography in Luce (1). Books 26–30 will have been published possibly by 26/5, certainly by 19; *per.* 59 refers to an event of 18 B.C. It is generally assumed that L. wrote an average of three books per year.

and which will have been published together with the first unit, is
roughly contemporaneous with Octavian's solidification of his
power.[20]

As a historian, L. is engaged in putting past events into an interpretative framework that not only explains but also legitimates them,
and that legitimates the authority of the state under whose rule
they have happened.[21] Small wonder, then, that his attitude toward
Augustus and *his* project has attracted more attention than any other
single issue. It has been argued that L. was completely committed
to Augustus;[22] a republican whose adherence to old-fashioned
politics and morality stood firm in the face of Augustan blandish-
ments, his independence respected;[23] a covert anti-Augustan;[24]

[20] Cf. *Praef.* 9 *labante deinde paulatim disciplina uelut dissidentes primo mores se-
quatur animo* [sc. *lector*], *deinde ut magis magisque lapsi sint, tum ire coeperint praeci-
pites, donec ad haec tempora quibus nec uitia nostra nec remedia pati possumus peruentum
est.* On L.'s Sallustian *aemulatio* see e.g. 18.5–15nn., 35.6n. and Moles 155–7,
159–62; on the date see *RICH* 132–8, especially 134: 'if it is right to date
the [writing of] the preface before the end of the civil war in 31 B.C., L. in
[*Praef.*] 9 is merely expressing a natural distaste both for the war itself and
for the prospect of dictatorship which alone would end the war. On this interpretation the preface fails to provide us with any evidence at all for L.'s
relationship with Augustus once the latter became *princeps.*'

[21] White (2) 11–14, 18–20 argues (following Hegel) that historiography is
written only when there is a need to 'moralize': 'narrative in general ...
from the annals to the fully realized "history," has to do with the topics of
law, legality, legitimacy, or, more generally, *authority* ... the more historically
self-conscious the writer of any form of historiography, the more the question of the social system and the law which sustains it, the authority of this
law and its justification, and threats to the law occupy his attention ... Unless at least two versions of the same set of events can be imagined, there is
no reason for the historian to take upon himself the authority of giving the
true account of what really happened' (at 13, 20). Even Tacitean, 'opposition' history does this: written from the safe vantage-point of a post-Domi-
tianic era, it reconstructs the anti-republic of the empire as bad authority in
a bad state, by implication moralizing the good authority that can be only
desired, not realized, under bad emperors.

[22] Syme (1) 463–5.

[23] Walsh 6, commenting on Tac. *A.* 4.34.3.

[24] H. J. Mette, *Gymnasium* 68 (1961) 269–85, cf. H. Petersen, *T.A.P.A.* 92
(1961) 440–52, arguing that in Book 1 L. was warning Augustus that Rome
would not tolerate monarchy. On Augustus and intellectual opposition see
K. A. Raaflaub and L. J. Samons II, *BRE* 436–47.

and a 'true' Augustan who found his republican values confirmed
and extolled by the emperor.[25]

This state of interpretative affairs is further complicated by the
fragile testimony of some MSS of *per.* 121, that that book (and so
the rest of the *AVC*) 'is said (*dicitur*) to have been published (*editus*)
after Augustus' death'. As a result, it has often been assumed that
L. had intended to end with Book 120 (43 B.C.), but added the later
books as an 'appendix'[26] which either was not published immediately because he died first, or was withheld for various reasons.[27]
The theorized existence of such an extension is as potentially unsettling to interpretation as the (possible) lack of an ending to the *AVC*
as a whole.[28] L.'s decision to keep writing has been taken as a *confessio imperii* by a historian who was converted by Augustus' achievement from his original vision that republican history came to a full
stop with the death of his hero, Cicero;[29] or as a supplement,

[25] Syme (3) 451–2; on the concept 'Augustan' see the articles and bibliography collected in *BRE*. This last interpretation has also been tainted by
'the senatorial historian' (n.17): only those who from lack of experience were
unable to read and record 'the real and secret history of the dynasty' could
avoid writing opposition history – unless, of course, they were mendacious
(Syme (3) 452, 446–7). L. thus becomes a benevolent incompetent (e.g.
Syme (3) 453) – clearly *not* the case. (For a sympathetic analysis of L. as
an encomiastic historian see *RICH* 128–40; for Augustan 'propaganda' see
Wallace-Hadrill (2) 222–7.)

[26] A prefatory fragment preserved at Plin. *NH praef.* 16 is often cited in
this context: *profiteor mirari T. Liuium, auctorem celeberrimum, in historiarum suarum
quas repetit ab origine urbis quodam uolumine sic exorsum: satis iam sibi gloriae quaesi-
tum et potuisse se desinere, ni animus inquies pasceretur opere.* Though there is no
evidence of where the remark came from, one can suppose that it is from a
late book (so Syme (3) 411, whose 'appendix' consists only of Books 134–42,
i.e. the books after the triumph of 29 B.C.), perhaps even 121 (so *RICH* 136).
Yet, though L. is given to talking about the size of his history and his relationship to it (e.g. at *Praef.* 4 it is *immensi operis*, at 31.1.5 it is like an increasingly deep sea into which he is wading), he nowhere, not even in Pliny's
fragment, says that he *wants* to stop; indeed, the way he tells us he 'could
have' done so is characteristically self-deprecating.

[27] On his death date see n.1; the reasons posited for an authorial refusal
to publish vary with the interpretations of the appendix's contents.

[28] The extension has precedents in Ennius and Polybius (*RICH* 155 n.94);
on its effects see Henderson.

[29] Cf. *RICH* 136–9 (with summaries of earlier arguments) and Henderson
78: 'L.'s history [on this view] is the authoritative machine for the recovery

primarily biographical, recounting the deeds of Augustus, whose assumption of the consulate and first exercise of power (Books 119–20) marked the end of one stage of Rome's history, as Romulus marked its beginning;[30] and as a subversive, anti-Augustan history that could not safely be published in its subject's – or its author's – lifetime.[31]

The real problem, however, lies in the attempt to read both L. and Augustus from their ends rather than from their beginnings – especially so in L.'s case, where the end does not survive. If all the extant books date from before (say) the middle of the second decade B.C. (and given the almost complete absence of contemporary references in those books),[32] then the nature of his 'Augustanism' can hardly be determined. More interesting, then, to consider the *AVC* as the gradual, often experimental construction of a written Rome, built on the histories that came before it, which is to save the real Rome by providing it with precedents to imitate and avoid. As such, of course, the historian's project parallels/rivals Augustus' own building of a new Rome via (re)construction of its past.[33] Both L. and Augustus promoted many of the same virtues, most of them with roots in republican ideology.[34] But a shared project does not necessarily mean a lack of independence. L.'s discernible atti-

---

of the Roman past, the authorised "renovation" of *imperium*, the reordering enabled by the new order.' On this argument, and if L. outlived Augustus, it is suggested that he may have withheld the books in sympathy for his less converted comrades in historiography (Syme (3) 449).

[30] Stadter 299–300; on the tendency of L.'s later books to concentrate on personalities – an anticipation of imperial historiography – see Stadter 303. Syme (3) 433–48 rightly stresses the tact that on any reckoning would be needed in writing the history of the years 42–9.

[31] See works cited n.24.

[32] Above, n.18.

[33] On Augustus' progress via trial and error see e.g. C. Meier, *BRE* 67 and W. Eder, *BRE* 71–122; on his related building programme see P. Zanker, *The power of images in the age of Augustus* (trans. A. Shapiro, 1988) and B. A. Kellum, *BRE* 276–307.

[34] *LHA* 11–19, *RICH* 156 nn.110–11; Syme (3) 435–6 is characteristically cynical: 'It is easy enough for a government to filch and furbish up the forms and phrases of its adversaries, and Caesar Augustus operated with dexterity.' But he goes on, 'There was also a genuine and tangible revival of the Republic – the old houses came back, to public honour and perhaps to hopes of power.' See 6.9n., 17.5n.

tude toward the new government is cool and detached,[35] and his heroes differ from those of Augustus.[36] Most importantly, the exemplary portraits of the extant books are ambivalent ones, and fragmentary evidence suggests that this detachment continued when L. dealt with more contemporary figures.[37] Like most ancient historians, he claims – allusively, as always – to write without bias (*Praef.* 5);[38] in what has survived of the *AVC* he has succeeded in masking his own political inclinations only too well.

2. LIVIAN HISTORIOGRAPHY[39]

Annales

According to tradition,[40] historiography at Rome began in the form of a chronicle, the yearly records of the Pontifex Maximus which

[35] He is conspicuously careful not to 'lend his services as historian to the consolidation of the Augustan regime' (Walsh 6); a telling point is that in the extant books L. (*qua* narrative voice) refers only rarely to the Romans as *nostri* (as e.g. 7.14.6, 28.1.3; cf. A. D. Leeman, *Orationis ratio* (1963) 1 196).

[36] On the Forum of Augustus and L.'s heroes see T. J. Luce, *BRE* 123–38.

[37] He considered whether Marius had been 'better in war or more destructive in peace' (*per.* 80), and whether the state would have been better off had Caesar never been born (Sen. *NQ* 5.18.4); his obituary appraisal of Cicero is shrewd, even critical (fr. 61: see *LCH* 155); see also Solodow on the Horatii and cf. 38n.

[38] For exx. of the topos see *RICH* 73–4; in general see *RICH s.v.* 'truth' and T. J. Luce, *C.P.* 84 (1989) 16–31.

[39] In what follows, no attempt is made to address the question of L.'s competence as a historian. I assume that the *AVC* has a rhetorical basis and didactic aims, and that those who castigate L. for not conceiving and writing history according to modern 'rules' have confused their categories. For a balanced view of L. the Historian see *LCH*, esp. xv–xxvii; for the rhetorical nature of historiography see the provocative analysis in *RICH* (with extensive bibliography); for L.'s didacticism see below.

[40] The tradition is primarily a modern one (e.g. McDonald 155–6), though Cicero saw a direct stylistic progression from the *annales maximi* to later historians (*De orat.* 2.51–4, *Leg.* 1.6–7); B. W. Frier argues that Fabius Pictor (late third century) imitated the pontifical chronicle in creating a sort of 'ritualistic structure,' but that the final collection was the work of an Augustan antiquarian (*Libri annales pontificum maximorum* (1979) 283–4, 179–200). Chronological organization is of course far older than *annales* (Fornara 28–9). For other types of ancient historiography see Fornara 1–46, and on the meaning of *annales* see G. P. Verbrugghe, *Philologus* 133 (1989) 192–230.

were believed to have been kept from an early period as a calendrical and ritual record. These *annales maximi* would record such
things as the names of magistrates, the price of grain, temple dedi-
cations, and prodigies.[41] Whether any such chronicle was consulted
by scholars has been questioned; still more doubtful is whether in its
final form it contained genuine 'archival' material from the early
republic.[42] But it gave the kind of historiography known as *annales*
its distinctive formal structure: a chronological sequence of the
eponymous magistrates by whom the Romans dated their year,
with an accompanying record of state business. This skeleton of
names and deeds was elaborated according to rhetorical principles
until *annales* reached their developed form, a rich, circumstantial
narrative full of the particularities of the past.[43]

The basic unit of Livian history, then, is the year, which begins
and ends as *annales* plain and simple.[44] It opens with the magis-

[41] *CAH*[2] 20–1. The records are said to have been kept on an *album* until
the pontificate of P. Mucius Scaevola, *Pont. max.* 130–*c*.115 B.C. (Cic. *De orat.*
2.52).

[42] In an influential paper Rawson 1–15 argues that the chronicle was *not*
used. Other possible sources of information for a first-century historian included family records (e.g. Atticus' research on noble families, Nep. *Att.*
18.3–4: *LHA* 112), magisterial and triumphal lists ('*Fasti*': *CC* 13–18), antiquarian scholarship (e.g. Cincius and Varro: *LCH* 160), and inscriptions:
these last were used only sporadically (*CAH*[2] 21–2), and the two adduced
in Book 6 (4.3, 29.9) are described in the past tense, and were probably in
L.'s literary source. Most of L.'s material came from other historical narratives, including Greek histories of Rome (e.g. Polybius: *LCH* 168–71), poetry
(e.g. Naevius, Ennius: Badian 32 n.52, Moles 142), *commentarii* (e.g. Caesar's
bella), memoirs (e.g. Sulla's: E. Badian, *J.R.S.* 52 (1962) 49), and Latin prose
histories. On L.'s working methods see *LCH* 185–229; for his sources for the
second pentad see *LHA* 117–23.

[43] Most of this detail was the product of rhetorical *inuentio* (*CC* 21–6,
RICH 83–95); on the 'expansion of the past' in post-Catonian historians
see Badian 11–13, Cornell, *PP* 70–2. Cicero's word for the rhetorical super-
structure of history is *exaedificatio* (*De orat.* 2.63); for an analysis of the process
by which such a chronological list may be 'narrativized' see White (2) 6–9.

[44] L.'s narrative of the regal period does not have an annalistic framework, its chronology being determined by a series of royal 'begats' (on display in an unelaborated form in the Alban king list, 1.3.7–9); the latest books
may have returned to this organization by personality, with the series of
dynasts (n.30).

trates' assumption of office and attendant protocol (e.g. provincial assignments, prodigies) and closes with 'archival' material (trials, deaths, obituaries, building projects etc.).[45] L. tends to relate these details in an unelaborated style that evokes the language of early chronicle (3.10n., 24.11n.). Between comes the narrative of the year proper, divided into *res internae* and *res externae*.[46] The simplest – and ideal – form of a year is one in which annalistic material (the record of the state at peace) frames the narrative of a foreign campaign; a textual rhythm is thus established which corresponds to the rhythm of the state, which is likewise subject to annual change in the form of elections and change of military command.[47] But matters are not always so simple: while external fear inhibits domestic trouble,[48] on the other hand, internal conflict can ruin external success. In addition, L. often manipulates the formulaic year-boundaries

[45] For year-opening and year-end see Ginsburg 10–14 and 31–4 respectively, and on the formal elements in the *AVC* see T. F. Carney, *P.A.C.A.* 2 (1959) 1–9 and McDonald. The year-end often attracts antiquarian material, whose collection was not the province of historians, but which was often drawn on by them; there was a vogue in antiquarian research starting in the fifties and extending through the Augustan period (E. Rawson, *Intellectual life in the late Roman republic* (1985) 233–49; cf. n.42). Elections, which bridge both textual and actual years, are hard to classify; Ginsburg 33 reasonably puts them at the end, though their results – often announced in the same sentence – are the names of the magistrates by whom the next year is inaugurated (cf. 1.60.3, the last sentence of Book 1 announces the first consuls of 2).

[46] Ginsburg 53–5. Variation on the pattern is desirable: a year may be short or long (4.7–11n.) or may contain only one type of material (e.g. 38–42.3). L.'s history is the earliest of which enough is preserved for this structure to be fully visible, though there are elements of it in Sallust's *Bellum Jugurthinum* (cf. the alternation between *res internae* (the scenes at Rome) and *externae* (in Africa), and the 'annalistic' ending of ch. 114: 12.6n.). The fragments of L.'s annalistic predecessors are collected in Peter; for sketches of the early historians see Badian.

[47] Ginsburg 86, see 27.6–8n., 36.5n. A striking and contemporary example of the powerful combination of these two themes is Augustus' Parthian arch (*c.* 18 B.C.), on which he had the republican *Fasti* inscribed: the triumphal arch contained and advertised the essence of Roman greatness, the unbroken sequence of magistrates (Wallace-Hadrill (2) 224).

[48] The theory of the *metus hostilis* (e.g. *LCH* 271–3, Harris *s.v.*, Paul on Sall. *J.* 41.2); the interplay of external success ∼ internal disorder is especially marked in Books 1–10.

themselves, which thereby take on added significance: for instance, he may displace prodigy notices to point Roman neglect of religion; or he may allow dissonant voices to break into the year-end material, challenging the structure of the state and of its record.[49]

Domestic and foreign affairs within this annalistic framework are (for the most part) related in L.'s most characteristic narrative unit, the 'episode',[50] an artistic composition which can range in length from several chapters (e.g. the second year of the *seditio*, 14–20) to a portion of one chapter (e.g. Fabia, 34.5–10). Ancient historiography aimed at the vivid re-presentation of events; in the hands of the rhetorical masters, L. and Tacitus, it refined the practice of Greek (especially Hellenistic) historiography to create plausible, circumstantial, and convincing narrative that would produce pleasure, fear, sadness etc. in the reader.[51] Stories with pictures and conversation are intrinsically more lifelike and interesting – and thus more effective – than stories without, and a classic Livian episode is no exception, being written more ornately than the annalistic notices and containing a mixture of speech (both direct and indirect) and narrative.[52] Speeches were of the historian's own composition; even when an oration was known to have been delivered and a published version was available, he would write his own.[53] Formal *orationes* were used to argue a position, analyse an event, or characterize an actor; shorter remarks, especially but not exclusively those

[49] On prodigies see Levene, e.g. 38–42 (displacement highlights the impiety of Flaminius); on the voices see 16.8–17.5n.; for other modifications of formulaic material see 1.8n., 6.3n. Tacitus was to exploit the conflict between the historiographical ictus and accent, the (annalistic) form of the republic and the reality of *dominatio* (Ginsburg 100, M–W 78).

[50] The conventional term is 'Einzelerzählung,' 'unit narration' (K. Witte, *Rh.M.* 65 (1910) 270–305, 359–419); it has been a primary focus of interest in Livian literary studies (Walsh 24–6 has preliminary bibliography).

[51] *LHA s.v.* 'Hellenistic historiography,' F. W. Walbank, *Polybius* (1972) 34–9; on *euidentia* see 1.3n., 17.4n.

[52] The division of narrative into speech and action dates back to Homer; on the historians see N. P. Miller, *G.&R.* 22 (1975) 45–57.

[53] See 26.4n. and cf. 34.1–8.3 with B., M–W 117–18. Famous *dicta* (e.g. last words, quips) could be included *uerbatim* (e.g. 9.16.18, fr. 60, Sall. *J.* 35.10: *RICH* 54 n.67), but convention and *inuentio* could operate in such contexts as well (see Badian 17 on Maharbal's famous words to Hannibal).

in indirect speech, may highlight a reaction (20.3), report a message (28.1), clarify a statement (34.10), explore a character's motivation (9.1, 22.9), or focus a scene (16.5, 35.2).[54] L. typically omits the verb of speaking to introduce short passages of indirect speech: the reported thoughts surface directly from the narrative, without authorial intervention, as it were.

'This means you'

It will be seen that in many respects this alternation of annalistic notices with mimetic episode is a remarkably artificial format. The (re)creation of a compelling picture of the past ultimately depends on the maintenance of narrative illusion. The more 'artistic' that recreation is, the less obtrusive the artifice, the more persuasive it will be.[55] But in L.'s history the narrative illusion is repeatedly broken by the structure of the narrative itself. The textual year, whose chronology does not match real time (could everyone important in Rome really have died at the end of the year?[56]), keeps intruding. The texture of the narrative corresponds to the various facets of L.'s puzzling *persona*: like him, it veers between assurance (perfect unchallenged mimesis, the *sub oculos subiectio* of vivid narration) and the need to document, to query, to list facts, to doubt (that is, to show the seams of the text). The result is to unsettle the authority both of the presentation and of the historian's own voice.[57] This decentralized authority has a specific end: the engagement of the reader in the historiographical project.

This participation is essential, for L. is writing history which

[54] For L.'s sophisticated use of indirect discourse see Lambert and *LHA s.v. 'oratio obliqua'*.

[55] This is not, of course, to deny the persuasive effect of a deliberate breaking of the illusion by a confidential appeal to the reader's trust, judgment etc. (12.2n.); but such tactics work best if used sparingly.

[56] Ginsburg 33–4.

[57] See above, p. 2 and 9.3n. on third-person narration. White (2) 185–213 analyses a similarly decentralized authorial voice; for other discussions of author-ity see F. Kermode, *The genesis of secrecy* (1979) and G. B. Conte, *The rhetoric of imitation* (ed. C. P. Segal, 1984) 141–84 (he emphasizes the necessary limits to such unsettling: the author has to remain in charge – as L. does).

teaches moral and ethical lessons.[58] It is thus a kind of pragmatic history, as Polybius recommended (9.1–2); but where Polybius addressed himself to other political professionals, L. is writing for an unidentified 'you': *hoc illud est praecipue in cognitione rerum salubre ac frugiferum, omnis te exempli documenta in illustri posita monumento intueri; inde tibi tuaeque rei publicae quod imitere capias, inde foedum inceptu foedum exitu quod uites* (*Praef.* 10). There is a direct, personal relationship between the *ego* of the text and this *tu*: history is understood – even made – in the space between them. The reader's job is to observe closely (*intueri*) not only the results (displayed in L.'s *illustre monumentum* as in a diorama) but also the workings of history. *Praef.* 9[59] singles out the constant change of the Roman state over time, while §10 describes the negative *exemplum* dynamically as something that begins and ends badly, drawing our attention to its cause and outcome, as well as to its nature (*foedum*). This movement of the past is matched by the reader's own acts: seizing and avoiding *exempla*, conjecturing (12.3), wondering (12.2), learning (20.5), inspecting (14.2). Reading history is as active a process as writing it – or even as making it.[60]

The author, for his part, offers guidance about how to read, sometimes outright (22.6n.), but more often implicitly by establishing a system of cross-references among characters and actions, both throughout the *AVC* and outside it, i.e. with other histories.[61] In Book 6, for instance, Manlius resembles his precursors (Cassius, Maelius) and his successors (Catiline, Caesar), while the clash between Furius and Camillus (22.5–26) evokes several past and future conflicts between a rash young man and a wiser, older one. While

---

[58] Basic discussion at *LHA* 39–40, 82–109; favourite didactic methods include the personification of virtues (e.g. 27.1; see O. p. 18) and the construction of spectacular scenes (Feldherr *passim*). On the reader's involvement in the Preface see Moles *passim*.

[59] Quoted n.20.

[60] L. is explicit at 10.31.15 *quinam sit ille quem pigeat longinquitatis bellorum scribendo legendoque quae gerentes non fatigauerunt?*, cf. 31.1.1 *me quoque iuuat, uelut ipse in parte laboris ac periculis fuerim, ad finem belli Punici peruenisse.* See the important discussion of Catin 127–36.

[61] L.'s procedure resembles Virgil's; for similar Tacitean practice see J. Henderson in A. J. Boyle, ed., *The imperial muse: Flavian epicist to Claudian* (1990) 167–210.

the existing density of tradition constrains both historian and reader (we already 'know' what has happened), L. can still operate with considerable freedom even within the weight of Rome's past, making new connections or highlighting neglected ones (is Manlius Cicero? 18.5n., 18.8n.), and avoiding stories he does not wish to tell (38n., 42.9–11n.). The interpenetration among periods of history implies that even *protoi heuretai*, the founding figures with which early Roman history abounds (11.7n.), act as their descendants do, since the behaviour or custom they inaugurate is something familiar: their pioneering act is the foundation of something already known.[62] Conversely, the past can facilitate change: re-citation of lessons learned leads to new interpretations of them, for L.'s characters and his readers.[63]

Commonplaces

These patterns of repeated behaviour and imitation of character are matched on the literary level by the commonplace, or topos. An intricate intertextual net is created by the historian's deployment of conventional motifs, e.g. the battle description (ch. 24), the exhortation (7.3–6), the restive crowd (16.5), the jealous wife (34.7–10), the proud patrician (40.2). One can expand the definition of topos to include the formulaic language that attaches to these scenes, which may then be used outside them to evoke their larger context by a sort of shorthand (e.g. 33.3 *arbitris … remotis* (n.)). Standard elements of the rhetorician's craft,[64] topoi help create the sense of familiarity with which ancient historians make the past recognizable: 'the formula, the "repeated," … creates in the hearer the suggestion that the actions being told are unfolding in a

---

[62] An analogous process obtains in the case of monuments: a place can generate a story ('this is the Tarpeian rock, which is so called because …') or vice versa ('there was a woman named Tarpeia and …'); for the interdependence of historical narratives and monuments see Gabba 60–1, Wiseman in *PP*.

[63] On this process, which often relies on the deployment of *exempla*, see 28.5–29n. and Chaplin *passim*.

[64] Lausberg §409, §§1126–8. For repeated scenes and variations in L. see e.g. Catin 93–115, *LHA* 191–9.

paradigmatic world, quite detached and different from everyday life, in the space of the code, beyond that of its manifestations in particular events of individual tales.'[65] But, like traditional stories, topoi not only create and reinforce the *mos maiorum*, they can also be used to question and modify it: by improving commonplaces the historian can display his superior talent as a writer and as an interpreter (*aemulatio*), while by combining them in unexpected or dissonant ways he can problematize a conventional analysis or theme.[66] Also as with the deployment of traditional stories, this process depends on the activity of the reader, who must recognize both the voice of the *maiores* and the historian's manipulation thereof.

Linguistically as well as ethically, history thus becomes a 'knot of different times',[67] in which theoretically unique, non-recurrent events are built from other episodes, other stories. Because so much Roman history is articulated as the history of individual actors (an alternative title is *res gestae*, 'deeds': 1.1–3n.), L.'s narrative can be compared to the funeral processions of *imagines*, in which by wearing the portrait masks of their ancestors the living members of a family graphically represent the continuity of tradition, both diachronically (the ancestors walk in chronological order, the oldest at the head of the parade) and synchronically (each man metaphorically takes on the characteristics of the ancestor whose *imago* he wears and whose deeds he is expected to emulate – a collapsing of generations in *imitatio*).[68] As the family unit subsumes and protects its individual members, who in turn add to the greatness of the whole, so L.'s history is a continuous narrative of the *res gestae* of individuals

[65] Bettini 288 n.25; see White (1) 81–100 for the argument that narrative history succeeds in making sense of the unselected, random data of history by shaping them to a familiar pattern which makes sense because it is already known (so Sallust's Rome is in melodramatic decline, Tacitus' Rome is savagely farcical). On the tension between 'specific' and 'general' truth see J. L. Moles, *LF* 107–10; more on history and fiction in White (1) 121–34, L. O. Mink, *Historical understanding* (1987) 42–60, 89–105, 182–203, and L. Gossman, *Between history and literature* (1990) 227–56, 285–324.

[66] E.g. 18.5–15nn.; see also Cairns *s.v.* 'inclusion.' The shock value of 'inappropriate' use of topoi is seen everywhere in Tacitus (Plass *passim*).

[67] Serres 268.

[68] On the procession see Bettini 167–83; related comments in Hardie 35–7, 88–93.

which taken together constitute the history of Rome, whose immortal body is formed of the countless mortal bodies of her citizens.[69]

3. LANGUAGE AND STYLE

The number of L.'s stylistic admirers has been enormous. Quintilian established the terms of the discussion: L., like Herodotus, is wonderful at expressing emotions and at writing speeches;[70] above all, he has a pleasant style (Quint. 10.1.32), a *lactea ubertas* that has (wrongly) been taken to describe prose of unremitting richness and creaminess[71] and has been connected with Cicero's recommendation of a fluid style for history.[72] While some attempts have been

[69] Explicit at 9.18.8–19 (see 23.7n.); Cato's alleged suppression of the names of individuals in his *Origines* may have underscored a similar concept (discussion at A. E. Astin, *Cato the censor* (1978) 232–3). For parades of history cf. Virgil's heroes in *A.* 6 with Feeney 5–6, and the Forum of Augustus.

[70] Quint. 10.1.101: i.e. L. the Moralizer and Psychologist (n.58) and L. the Orator (n.8).

[71] L. the Ice Cream Cone? S. Hays has persuasively argued that *lactea ubertas* refers rather to the nourishing qualities of L.'s history in Quintilian's curriculum (*C.J.* 82 (1987) 107–16).

[72] *De orat.* 2.64, on which see *RICH* 94–5 and cf. McDonald 160 'Cicero defined the programme, L. carried it out' (modified later, e.g. 163 L. 'applied the accepted methods of historical composition'); O. p. 4 'only Cicero commanded L.'s admiration'; B. (on Books 31–3) p. 16. In the past century, L. has been too often seen as a militant Ciceronian somehow outside the historiographical tradition. While he does meet Cicero's recommendations (at *De orat.* 2.63) for the content of historiography (e.g. chronology, topographical descriptions, analysis of causes and character), these are traditional elements found in other historians before and after (*RICH* 109 n.77, 183–4). His *style*, on the other hand, while admitting of influence from Cicero (as well as from Thucydides, Ennius, Cato, Claudius Quadrigarius, Sallust etc.) is historiographical, as most convincingly shown by H. Tränkle, *W.S.* 81 (1968) 103–52 (see also W. D. Lebek, *Verba prisca* (1970) 199–202). The results of efforts to show his 'allegiance' to Cicero include such misconceived theories as that of S. G. Stacey (*A.L.L.* 10 (1898) 17–82, following Wölfflin) that L.'s style evolved from 'Silver' to Ciceronian (*contra*, Gries, Adams (4)) and such self-contradictory judgments as Syme (3) 733: 'Livian words and expressions are frequent in the writings of Tacitus. The contrary would surprise. They had become the common stock of the Latin historical style. It is not helpful to talk of "borrowings" from L.'

made to demonstrate the pervasively varied nature of L.'s style(s),[73] the image of the unbroken stream has obscured the real nature of his Latin (and, correspondingly, of his history): quirky, difficult, engaging.[74]

L.'s insistence that the reader become engaged in the historiographical process (above, pp. 13–15) informs his choice of style, whose primary characteristic is a suppleness, an imbalance that can be almost combative.[75] This is in keeping with his announced project: to narrate the history of Rome's growth with the ever-present consciousness of its subsequent decline.[76] There was a tricky balance to be maintained: he was not writing simply to praise Rome (though in the early books there was more to praise than to blame: *Praef.* 11), but to illustrate where she went wrong; a varied style was therefore needed, neither Sallustian spikiness nor Ciceronian balance, but something in between.[77] Like Tacitus he uses intertextuality, *uariatio*, epigrams, inconcinnity, and paronomasia to force his readers both to think about the potential difference between the surface and the 'real' world (11.4n., 14.2n., 38.6n.) and to work at understanding the kind of men and *mores* that built Rome – and were destroying it. But L. was also himself constructing a Rome to save the 'real' one. Like the city he writes about, his text expands (sometimes relentlessly), accommodating difference within a framework in which tradition and stability still have redemptive value, and in which the *species rerum* is not all there is.

[73] See the studies of Kühnast, Riemann, and Catterall.

[74] For reasons of space, prose rhythm has not been treated in the Commentary. L.'s *clausulae* show the same variation as other elements of his style; see in general H. Aili, *The prose rhythm of Sallust and Livy* (1979).

[75] Cf. W. Kroll, *Studien zum Verständnis der römischen Literatur* (1924) 362 on the 'variety and restlessness' of L.'s language.

[76] Cf. *Praef.* 4 (Rome's greatness is a cause of its decline: *ut iam magnitudine laboret sua ... iam pridem praeualentis populi uires se ipsae conficiunt*), 5 *malorum quae nostra tot per annos uidit aetas*, 9 (quoted n.20), 11 *auaritia luxuriaque*, 12 *nuper diuitiae auaritiam et abundantes uoluptates desiderium per luxum atque libidinem pereundi perdendique omnia inuexere*. Cf. *LCH* 155 'In the last two-thirds of the history geniality gave way to pessimism, idealization to blunt criticism.'

[77] For the concepts of praise and blame and their relation to historiographical style see *RICH s.vv.*; for 'le style c'est l'homme même' and its application to Roman history see A. H. McDonald, *J.R.S.* 65 (1975) 1–10 and (more generally) P. Gay, *Style in history* (1974).

These points are illustrated throughout the Commentary. What follows here is a discussion of three particular features of Livian style.

Diction and syntax

Historiography exhibits considerable freedom in matters of word choice and syntax, partly owing to the feeling that the genre was akin to poetry,[78] partly because its persuasive effect did not have to rely on immediate aural comprehensibility.[79] L.'s taste for the modern and the experimental can be illustrated on every page of the *AVC*, and is encapsulated by a remark he is said to have made about orators who by chasing after archaic and low vocabulary think they have achieved *seueritas* when they have in fact achieved only *obscuritas*: quoting a Greek rhetorician, he said 'they are mad – but in the right direction'.[80] He tailors his language to suit his subject-matter, ranging from the grandiose (23.4–7) to the intimate (34.5–10), from the sarcastic (40.9–10) to the moving (14.3–8) – and even to the parodic (18.5–15). He will use technical vocabulary when needed (e.g. 4.12 *substructum*), but will just as readily modify or avoid it (1.2 *commentariis*, 38.4 *cooptat*, 42.12 *ludi maximi*). Consistent in this variety, however, is a liking for the choice (e.g. 3.4 *prouoluisset*, 11.7 *ferri* (hist. infin.), 37.8 *socordius*) and for figurative language; his metaphors are less arresting than Tacitus', but, like him, he prefers allusive vocabulary to explicit simile, suggesting an often extended metaphorical comparison by his choice of words

[78] E.g. Quint. 10.1.31; the comparison rests on the affinities of content between historical epic and historical prose (M–W 4 n.10).

[79] Cf. Quint. 10.1.32 *neque illa Sallustiana breuitas, qua nihil apud aures uacuas atque eruditas potest esse perfectius, apud occupatum uariis cogitationibus iudicem et saepius ineruditum captanda nobis est, neque illa Liui lactea ubertas satis docebit eum qui non speciem expositionis sed fidem quaerit.*

[80] Sen. *Contr.* 9.2.26 *Liuius de oratoribus qui uerba antiqua et sordida consectantur et orationis obscuritatem seueritatem putant aiebat Miltiaden rhetorem eleganter dixisse:* ἐπὶ τὸ δεξιὸν μαίνονται [Hertz, Madvig: ΤΟΝαεΞΙΟΝaaaΙΝΟΝΤΑΙ MSS]. *tamen in his etiamsi minus est insaniae minus spei est; illi qui tument, illi qui abundantia laborant, plus habent furoris, sed plus et corporis; semper autem ad sanitatem procliuius est quod potest detractione curari; illi succurri non potest qui simul et insanit et deficit* (see Winterbottom's n.).

(1.3–6, 22.7, 37.2 (n.); see M–W 22). He uses repetition to set up responsions between episodes (1.6n., 37.4n., 41.11n.) or to underscore a theme (5.2n.), while repetitive figures of speech (e.g. polyptoton, homoioteleuton) give point to epigrammatic expressions (18.13, 40.14, 18). Especially characteristic is his use of *traductio*, the repetition of a word in close proximity but in different senses.[81] His syntax too is varied, often in a proto-Tacitean manner (Index *s.v. uariatio*); but he tends to innovate in subtle ways, introducing new constructions modelled on old (25.9n.) and using several constructions with the same word (e.g. 2.9 (*ab*), 5.7, 18.4, 23.12, 40.12).

Sentence structure

Quintilian compared *historia* to a human chain: *historia non tam finitimos numeros quam orbem quendam contextumque desiderat. namque omnia eius membra conexa sunt … ut homines, qui manibus inuicem apprehensis gradum firmant, continent et continentur* (9.4.129). His metaphor aptly describes the historiographical period, a sentence built of discrete units, each describing a separate action, with the result that a single period can narrate an entire event, as 8.10 *quae postquam nulla eruptione impediri* <u>*uidet*</u>, *minus esse animi* <u>*ratus*</u> *in hoste quam ut in eo tam lentae spei uictoriam exspectaret,* <u>*cohortatus*</u> *milites ne tamquam Veios oppugnantes in opere longinquo sese tererent, uictoriam in manibus esse, ingenti militum alacritate moenia undique* <u>*aggressus*</u> *scalis oppidum* <u>*cepit*</u>. Each of the underlined verbs is logically a new 'main' verb, since each can be replaced by an indicative connected by *et* (he saw – he thought – he exhorted – he attacked – he captured).[82] Since the verbs move the action forward, their clauses are called 'continuative elements' or 'continuative narrative cola'.[83] Though these cola can theoretically be arranged in any order (subject to syntactical constraints), there are three dominant

---

[81] For this and other figures of speech and thought see the Index and W. Eckert, *De figurarum in Titi Livi ab urbe condita libris usu* (diss. Vratislaviae, 1911).

[82] So there is an equivalence between the verbal actions at Caes. *G.* 4.27.3 *hunc … comprehenderant atque in uincula coiecerant* and *G.* 7.13.2 *oppidani … comprehensos eos … ad Caesarem perduxerunt*.

[83] The fundamental study is that of Spilman, who gives exx. of each type of clause (participle, *cum*-clause, *dum*-clause, *postquam*-clause etc.) and its possible 'shading' (temporal, causal, adversative etc.).

patterns:[84] (1) the historiographical period proper, in which one or more grammatically subordinate clauses are followed by a main clause; any of the elements may be multiplied, but each will move the story forward (e.g. 8.3, 8.10 (quoted above), 15.1–2, 34.8–9);[85] (2) the 'phrase à relance', which starts again, as it were, by adding a second (etc.) period to an original one;[86] and (3) the 'phrase à rallonge', in which a main clause is followed by continuative elements, usually an abl. abs., as 27.1–2 *Camillus ... magistratu abiit creatis tribunis ... in insequentem annum*.[87] These narrative sentences differ fundamentally from the characteristic oratorical period, in which subordinate clauses serve primarily to elaborate or describe (as 17.1–2) rather than to move forward, and of which the chief characteristic is the suspension of syntax and meaning, resolved by one or more verbs at or near the end (as 40.3–5).[88]

Arrangement

A prominent feature of L.'s style is its interest in patterns, both on the level of the book and pentad and elsewhere.[89] These may be described as variations on patterns of two and of three. There is a well-documented tendency in Indo-European languages for pairs

[84] Codified and analysed by C-L 129–247 ('phrase narrative-type'), 253–82 ('phrase à relance'), 283–336 ('phrase à rallonge').

[85] Walsh 26 n.2 rightly suggests that the misleading designation 'period' not be applied to this kind of sentence.

[86] E.g. 25.5 *introductis in senatum captiuis cum bello persequendos Tusculanos patres censuissent Camilloque id bellum mandassent, adiutorem sibi ad eam rem unum petit, permissoque ut ex collegis optaret quem uellet contra spem omnium L. Furium optauit.*

[87] The shape lends itself as much to analysis of motives or reactions as to forward-moving narration, and was perfected by Tacitus; cf. 4.6, 6.5, 13.4 and see M–W 23–4; on the development of postpositive participles see Schlicher 298–300.

[88] For practical analyses of oratorical style see W. R. Johnson, *Luxuriance and economy* (1971), H. C. Gotoff, *Cicero's elegant style* (1979), both of whom rightly emphasize the variety of Cicero's sentence shapes; for L.'s oratory see Dangel, and for schematic representations of sentence-types in Latin see G–L §686–7. The best short analysis of narrative *v.* oratorical sentences is Wilkinson 167–88.

[89] For reasons of space, these patterns have generally not been noted in the Commentary; they are illustrated here with passages from Book 6.

and triads to be arranged in members of increasing length, often
unified by repeated sounds (e.g. 3.4 *luctum lacrimasque*, 14.4 *ciuem commilitonemque*, 17.4, 33.10 *Tusculanos ... uerterat*; 39.6 *et ... potestatis*;
17.2, a tricolon *auctum* with anaphora).[90] This kind of increasing pattern can also structure a paragraph or scene (1.10–12, 4.7–11; see
LCH 53–4, M–W 15–17 on Tacitean dyads and triads). Patterns of
two can be combined either in chiasmus (ABBA, e.g. 19.7 *accusatores de
plebe, patricium reum*) or interweaving (ABAB, e.g. 34.1 *uis patrum in dies
miseriaeque plebis crescebant*).[91] These can provide large-scale organization: so Book 6 is arranged in a predominantly interwoven pattern
(Camillus – Manlius – Camillus – Licinius and Sextius), while its
domestic episodes respond chiastically to the two city-captures in
Book 5 (Veii – Gauls ~ Manlius – Licinius and Sextius: 40–1n., cf.
31–32.2n.). The effects can equally be very local (cf. the chiastic
alliteration at 1.1, 9.12, 21.6 *spatium ... senatum*). Both arrangements
can expand a 'table of contents': so the Italian settlements of Antenor and Aeneas respond chiastically to their naming in the first
sentence (1.1.1–5, cf. 9.3 *Nepete ac Sutrio*, 41.4);[92] for interlaced expansion cf. 4.9, 9.11, 11.2, 22.6. A particularly common feature is the
sequential deployment of these patterns, e.g. chiasmus followed by
interweaving (ABBABA)[93] or vice versa (ABABBA).[94] Again, this can obtain on a local level, where a change of pattern often marks the end
of a series with variation (e.g. 16.4 *obuersatam ... turbam*, 41.9 *tradamus*

[90] Behagel's Law; for Latin, see Lindholm's copiously illustrated study
(117–73 on prose).

[91] Chiasmus, which is one of L.'s favourite devices, often produces significant juxtaposition of opposites (e.g. 3.4 *Sutrinos ~ Etruscis*, 15.12, 18.6–7,
20.8); interweaving suggests parallelism rather than antithesis (33.1n.).

[92] Chiastic expansion similarly structures the *Aeneid* (*arma* ~ Books 6–12,
uirum ~ Books 1–6); on Tacitus see A. J. Woodman, *C.Q.* 39 (1989) 203; and
cf. Thuc. 1.1.2 ~ 1.21.2–23.3 and 1.1.3 ~ 1.2–21.1 (*RICH* 7), Cic. *Pis.* 33, *B.
Afr.* 64, Hor. *C.* 1.12 (the opening triad *uirum* | *heroa* | *deum* expanded in
reverse order).

[93] Cf. 27.7 *nec ... contione*, 38.15.9, Cic. *Ver.* 4.78, *Mil.* 65 *credi popae, confes-
sionem ... audire, uulnus ... probari*, Tac. *A.* 4.3.3 with M–W. For these and
other patterns see the studies of R. B. Steele on anaphora and chiasmus in
L. (*T.A.P.A.* 32 (1901) 154–85), in the letters of Cic. Sen. Plin. Fro. (*Studies in
honor of Basil L. Gildersleeve* (1902) 339–52), and in Sall. Caes. Tac. Just. (diss.
Baltimore, 1891).

[94] Cf. 21.2 *praeter ... Latium*, 3.68.2 *agros ... tecta*, Cic. *Pis.* 63 *fructum ...
insignia*, Caes. *C.* 1.6.3.

... *nefas est*),[95] or on a larger one.[96] Finally, chiasmus and interweaving can be superimposed, frequently by the counterpoise of
vocabulary and case.[97]

Patterns of three show similar variation. The tricolon *auctum* has
been illustrated above;[98] also common are tricola with members of
alternating length: (1) XxX, as 3.5, 5.5, 17.4, 37.11;[99] (2) xXx, as
41.8 *si ... auis*.[100] In combination, triadic structures can mirror each
other (ABC ∼ CBA, a triple chiasmus, e.g. 14.11) or repeat each other
(ABC ∼ ABC, triple interweaving, e.g. 29.1); other responsions are ob-
viously possible, viz. ABC ∼ ACB;[101] ABC ∼ BCA (18.7, 24.9 *temeritati*

---

[95] 'Terminal modification' (Smith 53), cf. Adams (5) 82; on closure in classical literature see D. P. Fowler, *M.D.* 22 (1989) 75–122.

[96] E.g. 11.1 *bellum ... seditio* ∼ 11.2 (ABAB) ∼ 11.3–9 (B *seditio*), 12–13 (A *bellum*), 14–20 (B *seditio*); 18.2 *et patribus et plebi* ∼ *plebi ... patribus* (ABBA) ∼ 18.3–
16 (B *plebs*) ∼ 19 (A *patres*); cf. Cic. *Quinct.* 1 *gratia et eloquentia* (AB) ∼ *eloquentia
... gratia* (BA) ∼ 2 *disertissimo ... gratiosissimo* (BA) ∼ 3–4 [*eloquentia*], 5–9 *gratia*
(BA).

[97] Cf. 17.6 *in uno omnibus ... in tam multis uni*, 25.11 *omnia ... pace*, 33.10 *ex
ingenti metu ... in ... alacritatem* ∼ *ex ... fiducia ... in exiguam ... spem* (chiastic
content), Cic. *Arch.* 15 *naturam sine doctrina ... sine natura ualuisse doctrinam*,
Caes. *G.* 6.10.5, Vell. 117.2 *quem pauper diuitem ingressus diues pauperem reliquit*
with W. On a larger scale cf. 7.2, 8.3.

[98] The tricolon *diminutum* is less common (Lindholm 173), but cf. 16.2 *Iuppiter ... optime maxime Iunoque regina ac Minerua*; for decreasing length in dyads
cf. 17.2 *in libertatem ac lucem*, 33.7 *cum coniugibus ac liberis*, 23.9–11 (*quae ... paenituisse* ∼ *nunc ... praestantem; itaque ... regi* ∼ *collegae ... impedire*), 41.10 *quia ...
dant*.

[99] Cf. Quad. fr. 7 *et genere et ui et uirtute bellica*, Cic. *Inu.* 1.29 *et ad eorum qui
agent naturam et ad uulgi morem et ad eorum qui audient opinionem*, *Prou.* 1 *ac si ...
tribueretis*, Caes. *C.* 3.87.2.

[100] Cf. Cic. *Pis.* 22 *quis te illis diebus sobrium, quis agentem aliquid quod esset
libero dignum, quis denique in publico uidit?*, Hor. *C.* 1.29.1–5, Luc. 2.547–9 *ut
... Hiberos*. For *tetracola* with elements of different length cf. 7.2 (with Caes.
C. 3.78.1 *ad saucios ... relinquendum*, also with homoioteleuton) and 41.2 (with
Cic. 1 *Ver.* 2 *depeculatorem aerari, uexatorem Asiae atque Pamphyliae, praedonem iuris
urbani, labem atque perniciem prouinciae Siciliae*, also with alternation between
domestic and foreign content).

[101] This arrangement is quite popular, cf. 13.5 *missilibus ... teneri*, 24.5 *uestra ... haec*, 25.4 *aduersae ... Furium*, 25.5 *cum ... peperit*, Cic. *Balb.* 18 *cur potius
inuidia* (A) *uiolatura* (B) *uirtutem L. Corneli* (C) *quam aequitas uestra* (A) *pudorem eius*
(C) *adiutura* (B) *uideatur*, Caes. *G.* 7.14.9 *neu* [sc. *oppida*] *suis* (A) *sint ad detrectan-
dam militiam* (B) *receptacula* (C) *neu Romanis* (A) *proposita* (C) *ad copiam commeatus
praedamque tollendam* (B); for its use in expansion cf. 7.3 and 5.11.10–11 *senatu
... populo ... collegis* ∼ *senatus ... collegis ... populum*.

... *prudentiae*). Finally, triads tend to be subdivided; the arrangement is secured either by repetition of a word or sound in two of the three members (sometimes the outer members, as 41.1) or by a syntactical connection between them (as 17.2, 39.6).[102]

Such textual architectonics form the basis of L.'s *exaedificatio*, as he exploits varied rhythms both for ornament (e.g. the progressive series of sounds in the epigrammatic 2.40.13 *haud minus **pernicioso** quam **pertinaci certamine** confecit*[103]) and for point (e.g. the postponed 'punchline' at 20.14 (n.)). The structures of the text in turn construct the events related, as at 1.13.2 *soceri **generi**que **respergerent*** (linking the warring Romans and Sabines).[104] On a large scale (e.g.) without the responsion between Books 5 and 6, the significance of the plebeian capture of Rome would be diminished (above, p. 22). L.'s choice and meticulous deployment of diction, figures, and textual structures at once demonstrates and creates his authority as interpretative guide through his *Vrbs*.

4. *AB VRBE CONDITA* BOOK 6

This section briefly addresses three questions: the place of Book 6 in the *AVC* and its major themes; selected chronological and historical problems; the text. For other issues of interpretation the reader is referred to the Commentary.

Vrbs condenda

In contrast to many of his predecessors, and despite his claim to be more attracted by *prisca*, along with his readers L. hastens toward

---

[102] E.g. 2 + 1, as 2.7–8, 3.6 *conglobandi ... capiundi*, 16.7 *et paruum et paucis datum et **mercedem** esse prodendi **M. Manli***, 39.7; or 1 + 2, as 1.1 *sub ... consularibus*, 3.3 *opere uigiliis uulneribus*. See further L–H–S 722–3.

[103] Cf. Cat. 68.114 *perculit **imperio** deterioris **eri***, Caes. *G.* 3.23.7 *hostem et **uagari** et **uias** obsidere et **castris satis** praesidi relinquere*, Plin. *Ep.* 6.20.14 *ululatus feminarum, **infantum quiritatus, clamores** virorum* and H. James, *Washington Square* (1883) 5 'a **com**ely, **com**fortable, reason**able** woman'.

[104] Cf. Cic. *Pis.* 64 *Italia cuncta exsecratur, cuius idem tu superbissime decreta et preces repudiasti* (the spurned decrees and prayers come back to life in the curse).

the present:[105] his history expands as it moves forward, so that by
the end he covers approximately one year per book, while the six
centuries between Troy and the last of the kings are all contained
in Book 1.[106] The first two pentads have three important historical
and textual divisions: the beginning (1.1.1, the exodus from Troy),
the beginning of the republic (2.1.1), and the *secunda origo* after the
sack (6.1.1).[107] For practical reasons, each juncture is formally
marked: the Preface states L.'s programme and advertises Books 1–
5; Book 2 is the first new compositional unit – the first time the
formal structure of L.'s history is visible – and as such is marked
by a separate introduction; the preface of 6–10, the first separately
published unit, restates the history's title and its programme (1.1–
3n.).

Form echoes content: at each of these points a past destruction
gives way to future growth. Claudius Quadrigarius (early first century) began his *Annales* with the Gallic sack (frr. 1–5). L. chooses
instead to end Book 5 therewith and to begin 6 with the subsequent recovery. The same relationship obtains between the near-
destruction of Rome by the Gauls and its rebirth under Camillus
as between Books 1 and 2, the end of monarchy and the start of the
republic. The parallel is secured by quotation: in both cases a summary of past history (6.1.1–2 *quae ... interiere* ∼ 1.60.3) is juxtaposed
with a new table of contents (6.1.3 *clariora ... exponentur* ∼ 2.1.1);
there are, further, verbal echoes: 6.1.1 *ab condita urbe Roma ad captam* ∼ 1.60.3 *ab condita urbe ad liberatam*, 6.1.3 *laetius feraciusque* ∼ 2.1.2
libertas ... laetior. Both the start of the republic and the new *origo* in
390 in turn look back to the original foundation, establishing a historical continuity even across such cataclysmic events as the birth of
libertas and the near-death of Rome.[108] Finally, the foundations of

[105] *LCH* 155 n.27, cf. *Praef.* 4–5, and see Moles 146–7 on L.'s disingenuous
prefatory assertion and its modifications.

[106] The distribution varies: 43 B.C. takes five books, 42–9 B.C. only twenty;
in the first pentad, Book 2 covers 509–468, while 5 contains only fourteen
years (403–390). The general tendency, however, is clear (Stadter *passim*).

[107] There is a secondary preface at 7.29.1–2, the start of the Samnite
wars, but it does not coincide with a textual break.

[108] 6.1.1–3, a new foundation after the destruction of a mother city, also
evokes the passage from Troy to Italy (∼1.1.1 *satis constat Troia capta ... 10*

Books 2 and 6 are historiographical as well. At 2.1.1 L. makes his
forthcoming programme explicit: Roman *res gestae* and *annales*.[109]
The preface of 6 announces the same programme (1.1–3nn.), but
again with renewal. The burning of the real Rome also saw the
burning of her history (1.2): the fresh start in 390 redraws the limits
of the historically verifiable, which L. had previously defined as ex-
cluding events *ante conditam condendamue urbem* (*Praef.* 6).[110] In all
senses, then, we are starting over again.

The narrative of the 23 years following this new foundation falls
into four parts: two phases of military operations (in which Camillus
is the major figure) as Rome consolidates its power in Latium (1.4–
10, 21–33), the Manlian *seditio* (11–20), and the Licinio-Sextian rogations (34–42). L.'s interest in the world outside the senate led him to
combine a history of the élite with that of the plebs which was
'utterly innovative.'[111] In this book he sets in counterpoise the story
of Manlius, a patrician war hero who becomes a demagogue, and
that of the plebeian tribunes, who win the right to stand for election
as consul. In both cases, as he investigates the acquisition and handling of political power, L. pays close attention to the crowds, who are
both the raw material for and the instigators of change. He also
plays *res internae* off against *res externae*, continuing to exploit the ten-

oppidum condunt), though by refusing to abandon their city at 5.55.2 the Romans effectively refuse to repeat the Troy–Rome cycle, choosing instead to
refound on the spot (see also 4.5n.). For the idea that L. saw Roman history
as a series of inaugurations/refoundations see Serres 115, 158, 263 and Miles
(1) and (2).

[109] *Liberi iam hinc populi Romani res pace belloque gestas, annuos magistratus, im-
periaque legum potentiora quam hominum peragam*, cf. Cato 1 *si ques homines sunt,
quos delectat populi Romani gesta describere*, Sall. *H.* 1.1 (quoted on 1.3 *deinceps*);
for *res gestae* and *annales* see pp. 9, 16.

[110] In the months following the sack the idea of rebuilding is prominent
(5.55.2 *promisce urbs aedificari coepta*, 6.1.6 *reficiendae urbis*, 4.5 *aedificandi*, 4.6 *aedificiis*, 5.5 *aedificandi*). But L. also imagines his subject-matter and sources as
physical objects (1.2 *res … obscuras*; *monumenta*), and his frequent allusions to
the size of his history (n.26) suggest a metaphorical equivalence between the
physical city and his own literary *exaedificatio* (n.43). This equivalence is to the
fore at 6.1.1–3. For a similar analogy between Herodotus' travels through
life and through his book see Hartog 260–309, Moles, *LF* 96–7.

[111] Ridley, *SS* 132–3 (see also above, n.2, n.17); on the book's themes see
Pinsent (2) 2.

sion between external and internal affairs that characterized the first pentad, where Rome repeatedly faced an increase in civil conflicts during times of peace abroad.[112] Though the Romans tend to behave in an orderly, efficient manner in the military sphere, here too are raised issues of the proper handling of power that complement the questions posed by events *domi* (e.g. how should Camillus be limited/limit himself? what are the consequences of patrician military control?). These issues are extensively treated in the rest of the pentad, where the problems of Roman expansion, heroism, and the place of the plebeian order are all put under scrutiny.[113]

Who, what, and when

By the first century B.C., antiquarian research had produced a list of eponymous magistrates from the beginning of the republic; this is fullest for the years after 300 B.C., but there is close agreement among independent sources (e.g. L. and Diodorus) for earlier years as well.[114] Plebeian officers are mentioned less frequently, though Licinius Macer's *Annales* may have contained more data;[115] there were also separate lists of triumphators.[116] Ancient scholars as well as modern ones were cognizant of the tendentious nature of this evidence, which could be distorted by familial and political factors;[117] I have printed the names as in the OCT and refer the reader to *MRR* and *RE* for prosopographical discussions.

The individual actors are symptomatic of larger historical problems. The *AVC* exemplifies Cornell's contention that 'the historical tradition of the Roman Republic was not an authenticated

[112] Above, n.48. The alternation between peace and war serves narrative purposes, too (cf. 27.6–8n., 35.10n.).

[113] Particularly in the stories of single combat (e.g. 7.9–10), *deuotio* (e.g. 8.9–10), disobedience (e.g. 8.7), and struggles for plebeian equality (e.g. 9.33–4); for a preliminary analysis of the pentad see Lipovsky.

[114] For the magistrates and ancient refs. see *MRR*; specialized discussion of the consular tribunes in L. and Diodorus by A. Drummond, *Athenaeum* 58 (1980) 57–72.

[115] He was a Marian *popularis*, *tr. pl.* 73; on his history, which L. used and which emphasized the sovereignty of the people, see O. pp. 7–12; for the tribunician *fasti* see G. Niccolini, *I fasti dei tribuni della plebe* (1934).

[116] *CIL* I² 1.43–50.   [117] E.g. 8.40.4; see Wiseman 207–18.

official record or an objective critical reconstruction; rather, it was an ideological construct designed to control, to justify, and to inspire ... The functional role of tradition in the political and social life of the Republic meant that the generally accepted picture of Rome's history was subject to a process of continuous transformation as each generation reconstructed the past in its own image.'[118] Since much of L.'s description of early Rome is more applicable to his own day, in commenting on it I have tried to explain the customs to which he refers (usually triumviral or Augustan). Yet because of its highly coloured nature, the *AVC* presents enormous difficulties for modern historians trying to reconstruct the reality of ancient Rome.[119] The reliability of the historical tradition about the first centuries of the republic is a matter of intense current debate. I have followed what may be called the optimist line, which assumes that the outline we have in L. and others is basically correct, though details of battles, names etc. are probably not.[120] (For example, while the fourth century was clearly a time of Roman expansion and conquest, several of the military engagements reported in Book 6 appear to be doublets of one another (so ch. 2 ~ 7–8 ~ 22.6–24; ch. 3 ~ 9.7–12), a problem of which L. is aware: 12.2n.[121]) It is very possible that this approach is essentially mistaken,[122] but given that the didactic and moral value of the *AVC* is as an exemplary construction of Roman power, details of individual events hardly matter.[123]

Finally, the chronology of these years. Two matters require com-

[118] *SSAR* 58.

[119] While L. had a conception of historical change, he apparently conceived that change primarily as one of degree, not of kind: the possibility that early Rome was fundamentally other does not seem to have presented itself to him (see *CC* 42–5, Miles (2), and esp. *LCH* xx–xxi, 272–80, 248–9 (on 43.13.1–2): L. realizes that 'the milieu of the past is not that of the present').

[120] This is the approach taken by many of the contributors to *CAH*[2].

[121] Oakley (2) 10–11, 14–15.

[122] R. Saller, *J.R.S.* 81 (1991) 157–61 lays out the terms of the debate; see also Millar.

[123] Cf. Wiseman 293–6, arguing that history is likely to have been falsified to a greater degree precisely because 'the historical past of Rome was of direct political concern to the ruling élite' (at 294).

ment. By traditional dating, the years covered by Book 6 are (the end of) 364–387 *ab urbe condita* = 390–367 B.C.[124] But the traditional dating does not match Greek chronologies of the same period; comparison with events in other parts of the Mediterranean indicates that Rome was sacked in 386, not 390, B.C. This discrepancy arises from an ancient attempt to extend the chronology of the fourth century when it was realized that there were more years than there were recorded magisterial colleges. Two different methods of extension were used, both incorporated by the Varronian chronology;[125] instead of bringing the Roman dating in line with the Greek, they in fact moved it four years earlier.[126] (But, since the Romans dated events primarily by consular years, the confusion would have been considerably mitigated for a contemporary reader.) Secondly, during this period there is a difference between the magistrate year and the calendar year. The former had no fixed starting point in the early republic; during the period covered in 6, the consular tribunes (and later consuls) entered office on 1 July.[127] Each Livian year, then, spans half of two calendar years.

The text

Though the *AVC* was published in pentads, it was transmitted in groups of 10 books (decades), which have different textual histories. All the medieval codices of the first decade derive from a fifth-century 'edition' made by the Nicomachi and Symmachi, two of the last great pagan families of Rome. The subscriptions to these MSS, which describe the activity of these early *emendatores*, are of special

[124] Calculating from Varro's foundation date (=753 B.C.); other antiquarians dated the founding of the city to different years (Dion. Hal. 1.74.1–2; see Douglas on Cic. *Brut.* 72); for A.U.C. (=era) dating see Pinsent (2) 3–6.

[125] Insertion of the so-called 'dictator' years of 333, 324, 309, and 301 B.C., and the extension of the *solitudo magistratuum* (35.10) from one year (as in Diodorus) to five.

[126] See the discussion in *CAH*² 347–50, from which I have borrowed this explication. L. omits the dictator years *and* the consular college of 376 (35.3n.), making his chronology further discrepant from the Varronian.

[127] Beginning in 392 (5.32.1); the two years were synchronized from 153 B.C.

interest to the history of textual scholarship;[128] their descendants include Petrarch's copy (*A*).[129] A second strand of the tradition is represented by a fifth-century uncial MS containing fragments of Books 3–6.[130] The text printed here is that of the OCT, with the following modifications: (1) spelling has been regularized; (2) the paragraphing (a modern convention) has frequently been changed; (3) a score of different readings have been adopted, most significantly at 1.11, 6.8, 6.13, 9.10, 14.2, 18.13, 19.4, 27.3, 37.8, 40.16, 42.8, 42.12.

The following are the abbreviations of the MSS, their names, and their date(s) by century:

V	Veronensis rescriptus, V	*P*	Parisiensis, IX
M	Mediceus, X	*U*	Upsaliensis, X
Vorm.	Vormatiensis (now lost), X?	*A*	Agennensis, XII–XIV
		π	agreement of *EOPU*
H	Harleianus, X	**N**	agreement of the Symmachean MSS
E	Einsiedlensis, X		
O	Oxoniensis, XI	ω	agreement of all MSS

In the Apparatus, superscript 'c' indicates a corrector; square brackets ([ ]) indicate an editorial deletion (so also in the text), angle brackets (⟨ ⟩) an editorial addition.

128 J. E. G. Zetzel, *C.P.* 75 (1980) 38–59.
129 G. Billanovich, *J.W.I.* 14 (1951) 137–208.
130 In general L. D. Reynolds, 'Livy' in L. D. Reynolds, ed., *Texts and transmission: a survey of the Latin classics* (1983) 205–14.

TITI LIVI AB VRBE CONDITA
LIBER SEXTVS

TITI LIVI AB VRBE CONDITA
LIBER SEXTVS

Quae ab condita urbe Roma ad captam eandem Romani sub **1**
regibus primum, consulibus deinde ac dictatoribus decemuirisque ac tribunis consularibus gessere, foris bella, domi seditiones, quinque libris exposui, res cum uetustate nimia ob- **2**
scuras uelut quae magno ex interuallo loci uix cernuntur,
tum quod paruae et rarae per eadem tempora litterae fuere,
una custodia fidelis memoriae rerum gestarum, et quod
etiam si quae in commentariis pontificum aliisque publicis
priuatisque erant monumentis, incensa urbe pleraeque interiere. clariora deinceps certioraque ab secunda origine uelut **3**
ab stirpibus laetius feraciusque renatae urbis gesta, domi militiaeque exponentur.

Ceterum primo quo adminiculo erecta erat eodem innixa **4**
M. Furio principe stetit, neque eum abdicare se dictatura
nisi anno circumacto passi sunt. comitia in insequentem an- **5**
num tribunos habere quorum in magistratu capta urbs esset
non placuit; res ad interregnum rediit. cum ciuitas in opere **6**
ac labore assiduo reficiendae urbis teneretur, interim Q. Fabio, simul primum magistratu abiit, ab Cn. Marcio tribuno
plebis dicta dies est quod [legatus] in Gallos, ad quos missus
erat orator, contra ius gentium pugnasset; cui iudicio eum **7**
mors adeo opportuna ut uoluntariam magna pars crederet
subtraxit. interregnum initum: P. Cornelius Scipio interrex **8**
et post eum M. Furius Camillus [iterum]. is tribunos militum
consulari potestate creat L. Valerium Publicolam iterum
L. Verginium P. Cornelium A. Manlium L. Aemilium L.
Postumium.

Hi ex interregno cum extemplo magistratum inissent, nulla **9**

1.1 eandem *recc. aliq., Muretus*: urbem eandem π: e. u. *MH*   1.6 [legatus]
Cobet   1.8 [iterum] *Duker*

de re prius quam de religionibus senatum consuluere. in 10
primis foedera ac leges (erant autem eae duodecim tabulae
et quaedam regiae leges) conquiri, quae comparerent, iusserunt. alia ex eis edita etiam in uulgus; quae autem ad sacra
pertinebant a pontificibus maxime ut religione obstrictos haberent multitudinis animos suppressa. tum de diebus religio- 11
sis agitari coeptum, diemque a. d. XV Kal. Sextiles, duplici
clade insignem, quo die ad Cremeram Fabii caesi, quo
deinde ad Alliam cum exitio urbis foede pugnatum, a poster-
iore clade Alliensem appellarunt, insignemque nulla re publice priuatimque agenda fecerunt. quidam, quod postridie 12
Idus Quintiles non litasset Sulpicius tribunus militum neque
inuenta pace deum post diem tertium obiectus hosti exercitus Romanus esset, etiam postridie Idus rebus diuinis super-
sederi iussum; inde ut postridie Kalendas quoque ac Nonas
eadem religio esset traditum putant.

Nec diu licuit quietis consilia erigendae ex tam graui casu **2**
rei publicae secum agitare. hinc Volsci, ueteres hostes, ad 2
exstinguendum nomen Romanum arma ceperant; hinc Etruriae principum ex omnibus populis coniurationem de bello ad
fanum Voltumnae factam mercatores afferebant; nouus quo- 3
que terror accesserat defectione Latinorum Hernicorumque,
qui post pugnam ad lacum Regillum factam per annos prope
centum numquam ambigua fide in amicitia populi Romani
fuerant. itaque cum tanti undique terrores circumstarent ap- 4
pareretque omnibus non odio solum apud hostes sed contemptu etiam inter socios nomen Romanum laborare, placuit 5
eiusdem auspiciis defendi rem publicam cuius reciperata esset, dictatoremque dici M. Furium Camillum. is dictator C. 6
Seruilium Ahalam magistrum equitum dixit, iustitioque indicto dilectum iuniorum habuit ita ut seniores quoque quibus aliquid roboris superesset in uerba sua iuratos cen-

---

1.11 nulla re ... agenda A^c : rei nullius (nulli π) *VM Vorm.*π: agendae ω
(agenda *H*): nota rei nullius ... agendae *Watt 214 (alii alia)*

turiaret. exercitum conscriptum armatumque trifariam diuisit: 7
partem unam in agro Veiente Etruriae opposuit, alteram ante
urbem castra locare iussit. tribuni militum his A. Manlius, 8
illis qui aduersus Etruscos mittebantur L. Aemilius praepositus; tertiam partem ipse ad Volscos duxit nec procul a La-
nuuio (ad Mecium is locus dicitur) castra oppugnare est
adortus.

Quibus ab contemptu, quod prope omnem deletam a Gal- 9
lis Romanam iuuentutem crederent, ad bellum profectis tantum Camillus auditus imperator terroris intulerat ut uallo se
ipsi, uallum congestis arboribus saepirent, ne qua intrare ad
munimenta hostis posset. quod ubi animaduertit Camillus, 10
ignem in obiectam saepem coici iussit. et forte erat uis
magna uenti uersa in hostem; itaque non aperuit solum in- 11
cendio uiam sed flammis in castra tendentibus uapore etiam
ac fumo crepituque uiridis materiae flagrantis ita consternauit hostes, ut minor moles superantibus uallum militibus
munitum in castra Volscorum Romanis fuerit quam transcendentibus saepem incendio absumptam fuerat. fusis hosti- 12
bus caesisque cum castra impetu cepisset, dictator praedam
militi dedit quo minus speratam minime largitore duce, eo
militi gratiorem. persecutus deinde fugientes cum omnem 13
Volscum agrum depopulatus esset, ad deditionem Volscos
septuagesimo demum anno subegit. uictor ex Volscis in 14
Aequos transiit et ipsos bellum molientes; exercitum eorum ad
Bolas oppressit, nec castra modo sed urbem etiam aggressus
impetu primo cepit.

Cum in ea parte in qua caput rei Romanae Camillus erat **3**
ea fortuna esset, aliam in partem terror ingens ingruerat:
Etruria prope omnis armata Sutrium, socios populi Romani, 2
obsidebat. quorum legati opem rebus affectis orantes cum senatum adissent, decretum tulere ut dictator primo quoque
tempore auxilium Sutrinis ferret. cuius spei moram cum pati 3
fortuna obsessorum non potuisset confectaque paucitas oppi-
danorum opere uigiliis uulneribus, quae semper eosdem

urgebant, per pactionem urbe hostibus tradita inermis cum
singulis emissa uestimentis miserabili agmine penates relin-
queret, eo forte tempore Camillus cum exercitu Romano 4
interuenit. cui cum se maesta turba ad pedes prouoluisset
principumque orationem necessitate ultima expressam fletus
mulierum ac puerorum qui exsilii comites trahebantur excepisset, parcere lamentis Sutrinos iussit: Etruscis se luctum lacrimasque ferre. sarcinas inde deponi Sutrinosque ibi con- 5
sidere modico praesidio relicto, arma secum militem ferre
iubet.

Ita expedito exercitu profectus ad Sutrium, id quod rebatur, soluta omnia rebus (ut fit) secundis inuenit, nullam stationem ante moenia, patentes portas, uictorem uagum praedam ex hostium tectis egerentem. iterum igitur eodem die 6
Sutrium capitur. uictores Etrusci passim trucidantur ab nouo
hoste, neque se conglobandi coeundique in unum aut arma
capiundi datur spatium. cum pro se quisque tenderent ad 7
portas, si qua forte se in agros eicere possent, clausas (id
enim primum dictator imperauerat) portas inueniunt. inde 8
alii arma capere, alii, quos forte armatos tumultus occu-
pauerat, conuocare suos ut proelium inirent; quod accensum
ab desperatione hostium fuisset, ni praecones per urbem di-
missi poni arma et parci inermi iussissent nec praeter armatos quemquam uiolari. tum etiam quibus animi in spe ultima 9
obstinati ad decertandum fuerant, postquam data spes uitae
est, iactare passim arma inermesque, quod tutius fortuna fecerat, se hosti offerre. magna multitudo in custodias diuisa; 10
oppidum ante noctem redditum Sutrinis inuiolatum inte-
grumque ab omni clade belli, quia non ui captum sed traditum per condiciones fuerat. Camillus in urbem triumphans 4
rediit trium simul bellorum uictor. longe plurimos captiuos 2
ex Etruscis ante currum duxit; quibus sub hasta uenumdatis
tantum aeris redactum est ut pretio pro auro matronis persoluto ex eo quod supererat tres paterae aureae factae sint,

quas cum titulo nominis Camilli ante Capitolium incensum 3
in Iouis cella constat ante pedes Iunonis positas fuisse.

Eo anno in ciuitatem accepti qui Veientium Capenatium- 4
que ac Faliscorum per ea bella transfugerant ad Romanos
agerque his nouis ciuibus assignatus. reuocati quoque in ur- 5
bem senatus consulto a Veiis qui aedificandi Romae pigritia
occupatis ibi uacuis tectis Veios se contulerant. et primo fre-
mitus fuit aspernantium imperium; dies deinde praestituta
capitalisque poena, qui non remigrasset Romam, ex ferocibus uniuersis singulos, metu suo quemque, oboedientes fecit.
et Roma cum frequentia crescere, tum tota simul exsurgere 6
aedificiis et re publica impensas adiuuante et aedilibus uelut
publicum exigentibus opus et ipsis priuatis (admonebat enim
desiderium usus) festinantibus ad effectum operis; intraque
annum noua urbs stetit.

Exitu anni comitia tribunorum militum consulari potestate 7
habita. creati T. Quinctius Cincinnatus Q. Seruilius Fidenas
quintum L. Iulius Iulus L. Aquilius Coruus L. Lucretius Tri-
cipitinus Ser. Sulpicius Rufus exercitum alterum in Aequos,
non ad bellum (uictos namque se fatebantur) sed ab odio ad 8
peruastandos fines, ne quid ad noua consilia relinqueretur
uirium, duxere, alterum in agrum Tarquiniensem; ibi oppida 9
Etruscorum Cortuosa et Contenebra ui capta. ad Cortuosam
nihil certaminis fuit: improuiso adorti primo clamore atque
impetu cepere; direptum oppidum atque incensum est. Con- 10
tenebra paucos dies oppugnationem sustinuit, laborque continuus non die non nocte remissus subegit eos. cum in sex
partes diuisus exercitus Romanus senis horis in orbem succederet proelio, oppidanos eosdem integro semper certamini
paucitas fessos obiceret, cessere tandem locusque inuadendi
urbem Romanis datus est. publicari praedam tribunis place- 11
bat, sed imperium quam consilium segnius fuit: dum cunc-
tantur, iam militum praeda erat nec nisi per inuidiam adimi
poterat.

Eodem anno, ne priuatis tantum operibus cresceret urbs, 12
Capitolium quoque saxo quadrato substructum est, opus uel
in hac magnificentia urbis conspiciendum. iam et tribuni ple- 5
bis ciuitate aedificando occupata contiones suas frequentare
legibus agrariis conabantur. ostentabatur in spem Pomptinus 2
ager, tum primum post accisas a Camillo Volscorum res possessionis haud ambiguae. criminabantur multo eum infes- 3
tiorem agrum ab nobilitate esse quam a Volscis fuerit; ab
illis enim tantum, quoad uires et arma habuerint, incursiones eo factas; nobiles homines in possessionem agri pub- 4
lici grassari nec, nisi antequam omnia praecipiant diuisus sit,
locum ibi plebi fore. haud magno opere plebem mouerunt et 5
infrequentem in foro propter aedificandi curam et eodem exhaustam impensis eoque agri immemorem, ad quem instruendum uires non essent.

In ciuitate plena religionum, tunc etiam ab recenti clade 6
superstitiosis principibus, ut renouarentur auspicia res ad interregnum rediit. interreges deinceps M. Manlius Capitolinus
Ser. Sulpicius Camerinus L. Valerius Potitus; hic demum 7
tribunorum militum consulari potestate comitia habuit. L.
Papirium Cn. Sergium L. Aemilium iterum Licinum Menenium L. Valerium Publicolam tertium creat; ii ex interregno
magistratum occepere. eo anno aedis Martis Gallico bello 8
uota dedicata est a T. Quinctio duumuiro sacris faciendis.
tribus quattuor ex nouis ciuibus additae, Stellatina Tromen-
tina Sabatina Arniensis; eaeque uiginti quinque tribuum nu-
merum expleuere. de agro Pomptino ab L. Sicinio tribuno 6
plebis actum ad frequentiorem iam populum mobilioremque
ad cupiditatem agri quam fuerat. et de Latino Hernicoque 2
bello mentio facta in senatu maioris belli cura, quod Etruria
in armis erat, dilata est.

Res ad Camillum tribunum militum consulari potestate 3

5.5 eodem ω (eo dein *U*), *del. Wesenberg*: ex eodem *Watt*   5.7 Licinum
Walters (*v. MRR I 99–100*): -nium ω (L. Aemilium ... Menenium *om. H*)

rediit; collegae additi quinque, Ser. Cornelius Maluginensis
Q. Seruilius Fidenas sextum L. Quinctius Cincinnatus L.
Horatius Puluillus P. Valerius. principio anni auersae curae 4
hominum sunt a bello Etrusco, quod fugientium ex agro
Pomptino agmen repente illatum in urbem attulit Antiates
in armis esse Latinorumque populos iuuentutem suam summisisse ad id bellum, eo abnuentes publicum fuisse consilium 5
quod non prohibitos tantummodo uoluntarios dicerent militare ubi uellent.

Desierant iam ulla contemni bella. itaque senatus dis agere 6
gratias quod Camillus in magistratu esset: dictatorem quippe
dicendum eum fuisse si priuatus esset; et collegae fateri regimen omnium rerum, ubi quid bellici terroris ingruat, in uiro 7
uno esse sibique destinatum in animo esse Camillo summittere imperium nec quicquam de maiestate sua detractum
credere quod maiestati eius uiri concessissent. collaudatis ab
senatu tribunis et ipse Camillus confusus animo gratias egit.
ingens inde ait onus a populo Romano sibi, qui se [dicta- 8
torem] iam quartum creasset, magnum ab senatu talibus de
se iudiciis eius ordinis, maximum tam honorato collegarum
obsequio iniungi; itaque si quid laboris uigiliarumque adici 9
possit, certantem secum ipsum adnisurum ut tanto de se consensu ciuitatis opinionem, quae maxima sit, etiam constan-
tem efficiat. quod ad bellum atque Antiates attineat, plus ibi 10
minarum quam periculi esse; se tamen, ut nihil timendi, sic
nihil contemnendi auctorem esse. circumsederi urbem Roma- 11
nam ab inuidia et odio finitimorum; itaque et ducibus pluribus et exercitibus administrandam rem publicam esse. 'te' 12
inquit, 'P. Valeri, socium imperii consiliique legiones mecum
aduersus Antiatem hostem ducere placet; te, Q. Seruili, al- 13
tero exercitu instructo paratoque ad urbem castra habere,
intentum siue Etruria se interim, ut nuper, siue, noua haec

6.8 [dictatorem] *Madvig 130–1*   honorato *V*: -um **N**: -orum *Aldus*
6.13 ad urbem *V*: in urbe **N** (-m *A*)

cura, Latini atque Hernici mouerint; pro certo habeo ita
rem gesturum ut patre auo teque ipso ac sex tribunatibus
dignum est. tertius exercitus ex causariis senioribusque a L. 14
Quinctio scribatur, qui urbi moenibusque praesidio sit. L.
Horatius arma tela frumentum quaeque alia belli tempora
poscent prouideat. te, Ser. Corneli, praesidem huius publici 15
consilii, custodem religionum comitiorum legum rerum
omnium urbanarum, collegae facimus.' cunctis in partes 16
muneris sui benigne pollicentibus operam Valerius, socius
imperii lectus, adiecit M. Furium sibi pro dictatore seque ei
pro magistro equitum futurum; proinde, quam opinionem 17
de unico imperatore, eam spem de bello haberent. se uero
bene sperare patres et de bello et de pace uniuersaque re
publica erecti gaudio fremunt nec dictatore umquam opus 18
fore rei publicae si talis uiros in magistratu habeat, tam concordibus iunctos animis, parere atque imperare iuxta paratos
laudemque conferentes potius in medium quam ex communi
ad se trahentes.

Iustitio indicto dilectuque habito Furius ac Valerius ad **7**
Satricum profecti, quo non Volscorum modo iuuentutem
Antiates ex noua subole lectam sed ingentem Latinorum
Hernicorumque uim conciuerant ex integerrimis diutina
pace populis. itaque nouus hostis ueteri adiunctus commouit
animos militis Romani. quod ubi aciem iam instruenti Camillo 2
centuriones renuntiauerunt turbatas militum mentes esse,
segniter arma capta, cunctabundosque et resistentes egressos
castris esse, quin uoces quoque auditas cum centenis hostibus
singulos pugnaturos et aegre inermem tantam multitudinem,
nedum armatam, sustineri posse, in equum insilit et ante 3
signa obuersus in aciem ordines interequitans: 'quae tristitia,
milites, haec, quae insolita cunctatio est? hostem an me an
uos ignoratis? hostis est quid aliud quam perpetua materia
uirtutis gloriaeque uestrae? uos contra me duce, ut Falerios 4

Veiosque captos et in capta patria Gallorum legiones caesas
taceam, modo trigeminae uictoriae triplicem triumphum ex
his ipsis Volscis et Aequis et ex Etruria egistis. an me, quod 5
non dictator uobis sed tribunus signum dedi, non agnoscitis
ducem? neque ego maxima imperia in uos desidero, et uos
in me nihil praeter me ipsum intueri decet; neque enim dictatura mihi umquam animos fecit, ut ne exsilium quidem
ademit. iidem igitur omnes sumus, et cum eadem omnia in 6
hoc bellum afferamus quae in priora attulimus, eundem e-
uentum belli exspectemus. simul concurreritis, quod quisque
didicit ac consueuit faciet: uos uincetis, illi fugient.'

Dato deinde signo ex equo desilit et proximum signiferum **8**
manu arreptum secum in hostem rapit 'infer, miles' clamitans, 'signum.' quod ubi uidere ipsum Camillum iam ad mu- 2
nera corporis senecta inualidum uadentem in hostes, procurrunt pariter omnes clamore sublato 'sequere imperatorem'
pro se quisque clamantes. emissum etiam signum Camilli 3
iussu in hostium aciem ferunt idque ut repeteretur concitatos
antesignanos; ibi primum pulsum Antiatem, terroremque non 4
in primam tantum aciem sed etiam ad subsidiarios perlatum.
nec uis tantum militum mouebat, excitata praesentia ducis, 5
sed quod Volscorum animis nihil terribilius erat quam ipsius
Camilli forte oblata species; ita quocumque se intulisset uic- 6
toriam secum haud dubiam trahebat. maxime id euidens fuit,
cum in laeuum cornu prope iam pulsum arrepto repente
equo cum scuto pedestri aduectus conspectu suo proelium
restituit, ostentans uincentem ceteram aciem. iam inclinata 7
res erat, sed turba hostium et fuga impediebatur et longa
caede conficienda multitudo tanta fesso militi erat, cum repente ingentibus procellis fusus imber certam magis uictoriam quam proelium diremit.

Signo deinde receptui dato nox insecuta quietis Romanis 8
perfecit bellum. Latini namque et Hernici relictis Volscis

8.7 impediebatur *H*: -bat *M*(*Vorm.?*)π

domos profecti sunt, malis consiliis pares adepti euentus;
Volsci ubi se desertos ab eis uidere quorum fiducia rebel- 9
lauerant, relictis castris moenibus Satrici se includunt. quos
primo Camillus uallo circumdare et aggere atque operibus
oppugnare est adortus. quae postquam nulla eruptione impe- 10
diri uidet, minus esse animi ratus in hoste quam ut in eo tam
lentae spei uictoriam exspectaret, cohortatus milites ne tamquam Veios oppugnantes in opere longinquo sese tererent,
uictoriam in manibus esse, ingenti militum alacritate moenia
undique aggressus scalis oppidum cepit. Volsci abiectis armis
sese dediderunt.

Ceterum animus ducis rei maiori, Antio, imminebat: id **9**
caput Volscorum, eam fuisse originem proximi belli. sed quia 2
nisi magno apparatu, tormentis machinisque, tam ualida
urbs capi non poterat, relicto ad exercitum collega Romam
est profectus, ut senatum ad excidendum Antium hortaretur.
inter sermonem eius (credo rem Antiatem diuturniorem man- 3
ere dis cordi fuisse) legati ab Nepete ac Sutrio auxilium
aduersus Etruscos petentes ueniunt, breuem occasionem esse
ferendi auxilii memorantes. eo uim Camilli ab Antio fortuna
auertit. namque cum ea loca opposita Etruriae et uelut 4
claustra inde portaeque essent, et illis occupandi ea cum
quid noui molirentur et Romanis reciperandi tuendique
cura erat. igitur senatui cum Camillo agi placuit ut omisso 5
Antio bellum Etruscum susciperet; legiones urbanae quibus
Quinctius praefuerat ei decernuntur. quamquam expertum 6
exercitum assuetumque imperio qui in Volscis erat mallet,
nihil recusauit; Valerium tantummodo imperii socium depo-
poscit. Quinctius Horatiusque successores Valerio in Volscos
missi.

Profecti ab urbe Sutrium Furius et Valerius partem oppidi 7
iam captam ab Etruscis inuenere, ex parte altera intersaeptis
itineribus aegre oppidanos uim hostium ab se arcentes. cum 8
Romani auxilii aduentus tum Camilli nomen celeberrimum
apud hostes sociosque et in praesentia rem inclinatam susti-

nuit et spatium ad opem ferendam dedit. itaque diuiso exer- 9
citu Camillus collegam in eam partem circumductis copiis
quam hostes tenebant moenia aggredi iubet, non tanta spe
scalis capi urbem posse quam ut auersis eo hostibus et oppidanis iam pugnando fessis laxaretur labor et ipse spatium in-
trandi sine certamine moenia haberet. quod cum simul 10
utrimque factum esset ancepsque terror Etruscos circum-
staret et moenia summa ui oppugnari et intra moenia esse
hostem uiderent, porta se, quae una forte non obsidebatur,
trepidi uno agmine eiecere. magna caedes fugientium et in 11
urbe et per agros est facta: plures a Furianis intra moenia
caesi, Valeriani expeditiores ad persequendos fuere, nec ante
noctem, quae conspectum ademit, finem caedendi fecere.

  Sutrio recepto restitutoque sociis Nepete exercitus ductus, 12
quod per deditionem acceptum iam totum Etrusci habebant.
uidebatur plus in ea urbe recipienda laboris fore, non eo so- **10**
lum quod tota hostium erat sed etiam quod parte Nepesinorum prodente ciuitatem facta erat deditio. mitti tamen ad 2
principes eorum placuit ut secernerent se ab Etruscis fidemque
quam implorassent ab Romanis ipsi praestarent. unde cum 3
responsum allatum esset nihil suae potestatis esse, Etruscos
moenia custodiasque portarum tenere, primo populationibus
agri terror est oppidanis admotus; deinde, postquam deditio- 4
nis quam societatis fides sanctior erat, fascibus sarmentorum
ex agro collatis ductus ad moenia exercitus completisque fos-
sis scalae admotae et clamore primo impetuque oppidum
capitur. Nepesinis inde edictum ut arma ponant parcique 5
iussum inermi; Etrusci pariter armati atque inermes caesi.
Nepesinorum quoque auctores deditionis securi percussi; in-
noxiae multitudini redditae res oppidumque cum praesidio relictum. ita duabus sociis urbibus ex hoste receptis uictorem 6
exercitum tribuni cum magna gloria Romam reduxerunt.

9.9 non tanta **N**: montana *M*: non tam *Alschefski*   9.11 persequendos ω:
-dum *rec. unus, M. Müller*: -dos eos *Fügner*

Eodem anno ab Latinis Hernicisque res repetitae quaesi-
tumque cur per eos annos militem ex instituto non dedissent. responsum frequenti utriusque gentis concilio est nec 7
culpam in eo publicam nec consilium fuisse quod suae iuuentutis aliqui apud Volscos militauerint; eos tamen ipsos praui 8
consilii poenam habere nec quemquam ex his reducem esse;
militis autem non dati causam terrorem assiduum a Volscis
fuisse, quam pestem adhaerentem lateri suo tot super alia
aliis bellis exhauriri nequisse. quae relata patribus magis 9
tempus quam causam non uisa belli habere.

Insequenti anno, A. Manlio P. Cornelio T. et L. Quinctiis **11**
Capitolinis L. Papirio Cursore iterum Cn. Sergio iterum tribunis consulari potestate, graue bellum foris, grauior domi
seditio exorta, bellum ab Volscis adiuncta Latinorum atque 2
Hernicorum defectione, seditio unde minime timeri potuit, a
patriciae gentis uiro et inclitae famae, M. Manlio Capitolino.
qui nimius animi cum alios principes sperneret, uni inuideret 3
eximio simul honoribus atque uirtutibus, M. Furio, aegre ferebat solum eum in magistratibus, solum apud exercitus esse:
tantum iam eminere ut iisdem auspiciis creatos non pro col- 4
legis sed pro ministris habeat, cum interim, si quis uere aestimare uelit, a M. Furio reciperari patria ex obsidione hostium non potuerit nisi a se prius Capitolium atque arx
seruata esset; et ille inter aurum accipiendum et in spem pa- 5
cis solutis animis Gallos aggressus sit, ipse armatos capien-
tesque arcem depulerit; illius gloriae pars uirilis apud omnes
milites sit qui simul uicerint: suae uictoriae neminem omnium mortalium socium esse. his opinionibus inflato animo, 6
ad hoc uitio quoque ingenii uehemens et impotens, postquam inter patres non quantum aequum censebat excellere
suas opes animaduertit, primus omnium ex patribus popu- 7

11.1 ⟨iterum Cn. Sergio⟩ *MRR I 101–2* (*iam* ⟨iterum C. Sergio⟩ *Glareanus,
Sigonius*)

laris factus cum plebeiis magistratibus consilia communicare;
criminando patres, alliciendo ad se plebem iam aura non
consilio ferri famaeque magnae malle quam bonae esse.

Et non contentus agrariis legibus, quae materia semper tri- 8
bunis plebi seditionum fuisset, fidem moliri coepit: acriores
quippe aeris alieni stimulos esse, qui non egestatem modo
atque ignominiam minentur sed neruo ac uinculis corpus liberum territent. et erat aeris alieni magna uis re damnosis- 9
sima etiam diuitibus, aedificando, contracta. bellum itaque
Volscum, graue per se, oneratum Latinorum atque Hernicorum defectione, in speciem causae iactatum ut maior potestas quaereretur; sed noua consilia Manli magis compulere 10
senatum ad dictatorem creandum. creatus A. Cornelius Cossus magistrum equitum dixit T. Quinctium Capitolinum.

Dictator etsi maiorem dimicationem propositam domi **12**
quam foris cernebat, tamen, seu quia celeritate ad bellum
opus erat, seu uictoria triumphoque dictaturae ipsi uires se
additurum ratus, dilectu habito in agrum Pomptinum, quo
a Volscis exercitum indictum audierat, pergit.

Non dubito praeter satietatem tot iam libris assidua bella 2
cum Volscis gesta legentibus illud quoque succursurum, quod
mihi percensenti propiores temporibus harum rerum auctores miraculo fuit, unde totiens uictis Volscis et Aequis suf-
fecerint milites. quod cum ab antiquis tacitum praetermissum 3
sit, cuius tandem ego rei praeter opinionem, quae sua cuique
coniectanti esse potest, auctor sim? simile ueri est aut inter- 4
uallis bellorum, sicut nunc in dilectibus fit Romanis, alia atque alia subole iuniorum ad bella instauranda totiens usos
esse, aut non ex iisdem semper populis exercitus scriptos,
quamquam eadem semper gens bellum intulerit, aut innu- 5
merabilem multitudinem liberorum capitum in eis fuisse locis
quae nunc uix seminario exiguo militum relicto seruitia Romana ab solitudine uindicant. ingens certe, quod inter 6
omnes auctores conueniat, quamquam nuper Camilli ductu

atque auspicio accisae res erant, Volscorum exercitus fuit;
ad hoc Latini Hernicique accesserant et Circeiensium quidam et coloni etiam a Velitris Romani.

Dictator castris eo die positis, postero cum auspicato pro- 7
disset hostiaque caesa pacem deum adorasset, laetus ad milites iam arma ad propositum pugnae signum (sicut edictum
erat) luce prima capientes processit. 'nostra uictoria est, mili- 8
tes' inquit, 'si quid di uatesque eorum in futurum uident. itaque, ut decet certae spei plenos et cum imparibus manus
conserturos, pilis ante pedes positis gladiis tantum dextras ar-
memus. ne procurri quidem ab acie uelim sed obnixos uos
stabili gradu impetum hostium excipere. ubi illi uana in- 9
iecerint missilia et effusi stantibus uobis se intulerint, tum
micent gladii et ueniat in mentem unicuique deos esse qui
Romanum adiuuent, deos qui secundis auibus in proelium
miserint. tu, T. Quincti, equitem intentus ad primum initium 10
moti certaminis teneas; ubi haerere iam aciem collato pede
uideris, tum terrorem equestrem occupatis alio pauore infer
inuectusque ordines pugnantium dissipa.' sic eques, sic pe- 11
des, ut praeceperat, pugnant; nec dux legiones nec fortuna
fefellit ducem.

Multitudo hostium nulli rei praeterquam numero freta et **13**
oculis utramque metiens aciem temere proelium iniit, temere
omisit; clamore tantum missilibusque telis et primo pugnae 2
impetu ferox gladios et collatum pedem et uultum hostis ardore animi micantem ferre non potuit. impulsa frons prima 3
et trepidatio subsidiis illata; et suum terrorem intulit eques;
rupti inde multis locis ordines motaque omnia et fluctuanti
similis acies erat. dein postquam cadentibus primis iam ad
se quisque peruenturam caedem cernebat, terga uertunt. in- 4
stare Romanus; et donec armati confertique abibant, peditum labor in persequendo fuit: postquam iactari arma passim fugaque per agros spargi aciem hostium animaduersum
est, tum equitum turmae emissae, dato signo ne in singulorum morando caede spatium ad euadendum interim multi-

tudini darent: satis esse missilibus ac terrore impediri cursum 5
obequitandoque agmen teneri dum assequi pedes et iusta
caede conficere hostem posset. fugae sequendique non ante 6
noctem finis fuit. capta quoque ac direpta eodem die castra
Volscorum praedaque omnis praeter libera corpora militi
concessa est. pars maxima captiuorum ex Latinis atque Her- 7
nicis fuit, nec hominum de plebe, ut credi posset mercede militasse, sed principes quidam iuuentutis inuenti, manifesta fides publica ope Volscos hostes adiutos. Circeiensium 8
quoque quidam cogniti et coloni a Velitris; Romamque
omnes missi percontantibus primoribus patrum eadem quae
dictatori, defectionem sui quisque populi, haud perplexe
indicauere.

   Dictator exercitum in statiuis tenebat, minime dubius bel- **14**
lum cum iis populis patres iussuros, cum maior domi exorta
moles coegit acciri Romam eum gliscente in dies seditione,
quam solito magis metuendam auctor faciebat. (non enim 2
iam orationes modo M. Manli sed facta, popularia in speciem, tumultuosa eadem qua mente fierent intuenti erant.)
centurionem, nobilem militaribus factis, iudicatum pecuniae 3
cum duci uidisset, medio foro cum caterua sua accurrit et
manum iniecit; uociferatusque de superbia patrum ac crudelitate feneratorum et miseriis plebis, uirtutibus eius uiri fortunaque, 'tum uero ego' inquit 'nequiquam hac dextra Capi- 4
tolium arcemque seruauerim, si ciuem commilitonemque
meum tamquam Gallis uictoribus captum in seruitutem ac
uincula duci uideam.' inde rem creditori palam populo soluit 5
libraque et aere liberatum emittit, deos atque homines obtestantem ut M. Manlio, liberatori suo, parenti plebis Romanae, gratiam referant. acceptus extemplo in tumultuosam 6
turbam et ipse tumultum augebat, cicatrices acceptas Veienti
Gallico aliisque deinceps bellis ostentans: se militantem, se 7
restituentem euersos penates, multiplici iam sorte exsoluta,

14.2 intuenti *Gronovius*: intuenda ω

mergentibus semper sortem usuris, obrutum fenore esse; uidere lucem forum ciuium ora M. Manli opera, omnia parentum beneficia ab illo se habere; illi deuouere corporis 8
uitaeque ac sanguinis quod supersit; quodcumque sibi cum
patria, penatibus publicis ac priuatis, iuris fuerit, id cum
uno homine esse. his uocibus instincta plebes cum iam unius 9
hominis esset, addita alia commodioris ad omnia turbanda
consilii res. fundum in Veienti, caput patrimonii, subiecit 10
praeconi, 'ne quem uestrum' inquit, 'Quirites, donec quicquam in re mea supererit, iudicatum addictumue duci patiar.' id uero ita accendit animos, ut per omne fas ac nefas
secuturi uindicem libertatis uiderentur.

Ad hoc domi contionantis in modum sermones pleni crim- 11
inum in patres; inter quos omisso discrimine uera an uana
iaceret, thesauros Gallici auri occultari a patribus iecit nec
iam possidendis publicis agris contentos esse nisi pecuniam
quoque publicam auertant; ea res si palam fiat, exsolui plebem aere alieno posse. quae ubi obiecta spes est, enimuero 12
indignum facinus uideri, cum conferendum ad redimendam
ciuitatem a Gallis aurum fuerit, tributo collationem factam,
idem aurum ex hostibus captum in paucorum praedam cessisse. itaque exsequebantur quaerendo ubi tantae rei furtum 13
occultaretur; differentique et tempore suo se indicaturum dicenti ceteris omissis eo uersae erant omnium curae apparebatque nec ueri indicii gratiam mediam nec falsi offensionem fore.

Ita suspensis rebus dictator accitus ab exercitu in urbem 15
uenit. postero die senatu habito, cum satis periclitatus uolun-
tates hominum discedere senatum ab se uetuisset, stipatus ea
multitudine sella in comitio posita uiatorem ad M. Manlium
misit; qui dictatoris iussu uocatus, cum signum suis dedisset 2
adesse certamen, agmine ingenti ad tribunal uenit. hinc sena- 3
tus, hinc plebs, suum quisque intuentes ducem, uelut in acie

14.11 quos *rec. unus, Drakenborch*: quos cum ω

constiterant. tum dictator silentio facto, 'utinam' inquit, 4
'mihi patribusque Romanis ita de ceteris rebus cum plebe
conueniat, quemadmodum, quod ad te attinet eamque rem
quam de te sum quaesiturus conuenturum satis confido.
spem factam a te ciuitati uideo fide incolumi ex thesauris 5
Gallicis, quos primores patrum occultent, creditum solui
posse. cui ego rei tantum abest ut impedimento sim ut contra te, M. Manli, adhorter, liberes fenore plebem Romanam
et istos incubantes publicis thesauris ex praeda clandestina
euoluas. quod nisi facis, siue ut et ipse in parte praedae sis 6
siue quia uanum indicium est, in uincla te duci iubebo nec
diutius patiar a te multitudinem fallaci spe concitari.'

Ad ea Manlius nec se fefellisse ait non aduersus Volscos, 7
totiens hostes quotiens patribus expediat, nec aduersus Latinos Hernicosque, quos falsis criminibus in arma agant, sed
aduersus se ac plebem Romanam dictatorem creatum esse;
iam omisso bello quod simulatum sit in se impetum fieri; 8
iam dictatorem profiteri patrocinium feneratorum aduersus
plebem; iam sibi ex fauore multitudinis crimen et perniciem
quaeri. 'offendit' inquit, 'te, A. Corneli, uosque, patres con- 9
scripti, circumfusa turba lateri meo? quin eam diducitis a me
singuli uestris beneficiis, intercedendo, eximendo de neruo
ciues uestros, prohibendo iudicatos addictosque duci, ex eo
quod afluit opibus uestris sustinendo necessitates aliorum?
sed quid ego uos de uestro impendatis hortor? sortem reli- 10
quam ferte: de capite deducite quod usuris pernumeratum
est; iam nihilo mea turba quam ullius conspectior erit. at 11
enim quid ita solus ego ciuium curam ago? nihilo magis
quod respondeam habeo quam si quaeras quid ita solus Capitolium arcemque seruauerim. et tum uniuersis quam potui
opem tuli et nunc singulis feram. nam quod ad thesauros 12
Gallicos attinet, rem suapte natura facilem difficilem interrogatio facit. cur enim quaeritis quod scitis? cur quod in sinu
uestro est excuti iubetis potius quam ponatis, nisi aliqua
fraus subest? quo magis argui praestigias iubetis uestras, eo 13

plus uereor ne abstuleritis obseruantibus etiam oculos. itaque
non ego uobis ut indicem praedas uestras, sed uos id cogendi
estis ut in medium proferatis.'

Cum mittere ambages dictator iuberet et aut peragere **16**
uerum indicium cogeret aut fateri facinus insimulati falso
crimine senatus oblataeque uani furti inuidiae, negantem arbitrio inimicorum se locuturum in uincla duci iussit. arreptus 2
a uiatore 'Iuppiter' inquit, 'optime maxime Iunoque regina
ac Minerua ceterique di deaeque, qui Capitolium arcemque
incolitis, sicine uestrum militem ac praesidem sinitis uexari
ab inimicis? haec dextra, qua Gallos fudi a delubris uestris,
iam in uinclis et catenis erit?' nullius nec oculi nec aures 3
indignitatem ferebant; sed inuicta sibi quaedam patientissima
iusti imperii ciuitas fecerat, nec aduersus dictatoriam uim aut
tribuni plebis aut ipsa plebs attollere oculos aut hiscere aude-
bant. coniecto in carcerem Manlio satis constat magnam 4
partem plebis uestem mutasse, multos mortales capillum ac
barbam promisisse, obuersatamque uestibulo carceris maestam turbam.

Dictator de Volscis triumphauit, inuidiaeque magis trium- 5
phus quam gloriae fuit; quippe domi non militiae partum
eum actumque de ciue non de hoste fremebant: unum de-
fuisse tantum superbiae, quod non M. Manlius ante currum
sit ductus. iamque haud procul seditione res erat. cuius le- 6
niendae causa postulante nullo largitor uoluntarius repente
senatus factus Satricum coloniam duo milia ciuium Romanorum deduci iussit. bina iugera et semisses agri assignati.
quod cum et paruum et paucis datum et mercedem esse pro- 7
dendi M. Manli interpretarentur, remedio irritatur seditio.

Et iam magis insignis et sordibus et facie reorum turba 8
Manliana erat, amotusque post triumphum abdicatione dictaturae terror et linguam et animos liberauerat hominum.
audiebantur itaque propalam uoces exprobrantium multitu- **17**
dini, quod defensores suos semper in praecipitem locum
fauore tollat, deinde in ipso discrimine periculi destituat: sic 2

Sp. Cassium in agros plebem uocantem, sic Sp. Maelium ab
ore ciuium famem suis impensis propulsantem oppressos, sic
M. Manlium mersam et obrutam fenore partem ciuitatis in
libertatem ac lucem extrahentem proditum inimicis. saginare plebem populares suos ut iugulentur. hocine patien- 3
dum fuisse, si ad nutum dictatoris non responderit uir consularis? fingerent mentitum ante atque ideo non habuisse quod
tum responderet; cui seruo umquam mendacii poenam uincula fuisse? non obuersatam esse memoriam noctis illius 4
quae paene ultima atque aeterna nomini Romano fuerit?
non speciem agminis Gallorum per Tarpeiam rupem scandentis? non ipsius M. Manli, qualem eum armatum, plenum
sudoris ac sanguinis ipso paene Ioue erepto ex hostium manibus uidissent? selibrisne farris gratiam seruatori patriae rela- 5
tam? et quem prope caelestem, cognomine certe Capitolino
Ioui parem fecerint eum pati uinctum in carcere, in tenebris
obnoxiam carnificis arbitrio ducere animam? adeo in uno
omnibus satis auxilii fuisse, nullam opem in tam multis uni
esse? iam ne nocte quidem turba ex eo loco dilabebatur re- 6
fracturosque carcerem minabantur, cum remisso quod erepturi erant ex senatus consulto Manlius uinculis liberatur.
quo facto non seditio finita sed dux seditioni datus est.

Per eosdem dies Latinis et Hernicis, simul colonis Cir- 7
ceiensibus et a Velitris, purgantibus se Volsci crimine belli
captiuosque repetentibus ut suis legibus in eos animaduerter-
ent, tristia responsa reddita, tristiora colonis quod ciues
Romani patriae oppugnandae nefanda consilia inissent. non 8
negatum itaque tantum de captiuis sed, in quo ab sociis tamen temperauerant, denuntiatum senatus uerbis facesserent
propere ex urbe ab ore atque oculis populi Romani, ne nihil
eos legationis ius externo, non ciui comparatum tegeret.

Recrudescente Manliana seditione sub exitum anni comitia **18**
habita creatique tribuni militum consulari potestate Ser.
Cornelius Maluginensis iterum P. Valerius Potitus iterum
M. Furius Camillus quintum Ser. Sulpicius Rufus iterum C.

Papirius Crassus T. Quinctius Cincinnatus iterum. cuius 2
principio anni et patribus et plebi peropportune externa pax
data: plebi, quod non auocata dilectu spem cepit, dum tam
potentem haberet ducem, fenoris expugnandi; patribus, ne
quo externo terrore auocarentur animi ab sanandis domesticis malis. igitur cum pars utraque acrior aliquanto coorta 3
esset, iam propinquum certamen aderat.

Et Manlius aduocata domum plebe cum principibus
nouandarum rerum interdiu noctuque consilia agitat, ple-
nior aliquanto animorum irarumque quam antea fuerat.
iram accenderat ignominia recens in animo ad contumeliam 4
inexperto; spiritus dabat, quod nec ausus esset idem in se
dictator quod in Sp. Maelio Cincinnatus Quinctius fecisset,
et uinculorum suorum inuidiam non dictator modo abdicando dictaturam fugisset sed ne senatus quidem sustinere
potuisset. his simul inflatus exacerbatusque iam per se accen- 5
sos incitabat plebis animos: 'quousque tandem ignorabitis
uires uestras, quas natura ne beluas quidem ignorare uoluit?
numerate saltem quot ipsi sitis, quot aduersarios habeatis.
quot enim clientes circa singulos fuistis patronos, tot nunc
aduersus unum hostem eritis. si singuli singulos aggressuri 6
essetis, tamen acrius crederem uos pro libertate quam illos
pro dominatione certaturos. ostendite modo bellum; pacem 7
habebitis. uideant uos paratos ad uim; ius ipsi remittent. audendum est aliquid uniuersis aut omnia singulis patienda.

'Quousque me circumspectabitis? ego quidem nulli ues- 8
trum deero; ne fortuna mea desit uidete. ipse uindex uester,
ubi uisum inimicis est, nullus repente fui, et uidistis in uincula duci uniuersi eum qui a singulis uobis uincula depuleram. quid sperem, si plus in me audeant inimici? an 9
exitum Cassi Maelique exspectem? bene facitis quod abominamini. "di prohibebunt haec"; sed numquam propter me
de caelo descendent; uobis dent mentem oportet ut prohi-

18.5 quot enim ... eritis *post* habeatis *Walters*: *post* certaturos (6) ω

beatis, sicut mihi dederunt armato togatoque ut uos a barbaris hostibus, a superbis defenderem ciuibus.

'Tam paruus animus tanti populi est ut semper uobis auxi- 10
lium aduersus inimicos satis sit nec ullum, nisi quatenus imperari uobis sinatis, certamen aduersus patres noritis? nec
hoc natura insitum uobis est, sed usu possidemini. cur enim 11
aduersus externos tantum animorum geritis ut imperare illis
aequum censeatis? quia consuestis cum eis pro imperio certare, aduersus hos temptare magis quam tueri libertatem. ta- 12
men, qualescumque duces habuistis, qualescumque ipsi fuistis, omnia adhuc quantacumque petistis obtinuistis, seu ui
seu fortuna uestra. tempus est iam maiora conari. 13

'Experimini modo et uestram felicitatem et me, ut spero,
feliciter expertum; minore negotio qui imperet patribus im-
ponetis quam qui resisterent imperantibus imposuistis. solo 14
aequandae sunt dictaturae consulatusque, ut caput attollere
Romana plebes possit. proinde adeste; prohibete ius de pecu-
niis dici. ego me patronum profiteor plebis, quod mihi cura
mea et fides nomen induit: uos si quo insigni magis imperii 15
honorisue nomine uestrum appellabitis ducem, eo utemini
potentiore ad obtinenda ea quae uultis.' inde de regno 16
agendi ortum initium dicitur; sed nec cum quibus nec quem
ad finem consilia peruenerint satis planum traditur.

At in parte altera senatus de secessione in domum priua- **19**
tam plebis, forte etiam in arce positam, et imminenti mole
libertati agitat. magna pars uociferantur Seruilio Ahala opus 2
esse, qui non in uincla duci iubendo irritet publicum hostem
sed unius iactura ciuis finiat intestinum bellum. decurritur ad 3
leniorem uerbis sententiam, uim tamen eandem habentem,
ut uideant magistratus ne quid ex perniciosis consiliis M.
Manli res publica detrimenti capiat. tum tribuni consulari 4
potestate tribunique plebi – nam ei, quia eundem et suae
potestatis, quem libertatis omnium, finem cernebant, patrum

18.13 iam *Gronovius*: etiam ω (*om. O*)   19.4 ei *U*: et *MEOPH*

auctoritati se dediderant – hi tum omnes quid opus facto sit
consultant. cum praeter uim et caedem nihil cuiquam occur- 5
reret, eam autem ingentis dimicationis fore appareret, tum
M. Menenius et Q. Publilius tribuni plebis: 'quid patrum et 6
plebis certamen facimus, quod ciuitatis esse aduersus unum
pestiferum ciuem debet? quid cum plebe aggredimur eum
quem per ipsam plebem tutius aggredi est ut suis ipse oner-
atus uiribus ruat? diem dicere ei nobis in animo est. nihil 7
minus populare quam regnum est. simul multitudo illa non
secum certari uiderint et ex aduocatis iudices facti erunt et
accusatores de plebe patricium reum intuebuntur et regni
crimen in medio, nulli magis quam libertati fauebunt suae.'
approbantibus cunctis diem Manlio dicunt.   **20**

Quod ubi est factum, primo commota plebs est, utique 2
postquam sordidatum reum uiderunt nec cum eo non modo
patrum quemquam sed ne cognatos quidem aut affines, postremo ne fratres quidem A. et T. Manlios, quod ad eum diem
numquam usu uenisset, ut in tanto discrimine non et proximi
uestem mutarent: Ap. Claudio in uincula ducto C. Claudium 3
inimicum Claudiamque omnem gentem sordidatam fuisse;
consensu opprimi popularem uirum, quod primus a patribus
ad plebem defecisset.

Cum dies uenit, quae praeter coetus multitudinis seditio- 4
sasque uoces et largitionem et fallax indicium pertinentia
proprie ad regni crimen ab accusatoribus obiecta sint reo,
apud neminem auctorem inuenio; nec dubito haud parua 5
fuisse, cum damnandi mora plebi non in causa sed in loco
fuerit. illud notandum uidetur, ut sciant homines quae et
quanta decora foeda cupiditas regni non ingrata solum sed
inuisa etiam reddiderit: homines prope quadringentos pro- 6
duxisse dicitur, quibus sine fenore expensas pecunias tulisset,
quorum bona uenire, quos duci addictos prohibuisset; ad 7
haec decora quoque belli non commemorasse tantum sed
protulisse etiam conspicienda, spolia hostium caesorum ad
triginta, dona imperatorum ad quadraginta, in quibus in-

signes duas murales coronas, ciuicas octo; ad hoc seruatos 8
ex hostibus ciues [produxit], inter quos C. Seruilium magistrum equitum absentem nominatum; et cum ea quoque quae
bello gesta essent pro fastigio rerum oratione etiam magnifica, facta dictis aequando, memorasset, nudasse pectus insigne cicatricibus bello acceptis et identidem Capitolium 9
spectans Iouem deosque alios deuocasse ad auxilium fortu-
narum suarum precatusque esse ut, quam mentem sibi Capitolinam arcem protegenti ad salutem populi Romani
dedissent, eam populo Romano in suo discrimine darent, et
orasse singulos uniuersosque ut Capitolium atque arcem intuentes, ut ad deos immortales uersi de se iudicarent.

In campo Martio cum centuriatim populus citaretur et 10
reus ad Capitolium manus tendens ab hominibus ad deos
preces auertisset, apparuit tribunis, nisi oculos quoque hominum liberassent tanti memoria decoris, numquam fore in
praeoccupatis beneficio animis uero crimini locum. ita pro- 11
dicta die in Petelinum lucum extra portam Flumentanam,
unde conspectus in Capitolium non esset, concilium populi
indictum est. ibi crimen ualuit et obstinatis animis triste iudi-
cium inuisumque etiam iudicibus factum. sunt qui per duum- 12
uiros, qui de perduellione anquirerent creatos, auctores sint
damnatum.

Tribuni de saxo Tarpeio deiecerunt locusque idem in uno
nomine et eximiae gloriae monumentum et poenae ultimae
fuit. adiectae mortuo notae sunt: publica una, quod, cum do- 13
mus eius fuisset ubi nunc aedes atque officina Monetae est,
latum ad populum est ne quis patricius in arce aut Capitolio
habitaret; gentilicia altera, quod gentis Manliae decreto cau- 14
tum est ne quis deinde M. Manlius uocaretur. hunc exitum
habuit uir, nisi in libera ciuitate natus esset, memorabilis.
populum breui, postquam periculum ab eo nullum erat, per 15
se ipsas recordantem uirtutes desiderium eius tenuit. pestilentia

20.8 [produxit] *Rhenanus*

etiam breui consecuta nullis occurrentibus tantae cladis causis
ex Manliano supplicio magnae parti uideri orta: uiola- 16
tum Capitolium esse sanguine seruatoris nec dis cordi fuisse
poenam eius oblatam prope oculis suis, a quo sua templa
erepta e manibus hostium essent.

Pestilentiam inopia frugum et uulgatam utriusque mali fa- 21
mam anno insequente multiplex bellum excepit, L. Valerio
quartum A. Manlio tertium Ser. Sulpicio tertium L. Lucretio
L. Aemilio tertium M. Trebonio tribunis militum consulari
potestate. hostes noui praeter Volscos, uelut sorte quadam 2
prope in aeternum exercendo Romano militi datos, Circeiosque et Velitras colonias, iam diu molientes defectionem, et
suspectum Latium, Lanuuini etiam, quae fidelissima urbs
fuerat, subito exorti. id patres rati contemptu accidere, 3
quod Veliternis ciuibus suis tam diu impunita defectio esset,
decreuerunt ut primo quoque tempore ad populum ferretur
de bello eis indicendo. ad quam militiam quo paratior 4
plebes esset, quinqueuiros Pomptino agro diuidendo et trium-
uiros Nepete coloniae deducendae creauerunt. tum, ut 5
bellum iuberent, latum ad populum est et nequiquam dissuadentibus tribunis plebis omnes tribus bellum iusserunt. appar- 6
atum eo anno bellum est, exercitus propter pestilentiam non
eductus; eaque cunctatio colonis spatium dederat deprecandi
senatum et magna hominum pars eo ut legatio supplex Romam mitteretur inclinabat, ni priuato (ut fit) periculo publi- 7
cum implicitum esset auctoresque defectionis ab Romanis
metu, ne soli crimini subiecti piacula irae Romanorum de-
derentur, auertissent colonias a consiliis pacis. neque in senatu 8
solum per eos legatio impedita est sed magna pars plebis in-
citata ut praedatum in agrum Romanum exirent. haec noua
iniuria exturbauit omnem spem pacis. de Praenestinorum 9
quoque defectione eo anno primum fama exorta; arguenti-
busque eos Tusculanis et Gabinis et Labicanis, quorum in
fines incursatum erat, ita placide ab senatu responsum est

ut minus credi de criminibus, quia nollent ea uera esse,
appareret.

Insequenti anno Sp. et L. Papirii noui tribuni militum con- **22**
sulari potestate Velitras legiones duxere, quattuor collegis
Ser. Cornelio Maluginensi tertium Q. Seruilio C. Sulpicio
L. Aemilio quartum tribunis ad praesidium urbis et si qui
ex Etruria noui motus nuntiarentur (omnia enim inde sus-
pecta erant) relictis. ad Velitras aduersus maiora paene aux- 2
ilia Praenestinorum quam ipsam colonorum multitudinem secundo proelio pugnatum est ita ut propinquitas urbis hosti et
causa maturioris fugae et unum ex fuga receptaculum esset.
oppidi oppugnatione tribuni abstinuere, quia et anceps erat 3
nec in perniciem coloniae pugnandum censebant. litterae
Romam ad senatum cum uictoriae nuntiis acriores in Prae-
nestinum quam in Veliternum hostem missae. itaque ex sena- 4
tus consulto populique iussu bellum Praenestinis indictum;
qui coniuncti Volscis anno insequente Satricum, coloniam
populi Romani, pertinaciter a colonis defensam, ui expugna-
runt foedeque in captis exercuere uictoriam.

Eam rem aegre passi Romani M. Furium Camillum 5
sextum tribunum militum creauere; additi collegae A. et L.
Postumii Regillenses ac L. Furius cum L. Lucretio et M.
Fabio Ambusto. Volscum bellum M. Furio extra ordinem de- 6
cretum; adiutor ex tribunis sorte L. Furius datur, non tam e
re publica quam ut collegae materia ad omnem laudem esset
et publice, quod rem temeritate eius prolapsam restituit, et
priuatim, quod ex errore gratiam potius eius sibi quam
suam gloriam petiit. exactae iam aetatis Camillus erat, comi- 7
tiisque iurare parato in uerba excusandae ualetudini solita
consensus populi restiterat; sed uegetum ingenium in uiuido
pectore uigebat uirebatque integris sensibus, et ciuiles iam
res haud magnopere obeuntem bella excitabant. quattuor 8

legionibus quaternum milium scriptis, exercitu indicto ad
portam Esquilinam in posteram diem ad Satricum profectus.

Ibi eum expugnatores coloniae haudquaquam perculsi,
fidentes militum numero quo aliquantum praestabant, oppe-
riebantur. postquam appropinquare Romanos senserunt, 9
extemplo in aciem procedunt nihil dilaturi quin periculum
summae rerum facerent: ita paucitati hostium nihil artes imperatoris unici, quibus solis confiderent, profuturas esse.
idem ardor et in Romano exercitu erat et in altero duce, **23**
nec praesentis dimicationis fortunam ulla res praeterquam
unius uiri consilium atque imperium morabatur, qui occasionem iuuandarum ratione uirium trahendo bello quaerebat.
eo magis hostis instare nec iam pro castris tantum suis expli- 2
care aciem sed procedere in medium campi et uallo prope
hostium signa inferendo superbam fiduciam uirium ostentare.

Id aegre patiebatur Romanus miles, multo aegrius alter ex 3
tribunis militum, L. Furius, ferox cum aetate et ingenio, tum
multitudinis ex incertissimo sumentis animos spe inflatus. hic 4
per se iam milites incitatos insuper instigabat eleuando, qua
una poterat, aetate auctoritatem collegae, iuuenibus bella
data dictitans et cum corporibus uigere et deflorescere animos; cunctatorem ex acerrimo bellatore factum et, qui adue- 5
niens castra urbesque primo impetu rapere sit solitus, eum
residem intra uallum tempus terere, quid accessurum suis de-
cessurumue hostium uiribus sperantem? quam occasionem, 6
quod tempus, quem insidiis instruendis locum? frigere ac tor-
pere senis consilia. sed Camillo cum uitae satis tum gloriae 7
esse; quid attinere cum mortali corpore uno ciuitatis quam
immortalem esse deceat pati consenescere uires?

His sermonibus tota in se auerterat castra; et cum omnibus 8
locis posceretur pugna, 'sustinere' inquit, 'M. Furi, non possumus impetum militum, et hostis, cuius animos cunctando

23.6 instruendis *Gronovius*: instruentem ω

auximus, iam minime toleranda superbia insultat. cede unus
omnibus et patere te uinci consilio ut maturius bello uincas.'
ad ea Camillus, quae bella suo unius auspicio gesta ad eam 9
diem essent, negare in eis neque se neque populum Romanum aut consilii sui aut fortunae paenituisse; nunc scire se
collegam habere iure imperioque parem, uigore aetatis
praestantem; itaque se, quod ad exercitum attineat, regere 10
consuesse, non regi: collegae imperium se non posse impedire. dis bene iuuantibus ageret quod e re publica duceret:
aetati suae se ueniam etiam petere ne in prima acie esset; 11
quae senis munia in bello sint, iis se non defuturum. id a dis
immortalibus precari ne qui casus suum consilium laudabile
efficiat.

Nec ab hominibus salutaris sententia nec a dis tam piae 12
preces auditae sunt. primam aciem auctor pugnae instruit,
subsidia Camillus firmat ualidamque stationem pro castris
opponit; ipse edito loco spectator intentus in euentum alieni
consilii constitit. simul primo concursu concrepuere arma, **24**
hostis dolo non metu pedem rettulit. lenis ab tergo cliuus 2
erat inter aciem et castra; et, quod multitudo suppeditabat,
aliquot ualidas cohortes in castris armatas instructasque reliquerant, quae inter commissum iam certamen, ubi uallo appropinquasset hostis, erumperent. Romanus cedentem hos- 3
tem effuse sequendo in locum iniquum pertractus opportunus
huic eruptioni fuit. uersus itaque in uictorem terror et nouo
hoste et supina ualle Romanam inclinauit aciem. instant 4
Volsci recentes qui e castris impetum fecerant; integrant et
illi pugnam qui simulata cesserant fuga. iam non recipiebat
se Romanus miles sed immemor recentis ferociae ueterisque
decoris terga passim dabat atque effuso cursu castra repetebat, cum Camillus subiectus ab circumstantibus in equum et 5
raptim subsidiis oppositis 'haec est' inquit, 'milites, pugna
quam poposcistis? quis homo, quis deus est, quem accusare
possitis? uestra illa temeritas, uestra ignauia haec est. secuti 6

alium ducem sequimini nunc Camillum et quod ductu meo
soletis uincite. quid uallum et castra spectatis? neminem uestrum illa nisi uictorem receptura sunt.'

Pudor primo tenuit effusos; inde, ut circumagi signa 7
obuertique aciem uiderunt in hostem et dux, praeterquam
quod tot insignis triumphis, etiam aetate uenerabilis inter
prima signa ubi plurimus labor periculumque erat se offere-
bat, increpare singuli se quisque et alios, et adhortatio in
uicem totam alacri clamore peruasit aciem. neque alter tri- 8
bunus rei defuit sed missus a collega restituente peditum
aciem ad equites, non castigando (ad quam rem leuiorem
auctorem eum culpae societas fecerat) sed ab imperio totus
ad preces uersus orare singulos uniuersosque ut se reum fortunae eius diei crimine eximerent: 'abnuente ac prohibente 9
collega temeritati me omnium potius socium quam unius
prudentiae dedi. Camillus in utraque uestra fortuna suam
gloriam uidet; ego, ni restituitur pugna, quod miserrimum
est, fortunam cum omnibus, infamiam solus sentiam.' opti- 10
mum uisum est in fluctuante acie tradi equos et pedestri
pugna inuadere hostem. eunt insignes armis animisque qua
premi parte maxime peditum copias uident. nihil neque apud
duces neque apud milites remittitur a summo certamine animi. sensit ergo euentus uirtutis enixae opem et Volsci, qua 11
modo simulato metu cesserant, ea in ueram fugam effusi;
magna pars et in ipso certamine et post in fuga caesi, ceteri
in castris quae capta eodem impetu sunt; plures tamen capti
quam occisi. ubi in recensendis captiuis cum Tusculani ali- **25**
quot noscitarentur, secreti ab aliis ad tribunos adducuntur
percontantibusque fassi publico consilio se militasse.

Cuius tam uicini belli metu Camillus motus extemplo se 2
Romam captiuos ducturum ait, ne patres ignari sint Tusculanos ab societate descisse: castris exercituique interim, si uideatur, praesit collega. documento unus dies fuerat, ne sua 3
consilia melioribus praeferret. nec tamen aut ipsi aut in exer-

citu cuiquam satis placato animo Camillus laturus culpam
eius uidebatur, qua data in tam praecipitem casum res publica esset; et cum in exercitu tum Romae constans omnium 4
fama erat, cum uaria fortuna in Volscis gesta res esset,
aduersae pugnae fugaeque in L. Furio culpam, secundae decus omne penes M. Furium esse. introductis in senatum cap- 5
tiuis cum bello persequendos Tusculanos patres censuissent
Camilloque id bellum mandassent, adiutorem sibi ad eam
rem unum petit, permissoque ut ex collegis optaret quem
uellet contra spem omnium L. Furium optauit; qua modera- 6
tione animi cum collegae leuauit infamiam tum sibi gloriam
ingentem peperit.

Nec fuit cum Tusculanis bellum: pace constanti uim Romanam arcuerunt quam armis non poterant. intrantibus fines 7
Romanis non demigratum ex propinquis itineri locis, non
cultus agrorum intermissus; patentibus portis urbis togati
obuiam frequentes imperatoribus processere; commeatus exercitui comiter in castra ex urbe et ex agris deuehitur. Camil- 8
lus castris ante portas positis, eademne forma pacis quae in
agris ostentaretur etiam intra moenia esset scire cupiens, in- 9
gressus urbem ubi patentes ianuas et tabernis apertis proposita omnia in medio uidit intentosque opifices suo quemque
operi et ludos litterarum strepere discentium uocibus ac repletas semitas inter uulgus aliud puerorum et mulierum huc
atque illuc euntium qua quemque suorum usuum causae ferrent, nihil usquam non pauidis modo sed ne mirantibus qui- 10
dem simile, circumspiciebat omnia, inquirens oculis ubinam
bellum fuisset: adeo nec amotae rei usquam nec oblatae ad 11
tempus uestigium ullum erat sed ita omnia constanti tranquilla pace ut eo uix fama belli perlata uideri posset. uictus **26**
igitur patientia hostium senatum eorum uocari iussit. 'soli
adhuc' inquit, 'Tusculani, uera arma uerasque uires quibus
ab ira Romanorum uestra tutaremini inuenistis. ite Romam 2
ad senatum; aestimabunt patres utrum plus ante poenae an

62 TITI LIVI

nunc ueniae meriti sitis. non praecipiam gratiam publici beneficii; deprecandi potestatem a me habueritis; precibus euentum uestris senatus quem uidebitur dabit.'

Postquam Romam Tusculani uenerunt senatusque paulo 3
ante fidelium sociorum maestus in uestibulo curiae est conspectus, moti extemplo patres uocari eos iam tum hospitaliter magis quam hostiliter iussere. dictator Tusculanus ita 4
uerba fecit: 'quibus bellum indixistis intulistisque, patres conscripti, sicut nunc uidetis nos stantes in uestibulo curiae uestrae, ita armati paratique obuiam imperatoribus legio-
nibusque uestris processimus. hic noster, hic plebis nostrae 5
habitus fuit eritque semper, nisi si quando a uobis proque
uobis arma acceperimus. gratias agimus et ducibus uestris et
exercitibus, quod oculis magis quam auribus crediderunt et
ubi nihil hostile erat ne ipsi quidem fecerunt. pacem, quam 6
nos praestitimus, eam a uobis petimus; bellum eo, sicubi est,
auertatis precamur. in nos quid arma polleant uestra, si pa-
tiendo experiundum est, inermes experiemur. haec mens nostra est (di immortales faciant!) tam felix quam pia. quod ad 7
crimina attinet quibus moti bellum indixistis, etsi reuicta rebus uerbis confutare nihil attinet, tamen, etiamsi uera sint,
uel fateri nobis ea, cum tam euidenter paenituerit, tutum
censemus. peccetur in uos, dum digni sitis quibus ita satisfiat.' tantum fere uerborum ab Tusculanis factum. pacem in 8
praesentia nec ita multo post ciuitatem etiam impetrauerunt.
ab Tusculo legiones reductae.

Camillus, consilio et uirtute in Volsco bello, felicitate in **27**
Tusculana expeditione, utrobique singulari aduersus col-
legam patientia et moderatione insignis, magistratu abiit 2
creatis tribunis militaribus in insequentem annum L. et P.
Valeriis (Lucio quintum, Publio tertium) Cn. Sergio tertium
Licino Menenio iterum P. Papirio Ser. Cornelio Maluginense.

27.2 Publio tertium *A*: P. t. et *cett.*   Cn. *cf. 11.1 adn.*: C. ω   Licino *cf.*
5.7 *adn.*: -nio ω (lucio *A*)

censoribus quoque eguit annus, maxime propter incertam 3
famam aeris alieni, aggrauantibus summam eius inuidiosius
tribunis plebis, cum ab iis eleuaretur quibus fide magis
quam fortuna debentium laborare creditum uideri expediebat.
creati censores C. Sulpicius Camerinus Sp. Postumius Regil- 4
lensis, coeptaque iam res morte Postumi, quia collegam suffici censori religio erat, interpellata est. igitur cum Sulpicius 5
abdicasset se magistratu, censores alii uitio creati non gesserunt magistratum; tertios creari uelut dis non accipientibus
in eum annum censuram religiosum fuit.

Eam uero ludificationem plebis tribuni ferendam negabant: 6
fugere senatum testes, tabulas publicas census cuiusque, quia
nolint conspici summam aeris alieni, quae indicatura sit demersam partem a parte ciuitatis, cum interim obaeratam plebem obiectari aliis atque aliis hostibus; passim iam sine ullo 7
discrimine bella quaeri: ab Antio Satricum, ab Satrico Velitras, inde Tusculum legiones ductas; Latinis Hernicis Praenestinis iam intentari arma ciuium magis quam hostium
odio, ut in armis terant plebem nec respirare in urbe aut
per otium libertatis meminisse sinant aut consistere in contione, ubi aliquando audiant uocem tribuniciam de leuando
fenore et finem aliarum iniuriarum agentem. quod si sit ani- 8
mus plebi memor patrum libertatis, se nec addici quemquam
ciuem Romanum ob creditam pecuniam passuros neque dilectum haberi, donec inspecto aere alieno initaque ratione
minuendi eius sciat unus quisque quid sui, quid alieni sit,
supersit sibi liberum corpus an id quoque neruo debeatur.

Merces seditionis proposita confestim seditionem excitauit. 9
nam et addicebantur multi, et ad Praenestini famam belli
nouas legiones scribendas patres censuerant. quae utraque
simul auxilio tribunicio et consensu plebis impediri coepta;
nam neque duci addictos tribuni sinebant neque iuniores 10

27.3 eius *Watt*: etiam ω   inuidiosius *Madvig*: inuidiae eius ω: inuidiae
causa *Perizonius*

nomina dabant. cum patribus minor in praesens cura creditae
pecuniae iuris exsequendi quam dilectus esset (quippe iam a
Praeneste profectos hostes in agro Gabino consedisse nuntiabatur) interim tribunos plebis fama ea ipsa irritauerat magis 11
ad susceptum certamen quam deterruerat neque aliud ad seditionem exstinguendam in urbe quam prope illatum moenibus ipsis bellum ualuit. nam cum esset Praenestinis nuntiatum **28**
nullum exercitum conscriptum Romae, nullum ducem cer-
tum esse, patres ac plebem in semet ipsos uersos, occasionem 2
rati duces eorum raptim agmine facto, peruastatis protinus
agris ad portam Collinam signa intulere. ingens in urbe tre- 3
pidatio fuit. conclamatum 'ad arma' concursumque in muros
adque portas est; tandemque ab seditione ad bellum uersi
dictatorem T. Quinctium Cincinnatum creauere. is magis- 4
trum equitum A. Sempronium Atratinum dixit. quod ubi
auditum est – tantus eius magistratus terror erat – simul hostes a moenibus recessere et iuniores Romani ad edictum sine
retractatione conuenere.

Dum conscribitur Romae exercitus, castra interim hostium 5
haud procul Allia flumine posita. inde agrum late popu-
lantes, fatalem se urbi Romanae locum cepisse inter se iacta-
bant: similem pauorem inde ac fugam fore ac bello Gallico 6
fuerit; etenim si diem contactum religione insignemque nomine eius loci timeant Romani, quanto magis Alliensi die
Alliam ipsam, monumentum tantae cladis, reformidaturos?
species profecto iis ibi truces Gallorum sonumque uocis in
oculis atque auribus fore. has inanium rerum inanes ipsas 7
uoluentes cogitationes fortunae loci delegauerant spes suas.
Romani contra: ubicumque esset Latinus hostis, satis scire
eum esse quem ad Regillum lacum deuictum centum annorum pace obnoxia tenuerint; locum insignem memoria cla- 8
dis irritaturum se potius ad delendam memoriam dedecoris

27.10 ⟨in⟩ *post* minor *Strothius*   28.3 adque *Gronovius*: atque ω (ad *supra*
in *A*ᶜ)

quam ut timorem faciat, ne qua terra sit nefasta uictoriae
suae; quin ipsi sibi Galli si offerantur illo loco, se ita 9
pugnaturos ut Romae pugnauerint in repetenda patria, ut
postero die ad Gabios, tunc cum effecerint ne quis hostis
qui moenia Romana intrasset nuntium secundae aduersaeque fortunae domum perferret.

His utrimque animis ad Alliam uentum est. dictator Ro- **29**
manus, postquam in conspectu hostes erant instructi intentique, 'uidesne tu' inquit, 'A. Semproni, loci fortuna illos fretos ad Alliam constitisse? nec illis di immortales certioris
quicquam fiduciae maiorisue quod sit auxilii dederint. at tu, 2
fretus armis animisque, concitatis equis inuade mediam
aciem; ego cum legionibus in turbatos trepidantesque in-
feram signa. adeste, di testes foederis, et expetite poenas deb-
itas simul uobis uiolatis nobisque per uestrum numen
deceptis.' non equitem, non peditem sustinuere Praenestini.
primo impetu ac clamore dissipati ordines sunt; dein, post- 3
quam nullo loco constabat acies, terga uertunt consterna-
tique et praeter castra etiam sua pauore praelati non prius
se ab effuso cursu sistunt quam in conspectu Praeneste fuit.
ibi ex fuga dissipata locum quem tumultuario opere commu- 4
nirent capiunt, ne, si intra moenia se recepissent, extemplo
ureretur ager depopulatisque omnibus obsidio urbi inferre-
tur. sed postquam direptis ad Alliam castris uictor Romanus 5
aderat, id quoque munimentum relictum; et uix moenia tuta
rati oppido se Praeneste includunt. octo praeterea oppida 6
erant sub dicione Praenestinorum. ad ea circumlatum bellum
deincepsque haud magno certamine captis Velitras exercitus ductus; eae quoque expugnatae. tum ad caput belli 7
Praeneste uentum; id non ui sed per deditionem receptum
est. T. Quinctius, semel acie uictor, binis castris hostium, 8
nouem oppidis ui captis, Praeneste in deditionem accepto

29.4 dissipata *Madvig*: -ti ω

Romam reuertit triumphansque signum Praeneste deuectum
Iouis Imperatoris in Capitolium tulit. dedicatum est inter 9
cellam Iouis ac Mineruae tabulaque sub eo fixa, monumentum rerum gestarum, his ferme incisa litteris fuit: 'Iuppiter
atque diui omnes hoc dederunt ut T. Quinctius dictator oppida nouem caperet.' die uicesimo quam creatus erat dicta- 10
tura se abdicauit.

Comitia inde habita tribunorum militum consulari potes- **30**
tate, quibus aequatus patriciorum plebeiorumque numerus.
ex patribus creati P. et C. Manlii cum L. Iulio; plebes C. 2
Sextilium M. Albinium L. Antistium dedit. Manliis, quod 3
genere plebeios, gratia Iulium anteibant, Volsci prouincia
sine sorte, sine comparatione, extra ordinem data; cuius et
ipsos postmodo et patres qui dederant paenituit. inexplorato 4
pabulatum cohortes misere; quibus uelut circumuentis, cum
id falso nuntiatum esset, dum praesidio ut essent citati ferun-
tur, ne auctore quidem asseruato qui eos hostis Latinus pro
milite Romano frustratus erat ipsi in insidias praecipitauere.
ibi dum iniquo loco sola uirtute militum restantes caedunt 5
caeduntur que, castra interim Romana iacentia in campo ab
altera parte hostes inuasere. ab ducibus utrobique proditae 6
temeritate atque inscitia res; quidquid superfuit fortunae
populi Romani, id militum etiam sine rectore stabilis uirtus
tutata est. quae ubi Romam sunt relata, primum dictato- 7
rem dici placebat; deinde, postquam quietae res ex Volscis
afferebantur et apparuit nescire eos uictoria et tempore uti,
reuocati etiam inde exercitus ac duces.

Otiumque inde, quantum a Volscis, fuit; id modo extremo 8
anno tumultuatum quod Praenestini concitatis Latinorum
populis rebellarunt. eodem anno Setiam ipsis querentibus 9
penuriam hominum noui coloni ascripti; rebusque haud
prosperis bello domestica quies, quam tribunorum militum
ex plebe gratia maiestasque inter suos obtinuit, solacium fuit.

Insequentis anni principia statim seditione ingenti arsere **31**
tribunis militum consulari potestate Sp. Furio Q. Seruilio

iterum Licino Menenio tertium P. Cloelio M. Horatio L. Ge-
ganio. erat autem et materia et causa seditionis aes alie- 2
num; cuius noscendi gratia Sp. Seruilius Priscus Q. Cloelius
Siculus censores facti ne rem agerent bello impediti sunt.
namque trepidi nuntii primo, fuga deinde ex agris legiones 3
Volscorum ingressas fines popularique passim Romanum
agrum attulere. in qua trepidatione tantum afuit ut ciuilia 4
certamina terror externus cohiberet, ut contra eo uiolentior
potestas tribunicia impediendo dilectu esset, donec condiciones impositae patribus ne quis, quoad debellatum esset,
tributum daret aut ius de pecunia credita diceret. eo laxa- 5
mento plebi sumpto mora dilectui non est facta.

Legionibus nouis scriptis placuit duos exercitus in agrum
Volscum legionibus diuisis duci. Sp. Furius M. Horatius dextrorsus in maritimam oram atque Antium, Q. Seruilius et L.
Geganius laeua ad montes et Ecetram pergunt. neutra parte 6
hostis obuius [fuit]. populatio itaque non illi uagae similis
quam Volscus latrocinii more, discordiae hostium fretus et
uirtutem metuens, per trepidationem raptim fecerat sed ab
iusto exercitu iusta ira facta, spatio quoque temporis
grauior. quippe a Volscis timentibus ne interim exercitus ab 7
Roma exiret incursiones in extrema finium factae erant;
Romano contra etiam in hostico morandi causa erat, ut hostem ad certamen eliceret. itaque omnibus passim tectis 8
agrorum uicisque etiam quibusdam exustis, non arbore frugi-
fera, non satis in spem frugum relictis, omni quae extra moenia fuit hominum pecudumque praeda abacta Romam
utrimque exercitus reducti.

Paruo interuallo ad respirandum debitoribus dato, post- 32
quam quietae res ab hostibus erant, celebrari de integro iuris
dictio et tantum abesse spes ueteris leuandi fenoris, ut tributo
nouum fenus contraheretur in murum a censoribus locatum

31.1 Licino cf. 5.7 adn.: -nio ω   31.4 debellatum Moorstadt: bellatum
ω   31.5 ⟨in⟩ post dextrorsus Madvig   et Ecetram Madvig: et cetram H:
ecetram Mπ   31.6 [fuit]Walters: h.o.f. MH: h.f.o. π: o.h.f. Bibl. Vat. 3329

saxo quadrato faciundum; cui succumbere oneri coacta 2
plebes, quia quem dilectum impedirent non habebant tribuni
plebis.

Tribunos etiam militares patricios omnes coacta princi- 3
pum opibus fecit, L. Aemilium P. Valerium quartum C. Ve-
turium Ser. Sulpicium L. et C. Quinctios Cincinnatos. iis- 4
dem opibus obtinuere ut aduersus Latinos Volscosque, qui
coniunctis legionibus ad Satricum castra habebant, nullo impediente omnibus iunioribus sacramento adactis tres exercitus scriberent, unum ad praesidium urbis; alterum qui, si qui 5
alibi motus exstitisset, ad subita belli mitti posset; tertium
longe ualidissimum P. Valerius et L. Aemilius ad Satricum
duxere. ubi cum aciem instructam hostium loco aequo 6
inuenissent, extemplo pugnatum; et ut nondum satis claram
uictoriam, sic prosperae spei pugnam imber ingentibus procellis fusus diremit.

Postero die iterata pugna; et aliquamdiu aequa uirtute 7
fortunaque Latinae maxime legiones longa societate militiam
Romanam edoctae restabant. sed eques immissus ordines 8
turbauit; turbatis signa peditum illata, quantumque Romana
se inuexit acies, tantum hostes gradu demoti; et ut semel inclinauit pugna, iam intolerabilis Romana uis erat. fusi hostes 9
cum Satricum, quod duo milia inde aberat, non castra pete-
rent, ab equite maxime caesi; castra capta direptaque. ab 10
Satrico nocte quae proelio proxima fuit fugae simili agmine
petunt Antium; et cum Romanus exercitus prope uestigiis se-
queretur, plus tamen timor quam ira celeritatis habuit. prius 11
itaque moenia intrauere hostes quam Romanus extrema agminis carpere aut morari posset. inde aliquot dies uastando
agro absumpti nec Romanis satis instructis apparatu bellico
ad moenia aggredienda nec illis ad subeundum pugnae
casum.

Seditio tum inter Antiates Latinosque coorta, cum Anti- **33**
ates uicti malis subactique bello in quo et nati erant et consenuerant deditionem spectarent, Latinos ex diutina pace noua 2

defectio recentibus adhuc animis ferociores ad perseuerandum in bello faceret. finis certaminis fuit postquam utrisque apparuit nihil per alteros stare quo minus incepta persequerentur. Latini profecti, ab societate pacis, ut rebantur, inhonestae sese uindicauerunt; Antiates incommodis arbitris salutarium consiliorum remotis urbem agrosque Romanis dedunt. 3

Ira et rabies Latinorum, quia nec Romanos bello laedere 4 nec Volscos in armis retinere potuerant, eo erupit ut Satricum urbem, quae receptaculum primum eis aduersae pugnae fuerat, igni concremarent. nec aliud tectum eius superfuit urbis, cum faces pariter sacris profanisque inicerent, quam Matris Matutae templum; inde eos nec sua religio 5 nec uerecundia deum arcuisse dicitur sed uox horrenda edita templo cum tristibus minis ni nefandos ignes procul delubris amouissent. incensos ea rabie impetus Tusculum tulit ob 6 iram, quod deserto communi concilio Latinorum non in societatem modo Romanam sed etiam in ciuitatem se dedissent. patentibus portis cum improuiso incidissent, primo clamore 7 oppidum praeter arcem captum est. in arcem oppidani refugere cum coniugibus ac liberis nuntiosque Romam, qui certiorem de suo casu senatum facerent, misere. haud segnius 8 quam fide populi Romani dignum fuit exercitus Tusculum ductus; L. Quinctius et Ser. Sulpicius tribuni militum duxere.

Clausas portas [Tusculi] Latinosque simul obsidentium at- 9 que obsessorum animo hinc moenia Tusculi tueri uident, illinc arcem oppugnare, terrere una ac pauere. aduentus Ro- 10 manorum mutauerat utriusque partis animos: Tusculanos ex ingenti metu in summam alacritatem, Latinos ex prope certa fiducia mox capiendae arcis, quoniam oppido potirentur, in exiguam de se ipsis spem uerterat. tollitur ex arce clamor ab 11 Tusculanis; excipit aliquanto maior ab exercitu Romano. utrimque urgentur Latini: nec impetus Tusculanorum decurrentium ex superiore loco sustinent nec Romanos subeuntes

33.9 [Tusculi] *prius Madvig, alterum edd. vett., utrumque Conway*

moenia molientesque obices portarum arcere possunt. scalis 12
prius moenia capta, inde effracta claustra portarum; et cum
anceps hostis et a fronte et a tergo urgeret nec ad pugnam
ulla uis nec ad fugam loci quicquam superesset, in medio
caesi ad unum omnes. reciperato ab hostibus Tusculo exercitus Romam est reductus.

Quanto magis prosperis eo anno bellis tranquilla omnia **34**
foris erant, tanto in urbe uis patrum in dies miseriaeque plebis crescebant, cum eo ipso, quod necesse erat solui, facultas
soluendi impediretur. itaque cum iam ex re nihil dari posset, 2
fama et corpore iudicati atque addicti creditoribus satisfacie-
bant poenaque in uicem fidei cesserat. adeo ergo obnoxios 3
summiserant animos non infimi solum sed principes etiam
plebis, ut non modo ad tribunatum militum inter patricios
petendum, quod tanta ui ut liceret tetenderant, sed ne ad 4
plebeios quidem magistratus capessendos petendosque ulli
uiro acri experientique animus esset, possessionemque honoris usurpati modo a plebe per paucos annos reciperasse in
perpetuum patres uiderentur.

Ne id nimis laetum parti alteri esset, parua (ut plerumque 5
solet) rem ingentem moliundi causa interuenit. M. Fabi Am-
busti, potentis uiri cum inter sui corporis homines tum etiam
ad plebem, quod haudquaquam inter id genus contemptor
eius habebatur, filiae duae nuptae, Ser. Sulpicio maior,
minor C. Licinio Stoloni erat, illustri quidem uiro tamen plebeio; eaque ipsa affinitas haud spreta gratiam Fabio ad uulgum quaesierat. forte ita incidit ut in Ser. Sulpici tribuni 6
militum domo sorores Fabiae cum inter se (ut fit) sermonibus
tempus tererent, lictor Sulpici, cum is de foro se domum re-
ciperet, forem (ut mos est) uirga percuteret. cum ad id moris
eius insueta expauisset minor Fabia, risui sorori fuit miranti
ignorare id sororem. ceterum is risus stimulos paruis mobili 7
rebus animo muliebri subdidit. frequentia quoque prosequentium rogantiumque num quid uellet credo fortunatum
matrimonium ei sororis uisum suique ipsam malo arbitrio,

quo a proximis quisque minime anteiri uult, paenituisse. con- 8
fusam eam ex recenti morsu animi cum pater forte uidisset,
percontatus 'satin salue?' auertentem causam doloris (quippe
nec satis piam aduersus sororem nec admodum in uirum
honorificam) elicuit comiter sciscitando, ut fateretur eam 9
esse causam doloris, quod iuncta impari esset, nupta in domo
quam nec honos nec gratia intrare posset. consolans inde 10
filiam Ambustus bonum animum habere iussit: eosdem propediem domi uisuram honores quos apud sororem uideat.

Inde consilia inire cum genero coepit, adhibito L. Sextio, 11
strenuo adulescente et cuius spei nihil praeter genus patricium deesset. occasio uidebatur rerum nouandarum propter **35**
ingentem uim aeris alieni, cuius leuamen mali plebes nisi suis
in summo imperio locatis nullum speraret: accingendum ad
eam cogitationem esse; conando agendoque iam eo gra- 2
dum fecisse plebeios unde, si porro adnitantur, peruenire ad
summa et patribus aequari tam honore quam uirtute possent.
in praesentia tribunos plebis fieri placuit, quo in magistratu 3
sibimet ipsi uiam ad ceteros honores aperirent. creatique tri- 4
buni C. Licinius et L. Sextius promulgauere leges omnes
aduersus opes patriciorum et pro commodis plebis: unam de
aere alieno, ut deducto eo de capite quod usuris pernumeratum esset, id quod superesset triennio aequis portionibus
persolueretur; alteram de modo agrorum, ne quis plus quin- 5
genta iugera agri possideret; tertiam, ne tribunorum militum
comitia fierent consulumque utique alter ex plebe crearetur;
cuncta ingentia et quae sine certamine maximo obtineri non
possent.

Omnium igitur simul rerum quarum immodica cupido in- 6
ter mortales est, agri pecuniae honorum, discrimine proposito conterriti patres, cum trepidassent publicis priuatisque
consiliis, nullo remedio alio praeter expertam multis iam
ante certaminibus intercessionem inuento collegas aduersus

35.4 portionibus ω: pensionibus *Cuiacius*

tribunicias rogationes comparauerunt. qui ubi tribus ad suf- 7
fragium ineundum citari a Licinio Sextioque uiderunt, stipati
patrum praesidiis nec recitari rogationes nec sollemne quicquam aliud ad sciscendum plebi fieri passi sunt. iamque frus- 8
tra saepe concilio aduocato, cum pro antiquatis rogationes
essent, 'bene habet' inquit Sextius; 'quando quidem tantum
intercessionem pollere placet, isto ipso telo tutabimur plebem. agitedum comitia indicite, patres, tribunis militum 9
creandis. faxo ne iuuet uox ista "ueto," qua nunc concinentes collegas nostros tam laeti auditis.' haud irritae ceci- 10
dere minae. comitia praeter aedilium tribunorumque plebi
nulla sunt habita; Licinius Sextiusque tribuni plebis refecti
nullos curules magistratus creari passi sunt. eaque solitudo
magistratuum et plebe reficiente duos tribunos et iis comitia
tribunorum militum tollentibus per quinquennium urbem
tenuit.

Alia bella opportune quieuere: Veliterni coloni gestientes **36**
otio quod nullus exercitus Romanus esset, et agrum Romanum aliquotiens incursauere et Tusculum oppugnare adorti
sunt; eaque res Tusculanis, ueteribus sociis, nouis ciuibus, 2
opem orantibus uerecundia maxime non patres modo sed
etiam plebem mouit. remittentibus tribunis plebis comitia 3
per interregem sunt habita; creatique tribuni militum L.
Furius A. Manlius Ser. Sulpicius Ser. Cornelius P. et C.
Valerii. haudquaquam tam oboedientem in dilectu quam in
comitiis plebem habuere; ingentique contentione exercitu 4
scripto profecti non ab Tusculo modo summouere hostem
sed intra suamet ipsum moenia compulere, obsidebanturque 5
haud paulo ui maiore Velitrae quam Tusculum obsessum
fuerat.

Nec tamen ab eis, a quibus obsideri coeptae erant, ex-
pugnari potuere. ante noui creati sunt tribuni militum, Q. 6
Seruilius C. Veturius A. et M. Cornelii Q. Quinctius M.
Fabius. nihil ne ab his quidem tribunis ad Velitras memorabile factum.

In maiore discrimine domi res uertebantur. nam praeter 7
Sextium Liciniumque latores legum, iam octauum tribunos
plebis refectos, Fabius quoque tribunus militum, Stolonis socer, quarum legum auctor fuerat, earum suasorem se haud
dubium ferebat; et cum octo ex collegio tribunorum plebi 8
primo intercessores legum fuissent, quinque soli erant, et (ut
ferme solent qui a suis desciscunt) capti et stupentes animi
uocibus alienis id modo quod domi praeceptum erat intercessioni suae praetendebant: Velitris in exercitu plebis mag- 9
nam partem abesse; in aduentum militum comitia differri debere, ut uniuersa plebes de suis commodis suffragium ferret.
Sextius Liciniusque cum parte collegarum et uno ex tri- 10
bunis militum Fabio, artifices iam tot annorum usu tractandi
animos plebis, primores patrum productos interrogando de
singulis, quae ferebantur ad populum, fatigabant: aude- 11
rentne postulare ut, cum bina iugera agri plebi diuiderentur,
ipsis plus quingenta iugera habere liceret ut singuli prope
trecentorum ciuium possiderent agros, plebeio homini uix
ad tectum necessarium aut locum sepulturae suus pateret
ager? an placeret fenore circumuentam plebem, [ni] potius 12
quam sortem [creditum] soluat, corpus in neruum ac supplicia dare et gregatim cottidie de foro addictos duci et repleri
uinctis nobiles domus et, ubicumque patricius habitet, ibi
carcerem priuatum esse?

Haec indigna miserandaque auditu cum apud timentes **37**
sibimet ipsos maiore audientium indignatione quam sua
increpuissent, atqui nec agros occupandi modum nec fenore
trucidandi plebem alium patribus umquam fore affirmabant, 2
nisi alterum ex plebe consulem, custodem suae libertatis,
[plebi] fecissent. contemni iam tribunos plebis, quippe quae 3
potestas iam suam ipsa uim frangat intercedendo. non posse 4
aequo iure agi ubi imperium penes illos, penes se auxilium

36.12 [ni] *Glareanus*   [creditum] *Conway*   37.2 plebi ω, *del. Walters*:
plebes *recc., Drakenborch*: plebs *A^c*: plebei *Weissenborn*: plebeii *Bayet*   fecissent
M^c: fecisset ω

tantum sit; nisi imperio communicato numquam plebem in
parte pari rei publicae fore. nec esse quod quisquam satis
putet, si plebeiorum ratio comitiis consularibus habeatur;
nisi alterum consulem utique ex plebe fieri necesse sit, neminem fore. an iam memoria exisse, cum tribunos militum id-   5
circo potius quam consules creari placuisset ut et plebeiis pateret summus honos, quattuor et quadraginta annis neminem
ex plebe tribunum militum creatum esse? qui crederent duo-   6
bus nunc in locis sua uoluntate impertituros plebi honorem,
qui octona loca tribunis militum creandis occupare soliti sint,
et ad consulatum uiam fieri passuros, qui tribunatum saeptum tam diu habuerint? lege obtinendum esse quod co-   7
mitiis per gratiam nequeat, et seponendum extra certamen
alterum consulatum ad quem plebi sit aditus, quoniam in
certamine relictus praemium semper potentioris futurus sit.

Nec iam posse dici id quod antea iactare soliti sint, non   8
esse in plebeiis idoneos uiros ad curules magistratus. numqui
enim socordius aut segnius rem publicam administrare posse
post P. Licini Calui tribunatum, qui primus ex plebe creatus
sit, quam per eos annos gesta sit quibus praeter patricios
nemo tribunus militum fuerit? quin contra patricios aliquot   9
damnatos post tribunatum, neminem plebeium. quaestores
quoque, sicut tribunos militum, paucis ante annis ex plebe
coeptos creari nec ullius eorum populum Romanum paenituisse. consulatum superesse plebeiis; eam esse arcem liber-   10
tatis, id columen. si eo peruentum sit, tum populum Romanum
uere exactos ex urbe reges et stabilem libertatem suam exis-
timaturum; quippe ex illa die in plebem uentura omnia qui-   11
bus patricii excellant, imperium atque honorem, gloriam
belli genus nobilitatem, magna ipsis fruenda, maiora liberis
relinquenda.

Huius generis orationes ubi accipi uidere, nouam rogatio-   12

nem promulgant, ut pro duumuiris sacris faciundis decemuiri
creentur ita ut pars ex plebe, pars ex patribus fiat; omniumque earum rogationum comitia in aduentum eius exercitus
differunt qui Velitras obsidebat. prius circumactus est annus **38**
quam a Velitris reducerentur legiones.

   Ita suspensa de legibus res ad nouos tribunos militum
dilata; nam plebis tribunos eosdem, duos utique quia legum
latores erant, plebes reficiebat. tribuni militum creati T. 2
Quinctius Ser. Cornelius Ser. Sulpicius Sp. Seruilius L.
Papirius L. Veturius. principio statim anni ad ultimam dimi- 3
cationem de legibus uentum. et cum tribus uocarentur nec
intercessio collegarum latoribus obstaret, trepidi patres ad
duo ultima auxilia, summum imperium summumque ad ciuem
decurrunt. dictatorem dici placet; dicitur M. Furius Camillus, 4
qui magistrum equitum L. Aemilium cooptat. legum quoque
latores aduersus tantum apparatum aduersariorum et ipsi
causam plebis ingentibus animis armant concilioque plebis
indicto tribus ad suffragium uocant.

   Cum dictator, stipatus agmine patriciorum, plenus irae 5
minarumque consedisset atque ageretur res solito primum
certamine inter se tribunorum plebi ferentium legem intercedentiumque et, quanto iure potentior intercessio erat, tantum
uinceretur fauore legum ipsarum latorumque et 'uti rogas'
primae tribus dicerent, tum Camillus 'quandoquidem' inquit, 'Quirites, iam uos tribunicia libido, non potestas regit 6
et intercessionem, secessione quondam plebis partam, uobis
eadem ui facitis irritam qua peperistis, non rei publicae magis uniuersae quam uestra causa dictator intercessioni adero
euersumque uestrum auxilium imperio tutabor. itaque si C. 7
Licinius et L. Sextius intercessioni collegarum cedunt, nihil
patricium magistratum inseram concilio plebis; si aduersus
intercessionem tamquam captae ciuitati leges imponere ten-
dent, uim tribuniciam a se ipsa dissolui non patiar.' aduersus 8
ea cum contemptim tribuni plebis rem nihilo segnius peragerent, tum percitus ira Camillus lictores qui de medio

plebem emouerent misit et addidit minas, si pergerent, sacramento omnes iuniores adacturum exercitumque extemplo ex urbe educturum. terrorem ingentem incusserat plebi: 9 ducibus plebis accendit magis certamine animos quam minuit.

Sed re neutro inclinata magistratu se abdicauit, seu quia uitio creatus erat (ut scripsere quidam), seu quia tribuni plebis tulerunt ad plebem idque plebs sciuit ut, si M. Furius pro dictatore quid egisset, quingentum milium ei multa esset. sed 10 auspiciis magis quam noui exempli rogatione deterritum ut potius credam, cum ipsius uiri facit ingenium, tum quod ei suffectus est extemplo P. Manlius dictator (quem quid creari attinebat ad id certamen quo M. Furius uictus esset?) et 11 quod eundem M. Furium dictatorem insequens annus habuit, haud sine pudore certe fractum priore anno in se imperium repetiturum; simul quod eo tempore quo promulgatum de 12 multa eius traditur aut et huic rogationi, qua se in ordinem cogi uidebat, obsistere potuit aut ne illas quidem propter quas et haec lata erat impedire; et quod usque ad memoriam 13 nostram tribuniciis consularibusque certatum uiribus est, dictaturae semper altius fastigium fuit.

Inter priorem dictaturam abdicatam nouamque a Manlio **39** initam ab tribunis uelut per interregnum concilio plebis habito apparuit quae ex promulgatis plebi, quae latoribus gratiora essent. nam de fenore atque agro rogationes iubebant, 2 de plebeio consule antiquabant; et perfecta utraque res esset, ni tribuni se in omnia simul consulere plebem dixissent. P. 3 Manlius deinde dictator rem in causam plebis inclinauit C. Licinio, qui tribunus militum fuerat, magistro equitum de plebe dicto. id aegre patres passos accipio: dictatorem propin- 4 qua cognatione Licini se apud patres excusare solitum, simul negantem magistri equitum maius quam tribuni consularis imperium esse.

Licinius Sextiusque, cum tribunorum plebi creandorum in- 5 dicta comitia essent, ita se gerere ut negando iam sibi uelle continuari honorem acerrime accenderent ad id quod dissi-

mulando petebant plebem: nonum se annum iam uelut in acie 6
aduersus optimates maximo priuatim periculo, nullo publice
emolumento stare. consenuisse iam secum et rogationes promulgatas et uim omnem tribuniciae potestatis. primo interces- 7
sione collegarum in leges suas pugnatum esse, deinde ablegatione iuuentutis ad Veliternum bellum; postremo dictatorium
fulmen in se intentatum. iam nec collegas nec bellum nec dic- 8
tatorem obstare, quippe qui etiam omen plebeio consuli magistro equitum ex plebe dicendo dederit: se ipsam plebem et
commoda morari sua. liberam urbem ac forum a creditori- 9
bus, liberos agros ab iniustis possessoribus extemplo, si uelit,
habere posse. quae munera quando tandem satis grato animo 10
aestimaturos, si inter accipiendas de suis commodis rogationes spem honoris latoribus earum incidant? non esse modestiae populi Romani id postulare ut ipse fenore leuetur et in
agrum iniuria possessum a potentibus inducatur, per quos ea
consecutus sit senes tribunicios non sine honore tantum sed
etiam sine spe honoris relinquat. proinde ipsi primum statue- 11
rent apud animos quid uellent; deinde comitiis tribuniciis declararent uoluntatem. si coniuncte ferri ab se promulgatas
rogationes uellent, esse quod eosdem reficerent tribunos plebis; perlaturos enim quae promulgauerint. sin quod cuique 12
priuatim opus sit id modo accipi uelint, opus esse nihil inuidiosa continuatione honoris; nec se tribunatum nec illos ea
quae promulgata sint habituros.

Aduersus tam obstinatam orationem tribunorum cum prae **40**
indignitate rerum stupor silentiumque inde ceteros patrum
defixisset, Ap. Claudius Crassus, nepos decemuiri, dicitur 2
odio magis iraque quam spe ad dissuadendum processisse et
locutus in hanc fere sententiam esse: 'neque nouum neque 3
inopinatum mihi sit, Quirites, si, quod unum familiae nostrae semper obiectum est ab seditiosis tribunis, id nunc ego
quoque audiam, Claudiae genti iam inde ab initio nihil anti-

39.10 relinquat ω : -quere *Gronovius*

quius in re publica patrum maiestate fuisse, semper plebis
commodis aduersatos esse. quorum alterum neque nego ne-   4
que infitias eo: nos, ex quo adsciti sumus simul in ciuitatem
et patres, enixe operam dedisse ut per nos aucta potius quam
imminuta maiestas earum gentium inter quas nos esse uoluistis dici uere posset; illud alterum pro me maioribusque meis   5
contendere ausim, Quirites, nisi, quae pro uniuersa re publica fiant, ea plebi tamquam aliam incolenti urbem aduersa
quis putet, nihil nos neque priuatos neque in magistratibus
quod incommodum plebi esset scientes fecisse nec ullum factum dictumue nostrum contra utilitatem uestram, etsi quaedam contra uoluntatem fuerint, uere referri posse.

'An hoc, si Claudiae familiae non sim nec ex patricio san-   6
guine ortus sed unus Quiritium quilibet, qui modo me duobus ingenuis ortum et uiuere in libera ciuitate sciam, reticere
possim L. illum Sextium et C. Licinium, perpetuos, si dis pla-   7
cet, tribunos, tantum licentiae nouem annis quibus regnant
sumpsisse, ut uobis negent potestatem liberam suffragii non
in comitiis, non in legibus iubendis se permissuros esse? "sub   8
condicione" inquit, "nos reficietis decimum tribunos." quid
est aliud dicere "quod petunt alii, nos adeo fastidimus ut
sine mercede magna non accipiamus"? sed quae tandem ista   9
merces est qua uos semper tribunos plebis habeamus? "ut
rogationes" inquit, "nostras, seu placent seu displicent, seu
utiles seu inutiles sunt, omnes coniunctim accipiatis." obse-   10
cro uos, Tarquinii tribuni plebis, putate me ex media contione unum ciuem succlamare "bona uenia uestra liceat ex
his rogationibus legere quas salubres nobis censemus esse,
antiquare alias." "non" inquit, "licebit tu de fenore atque agris   11
quod ad uos omnes pertinet iubeas et hoc portenti non fiat
in urbe Romana uti L. Sextium atque hunc C. Licinium consules – quod indignaris, quod abominaris – uideas. aut om-

40.11 licebit tu ω: licebit. tu … uideas. *H. J. Müller*: licebit. (tu … uideas.)
Bayet: licebit. tu uideas? *Alschefski*: licebit ut *Madvig*

nia accipe, aut nihil fero"; ut si quis ei quem urgeat fames 12
uenenum ponat cum cibo et aut abstinere eo quod uitale sit
iubeat aut mortiferum uitali admisceat. ergo si esset libera
haec ciuitas, non tibi frequentes succlamassent "abi hinc
cum tribunatibus ac rogationibus tuis!"? quid? si tu non tu-
leris quod commodum est populo accipere, nemo erit qui
ferat? illud si quis patricius, si quis (quod illi uolunt inuidio- 13
sius esse) Claudius diceret "aut omnia accipite, aut nihil
fero," quis uestrum, Quirites, ferret? numquamne uos res 14
potius quam auctores spectabitis sed omnia semper quae magistratus ille dicet secundis auribus, quae ab nostrum quo dicentur aduersis accipietis?

   ' "At hercule sermo est minime ciuilis!" quid? rogatio qua- 15
lis est, quam a uobis antiquatam indignantur? sermoni, Quirites, simillima. "consules" inquit, "rogo ne uobis quos uelitis
facere liceat." an aliter rogat qui utique alterum ex plebe fieri 16
consulem iubet nec duos patricios creandi potestatem uobis
permittit? si hodie bella sint, quale Etruscum fuit cum Por- 17
senna Ianiculum insedit, quale Gallicum modo cum praeter
Capitolium atque arcem omnia haec hostium erant, et consulatum cum hoc M. Furio et quolibet alio ex patribus L.
ille Sextius peteret, possetisne ferre Sextium haud pro dubio
consulem esse, Camillum de repulsa dimicare? hocine est in 18
commune honores uocare, ut duos plebeios fieri consules
liceat, duos patricios non liceat? et alterum ex plebe creari
necesse sit, utrumque ex patribus praeterire liceat? quaenam
ista societas, quaenam consortio est? parum est, si, cuius pars
tua nulla adhuc fuit, in partem eius uenis, nisi partem
petendo totum traxeris?

   ' "Timeo" inquit, "ne, si duos licebit creari patricios, nemi- 19
nem creetis plebeium." quid est dicere aliud "quia indignos
uestra uoluntate creaturi non estis, necessitatem uobis
creandi quos non uultis imponam"? quid sequitur, nisi ut ne 20
beneficium quidem debeat populo, si cum duobus patriciis
unus petierit plebeius et lege se non suffragio creatum di-

cat? quomodo extorqueant, non quomodo petant honores **41**
quaerunt; et ita maxima sunt adepturi, ut nihil ne pro minimis quidem debeant; et occasionibus potius quam uirtute petere honores malunt. est aliquis qui se inspici aestimari 2
fastidiat, qui certos sibi uni honores inter dimicantes compe-
titores aequum censeat esse, qui se arbitrio uestro eximat,
qui uestra necessaria suffragia pro uoluntariis et serua pro
liberis faciat. omitto Licinium Sextiumque, quorum annos in 3
perpetua potestate tamquam regum in Capitolio numeratis:
quis est hodie in ciuitate tam humilis cui non uia ad consulatum facilior per istius legis occasionem quam nobis ac liberis
nostris fiat, siquidem nos ne cum uolueritis quidem creare
interdum poteritis, istos etiam si nolueritis necesse sit?

'De indignitate satis dictum est (etenim dignitas ad homines 4
pertinet); quid de religionibus atque auspiciis, quae propria
deorum immortalium contemptio atque iniuria est, loquar?
auspiciis hanc urbem conditam esse, auspiciis bello ac pace
domi militiaeque omnia geri, quis est qui ignoret? penes
quos igitur sunt auspicia more maiorum? nempe penes pa- 5
tres. nam plebeius quidem magistratus nullus auspicato creatur; nobis adeo propria sunt auspicia, ut non solum quos po- 6
pulus creat patricios magistratus non aliter quam auspicato
creet sed nos quoque ipsi sine suffragio populi auspicato interregem prodamus et priuatim auspicia habeamus, quae isti
ne in magistratibus quidem habent. quid igitur aliud quam 7
tollit ex ciuitate auspicia qui plebeios consules creando a patribus, qui soli ea habere possunt, aufert? eludant nunc licet
religiones: "quid enim est, si pulli non pascentur, si ex cauea 8
tardius exierint, si occecinerit auis?" parua sunt haec; sed
parua ista non contemnendo maiores uestri maximam hanc
rem fecerunt; nunc nos, tamquam iam nihil pace deorum 9
opus sit, omnes caerimonias polluimus. uulgo ergo pontifices
augures sacrificuli reges creentur; cuilibet apicem Dialem,
dummodo homo sit imponamus; tradamus ancilia penetralia

deos deorumque curam, quibus nefas est; non leges auspi- 10
cato ferantur, non magistratus creentur; nec centuriatis nec
curiatis comitiis patres auctores fiant; Sextius et Licinius tamquam Romulus ac Tatius in urbe Romana regnent, quia pecunias alienas, quia agros dono dant. tanta dulcedo est ex 11
alienis fortunis praedandi, nec in mentem uenit altera lege
solitudines uastas in agris fieri pellendo finibus dominos, altera fidem abrogari cum qua omnis humana societas tollitur? omnium rerum causa uobis antiquandas censeo istas roga- 12
tiones. quod faxitis deos uelim fortunare.'

   Oratio Appi ad id modo ualuit ut tempus rogationum iu- **42**
bendarum proferretur. refecti decimum iidem tribuni, Sextius 2
et Licinius, de decemuiris sacrorum ex parte de plebe creandis legem pertulere. creati quinque patrum, quinque plebis;
graduque eo iam uia facta ad consulatum uidebatur. hac uic- 3
toria contenta plebes cessit patribus ut in praesentia consulum mentione omissa tribuni militum crearentur. creati A.
et M. Cornelii iterum M. Geganius P. Manlius L. Veturius
P. Valerius sextum.

   Cum praeter Velitrarum obsidionem, tardi magis rem exi- 4
tus quam dubii, quietae externae res Romanis essent, fama
repens belli Gallici allata perpulit ciuitatem ut M. Furius dictator quintum diceretur. is T. Quinctium Poenum magistrum
equitum dixit. (bellatum cum Gallis eo anno circa Anienem 5
flumen auctor est Claudius inclitamque in ponte pugnam,
qua T. Manlius Gallum cum quo prouocatus manus conseruit in conspectu duorum exercituum caesum torque spoliauit, tum pugnatam. pluribus auctoribus magis adducor ut 6
credam decem haud minus post annos ea acta, hoc autem
anno in Albano agro cum Gallis dictatore M. Furio signa
collata.) nec dubia nec difficilis Romanis, quamquam ingen- 7
tem Galli terrorem memoria pristinae cladis attulerant, uictoria fuit. multa milia barbarorum in acie, multa captis castris caesa; palati alii Apuliam maxime petentes cum fuga se 8

longinqua tum quod passim eos simul pauor errorque distulerant, ab hoste [sese] tutati sunt. dictatori consensu patrum
plebisque triumphus decretus.

Vixdum perfunctum eum bello atrocior domi seditio exce- 9
pit, et per ingentia certamina dictator senatusque uictus ut
rogationes tribuniciae acciperentur; et comitia consulum
aduersa nobilitate habita, quibus L. Sextius de plebe primus
consul factus. et ne is quidem finis certaminum fuit. quia pa- 10
tricii se auctores futuros negabant, prope secessionem plebis
res terribilesque alias minas ciuilium certaminum uenit cum 11
tandem per dictatorem condicionibus sedatae discordiae sunt
concessumque ab nobilitate plebi de consule plebeio, a plebe
nobilitati de praetore uno qui ius in urbe diceret ex patribus
creando. ita ab diutina ira tandem in concordiam redactis 12
ordinibus, cum dignam eam rem senatus censeret esse meri-
toque id (si quando umquam alias) [deum immortalium
causa libenter facturos] fore, ut ludi maximi fierent et dies
unus ad triduum adiceretur, recusantibus id munus aedilibus 13
plebis, conclamatum a patriciis est iuuenibus se id honoris
deum immortalium causa libenter facturos [ut aediles fierent].
quibus cum ab uniuersis gratiae actae essent, factum senatus 14
consultum ut duumuiros aediles ex patribus dictator populum rogaret, patres auctores omnibus eius anni comitiis
fierent.

42.8 errorque *Harant*: terrorque ω   [sese] *Crevier*   42.12 [deum ... fac-
turos] *Kraus* (iam [causa ... facturos] *Madvig*)   42.13 [ut ... fierent] *Conway*

COMMENTARY

1.1–3 Preface

A new publication should announce its title, author, genre, and contents (D. C. Earl, *A.N.R.W.* 1 2 (1972) 842–56). The 'incipit' of Book 6 (*ab condita urbe*) is a variant of the history's general title (*Ab urbe condita*: cf. *Praef.* 6 *ante conditam ... urbem*, 2.1.2 *conditores ... urbis*, 31.1.4 *a condita urbe*), while the ref. to the first pentad (*quinque libris exposui*) identifies the author (above, pp. 1–2). Variations on *populi Romani res gestae* indicate the genre, Roman history (*CC* 12 n.24, cf. *Praef.* 1, 21.1.1, 31.1.2), while the list of magistrates (1) fixes the subgenre as *annales* (above, pp. 9–13). L.'s subject-matter in Books 1–5 (1) has been full of the exciting elements that constituted the primary topics of ancient history (cf. Tac. *A.* 4.32.1 *ingentia ... bella, expugnationes urbium, fusos captosque reges aut ... discordias consulum aduersum tribunos, agrarias frumentariasque leges, plebis et optimatium certamina* with M–W). He now promises even better history to come (3). The preface is circular: 1 *ab condita urbe* ∼ 3 *ab secunda origine ... renatae urbis; gessere* ∼ *gesta; foris ... domi* ∼ *domi militiaeque; exposui* ∼ *exponentur*. The ring composition establishes ties between the books L. has published and those he is now presenting, implying that the latter will have a similar content. Similar, but in fact better. It was a historiographical convention to claim that one's work surpassed that of one's precursors (*RICH s.v.* 'rivalry'). L. unconventionally treats his *own* work as his precursor, strengthening his explicit claim of the new books' superiority (3) by an inner ring of contrasts (2 *obscuras* ∼ 3 *clariora; rarae et paruae ... litterae* ∼ *certiora*).

1.1 Quae ... (2) interiere: this long period has a simple structure, hinged on the main verb *exposui*: the first part of the sentence is its dir. obj., the second – slightly longer, as often (above, pp. 21–2) – in apposition to that object. Each part comprises a statement qualified in three ways: *Quae ... Romani ... gessere* is further specified by (*a*) *ab ... eandem* (the time period), (*b*) *sub ... consularibus* (the magistrates), and (*c*) *foris ... seditiones* (the kind of events, appositional to *Quae*). Three explanations of *res ... obscuras* then follow (2), each

83

with a dependent construction; the tripartite arrangement is contained within a bipartite one (*cum ... tum*). The meticulously organized period is framed by the repeated *urbe* ~ *urbe*.   **ab condita urbe:** the textbook ex. of the idiomatic use of participle + noun as the equivalent of a noun-clause ('from the founding of the city': *NLS* §§95–6, Laughton 84–99). Though attested early (*OLD occido*[2] 4b), the 'AUC participle' is most frequent and flexible in L. and Tacitus.   **ad captam eandem:** for the non-repetition of *urbem* cf. 39.1 and see Kraus (1) 215–17.   **sub ... consularibus:** a tricolon *auctum* contained within the pair *primum ... deinde* (above, p. 24).   **consulibus ... consularibus:** sc. *sub* with each abl. For the chiastic alliteration see above, p. 22 with W. on Vell. 115.5. **decemuirisque ac tribunis:** coupled because each comprises a group, as opposed to the pairs of consuls or single dictators. Chiastic arrangement with the previous colon hints at a kinship between dictator and decemvir (16.3nn.), while the pairing opens the possibility that the decemvirs and consular tribunes have more in common than numbers alone (37.6n.).   **tr. consularibus:** first elected in 445 as substitutes for consuls, whom they replaced regularly until 367; each college consisted of from four to eight men (37.6n.). Plebeians were eligible from the start, though according to L. the first elected was in 400 (5.12.9–12; see *MRR* 1 52, 84 n.1). L.'s plebeians claim that the office was instituted so as to give them a chance to share the supreme power (cf. 37.5 and *CAH*[2] 192–5).   **gessere** i.e. *gesserunt*. This archaizing alternative 3rd plur. ending, a historiographical mannerism since Sall., declines in L. after Book 6 (E. B. Lease, *A.J.P.* 24 (1903) 408–22).   **foris ... domi** varies the polar expression *domi militiaeque*; for a similar play in a programmatic passage cf. Sall. *H.* 1.1 *militiae et domi*.   **bella ... seditiones:** cf. Tac. *A.* 4.32.1 *bella ... discordias* (quoted on 1–3); they reappear as an organizatory rubric at 11.1–2, 14.2, 27.11, 31.1–2, 42.9. L.'s singling out of these as his subject is a reminder that 'periods of human happiness and security are blank pages in history (White (2) 11, quoting Hegel).   **seditiones:** with *gessere* (above) by zeugma; *sed. gerere* is attested only once in Cassiodorus (*TLL* VI 1943.38–54).   **libris:** abl. of place where, indicating a citation (G–L §387).

  1.2 res ... cernuntur: an adaptation of Thuc. 1.1.3 (W–M):

'for the things before [the war], and those still older, it was impossible to find them out clearly (σαφῶς: *obscuras*) because of the length
of time (διὰ χρόνου πλῆθος: *uetustate nimia*); but on the basis of the
evidence (τεκμηρίων, cf. *litterae, monumentis*) which I can trust
(πιστεῦσαι, cf. *fidelis*) looking from a very great distance (ἐπὶ
μακρότατον σκοποῦντί μοι: *magno ... cernuntur*), I believe they
were not great'. *res* is part of the complex of refs. to *res gestae* (1–
3n.), but its meaning slides here to encompass past events conceived of as physical things (above, p. 26). The whole passage bears
comparison with *Rhet. Her.* 3.32, part of a discussion of the optimal
'memory background': *nec nimis illustres nec uehementer obscuros locos habere oportet ... interualla locorum mediocria placet esse ... nam ut aspectus
item cogitatio minus ualet siue nimis procul remoueris siue uehementer prope
admoueris id quod oportet uideri.*   **cum ... obscuras:** *cum* is a conjunction, *uetustate nimia* an unaccompanied causal abl.; for the inconcinnity *cum* [abl.] ~ *tum* [*quod*] (below) cf. 42.8, Caes. *C.* 3.42.5 and
see Catterall 316–17.   **ex interuallo** 'from a (physical) distance'
is first attested here (*TLL*). For a literary artifact (imaginatively)
seen from afar cf. Hor. *Ars* 361–3 *erit* [sc. *poesis*] *quae si propius stes |
te capiat magis, et quaedam si longius abstes. | haec amat obscurum, uolet haec
sub luce uideri*; for the claim that the distant past is intrinsically difficult to verify see 12.2n.   **cernuntur:** 3n.   **paruae** 'insig-
nificant' (*OLD* 5), further specified by *rarae*. Emendation (e.g. to
parcae: Watt 213) is unnecessary; for the combination of ideas cf.
21.35.10 *parua furta per occasionem temptantibus*, Cic. *De orat.* 2.320 *paruis atque infrequentibus*.   **per eadem tempora:** cf. 7.3.6 *quia rarae
per ea tempora litterae erant*. This weakened sense of *idem* (= *is*) is fairly
common in expressions of time, where *eo anno* and *eodem anno* may
be interchangeable (as 10.13.1 ~ 10.13.14, cf. Tac. *D.* 21.6 with
Gudeman). See L. R. Palmer, *The Latin language* (1961) 169 on later
Latin's preference for 'bulkier' forms (e.g. compound verbs,
pleonasms), a tendency already visible in L.   **litterae:** 'written
records' (Radice). Historiographical prefaces sometimes appealed to
the reliability of their sources (cf. Sen. *Apoc.* 1.1–3, *HA Aur.* 1–2); L.
suggests by implication that his next books will be based on better
evidence (3n. *certiora*).   **una** 'the only'.   **custodia fidelis**
'trustworthy place for safe-keeping'. The idea of a loyal guard is
common, but this particular expression occurs elsewhere only at

5.40.7, of the *locus* in which the *sacra* are buried to protect them from the Gauls (it has elevated literary associations, cf. Enn. *scen.* 237 J *fida custos*, Cic. *ND* 2.158 *canum … fida custodia*, Virg. *A.* 9.648, Plin. *Pan.* 49.3). The epithet, which appears to be applied to literature in general, in fact pushes the *AVC* into the limelight: like the place in the Forum, L.'s history proves to be a safe place, each of them unexpectedly preserving Roman tradition from the Gauls, who destroy the city and its records. **memoriae … gestarum** 'history' (*OLD memoria* 7). **quae:** sc. *litterae.* **in commentariis pontificum:** procedural handbooks (O. on 1.60.4), though L. may be using the phrase non-technically of the pontifical *annales* (above, pp. 9–10): *commentarius* was the name for the 'unelaborated' sketch (as Caesar's *bella*) which was then written up into a historical narrative (*RICH* 90, 92). **publicis … monumentis:** cf. 9.6.7 *priuatisque et publicis fungitur officiis.* The separation of an attributive adj. (or possessive gen.) from its noun by a verb is an artistic mannerism which, though common in poetry, is selectively distributed in prose. Cic. liked it, especially in the more ornately written speeches; in historical narrative it was favoured by L., Sis., Caes. in the later books of *G.* and in *C.*, and by Nepos. It can lend emphasis (6.4n., 12.4n.), improve a clausula, or add stylistic flavour, as here (Adams (1) 2–5). See also 2.12n. **monumentis:** L. uses *monumentum* both of physical objects like tombs (38.56.3) and of written records (often with a defining gen. as 7.21.6 *omnium annalium monumenta*). Sometimes, as at *Praef.* 6, the meanings overlap, as in the common comparison of a literary *monumentum* to a physical one (most famously at Hor. *C.* 3.30.1). The present juxtaposition with *incensa urbe*, together with the corporeal sense of *res* above (n.), suggests that both meanings are felt. Written *monumenta* are the verbal representation of Roman *gesta*, as the *monumenta* of the city are their visual incarnation (above, p. 15 n.62); for the types of evidence envisioned here see *CC* 9–26, *CAH*² 16–24. **ĭntĕrĭērĕ:** a hexameter ending (cf. *sēdĭtĭōnēs* above), emphatically marking the genre as historiography (Goodyear on Tac. *A.* 1.1.1); for L.'s *clausulae* see above, p. 18 n.74.

1.3 clariora … exponentur: the announcement of the material to come contrasts in length and pace with the preceding period. This technique of slowing the narrative down with a long,

relatively involved sentence in order to give more weight to a
shorter following statement is the large-scale reflection of a common historiographical sentence-shape (above, p. 21). The proportion
of 1–2 to 3 is duplicated in the structure of 3, whose weighted subj.
clariora . . . gesta makes the sentence top-heavy.   **clariora** caps the
light imagery in 2 (*obscuras*, *cernuntur*): what was previously barely
visible will henceforth be 'brighter.' L. allusively deploys the prefatory 'autopsy' topos, referring not to his own eye-witness but to the
metaphorical autopsy afforded by literary memory; for the combination with *certiora* cf. Sen. *Apoc.* 1.3 *ab hoc ego qui tum audiui, certa clara
affero* (the end of the preface) and *OLD clarus* 4. But *clarus* is also an
epithet of literary style (*OLD* 2d), and ancient historians strove for
vividness (*enargeia* or *euidentia*) in their narratives (17.4n., 20.6–9n.:
LHA 181–7, *RICH s.v.* 'vivid description'); for *euidentia* in rhetoric
cf. Quint. 8.3.61–71, esp. 62 *magna uirtus res de quibus loquimur clare
atque ut cerni uideantur enuntiare.* Finally, the comparative proclaims
that the forthcoming narrative will make L. 'more famous' (*OLD* 6)
than his predecessors: in this case both himself (1–3n.) and his
rivals; for this claim cf. *Praef.* 2 *scribendi arte rudem uetustatem supera-
turos credunt* and for the theme of sight in Book 6 see further
12.1n.   **deinceps** 'from then on' (*OLD* 3a) identifies the time
frame with which the next part of the history will be concerned;
cf. Sall. *H.* 1.1 *res populi Romani M. Lepido Q. Catulo consulibus ac
deinde militiae et domi gestas conposui.*   **certiora** refers to factual ac-
curacy (*OLD* 4–5, cf. 2 *fidelis*), a second way in which a historian
typically hopes to surpass his precursors (cf. *Praef.* 2 *certius aliquid*
with J. L. Moles, *LF* 88–121).   **ab . . . origine:** saving a city
was equivalent in glory to founding one (e.g. Cic. *Rep.* 1.12); hence
C., who rescued Rome from the Gauls, is twice styled her second
founder (5.49.7, 7.1.9), and Rome is here said to be reborn. See
Weinstock 175–99; for this rebirth see above, pp. 25–6 and cf. 41.8n.,
10n.   **uelut ab stirpibus** 'as if from the stalk,' cf. 26.41.22 *nomini Scipionum, suboli imperatorum . . . uelut accisis recrescenti stirpibus.*
The extended agricultural imagery in this section and below (4, 6)
evokes theories of the biological growth of states (e.g. Polyb.
6.4.11–13, Sen. *Hist.* fr. 1); for Book 1 see M. Ruch, *Studii clasice* 10
(1968) 123–31 and in general above, p. 25.   **laetius feraciusque:**
cf. 2.1.2 *laetior libertas.* The precise sense of *laetius* ('fertile,' *OLD* 1) is

given by its near synonym *feracius*, an adv. first attested here (cf. 37.8n.); for the combination cf. Sen. *Helu.* 9.1 *terra laetarum arborum ferax*. It was believed that burning over a field of wheat or pasturage (cf. 2 *incensa urbe*) would make subsequent crops grow better: Virg. *G.* 1.84–93 with Mynors, Plin. *NH* 17.253–4, and M. S. Spurr, *Arable cultivation in Roman Italy ca. 200 B.C.–ca. A.D. 100* (1986) 69, 122. For the thought cf. Sen. *Ep.* 91.13 *Timagenes, felicitati urbis inimicus, aiebat Romae sibi incendia ob hoc unum dolori esse, quod sciret meliora surrectura quam arsissent*, to which L. may allude; cf. Luce (1) 226 n.49.   **renatae:** a technical agricultural sense (cf. Gaius, *Dig.* 50.16.30 *quae* [sc. *silua*] *succisa rursus ex stirpibus aut radicibus renascitur* and *OLD* 2a), used in a metaphor 'unique not only in [L.'s] history, but in all extant literature of the preclassical and classical periods' but with 'virtual equivalents' in late-republican political propaganda (Miles (1) 25); see further above, p. 8.   **gesta** 'deeds'. **exponentur** ~ 2 *exposui*, a kind of verbal polyptoton (for its pointed use see 15.4n.); for the prefatory fut. cf. *Praef.* 1, 2.1.2, 7.1.1, Cato *Agr. praef.* 4, Sall. *J.* 5.1, Tac. *H.* 1.1.1.

1.4–8 The year 390 B.C.

The close connection between Books 5 and 6 is manifest in the narrative holding over of this 'end-of-year' material from 5, where the rest of 390 was related (on these 'archival' notices and the division of the year into *res internae* and *externae* see above, pp. 10–11). As with the break between monarchy and republic (Books 1–2), L. here makes the transition with a single dominant figure who liberates and then supports the city (Brutus and C., respectively: see further above, pp. 25–6). The state's insistence that C. not resign is opposed via chiasmus to its refusal to allow the tribunes of this disastrous year to hold new elections (4–5 *M. Furio ... anno circumacto ~ in insequentem annum tribunos*).

1.4 Ceterum 'dismisses what is of the nature of a digression, and resumes the main narrative' (Stephenson); it is first common in Sallust and L. (*TLL*).   **primo:** adv.; it is taken out of its clause (*quo ... erat*) for emphasis. The disjointed word order draws attention to the etymological play with *principe* (below); cf. Cic. *Fam.* 12.24.2 *ut primum occasio data est, meo pristino more rem pub. defendi, me*

principem senatui populoque Romano professus sum and see L–H–S 790–
3.   **quo ... innixa:** the ideal leader not only rescues but continues to protect his charge, cf. Plin. *Pan.* 50.4 *ingentia opera eodem
quo exstructa sunt animo ab interitu uindicare*; for the state leaning on a
single leader, an image that recurs in panegyric, cf. *Pan. Lat.* 7.10.1
*aut etiam di immortales probare uoluerunt tibi innixam stetisse rem publicam,
cum sine te stare non posset* (Béranger 169–70, 175–80).   **adminiculo:** often used of a stake for plants (e.g. Plin. *NH* 12.112) and
probably technical, though its fig. use is attested earlier (as Var. *R.*
1.17.1 'tools,' Cic. *Off.* 3.34 'help'). For the state as a weak body
needing support cf. Sen. *Hist.* fr. 1 *amissa enim libertate ... ita conse-
nuit tamquam sustentare se ipsa non ualeret nisi adminiculo regentium nitere-
tur.*   **erecta erat:** of staking plants at e.g. Col. 5.5.16 *palmites
... ad arundines erigere* (*OLD* 3c).   **M. Furio:** Camillus, one of
L.'s most important early heroes, and one who shares many traits
with the later Augustus, probably because they are both cut from
the same late-republican cloth (above, p. 8; see O. on 5.51–4).
Though he dominated the narrative of Book 5, his role in the
post-sack world is curiously and increasingly downplayed, esp. in
domestic situations (11.4n., 38n.); see further Miles (1) 14–18, (2)
193–204.   **principe** 'leading citizen,' 'the language of first century politics' (O. on 3.1.3; see *VL* 327–37, 441–2).   **stetit:** sc.
urbs, cf. Enn. *Ann.* 156 Sk *moribus antiquis res stat Romana uirisque,*
also alluded to at 3.1 (n.). For *stare* of vegetation (*OLD* 4) cf. Enn.
Ann. 223–4 Sk, Plin. *NH* 17.165 *sine adminiculo uitis per se sta-
bit.*   **abdicare:** cf. 5.49.9 (C. is asked not to abdicate immediately after his triumph); an equally anachronistic popular consensus
appointed him dictator in 390 (O. on 5.43.6–46). See further
6.9n.   **dictatura:** the etymological play with *abdicare* is very
common (2.5n.).   **nisi ... circumacto** 'until a year had
passed'; for *nisi* 'except' + abl. abs. see *OLD nisi* 6b. *circumagere* of
time, first at Lucr. 5.883, is almost exclusively Livian (*TLL*).
passi sunt: the subj. shifts to the plur. (sc. *ciues* or *Romani*).

1.5 comitia 'elections' (*OLD* 2). Their conventional placement
with 'end-of-year' material reinforces the overlap of *res gestae* as
text and as history; for their transitional force see above, p. 11 n.45.
in insequentem annum 'for the following year,' a transitional
formula which L. varies in case (nom. at 5.24.1, gen. at 31.1, abl.

at 11.1), as he does the formulaic introduction of a year by the consuls' names (8n.). It is not common elsewhere.   **tribunos:** sc.
militum (1n.); they are the subj. of *habere*.   **res ... rediit:** *res* for
res publica, as often. The force of the preverb in *rediit* is weak, but
present (*OLD* 10a): the *patres* are the default caretakers of the state.
So in the case of the death or resignation of all the chief magistrates
a five-day *interregnum* was declared; the *interrex*, who was chosen by
the highest-ranking patrician senators, renewed the auspices (2.5n.)
and held elections (J. Linderski, *SS* 38–9).

1.6 opere ac labore: virtual synonyms, here forming a hendiadys ('the laborious activity'); cf. 32.3.5 *confectos iam se labore opere*,
Virg. *A.* 6.129 with Austin, Tac. *H.* 5.12.1 with H.   **reficiendae:** cf. 33.38.14 *in operibus reficiendae urbis*. The verb is used of re-
pairing damaged structures (*OLD* 1a) as well as of revitalizing
plants or soil (*OLD* 5c, add Plin. *NH* 17.144, quoted at *OLD* 2a); it
bridges between the agricultural language of 3–4 and the theme of
building which continues through the next chh. *reficere* next recurs in
a cluster during the rogations (35.10 *bis*, 36.7, 38.2, 39.11, 40.8, 42.2)
in another technical sense, of re-electing magistrates (*OLD* 4). L.
thus creates a link between the city's recovery from the sack and
the plebeians' achievement of their political aims that may be
(re)read ironically (Rome's rebirth is reinterpreted as the threatening presence of Licinius and Sextius, reappointed year after year)
or positively (Rome's rebirth foreshadows plebeian access to greater
power within the state).   **Q. Fabio:** three Fabii were sent as
ambassadors to Clusium to deal with a Gallic military threat in
391 (5.35.5); their fierce behaviour provoked the Gallic attack.   **simul primum:** an unusual but not unparalleled combination (35.44.5, Hor. *Ep.* 2.2.49 with Brink).   **tr. plebis:** in this
phrase L. uses the gens. *plebis* and *plebi* (from the archaizing nom.
plebes) interchangeably, though unlike Sallust he prefers the former
(M–W on Tac. *A.* 4.6.4).   **dicta dies est:** an indictment or
summons (*OLD dies* 7b). This is the first act of plebeian aggression
in Book 6. It may be significant that L. reports it between the two
logically coherent notices about the *interregnum:* the plebeian tribune
interrupts the narration of patrician activities in a small way here,
as Licinius and Sextius will interrupt the operation of the state as
a whole later on (35.10n.); cf. 5.6, where there is no break between

res ... rediit and the naming of the *interreges*.   **orator** 'ambassa-
dor' (*OLD* 1).

1.7 cui iudicio ... subtraxit anticipates the frequent description by imperial writers of death as a last-minute reprieve or (more
regularly) as an escape from deserved punishment. *subtrahere* seems
to attach itself to such formulations, cf. 8.39.14 *ipse morte uoluntaria
ignominiae se ... subtraxit*, 9.26.7, Plin. *Ep.* 2.11.9 *cognitioni ... mors
opportuna subtraxit*, Sen. *Marc.* 26.2, Tac. *H.* 1.45.2.   **mors ...
opportuna** varies Cicero's *opportunitas mortis* (*De orat.* 3.12, *Brut.* 4)
a theme that became a commonplace in its own right (W. on Vell.
66.4). L. imbues Cicero's image with a cynical tone, cf. 23.30.12
mors adeo opportuna ut patrem quoque suspicione aspergeret.

1.8 is: the resumptive pronoun, regular in reports of appointments, contributes an annalistic flavour (above, p. 11). Official language continues in the asyndetic tribune list following; cf. 5.8
(tribes), *CIL* I² 2 p. 825 (index of magistracy titles), and the formulaic asyndeton in consular dates (e.g. Sall. *H.* 1.1, quoted on 3).
tribunos ... potestate: in. L. varies his recording of the yearly
transfer of power from one set of magistrates to another: (1) the announcement of an electoral assembly or *interregnum* is followed by its
results, the change of year marked by the process as well as by the
magistrates (as here); (2) a list of new magistrates is followed by
a phrase like *principio anni*, the change of year denoted simply by
naming the eponymous officials (as 6.3–4); (3) the names of the
new officials are worked into the narrative of a specific event (as
7.11.2 *ea fuit causa cur proximo anno C. Poetelius Balbus consul, cum collegae eius ... Hernici prouincia euenisset, aduersus Tiburtes ... exercitum duceret*). This flexibility contrasts with Thucydides' formulaic
recording of year-end (cf. 2.46.1) and with Tacitus' habit of beginning the year with the consuls' names in the abl. (Ginsburg 11). See
LHA 174 n.3 and above, pp. 11–12.

1.9–4.6 The year 389 B.C.

1.9–12 Internal affairs

The *res internae* are subdivided into two parts (10 *in primis*, 11 *tum*).
L.'s attention is more engaged by the matter of the *dies religiosi*,

which he accordingly discusses second, at greater length (above, p. 22), a modulation from short to long repeated within 10 (*alia ... uulgus ∼ quae ... suppressa*). The physical rebuilding of Rome began at 5.55.2–5 with little consideration for formal matters (2 *promisce*, 4 *omisso sui alienique discrimine*). Now, as if in response to the formal narrative reorganization of the new book, the state authorities turn to cleaning up in the legal and sacral realms.

1.9 de religionibus: very generally, matters involving due observance of laws relating to the supernatural (*OLD* 3b). The specific sense changes throughout the paragraph (nn.).

1.10 foedera: antiquarians and historians alike were interested in treaties as documentary material (O. on 2.33.4 and 4.4.10; see above, p. 10).   **erant ... leges:** i.e. the Twelve Tables, believed to have been preserved on bronze (3.57.10 with O.), and regal decrees (*CAH*[2] 107) of which the sixth-century *cippus* from the Forum may be an example (A. E. Gordon, *Illustrated introduction to Latin epigraphy* (1983) 78–80 with Pl. 3).   **autem** marks the parenthesis (*OLD* 4).   **conquiri** connotes going out of one's way to hunt out information, esp. of a verbal or documentary nature (cf. 34.5.6, 40.37.2, Cic. *Rab. perd.* 15 *ex annalium monumentis atque ex regum commentariis conquisierit*, Tac. *H.* 2.50.2).   **quae comparerent** 'such as could be found.'   **alia ex eis:** sc. *legibus. alia* is a 'summary priamel,' clearing away other information to focus attention on the sacral laws. It is a common narrative device in L. (cf. 15.4, 40.1, 1.1.1 *in ceteros saeuitum esse Troianos*); for the term see W. H. Race, *The classical priamel from Homer to Boethius* (1982) 10–17.   **edita:** sc. *sunt*, 'were presented for inspection,' often of documents (*OLD* 10a); for early Roman literacy see W. V. Harris, *Ancient literacy* (1989) 151–4. Omission of *est* or *sunt* with the perf. participle, though a natural and ancient feature of Latin, is surprisingly rare in 'classical' authors; Sall., L., and Tac. favour it, esp. in narrative (Schlicher 294–5), and it is a Virgilian mannerism (Austin on *A.* 2.2). The ellipse is easiest when the participle is sentence-final (as 42.8); for deponents (as 22.8) see Goodyear on Tac. *A.* 1.8.1 with App. 5. **etiam in uulgus:** for the political manipulation of documents cf. 9.46.4–5 (Cn. Flavius publishes the *ciuile ius*, an act exemplifying his *contumacia aduersus contemnentes humilitatem suam nobiles*). The effects of the archaic codification and dissemination of the law are debated, though they certainly extended beyond the simple provision

of information. Publication of rights and responsibilities could clarify certain social ground rules for those who could read or find
someone to read for them (last n.); W. Eder suggests that it was
designed to increase aristocratic power (*SSAR* 262–300). Withholding such information, however (*suppressa* below), ensures continued
control by those who possess the secret over those who are given
only select access to it. The non-availability of information will
play a key role in Tacitus' vision of the deceptive, manipulative
quality of *principatus* (cf. *A.* 1.6.3, 2.36.1 with Goodyear, and *H.*
1.4.2 for the danger of revealing *arcana imperii*).   **autem:** adversative (*OLD* 2).   **religione:** almost 'superstition' (*OLD* 6); for *rel.
obstringere* cf. Cic. *Ver.* 4.114, Caes. *C.* 1.11.12 *nulla tamen mendaci religione obstrictus*, Tac. *A.* 12.34. As *obstringere* literally means 'to bind',
L. plays on a popular derivation of *religio* from *re-ligare* (Maltby
522–3), cf. Lucr. 1.931–2 *et artis religionum nodis animos exsoluere pergo*
with Friedländer 19. The etymological play is reinforced by the interlaced word order of *ut ... animos*, which reproduces the coils of
religio.   **obstrictos ... animos:** for religious fear as a form of
social control cf. 5.14.1–5 (the patricians distort *religio* to defeat the
plebeians); Polybius singles it out as characteristic of Rome (6.56.6–
15; on the topos see Liebeschuetz 4–7, Levene 137 n.47). L.'s own
religious position is as elusive as his political one (above, pp. 6–9),
and the opinions he expresses are contextually determined (Levene
241–3); see further J. H. W. G. Liebeschuetz, *J.R.S.* 57 (1967) 45–55.

1.11 de diebus religiosis: after assembling existing ordinances
(10) the senate creates new ones.   **agitari:** here virtually synonymous with *agi* (*OLD* 18 ∼ *OLD ago* 40). The distribution of frequentative verbs in L. does not bear out the hypothesis of a stylistic
change in his writing (above, p. 17 n.72) but is 'determined by the
subject matter' (Adams (4) 57–9).   **coeptum:** sc. *est* (impers.), idiomatically attracted into the passive by the dependent passive infin.
(O. on 5.17.10).   **diemque ... Sextiles:** 18 July (Scullard 166).
Sextilis was renamed Augustus in 8 B.C. (A. B. Bosworth, *H.S.C.P.*
86 (1982) 164–70); here and in 12 L. uses the old name to avoid anachronism.   **duplici clade:** synchronism of notable events was
popular (cf. Tac. *A.* 15.41.2, the fires of Rome in 390 B.C. and A.D.
64; Plut. *Cam.* 19, the battles of Mycale, Plataea, and Marathon); for
the Fabii cf. 2.48–50, for the Allia, 5.38. They are later (9.38.15)
connected with Caudium. On significant days see A. T. Grafton

and N. M. Smerdlow, *J.W.I.* 51 (1988) 14–42.   **quo die ... pug-natum:** paired, parallel phrases, the second extended by *cum ...
urbis*; the descriptive expansion has an oratorical flavour (Dangel
31, cf. 40.2n.). The repetition of *dies* in this section is in an archaic
or legalistic manner (Adams (5) 87).   **insignemque:** repeated for
emphasis: the disaster of a single day will be perpetuated in the
yearly calendar (28.5–29n.). The repetition replays in miniature the
mise en abîme that history enacts: the battle, the chronicle, and the
narratives elaborating the chronicle are all *res gestae*.   **re ...
agenda:** for *insignis* + abl. of the gerundive cf. Tac. *A.* 6.29.3
Scaurus ... insignis nobilitate et orandis causis, and for L.'s flexibility in
using abls. to qualify adjs. see 14.11n., 31.4n. On the prohibitions
involving *dies religiosi* see Nisbet–Hubbard on Hor. *C.* 2.13.1.
priuatimque: slightly disjunctive (=*priuatimue*): *OLD -que* 7.

1.12 quidam ... putant: the second item under *dies religiosi* is
accorded the same space as the first, but L. reports the two less important matters as additional material found in his sources (*quidam*
sc. *auctores*). The verbal action becomes increasingly less direct from
11 (*appellarunt ... fecerunt*) to 12 (*iussum ... traditum putant*), mimicking
the process by which the *religio* was extended by analogy.
postridie Idus Quintiles: 16 July (Scullard 46); the month was
renamed in 44 B.C. (K. Scott, *Y.C.S.* 2 (1931) 221–4).   **neque ...
deum** 'and because the gods' blessing was not obtained'. The *pax
deorum* was a 'semi-legal and contractual' notion: 'if the worshippers
scrupulously did their part, it was hoped or even assumed that the
deities would do theirs' (Scullard 19). This disaster ensued because
Sulpicius did not follow correct ritual (*non litasset* = did not obtain
favourable omens; see Pease on Cic. *Diu.* 2.36).   **deum:** an old-
fashioned gen. plur., at this period mostly in formulae; L., like Tacitus, uses it with considerable latitude (Adams (4) 56), cf. 33.5.
post diem tertium = *tribus post diebus*: two, on our reckoning.
religio 'taboo' (*OLD* 2).   **traditum:** sc. *esse*: 'that ... it became
traditional' (*OLD* 4).

2–4.3 Affairs abroad

Military events in the first quarter of Book 6 are dominated by two
episodes (above, p. 12) in the *aristeia* of C., in each of which he faces

three enemies (2–4.3, 6.3–10.6); the first tricolon (Volsci–Aequi–
Etrusci) has a diminished second member and elaborated third
(above, p. 23). The story-shape is conventional: (1) report of external
threat, [(2) appointment of dictator and *magister equitum*], (3) field assignments, (4) engagement(s), (5) re-entry into city [with triumph].

Throughout this period hostile encounters between Romans and
their neighbours tend to be provoked by the latter, usually out of
the (vain) hope that the sack had significantly impaired Rome's
strength (on the scenario of Roman retaliation for an enemy attack, the so-called 'just war,' see Brunt (2) 305–8, and on the degree of destruction caused by the Gauls see *CAH*[2] 308). Instead,
Roman aggressiveness – additionally motivated by the pressing
need to acquire land (cf. 5.1 (n.), 36.11) and reduce internal debt
(11.8 (n.), 34.1–2: Oakley (2) 18–22) – results by the end of the
book in a series of victories which solidify Rome's position and allow it to begin the annexation of Italy.

2.1 Nec 'but ... not' (*OLD* 5).   **quietis** 'in peace,' sc. *Romanis*.
consilia ... agitare: the expression is first attested in L.
erigendae ∼ 1.4 *erecta erat*, continuing the physical language used
to describe the state. The gerundive suggests that that first upright
motion was a preliminary step in a long process – as indeed proves
to be the case. For *erigere rem pub.* cf. Pompey *apud* Cic. *Att.* 8.12c.3
possumus etiam nunc rem pub. erigere, V. Max 5.6 *ext.* 5 (*patria*), Sen.
Tro. 740 *Troiam erigent?* with Fantham.   **casu** 'fall': both lit. and
fig. senses are felt (last n.).

2.2 hinc ... afferebant: the two enemies are made parallel by
anaphora (Lausberg §§629–30) and homoioteleuton (Lausberg
§§725–8). L. upsets the balance by making the subj. of the second
element not the enemy but the merchants and by changing the
verb tense (*ceperant* ∼ *afferebant*).   **Volsci:** with their allies,
Rome's most persistent threat in this period (cf. 12.2–6 with *CAH*[2]
315–18). L. likes to flag stages in the narrative with 'headings,' often
(as here) using proper names (cf. *Etruriae* below: Luce (2) 285–7, C-L
18–24).   **ad exstinguendum nomen:** the expression (also at
28.30.10) is hyperbolic and Ciceronian, cf. *Cat.* 4.7 *populi Romani nomen exstinguere*, *Mur.* 80 *consilia ... nominis Romani exstinguendi* (both of
Catiline).   **ceperant:** a typical use of the pluperf. (with 3 *accesserat*) to set a scene economically by compressing background infor-

mation (*LHA* 179).   **Etruriae ... factam:** periodic suspension
creates a close-knit phrase whose key terms *Etruriae ... coniurationem
... factam* are located at beginning, middle, and end.   **fanum
Voltumnae:** a cult centre and political meeting place for the
Etruscan cities (O. on 5.33.9).   **afferebant** 'kept bringing.'

2.3 nouus ... fuerant: L. varies the form of his report of the
third threat (above, p. 23 n.95).   **Latinorum Hernicorumque:**
the so-called Latin League, a confederation of Latin communities
(*CAH*² 264–74), and the Hernician tribe are often linked; the *foedera* allying them with Rome were both traditionally signed by Sp.
Cassius (*CAH*² 276).   **pugnam ... factam:** probably in 496
(O. on 2.19–20).   **ambigua fide:** abl. of manner, cf. 36.35.8
quos non sincera fide in amicitia fuisse satis constat.   **in amicitia ...
fuerant:** the official phrase was *in amicitia p. R. permanere* (Powell
on Cic. *Sen.* 41).

2.4 itaque ... (5) Camillum: L. moves the reader from the
emotional circumstances of the threatened conflict to the decision
to appoint a dictator, from the vague *tanti undique terrores* to the specific *M. Furium Camillum.* Though the bipartite *cum*-clause increases
in length, expanding the enemies' hatred, the sentence as a whole
is built of progressively shorter units (*cum ... laborare ∼ placuit ...
C.*, itself subdivided into *placuit ... esset ∼ dictatoremque ... C.*), an increasing terseness focusing attention on the significant name at the
end (Marouzeau II 90; see also 1.3n.).   **cum ... circumstarent:** cf. Cic. *Phil.* 10.20 *dies et noctes omnia nos undique fata circumstant*
and other parallels (largely Livian) cited by Austin on Virg. *A.*
2.559 *saeuus circumstetit horror.*   **odio ... contemptu:** emotions
characteristically felt for a tyrant by his subjects in response to his
identical feelings about them. When the accompanying fear is over-
ridden, hatred and contempt motivate rebellion; cf. 9 and see M–W
on Tac. *A.* 4.40.2 (hatred and fear), Arist. *Pol.* 1311b36–12a17 (contempt). L. not infrequently hints at the emotions of those who found
themselves in the path of Roman expansion, first at *Praef.* 7, cf. 6.11
(*inuidia et odio*), 33.3–6. Like other Roman historians, he can put a
sympathetic speech into the mouth of an enemy, as 9.1.3–11,
21.19.9–10 (*LHA* 84; see Ogilvie–Richmond on Tac. *Ag.* 30–3 and
Balsdon 161–92); he will similarly change the focalization to show
things from the plebeian point of view (e.g. 16.3n.; see I. J. F. de

Jong, *Narrators and focalizers* (1987)). **apud ... inter:** typical Livian *uariatio* of prepositions, as 8.4, 9.11, 25.4, 34.5, 8: Catterall 300–1, Sörbom 46–9.

2.5 eiusdem auspiciis ... cuius: for the brachylogy cf. 2.20.1 *domestica etiam gloria accensus ut cuius familiae decus eiecti reges erant, eiusdem interfecti forent.* As at 1.4, C. represents continuity between rescue and recovery; for his embodiment of the state's good fortune see also 3.1n. **auspiciis:** abl. of attendant circs. (Roby §1246). The chief magistrate(s) took the auspices before any important action 'to test the rightness of a preconceived plan by looking for a sign of divine encouragement or warning' (Scullard 27; see also Rykwert 44–8). The possession of *auspicia* and the authority they convey will be a crucial issue in the rogations (41.4–5nn.). **reciperata esset** 'had been recaptured,' L.'s word of choice to describe C.'s recovery of Rome (5.49.3, 49.7, 51.3 *bis*, 7.18.1, 22.14.9, 25.6.11); see further 11.4n. **dictatoremque dici:** a *figura etymologica*, the dictator's title being traditionally explained by his being appointed, not elected (e.g. Var. *L.* 5.82 *dictator quod a consule dicebatur, cui dicto audientes omnes essent*: Maltby 186–7). The title itself is an agent noun meaning one who prescribes, a meaning reflected in the dictator's first action, the appointment of a *magister equitum* (6 *dictator ... dixit*). The play between active and passive encapsulates the process by which the dictator is chosen, invested with (theoretically) absolute powers, but expected eventually to resign those powers (*CAH*[2] 190–2).

2.6 is: 1.8n. **iustitioque:** in times of emergency the city suspended all business, public and private. *indicto* 'proclaimed' continues the play with *dicere* (5n.); for the sentence shape ('phrase à relance') see above, p. 21. **dilectum ... iuratos centuriaret:** three stages of a military levy: the *dilectus* or choosing of those eligible, the oath-taking (*OLD iuro* 5a), the division into fighting units (*IM* 625–44). L.'s precise description, which continues in 6, conveys the Roman orderliness and vitiates in advance the fond enemy expectation (9) that the recently defeated Rome will not be able to mount a defence. **ita ut** introduces a slight concession (*OLD ita* 19): the levy of *iuniores* (men aged from 17 to 45) was conducted so as not to exclude some *seniores* (those aged 46 and over); cf. 4.54.2 *tunc primum plebeiis quaestoribus creatis ita ut in quattuor creandis uni patricio ...*

relinqueretur locus. Wholesale call-ups such as this were made in response to extreme emergencies (*IM* 21, 639)   **centuriaret:** surprisingly rare in this technical sense, of dividing soldiers into groups of 100 (cf. 10.21.4, fr. book 11 (*Athenaeum* 56 (1988) 447–521 at 471–2), Cic. *Red. pop.* 13.1); on its figurative use in comedy (= 'marshal') see Fantham 29.

2.7 conscriptum armatumque: recording of names and distribution of arms; for the continuative participles see above, p. 20. **trifariam:** a Livian coinage modelled after the common *bifariam* and not found again before the second century A.D. L. seems to have liked coining or appropriating numeral forms, cf. *octiplicatus* (only at 4.24.7), *octoiugis* (of tribunes at 5.2.10; compounds of a numeral + *-iugis* are otherwise applied to teams of animals); on his advs. see also 36.7n., 36.12n.   **unam ... alteram:** L. links the Etrurian and urban armies by arranging them and their tribunes chiastically (∼8 *his ... illis*); the third army, which C. commands, is added at the end (8 *tertiam ... adortus*: above, p. 24) to lead into C.'s successful campaigns. Manlius and Aemilius are not heard of again.   **Veiente Etruriae:** a jingoistic juxtaposition, reminding us that Veii is no longer part of Etruria (4.4n.). For the adjectival abl. sing. in *-e* see G–L §83 R. and cf. 14.13 (n.), 21.1.

2.8 tribuni ... Manlius ... Aemilius: partitive apposition (G–L §322); the verb (*praepositus*) agrees with the nearer of the subjs. The magistrates remained in office but took instructions from the dictator; cf. 6.12–15.   **ipse** frequently designates a commander (M–W on Tac. *A.* 4.24.3). Caesar is especially fond of referring to himself as 'himself' (cf. Hirt. *G.* 8.46.1, 3, 5 – a somewhat wicked imitation?).   **ad** = *aduersus* (*OLD* 31).   **ad ... dicitur:** if the text is right, this means 'the place is called "near [the?] Mecius"'; cf. Var. *L.* 5.154 *intimus circus 'ad Murciae' uocatur* (Richardson 260), and for the play in meanings of *ad* see 3.5n.   **oppugnare est adortus:** a cliché of military narrative.

2.9 Quibus ... intulerat: the terms of the rel. clause are reversed in the main clause: enemy confidence owing to supposed Roman weakness ∼ enemy fear owing to actual Roman strength. *quibus ... profectis* is dat., though the habitual shape of the historiographical period (above, p. 21) leads one to expect an abl.; for continuative dat. participles see Spilman 198.   **ab** 'as a consequence of' (*OLD*

15), a usage extended by L. (Gries 87–90); he also uses the (equivalent) unaccompanied causal abl. (as 4, 21.3). **crederent:** verbs of speaking (etc.) when introducing reasons commonly go into the subjunc. by an idiomatic extension of the subjunc. of alleged reason (*NLS* §242 *Note* ii). **tantum** goes with *terroris* below; for similar hyperbata with the partitive gen. cf. 4.8, 10.1, 14.8, 19.3. **C. ... imperator** 'the report that C. was general'; for the AUC participle (1.1n.) cf. Ov. *Ars* 3.684 *audita paelice.* The power of a ruler's name was a panegyrical motif (W. on Vell. 94.4), cf. 9.18.6, Caes. *C.* 3.13.2, Luc. 2.600 *iam uictum fama non uisi Caesaris agmen.* See also 8.5n. **imperator terroris intulerat:** this cluster of similar sounds reinforces the connection between the general and the fear he inspires. In prose as in verse, alliteration and assonance frequently highlight a phrase or the organization of a sentence (J. Marouzeau, *Traité de stylistique latine* (1954) 45–50, Goodyear on Tac. *A.* 1.3.2 with App. 3); see further above, p. 24. **uallo ... uallum:** cf. 22.60.23 *obsessi uallum armis, se ipsi tutati uallo sunt.* The polyptoton (Lausberg §§643–4) is picked up by the verbal doubling *fuerit ... fuerat* in 11 (= epiphora, Lausberg §§631–2). **intrare ad:** very rare with an inanimate obj. (cf. Phaedr. 5.9.2). **hostis:** focalized by the Volsci; cf. 3.3n. (*hostibus*).

2.10 quod: connective (*NLS* §230 (6)). **et forte ... uersa:** C. takes advantage of a chance occurrence to turn the battle into a terrifying rout. The weight of L.'s description, enhanced by alliteration (9n.), is on the effects of the wind, giving it the status of an unstoppable natural force. Plutarch's C., on the other hand, anticipates the wind and plans his attack the night before (*Cam.* 34.4–5, cf. Plut. *Sert.* 17.7 for the stratagem). For the form of expression cf. 3.7.3, 26.4.1 *uis omnis belli uersa in Capuam*; for wind helping fires burn cf. 21.37.2.

2.11 aperuit ... uiam is choice, cf. 35.3, Virg. *A.* 10.864 with Harrison; C. is the subj. **uapore ... crepituque:** *-que* joins a related third element to a natural pair, cf. 1.28.7 *populo Romano ac mihi uobisque, Albani,* 22.9.4 *miles hibernis itineribus ac palustri uia proelioque ... affectus.* The sensory vividness of the description increases: steamy heat – smoke – crackling noise. **uiridis** is scarce in L. (four times, always of vegetation) though not rare elsewhere; cf. 22.7nn. **flagrantis** in a lit. sense is predominantly poetic

and historiographical (*OLD* 1).   **consternauit:** a strong verb
with which Ovid characterizes his personified *Terrores* (*M.* 12.60)
and attested only rarely before L., who promotes it.   **moles:** by
a kind of syllepsis this has a choice fig. sense ('effort', *OLD* 8, cf.
Virg. *A.* 1.33, Vell. 121.1, Tac. *A.* 2.78.1) with *superantibus ... in castra*
but its lit. meaning with *transcendentibus ... absumptam* below ('pile',
esp. of a defensive structure, *OLD* 3).   **superantibus ... Ro-**
manis: the word order imitates the Roman progress over the *ual-*
lum into the Volscian camp, a sort of verbal hurdles; the postponed
Romanis are juxtaposed with their enemies.   **uallum ... muni-**
tum ∼ *saepem ... absumptam* below.   **fuerit:** the perf. subjunc.
stresses that the result actually happened (*NLS* §164).

  2.12 fusis ... cepisset: alliteration of *s* and *c* continues the
striking sound patterns (previously of *f, u,* and *m*) that characterize
the incident (9n.).   **militi:** this collective sing. (=*militibus*), an
ex. of synecdoche (*Rhet. Her.* 4.44–5) is common only in L., Tac.,
and Amm. (M–W 88); *inermis* (3.8) is analogous. L. similarly favours
the sing. of nationalities (e.g. 13.4 *Romanus*, 31.6 *Volscus*).   **quo**
... gratiorem: an attributive phrase modifying *praedam* and separated from it by the verb. This type of hyperbaton is a Sallustian
stylistic development probably in imitation of Thucydides and imitated by Tacitus (Adams (1) 8–9); for L. cf. 3.10, 5.5, 6.13, 18, 14.5,
23.9, 34.6.   **minus ... minime:** L. habitually uses the positive
and comparative degrees in such plays (11.1n.), but cf. 4.11.2 (*maiori*
... maxime).   **minime ... duce** 'because their leader was hardly
given to generosity'. C.'s reputation for stinginess comes partly from
his insistence that one tenth of the *praeda Veientana* be given to
Delphic Apollo, a politically insensitive move generating such re-
sentment that he was eventually forced into exile (5.23.8–11, 32.8–
9). Domestic *largitio* tended to be perceived as a revolutionary
move (17.5n.), and in refusing it C. is distinctly Catonian (Sall. *C.*
54.3 *nihil largiundo*: 11.7n.); but distribution of booty – which could
also be made state property (4.11) – was an accepted way of increasing soldiers' pay. On the general's authority over *praeda* see Paul on
Sall. *J.* 41.7; on the economic benefits of war see Oakley (2) 22–8.

  2.13 persecutus ... depopulatus esset: continuative cola
('he pursued ... and ravaged'): above, p. 20. Deponent perf. participle + *cum*-clause is an order favoured by L. but avoided by Caesar

(Spilman 213 n.96). **septuagesimo:** a rhetorical number (A. Dreizehnter, *Die rhetorische Zahl* (1978) 86–8); see also 20.6n., 42.6n. **subegit** is optimistic, as the Volsci are again a threat only three years later (cf. 12.2–6), but cf. C.'s (Augustan) *elogium, CIL* I² 1 p. 191 *Aequis et Volscis subactis.*

2.14 Aequos: the Aequi serve as a hinge to move C. from Lanuvium to Sutrium; for L.'s use of physical motion to effect narrative transition (also at 9.3, 26.2–3, 33.4 etc.) see *LHA* 180–1 and cf. 6.2n. **et ... molientes** 'who were also engineering war'. *bellum m.* is first in L. (but cf. Cic. *Clu.* 176 *insidias m., Att.* 7.11.1 *scelera m.*); *moliri* is 'a good verb' which implies 'the skill needed to engineer something effective in a difficult situation' (Austin on Virg. *A.* 2.109). L. is also the first to use it in the sense 'force out of position' (metaphorically at 11.8, lit. at 33.11: Tac. *A.* 1.39.3 with Goodyear) and of non-physical disturbance (33.49.7 *ad animum eius moliendum*). **oppressit** 'surprised' (military jargon: *OLD* 7a). **impetu primo:** capture at the first charge is a mark of a good general (as 4.9, 23.5, 33.7 etc.), analogous to the efficacy of his name (9n.) or appearance (8.5n.).

3–4.3 Sutrium. L. transforms the threatened Etruscan attack on Rome (2.2) into an attack on its allies. Rather than having to defend themselves, the Romans assume their self-appointed role as guardians of world peace (as 33.8, but cf. their refusal to intervene at 21.9); the first Samnite and Second Punic wars e.g. allegedly began with just such situations (see Weinstock 267–9, Brunt (2) 170–2, 433–80). The narrative pits helpless allies against greedy invaders in a twice-told siege, in which the townspeople's exodus and rescue is doubled and reversed by the Etruscan looting and punishment (5–10nn.): cf. 6 *iterum ... eodem die Sutrium capitur.* The episode is bracketed by an introduction (1–4) and epilogue (4.1–3), both framed by repetitions of C.'s name, in whose centres we see a brief glimpse of Rome itself: the senate making a decision (2), gold being returned to the matrons (4.2). The structure thus reinforces the opening statement that C. embodies Roman power (*cum ... esset*).

3.1 cum ... esset: the panegyrical topos that the state's well-being is where its leader is (8.5n.); for the form of expression cf. Laelius' eulogy of Scipio Aemilianus (*orat.* 23) *necesse enim fuisse ibi esse terrarum imperium ubi ille esset, Pan. Lat.* 7.10.2 *ibi uero paene funditus*

corruit unde tu, Maximiane, discesseras.   **caput rei Rom.:** a striking
epithet combining the hyperbolic *caput rerum* (= Rome, an Augustan
formulation: Nicolet (2) 192 with nn. 9–10) with the Ennian *res Romana* (e.g. *Ann.* 156 Sk, quoted on 1.4); for it see Pinsent (1). The
metaphor, which became common in panegyric (W. on Vell. 101.2
duo rei publicae capita), draws on the comparison of the state to a
body with one governing entity and co-operating limbs which can
neither become outsized (Sen. *Contr.* 7 *praef.* 2) nor rebel (2.32.9–12)
if the health of the whole is to be maintained (for state ~ body see
Béranger 218–37, Fantham 122–3, 128–9). The present expression
recalls the army's plight during the Gallic invasion (5.46.5 *corpori
ualido* [sc. *exercitui*] *caput deerat*), a situation saved by C.'s intervention. See A. Wallace-Hadrill, *J.R.S.* 76 (1986) 68, 70–3 and for challenges to this heady authority see 5.6n., 37.4n.   **ea ... esset**
'this is how things were going'. C.'s favourable luck, which is in
counterpoise to the Sutrini's bad fortune (3), will result in (*mala*) *fortuna* for the Etruscans (9n.).   **terror ingens:** a Livian commonplace.   **ingruerat** 'had fallen menacingly'; for the pluperf. see
2.2n. *ingruere* is a significant player in the debate about the evolu-
tion of L.'s vocabulary (Gries 43–4). It occurs once at Pl. *Amph.*
236, next in Virg. (Austin on *A.* 2.301), but is most frequent in L.
(14) and Tac. (28). L. regularly construes it with *in* (as here), elsewhere only at Tac. *H.* 3.34.1 *ingruente in Italiam Hannibale* – a Livian
nod doubly appropriate in a context involving Hannibal and an
obituary notice for a city (cf. 5.22.8, Veii). See also 24.10n.

3.2 Sutrium: a strategically important town (9.4) colonized
probably in 383 with Nepet (21.4: *CAH*[2] 312).   **socios:** in apposition to *Sutrium*, cf. 21.2, 9.21.6 *Plisticam ... socios Romanorum*; for the
political connotations of *socius* see B. on 31.1.9–10.   **quorum:**
the antecedent is *socios*.   **affectis** anticipates 3 *confecta*: the change
in prefix encapsulates the passage from partial to total disaster.
ut ... ferret: the content of the decree. The army stationed in
Veian territory (2.7) could have reached Sutrium much faster, but
this is C.'s show.   **primo quoque tempore** 'at the soonest possible moment' ~ 4 *eo forte tempore*: the dictator's earliest convenience
will be the moment of Sutrium's greatest despair. The synchronism
elevates both C.'s importance and the magnitude of the military
rescue.

3.3 cuius ... (4) interuenit: a historiographical period (above, p. 21) whose first element (*cuius ... potuisset*) provides a backdrop ('they could not wait, and so ...'). Description of the siege and capture of cities was a popular declamatory and historiographical motif (G. M. Paul, *Phoenix* 76 (1982) 144–55; see further 4.10nn., 33.7nn., 34.4n.); on L.'s use of such formulaic scenes see above, pp. 15–16. **spei moram** 'the delay of their hope', also at Vell. 67.2, Tac. *A.* 16.19.1. Shifting hope is perhaps the clearest illustration of the reciprocity between conquerer and conquered that is highlighted throughout the episode by changes in viewpoint. The *spei mora* that the Sutrini cannot endure finds its complement in the Etruscans' *desperatio* (8); their response, the *spes ultima* of battle (9), turns within the sentence to *spes uitae*, whose acceptance entails relinquishment of the title *uictor* (5 *uictorem uagum*, 6 *uictores Etrusci*, 4.1 *Camillus ... uictor*). On this 'alternation of action represented syntactically' see McDonald 165.   **fortuna** 'condition' (*OLD* 11a); see 1n. Abstract (*fortuna, paucitas*) and impers. nouns (*agmen*, 4 *turba, fletus*) heighten the pathos of the surrender.   **confecta:** conventional in such contexts, cf. 42.54.3 *oppidanos diem noctem eosdem tuentes moenia non uulnera modo sed etiam uigiliae et continens labor conficiebat*, Caes. *C.* 2.41.3 *equitibus ut paucis et labore confectis.*   **paucitas:** abstract for concrete (=*pauci*), regular in military narrative (*TLL*).   **opere ... uulneribus:** abls. of instrument; the asyndeton piles on the hardships.   **quae ... urgebant:** for the topos of fresh besiegers wearing down the limited resources of the besieged cf. 4.10, 5.19.11, 42.54.3 (quoted above), Caes. *C.* 3.40.1; for *urgere* in sieges cf. 5.4.10, 25.27.9.   **hostibus:** the referent of *hostis* changes throughout the episode: *Etrusci* (3, 8), *Sutrini* (5), *Romani* (6, 9); see *LHA* 193 and on *spei moram* above.   **inermis ... uestimentis:** the interlaced word order is a decorative touch for which cf. 25.11, 27.9 (n.), 32.1, 2, 34.7, 38.13, 42.13 (n.) and see W. on Vell. 100.1. *inermis ... emissa* agree with *paucitas* above; for the single piece of clothing see B. on 31.17.3.   **miserabili agmine:** abl. of manner; for the scene cf. 1.29.5 *iam continens agmen migrantium impleuerat uias*, Tac. *A.* 1.40.4 *incedebat muliebre et miserabile agmen ... lamentantes ... coniuges quae simul trahebantur*, an 'intensely pathetic mode of description' (Goodyear).   **penates** 'home' (*OLD* 3).

3.4 eo forte tempore resumes *cum* above, emphasizing the mo-

ment of C.'s arrival on to L.'s elaborately set scene. For pleonasm
with expressions of time see Vell. 78.2 with W.; for *forte* see
9.10n. **interuenit:** C.'s entrance recalls his appearance in
Rome in 390: *nam forte quadam priusquam infanda merces perficeretur ...
dictator interuenit* (5.49.1). This sense of timing is both strategically
(23.6n.) and narratively important: by arriving at the moment of
concentrated despair C. effects a peripeteia (cf. 8.2n., 12.11n.,
21.6n., 22.7n. and see *LHA* 201–4, 209–10). A significant difference
between domestic and foreign affairs in Book 6 is the pronounced
absence of such skill among the authorities at home: only the rebels
have comparable timing (esp. Manlius, 14.3–10, but Licinius and
Sextius have a sense of occasion as well at 35.10, cf. 36.1). **cui
... ferre:** like the previous sentence, this one juxtaposes the lei-
surely recapitulation of the connective rel. + *cum*-clauses with C.'s
quick military decisions (Luce (2) 287–8). **cui:** sympathetic dat.
with *ad pedes* (*NLS* §63). **prouoluisset:** a choice historiographical favourite (e.g. Sis. fr. 104 *mare persubhorrescere caecosque fluctus in se
prouoluere ... occepit*, Tac. *H.* 1.41.2 with H.); for personal supplica-
tion cf. Curt. 3.12.11 *prouolutae ad pedes*, [Quint.] *Decl.* 5.9.2 *ad tua
genua prouoluor*, Tac. *A.* 11.30.1 *genibus Caesaris prouoluta*. **orationem
... expressam:** cf. 8.2.6 *ultima ... necessitate expressam* [sc. *deditionem*], Curt. 9.3.6 *uoces ... necessitate ultima expressas*. **fletus:**
nom. sing. Lamentation is a standard feature of the captured city,
cf. 1.29.5, 5.21.11 *mixto mulierum ac puerorum ploratu*; for weeping
women in L. see Santoro L'hoir (2) 83–5. **exsilii comites:** the
topos of women accompanying their men into exile recurs in imperial literature (H. on Tac. *H.* 1.13.1); for the form of expression
see W. on Vell. 100.5. **trahebantur:** conventional in such contexts (*OLD* 2), cf. 9.17.16 *mulierum ac spadonum agmen trahentem*, Tac.
A. 1.40.4 (quoted 3n.), *A.* 3.33.2 *placitum olim ne feminae in socios ...
trahebantur*. **excepisset** 'followed' (*OLD* 16), cf. 33.11, 7.13.11 *orationem ... exceperunt preces multitudinis*. **parcere ... ferre:** the
chiastic arrangement centred on *iussit* underscores the shift from
Sutrium's grief to that in store for Etruria. With *se ... ferre* sc.
dixit, a common and mild zeugma (Bell 310). **luctum lacrimasque:** abstract + concrete. For the alliterative combination cf.
22.49.9 *lacrimarum satis luctusque est*, Cic. *Pis.* 89 *lamentis luctuque* and
see above, p. 22. **ferre** 'to inflict on' (*OLD* 30a–b = *OLD* afferre

16), a sense which, with a personal subj. and a pejorative obj., is almost exclusively poetic (*TLL* VI 546.52–7), cf. Tac. *D.* 5.5 *inimicis metum et terrorem ultro ferat* with Gudeman. The substitution of a simple for a compound form is a mark of elevated style (W. on Vell. 91.1; see Bell 330–3, Riemann 191–200).

3.5 inde 'then' (*OLD* 5).   **ferre** 'bring' ~ 4 *ferre*, with a change of meaning. This kind of repetition with varied meaning (*traductio*) is a Livian mannerism; cf. 9, 2.8, 26.7, 31.6, 40.13 (nn.). He tends to use it with ordinary words, as 5.46.7 *discriminaque rerum prope perditis rebus seruabant*; it is equally a feature of Virgil's style (Austin on *A.* 1.85, 2.505) and should perhaps be recognized in Caesar in cases where carelessness or inelegance have been alleged (as by Eden 84–5).   **iubet:** the first in a series of hist. presents running through 8 when the fighting begins and L. switches to hist. infins. For this typical verbal *uariatio* see *LHA* 195–6 (this episode), C-L 369–410 (historiography in general).   **Ita ... profectus:** C.'s procedure is conventional, cf. Caes. *C.* 1.64.5, *B. Afr.* 9.1. **ad** 'to the neighbourhood of', regular with town names in military narratives (G–L §337 R.4).   **id ... rebatur** looks forward, cf. 33.3, Virg. *A.* 6.97 *uia ... quod minime reris, Graia pandetur ab urbe*, Tac. *A.* 4.71.3 and see 24.9n.   **soluta** 'lax' of conditions is first in L. (*OLD* 6a).   **omnia:** the neut. plur. in battle scenes and other vivid descriptions is characteristically Livian (Walsh on 21.11.6), cf. 13.3 *mota ... omnia*, 1.29.2 *omnia ... miscet*, 9.43.16 *omnia obtinet caedes*. It appears to be an extension of Caesar's fondness for *omnia* with expressions of fullness in battle scenes (e.g. *G.* 5.33.6, *C.* 2.41.8); cf. 24.26.14 *tandem uolneribus confectae, cum omnia replessent sanguine, exanimes corruerunt*, Hirt. *G.* 8.25.1 *cum omnia caedibus ... uastasset*, Sall. *J.* 92.3, 101.11, Tac. *A.* 1.70.3 *cuncta pari uiolentia inuoluebantur*, *A.* 4.49.3. **ut fit** marks a proverb or commonplace (*OLD* 3b); see also 34.7n. For the idea that good fortune makes its possessor incautious cf. 5.44.6, 21.61.2 *ferme fit ut secundae res neglegentiam creent* and see Otto 142, 145; it informs admonitions to be prepared for trouble even in prosperity (Nisbet–Hubbard on Hor. *C.* 2.10.13–14).   **inuenit ... egerentem:** as C. arrives, the scene is reset for a second siege. Instead of beaten *oppidani* leaving with their possessions, he finds a victorious army looting (*praedam ... egerentem* ~ 3 *emissa uestimentis*); the latter's carelessness is displayed in an asyndetic tricolon which ironically answers 3 *opere ... uulneribus* (esp. *nullam statio-nem* ∼ 3 *uigiliis*). The perspective is that of C. arriving outside Su-trium: the eye moves from city outskirts to gates to the homes of the dispossessed; for other exx. of 'graphic presentation' (*LHA* 181) cf. 23.2 (n.), 3.42.6–7 (moving outward from Rome), Cato fr. 83 (with von Albrecht 28), Virg. *A.* 1.159–69 (entering a harbour). **nullam ... egerentem:** appositional to *soluta omnia* above; for the shape of the tricolon see above, p. 23. **stationem:** conven-tional of the careless enemy (e.g. 5.39.2, 9.45.15, 25.38.16, all in reconnoitring reports): M–W on Tac. *A.* 4.48.1. **egerentem:** first at Cato *Agr.* 37.3 *stercus egerito*; L. and Ovid develop its use in non-agricultural contexts (previously at *B. Alex.* 21.5); for *praedam egerere* cf. Tac. *H.* 3.33.2 with H. L. favours uncommon or vivid compound verbs, e.g. *concrepare* (24.1n.), *emouere* (38.8n.); on com-pounds of *equitare* see 7.3n.

3.6 iterum: a signal that what follows is like what has preceded (3–4.3n.); for the narrative self-referentiality see 39.5n. *iterum ... spa-tium* summarizes the battle that ensues, the narrative of which chi-astically expands this 'blurb': *eodem die ... capitur* ∼ 10 *oppidum ... captum*; *conglobandi ... in unum aut arma capiundi* ∼ 8 *arma capere ... con-uocare suos* (above, p. 22). **eodem die:** the coincidence enhances the peripeteia; cf. Sall. *J.* 66–9 (Vaga retaken on the next day), Virg. *A.* 10.508 *haec te prima dies bello dedit, haec eadem aufert*; see also 20.12n. **ab nouo hoste:** C.'s second intervention (4n.). **neque ... spatium:** an accumulation of gerund(ive)s typical of military narrative; cf. 9.4, Caes. *G.* 2.20.1 (nine), 4.24.2, *C.* 3.38.2, Tac. *H.* 1.32.2, *A.* 1.67.1 (four). **conglobandi:** cf. Sis. fr. 64 *con-globati et collecti concrepant armis*, Sall. *J.* 97.4; the verb is favoured by L. and Tacitus. **coeundique in unum:** virtually synonymous with *conglobandi*, a phenomenon known as *congeries uerborum* (cf. Laus-berg §406, 'horizontal amplification'); cf. 4.10, 11.8, 24.9, 40.4 and see *LHA* 240.

3.7 quisque tenderent: a plur. verb in agreement with a col-lective noun is common in early Latin; Cicero admits it when the noun and the verb are in different clauses (as 17.6 *turba ... dilabeba-tur [et] minabantur*), and there are a few exx. in Caes. and Sall. L. uses it 'd'une manière très hardie' (Riemann 255–6). **portas ... portas:** the repetition, which is characteristic in the neighbour-

hood of a parenthesis (see below), iconically represents the gates'
dual function, as (possible) escape and as trap. Many class such repetition as subconscious (e.g. B. on Books 34–6, p. 13); but like
sound patterns (2.9n.), it can highlight or unify an expression or
a section of narrative.   **si** 'to see if' (*OLD* 11).   **se … ei-**
cere: a panicky reaction, cf. 9.10, 28.3.10 *patefacta repente porta … ex*
oppido sese eiecerunt, Caes. *G.* 4.15.1 *armis abiectis … se ex castris eiecerunt.*
Where the *oppidani* had been 'sent out' (3 *emissa*), the Etruscans cannot escape; for besiegers besieged inside locked gates cf. 33.9–12.
id … imperauerat: the parenthesis heightens the emphasis on
clausas and focuses attention on C.'s order; for the demonstrative
pronoun cf. 19.4 and see M. von Albrecht, *Die Parenthese in Ovids*
Metamorphosen und ihre dicterische Funktion (1964) 96–7, with 84–9 on
the repetition of a word before and after the parenthesis (*portas ~*
portas).   **enim** marks the parenthesis (*OLD* 3).

3.8 alii … alii: description of the activity of different groups
headed by forms of *alius, pars* etc., a staple of historiographical narrative, is the small-scale reflection of L.'s 'unit narrations' (Luce (2)
285; above, p. 12). See also 10.3n.   **capere:** hist. infin. with conative or inceptive force (so *conuocare* below): *NLS* §21.   **tumultus**
'sudden attack' (*OLD* 2b).   **conuocare … ut:** cf. 44.12.3 *conuo-*
cabanturque ut signa … inferrent. conuocare is generally used absolutely
and paired with a verb of commanding or exhorting, as Nep. *Han.*
10.5 *classiarios conuocat iisque praecipit omnes ut … concurrant.*
desperatione ~ 3 *spei moram* (n.).   **ni:** an archaism; L. increasingly prefers *nisi*, a trend in which he is followed by Tacitus
(Adams (4) 60). The peripeteia introduced by *ni* is typically Livian,
a device borrowed from Hellenistic historiography (O. on 3.5.8); for
the '*ni* de rupture' see C-L 597–616.   **poni … parci** ~ 4–5 *par-*
cere … deponi (chiastic with *uariatio* of voice and prefix); C.'s orders
again put an end to emotional and physical distress (5n.).   **parci**
… uiolari recalls the most celebrated expression of Rome's
foreign policy, Virg. *A.* 6.853 *parcere subiectis et debellare superbos*; for
prose parallels see Austin's n.   **inermi:** collective sing. (2.12n.).
For the common pairing with *armatus* (below) cf. 26.6 *quid arma pol-*
leant uestra … inermes experiemur and see McKeown on Ov. *Am.*
1.2.22, W. on Vell. 80.4.

3.9 animi … obstinati: an old-fashioned expression that L.

likes (e.g. 20.11, 5.41.1); see H. on Tac. *H.* 2.101.2. *obstinatus ad* is
first in L. (*TLL*).   **spe ultima** ~ 4 *necessitate ultima*.   **iactare
... offerre:** hist. infins. close the abortive fighting, as they began
it (8); in each case they sketch in what immediately follows the turning point of the action (Viljamaa 59–60). Tacitus echoes this passage with its uncommon reflexive form at *Ag.* 37.3 *inermes ultro ruere
ac se morti offerre*; see further 11.7n.   **fortuna** has a 'casual and
conventional' sense (*LHA* 57 n.2) = 'the way things fell out' (*OLD*
5). But its third occurrence in one chapter is not casual: both sides
owe their condition to the good luck that C. brought with him (1n.).

3.10 diuisa ... redditum: passive verbs and short sentences
are characteristic of 'military communiqué' style (O. on 2.26.6, following Fraenkel II 69–73), cf. 10.5, 32.9, 42.7; for the choice *diuidere
in* see Tac. *A.* 2.67.2 with Goodyear.   **inuiolatum integrum-
que:** for the assonant synonyms (6n.) cf. Cic. *Ver.* 4.130, *Cael.* 11,
Col. 3.18.2; for the attribute's separation from its noun (*oppidum*)
see 2.12n.   **ui captum:** a military cliché, e.g. 1.11.7, 24.20.8,
Cato fr. 136, Cic. *Ver.* 4.120, *B. Hisp.* 1.4, Fron. *S.* 3.8.1.   **ui** ~ *per
condiciones* below (Catterall 305–6, Sörbom 84–7).   **traditum** ~ 3
per pactionem urbe ... tradita (5n.).

4.1 Camillus ... uictor: for those who believe C. imitates Augustus, this triple triumph recalls the most famous one in recent
memory, that of Augustus in 29 (e.g. Burck (2) 360). C. and Augustus share some qualities (1.4n.), but L. never explicitly compares Augustus to *any* republican hero; moreover, the early books of the *AVC*
were written well before Augustus' propaganda of images was fixed
(above, p. 8).   **in urbem ... rediit:** returning to Rome or Italy
is a favourite closural device in military narrative, cf. 10.6, 26.8,
33.12, 38.1 (n.), Caes. *G.* 6.44.3, *B. Alex.* 78.5, *B. Afr.* 98.2, Sall. *J.*
114.3, and see Smith 175–8.   **triumphans:** regular in L.'s formulaic triumph notices, though the participle is less frequent than
the perf. (Phillips 269). The language echoes official reports, cf. *CIL*
VI 331.4–5 *Romam redieit triumphans*.   **trium ... uictor:** the post-
ponement of the appositive phrase creates a diptych-like sentence
with isocolonic elements hinged on *rediit*.   **bellorum:** gen. of respect; cf. Tac. *H.* 2.28.2 *tot bellorum uictores* with H.

4.2 ante ... duxit: the standard phrase (Phillips 271).   **quibus
... uenumdatis:** for slavery in the early republic see Oakley (2)

23–6.   **redactum est:** the official expression (W. on Vell.
92.2).   **pretio ... persoluto:** the women contributed jewelry
to make up the amount needed for Apollo's gift after Veii's capture
(5.25.8) and for the Gallic ransom (5.50.7); L. does not here specify
which he means. The unsolicited return of this gold partly contradicts Manlius' later accusations that the *pauci* are hoarding the ransom (14.11–12, 15.12–13).

4.3 quas ... positas: the rel. clause incorporates four prep.
phrases, each consisting of noun + proper name; the content of
each pair (*cum ... incensum, in ... Iunonis*) is chiastic.   **cum titulo
... Camilli** 'inscribed with the name Camillus'.   **ante ... incensum:** 6 July 83, during the Sullan civil wars (Tac. *H.* 3.72.1
with Wellesley). The incendiary was not identified. By marking the
date in this way L. makes a glancing allusion to recent troubles and
invites a contrast between C.'s empire-building and the destructive
behaviour of the last century; the reminder of the recent violence in
contemporary Rome also serves as an ironic foil for the city's sudden rise from its own ashes (6).   **ante pedes Iunonis:** the temple of Jupiter Optimus Maximus, the endpoint of triumphal processions from the time of the Etruscan kings (L. Bonfante Warren,
J.R.S. 60 (1970) 49–66), was built in Etruscan style by Tarquinius
Superbus and had three *cellae*, of Jupiter, Juno, and Minerva
(Richardson 221–4). This statue, however, seems to have been an
additional one perhaps set next to the cult image of Jove (Bayet).

4.4–6 End of the year

4.4 eo anno with *nouis ciuibus* (below) ~ 6 *intraque annum noua urbs*
(frame).   **in ciuitatem** 'into citizenship'. From its beginnings,
Rome had a policy of enfranchising immigrants and refugees alike,
the most famous early exx. being Romulus' asylum (1.8.4–6), the
assimilation of the Sabines and Albans (1.13.4, 28.7), and the immi-
gration of the Claudii (40.4n.). Such amalgamations not infrequently necessitated enlarging either the physical city (e.g. 1.30.1
Caelius additur urbi mons) or the organizational units of its inhabitants
(e.g. 5.8). On the consequences of this tradition of multiplicity in
Rome's self-definition see 40.4n., 41.10n.   **Veientium** and the
following partitive gens. depend on *qui*, a favourite Livian idiom

(G–L §371 N).   **per ea bella:** Veii came under Roman control
in 396 B.C., Capenae in 395, Falerii in 394; all three Roman campaigns were led by C.

4.5 reuocati: sc. *sunt* (1.10n.).   **qui ... contulerant** 'who,
being too lazy to build at Rome, since the empty houses there had
all been occupied, had migrated to Veii'. If *ibi*, as is generally assumed, refers to Veii, the only logical translation is 'people who
... had gone off to Veii and occupied vacant houses there' (Radice), taking *occupatis* as a continuative participle (above, p. 20). But
such abl. participles follow the verb to whose action they are logically consequent, as 4.10.5 *oppressi dederunt poenas, uix nuntiis caedis relictis* (= *et uix nuntii relicti sunt*). The Romans began rebuilding a year
ago (5.55.2), creating *uacua tecta* which were then occupied by the
builders or their tenants (Kraus (1) 217–19). The antithetical logic
is reinforced by chiasmus: *a Veiis ~ Veios, aedificandi ~ uacuis tectis,
Romae ~ ibi, pigritia ~ occupatis*.   **aspernantium** 'of those refusing to accept the order' (*OLD aspernor* 4, *imperium* 8).   **dies ...
praestituta:** the appointed deadline, by which they had to have
returned. The fem. indicates that the time leading up to the *dies* is
also meant: when referring to a specific day L. generally has the
masc. (see B. on Books 34–6, p. 396, refining Fraenkel 1 27–72).
capitalisque poena: sc. *decreta* (zeugma): *poenam praestituere* is not
attested. *capitalis* refers not to death but to loss of civil rights (*OLD*
1b). The senate may have been opposed to individuals moving to
Veii out of fear of repopulating a once dangerous enemy site
(Bayet 9). But there is more to it than that. Twice in the past ten
years the *tr. pl.* proposed that the Romans migrate to Veii (5.24.4–
8, 49.8–9), proposals that were defeated only by concentrated patrician opposition. Veii has thus come to be perceived as a potential
new Rome for the plebs (cf. 5.24.11 *conditorem Veios sequantur, relicto
deo Romulo*), who already form a separate city within the state
(11.7n.), and who are repeatedly compared to foreign enemies
(31.2n., 34.3n.). Moving to Veii would realize the threat implicit in
the plebeian organization and would undo the Roman policy of incorporation (4n.). For fears of a *secessio plebis* see 19.1n., 42.10n.; for
late-republican and triumviral worries about an *altera Roma* see P.
Ceauşescu, *Historia* 25 (1976) 79–107.   **qui ... remigrasset** 'for
anyone who had not returned', the protasis of a fut. logical condi-

tion in virtual *o.o.*, representing the text of the decree (Roby §1752). For *qui = ei qui* cf. Cic. *Tusc.* 5.20 *praemium proposuit qui inuenisset nouam uoluptatem.*   **ferocibus** 'defiant' (*OLD* 3). '[*F*]*erocia* is a trait that incites or exacerbates civil strife .... [but] an admirable *ferocia* drives the fight against tyranny and for *libertas*' (R. J. Penella, *C.Q.* 40 (1990) 213 n.13). Disobedient citizens are not admirable; but exacting obedience with fear is a patrician habit (16.3nn.) that the plebs eventually resist (34–42).   **uniuersis singulos:** the first appearance in Book 6 of the contrast between the multitude and the individual (11.3–5nn., 15.11n., 23.8n., 24.8n., 40.10n.). Here fear diffuses the crowd by turning it into a collection of singletons; see also 25.9n.   **quemque:** in apposition to *singulos.*

4.6 Roma ... exsurgere: the crowd enlarges the city which in turn suddenly shoots upward; *crescere* and *exsurgere* are hist. infins. This snapshot of the busy Romans evokes other descriptions of energetic building, as the Tyrians at Virg. *A.* 2.418–40 (cf. 437 *fortunati quorum iam moenia surgunt*), while rebuilding cities is the hallmark of a good leader (W. on Vell. 124.4, adding *Pan. Mess.* 174 *structis exsurgunt oppida muris*).   **exsurgere** of physical structures is extremely rare (cf. *Pan. Mess.* 174 (last n.), Amm. 19.5.4); the unusual language, however, recalls the common expression *surgit opus* of a literary work (cf. J. Masters, *Poetry and civil war in Lucan's Bellum Civile* (1992) 33): the 'real' Rome grows as L.'s text does (1.2n., 1.11n.).   **et re publica ... operis:** an appendix of abl. abs. (above, p. 21) explaining the conditions under which the *aedificia* rise. The objs. of the participles in this tricolon *auctum* move gradually out of their ablatival frames, mimicking the urban growth (*re pub. impensas adiuuante ... aedilibus uelut publicum exigentibus opus ... priuatis ... festinantibus ad effectum operis*). L. uses the converse of this pattern at 1.28.6 *Mettius ille est ductor itineris huius, Mettius idem huius machinator belli, Mettius foederis Romani Albanique ruptor*: Hostilius gradually delimits the responsibility for Alba's treachery, enclosing the broken *foedus* inside its betrayer.   **re pub. ... priuatis:** the three parties are listed in order of decreasing public importance; the aediles, who were in charge of various urban activities, esp. public building and games (42.13), form a middle term by supervising the publicly subsidized private construction. The progression implies co-operation and similarity between state and citizens, another ideal (cf. 26.8, 5.28.4 and

see W. on Vell. 126.5). The reluctant builders (5) have apparently
been forgotten, but discontent soon reappears (5.5, 6.1, 11.9).
festinantibus: cf. 5.55.4 *festinatio curam exemit uicos derigendi, dum
omisso sui alienique discrimine in uacuo aedificant.*   **admonebat ...
usus** 'for the desire to enjoy it urged them on'; *usus* is objective
gen.   **noua ... stetit** closes the large frame which opened at
1.4 *innixa ... stetit*: the second founding is complete.

4.7–5.5 The year 388 B.C.

4.7–11 Affairs abroad

L.'s short accounts of this year and the next (5.6–6.2) provide a lull
between C.'s two appearances, a typically varied narrative pace.
The account of 388 is balanced between *res externae* and *internae*; in
both sections L. shows a group of people worn down by Roman
power and forced to cede their territory. The juxtaposition of Roman victory over Contenebra (10–11) and patrician victory over the
plebs (5.3–5) raises questions about the nature of Roman authority
– should it be the same at home as abroad? – that are addressed
throughout Book 6 (e.g. 15.7, 16.5, 34.3).

   4.7 Exitu anni: 1.5n.   **comitia tribunorum:** L. construes
comitia + objective gen., + the dat. gerundive (expressing purpose,
as 35.9), and + adj. (37.4).   **creati ... Rufus:** for the tribune
list to be the subj. of a verb is unusual, though analogous to the
common *creatus dictator magistrum equitum dixit* (as 11.10); cf. 31.2 and
1.8n.   **creati:** *aliquis creatur* with ellipse of the magistracy title is
a Livian idiom (*TLL*).   **exercitum:** the noun common to the
two following phrases is placed first, a position sometimes called
'Basis' (E. Fraenkel, *Leseproben aus Reden Ciceros und Catos* (1968) *s.v.*);
cf. 6.18, 8.7, 10.5, 15.7, 18.4, 41.8.   **ad** 'for' (*OLD* 40).   **uictos
... fatebantur:** the so-called *confessio imperii*, found as early as
Enn. *Ann.* 513 Sk *qui uincit non est uictor nisi uictus fatetur* (see W. on
Vell. 90.1).   **namque:** an elevated equivalent of *nam*, esp. mannered when used (as here) before a consonant; L., like Tac., becomes increasingly less fond of it (Adams (4) 60).

   4.8 ab odio: a rare instance of Rome's making a violent un-
provoked attack on its neighbours (2–4.3n.); for *ab* see 2.9n.

peruastandos: a Livian favourite first attested here, and elsewhere found at Tac. *A.* 1.51.1, 15.45.1, *HA Opel. Macr.* 14.5. The *per-* here has little force; on *per-*compounds, perhaps 'too colloquial for literary use,' see Kenney on Lucr. 3.179–80.   **noua** 'revolutionary' (*OLD* 10).   **alterum:** by postponing the second army until after the main verb L. turns decisively away from the Aequi toward the significantly longer Etruscan campaign.

4.9 Cortuosa et Contenebra: a table of contents; cf. 11.1–2. **ad Cortuosam** ~ 10 *Contenebra* (*uariatio*); for the 'headings' see 2.2n. **clamore atque impetu:** military jargon (e.g. 3.60.10, 7.40.10, Flor. 1.7.14, Tac. *H.* 4.23.2) and often varied, as Pl. *Amph.* 245 *cum clamore inuolant impetu*, *B. Hisp.* 25.8 *clamore facto impetum dederunt* (see also 24.11n., 29.1n.). For the psychological importance of shouting cf. Onas. 29.1, Fron. *S.* 2.4.3, 8.   **direptum ... atque incensum:** another conventional pair, in L. nearly always in this logical order (B. on 32.15.3): first you pillage, then you burn (when the two are part of a longer list the order is freer, as 2.23.5, Cic. *Dom.* 25, [Quint.] *Decl.* 272.13). For the passives see 3.10n.

4.10 oppugnationem: the recent pathetic picture of Sutrium under siege must colour the way we read this Roman victory over equally helpless *oppidani*; for the motifs see 3.3–4nn.   **laborque continuus:** cf. 5.19.11, Caes. *C.* 1.62.1 *summo labore ... continuato diem noctemque opere*, 3.97.4 *totius diei continenti labore erant confecti noxque iam suberat.*   **non die non nocte:** cf. 21.11.5, 32.15.2. Perhaps in imitation of Cato, Sall. made asyndeton *bimembre* a feature of historiographical style (L–H–S 829); cf. 29.2, 31.8, 41.2, 7.17.9 *uagos palantes*, 9.14.11 *seruos liberos*, 41.3.1 *terra mari* and see B. on Books 34–7, p. 11.   **non ... remissus** repeats and intensifies *continuus* (3.6n.).   **eos:** the sentence ends with a thud. Many prose authors do not admit the acc. of *is* or *se* at the end of a major colon (so Hirt., Sall. *C.* and *J.*, Vell., Tac. outside *A.* 2.45.1), others allow only *se* (Nep., Caes., Cic. *orat.* outside *Ver.* 4.49). L.'s practice is more flexible; see also 32.9n.   **senis ... orbem** 'for six hours apiece in rotation'; for the stratagem cf. Onas. 42.7–13.   **succederet:** idiomatic of military relief (*OLD* 4b); for *succ. proelio* cf. Virg. *A.* 10.690 (*pugnae*) with Harrison. This is the third *sub-*compound in 10: the Etruscan effort to hold up the siege (*sustinuit*) defeats them (*subegit*) because the Romans can come up fresh each time.   **oppidanos eosdem:** adversative asyndeton; for the topos see 3.3n.   **fessos:** choicer than *lassus*, which L. (with Sall. and Tac.) avoids; on such synonyms see P. Watson, *C.Q.* 35 (1985) 430–48.   **cessere** ∼ *succederet* above, an ironic echo. The losers disappear once the town is taken: only *praeda* is left (11 *bis*).   **locus ... datus est:** the shift to the non-personal subj. underscores the disappearance of all Etruscan resistance. **inuadendi urbem:** it is said that a gerund takes a direct obj. only when that obj. is a neuter pronoun or adj. (as 6.10) or when the corresponding gerundive construction would produce the 'jingling' *-orum -orum* (as 21.28.5 *elephantorum traiciendorum ... consilia*). But L. – and others – are considerably freer than that (C. Macdonald, *G.&R.* 8 (1961) 188–9).   **urbem:** a common synonym for *oppidum*, cf. 7.19.1 *urbs capta ceteraque oppida* (*TLL* ix 2.755.2–6).

4.11 publicari: 2.12n.   **sed ... poterat:** emphatic word order (next n.) enhances the cynical realism with which L. describes the soldiers' power (cf. 3.31.4, 4.49.9–10). Their eagerness for *praeda* cuts two ways: it illustrates their poverty (5.5) but also shows them behaving like the grasping *patres* (5.4).   **quam ... segnius:** emphatic inversion (Adams (5) 83–6).   **consilium** 'intention' (*OLD* 5).

4.12–5.5 Internal affairs

4.12 An archival detail (above, p. 11) separates *res externae* from *internae*. That the substruction of the Capitoline (Richardson 31–2) was remarkable in the late republic is confirmed by Plin. *NH* 36.104; cf. 1.56.2 *duobus operibus* [the Cloaca Maxima and Circus] *uix noua haec magnificentia ... adaequare potuit*.   **saxo quadrato:** large squared-off blocks.   **substructum** 'supported from underneath' is technical (cf. Vitr. 2.8.20).   **hac** breaks the narrative illusion by appealing to the reader's experience; cf. 12.4 *nunc* and see above, pp. 13–15.   **conspiciendum** 'worth looking at', cf. Juv. 4.115 *grande et conspicuum nostro quoque tempore monstrum*. The historian acts as tour guide (Gabba 60–2, Hartog 263–5); for the visual in Book 6 see 1.3n., 8.6n., 12.1n., 20.6–9nn.

5.1 iam: sentence-initial *iam* brings one into the centre of the action, an epic technique developed in prose by L. (C-L 497–516).

The insistent particle is followed in 2–3 by sentence-initial verbs which speed the narrative along (Marouzeau II 64–72).   **et** 'also'. The sense (by implication from 4.12) seems to be that the *tr. pl.*, who are here taking their first action since 390 (1.6n.), must compete with the rest of the state for plebeian attention. Their vain attempt to force the aristocracy to cede some territory heralds the *seditio* and the rogations, both partly based on land reform.   **ciuitate** = *ciuibus* (*OLD* 2). The abl. abs. is concessive.   **contiones:** either public assemblies or the speeches there delivered, both associated with demagoguery (Seager (1) 334); on them see Taylor 15–33, F. Millar, *J.R.S.* 76 (1986) 1–11.   **legibus agrariis:** instrumental. Measures insuring equitable distribution of land or laws limiting individual holdings were from the aristocratic point of view one hallmark of seditious behaviour (Seager (1) 332–3); on the need for them see Brunt (1) *s.v.* 'agrarian legislation'.

5.2 ostentabatur in spem: cf. 30.33.9 *campi ... in spem uictoriae ostentabantur* (the only other ex. of *ostentare in*), Cic. *Clu.* 22 *spes ... ostentata*, Sall. *J.* 66.1 *ostentando praedam*, Tac. *A.* 12.44.4 *in spem trahere et Armeniam ostendere.*   **Pomptinus ager:** also discussed in 387 (6.1) and 383 (21.4). *ager/agr-* run throughout the paragraph, discreetly underscoring its theme; cf. 21.13 (an attempt to persuade Saguntum of its best interests: 25 forms of *uos/uestr-* in 27 lines), Sall. *J.* 14 (Adherbal pleads for his family's rights: 46 forms of *pater, frater* etc. in four pages) and see von Albrecht 6 (on Cato).   **tum ... ambiguae:** the weight of the sentence falls on this long attribute.   **post ... res:** bracketing word order in which C. and the Volsci meet (cf. 2.11n.). The fig. use of *accidere* is relatively rare (*TLL*).   **possessionis:** descriptive gen., 'under military control' (*OLD* 2a); cf. 34.62.4 *regionem ... ex quadam parte dubiae possessionis.*

5.3 criminabantur introduces an ascending scale of wrongs: the *nobiles* progress from hostility (*infestiorem*) to occupation (4 *in possessionem*) to unchallenged possession (*nec ... locum*) of the *ager*.   **multo:** abl. of degree of difference.   **infestiorem ab** 'more threatened by'; the construction with *ab* is only here and 10.46.9.   **nobilitate ... Volscis:** picked up chiastically by what follows.   **fuerit:** the tribunes use primary tenses of the subjunc., despite the imperf. 'head' verb. L. has a habit of abandoning secondary sequence in clauses subsequent to the one containing a historic governing verb; as a rule, he tends to 'reproduce' the tenses used by the speaker (*repraesentatio*: *LHA* 265–6, *NLS* §284).   **tantum ... incursiones:** the attacks on this land (with 4 *grassari*) are imaged as a disease, cf. Cels. 3.22.10 *febris ... incursat* and see *OLD infestus* 4, *grassari* 4 with M–W 240–1.   **eo** 'thither' (*OLD eo*² 1).

5.4 nobiles homines: a tepid Ciceronian compliment (Santoro L'hoir (2) 18) given a bite by being placed in counterpoise to the harmless enemy (3 *illis*); the pleonastic *homo* weights the phrase (Opelt 261).   **possessionem:** legal control of land (*OLD* 1) guaranteed by occupation thereof, and misused by the *nobiles* (Eder, *SSAR* 296–7).   **agri publici:** land confiscated from defeated towns (*OCD*).   **grassari:** a good historiographical word, choice and predominantly poetic; in prose it is promoted by Sall. (3), L. (8), Plin. *NH*, Tac. (*TLL*). Here the sense of sneaky but relentless encroachment is uppermost; cf. 45.23.9 *qui assentando multitudini grassarentur* and for the frequentative see 1.11n.   **praecipiant** 'seize first' (*OLD* 1).   **diuisus sit** = fut. perf. indic. in *o.r.* (*NLS* §280.2). *diuidere* occurs in Book 6 only of groups of combatants (2.7, 3.10, 9.9, 31.5) and of dividing the *ager* among the plebs (also 21.4, 36.11). The difficulty of apportioning the land here contrasts with the easy division of the army at 4.10, a strategy that led inexorably to victory.   **locum** 'room for' (*OLD* 13), cf. 36.11n.

5.5 haud magno opere: a Livian combination (also at 22.7, 24.5.7).   **et ... essent:** a tricolon of postponed attributive phrases (2.12n.).   **infrequentem ... aedificandi** ∼ 1 *aedificando ... frequentare* (frame).   **in foro:** where the *contiones* would be given (15.1n.).   **eodem** refers to *aedificandi*. The two abls. with *exhaustam* are awkward, and one should perhaps write *ex eodem* (Watt 214): 'since they were scarce in the Forum on account of their preoccupation with building and as a result of *that* had been drained by expenses'. For the debilitating effects of building expenses see 11.9n.   **exhaustam:** cf. 27.9.2 *stipendiis ... exhaustos*, Cic. *Att.* 6.1.2 *exhaustam ... sumptibus prouinciam*. For the short central element see above, p. 23.   **immemorem:** the adjs. describing plebs become progressively less physical.   **instruendum:** to fit out with livestock etc. (*OLD* 6).   **uires** 'resources', mental, physical, and financial (*OLD* 21, 22, 26).   **essent:** sc. *plebi*.

5.6–6.2 The year 387 B.C.

5.6 plena religionum 'full of religious fears' recalls C.'s argument that the Romans should remain in their city (5.52.2): *nullus locus ... non religionum deorumque est plenus.*   **etiam:** with *principibus.*   **ab** 'after and because of' (*OLD* 14).   **superstitiosis:** only here in L. The adj. regularly has the sense of 'credulous' (*OLD* 2) and may both suggest that the leaders are normally unaffected by the *religio* that binds the plebs (1.10) and cast doubt on the reasonableness of that *religio*. But *superstitio/-osus* are sometimes hard to distinguish from *religio/-osus* (as Cic. *Ver.* 4.113), and the adj. here ∼ *plena religionum*, as *principibus* ∼ *ciuitate* (chiasmus). See further on 1.10.   **re-nouarentur:** of the auspices (2.5n.) in L. only here and 5.31.7, 52.9 *auspiciorum renouatio* (both of the year in which the Gauls sacked Rome). By repeating the unusual expression L. opposes this new beginning, which the Romans will later ratify by reversing the disaster at the Allia (28.5–29), to the earlier, disastrous one. *a. renouare* is attested elsewhere only at Serv. on Virg. *A.* 2.178 and may have been technical; more common is *a. repetere* (e.g. 5.17.3). On L.'s technical vocabulary see McDonald 157–8; on foundation in Book 6 see 1.3n.   **deinceps** 'in succession' (*OLD* 1a).   **Capitolinus:** the first time Manlius is given his cognomen since his introduction (5.31.2 *cui Capitolino postea fuit cognomen*). The nickname will later be allusively explained as deriving both from Manlius' having saved the Capitol (11.2, 17.5) and from his having a house there (19.1, probably the historical reason: O. on 5.31.2), while Manlius is not shy about recalling his achievement (11.2n.). But Manlius is not the only Capitol hero in Books 5–6: it is C. who first monopolizes the word *Capitolium* (10 times in 5.51–4), and who is accorded the striking epithet *caput rei Romanae* (3.1n.). This textual rivalry will become 'real' rivalry in 385 (11.3n.; Jaeger 354).

5.7 tribunorum: 4.7n.   **occepere:** a recherché synonym for *inire* and *incipere*, after the second century B.C. almost exclusively historiographical (Sis. Sall. L. Tac.); the archaizing Apul. revives it. L. has it + infin. (1.49.1), absolutely (29.27.6), and (most often) + *magistratum.*

5.8 aedis Martis: outside the Porta Capena (Richardson 244–

5). **duumuiro:** they were in charge of keeping and consulting the Sibylline books and performed other religious functions as needed (Scullard 29–30). The college was enlarged and admitted plebeians in 367 (42.2).   **tribus:** civilian units for some assemblies (esp. those that elected plebeian officials), taxation, and military service (Taylor 64–70). For the asyndeton in this list see 1.8n. **uiginti ... expleuere** 'brought the number of tribes up to 25' (*OLD expleo* 4); see 4.4n.

6.1 L. Sicinio: there was an old association of the *gens Sicinia* with the tribunate (O. on 2.32.2).   **actum ad ... populum** varies the technical *agere cum populo* 'to transact business with the people' (*OLD ago* 39c).   **frequentiorem** ~ 5.1 *frequentare*, 5.5 *infrequentem*.   **mobilioremque** ~ 5.5 *plebem mouerunt.* L. alludes to the topos of the easily swayed crowd (Otto 378); see also 27.7n. (*in contione*). *mobilis ad* is first here, cf. 29.3.13, Sen. *Ep.* 92.29.

6.2 mentio ... dilata: the displacement of one item on the senatorial agenda by the sudden intrusion of another, repeated at 4 and at 9.3, is a transitional device resembling L.'s use of a journey to effect a shift of scene (2.14n.).

6.3–10 The year 386 B.C.

6.3–18 Internal affairs

These *res internae* are an expanded version of the simple report of C.'s dictatorial appointment at 2.4–5. The speech in which C. accepts the appointment and assigns provinces to the other military tribunes (8–15) is framed by pictures of the tribunes, senate, and people willingly yielding to his greater authority (6–7 ~ 16–18). Together with the story of C. and Furius (22.5–26), this episode illustrates the proper handling of power; they frame the negative *exemplum* of Manlius (11–20).

6.3 Res ... rediit: a rare instance in L. of *res redire ad* + personal obj. (cf. 7.25.10, of C.'s son); he otherwise has *ad interregnum* (as 1.5) or *ad patres* (as 1.32.1). The form of expression implies that C. is practically an institution. Accompanying the unusual diction is a dislocated tribune list in which the most important member is given separate mention; cf. 22.1, 22.5 and see Drummond (1) 88.

6.4 principio anni: 1.8n.   **auersae curae:** 2n.   **fugientium ... in urbem:** for refugees bringing disastrous news cf. 33.3 (n.), 1.14.5 *tumultusque repens ex agris in urbem illatus pro nuntio fuit,* 34.11.11, Caes. *C.* 2.25.2, Curt. 3.8.14, and see Pritchett v 348–52. The flight of *agrestes* was a topic for rhetorical description (Sen. *Contr.* 1.6.12).   **repente:** a stylistically elevated synonym for *subito* of which L. grew increasingly fond (Adams (4) 59). While L. likes to introduce events with 'suddenly' (*LHA* 193–4), it was also, along with *improuiso* (33.7), technical for a surprise attack (Wheeler 82).   **Antiates ... (5) uellent:** the content of the message is itself a complex sentence extended by a participial appendix (*eo ... uellent*) examining the Latins' state of mind.   **Antiates:** Volsci from Antium.   **summisisse** 'had sent secretly', regular of sending reinforcements with or without the implication of furtiveness, cf. 44.4.9, Caes. *G.* 7.85.1, Fron. *S.* 2.3.8.

6.5 eo ... uellent 'denying this was official policy on these grounds, by saying that [the youths], who had merely not been forbidden to, were fighting as volunteers where they wished'. *eo* looks forward to *quod*: lit. by this means, that they said (Stephenson).   **abnuentes:** an appended 'participle de mise en scène' turns the narrative attention to the Latins (cf. 14.5 *obtestantem,* 23.4 *dictitans*); the construction is commonest in L. and Tac. (C-L 311–14).   **publicum ... consilium:** the hyperbaton emphasizes the adj. (1.2n.); for the excuse cf. 10.7, Caes. *G.* 5.1.7, Dion. Hal. 3.37.3, 9.60.3–4, and for the reverse cf. 13.7–8, 25.1 (n.). In such cases those responsible might be the only ones punished (10.5n.). **uoluntarios ... uellent:** *figura etymologica,* cf. 39.11, Sen. *Ep.* 81.13 and for similar play in L. cf. 1.14.7 *subsidere in insidiis,* 42.53.4 *uehicula tantum imperata ut ... ueherent.*   **dicerent:** 2.9n.

6.6 Desierant ... bella 'at this point all wars had ceased being belittled'.   **ulla** heightens the emphasis after the virtual negative *desierant.* Adjs. expressing quantity and size are esp. likely to be disjoined in this way (Adams (1) 2); for the verbal hyperbaton see 1.2n.   **senatus ... collegae** ~ 7 *ab senatu tribunis* (frame). Both senate and tribunes elevate C. to a position of extraordinary authority, though the senate speaks in procedural terms (*magistratus, dictator, priuatus*), the tribunes in more affective images of Roman power (*regimen, imperium, maiestas*). In each case the expression moves from the

general to the specific (*in magistratu* ∼ *dictatorem*; *in uiro uno* ∼ *Camillo*).
agere: hist. infin. (so also *fateri* below).   **gratias** ∼ 7 *gratias*
(frame). L. usually expresses thanks to gods with the elevated *grates*,
to humans with *gratia* (Moussy 85–6).   **dictatorem ... fuisse**
'for he would have had to be made dictator'. Postposition of *quippe*
is rare (Adams (2) 366 n.3) and usually in *o.o.* in L. (e.g.
11.8).   **priuatus:** i.e. not in office. The senate articulates a republican ideal, that a *priuatus* not have the same power as an appointed
official; for the opposition with *magistratu* see *VL* 310 and cf. Cic.
Phil. 11.17–18. Since C. is already tribune, he does not pose the
same threat as the dynasts, who acted *priuato consilio* (17.2n.); he
does, however, receive authority out of proportion to his role as
one of six. The whole scene has been read as an allegory of Augustus' veiled assumption of power (Hellegouarc'h).   **regimen ...**
(7) esse: a statement of good military policy (it lies behind the
creation of the dictatorship: *CAH*^{2} 191) and the core of the auto-
cratic crisis of the first century B.C.: when does *unus uir*, the top of
the competitive republican heap (11.3n.), become dangerous? L.'s
form of expression here echoes contemporary political language
that passed into imperial self-definition, cf. Quint. 3.8.47 (how to
argue a bad position) *et C. Caesari suadentes regnum affirmabimus stare
iam rem publicam nisi uno regente non posse*, Tac. *A.* 1.9.4 *non aliud discor-
dantis patriae remedium fuisse quam ut ab uno regeretur* with M–W 173; for
the imperial balance of 'one of many' with 'the one and only' see
Wallace-Hadrill (1).   **regimen** has a 'poetic and somewhat archaic flavour' (Skutsch on Enn. *Ann.* 407); it is first in prose in L.
Like *caput* (5.7n.), *unus* (next n. but one) and *solus* (11.3n.), the meaning and possession of the root *reg-* is disputed between C. and Manlius (23.10n.): does it denote military command or monarchical rule?
Cf. 3.33.7, 24.4.3 *nomen regium penes puerum* ∼ *regimen rerum ... penes se.*
See also 11.4n., 41.10n.   **ubi ... ingruat:** cf. Tac. *A.* 4.2.1 *si quid
subitum ingruat*; *quid = aliquid* (*OLD quis*^{2} 1b).

6.7 uiro uno: for the laudatory formulation see Santoro L'hoir
(1) 230–2, Weinstock 169, 219–20; for *uir* as a heroic epithet see
Santoro L'hoir (2) 63–9. Manlius wants to be *unus uir* (11.3–4nn.),
though it is C. who repeatedly receives the appellation (23.1n.); for
the problems attaching to being 'one' see 14–16.4n., 35.4n., and
Hardie *s.v.* 'one and many'.   **sibique ... animo** 'and that it

was their intention'. *d. in animo* is attested elsewhere only at 21.44.9; in both cases the preposition removes any ambiguity with an accompanying sympathetic dat. (Walsh).   **Camillo ... imperium** 'to make their *imperium* subordinate to C.', a sense of *summittere* apparently first here (*OLD* 10a). *summ. imperium* is modelled on *summittere fasces*, an official recognition of superior *maiestas* (Vell. 99.4 with W.); cf. the related *subicere imperio*, as 28.21.9 *mortem in certamine quam ut alter alterius imperio subiceretur praeoptantes*, Cic. *Off.* 2.2.2. **nec ... concessissent:** an epigrammatic expression graphically illustrating the balance of power. *maiestas* (lit. 'bigness', cf. 40.4n., Caes. *C.* 3.106.4 *maiestatem regiam minui*) was the quality of authority and power possessed both by the Roman people (vis-à-vis other states) and by politically powerful men within the Roman state (*VL* 314–20). Like *dignitas* it had to be carefully guarded and respected, and the tricky balance between one man's *maiestas* and another's had to be maintained in order to preserve the oligarchical government's self-esteem and smooth functioning. See N. Mackie in A. Powell (ed.), *Roman poetry and propaganda in the age of Augustus* (1992) 88–91.   **quicquam ... detractum** 'had there been any diminishment' (*OLD detraho* 7b).   **eius uiri:** slightly tautological (cf. *OLD uir* 6) and therefore slightly emphatic: all of *is uir* is needed to balance *sua* (above).   **concessissent** 'they had deferred' (*OLD* 3); for its diplomatic use cf. Sall. *J.* 11.4 *aetati concederet* 'deferred to his age', Tac. *A.* 2.74.1 with Goodyear.   **collaudatis** ~ 18 *laudemque conferentes ... in medium. conlaudatis ... gratias* reflects official senatorial language, cf. Cic. *Cat.* 3.14 (the S.C. concerning the conspirators) *primum mihi gratiae uerbis amplissimis aguntur ... deinde ... praetores ... merito ac iure laudantur*; for formal expressions of thanks see Cairns 74 n.12, Talbert 227–8.   **confusus** 'overcome' (Stephenson); in this specialized sense *confusus* describes moments of considerable anxiety (cf. 34.8 and Vell. 124.1 *populi confusio* with W.). C.'s momentary dismay has been compared (by Hellegouarc'h 123) with early imperial refusals of power, gestures 'designed to substantiate an elaborate pretence that things are not as they seem' (Wallace-Hadrill (1) 37), cf. Tac. *A.* 1.12.2 *perculsus improuisa interrogatione paulum reticuit*. But one cannot fairly speak of a *recusatio* here: C.'s reluctance is neither feigned nor obtrusive, nor does he force the senate to insist that he take power. His behaviour instead illustrates the quality of *moderatio* (18n. (*in medium*), 25.6n.): caught in the position familiar to L.'s contemporary readers, of a strong man offered unlimited power, he shows a strong sense of the limits within which he should operate.

6.8–15. Form and content of the book's first *oratio* together reflect C.'s judicious handling of power. The speech falls into two sections of equal length, the first in *o.o.*, the second in *o.r.*; modulation from one to the other is a common device in historiography, used both for *uariatio* and emphasis (Lambert 38–41). Here the contrast between the forms of discourse harmonizes with the thematic movement from reflection to action, from C.'s description of the situation (8–11) to the military assignments (12–15). His modest pose likewise plays with the possibilities of the shift to *o.r.* He speaks about himself in 8–11; but once he assumes a direct voice at 12–15 (thereby becoming present in the narrative), he concentrates on his colleagues, to his own almost complete exclusion (12 *mecum* and 13 *habeo* are the only traces of him). Finally, he makes his assignments in impersonal (12 *placet*), hortatory (14 *scribatur ... prouideat*), and collective (15 *facimus*) language: this is an official distribution of power conveying impersonal, public authority. But working against C.'s self-effacement is the remarkable tension between the speech and the framing narrative. While C. retreats behind the needs and traditional powers of the republic, the frame insists on the unusual circumstances and character of this appointment (6–7, 16, 18), compelling attention on to the speech itself and, of course, on to the reluctant speaker who is 'the more *princeps* because the more *ciuis*' (Momigliano 111).

6.8 ingens ... (9) efficiat: the *captatio beneuolentiae*: C. acknowledges the responsibility he faces (8), and promises to live up to it (9). Compliments to the audience reinforce his *modestia* (but see 9n.).   **ingens ... magnum ... maximum:** the sequence produces a suggestion of crowd-pleasing exaggeration in *ingens* ('an *enormous* responsibility'); that the tribunes and senate are of a different order is shown by the change of adj. (above, p. 24).   **onus ... iniungi:** the idea that governing the state is burdensome is conventional, cf. 2.49.1, Xen. *Cyr.* 7.5.37–57, Ael. *Hist.* 2.20, Hor. *Ep.* 2.1.1 with Brink, Ov. *M.* 15.1 with Bömer, Vell. 124.2 with W. For the wordplay in *onus* ∼ *honorato* (below) see Otto 167.   **a populo:** C.

first considers people, senate, and magistrates separately, in the order in which the emergency affected them (4 *hominum*, 6 *senatus*, 6–7 *collegae*); he then unites them (9 *ciuitatis*) in promising to meet their challenge.   **qui:** causal; for the *uariatio* with *iudiciis* and *obsequio* below (causal rel. ∼ causal abl.) see Catterall 316–19, Sörbom 119.   **ab senatu:** a respect for the senate that would become 'studied' and ritualized under the empire (Wallace-Hadrill (1) 37–8).   **eius ordinis:** the demonstrative phrase weights the colon. Cf. 2.1.10 *quo plus uirium in senatu frequentia etiam ordinis faceret*, 9.30.1–2, Sall. *C.* 46.6 *eo senatum aduocat magnaque frequentia eius ordinis Volturcium ... introducit*. In all these passages there is a slight but clear distinction made between the *senatus* as the governing body and the *senatorius ordo* as the individuals comprising that body. **honorato** = *honorans*, cf. 27.10.6 *honoratissimo decreto*, Ascon. *in Pis.* 3; the active sense is frequent in V. Max. (*TLL*).   **honorato ... obsequio:** C. acknowledges and returns the compliment paid him by his colleagues in 7. *honor, maiestas*, and *obsequium* are interrelated: Ovid makes *Honor* one of the parents of *Maiestas* at *F.* 5.23–7, while *obsequium* like *honor* is part of the complex of proper behaviour due to one invested with *maiestas*. So allied states, who are often bound by treaty to preserve the *maiestas* of the Roman people, show *obsequium* to Rome (as 7.30.19, *CIL* XIII 1.1.1668.2.34 *immobilem fidem obsequiumque*). *obsequium* is, further, the *uox propria* of the obedience due to a military superior (cf. 41.10.12, Tac. *Ag.* 8.1, 42.4), from which it is clearly distinguished when used to describe toadyism (as 23.4.2–5 *senatores ... plebem adulari ... ciuitas ... obsequio principum et licentia plebei lasciuire*; Tac. *A.* 4.20.3 *deforme obsequium*): see Syme (2) 28.

6.9 itaque: C. turns to the response required by the state's confidence in him, repeating in miniature the speech's general move from reflection to action (see above); the same shift recurs in 10–11, where he follows description of the current threat with a call for military action.   **laboris uigiliarumque:** withstanding these (often + *periculum*, cf. 24.7) is typical of the ideal general, cf. 34.18.5 *parsimonia et uigiliis et labore cum ultimis militum certaret*, Vell. 79.1 *labore uigilia periculo inuictus* with W.   **adici:** i.e. to the existing talent that C. brings to his job. The expression is odd; for *adicere* used absolutely cf. Tac. *A.* 12.10.1 (an easier passage) and cf. the military sense 'add as reinforcement' (*OLD* 8).   **certantem se-**

cum: having no rivals, C. can vie only with himself – precisely the ground for Manlius' complaint against him at 11.3–5. While competition was the essence of republican public life (11.3n.), *secum certare* is a panegyrical motif, and it is somewhat surprising to find C. using it of himself; cf. Cic. *De orat.* 3.3 *omnium consensu sic esse tum iudicatum ceteros a Crasso semper omnis, illo autem die etiam ipsum a se superatum, Fam.* 9.14.6 *te imitere oportet, tecum ipse certes* and Plin. *Pan.* 13.5 *sine exemplo secum certare, secum contendere.* **ut ... efficiat:** C. unites the elements of the opening tricolon in the *ciuitas* considered as a whole (*tanto ... consensu* ∼ 8 *talibus ... iudiciis, maxima* ∼ 8 *maximum*); the ring, whose closural force is underscored by the absolute *maxima* and *constantem* (11.5n.), elegantly divides this part of the speech from the rest.   **tanto ... ciuitatis:** 'since there was such consensus about him among the citizens'; the abl. is one of attendant circs. (Roby §§1240–2), cf. Cic. *Arch.* 3 *hoc concursu hominum litteratissimorum, hac uestra humanitate, hoc denique praetore exercente iudicium.* **consensu** has strong roots in the republican tradition, esp. in the Ciceronian *consensus bonorum omnium* (as *Dom.* 94, *Sest.* 36); the notion is already present in L. Cornelius Scipio's epitaph (*CIL* I² 2.9, second century B.C.) *honc oino ploirume cosentiunt Romai | duonoro optumo fuisse uiro* (*VL* 123–7). As with many republican slogans, together with *concordia* the concept was adopted by Caesar (Weinstock 160–6) and by Augustus to express the unity of the state behind his leadership (e.g. *RG* 34.1: Syme (1) *s.vv.* 'concordia ordinum' and 'consensus Italiae'). L. is aware of the potential difficulties with such agreement (20.3n.).   **opinionem:** this is by nature subject to change (e.g. Cic. *Mur.* 35 *totam opinionem parua non numquam commutat aura rumoris*); by saying that he will try to make it permanent C. implies not that the *populus* is fickle, but that his own efforts may not be good enough to keep their good opinion.   **quae ... sit** 'though it is already highly favourable'.   **constantem** 'unchanging' (cf. 25.4, 6), a military and political virtue (M–W 189); the connection of *constans* and *consensus* is Ciceronian (*Sest.* 87, *Parad.* 22).

6.10 quod ... attineat: an oratorical flourish (over 75 per cent of L.'s exx. are in speeches) apparently favoured by Cato (four exx. preserved) and Cicero. It is common in Plautus, and may have had colloquial force. The phrase is weighted by the repeated sounds in *atque Antiates attineat* (2.9n.)   **bellum atque Antiates:** hendiadys;

cf. Tac. *Ag.* 25.1 *terra et hostis* (= *terrestris hostis*).   **minarum ...
periculi** ~ *timendi ... contemnendi* (chiasmus). Such fearless caution
is the hallmark of the ideal general (Vell. 118.2 with W.).   **esse
... esse:** the repetition may be 'invisible' (as probably in 6–7),
though it does highlight the almost pedantic subdivisions of C.'s
thought (*plus ... quam, ut ... sic*).   **ut ... sic** 'while ... at the
same time' (*OLD ut* 5b).   **timendi ... contemnendi:** the contrast of simple with compound verbs is a type of *adnominatio*, wordplay involving a change of spelling (Lausberg §§637–8), cf. 28.41.7
quem non magis timuisse uideatur quam contempsisse, Tac. *H.* 3.9.5 (*timens
... contemptim*) and see Bonner (1) 69–70 on the trick in the declaimers. An analogous play occurs at 18 (n.).

6.11 circumsederi may have been technical (cf. *B. Hisp.* 26.4,
Fron. *S.* 2.9.1, 3.6.5) or for some reason was not to most authors'
taste; L. and Cicero alone use it with any frequency, though both
far prefer *obsidere* (Cic. e.g. restricts *circumsedere* almost entirely to descriptions of Mutina). L. last used it of the Gallic siege (5.53.5), a
disaster that mirrored the siege of Veii (5.6.8, 22.8). Its initial position here, which marks a transition in the argument, also emphasizes its unfortunate textual associations; for these city captures in
Book 6 see 40–1n.   **urbem Rom.:** more emphatic, and in this
context more pathetic, than *urbem* alone; cf. 40.11, 41.10.   **ab inuidia ... finitimorum** 'by envious and hostile neighbours', abstract for concrete. *ab* is of the agent with the personified emotions
(G–L §401 R.2).   **inuidia:** it was a commonplace that excellence
attracted *inuidia*, so much so that the *inuidia* attaching to great men
was a declamatory topic (W. on Vell. 44.2); see *VL* 195–9, *RICH* 74
and Otto 176, adding Pind. *P.* 11.29, Soph. *Ai.* 157, Lucr. 3.74–6
with Kenney, Virg. *A.* 11.335–7, Sen. *Contr.* 1.8.10, Onas. 42.24–6.
Envy joins naturally with *odium*: cf. Thuc. 2.64.5 with Rusten, Cic.
Marc. 29, Plut. *Alex.* 11.1, Dio 53.8.6 (*misos* and *phthonos* directed at
Augustus and other *aristoi*). See also 2.4n., 11.3n.   **ducibus ...
exercitibus:** an ideal general relies on the advice and aid of
others (Onas. 3, cf. Tac. *A.* 1.11.1 *plures facilius munia rei pub. ... exse-
cuturos*, Suet. *Tib.* 25.1 *sufficere solus nemo posset nisi cum altero uel etiam
cum pluribus*, Dio 53.8.7, Augustus declares that many hands are
needed to administer the state). For the negative reaction brought
about by a refusal to share cf. Nep. *Dion* 6.4 *uersum illum Homeri*

rettulit ... non posse bene geri rem pub. multorum imperiis. quod dictum magna inuidia consecuta est: namque aperuisse uidebatur omnia in sua potestate esse uelle. See further 12n.   **pluribus:** the word order sets the *duces* off from their armies, who are added as a sort of afterthought; cf. 26.5.

6.12 'te ... P. Valeri': for the transition to *o.r.* cf. 15.9, 1.13.3 with W–M and see Lambert 40 n.1. C. indicates each of the tribunes in turn by a heading (*te ... tertius ... L. Horatius ... te* below); for the general's naming of his subordinate cf. 12.10, 29.1, 8.38.14.   **socium imperii:** cf. 10.26.2 *si sibi adiutorem belli sociumque imperii darent,* Cic. *Mur.* 83 *adiutorem, defensorem, socium in re publica.* There is a later parallel in Tacitus' description of Seianus as *adiutor imperii* and *socius laborum* (M–W 90); for the need for helping hands see 11n.   **consiliique:** both 'deliberation' and 'strategy' (*OLD* 7); the meaning changes in 15 (3.5n.).   **Antiatem:** C. deals with the three enemies (cf. 13 *Etruria ... Latini*) in reverse order to their introduction in 2–4.   **placet** governs *ducere* here and *habere* in 13, linking the first two tribunes.

6.13 castra habere 'encamp,' common in L. and Caesar (e.g. *G.* 1.44.3, *C.* 1.43.1, *B. Afr.* 34.5) but not elsewhere, may be part of the *sermo castrensis;* cf. Ov. *Am.* 1.9.1 *habet sua castra Cupido.*   **intentum** agrees with *te* (12); for the postponed attributive participle see 2.12n.   **siue ... siue:** parallel members with chiastic content (*Etruria ... nuper ∼ noua ... Latini*); for the *uariatio Etruria ∼ Latini* cf. 7.4, 12.6, and see Catterall 295–6.   **cura:** the personification is poetic (*OLD* 1b *ad fin.*, 8).   **pro certo ... dignum est:** Servilius is amplified by a combination of familial prestige and personal experience.   **gesturum:** sc. *te esse.*   **patre ... dignum:** cf. Cic. *Phil.* 3.25 *uir patre auo maioribusque suis dignissimus.* Ancestors lent an aristocrat prestige and glory, but it was his duty to surpass their deeds, thereby garnering more glory for himself and for his descendants (cf. the Scipionic epitaphs, *CIL* I² 2.10 *facile facteis superases gloriam maiorum,* 2.15 *facta patris petiei*); see further 30.3n., 37.11nn.   **ac** joins a new element to the list of family members, cf. 5.2.12 *parentes liberosque* [direct relation] *ac coniuges* [collateral].

6.14 tertius: the central term in this list of five is the most varied in form, having as subj. not the tribune but the army (above, p. 23); it is balanced within itself (*causariis senioribusque ~ urbi moenibusque*), while the tribunes on either side form pairs (two facing external foes ~ two in charge of administrative needs).   **causariis:** soldiers who have received medical discharges, a technical term first here (Dutoit (1) 122); for *seniores* see 2.6n.   **scribatur:** technical of drafting soldiers (*OLD* 7b).   **qui ... sit:** purpose. **praesidio:** predicative dat. (*NLS* §68).   **quaeque alia** = *et alia quae*. The list of essentials varies (though it generally includes *frumentum*) but its form is virtually set, cf. 34.6.13 *pecuniae frumentum et cetera quae belli usus postulabant*, Caes. *G.* 2.3.4, *B. Afr.* 36.4, Sall. *J.* 47.2, 86.1, *H.* 2.47.6.   **belli tempora** 'war-time emergencies'. For *tempus* = 'dangerous/critical time' see *OLD* 11a.   **prouideat:** like *prudentia* (24.9), *prouidentia* is a predominantly military virtue conveying experience and wisdom. For them in L. see Moore 110–13, 118–20; on the development of *prouidentia* see W. on Vell. 115.5.

6.15 praesidem ... consilii ~ 12 *socium imperii consiliique*, framing the *o.r.*   **huius ... consilii** i.e. the senate, cf. Cic. *Phil.* 4.14 *senatum, id est orbis terrae consilium.*   **custodem ... urbanarum:** 'a central theme of Roman political feeling finds its expression in the formula *custos patriae* (*urbis, ciuitatis, rei publicae*, etc.)' (Skutsch on Enn. *Ann.* 107); it is esp. frequent in the late republic (as Cic. *Dom.* 40 *me custodem urbis*) and after (cf. 2.1.8 *libertatis custos*, Hor. *C.* 4.15.17 *custode rerum Caesare*, Vell. 98.1, 104.2 with W.). See further 14.5n. (*parenti pl. R.*).   **religionum comitiorum legum:** the three chief spheres of Roman public life, sacral, civic, and legal; cf. 5.6.17 *senatum ... magistratus ... leges ... mores maiorum ... instituta patrum* and Tacitus' imitation at *A.* 1.2.1 *munia senatus magistratuum legum.*   **rerum ... urbanarum** sums up the preceding list with the asyndeton regular in such cases (G–L §474 N.). The list as a whole ~ 14 *arma ... poscent*, linking the two assignments (14n. *tertius*).   **collegae facimus:** the plur. reinforces C.'s self-effacement behind the structures of the republic (8–15n.).

6.16 cunctis 'was artificial at all periods' (Adams (4) 61); by this time it was in prose virtually restricted to fixed phrases, esp. (as here) in conjunction with a pres. participle.   **in partes muneris sui** 'for the tasks [*OLD pars* 10] appertaining to their [collective] duty'.   **pollicentibus:** i.e. the tribunes; the senate responds at 17 (*patres*), forming a chiastic frame around C.'s speech (*pollicen-*

tibus ... patres ~ 6 *senatus ... collegae*).   **pro** 'the equivalent of' (*OLD* 9b). Valerius reintroduces the idea that C.'s is an extraordinary appointment (*dictatore* ~ 6 *dictatorem*); see 8–15n.

   6.17 proinde introduces the following exhortation (*OLD* 3a), cf. 18.14, 39.10.   **opinionem** ~ 9 *opinionem*. The focus returns to C.: instead of his trying to justify the state's opinion of him, *opinio* will determine Rome's hope for the war's outcome.   **unico imperatore** also occurs in Catullus' invectives against Caesar (29.11, 54.7), suggesting that it was in common use and, like our 'brilliant', could be sincere or heavily ironic. L.'s use of *unicus* 'exceptional' varies accordingly (E. Dutoit, *Latomus* 15 (1956) 481–8). C., who is *unicus* three times (also 22.9, 7.1.9), as he is *unus uir* (Pinsent (1) 15; see 6n.), embodies the positive sense of the adj.; most of the generals to whom L. later applies it are connected with C., though not always favourably: Fabius Maximus is *hic nouus Camillus, nobis dictator unicus* – sarcastically – at 22.14.9 (echoed at 22.27.3); the avenger of Caudium is compared with C. (9.15.10); Sulpicius, *unicus dux* (again sarcastic) at 7.12.13, has a triumph which recalls C.'s (7.15.8).   **se ... (18) trahentes:** the postponed subj. *patres* separates the first colon, an infin. clause dependent on *fremunt*, from the triad of prep. phrases dependent on *bene sperare*; *fremunt* is then followed by a second dependent clause comprising a condition + extended tripartite attributive phrase. The weight of the sentence falls on the two tricola, whose repeated, syntactically identical elements are characteristically oratorical (40.2n.).   **bene sperare** ~ 16 *spes*; the repetition indicates an affirmative response (*NLS* §171).   **erecti gaudio:** only here, cf. Sen. *Const.* 9.3 *erectus laetusque ... continuo gaudio elatus*; more conventional complements of *erectus* are *exspectatione* (2.54.8, 36.34.8) and *in spem* (3.1.2, Tac. *H.* 1.4.3).   **fremunt:** an onomatopoeic verb ('to hum', cf. Var. *L.* 6.67) favoured by Virg. (38), L. (39), and Tac. (13). L. has it of both positive and negative emotions.

   6.18 talis: specified by the adjs. following *habeat*; for the hyperbaton see 2.12n.   **habeat:** the subj. is *res publica*. For the thought cf. Cic. *Cat.* 4.15.   **tam ... trahentes** ~ 17 *et de bello ... re publica*; in each tricolon *auctum* the third member caps and explains the first two: the polar terms war and peace are the essence of the Roman state (as 1.1); C. and Valerius show their harmonious and co-

operative spirit by refraining from self-aggrandisement. For tricola
rounding off a section of narrative see Eden 110.   **tam** ~ *talis*
above.   **concordibus:** 8n. *(consensu).*   **iunctos** ~ *iuxta* below,
linking the first two cola.   **parere ... imperare:** this give and
take is a necessary condition for *libertas*, cf. 4.5.5 *si, quod aequandae
libertatis est, in uicem annuis magistratibus parere atque imperitare licet* with
Wirszubski 9–24. For the paronomastic combination (usually in antithesis) cf. 21.4.3, Cic. *Fin.* 2.46, Hor. *Ep.* 1.2.62–3, Vell. 79.1 with
W., Tac. *Ag.* 32.3 *inter male parentes et iniuste imperantes* with Otto 295–
6, and see 23.10n.; for the figure involved see 10n.   **iuxta paratos** continues the wordplay with a third verb and a change of vowel
quantity (*părere* ~ *păratos*); cf. 26.4, Caes. *C.* 3.95.2 *parati imperio par-
uerunt*, Sall. *C.* 20.17 *imperare parati*, Virg. *A.* 4.238 *parere parabat* with
Austin. The expression may strike a 'heroic note' (W. on Vell. 43.2
alterutri se fortunae parans), cf. Virg. *A.* 2.61 *in utrumque paratus* and for
iuxta = pariter see H. on Tac. *H.* 1.10.1.   **laudemque:** 'Basis'
(4.7n.). The following colon is framed by rhyming participles enclosing the antithesis *in medium* ~ *ex communi*; the structure of the whole
is chiastic. For such balance at period-end see Wilkinson 216–
17.   **in medium:** located precisely in the middle of its clause;
cf. Virg. *A.* 8.675 (*in medio* in the middle of the shield and of the
description of the shield) with R. F. Thomas, *H.S.C.P.* 87 (1983)
179–80. The idea of a common good available to all is characteristic of Golden Age communities (Virg. *G.* 1.127 with Thomas); for
the need to co-operate in an emergency cf. 5.44.1 *periculum commune
cogit quod quisque possit ... praesidii in medium conferre* with O.   **ad se
trahentes:** cf. Tac. *H.* 1.79.5 *gloriam in se trahente* with H. and see
8.6n.

7–10.6 Affairs abroad

C. leads a triple expedition against the Volsci, Antium (forestalled
at 9.1–3), and Etruria. The structure is similar to that of 2–4.3,
where the Aequi served as a hinge between longer engagements
(2.14n.). This time, however, the first battle rather than the last is
the most elaborate; the third is itself a diptych, illustrating Nepet's
and Sutrium's different responses to an Etruscan invasion (9.7–
11 ~ 10.1–6). Many of the features of the battle at Satricum (7–8)

will recur in C.'s last major military appearance (22.5–26); on the formulaic composition see above, pp. 15–17.

7.1 Iustitio: 2.6n.   **Satricum:** an important and ancient Latin city colonized in 385 (16.6), burnt in 377 (33.4n.), recolonized and rebuilt in 348 (7.27.2).   **profecti:** sc. *sunt* (1.10n.).   **quo ... populis:** subj. (*Antiates*) and verb (*conciuerant*) each bisects an element of the *non modo ... sed* construction; the second half of each part of the antithesis consists of a prep. phrase.   **quo** 'whither'.   **noua** ~ *integerrimis* below.   **subole** 'generation', an elevated word (M–W 120); it refers here to the stock needed to keep a race going (*OLD* 2c, 3), cf. 12.4.   **lectam:** technical of recruiting soldiers (*OLD* 6d).   **sed:** sc. *etiam*.   **uim:** a necessary supplement: the triple ellipse *non modo iuuentutem ... lectam* [sc. *conciuerant*] *sed ingentem* [sc. *iuuentutem*] *... conciuerant* [sc. *lectam*] *ex ... populis* would be bold even for L.   **conciuerant:** archaic and rare in prose outside L. and Tac.; the latter drops its synonym *concitare*, for which L. shows an increasing preference (Adams (4) 58–9).   **integerrimis:** the Ciceronian superlative, which L. has elsewhere only at 10.28.5, contributes to the exaggerated picture of the hordes waiting to attack. For the thought see 33.2n.   **nouus ... ueteri:** for the topos of piling new on old cf. 4.45.3 *nouos hostes ... consilia cum ueteribus iungere*, Aesch. *Sept.* 739–41, *Ag.* 764–6, Eur. *Med.* 76–9, Sen. *Suas.* 1.13, Curt. 10.5.13 *nouis uulneribus ueteres rumpendas cicatrices* (modelled on Aesch. *Ag.* 1480?), Sen. *Ep.* 113.30 *nouas ueteribus adiungunt*, [Quint.] *Decl.* 5.16. The new enemy, paradoxically, is from the long-peaceful Latins, the old from the *noua suboles* at Antium.   **militis:** collective sing. (2.12n.).

7.2 quod: obj. of *renuntiauerunt* with connective force; it is appositionally expanded by *turbatas ... posse* (below). That tetracolon reports rebellious actions of increasing severity, culminating in the extended final colon in which the soldiers actually speak (in *o.o.*). The content is chiastic (*mentes ... arma capta* ~ *egressos castris ... uoces*); on the shape see above, p. 23 n.100 and for the scene cf. Caes. *G.* 1.39.7.   **turbatas ... mentes** 'mentally unbalanced' (*OLD turbo* 5b); for *turbata mens* of panic cf. 3.60.10, 7.26.5. That C. agrees with the centurions' diagnosis is shown by his question *hostem ... ignoratis?* (3), failure of recognition being a sign of madness (Nisbet on Cic. *Pis.* 47).   **segniter:** first attested in L. and after him favoured only by Tacitus (6), though the comparative (37.8) is found as early as Cato.   **cunctabundos:** glossed by *resistentes*, cf. 33.8.2 *inuitum et cunctabundum*. For L.'s and Tacitus' fondness for adjs. in -*bundus* see Goodyear on Tac. *A.* 1.17.1 *contionabundus*.   **egressos:** sc. *milites* from *militum* above.   **quin** 'in fact' (*OLD* 2).   **uoces** introduces the following *o.o.*; cf. 17.1–2.   **cum centenis ... singulos:** the soldiers should believe that one Roman is a match for many foreigners (cf. Herod. 7.102.3, Xen. *Anab.* 1.7.3, Pl. *Mil.* 42–7, Caes. *C.* 1.58, *HA Aurel.* 6.4 *mille mille mille decollauimus*). Barbarians conventionally come in hordes, cf. 5.34.2, Herod. 4.172, Xen. *Anab.* 1.7.4, 3.2.16, Cic. *Arch.* 21, Vell. 106.1 with W.   **pugnaturos:** sc. *se esse*. Omission of *se* is esp. common with the fut. infin. (Adams (2) 370–1).   **inermem ... armatam:** for the paronomasia see 3.8n.   **sustineri posse:** a periphrasis for the fut. infin. pass. (*NLS* §154 *Note* i).

7.3 in equum insilit: cf. Sall. *H.* 5.5. C. leaps ostentatiously on and off his horse throughout this episode, energetic leadership characteristic of a good general (cf. 8.1, 6 with Lipovsky 93 n.4), though he will not be able even to mount at 24.5. For the general's exhortation from horseback, a subset of his walking along the ranks (Hansen 169–71), cf. *B. Afr.* 58, Dion. Hal. 3.25.1, Onas. 33.6, Arr. *Anab.* 2.10.2, Just. 11.9.3.   **et** does not actually connect anything: one expects a *uerbum dicendi*, but in the event C.'s speech just starts (cf. 3.11.12 with W–M).   **ante:** C.'s progress among the soldiers is described with precision: *ante signa* ... *in aciem* ... *ordines interequitans* (W–M).   **interequitans:** only in L. and Curtius; it may have been technical (B. on 34.15.4). Compounds of *equitare* seem to have been freely coined as needed: *adeq.* and *pereq.* are relatively common in the historians and military writers; L. alone has *praetereq.* (3.61.10), *circumeq.* (29.7.5), *abeq.* (24.31.10) and the first attestation of *obeq.* (2.45.3).

7.3–6. The pre-battle *hortatio*, a sub-genre of historiography with roots in Homer (Keitel (1), cf. Quint. 10.1.47), is a stylized feature of military narratives, often dropped into the proceedings with all the verisimilitude of a song in a movie musical: the action stops while elaborate exhortations are delivered by ideal generals, who were expected to be good speakers (Onas. 1.13–16; cf. 21.40–1 ~ 43–4, Scipio and Hannibal). Whatever historical reality these speeches reflect (there may have been some sort of brief pep talk: Hansen 171), historians deploy them to various purposes, e.g. to raise the energy level (as here), spark a peripeteia (24.5–6), pit two sides against one another (28.5–6 ∼ 7–9), show an anti-Roman viewpoint (2.4n.), or – by transferring them to the domestic sphere – to crystallize tensions between political factions (17.1–5, 18.5–15, 39.5–12).

quae ... est?: C. opens with a barrage of rhetorical questions, a combative tactic that challenges his audience to fight back (15.9n., cf. 17.3–5, 24.5–6 and see Ullmann (2) 53–6). Both parts of this question have the same number of syllables (isocolon, Lausberg §§719–24); for the device in L.'s speeches see Ullmann (2) 83–5. **quae ... haec:** the demonstrative is strikingly postponed, the disjunctive word order emphasized by the intrusive voc. *milites*; cf. 27.13.3 *qui pauor hic, qui terror, quae repente, qui et cum quibus pugnaretis, obliuio animos cepit?*, and for the conventional place of rebuke in a *hortatio* see Keitel (1) 163. **tristitia** 'moroseness' is associated with defeat or slavery (1.29.3, 3.6.6, 26.49.8) and with bad omens (*OLD tristis* 5, cf. 12.7n. (*laetus*)); it is the last thing one wants one's soldiers to display. **cunctatio** ∼ 2 *cunctabundos*. *cunctatio* is tantamount to cowardice: its connotations of prudence are missing here (23.5n.). But *insolita* softens the taunt and suggests C.'s next topic, the soldiers' usual courage. **hostem ... me ... uos:** a table of contents, which C. will pick up in a tricolon *auctum* (3–5) in the order ACB, allowing him to end with himself (above, p. 23). **ignoratis** 'are you unfamiliar with' (*OLD* 2), cf. 21.40.5 *ne genus belli neue hostem ignoretis*; for the connection with madness see 2n. **hostis ... aliud:** cf. Thuc. 3.30.4 ('what is war but'), Tac. *H.* 4.76.1 *Gallos quid aliud quam praedam uictoribus*. This is the figure *definitio* (Lausberg §782) which sets out the nature of something *dilucide ... et breuiter* (*Rhet. Her.* 4.35, see further 40.8n.); for the parainetic motif of the despicable enemy cf. 12.8, 18.4n., 21.10.9 *effigies immo, umbrae hominum ... cum hoc equite, cum hoc pedite pugnaturi estis, reliquias extremas hostium, non hostem habetis*, Onas. 14.3, Fron. *S.*1.11.17–18 and see Keitel (2) 74. **materia** occurs five times in Book 6, in its lit. sense (2.11), then twice of fuel for military glory (also at 22.6, cf. Cic. *Mil.* 35 *Clodium ... segetem ac materiam suae glo-*

riae), twice of fuel for domestic *seditiones* (11.8, 31.2). The repetitions link the two spheres of action (see also 1.6n. (*reficiendae*)).

7.4 uos ... me duce: C. interweaves the soldiers with himself (so 5 *me ... uobis ... ducem*); see Keitel (2) 74 on the 'symbiotic relationship' between a general and his troops.   **ut** 'even if' (*OLD* 35).   **Falerios ... caesas:** the three chief military episodes in Book 5, the first two picked up in reverse order (4.4n.; see above, p. 23). Exhortation by appeal to past victories and tested courage was the rule (Keitel (2) 75, cf. Thuc. 6.68.4, 7.66.1, Xen. *Anab.* 3.2.14–15, Caes. *G.* 1.40.5, Sall. *C.* 58.18–19, *J.* 49.2 with Paul, Luc. 7.285–7); for its combination, as here, with the 'same enemy' topos (below) cf. Tac. *Ag.* 34.1 *si nouae gentes atque ignota acies constitisset, aliorum exercituum exemplis uos hortarer: nunc uestra decora recensete, uestros oculos interrogate.*   **captos ... caesas:** AUC participles (1.1n.).   **capta patria** has great pathetic force (cf. 5.53.5, 26.15.14) which heightens the significance of the Roman victory: they saved the city even after it had fallen.   **taceam:** the figure *praeteritio*, which by refusing to mention something both brings it into play and makes it into a foil for something else (Lausberg §§882–6); see also 40–1n.   **trigeminae ... triplicem:** emphatic repetition with *uariatio*; the gen. with *triumphus* is descriptive.   **ex his ipsis:** the 'same enemy' topos; cf. 21.40.5, 27.13.3–4, Thuc. 5.9.1, 7.63.4, Caes. *G.* 1.40.7, *C.* 3.87.1, Dion. Hal. 3.23.19.   **Volscis ~ *Etruria*** (6.13n.).

7.5 me ... ducem frames the sentence, *ducem* postponed until the very end for emphasis ('don't you recognize me – that I am your leader?').   **non dictator ... sed tribunus:** the relationship between troops and men is further specified by the 'name' motif, which either establishes the leader's position (cf. 18.15, Xen. *Anab.* 3.1.25, Caes. *C.* 2.32.13, Sall. *C.* 20.16 with McGushin, Luc. 7.84–8) or the soldiers' (Keitel (2) 74).   **non agnoscitis ~ *ignoratis*** above (*uariatio*: Catterall 298–9, cf. 12.10n.).   **maxima imperia:** cf. Cic. *Balb.* 9, *Phil.* 5.44, *Fam.* 3.7.5; it is a variant on *summa imperia* (i.e. consulship, dictatorship, praetorship).   **in uos** 'over you'.   **in me** 'in my case'.   **intueri** strongly suggests looking at for guidance, or as a model (*OLD* 3, 6); it is the *uox propria* for looking at the *imagines*, cf. Cic. *Arch.* 14, Sall. *J.* 4.5 (above,

p. 14). **neque ... ademit:** C.'s claim to be unchanged by good
or bad fortune is characteristic of several ancient philosophical
schools, including Stoicism. **dictatura:** neither the fact of command nor the title 'Dictator'. For the idea that words cannot produce *uirtus* cf. Xen. *Cyr.* 3.50, 51, Sall. *C.* 58.1 with Vretska, *J.*
85.50. **animos fecit** 'gave courage,' in this sense apparently
only in L. (e.g. 1.34.4, 22.26.1); Ov. *Tr.* 5.8.3 is different ('make angry'). **ut ne ... quidem** 'any more than' (Radice). **exsilium:** 2.12n.

7.6 iidem ... exspectemus: cf. Tac. *H.* 1.38.1 *idem senatus, idem
populi Romani animus est: uestra uirtus exspectatur.* C. sounds more than
slightly exasperated as he summarizes his argument with exaggerated care. **iidem ... eadem ... eundum:** tricolon with
anaphoric polyptoton and an elaborated central member (above, p.
23). **euentum** ∼ 8.8 *euentus*; its placement suggests the conventional prayer at the start of an enterprise for *boni euentus* (Appel 130–
1). **simul** 'as soon as' (*OLD* 11a), which L. prefers to *simul ac.* In
these concluding sentences C. gives instructions for the battle
ahead; for a more elaborate version cf. 12.8–9 (nn.). **uos ...
fugient:** terse and to the point. For the short sentences describing
the actions of complementary groups cf. Caes. *C.* 1.15.2 *milites im-
perat: mittunt.*

8.1 ex equo desilit: so Caesar at the battle of Munda dismounted
and turned his retreating soldiers around (Vell. 55.3, cf. also Caes.
G. 2.25.12–3). **proximum ... rapit:** as he later drags victory
with him (6), C. here pulls the standard-bearer into battle, a hyperbolic variation on the general's snatching up the *signum* (often actually throwing it into the enemy ranks), cf. 3.70.10 *arrepta signa ab
signiferis ipse inferre*, Fron. *S.* 2.8.1–6, 4.5.3. **signiferum ...
'infer ... signum':** C. tells the *signifer* to do his (etymological)
job – chiastically, of course. Cf. 5.55.2 *signifer, statue signum*, 41.4.1
signiferum suum ... inferre signum iussit and Petr. 36.5–8 *carpe, Carpe*
(to the carver named Carpus). **arreptum ... rapit:** a subtype
of the figure 'resumption' (32.8n.). For the relatively uncommon
placing of the participle first cf. 5.49.8 *seruatam ... bello patriam iterum in pace ... seruauit*, Catul. 64.43 *nomine dicentem quos diximus*; for
the shift between compound and simplex (here with slight change
of meaning) cf. Caes. *C.* 2.11.2 *inuolutae labuntur, delapsae ... remouen-*

tur, Ov. *Am.* 2.16.26 *fundit et effusas ore receptat aquas* with B. on
31.37.7 *conuertit … uersaque.*   **rapit** 'compelled along' (*OLD* 7a).
clamitans: see on *clamantes* below.

8.2 munera corporis: cf. Cic. *Amic.* 22 *muneribus fungare
corporis.*   **senecta:** a choice and historiographical substantive
found overwhelmingly in the abl., as here (Adams (2) 352). Tacitus
favours *inualidus senecta* (*H.* 1.9.1, *A.* 3.43.3, 13.6.3).   **inualidum:**
ironic: 'this "invalid" general'; it foreshadows the description of
the aged C. at 22.7, while C. will repeat his inspiring behaviour at
24.7.   **uadentem** 'is employed by L. to give point to striking
episodes' (O. on 1.7.7); it denotes huge, dramatic motion, cf.
26.6.10 *elephanti … uadentes*, Enn. *Ann.* 253 Sk *uadunt solida ui*, Sall.
J. 94.6 (its first appearance in artistic prose) *super occisorum corpora
uadere, auidi gloriae.*   **in hostes:** a general was supposed to share
his soldiers' danger (W. on Vell. 114.13, Miniconi 168), though
Onas. 33 argues that he should stop short of entering battle.
procurrunt: the battle's major peripeteia (3.4n.); there is a minor
one at 6 *cum … restituit.*   **clamore sublato:** action contemporaneous with the main verb: 'they charged, raising a shout' (M–W on
Tac. *A.* 4.64.1). It is hard to see the point of the repetition with
clamantes below.   **'sequere imperatorem':** these bits of *o.r.*
are characteristic of battle narratives (e.g. Caes. *C.* 2.34.4, *B. Alex.*
15.3–4, *B. Afr.* 16.1–3).   **clamantes** ~ 1 *clamitans* (they are synonyms: Adams (4) 58); the echo embodies the desired harmony between general and soldiers (7.4n.).

8.3 emissum … signum ~ *concitatos antesignanos* below (ABAB);
the second part of the sentence (4) is chiastic (*pulsum Antiatem* ~
terrorem … perlatum). The Roman onslaught (*emissum … in host.
aciem … antesig.*) matches the enemy retreat step by step (*pulsum
… in … aciem … ad subsidiaries*).   **ferunt** 'they say', sc. *auctores*
(12.2n.).   **antesignanos** ~ 4 *primam … aciem.*

8.4 Antiatem: collective sing. (2.12n.).   **terroremque** ~ 5
terribilius.   **in … ad:** 2.4n.

8.5 uis … militum: 'military force' (*OLD uis* 5), a common
expression made uncommon by the addition of *excitata* ('though it
was spurred on'), which logically modifies the soldiers themselves.
The abstracts *praesentia* and *species* (below) contribute to the slightly
mannered language.   **praesentia:** for the leader's beneficial

presence, a panegyrical topic, see Brink on Hor. *Ep.* 2.1.15 *praesenti tibi*, W. on Vell. 92.2 *circumferens ... praesentia sua pacis suae bona* (both of Augustus).   **quod** 'the fact that' ~ *uis* above (Catterall 316). **terribilius** 'more terror-inspiring'; the adj. is Ennian (*Ann.* 309, 451 Sk), the comparative attested first at Cic. *Phil.* 2.65, next in L.   **ipsius ... species:** C.'s appearance works on the enemy as on his own men (cf. 8.9.9–14, the double effect of Decius' *deuotio*); for the decisive power of the leader's appearance see W. on Vell. 75.1 and cf. 2.9n.   **forte oblata species** 'a chance sighting'; for the participle see 1.1n.

8.6 ita ... trahebat: cf. 4.13.3 (quoted on 15.9) and for the motif cf. 9.18.16 *domini rerum ... trahunt consiliis cuncta*, 9.40.10, Prop. 4.9.65 *fata trahentem*, Sen. *Suas.* 2.1 *licet totum classe Orientem trahat*, V. Max. 3.2.24 *ut maiorem semper uictoriae partem traxisse uideatur*, Tac. *H.* 3.20.3 *uim uictoriamque nobiscum ferimus*. C. lit. brings the word 'victory' with him wherever he goes: it occurs seven times during this engagement (7.4, 6, 8.6 *bis*, 7, 10 *bis*).   **se intulisset:** frequentative subjunc. ('anywhere he might appear'), a usage widespread in the historians (*NLS* §196; Riemann 294–8).   **euidens:** L. demonstrates the illustrative quality of C.'s decisive appearance, which produces clarity both on the level of story (i.e. for the characters) and discourse (he provides an occasion for narrative *euidentia*: 1.3n.). **equo ... pedestri:** C. has both infantry and cavalry equipment; the detail highlights his ability to encourage both parts of his army.   **conspectu suo** ~ *ostentans* below: C. is himself seen and displays things to others. For *conspectus* 'sight of' (*OLD* 2) cf. Caes. *C.* 3.51.2 *neque uero conspectum aut impetum nostrorum tulerunt*; for the motif see 5n.   **restituit** 'retrieved (the fortune)' (*OLD* 3c). **uincentem:** completive participle after a verb of perception (*NLS* §94); the participle gives a greater sense of immediacy than the infin.

8.7 iam ... erat 'at this point a rout had already begun'. *inclinare* is a calque on ἔγκλιμα, technical for 'rout' from Xen. *Hel.* on (Pritchett IV 69–70); for *iam* see 5.1n.   **sed** introduces a qualification, not a contradiction (*OLD* 7), the unexpressed thought being, 'and the Romans would have mopped things up quickly, but ...'. The *multitudo* whose weight the Romans had feared (7.2) turns out to be unwieldy in an unexpected way.   **turba ...**

erat 'because of the crowd of enemies, on the one hand their [i.e. the enemy's] flight was impeded, on the other accomplishing the slaughter of such a great multitude was a long business for the exhausted soldiers'. *et* is postponed because *turba* is common to both subsequent clauses (4.7n.). For crowds impeding themselves cf. 9.23.16, 34.15.8, Caes. *C.* 2.35.3; for 'too many to slaughter' cf. *B. Afr.* 19.3 *tantam se multitudinem … sumministraturum ut etiam caedendo in ipsa uictoria defatigati uincerentur*, Luc. 7.534–5; a similar idea is called to mind by Caligula's wish that the Roman people had only one neck (Suet. *Cal.* 30.2).   **fuga … caede:** a conventional pair (Xen. *Hel.* 4.6.11 'died trying to escape', Caes. *G.* 7.67.6, *C.* 2.34.6, *B. Alex.* 18.3, Sall. *J.* 3.2, *H.* 1.55.17, Tac. *A.* 14.64.3) and the inevitable results of victory, though here neither is possible.   **longa:** *caedes* is more often qualified by *magna* (as 9.11); but cf. *continua c.* (Tac. *A.* 6.29.1), *infinita c.* (Cic. *Cat.* 3.8, 25), *quanta c.* (Virg. *A.* 8.537).   **conficienda:** the gerundive works like an AUC participle (1.1n.), a Livian innovation (*NLS* §95).   **cum … diremit:** inverted *cum* following imperfs., as usual (*NLS* §237); on the '*cum* de rupture', which suspends one action in order to introduce a second, unexpected one, see C-L 561–95.   **ingentibus … imber:** for rain interrupting a battle (often with *dirimere*) cf. 32.6, 23.44.4 *i. p. effusus imber*, 26.11.2, 28.15.11–12, Polyb. 18.20.7–9 (mist after rain halts a march), Tac. *H.* 5.18.2, *A.* 2.7.2 (battle cannot be started). For the related motif of night stopping a battle see 9.11n. and for the language see H. on Tac. *H.* 3.69.4.   **uictoriam … proelium:** cf. 5.44.7 *me sequimini ad caedem, non ad pugnam*, Tac. *H.* 3.77.1 with H.

8.8 quietis 'making no move' (*OLD* 2a).   **Latini … relictis Volscis** ~ 9 *Volsci … relictis castris*, a bipartite *gradatio* (Lausberg §§623–4), cf. 27.7. The complete (i.e. tripartite or more) figure is rare in prose; cf. 1.3.8 *Latino Alba ortus, Alba Atys, Atye Capys, Capye Capetus, Capeto Tiberinus*, 8.34.7, 23.43.4, Cic. *Mil.* 61.   **malis … euentus** ~ 7.6 *euentum*. For the topos bad start ~ bad end see Otto 206, 287.   **malis consiliis:** the idea that a bad plan wreaks its worst effects on the planner is proverbial, cf. Hes. *Op.* 265–6 with West.   **pares … euentus:** for the hyperbaton see 1.2n.

8.9 quorum: objective gen., 'relying on whom'. For the fickleness of allies in adversity see W. on Vell. 53.2.   **operibus:** siege

works (*OLD* 10b). For these and the specific siege engines in 9.2 see
G. Webster, *The Roman imperial army* (1969) 231–6.

8.10 quae ... cepit: the sentence is built almost exclusively
from continuative cola (above, p. 20).   **postquam ... uidet:**
postquam + hist. pres. is rare outside of the historians, who use it
primarily with verbs of perceiving (*NLS* §217 (3)).   **eruptione**
'sortie' (*OLD* 1).   **animi** 'courage'; the gen. as with *nihil, satis*
etc.   **quam ut ... exspectaret** 'for him in this [enemy's] case
to wait for a victory that would require such slow-working hope'. A
final subjunc. after comparative *quam* is required 'when the compared action is one that is to be, or was, *purposely rejected*' (*NLS*
§253 *Note* ii); the superfluous *ut* is first common in L., esp. after a
main clause in the acc. + infin. (as here).   **lentae spei:** gen. describing 'what a person or thing is capable of, requires, or involves'
(*NLS* §85 1 (c)); for the form of expression cf. 5.5.7 *lentiorem spem*, 6.2
serae spei (both of Veii: see below), 30.28.8, Ov. *Ep.* 2.3.   **spei
... exspectaret:** though the Romans did not explicitly derive
(*ex*)*spectare* from *spes* (Maltby 576), the paronomastic collocation is
common; cf. 18.9, Cic. *Cael.* 66 *spe delectationis expecto*, *Att.* 3.20.1 *spei
et expectationi*, Tac. *H.* 2.78.3, *A.* 3.29.4 *suspectumque iam nimiae spei
Seianum.*   **tamquam ... oppugnantes:** the comparison with
Veii, a siege that took ten years, combines the motifs of 'former
victories' (7.4n.) and (by implication) 'despicable enemy' (7.3n.):
'these Volsci are nothing like the Veians, whom you once beat; victory is at hand'.   **opere** 'effort' (*OLD* 5a): the brief push required will save them from having to mount a siege (∼9 *operibus*).
sese tererent 'wear themselves down'.   **esse:** a mild zeugma
after *cohortatus* (3.4n.).

9.1 animus as subj. is slightly more mannered than *dux*, cf.
34.33.9 *ipsius imperatoris animus ad pacem inclinatior erat*; for *a. imminet*
cf. Sen. *Vit.* 6.1.   **imminebat** 'was intent on' (*OLD* 3a), cf.
3.51.9 *imminens ... ei potestati*, *Culex* 90–1 *huic imminet, omnes | derigit
huc sensus*. The regular use of *imminere* in martial contexts (as
9.31.14, 26.13.11, 42.10.11) firmly establishes this 'looming' as a
threat.   **id ... eam:** a demonstrative is commonly attracted
into the case of its defining substantive (Roby §1068); for L.'s form
of expression cf. Virg. *A.* 12.572 *hoc caput ... haec belli summa*

nefandi.   **caput:** sc. *esse.*   **fuisse:** for the omission of a *uerbum dicendi* see above, p. 13.

9.2 tormentis machinisque: 8.9n.   **ualida urbs:** a 'stock expression in history'; the adj., 'common in poets and writers of artificial prose', outnumbers its synonym *firmus* throughout the *AVC* (Adams (4) 59–60).   **ad exercitum** 'with the army' (*OLD ad* 18b).   **ad excidendum Antium:** for the violent image cf. 2.2 *ad exstinguendum nomen Romanum* (n.). *excidere* is regular in military contexts (*OLD* 5, Powell on Cic. *Sen.* 18), but in this sense only twice in L. (also 21.19.1).

9.3 inter sermonem eius 'while he was speaking'; for *sermo* of addresses in the senate cf. Cic. *Fam.* 3.8.2, Tac. *H.* 1.19.1, also of a soldier (Galba). As the legates arrive in the midst of C.'s speech, so L.'s parenthetical explanation for the interruption itself disturbs the narrative.   **credo** 'I suppose'. Authorial intervention is common practice in ancient historiography, though its frequency varies, L. and Herodotus being among the chattiest writers; for L.'s personal interventions see Steele 21–3 (refs. to himself and his sources), 42–3 (refs. to the reader). The 'invisible' narrator was not a critical desideratum; instead, a historian was expected to pass judgment on his subject (cf. Cic. *De orat.* 2.63, *Fam.* 5.12.4). There were historians who effaced themselves as far as they could, the most notorious exx. being Thucydides (cf. 1.1.1 with Hornblower, 4.104.4) and Caesar (cf. his sleight of hand at *C.* 3.1.1 *dictatore habente comitia Caesare consules creantur Iulius Caesar et P. Seruilius*, from which it would appear that there are *two* Caesars, neither of them the author). Consistent use of the third person enhances authority by simultaneously masking signs of hesitation or doubt (on Thucydides see *RICH* 16–23) and giving the impression that the story is telling itself, an obvious advantage in creating a coherent and persuasive re-presentation of events (Booth 3–19, White (2) 2–3, 18–19). L.'s frequent first-person intrusions, which engage the reader in his project (above, p. 13), have helped diminish his *auctoritas* in the eyes of some (cf. Quint. 2.5.19). Yet 'frank' intervention can also inspire trust (12.2n.).   **rem Antiatem:** 3.1n. *rem ... manere* is treated as a neuter noun and forms the subj. of the *o.o.* (G–L §422).   **dis ... fuisse:** L. not infrequently appeals to supernatural forces, often in the form of a vague *fors* or *fatum* (21.2n.), to explain a sudden turn of events. These *di* slide imperceptibly into *fortuna* (below), who, though perhaps wearing 'the conventional garb of Hellenistic Tyche' (*LHA* 58), is a most appropriate protector for Antium, since she had a major cult there (Champeaux 95 n.43, 149–91). **cordi:** predicative dat. *c. esse* 'to be dear to' occurs across the extant corpus of literary Latin; L. is among those who are fondest of it. *dis cordi esse* may have been a stock expression in prayers (Nisbet–Hubbard on Hor. *C.* 1.17.14).   **Nepete** indeclinable (it is acc. in 12). The town was colonized in 383 (21.4); for Sutrium see 3.2n. **petentes** = *qui petant*, cf. 5.33.1, 21.6.2 *missi auxilium ... orantes*. The pres. participle of verbs of seeking and avoiding is used to express purpose in Cicero's latest works (Laughton 30–1); L. so employs it freely (L–H–S 387).   **memorantes:** a postponed participial colon of an old type, expressing a state of mind (C-L 306–11). *memorare* is an old-fashioned word gradually replaced in the *AVC* by *commemorare*; it is favoured by historians (Adams (4) 55).   **uim Camilli** is in imitation of the epic periphrasis Ἡρακλῆος βίη 'mighty Heroclès' (*et sim.*, e.g. Hom. *Il.* 3.105, 18.117). *uis* can designate the power of a deity (*OLD* 12a), a sense perhaps present here.

9.4 opposita 'facing'; what follows suggests two ways of reading this, either as expressing hindrance (*OLD* 2) or availability (*OLD* 1b), depending on whether the towns are seen as *claustra* or *portae* (next n.).   **claustra ... portaeque:** the metaphorical equation of a geographical feature with a doorway is common; here metaphor is combined with synecdoche (*claustra* for *ianua*, as 31.48.7, Curt. 4.8.4, Tac. *A.* 2.59.3 with Koestermann). *claustra ... portaeque* correspond chiastically to *illis ... molirentur* (the Etruscans want the gates open; for *porta* implying the possibility of passage see *OLD* 2) and *Romanis ... erat* (the Romans want to bolt the door).   **inde** qualifies the nouns (almost = *eius*, cf. Virg. *Aen.* 1.13 *longe* with Austin), apparently an extension of its use in indicating geographical proximity (*OLD* 3), as 5.34.6 *Alpes inde oppositae erant*.   **illis:** sc. *Etruscis* from *Etruriae* above.   **cum ... molirentur:** frequentative (8.6n.); for *noua moliri* cf. Vell. 129.2 with W., Tac. *H.* 4.38.1 with H.

9.5 igitur: Cicero rarely begins a sentence with this confirmatory particle; the tendency to do so is a historiographical affectation traditionally associated with the iconoclastic style of Sallust. L. has initial *igitur* 26 per cent of the time (Adams (4) 61, *TLL* v 2.760–1). **cum ... agi** 'to make arrangements with'; for the following subjunc. cf. 8.23.12 *actum cum tribunis est ad populum ferrent.* **Antio ... Etruscum:** *uariatio* (noun ~ adj.): Catterall 306–7, Sörbom 92–4.

9.6 expertum ... adsuetum: the word order (adj. – noun – adj.) is a version of the figure *coniunctio* (*Rhet. Her.* 4.38), cf. 1.19.7 *nefastos dies fastosque,* 44.1 *cum uinculorum minis mortisque. expertum* is passive ('that he was used to', *OLD* 5), a sense that L. introduced into prose (*LHA* 266), cf. 18.13. **mallet** 'he would have preferred', potential subjunc.; the imperf. designates unfulfilled action (*NLS* §121). **Valerium:** C.'s desire to have Valerius continue as his partner foreshadows his request that L. Furius, despite his insubordination, be reassigned to him (25.5–6). **imperii socium:** 6.12n. **successores Valerio:** *successor* + dat. (by analogy with *succedere*) is unusual and unattested in literary Latin before L.

9.7–12 Sutrium. The tribunes' partnership is underscored by correlative and parallel constructions: the town is partly in Etruscan hands, partly free (7); the Roman intervention gives both immediate and future hope (8); the battle has two fronts and two locales (9–11). In all, there are five sets of formal correlations (7 *partem ... parte,* 8 *cum ... tum, et ... et,* 9 *et ... et,* 11 *et ... et*); in contrast the fight at Satricum (chh. 7–8) has only 8.7 *et ... et.* For a similar reinforcement of theme by grammar cf. 1.23–5 with Konstan 209.

9.7 Sutrium: acc. of end of motion. **partem** ~ *ex parte* below, minor *uariatio* reinforced by *captam* ~ *arcentes* and graphically illustrating the division in the town. **arcentes:** the participle as after verbs of perception (8.6n.). **itineribus:** the town streets, cf. Thuc. 2.3.3.

9.8 aduentus: 8.5n. **Camilli nomen:** 2.9n. **celeberrimum:** *celeber* 'famous, celebrated' is first in prose at Cic. *Ver.* 3.61 *celeberrima atque notissima,* where *notissima* glosses the new sense (cf. *Arch.* 5 *celebritate famae ... notus*), then in L. (*TLL*).

9.9 circumductis copiis is part of the acc. + infin. clause: 'ordered his colleague to lead his troops around ... and attack the walls'. Valerius is to create a diversion, for which cf. 5.21.4, 32.24.3–6, Onas. 42.6, Fron. *S.* 3.6. **tanta ... quam:** for the inconcinnity cf. Virg. *Aen.* 6.351–4 *iuro | non ullum pro me tantum cepisse timorem | quam tua ne ... deficeret ... nauis.*   **ut:** purpose. For causal abl. (*spe*) ~ final clause cf. Catterall 315 (nom. (etc.) ~ final clause), Sörbom 114.   **auersis eo hostibus** 'by making the enemy turn in that direction'.   **et ... haberet:** C.'s two aims correspond to the effects his arrival had in 8 (*rem ... sustinuit ~ laxaretur labor, spatium ad opem ferendam ~ spatium intrandi moenia*). In each case the first clause describes a lull in the action, the second a decisive Roman move.   **oppidanis** ~ *ipse* (below): the *uariatio* brings out the fact that the townspeople have lost the power of self-regulated action, while C. acts forcefully in the nom.   **labor:** for the expression cf. 9.16.15 *ut sibi ... laxaret aliquid laboris*; for L.'s habit of putting the subj. late in the sentence see Kühnast 310–11.   **intrandi ... moenia:** 4.10n.

9.10 quod cum ... factum esset: a historiographical 'cliché de liaison' which takes various forms (e.g. 17.6 *quo facto*, 20.1 *quod ubi est factum*); it is esp. at home in Caesarian narrative (C-L 65–72).   **et ... et:** the first *et* links *uiderent* with what precedes, the second joins the two elements of the *uiderent* clause.   **moenia ... intra moenia:** a type of repetition resembling the 'Priam' figure (16.3n.).   **porta ... eiecere:** the elements of this quasi-miraculous escape can be paralleled: for part of a town being untouched in a siege cf. 5.29.4, 36.24.5, Thuc. 2.4.4 (one gate is deserted); for deliberately letting the enemy out cf. 2.47.8 *ad extrema uentum foret ni legati ... patefecissent una porta hostibus uiam*; for escape at the last moment from a besieging army cf. Caes. *C.* 3.96.3 *decumana porta se ex castris eiecit*, Tac. *A.* 1.66.1. More often an attacking force finds a single unguarded means of approach (5.47.2, 37.11.15 (one gate is betrayed), Herod. 1.84, Sall. *J.* 93.2 with Paul).   **se:** an unemphatic personal pronoun in second position (Wackernagel's law).   **forte** often appears in these stories of happy coincidence, e.g. 2.10, 3.4, 34.6, 34.8, 1.24.1 (there 'chance' to be valorous triplets in both the Roman and Alban armies), 1.58.6 (Collatinus and Lucretius 'chance' to meet Brutus); see J. Champeaux, *R.E.L.* 45 (1967) 369–71.

9.11 et in urbe et per agros: expanded by the next sentence (ABAB), where the parallelism is upset by L.'s typical imbalance (*a Furianis* ~ *Valeriani*).   **plures ... expeditiores:** each tribune has his own area of superiority. For *expeditus ad* + gerund(ive) cf. Cic. *De orat.* 2.131, Var. *R.* 3.9.15, Nep. *Dat.* 6.2, Vitr. 4 *praef.* 10, Petr. 114.14. **persequendos** is difficult but may be right; its noun must be supplied from *fugientium* above. Cf. 35.25.9 *plus ea oratio momenti ad incitandos ad bellum habuit*, 38.29.3 *plerumque his proeliis superiores erant. una ad coercendos inuenta ... res est*, Caes. *C.* 3.83.3 *unam fore tabellam* [sc. *eis*] *qui liberandos omni periculo censerent*. **noctem:** for night stopping a battle see *RICH* 193 n.42 and add 13.6, Caes. *G.* 2.6.4, *B. Alex.* 11.5, Sall. *J.* 38.8, Sen. *Contr.* 1.5.9 *finem rapiendi*, Fron. *S.* 2.9.1, Tac. *A.* 12.16.2; Pritchett IV 46–51 has Greek exx. See also 8.7n.

9.12 Sutrio ... sociis: chiastic alliteration rounds off the Roman job at Sutrium. **Nepete:** in contrast to the physical division between Sutrini and Etruscans, some Nepesini are in collaboration with the enemy, resulting in a complete loss of the town (*totum* below, 10.1 *tota*). Narrative devices mirrored the physical separation at Sutrium (9.7–12n.); the ideological split at Nepet will be reflected in the narrative only after C.'s victory, when he scrupulously divides the captives into Etruscans and Nepesini, then separates the latter into the guilty leaders and the innocent *multitudo* (10.5). **quod:** rel. pronoun. **acceptum** is causal.

10.1 plus ... laboris: this narrative will be more exciting than the last, for those who like *expugnationes urbium* (cf. Tac. *A.* 4.32.1, quoted on 1.1–3). **parte ... ciuitatem** 'by the betrayal of the state by a faction [*OLD pars* 16] of the Nepesini'.

10.2 mitti ... placuit: C. tries two stratagems to avoid a full-scale attack, first attempting unsuccessfully to induce treachery (on which see Fron. *S.* 3.3). **secernerent ... praestarent:** the content of the message is bracketed between its verbs, an elegant word order that heightens the correspondence between the desired actions (C-L 365–8). In answer (3) the Nepesini use a different order (*nihil ... esse, Etruscos ... tenere*); see also 32.2n. **fidem** 'loyalty' (*OLD* 8); for *fides* in treaties (etc.) between cities see Moore 35–40.

10.3 unde 'from whom'; the connective use is rare (*OLD* 10b). **suae potestatis:** defining gen., sometimes classed as possessive (Roby §1282). **Etruscos** ~ *suae* above; the *principes* put the emphatic proper name first lest there be any misunderstanding about the situation (see further 5n.). **primo:** L. is famous for carefully delineating the stages of an action (*LHA* 198–9), cf. 4 *deinde*, 13.3, 39.7; it is an organizational feature he may have picked up from Caesar (cf. *G.* 2.30.1–3, 3.20.3–4, *C.* 3.45.3). On other Caesarian tidiness see Eden 110–11, von Albrecht 59–64.   **populationibus:** for devastating the countryside in order to provoke either surrender or a sortie cf. 5.26.4, 42.1 (Rome itself becomes the countryside as the garrison is trapped in the *arx*), 8.29.11, 43.23.4, Thuc. 1.81.6, 143.5 with Hornblower, Fron. *S.* 3.10.6–7.   **terror ... admotus:** first attested here. *admouere* often denotes hostile motion; it was technical of fire and war machines (as *scalae admotae* below: *TLL* I 771.42–76).

10.4 postquam ... erat: the imperf. with *postquam* and other temporal conjunctions is regular only in historiography; the continuative tense has a causal flavour: 'after [and since] the treason proved more binding' (*NLS* §217 (5)).   **deditionis ... societatis:** objective gens.   **quam ... sanctior:** 4.11n.   **fides sanctior:** cf. 8.37.2, Enn. *scen.* 320 J *nulla sancta societas nec fides regni est*, Cic. *Ver.* 3.6, Virg. *A.* 7.365, Vell. 2.18.4; on *sanctus* here see Moore 124 n.11.   **ex agro ... admotae** ~ 3 *populationibus agri terror ... admotus*: the harvest of destruction becomes a means for bringing real danger inside Nepet.

10.5 Nepesinis ... Etrusci ... Nepesinorum: the clarity of exposition produced by these headings (2.2n.) recalls the collaborators' use of a similar device as they tried to insulate themselves from responsibility (3n.).   **parci ... inermi:** 3.8n.   **iussum:** sc. *Romanis*. For the military passive and communiqué style see 3.10n. **Nepesinorum** 'among the Nepesini' (partitive gen.) qualifies both *auctores* and *multitudini* below (4.7n.).   **auctores deditionis:** technical (W. on Vell. 119.4). C. imposes the distinction that he wished the Nepesini to make themselves (2). For punishment of ringleaders only cf. 21.7, 9.16.10, 28.29.7–12 (mutineers) and see Lintott 42–3; on capital penalties see also 20.12n.   **securi percussi** 'beheaded', a 'republican and consecrated phrase' (Syme (2) 725).

10.6 uictorem ... reduxerunt: it is L.'s practice in Book 6 to mention only briefly the return of armies *not* under dictatorial command (26.8, 31.8, 33.12; contrast C.'s return at 4.1–3, Quinctius' at 29.8–9). The elaboration here, in which re-entry into Rome entails *uictoria* and *gloria*, is elsewhere associated with triumphs, although no cons. trib. triumphed (*CAH*² 193, cf. Sall. *J.* 114.3, Tibul. 2.1.33–4, Vitr. 1 *praef.* 1 *triumpho uictoriaque tua ciues gloriarentur*, Sil. 15.98–100, Plin. *Pan.* 16.3–4); it reminds us both that C. is a dictator in all but name (6.6, 16) and that his respect for Valerius' *dignitas* is such that he allows him full partnership in this 'triumphal' entry.   **Romam:** 4.1n.

10.6–9 End of the year

res repetitae: the first step in declaring war (*CAH*² 292–3, Harris 166–75).   **ex instituto:** by the *foedus Cassianum* (2.3n.).

   10.7 frequenti: technical of full assemblies (*OLD* 4a).   **in eo** 'in this matter', picked up by *quod*.   **publicam** qualifies both *culpam* and *consilium* but agrees with the noun in its own half of the *nec ... nec* construction (technically if not lit. the nearer: G–L §290). On the word order see 9.6n.; for the topos see 6.5n.   **apud** 'on the side of' (*OLD* 4c).

   10.8 praui ... poenam: on paying in kind for bad *consilium* see 8.8n.   **nec** 'for', epexegetic and inferential.   **his:** L. often retains forms of *hic* and *nunc* in *o.o.* (an element of *repraesentatio*: 5.3n.).   **militis ... non dati causam** 'the reason that they had not provided soldiers'.   **quam pestem:** regular incorporation of an appositional substantive into the rel. clause (G–L §616.2).   **pestem** images a clinging poison or beast, cf. Cic. *Tusc.* 2.20 (the poison of Nessus), Virg. *G.* 3.419 (a snake), Col. 9.14.2 *pestes ... fauis adhaerentes* (insects). For *pestis* in invective see Opelt 135–8 (politicians), 182–6 (foreigners).   **adhaerentem lateri:** cf. 34.41.4, 39.25.11, and see W. on Vell. 129.3; for the thought cf. Cic. *Tusc.* 4.24 *inhaeret in uisceribus ... malum exsistitque ... aegrotatio quae euelli inueterata non possunt.*   **tot ... bellis** 'by means of so many wars, one on top of another'.   **exhauriri** 'be drawn off', perhaps 'gouged out' as a leech: *exhaurire* here approaches one sense of *haurire*, cf. Lucr. 6.141 *arbusta ... radicibus hauriat ab imis* with D. A. West, *C.Q.* 25 (1965) 275–6.

   10.9 quae ... habere 'but when this answer was relayed, it seemed to the senate to afford [*OLD habeo* 14] a reason for war but not an opportune moment'. This epigram, whose closural force is enhanced by interlaced word order and pervasive (though not very successful) point, rounds off the first major division of Book 6. For *epiphonemata* see Lausberg §879, Smith 192–210; see further 6.18nn., 16.7n., 17.6n., 37.11n., M–W 98, W. on Vell. 48.5, 112.6.

magis ... quam: a *magis quam*-epigram can point to a reality underneath a surface (e.g. 8.7 *magis uictoriam quam proelium*) or to an illogicality: why did the senate *not* have time for war? there was nothing else on the books at the moment (cf. 21.9 for a cynical appraisal of a similar situation). The persuasiveness of comparative expressions is discussed by Arist. *Rhet.* 1363b–1365b; their pointed deployment is a staple of the declaimers' paradoxical language (e.g. Sen. *Contr.* 1.5.9, 2.2.2, 7.3.5, [Quint.] *Decl.* 8.14, 251.3, 289.1) but reaches its full potential in Tacitus (Plass 50–4, Voss 126–8).

11–17 The year 385 B.C.

11 Internal affairs

The *seditio* of M. Manlius Capitolinus (11–20) is the last and most elaborate of a triad of demagogue narratives in the first decade (with Sp. Cassius at 2.41, Sp. Maelius at 4.12.6–16). *Populares* tended to imitate the actions of their precursors (Seager (1) 332–3); Manlius, no exception to the rule, invokes the tradition *he* is following (18.9n.). Literary accounts of *popularis* behaviour also show a high degree of intertextual dependence. Manlius' story, which is dense with conventional elements, owes a particular debt to Sallust's and Cicero's portraits of Catiline. (For other traditional strands – Gracchan, Sullan, Clodian, and Caesarian – see Valvo in general; on the history see *CAH*[2] 331–2 and P. M. Martin, *SS* 49–72.)

Though conventional, Manlius is not simple. His demagoguery provokes a moderately hostile response from L. (Valvo 9), who points out Manlius' hidden motives (14.2, 11, 20.4–5). Yet it is characteristic of L.'s narratives of domestic conflict that sympathy tends to lie with both sides: the historian is interested in moral complexity (Levene 204–8, Solodow in general), in which he engages his readers by inviting them to question traditional interpretations of his characters' motives and actions (see nn. on 11.4, 9, 16.5, 20.3, 10, 15–16). In this episode L.'s even-handedness exceeds his customary synthesis of incompatible strands of the narrative tradition (*CC* 50–1): he allows Manlius to set himself up as a rival historian (11.4nn.) while himself doubting the basic premise of the story (18.16, 20.4). Manlius' death is a solution from which neither the political nor the narrative authority fully recovers (18–20.12n., cf. Bayet 111–13 on Manlius' different sides which 'déconcertent le jugement et créent chez le lecteur une sorte de malaise'). The narrative itself is preoccupied with the same issues as the story it tells: power, deception, and above all, authority – whose version of history is finally to be believed?

11.1 Insequenti ... exorta: the prefatory chapter, which touches on nearly all the issues of the forthcoming conflict (Valvo 8), is delineated by triple ring structure: it opens and closes with official appointments (1 ∼ 10, outer ring), inside of which the year's events are resumed (1–2 *graue bellum ... adiuncta ... defectione* ∼ 9 *bellum ... graue ... oneratum ... defectione,* second ring), in their turn enclosing the sketch of Manlius (2 *patriciae gentis ... famae* ∼ 7 *plebem ... famae,* inner ring). **A. Manlio ... potestate:** 1.8n. **graue ... grauior:** an intensifying polyptoton common in L. by which he simultaneously compares two items which share a quality, and distinguishes them in degree. The similarity between events *domi* and *foris* will be highlighted by the military language with which L. describes the former (12.1, 15.2–3, 38.3–4); their difference, by the fact that, as the book progresses, events in the field are increasingly organized and predictable, while those at home are chaotic and dangerous. The present distinction provides a transition, turning our attention from what has heretofore been the book's main focus (*bellum*) to a new area (*seditio*); see also 6.2n. **seditio:** each main 'act' of the episode is tagged, cf. 14.1 *gliscente ... seditione,* 18.1 *recrudescente ... sed.* (Lipovsky 35; see also 34.5n.).

11.2 ab 'at the hands of' (*OLD* 18a). **unde ... potuit** 'whence it could have least been expected'; for the potential indic. of *posse* see *NLS* §125. Like Sallust in *C.*, L. begins with a character sketch of his hero (E. Burck, *Gymnasium* 73 (1966) 95): but where Catiline had revelled in civil strife *ab adulescentia* (*C.* 5.2), Manlius' behaviour is a surprise; nor does L. choose, with Quad. (fr. 7) and

later Dio (7.26.2) to exploit the contrast between his two 'halves'
by focusing on the problem of transferring excellence from the military to the civic sphere (Wiseman 234, cf. Solodow 255 on Horatius). Instead, L. will rarely allude to his heroism (20.5, 12), letting
Manlius blow his own horn (4–5nn., 14.4, 15.11, 16.2, 20.7–9nn.).
a ... famae: for the word order see 9.6n.   **uiro ... M.
Manlio:** the appositive combination of proper name + *uir* is something of a Livian mannerism (e.g. 34.5, 3.44.3, 24.40.8; cf. W. on
Vell. 129.1). Here the pattern is reversed: L. defines Manlius first
by his qualities, which make his actions so startling, then by his
name.   **inclitae famae:** a rather free descriptive gen. (also at
7), cf. 45.27.11 *Athenas ... uetustae famae*. As *inclitus* lit. = 'something
heard of', the expression is tautologous: 'famous report' (Woodman 252 n.9); cf. Virg. *A.* 2.82 with Austin, Sil. 16.607–8, Tac. *H.*
4.61.1 with H.   **M. Manlio Capitolino:** the most important
piece of information is saved for the end (cf. 2.5). Manlius' *cognomen*
is a pointed reminder of his achievement (∼ *inclitae famae* above):
5.6n.

11.3 nimius animi 'overweening in spirit'; for the choice
gen. + adj. see *NLS* §73 (6), Gries 37–40. The epithet is modelled
on Sall. *H.* 4.73 *impotens et nimius animi est*, which has also influenced
6 below and which itself draws on Sis. fr. 50 *sublatus laetitia nimia
atque impotentia commotus animi*; cf. also Sall. *C.* 5.6 *animus ... nimis
alta semper cupiebat*, Vell. 33.1 *praeclarum Cn. Pompeium sed nimium iam
liberae rei pub.*, Tac. *H.* 3.52.1 *nimius iam Antonius*. The Roman aristocratic code put the highest value on personal *gloria* acquired in the
service of the state; over-preoccupation with status, however, could
twist the ideal of aristocratic pre-eminence into a desire for *potentia*
(Earl 52–8); see also 6.7n., 35.6n.   **alios ... uni:** cf. Vell. 79.1
on Agrippa: *parendique (sed uni) scientissimus, aliis sane imperandi cupi-
dus.*   **sperneret:** 14.3n. (*superbia*); for Manlius' superior attitude
cf. Quad. fr. 7 *is genere et ui et uirtute bellica nemini concedebat.*   **uni:**
6.7n. Manlius envies one man because that man is the 'one above
all others' (*OLD* 8a), a position that Manlius himself wants. For C.
to be the target of Manlius' *inuidia* is perfectly natural, esp. since
the two are akin in many ways (4n., 7nn., 8n. (*materia*), 14.8n., 16.8n.,
17.5n.). What is less natural is that L. gives C. no part in the *seditio*
and yet adopts a two-year version that dates its resolution to C.'s

tribunate in 384 (Wiseman 238; see also 12.6n.). L. uses C. almost
exclusively in military contexts in Book 6 (see also 22.5–26n.).
inuideret: 6.11n. *inuidia* is a leitmotif of the *seditio* (16.1, 5, 18.4,
20.5, 11), connected with the theme of sight (20.5n.).   **eximio:**
of persons only at Pl. *Bac.* 943 before L. (*TLL*). For the abls. of
respect following cf. Vell. 2.18.1 *uirtute eximius*, Plin. *NH* 7.56.
honoribus 'offices' (∼ *in magistratibus* below); on its political connotations see *VL* 383–7.   **uirtutibus:** military qualities (∼ *apud ex-*
ercitus): *OLD* 1b, Moore 5–14.   **ferebat** introduces accs. + infin.
(*OLD* 18), exploring Manlius' thoughts.   **solum:** cf. 45.31.5 *soli*
tum in magistratibus soli in legationibus erant. solus was technical of acting single-handed (*OLD* 4), which, though acceptable in war (within
certain guidelines: cf. 7.9.3–10, 8.6.16–7), in political terms meant
ruling without a colleague, a condition antithetical to *libertas* (cf.
Vell. 33.3 *in quibus rebus primus esse debebat, solus esse cupiebat* (Pompey)
and see 6.7n., 35.4n.). Manlius claims *solus* status for himself at 15.11;
on its connection with the *primus* motif (7n.) see Vell. 66.5 with W.
in ... apud: 2.4n.

11.4 tantum ... habeat: he refers first to the events of the last
year (6.3–10), turning at *cum interim* (below) to the Gallic war. Manlius effectively accuses C. of *regnum*, a charge to which all powerful
politicians were liable (Weinstock 134–5, Erskine 113–5; for L. see
Bruno (1)). His challenge seems absurd given the way in which L.
told the story – but the C. we finally see acting politically is arrogant enough to lend credence to Manlius' claim (ch. 38).   **emi-**
nere: given his Capitoline feat, Manlius naturally gravitates toward
images of height and climbing. The association of height and (destructive) pride is common (Nisbet–Hubbard on Hor. *C.* 1.18.15),
cf. Cic. *Off.* 1.65 *facillime ... ad res iniustas impellitur ut quisque altissimo*
animo est gloriae cupiditate; for height and *inuidia* see Nisbet–Hubbard
on Hor. *C.* 2.10.9.   **non pro ... sed pro:** Manlius introduces a
favourite theme of ancient historians, the contrast between surface
and reality, which, in various forms, will run throughout the episode (14.2n.). The original formulation is linguistic: the historian
draws attention to the gap between what things are called and
what they are (Thuc. 3.82.4 with Hornblower; for Latin adapta-
tions see M–W 83, 94–5, Plass 45–7). The tactic is recommended
by rhetoricians in attacking an opponent (*Rhet. Her.* 3.6); for *pro* in

such contexts see *OLD* 9.   **ministris:** contemptuous both of C.
and of the 'attendants' (*OLD* 3b, Opelt 147–8), cf. Cic. *Ver.* 3.21 *nomine decumanos, re uera ministros . . . cupiditatum suarum.*   **habeat:** for
the tense see 5.3n.   **cum interim** 'while in fact'. The inverted
cum clause which occupies most of the sentence (through 5 *uicerint*)
is effectively in *o.o.*; elsewhere in L. such clauses can go into acc. +
infin. (as at 27.6: *NLS* §237 *Note*).   **si quis . . . uelit:** a standard
expression of objective viewpoint, such as a historian might use (cf.
37.58.8, Scipio corrects an interpretation of his *res gestae*; fr. 61 (L.
on Cicero) *quae uere aestimanti minus indigna uideri potuit*); the absolute
use of *aestimare*, as here, is particularly characteristic of the historian (Sall. *C.* 8.2 with Vretska, Curt. 10.5.26, Tac. *Ag.* 11.3, *G.* 6.3).
Manlius goes on to compare C.'s deeds with his own, using a standard historiographical technique for evaluating great men (*syncrisis*:
J. L. Moles, *Plutarch: the life of Cicero* (1988) 19–26; on the interaction
between him and C. see Burck (2) 361, 373–4). While his reliability
is at best doubtful, owing to his patent bias, Manlius repeatedly
challenges the 'official' story (14.11, 20.6–9n.), raising doubts which
are never fully resolved (18.16n.).   **a M. Furio . . . nisi a se:**
Manlius reverses the order of protasis and apodosis in order to
end with himself, an order he maintains throughout the *syncrisis*.
He claims superiority on the grounds of temporal priority, greater
degree of difficulty, and the fact that he acted alone (5). There
could indeed have been no ransom, let alone a rescue, if Manlius
had not repelled the Gallic sneak attack; and as L. stresses, he was
the only one who woke in time to do so (5.47.4; at Dion. Hal. 13.7.3,
Plut. *Cam.* 27.3, the geese wake everyone up). But Manlius did not
eliminate the Gauls altogether; their defeat required the efforts of
both men, one from inside, the other from outside the citadel (N.
Horsfall, *C.J.* 72 (1980–1) 298–311).   **reciperari patria:** a striking phrase, also at 5.49.1 and Nep. *Pel.* 2.1. *urbs reciperata* may have
been the official description of Rome's rescue from the Gauls, cf.
CIL I² 1 p. 191 [*urbe recup*]*erata sacra . . .* [*reu*]*exit*, Var. *L.* 5.157 *Roma
rec.*, Tac. *A.* 2.52.5 *illum reciperatorem urbis* (i.e. C.), Gell. 5.17.2 (quoting the Augustan antiquarian Verrius Flaccus), 17.21.25. In Manlius'
mouth it has a bitter sound, as if he is echoing an oft-heard slogan
(cf. 2.5n.).   **Capitolium atque arx:** L. tends to join these near-
synonyms (Richardson 69) in this order and with this connective (O.

on 5.53.9) but the sheer number of refs. to them in the *seditio* calls
for *uariatio*: the reverse order is found at 20.13; *-que* at 14.4, 15.11,
16.2.   **seruata esset:** for the tense see *NLS* §272 (2).

11.5 ille: for demonstrative pronouns in *syncrises* (generally
hic ~ ille) cf. Cic. *Cat.* 2.25, Sall. *C.* 54.2–3, Vell. 44.2, 84.1, Plin.
Ep. 5.8.9–10 (*historia ~ oratio*).   **inter ... accipiendum ~** *solutis
animis* below (3.10n.). For the uncommon *inter* + gerund(ive) cf. 39.10
(Fletcher (1) 166).   **solutis animis** 'once their minds had been
relaxed'; for *in spem soluere* (*OLD soluo* 8c) cf. Tac. *H.* 2.99.2 *soluti in
luxum* with H.   **illius ... esse:** the last item in the tricolon is
adorned with wordplay (*uicerint ... uictoriae*), chiasmus, and polyptoton; for the closural 'authority of unqualified assertion' reinforced by
an accumulation of formal devices see Smith 157–63.   **illius** 'his'.
pars uirilis 'the lion's share'.   **neminem ... esse:** Manlius
reverts to the acc. + infin. with which he began (3–4).   **neminem
... socium:** the *solus* motif (3). Manlius is quoting (somewhat
ominously: R. R. Dyer, *J.R.S.* 80 (1990) 29) Cic. *Marc.* 7 *at uero
huius gloriae, C. Caesar, quam es paulo ante adeptus socium habes neminem*, cf. also *Marc.* 11, Ov. *Am.* 2.12.9–14 (a humorous adaptation).
mortalium 'was favoured by historians for its impressiveness' (O.
on 1.9.8). Manlius may be implying that only the gods could have
helped him; see further 17.5n.

11.6 his ... impotens: only here does L. offer a direct explanation of Manlius' behaviour, that his aristocratic *inuidia* was exacer-
bated by a flaw in his character (*uitium ingenii*: C. Gill, *C.Q.* 33
(1983) 485); but doubts about this unfavourable and conventional
picture resurface in 9.   **opinionibus inflato:** cf. Cic. *Off.* 1.91.
L.'s description – which continues with 7 *aura ... ferri* – combines
the venerable connection between political/mental turbulence and
winds or storms (Fantham 25–6, 128) with the idea that *populares*
politicians were *leues* (Seager (1) 336), cf. Cic. *Phil.* 11.17 *populare
atque uentosum ... minime nostrae grauitatis.*   **inflato animo:** cf.
Quad. fr. 61, Curt. 5.10.3, Sen. *Ep.* 87.31. It is an etymological
pun, *animus* being popularly derived from ἄνεμος, 'wind' (Maltby
37); for wind and pride see Nisbet–Hubbard on Hor. *C.* 2.10.21.
Manlius is *inflatus* again at 18.5, immediately before his *hortatio*;
both contexts suggest a secondary metaphor, of puffed-up speaking
style (*OLD inflatus* 2b, continued with *uehemens* below, *OLD*

4c).   **ad hoc:** a Sallustian mannerism that L. deploys frequently
(Sall. *C.* 14.3 with Vretska); in Book 6 it occurs only in the *seditio*
(also at 12.6, 14.11, 20.7 *ad haec*, 20.8). Here he is quoting Sall. *H.*
4.73 (3n.).   **uehemens:** a Ciceronian favourite (500+) which L.
uses sparingly (13), usually to describe patrician force directed
against plebeians (here, paradoxically, of a patrician turning on his
own class); for its application to desperadoes cf. Sall. *C.* 43.4, Cic.
Phil. 11.1 (Sulla). With *inflato* and *aura* (below) it extends the image
of Manlius being so puffed up by wind that he takes on its violent
nature; for *uehemens* of wind cf. Lucil. 998, Var. *Men.* 472, Cic. *S.
Rosc.* 136, *B. Alex.* 65.3, Col. 4.19.3, Curt. 4.3.6.   **impotens:**
lacking in self-control (*OLD* 3), a good insult for tyrants and tyrannical politicians (Opelt 163, 167); like *uehemens* it can be used of natural forces (*OLD* 3c). To the plebs Manlius will appear *potens*
(18.2).   **non:** sc. *tantum.*   **aequum censebat** ~ 4 *si quis ...
uelit*; Manlius is again evaluating. The combination of *aequum* and
excellere (below) is paradoxical: there should be a contrast between
the two, as at Cic. *Inu.* 1.3 *ut inter quos posset excellere, cum iis se pate-
retur aequari,* Vell. 124.2 *potius aequalem ciuem quam eminentem.*   **suas
opes** '(political) force' (*OLD* 2b, *VL* 237–8). With Manlius' attitude
one can compare Catiline's 'obsession with *dignitas*' (Seager (2) 383)
– to say nothing of Caesar's (e.g. *C.* 1.9.2), an analogy that did not
escape Cicero: *in perditis impiisque consiliis quibus Caesar usus est nulla
potuit esse felicitas; feliciorque meo iudicio Camillus exsulans quam temporibus
isdem Manlius etiam si, id quod cupierat, regnare potuisset* (*Ep.* fr. 2.5).

   11.7 primus: there was much ancient interest in identifying in-
ventors and founders (*protoi heuretai*), partly from purely antiquarian
interest, partly as a means of tracing the roots of contemporary
practices (above, p. 15); on L. see Steele 38–9 and J. Poucet, *Latomus*
51 (1992) 281–314. Describing someone as acting *solus ... aut primus
at certe cum paucis* is also a means of pleasing an audience, esp. in
encomium (Quint. 3.7.16).   **popularis** indicates a support of
the *populus*, which in practice generally means the plebs (but see
19.7n.); its tone depends on who is using it. It is regularly applied
to politicians who were opposed to the self-described *boni* or *optimates* and who were therefore 'criminal, naturally wicked, mad, or
poor' (Seager (1) 328; in general *VL* 518–41).   **popularis factus:** probably 'took up the popular cause' (Radice), though he is

not the first Livian patrician to be called *popularis* (cf. 2.8.2, 2.41.7); if it refers to a formal renunciation of patrician status (*transitio ad plebem*: so Valvo 13–15), it is anachronistic (Cornell 110–11; cf. Cic. *Brut.* 62 on falsified *transitiones*). The thoroughgoing nature of Manlius' defection is shown by the fact that the authorities think they can defeat him only by proving he is still a patrician (19.7). The present situation is later reversed when Licinius and Sextius threaten patrician exclusivity by demanding plebeian consuls. **plebeiis magistratibus:** though the *tr. pl.* were not senatorial magistrates until the third century (*OCD*), they were often called 'magistrates' before then as well, as if the plebs inhabited a second city (Cornell 106, 'a fully articulated alternative state'), cf. 2.33.1 (quoted on 42.11), 24.1 *adeo duas ex una ciuitate discordia fecerat* and see 4.5n., 20.3n. **consilia** 'schemes'; it is used in a different sense below (3.5n.). **communicare:** following the report of Manlius' thoughts (6) L. narrates his actions with hist. infins. (for the pattern see Viljamaa 45–7); for *comm. consilia* of conspiracy cf. 23.34.9, Caes. *G.* 6.2.3, Sall. *C.* 18.5. **criminando ... alliciendo:** instrumental gerunds describing action accompanying that of the main verbs and equivalent in sense to pres. participles; their use is widespread in L. (*NLS* §205, Riemann 308). **criminando:** the *mot juste* for tribunician complaints against aristocratic behaviour, cf. 5.3, 3.9.2, 8.12.14 *dictatura popularis ... orationibus in patres criminosis fuit*, Cic. *Mil.* 12, Sall. *C.* 38.1 with Vretska. In Book 6 *crimi(e)n-* is concentrated in the *seditio* and in complaints about allied defection (17.7, 21.7, 9, 26.7); its absence from the rogation narrative underscores that episode's greater complexity: political action can no longer rely simply on invective. **alliciendo** need not have a negative connotation (cf. Cic. *Off.* 1.56 *uirtus nos ad se allicit*, Paul. *Fest.* 117 *lectus ... quod fatigatos ad se alliciat*); in the present context, however, it certainly does, cf. 1.47.7, Tac. *H.* 1.78.2, *A.* 5.10.1 (all of preparations for a coup d'état) and the similar action of Augustus at Tac. *A.* 1.2.2 *populum annona, cunctos dulcedine otii pellexit*. **aura ... ferri:** continues the imagery of 6 (nn.); for the breezes of popular support cf. 3.33.7, Cic. *Har.* 43, Luc. 1.131–3 *famaeque petitor ... popularibus auris | impelli*, [Quint.] *Decl.* 352.1 *non iudicio sed ... incerta populi aura*; for the (rarer) unqualified use of *aura* in this sense see *OLD* 3b. **consilio** 'exercise of judgment'

(*OLD* 7), cf. 26.25.10 *ira* ~ *consilio*, Hor. *C.* 3.4.65 *uis consili expers mole ruit sua*, Prop. 1.1.6 *nullo uiuere consilio*. In this and the related sense, 'intelligence' (*OLD* 8), *consilium* in L. is most often associated with the military sphere (Moore 107–9), and is a dominant characteristic of C. in the next war narrative (23.1, 9, 11, 27.1). **ferri ... malle:** hist. infins. The passive, whose use L. affects (Viljamaa 17–19), is choice and historiographical. **famaeque ... esse:** an epigrammatic flourish pointing to the gap between specious appearance (*magnae* = quantity) and true worth (*bonae* = quality), see 4n., 10.9n. It recalls Sall. *C.* 54.6 on Cato Uticensis, *esse quam uideri bonus malebat* (based on Aesch. *Sept.* 592); in the same vein cf. Sall. *C.* 10.5 *magisque uoltum quam ingenium bonum habere*, Sen. *Ep.* 123.11 *nec dubitaueris bonam uitam quam opinionem bonam malle*, Tac. *Ag.* 5.3 *nec minus periculum ex magna fama quam ex mala*. The implied contrast with Cato is also a contrast with C. (who has Catonian attributes: 2.12n., 25.6n., 40.17n.) and a further link in the association of Manlius with Caesar (14.5n., 14.7n. (*opera*), 14.10n.). **famae:** 2n.; on *fama popularis* see Seager (1) 330.

11.8 Et ... coepit: at the end of the character sketch L. introduces the issues that will be in play, agrarian legislation (5.1n.) and debt relief, Manlius' primary interest. The need for debt reform is prominent in the struggle of the orders (Brunt (1) *s.v.* 'debt problem'), as it is in one of Manlius' more contemporary contexts, the Catilinarian conspiracy (e.g. Cic. *Cat.* 2.8, 10, 18, Sall. *C.* 14.2, 21.2). It becomes a secondary theme after Manlius' imprisonment. **quae ... fuisset** 'the sort of raw material for sedition that had always been on hand for the plebeian tribunes'; for the incorporated antecedent see 10.8n. and for the characterizing subjunc. see *NLS* §155. The tribunate was naturally linked with *seditio* (Seager (1) 336), cf. Cic. *Leg.* 3.19 *in seditione et ad seditionem nata*. **materia:** 7.3n. **fidem moliri coepit:** 'began to disturb [the institution of] credit' (*OLD fides* 5); for the metaphor cf. Luc. 1.182 *concussa fides*. **acriores ... territent:** *o.o.* explains Manlius' motives (above, p. 13). *acr(ior)es stimuli* is first here in prose; cf. Hor. *S.* 2.7.93–4 (wielded by a *dominus*), Virg. *A.* 9.718 (by Mars), Tac. *H.* 1.15.3 with H. and see 34.7n. **aeris alieni** 'debt' (lit., 'other people's money'). Manlius' chosen direction of attack is shrewd: as economic insecurity threatens the very real possibility of social or physical disaster (next nn.), endless opportunities for emotional manipulation present themselves.   **egestatem ... ignominiam:** combined also at Sall. *C.* 21.4. Destitution and disgrace were marks of shame (e.g. Cic. *Cat.* 2.24–5 on the *egestas* of the conspirators) that could drive men to rebellion (so exploited by Catiline at Sall. *C.* 20.8, 21.4, 58.6; *ignominia* leads to violence e.g. at Tac. *A.* 12.40.3 *stimulante ignominia*). Technical *ignominia* will befall Manlius after his death (20.14).   **neruo ac uinculis:** debtors could be enslaved, either in debt-bondage (*nexum*) or as punishment for defaulting (*CAH*² 215–16, 329–33); the threat is realized in the case of the centurion (14). For *neruus* 'bond' see *OLD* 4; for the *congeries* (3.6n.) see Lindholm 31.   **corpus liberum** 'a free man'. *liber-* is a leitmotiv in the *seditio* (15 times) and in the rogations (8), a rallying cry for both sides; it appears only twice (12.5, 13.7) in non-domestic contexts.   **territent:** 1.11n.

    11.9 et erat 'and in fact there was' (*OLD et* 2). This use of *et era(n)t* to vouch for part of a statement stemming from a (possibly) unreliable source is also a Tacitean trick (Develin 73). By confirming the existence of this private debt L. strengthens Manlius' case: building is often a symptom of avarice (Nisbet–Hubbard on Hor. *C.* 2.18), but the state has encouraged this expenditure (4.6). **aeris alieni ... uis:** L. likes this slightly mannered expression (cf. 35.1, 7.21.8, 42.5.7); the boldness is tempered by the fact that *aes* is a physical substance (cf. Cic. *Parad.* 48 *uis auri*).   **re ... aedificando:** cf. Nep. *Att.* 13.1, Plin. *Pan.* 51.1, Suet. *Nero* 31 *non in alia re damnosior quam in aedificando*, Plut. *Cras.* 2.5, and the Spartan curse 'may house-building seize you ... and may your wife take a lover' (W–M). The appositive use of the gerund(ive) is uncommon (L–H–S 428).   **damnosissima:** a rare superlative, also at Pl. *Bac.* 117, Plin. *NH* 9.104.   **contracta:** nom. sing. *contrahere* is technical of a formal bond (*OLD* 6a), cf. 32.1, 36.7.4 *magnitudo aeris alieni ... contracti*; in L., however, it regularly = 'incur, catch' as an illness (*OLD* 8b), a sense also felt here.   **itaque:** L. started a fashion for postponing *itaque* (*OLD* Intro.), though he does not do so consistently (*TLL* v 2.760–1); see also 9.5n. It is partly this play with the placement of little words that gives L.'s prose its slightly unbalanced feel, though he 'tended to tone down the artificiality of the first decade in the later books' (Adams (4) 61–2).   **oneratum**

'made worse' (*OLD* 8), a fig. sense not attested before L. (*TLL*); that of *onus*, however, is very early (*OLD* 5, 6).   **in speciem ... quaereretur** '[the war] was bruited about so as to produce [*OLD in* 21] the appearance of a reason for needing a greater power'. This admission that the dictator was created under false pretences (15.7n.) further exemplifies the narrator's reluctance to take sides, and tends to confirm Manlius' belief that there is something going on under the surface of the *species rerum* (4n.); on the deceitfulness of *species* see Otto 329, and on L.'s liking for *in speciem* 'for (mere) show' see O. on 3.9.13.   **iactatum** has a strong connotation of deception, as 4.42.4 *quae in speciem ... iactentur*, 26.51.14. Cicero and others associated *iactatio* with the *popularis* image (cf. 14.11 with Seager (1) 329, 336): here the *patres* behave no better than their opponents.

11.10 noua: 4.8n.   **compulere:** first attested here with *ad* + gerund(ive) (*TLL*). For the idea that the senate is forced into taking unpopular positions see 40.6n.   **creandum. creatus:** repetition evoking official, 'curial' style (von Albrecht 149); see also 32.8n.

12–13 Affairs abroad

Scholars have treated Cossus' military engagement as separate from the *seditio*, another of the sometimes unconnected skirmishes scattered through Book 6 (Lipovsky 89–92, Valvo 22–3). Yet it serves as a foil to the *res internae* narrative: Cossus uses the war to increase the power of his office before dealing with Manlius (12.1). Shared elements link the episodes: absolute dictatorial authority meets with obedience in the field, defiance at home; the gods work reliably in the one, seeing clearly into the future, but are absent or capricious in the other; deceit and misapprehension are present in the field only among the enemy, omnipresent at home; finally, military traitors are clearly recognizable whereas political identities and purposes are dangerously confused.

12.1 Dictator ... pergit: this narrative unit and the next (14–16.4) each begin with Cossus postponing one job in favour of another: here he reckons the *seditio* is more important but opts for war; at 14.1 he is sure he will be asked to finish the war but is called home. This variation on L.'s usual transitional device (2.14n.) unambiguously establishes that the *res externae* and *internae* are not only parallel to but comment on each other.   **dimicationem** is stronger than *certamen*, implying actual violence (as at 19.5); for the regular description of the struggle between the orders as a military conflict see Bruno (2) 121–4.   **propositam** 'was threatened' (*OLD* 7c), cf. 4.48.4 *atrox plebi patribusque propositum ... certamen*, 10.24.14 *cum periculum, cum dimicatio proposita sit.*   **cernebat** 'saw clearly' occurs only thrice in Book 6 after 1.2 (also 13.3, 19.4). Though an ordinary word in L. and elsewhere, this restricted use is suggestive. Perception is all-important in the *seditio*: Manlius tries to bring a patrician secret into the open (14.11, 15.12–13) as he brought the plebs out of the darkness (14.7, 17.2); the dictatorial power removes any ability to see (15.13, 16.3); finally, spectacle is used to determine or to question the reliability of interpretation (14–16.4n., 20.6–9n.). In this visual jumble, *cernere* marks efficient, 'true' sight like that of the historian (1.3n.): Cossus' clear sight leads him to get the easier of his tasks out of the way first; at 13.3 and 19.4 the clear perception of danger causes first the enemy, then the *tr. pl.* to take decisive action for their own preservation.   **seu ... seu:** patrician duplicity is reflected by the form in which L. couches his analysis of Cossus' motives, the so-called 'loaded alternative' (D. Whitehead, *Latomus* 38 (1979) 474–95), with which the historian offers two or more explanations of an event (typically comprising a factual reason, e.g. *quia celeritate ... opus erat*, and a supernatural or psychological one, e.g. *ratus*) while declining to choose among them. In Tacitus the device figures the ironic, dangerous world the historian is recording/creating (M–W 32); L. uses it to illuminate duplicity (e.g. 1.4.2, 26.19.3–4) and to open up possible interpretations, underscoring the fact that in writing/reading history several readings of a given event may be possible. For early exx. cf. Quad. fr. 89 (*utrum ... an*), Caes. *C.* 2.27.2, *B. Afr.* 85.1; for the historian and causation see 34.7n. (*credo*).   **quia ... erat** ~ *ratus*, cf. 1.4.2 *seu ita rata seu quia*, 38.5.10 *seu ... deterrito ... seu quia* (Sörbom 125–6); see also 1.2n.   **uires:** even the extraordinary dictatorial power is at risk when unsupported by popular consensus (further 16.3n., 38.2n., 38.13n.).   **pergit:** L. gradually abandons the simple verb

in favour of *pergit ire*, a 'curious change of taste which resists classi-
fication in stylistic terms' (Adams (4) 56).

12.2–6. Digression. This is one of three extended passages in Book
6 where L. discusses a scholarly question *in propria persona*, here
ostensibly in order to maintain his readers' interest and trust in
the face of an implausibility in the traditional story. Yet the digression's discordant position – it interrupts Cossus just as his war story
is about to start, the usual position for plot variants being at the
end of an episode (Luce (1) 217) – together with its length and apparent pointlessness (6n.), suggests that its ostensible purpose masks
a deeper one. The passage shares conventional elements with other
such interventions that function as pre-emptive strikes in which a
writer takes the reader into his confidence, thereby forestalling objections to his narrative and establishing his superior authority (2n.,
3n.; see M–W 123–32, Booth 184 n.16). L. does this and more.
Manlius' bid for narrative control in ch. 11 and the resultant tensions among points of view are reflected in L.'s attempt to find a
reliable narrative among his sources; further, he uses his doubting
persona to engage the reader in the historiographical process (4n.),
teaching lessons about the difficulties involved in evaluating any
historical narrative that will be needed in reading the *seditio* (14–
16.4n., 20.5n.).

The digression has a structure similar to that of a deliberative
speech (on which see *inter alia* Quint. 3.8). A *captatio beneuolentiae* appeals to the reader's experience on the basis of L.'s own, establishing a camaraderie between them (*principium a propria persona* and *ab
auditoribus*, 2). After establishing this solidarity he introduces the problem (*propositio*, 2–3), whose solution is also a co-operative effort.
The arguments follow, two with counter-arguments (as if anticipating an opponent's objections: *refutatio*, 4–5), and are capped with
a *conclusio* whose nearly total inconclusiveness is offset by strong
closural signals (6n.).

12.2 Non dubito: though L. goes on to record his doubts about
the tradition, this strong *non dubito* registers sympathy with the
reader. For doubt as a way of increasing trust cf. Quint. 9.2.19 *ad-
fert aliquam fidem ueritatis et dubitatio* with 2–6n.; on the first person see
9.3n.   **praeter satietatem** ∼ *illud … succursurum* below: like L.,
the reader feels at once sated and perplexed. Concern for one's

audience is at least as old as Pindar, where it is similarly expressed
as a fear that the listener will be over-full (e.g. *P.* 8.29–32); in Latin
cf. Sis. fr. 127, Nep. *Pel.* 1.1 *satietati ... lectorum*, Tac. *A.* 4.33.3 *obuia
rerum similitudine et satietate*, 6.38.1, 16.16.1. One remedy was to introduce *uarietas* in the form of digressions (M–W 170, cf. *Rhet. Her.*
4.16); cf. 9.17.1 *uarietatibusque distinguendo opere et legentibus uelut deuerti-
cula amoena et requiem animo meo quaererem.*   **tot iam libris:** 1.in. L.
mentions such difficulties most frequently in Books 1–10 (Steele 21–
2), and he is well aware of the problem of doublets (29.35.2).
assidua ... gesta: the eternal return of the Volsci is something
of a running joke in the *AVC* (cf. 21.2, 3.10.8, 7.30.7; on their re-
volts see *CAH*² 316–19). By instilling these doubts in the reader
about the size (and consequent threat) of the Volscian army L. implicitly supports Manlius' denunciation of the war as a sham (15.7).
gesta legentibus ~ *percensenti ... auctores* (chiastic). Reader and
author share an activity, though the former deals with the literary
product (*gesta*), L. with the producers (*auctores*); the reader thus becomes 'a quasi-associate to witness and pass judgment on what is
presented' (Steele 44; above, pp. 13–15).   **legentibus** 'readers';
replacement of an existing agent noun (i.e. *lector*) by a substantive
pres. participle is increasingly common under the empire (Adams
(3) 129).   **succursurum:** sc. *esse.* L. tends to construe *non dubitare*
'not to doubt' with acc. + infin.; after (*non*) *dubius* he favours *quin* +
ind. quest. (Riemann 283–4).   **percensenti** 'as I was making a
thorough survey': L.'s doubts about the Volscian manpower would
have arisen as he was reading earlier narratives (above, p. 10 n.
42). For intensifying *per-* in refs. to L.'s activity cf. *Praef.* 1 *perscripserim* (also at 31.1.2), 9.18.12 *percurrere*, 41.25.8 *persequi.*   **propiores:**
the idea that historians living closer in time to the events they describe have more trustworthy information about them recurs at
1.55.8, 22.7.4 etc. (Steele 16, *LCH* 149). It is part of the 'autopsy'
topos (1.3n.; cf. Fehling 167–8 on the reliability of old people).   **auctores:** citation of sources was part of the annalistic
manner (above, p. 11), and seems at times to be used primarily to
convey a reassuring authority (*LHA* 142, Develin 69–70, 79); for
auctores, which may or may not be a true plur., see Steele 25, M–
W 125.   **miraculo:** historiographical digressions often report
thaumata (= *miracula*), 'amazing' or 'surprising' things that entertain

the reader and provide an instructive comparison with the familiar (e.g. Hartog 230–7, esp. 233–4 on θώματα and digressions; in general see Gabba). One can incorporate *miracula* by denying that one is doing so (as 1.4.6–7, 5.21.8–9) or by writing about real events in language appropriate to thaumatological literature (M–W 130–1 and Woodman). L. here announces a *miraculum* but then reveals that it is a scholarly one (cf. Tac. *A.* 2.59–61, 6.28 (the phoenix): *miraculum* marks antiquarian digressions). Like many Herodotean *thaumata*, this one has to do with size (6 *ingens*: Hartog 235–6). **unde ... milites:** appositional to *illud* above; for the postponed subj. see 9.9n.

12.3 quod ... sim?: Quintilian singles out L.'s propensity to doubt from the habitual wrangling among historians (2.4.19 *saepe etiam quaeri solet de tempore, de loco, quo gesta res dicitur, nonnumquam de persona quoque, sicut Liuius frequentissime dubitat et alii ab aliis historici dissentiunt*). It has produced reactions ranging from barely veiled exasperation (*LHA* 143) to admiration (Develin 79 'honest and straightforward, as well as critical'). This apparent abrogation of authority cuts two ways: it is part of a pervasive unease in this section about the historical tradition that compels L.'s readers to exercise their critical functions (2–6n., 18–20.11n.); on the other hand, by taking a critical attitude toward his own text L. highlights his role as an enquirer into and interpreter of inherited stories (Levene 29). It is important not to take L. too much at his word in such passages. Luce perceptively compares this mannerism to Tacitus' complaints about the dull nature of his own material: each is a pose (*LCH* 44 n.20, cf. Steele 19 'while such statements are fairly common, in most instances Livy gives an indication of his own position'). L. is, in short, having his cake and eating it too.   **tacitum** 'in silence'. For the 'unsuccessful enquiry' topos see Fehling 125–7 and 168: 'for the trusting sort of reader there is nothing less suspicious-looking than an admission by an author that there is something he does not know "because no one says anything about it"' (125).   **cuius ... rei:** objective gen. with *auctor* ('what can I vouch for?').   **tandem** 'after all' (*OLD* 1b).   **quae ... potest** 'which anyone may have if he draws his own conclusions'. *sua* is predicative; the dat. is of the possessor (*NLS* §63).   **coniectanti:** *coniectura* is a kind of reasoning that infers the existence or nature of a thing not evident from something present; in litigation, a *coniectur-alis causa* is one in which the *factum* is questioned, forcing the orator to argue from circumstantial evidence and from probability (Lausberg *s.v.* '*coniectura*', cf. *Rhet. Her.* 1.18). For *coniectura* as a deductive method in historiography cf. 4.20.8–11 *quis ea in re sit error ... existimatio communis omnibus est ... ea libera coniectura est*, Sall. *H.* 3.74, Curt. 6.11.21, Tac. *A.* 1.32.3 with Goodyear. When L.'s sources, which constitute his evidence for this period (*LCH* 143–4), cannot solve a problem, like other ancient historians he relies on a combination of common sense and arguments from analogy or verisimilitude (4). Under such circumstances it is nearly true that each (informed) reader can be an *auctor*. But L. does not relinquish control (see above on *tacitum* and 2–6n.).

12.4 simile ueri est: appeal to verisimilitude was a basic critical stance in historiographical and legal argument (*RICH s.v.* 'plausibility and credibility') and like *quae ... sim?* (above) makes the reader an accomplice in the historical endeavour: 'like the truth' implies a notion of what is *uerum* or 'realistic' that relies on the experience and judgment of L.'s audience.   **ueri:** L. has *ueri* and *uero simile* in about equal proportion and with little apparent difference in sense (G–L §359 N.4). He equally varies the order, *u. simile* being inherited, *simile u.* the innovation (Adams (5) 75).   **sicut nunc ... fit:** the first plausible reason relies on a hypothetical likeness with contemporary practice: 'we know how it is today; perhaps it was like that then'. This appeal to analogy is quite different from asserting that circumstances have not changed from ancient times to the writer's own day (above, p. 28).   **in dilectibus fit Romanis** 'in *Roman* levies'. While determinative adjs. like *Romanus* tend to follow their nouns, after Cicero the adj. rarely follows the verb in this kind of hyperbaton (on which see 1.2n.): when it does, it is stressed (Adams (1) 12–13).   **alia ... iuniorum** 'one generation of young men after another'. For *alia atque alia* cf. 1.8.4, Catul. 68.152 with Fordyce (*OLD alius* 4).   **usos esse:** sc. *eos*; the acc. + infin. clause is the subject of *s.u. est* above, as are *scriptos* and *fuisse* below (*NLS* §25).   **aut ... intulerit:** though parallel in form (*iis-dem* ~ *eadem*), the second reason no longer appeals to similarity of meaning but depends on a distinction between the meaning of the near-synonyms *populus* 'tribe' and *gens* 'nation', a kind of argumentation associated with the sophist Prodicus (G. B. Kerferd, *The Sophistic movement* (1981) 68–77).

12.5 aut ... uindicant: L. finally asks the reader to assume that the situation in 369 A.U.C. was the opposite of the present both in form and in meaning, as it were: *nunc* appeals now not to similarity but to difference. For the idea that one cannot tell from present appearances what a city (*vel sim.*) used to be like cf. Thuc. 1.10.1–2 with Hornblower (W.).   **nunc** with *Romana* below ∼ 4 *nunc* ... *Romanis*, framing the list.   **seminario ... relicto:** i.e. only a few who were eligible for the army still lived in rural areas (next n.). *seminarium*, a metaphor that Cic. liked (e.g. *Cat.* 2.23, *Pis.* 97, *Phil.* 13.3), occurs elsewhere in L. only at 42.61.5. The underlying imagery is agricultural (so also 4 *suboles*, 6 *accisae*).   **seruitia** 'slaves', by metonymy, and in regular use since Cicero (Vell. 73.3 with W.). The slaves referred to – who in the republic could not normally serve in the army – were those on large estates (*latifundia*: *IM* 128, 345–75); for the complaint cf. 7.25.8–9, Var. *R.* 1.2.6, Plin. *NH* 18.36. Depopulation of rural areas due to war deaths was also a problem in the late republic (Paul on Sall. *J.* 5.2).   **ab solitudine uindicant** 'keep from being a desert'; for *solitudo Italiae* cf. Cic. *Att.* 1.19.4. *uindicare*, associated with *libertas* in political slogans, is a significant theme in the *seditio* narrative (14.10n.), and is used of slavery here with conscious irony.

12.6 ingens ... Romani: the discussion is so far from coming to a resolution that L. repeats the original problem (*quamquam ... erant*; see also next n.). Yet the accumulation of closural gestures creates a sense of finality: mention of *consensus* and the universality of *inter omnes auctores* (11.5n.), ring composition (*auctores* in 2 ∼ 6), and specific factual information. (For 'temporal punctuation' see Smith 130 and cf. Caes. *G.* 7.90 (military postings); *B. Afr.* 98, two dates as Caesar returns to Rome; Sall. *J.* 114.3, the only genuine date (i.e. month + day) in the monograph; Nep. *Att.* 22.3, precise date of Atticus' death.)   **omnes auctores:** L. cites as supporting evidence the very *consensus* that caused the original problem. For this use of *consensus* as a weapon see further 20.3n., 20.4–12n. **conueniat:** the subjunc. is restricting after the rel. *quod* (cf. 5.34.6, Roby §§1692–4), a sense reinforced by *certe* (*OLD* 2): 'it was enormous, at all events – on *that* all are agreed'. For the authority of consensus in historiography see e.g. Fehling 113–15, 165–6 (in source citations) and White (2) 11–14, 24–5. **Camilli ... accisae res** ~ 5.2. By alluding in this context to that emphatic statement about the Volscian defeat L. questions the efficacy of C.'s conquest, a questioning reinforced here by the rather grand official phraseology (next n.). But the mention also brings C. back into the story, challenging Cossus – will he do as well? or better? – and increasing the perplexity occasioned by C.'s absence from the political scene, despite Manlius' *inuidia* (cf. *CAH*² 332, C. 'plays a prominent but scarcely comprehensible role in the affair' – in fact in L.'s narrative he plays no part at all). **ductu atque auspicio:** technical (O. on 3.1.4). It was already officialese in the second century (Pl. *Amph.* 196, 657) and could be used playfully even to an emperor (Fro. *Ver.* 2.1.4 van den Hout). **Circeiensium** ~ *a Velitris* below (6.12n.). Circeii was traditionally colonized by Tarquinius Superbus, then again in 393 (*CAH*² 253, 301). **Velitris:** a Latin city first colonized in the 490s (*CAH*² 282), recaptured in 380 (29.6) and in 367 (42.4).

12.7 Dictator ... laetus ... processit: the elements of the main clause are placed strategically at beginning, middle, and end (cf. 2.2), the battle preliminaries reported in subordination (15.1n.). **eo die:** i.e. the day he arrived; the anaphoric demonstrative marks 2–6 as a digression. **postero:** sc. *die.* **auspicato** 'after taking the auspices', a modal abl. of the unaccompanied perf. participle attested from Plautus on (Roby §§1253–4); L. greatly extends their use (Gries 80–1). **prodisset ... adorasset ... processit:** near-homoioteleuton; the *pro*-compounds contribute to the pervasive alliteration with *p.* **pacem deum:** 1.12n.; for sacrifice before battle see Pritchett 1 109–15. **adorasset** 'pray for' is rare (*TLL*), cf. Virg. *A.* 3.370 *exorat pacem diuum.* Ritual correctness receives a lot of play here, as does the correspondence between Roman piety and success (Levene 208), in contradistinction to the problematic divine presence in the *seditio* (16.2n.). **laetus** 'propitious' (*OLD* 6); after his successful sacrifice Cossus takes on one of its attributes, cf. 7.26.4, 10.40.5, 14 (Feldherr 222–3). **ad** 'in preparation for' (*OLD* 32). **propositum ... signum** 'the setting up of a signal for battle' (presumably a flag, cf. Caes. *G.* 2.20.1, *B. Hisp.* 28.2). The expression does not occur outside of L.;

for the AUC participle see 1.1n.   **processit:** Cossus' *hortatio* (8–10) differs in several respects from C.'s (7.3–6), primarily because its audience is in a very different frame of mind. New are the ref. to the gods (8) and the detailed tactical instructions.

12.8 nostra ... uident: assuring the army of good omens is not only an effective *captatio beneuolentiae*, it is also good military tactics; cf. 10.40.5, Onas. 10.26, Fron. *S.* 1.11.11, 14 (Alexander manufactures a favourable omen) and see O. p. 510, Keitel (1) 154–5.   **nostra:** predicative.   **si** 'as sure as', cf. Virg. *A.* 1.603 with Austin.   **in futurum:** the substantive fut. participle is rare even in the historians (*NLS* §101 'hardly ever so used'). *futurum* is found in late Cicero (Laughton 123); cf. *conserturos* (below).   **uident:** 12.1n.   **itaque ... excipere:** Cossus speaks in increasing pairs (above, p. 22), securing parallelism with homoioteleuton (*plenos ... conserturos*), antithesis (*pilis ∼ gladiis, pedes ∼ dextras*), and framing verbs (*procurri ... excipere*: 10.2n.).   **cum imparibus:** not in number but in ability (the enemy army is in fact larger than the Roman, 13.1); for the topos see 7.2n.   **conserturos:** see on *in futurum* above.   **pilis ... positis:** given their usefulness as forward-moving cola, the natural place for abl. abs. is in the narrative, and in fact they are rare in Livian speeches (Dangel 28 n.60). For laying down spears cf. 7.16.5, 9.13.2, Caes. *G.* 1.52.4, 7.88.2, Sall. *C.* 60.2, Tac. *A.* 14.36.2.   **procurri ∼ excipere,** typical Livian *uariatio* in voice of the parallel infins. (Catterall 311–12, Sörbom 110). The impers. passive concentrates on the action (Pinkster 174): not 'I do not want *you* to' but 'I do not want there to be any'.   **obnixos ... excipere** 'take a stand ... and receive'; *stabili gradu* (for which cf. Tac. *H.* 2.35.1 with H.) qualifies *excipere*. For the tactic cf. Nep. *Chabr.* 1.2, Fron. *S.* 2.3.15; for the predominantly poetic *obniti* see Gries 52–3.

12.9 ubi ... miserint: Cossus continues to use increasing pairs (8n.), decorating them with parallel verbs (*iniecerint ∼ intulerint; micent ∼ ueniat*) and anaphora (*deos ... deos*).   **uana:** proleptic.   **micent gladii ∼** 13.2 *uultum ... micantem*. For the topos of the *fulgor armorum* see Nisbet–Hubbard on Hor. *C.* 2.1.19, Miniconi 164 and cf. Onas. 29.2 'The polished spear-points and flashing swords ... send ahead a terrible lightning-flash of war. If the enemy should also do this, it is necessary to frighten them in turn, but if not, one should frighten them first' (Loeb).   **deos esse** 'it is the gods who'. The repetition of *deos* evokes hymnic style (cf. Virg. *A.* 6.46 *deus ecce deus* with Austin).

12.10 tu, T. Quincti: 6.12n.   **intentus ... teneas:** for the wordplay cf. 9.24.8 *uos arcem intenti tenete*, 36.38.2, Virg. *A.* 2.1 *intentique ora tenebant*.   **primum initium:** pleonasm with 'beginning' words is common (L–H–S 793–4); for *p. initium* cf. 3.54.9 *prima initia inchoastis*, Lucr. 1.383, Cic. *Cael.* 11.   **moti certaminis** 'of the battle once it has been set in motion'. The choice expression, first attested here, seems to have been modelled on *bellum m.* (as 25.28.7, Cic. *Fam.* 9.13.1, Sall. *C.* 30.3, Tac. *H.* 2.67.1); *m. certamen* is also at [Ov.] *Ep.* 16.374, Luc. 3.121, Sil. *Pun.* 1.6, 2.430, 9.282. L. similarly innovates with *arma mouere* (Walsh on 21.5.3).   **teneas:** address of the 2nd sing. pres. jussive subjunc. to a definite person is rare in prose outside Cic. *epist.* (Fordyce on Catul. 8.1). Most of the Livian exx. quoted are put into the mouths of soldiers (cf. 3.48.4, 22.30.5, 26.50.7), suggesting an informal tone.   **haerere** 'is locked', cf. 38.22.9 *inter se conserti haerebant*, Virg. *A.* 10.361 *haeret pede pes densusque uiro uir* with Harrison, Flor. 1.45.5 *haerebat ... pugna*.   **collato pede** 'once they have engaged at close quarters' (*OLD confero* 15d).   **terrorem equestrem:** a slightly elevated expression in which the adj. is substituted for *equitum* or *equorum*. Such substitutions (and vice versa, the adj. for the gen.) are very much in Tacitus' manner (*A.* 1.3.7 with Goodyear); in L. cf. 27.2, 3.28.4 *ciuilem ... clamorem*, 8.13.15 *sociali ... exercitu*, 30.18.4 *equestrem procellam*, 42.39.2 *comitatus ... regius*.   **terrorem ... pauore:** *uariatio* (Catterall 297–8, Sörbom 16–29), cf. 10.28.9–10, 22.48.4–5, 30.21.6, 38.5.7. L.'s interest in the psychological aspects of war, especially fear, has long been noted (*LHA* 191–7).   **occupatis** introduces a metaphor of disease (*OLD* 4a, b) continued by *infer* below (*OLD* 9a *ad fin.*); for *pauor o.* cf. Ov. *M.* 12.135, and for the contagion of fear cf. Tac. *H.* 3.16.2.   **pauore:** 'a word of some elevation' (Jocelyn on Enn. *scen.* 17), also at 28.6, 29.3, 42.8.   **infer:** on using cavalry to effect a decisive rout cf. 29.2, 7.15.3, 10.28.7–10, Fron. *S.* 2.2.11, 3.17 and see 23.12n.   **infer inuectusque** ~ 9 *iniecerint ... intulerint.* This is a variation on the figure 'resumption' (32.8n.), cf. 5.13.11 *intulit terrorem trepidantesque ... auertit*, 9.37.10 *fundit ... fugatosque persequitur*, Cic. *S. Rosc.* 32 *patrem ... iugu-*

lastis, occisum ... rettulistis (Laughton 18), V. Max. 6.1 (ext. 2). The participle generally picks up the obj. of the verb in the preceding clause: so Quinctius takes the place of the *terror* he is meant to bring in.

12.11 sic ... pugnant: anaphora and alliteration combine with a certain military bluntness. *sic ... sic* ∼ 13.1 *temere ... temere*: the Romans act on instructions, the enemy without thought.   **ut prae-ceperat** ∼ 7 *sicut edictum erat*. The troops' obedience is manifest in the repetition during the battle of key points of the *hortatio*: 8 *cum imparibus* ∼ 13.1 *numero*; 9 *missilia ... micent gladii* ∼ 13.2 *missilibus ... gladios ... micantem*; 10 *collato pede* ∼ 13.2; 10 *terrorem equestrem ... in-fer* ∼ 13.3.   **nec ... ducem:** cf. Caes. *G.* 5.34.2 *tametsi ab duce et a fortuna deserebantur*. L. often forsakes peripeteia (3.4n.) and suspense at critical moments (as 5.21, Veii; 5.33.1, 37.1–2, the Allia; 9.1.1, 2.1, Caudium), a technique he shares with Virgil (e.g. *A.* 4.169, 9.312–16, 10.438). The contrast of this narrative clarity with the layers of deceit in the *seditio* is pointed (cf. 14.13, 15.6, 7, 16.1, 20.4).   **for-tuna** ∼ 7 *deum* (for the slide cf. 9.2–3). Together with *felicitas* (18.13), *Fortuna* accompanies successful generals (e.g. Thuc. 3.97.2 with Hornblower), most famously Caesar; usually she helps his *uirtus*, but sometimes simply keeps him company (e.g. Vell. 55.1, 55.3 *sua Caesarem ... comitata fortuna* with W. on 97.4). For *fortuna* in L. see Levene 30–3; in Book 6 she actively intervenes, in one guise or another, at 9.4, 21.2 (n.), 34.5.

13.1 nulli rei ... freta: *fretus* + dat. is only in L.; he also has it + abl. (H. C. Nutting, *U.C.P.C.P.* 8 (1927) 305–30). On the 'bar-barian horde' motif see 7.2n.   **praeterquam numero:** contests between great and small in which the small are victorious are a mo-tif of folklore (esp. in single combat: Oakley (1) 408).   **oculis ... metiens:** quite mannered (cf. Hor. *S.* 1.2.103, Sen. *Tro.* 23, Apul. *Pl.* 1.14); for the interlaced word order see 3.3n. Stratagems using false appearances to convey a deceptive sense of one's own strength are legion (e.g. Fron. *S.* 2.4.1, 6, 8, 20; 4.7.20). Here we have the con-verse: the Volsci accurately estimate the number of Romans but fail to appreciate their value. See also 12.1n.   **temere:** *temeritas* is as-sociated with barbarians (Opelt 188–9, cf. Caes. *G.* 1.31.12) and pride (*VL* 247, 558, cf. Ov. *M.* 6.32, Vell. 68.3 *ultra fortem temera-rius*). Apart from this passage, in Book 6 L. reserves it for Roman

rashness, esp. that of L. Furius (22.6n.). **temere ... omisit:**
cf. Tac. *H.* 4.67.1 *Sabinus festinatum temere proelium pari formidine deser-*
uit. **proelium ... omisit:** also at 3.63.1, Curt. 5.2.5, Tac. *A.*
3.20.2. Like *certamen mouere* (12.10) it seems modelled on other expressions, e.g. *bellum omittere* (itself almost exclusively Livian: *TLL* IX
2.583.26–39).

13.2 clamore ... ferox ∼ *gladios ... micantem* below; each tricolon increases in immediacy (shouting ∼ charge, swords ∼ eyes) as
well as length. For the second triad cf. Hor. *C.* 1.2.38–40 (*clamor*
galeaeque ... et ... uultus). **ardore:** Roman enthusiasm (*OLD*
5) is literalized in the flash (*OLD* 2) of their eyes, cf. Lucr. 3.289,
Cic. *Marc.* 24 *ardor armorum atque animorum* and see Feldherr 156–7.
For *ardor animi* cf. Vell. 118.2 with W. and for the idea that one's
face shows one's emotions, character, etc. see Otto 147 *frons*
(1). **micantem:** the eyes' flash extends to the whole face; cf.
Sen. *Ep.* 115.14 *dulce si quid Veneris in uultu micat,* V. Fl. 6.606 *ora ...*
saeua micant. See also 8.5n.

13.3 impulsa ... uertunt: the rout is described first in the passive; with *cadentibus* the enemy takes its first active step – but only to
die or flee. **frons** 'front line' (*OLD* 6a). **prima ... inde**
... dein: 10.3n. **trepidatio:** 12.10n. **illata** 'inflicted' (*OLD*
9), in this sense often used of disease *et sim.* (*TLL* VII 1.1385.16–38).
suum 'its distinctive' (*OLD* B 11). **omnia:** 3.5n. **fluctu-**
anti: sc. *aciei.* For the participle used alone cf. Sen. *Thy.* 697–8 *nu-*
tauit aula ... fluctuanti similis; for *fluctuare* of battle lines (etc.) cf. 24.10,
8.39.4, Curt. 3.10.6, Tac. *H.* 1.40.1 with H. **dein:** an equivalent
to *deinde* 'common only in a few archaizers and writers of mannered
prose' (Adams (4) 61). L. employs it steadily but not ostentatiously.
peruenturam: *caedes* lends itself to this mild personification (the
activity for the agents), cf. 9.43.16, 10.41.5, 25.39.11. **cernebat:**
the enemy's vision is now absolutely clear: facilitated, of course, by
the grisly fact that as the soldiers in front fell those behind could lit.
see the Romans better.

13.4 instare: the hist. infin. marks a decisive turn in the situation (Viljamaa 41–5). It is said that hist. infins. 'are seldom used
singly' (*NLS* §21), but L. shows no reluctance to do so, nor does
Tac. When L. does arrange them in series, he prefers groups of two
or three (as at 3.8, 9) to the extended series found in Sall. and Tac.

(C-L 374–8).   **Romanus:** 2.12n.   **donec** 'as long as', a sense
first at Lucr. 5.178, introduced into prose by L., and affected by him
and Tacitus. *donec* was generally avoided in classical prose (L–H–S
629).   **peditum:** for the anteposition of the gen. see below (*in
... caede*).   **spargi:** of people first at Sall. *H.* 3.84, cf. Virg. *A.*
1.602 (*gens*).   **dato signo** 'with orders' (Radice). For the sentence shape see above, p. 21.   **ne ... darent:** the content of the
signum, further expanded by the following *o.o.* (cf. 3.4, 8.10).   **in
... caede** 'by delaying in the slaughter of individuals'. *singulorum*
is fronted to point the antithesis with *multitudini* below (Adams (5)
78), while the gerund lingers inside its dependent prep. phrase; cf.
3.70.4 *in auersam incursando aciem*, 26.5.7 *ad unam concurrendo partem*.
The structure of the whole (*in ... multitudini*) is chiastic.

13.5 missilibus ∼ *obequitando* (below); for the typical *uariatio* cf.
19.2 (Catterall 313, Sörbom 111–12).   **missilibus ac terrore:**
concrete + abstract, producing a kind of syllepsis (Lausberg §707.4);
cf. Tac. *G.* 1.1 *Germania ... a Sarmatis Dacisque mutuo metu aut montibus
separatur* (Catterall 304, Sörbom 75).   **assequi** 'catch up' (*OLD*
2).   **iusta** 'regular' (*OLD* 7b).

13.6 fugae sequendique: cf. 3.40.1 *nec irae nec ignoscendi modum*,
29.34.13 *fuga* (abl.) *... cedendo* with 5n.   **non ante noctem:** 9.11n.
praedaque ... concessa est: 2.12n.

13.7 pars maxima ∼ 8 *quidem*. Each group unambiguously announces its treachery, the first by the presence of *principes iuuentutis*,
the second by its own declaration (*indicauere*).   **nec** = *et non.*
hominum: in apposition to *captiuorum*.   **principes ... iuuen-**
tutis: the young aristocrats are unhesitatingly identified with the
state (*publica ope* below: 6.5n.) – very much not the case in the *seditio*, where the aristocratic Manlius may or may not be acting in the
interests of the *res publica* or the *populus* (19.7n.).   **manifesta**
fides: appositional to *principes*, cf. 6.13. *m. fides* is confined to epic
outside of this passage (Austin on Virg. *A.* 2.309); for *fides* 'evidence' see *OLD* 4.

13.8 Cerceiensium ... Velitris: information imparted in the
digression (12.6), but not to the Romans.   **Romamque ... in-**
dicauere 'and after they had all been sent to Rome, in response
to the questions of the leading senators they unambiguously declared the same thing that they had told the dictator, each [declar-

ing] his own tribe's revolt'. For the senate session cf. 10.9; for the shift to Rome see 4.1n. **defectionem:** in apposition to *eadem*. **haud perplexe:** litotes (Lausberg §§586–8). *perplexe* is attested earlier only at Ter. *Eun.* 817. **indicauere:** the *res externae* end with the innocent use of a word that will resound in the difficult and ambiguous context of the *seditio* (for Manlius' *indicium* cf. 14.13 *bis*, 15.6, 13, 16.1, 20.4).

14–16.4 Internal affairs

The problems of the Gallic *thesauri* and the *turba* which dominate these *res internae* reflect Manlius' grievance against C., who by misrepresenting his role in recovering the ransom gold (11.5) has reached unnatural pre-eminence at the centre of a group of subservient followers (11.4). The image of an object within a dense ring informs the picture of the senators hiding the gold (15.5), of the *turbae* around Manlius and Cossus (15.1, 9, 16.4), and of the metaphor, deployed by each side, of twisting verbal snares (15.12n., 16.1n.). It gradually becomes evident that the important secret is not the gold's whereabouts but Manlius' true nature, the decipherment of which is hampered by the dense narrative web surrounding it. Four possible 'readings' of the figure at the centre of the crowd are offered: he is a king (18.16, 19.6–7, 20.5), one *patronus* among many (15.10, 18.14), a plebeian agitator (though in this role he always has an intermediary/accomplice: 14.3–10n., 17.1n.), or a victim (20.3). These readings are not mutually exclusive (Serres 90–117, 231–62), but for Manlius' story to come to a satisfactory end, one must be validated.

The figure of the circle around a single point is also operative in the contest to determine whether Manlius or the state will ultimately have power. This takes place in the metaphorical arena of the spectacle, which L. often uses to 'act out' a lesson and to inspire the percipient watcher (including the reader) to morally correct action. The outcome tends to confirm the *status quo*, though not always without ambivalence (Solodow 259–60, Feldherr). There are four 'spectacular' scenes in the *seditio* (14.3–10, 15–16.4, 17.1–6, 20.1–11), each of which has two audiences: the emotionally manipulable *uulgus*, and those who know that it is dangerous to accept surface meanings (14.2n.). In Manlius' case both sides claim to see the truth under a deceptive surface and both sides are to some extent justified (15.7n., 20.4n.). Further, Manlius (11.4nn., 20.8nn.) and the historiographical tradition have conflicting interpretations of his actions, neither of which is completely satisfactory, Manlius' owing to his bias and dangerous behaviour, the tradition's owing to L.'s own doubts (18.16n., 20.4–5n.). Though the state succeeds in suppressing Manlius, it is far from certain that the authority which ultimately controls appearances – be it Cossus, the senate, or the historical tradition – has the last word on their truth.

14.1 Dictator ... faciebat: the logical subj. changes from *dictator* to *moles*, *seditione*, and finally *auctor*, a series ending with Manlius (cf. 2.5); Cossus does not reappear until 15.1.   **bellum ... seditione** ~ 11.1–2.   **iussuros:** sc. *esse*.   **cum ... coegit:** inverse *cum* (*NLS* §237).   **exorta moles:** cf. 11.1 *seditio exorta*, Tac. *A*. 3.43.1. *moles* = 'danger' (*OLD* 7): with *gliscente* (next n.) the metaphor is of a storm, cf. 4.43.3 *ex tranquillo necopinata moles discordiarum ... exorta*, Sall. *H*. 3.56 *uento gliscente*. Manlius' house is a lit. *moles* at 19.1.   **gliscente:** 'a choice and colourful replacement for *crescere* ... mainly domiciled in verse and history' (Goodyear on Tac. *A*. 1.1.2); for this expression cf. 42.2.2, *Dirae* 6, Tac. *A*. 4.17.3 (*discordia*) and see C. Moussy, *R.Ph.* 49 (1975) 49–66.   **solito:** abl. of comparison with *magis*; on the word order see 4.11n.   **auctor:** the person responsible (*OLD* 12a); see 36.7n.

14.2 non ... erant 'For now not only M. Manlius' speeches, but his actions as well, which appeared popular, were revolutionary in the eyes of someone who took into consideration the intention with which they were performed.'   **orationes ... facta:** the ancient polarism 'word ~ deed' (e.g. Otto 112, cf. Thuc. 2.35.11 with Hornblower) incidentally also represents the contents of historiography, i.e. speeches and narrative. The first year of the *seditio* concentrates on action, the second on words; the two are reunited in Manlius' last speech (20.8).   **in speciem:** Manlius' actions are open to the same charge of duplicity as the other patricians' (11.9n.). But L. sidesteps that charge: the contrast is not between *species* and *res* but between *species* and Manlius' *mens*, which remains an unresolved problem (cf. 18.16, 20.4).   **tumultuosa:** a Catonian and vivid word (Cato *orat.* 44, Sall. *H*. 2.87D).   **eadem** 'yet at the same time' (*OLD* 10). **qua ... fierent:** for the ind. ques. dependent on *intueri* cf. 7.32.10 *intueri cuius ductu auspicioque ineunda pugna sit*; the abl. is one of manner (Roby §1235.3). A person's state of mind or intention (*OLD mens* 7) was a recognized subject of rhetorical *coniectura* (Quint. 7.2.6; see 12.3n.). **intuenti:** L. warns us not to take things at face value with a participial dat. idiomatic in such appeals to the reader's perceptions (cf. 11.4n. (*si quis* ... *uelit*), 12.3, 9.17.4 *intuenti*, Thuc. 1.2.3 σκοποῦντί μοι with Hornblower, 1.21.2 σκοποῦσι, Cic. *Fam.* 5.12.5 *intuentibus*, Sen. *Apoc.* 5.4 *intuenti*, Tac. *A.* 1.32.3 *coniectantibus*); on the dat., first in L. of mental activity, see G–L §353. The warning confirms the joint role of the narrative audience and L.'s own readers as spectators of Manlius' first public bid for power; with it, the theme of 'clear sight' (12.1n.) is focused on the manipulation of appearances and the importance of distinguishing *species* from truth (11.4n., 11.9n.; on L.'s direction of our gaze/interpretation see Solodow 258–9, Feldherr 52).

14.3–10. Manlius and the centurion. This scene anticipates in a 'troubled and romantic way' the economic necessities that will force the pro-plebeian outcome of the rogations (Bayet 125–6). The episode resembles the prelude to the first *secessio plebis* (2.23.2– 7), in which the sight of a veteran being led into *nexum* spurs the populace to action (Bayet 125 n.1; see also 19.1n.). There are significant differences, however. The fifth-century soldier's misfortune and his physical distress are 'conspicuous', emblematic of the plebeian experience (2.23.2–3 *insignis unius calamitatis* ... *cum* ... *malorum suorum insignibus*): the rebellion he inspires arises from within the crowd, which remains leaderless (2.23.7, 27.7–8, 32.4). The centurion, on the other hand, has a precise rank, is known (3 *nobilem*) from the start, and his only marks are those of war glory (6): as a spectacular object he is a mirror-image of Manlius, whose gestures he replicates (6n.), and toward whom he turns the crowd's attention (see also 17.1n., 35.4n.).

14.3 centurionem: a heading (2.2n.). **nobilem** 'distinguished'; for the accompanying abl. of cause cf. 8.29.10 *par nobile rebus* ... *gestis*, 42.52.16, [Sall.] *Rep.* 2.5.3 *bona fama factisque fortibus nobilis*. **iudicatum ... duci:** the combination is archaic and legal (e.g. *Lex XII* 3.1–2); *duci* = 'be taken into possession' (*OLD* 4a;

see 11.8n.).   **pecuniae** 'debt' (i.e. *pecuniae mutuae*); the gen. is of
the charge (G–L §378).   **medio foro:** as the political centre of
Rome – and incidentally a place of entertainment (*OLD* 2b) – the
Forum matches the flamboyant public posturing of 385 (cf. 15.1–2).
Next year, meetings are less open (18.3, 19.1), the people asked only
to ratify an inevitable result (20.11). In non-archival contexts, L.
tends to provide urban topographical details only when the information is needed (19.1nn., 20.11n.; cf. 2.7.6, Publicola lives *in summa
Velia*; 5.41.4, the Gauls enter by the Porta Collina); see further 36.12n.
cum caterua sua: a characteristic entrance of a powerful figure
(Austin on Virg. *A.* 2.40), cf. 15.1, 35.7, 38.5. Manlius' *caterua* ('personal retinue') includes young aristocrats (Lintott 59–60) and *clientes*
(Drummond (2) 105); it will be augmented by the plebeian crowd
(15.2).   **accurrit:** Manlius is given to cheap dramatics (4, 16.2,
20.8, 10); here he restages C.'s nick-of-time rescue of Rome (3.4n.).
For the 'narrow-escape' topos cf. 9.10n., 17.4, Hom. *Il.* 5.311–17,
Thuc. 3.49.4 with Hornblower, Sall. *J.* 101.9.   **manum iniecit:**
Manlius counteracts the legal *manus iniectio* performed by the man
taking possession of the centurion (Lintott 26–7); the single visual
detail concentrates attention on the 'almost talismanic' gesture with
which Manlius asserts his power (Feldherr 12).   **superbia ...
crudelitate:** cf. Sall. *C.* 33.1 *miseri egentes, uiolentia atque crudelitate
faeneratorum ... expertes*, 33.3 *superbia magistratuum* (Valvo 24–5). Arro-
gance and cruelty are standard attributes of kings, patricians etc.;
cf. 2.4n. and on *superbia* in L. see Bruno (1).   **ac** 'and what is
more' (*OLD* 1a): the usurers add insult to the patrician injury.
et connects the following list, itself in the form ABC*que* (*OLD -que*
2b).   **miseriis plebis:** 34.1n. Manlius sounds like Catiline, cf.
Sall. *C.* 35.3 *publicam miserorum causam ... suscepi.*   **uirtutibus ...
fortunaque:** in a successful man these are complementary (W. on
Vell. 97.4, Moore 11). Here the close connection made by *-que* is
ironic: his excellence and his luck are tragically dissimilar. For the
word order see 9.6n.

14.4 tum uero 'in *that* case' (*OLD tum* 5b); the emphasis is considerably heightened by the anteposition of the apodosis, cf. Pl.
Pseud. 910 *tum pol ego interii, homo si ille abiit.*   **nequiquam:** a 'pathetic adverb' favoured by Virg. and L., after whom it 'disappears
almost entirely from prose' (Fordyce on Virg. *A.* 7.652).   **hac**

dextra: i.e. the one with which he rescued the man and which he is now doubtless waving in the air. For *hic* of a speaker's own body see *OLD* 1b; for the theatrical gesture cf. 7.32.12 *hac dextra mihi tres consulatus … peperi.* **seruauerim:** completed action in an ideal condition (*NLS* §197): 'it would seem that I have saved the *arx* to no purpose'. **ciuem … duci:** a defaulting debtor forfeited most citizen rights (*CAH*² 214–16). Manlius exploits the emotional effects of *ciuis*; cf. 2.12.9 with O. and, most famously, Cic. *Ver.* 5.162 *caedebatur … in medio foro Messanae ciuis Romanus … nulla uox alia illius miseri … audiebatur nisi haec 'ciuis Romanus sum'.* **commilitonem** can be used by one *miles* of another (e.g. 29.26.8) or in a flattering address to one's troops (cf. 2.55.7 with O.). Caesar regularly so employed it, though Augustus considered it too popular (Suet. *Jul.* 67.2, *Aug.* 25.1); Piso, Galba, and Otho all deploy it in playing for the army's loyalty (Tac. *H.* 1.29.2, 35.2, 37.1). The present case allies Manlius with previous revolutionaries: in the sense 'fellow-soldier' it is used elsewhere in the first decade only by plebeians in violent conflict with the patriciate (2.55.7, 3.50.5, 7). **tamquam … uictoribus:** Manlius repeatedly associates patrician control of the city with the Gauls' capture of it, an analogy indicative of his unwillingness or inability to think in non-military terms (11.2n., 15.7–13nn., 19.1n.); in performing economic rescues, then, he repeats his heroic deed of 390 (3n. (*accurrit*), 15.11, 18.9). **seruitutem ac uincula:** abstract + concrete (cf. 3.4, 13.5).

14.5 rem … soluit 'made payment' (*OLD soluo* 18b). **palam populo:** prepositional *palam* occurs first here in prose (*TLL*), cf. 10.13.3, Petr. 49.8, Flor. 2.4.1. **libraque et aere:** instruments used in the transfer of property (A. Berger, *Encyclopaedic dictionary of Roman law* (1953) *s.v.* '*Per aes et libram*'). **liberatum:** sc. *centurionem. liberare* is technical of freeing from a legal obligation (*OLD* 9), a meaning enhanced by its etymological connection with *libra* (Maltby 339). **emittit:** technical of releasing from custody (*OLD* 2). **deos … referant:** like a victorious soldier, the centurion bestows titles on his leader. The most recent case in the *AVC* is C. after defeating the Gauls (5.49.7: see below and for the custom see O. on 3.29.5). **obtestantem:** participial appendix (6.5n.); for the hyperbaton see 2.12n. **M. Manlio … suo …**

plebis: the elements of the tricolon *auctum* increase in universality.   **liberatori** has both pro- and anti-*popularis* resonances.
Caesar was awarded the then new title in 45, but Cicero laid it
liberally under contribution when speaking of Brutus and Cassius,
and L. calls the first Brutus *liberator urbis* (1.60.2); see Weinstock
137–48 and *FRR* 281–350 for *libertas*. Manlius is throughout described with such ambiguous language; see also 18.5–15n.   **parenti pl. R.:** a pointed reworking of *parens urbis/patriae*, which
L. bestows only on Romulus (e.g. 1.16.3) and C. (5.49.7, spoken
by his soldiers) in the extant *AVC*. It is also a Caesarian title (last
n.), though attested earlier (first at Cic. *Rab. perd.* 27 (of Marius), cf.
Pis. 6 (of Cicero) with Nisbet); see also 20.7n. The image of the
ruler *qua* benevolent father, exploited by Augustus, became a panegyrical topos (cf. *Dom.* 94, of Cicero by Cicero, Plin. *Pan.* 2.3, *Pan.
Lat.* 9.15.3 and see Weinstock 200–5, Stevenson).   **gratiam referant** implies making a tangible return for services rendered
(Moussy 262–80).

14.6 acceptus ... augebat: chiastic. As the centurion is received into the crowd he transfers his own energy to it (Feldherr
34), using physical and verbal display to direct attention back to
Manlius. For the practical help afforded by the *uoluntas militum* cf.
e.g. Cic. *Mur.* 38 (soldiers' testimonials in elections), Tac. *H.* 1.4.2.
acceptus ∼ *acceptas* below, in slightly different senses ('admitted'
OLD 12–14, 'sustained' *OLD* 7–8): for the play see 3.5n.   **tumultuosam ... tumultum** ∼ 2 *tumultuosa*; the crowd takes on Manlius'
nature (cf. 16.8 (n.)). For *tumult-* + *turba* cf. 2.59.7, 24.15.4 *capite aegre
inter turbam tumultumque abscidendo terebat tempus*, 30.10.5, Luc. 1.297,
[Quint.] *Decl.* 265.15, Tac. *H.* 1.55.4 *in tumultu ... turbantibus*.
cicatrices: as Manlius showed his hand, so the centurion shows his
scars; for the display of wounds to inspire pity and/or action cf.
20.8 (n.), 2.23.4 with O., Herod. 1.59.4, Sall. *J.* 85.29 with Paul,
Diod. 13.95.5–6, Tac. *A.* 1.35.1.   **deinceps** qualifies *bellis*, an attributive use of the adv. modelled on Greek practice (Riemann 242–
5), cf. 9.4 (n.), 15.7, 24.7.   **ostentans:** of displaying scars *et sim.*
at e.g. 2.23.4, Ter. *Eun.* 482–3 *neque pugnas narrat neque cicatrices suas |
ostentat*, Sall. *J.* 85.29, *H.* 1.88, Curt. 10.2.12.

14.7 se ... (8) esse: the centurion is logical and bipartite, de-
tailing his economic miseries at war and at home (*se ... se ... sorte*

... sortem), what he has received from Manlius (in public and private spheres), and what he owes Manlius (8, physical and legal). The speech forms a tricolon of the shape XxX (above, p. 23).   **militantem:** for debts incurred at home while a soldier was on campaign cf. 2.23.5, 7.38.7, Dion. Hal. 15.3.6, Val Max. 4.4.6 (see *IM* 311, 641–3).   **se restituentem ... esse:** he has been trying, but with little success, to do what C. exhorted all Rome to do after the sack (5.52.1 *e naufragiis ... emergentes*, 53.5 *desereremus penates nostros ... et Galli euertere potuerunt Romam quam Romani restituere non uidebuntur potuisse?*). Manlius' intervention is thus a direct answer to C.'s pretty – but pretty vacant – words.   **multiplici ... exsoluta** 'though he had paid off the principal [*OLD sors* 7] many times over'.   **obrutum fenore:** cf. 17.2, 35.7.2. The image has special resonance for one who fought in the Veian and Gallic wars (6), cf. 5.2.7 *niuibus pruinisque obrutum*, 42.7 *tot ... obruti malis*, 48.7 *prope obruentibus infirmum corpus armis.*   **uidere:** sc. *se.* The sentence-initial verb enhances the peripeteia (Marouzeau II 78–9); for the bracket *uidere ... habere* see 10.2n.   **lucem forum ciuium ora:** the most important elements of civic life; cf. 7.4.4 *foro luce congressu aequalium*, 23.10.7 *foro medio, luce clara, uidentibus uobis*, Cic. *Att.* 1.14.3 (the whole passage bears comparison), *Vat.* 24, *Phil.* 3.24 *uitatio oculorum lucis urbis fori*, Var. *Men.* 512. For asyndeton in 'emphatic enumeration' see G–L §481.2.   **opera** 'thanks to' (*OLD* 1c). Like Caesar, Manlius provides a *miseris perfugium* (Sall. *C.* 54.3: Valvo 28); for summoning help from one's fellow citizens (*'Quiritatio'*), explicit at 2.23.8 and implied here, see Lintott 11–16.   **parentum:** subjective gen. Children were expected to make active return for their parents' *beneficia* (Stevenson 427–9); Stephenson compares Soph. *Ai.* 518 (Ajax is Tecmessa's protector in place of her parents), cf. Hom. *Il.* 6.429–30, Xen. *Anab.* 1.3.6. For the relation between a patron and a parent cf. Pl. *Rud.* 1266 *mi patrone, immo potius mi pater* and see 5n.

14.8 deuouere implies a willingness to sacrifice his life (Skutsch on Enn. *Ann.* 74), even that Manlius is godlike in his eyes; for the figurative use see *OLD* 4b.   **corporis ... sanguinis** ~ 7 *uidere ... ora* (physical recompense for physical benefit). For the comprehensive expression cf. Var. *Men.* 405.1–3, Ov. *M.* 2.610–11, cf. Cic. *Quinct.* 39 *sanguinem uitamque, Cat.* 3.24 *aceruis corporum et ciuium sanguine.*   **corporis ... quod supersit** ~ *quodcumque ... iuris* below (chiastic).   **quodcumque ... iuris** ∼ 7 *parentum beneficia* (natural bonds). For *ius* ('bond' *OLD* 9) *cum aliquo* cf. 41.24.10, Cic. *Fam.* 13.14.1, Plin. *Ep.* 7.11.4; for the hyperbaton see 2.9n.   **sibi:** dat. of the possessor.   **penatibus ... priuatis** expands and explains *patria. penatibus* ∼ 7 *penates*; for the change of meaning see 3.5n.   **uno homine** 'one man only': Manlius has achieved C.'s position (11.3) and more: a single human being = the *patria* (23.7n.). **14.9 instincta:** the language of divine possession (*OLD* 1b); *instinctus* of enthusiasm generated by words is first in L.   **cum iam ... addita:** new excitement added to existing frenzy is a familiar detail in L.'s crowd scenes, cf. 18.5, 23.4, 2.23.2, 4.58.11, 31.6.3.   **unius hominis:** a kind of possessive gen. (G–L §366 R.1). The obtrusive repetition of the phrase from 8 intensifies the relationship between the centurion and the plebs.   **addita:** sc. *est.*   **alia ... res:** disjunction emphasizes the adj. ('something *else*'). *alius* is relatively detachable from its noun; here it brackets a second hyperbaton (cf. 35.6).   **commodioris ... consilii** 'involving a scheme better suited for throwing everything into confusion'; the gen. is descriptive. *commodus ad* + gerund(ive) is only here and Caes. *C.* 3.100.3 (*TLL*).   **ad ... turbanda:** cf. 1.46.7 *initium turbandi omnia*, Sall. *H.* 1.77.1 *seditionibus omnia turbata sunt.* The expression derives from 'civil war' language (Vell. 74.3 with W.); for *omnia* see 3.5n.

14.10 fundum: the donation of the *fundus* doubles Manlius' payment of the centurion's debts. Movement from individual plights to the universal is signalled by the shift from specific to general (4 *seruauerim* ∼ 10 *donec ... supererit,* 5 *liberatori suo* ∼ 10 *uind. libertatis*), while the doubling itself substantiates in advance Manlius' claim to care for *singuli* and *uniuersi* (15.11). There is however a concomitant move, slight but significant, from actual (the debt is paid there and then) to potential (the *patrimonium* is offered for auction). From now on, Manlius relies increasingly on symbols (11n., 20.6–9n.). **Veienti:** sc. *agro*; the substantival abl. in *-i* recurs in 13; see 2.7n. **patrimonii:** waste of familial fortune was a leading characteristic of the Catilinarian conspirators (e.g. Cic. *Cat.* 2.10, Sall. *C.* 14.2) and of aristocratic youths in general (C. Edwards, *The politics of immorality in ancient Rome* (1993) 173–90). Manlius behaves both as expected and in exactly the opposite way: he spends the chief part of his property not on himself but on others (cf. Octavian at Cic. *Phil.* 3.3 *patrimonium ... suum effudit*). **subiecit praeconi** 'put up for auction' (*OLD subicio* 6b). **ne ... patiar:** triggered by '*subicio fundum*' implicit in *fundum ... subiecit*, a striking dependence of an *o.r.* construction on the narrative. **Quirites:** 38.6n. **donec ... supererit:** cf. Sen. *Contr.* 1.8.14 *quamdiu uires fuissent, non defuturum rei pub. uirum fortem.* **iudicatum ... duci** ∼ 3 (n.). **accendit:** cf. 18.5. There was a widespread tendency to express enthusiasm with metaphors from fire (Fantham 7–11); on fire and crowds see Canetti 75–80. **per omne ... secuturi:** cf. Luc. 5.313–14 *per omne | fasque nefasque rues.* The doublet is proverbial (Häussler 160, Tac. *H.* 2.56.1 with H.); for the type (x + non-x), which is very old, see Donatus *ad* Ter. *And.* 214, Lindholm 4. **uindicem libertatis:** bestowed on Augustus after Actium, but long familiar from propaganda issued by both sides in civil conflicts (Weinstock 139, 143, Seager (1) 337–8), cf. Cic. *Brut.* 212 *ex dominatu Ti. Gracchi ... in libertatem rem. pub. uindicauit*, Sall. *C.* 20.6 (Catiline: *nosmet ... uindicamus in libertatem*). Though Manlius has performed legal *uindicatio* (3–5), this acclamation must be considered in the light of the plebeian inability to distinguish *fas* from *nefas* and the knowledge that such phrases 'were used primarily to obscure political issues and not to enunciate positive programmes' (Wirszubski 106).

14.11 Ad hoc ... (13) fore repeats the narrative pattern of 3–10: Manlius attacks the patricians, offers an economic solution, and so inspires the plebs that they are willing to go to extremes (13 *exsequebantur* ∼ 10 *secuturi*). But instead of being in public, he is at home; and at the heart of the scene we find not action but a claim that if a patrician secret is revealed, relief is inevitable (11 *res ... palam ... exsolui* ∼ 5 *rem ... palam ... soluit*). This retreat from the real to the symbolic, which continues throughout the *seditio* (10n., 20.6–9n.), is epitomized by the change in meaning from *soluit* 'paid' to *exsolui* 'be released from'. **domi ... patres** 'he held forth at home in the manner of one speaking in the public assembly, full of accusations against the patricians'; with *sermones* sc. *ei erant.* **domi:** meeting in secret implies conspiracy (*Lex XII* 8.26, Sall. *C.* 20.1; see Seager (2) 383), and Manlius' talk is all about secrets. There is an inherent dissonance in the juxtaposition *domi* ∼ *contionantis*; cf. 18.5–15, which doubles this on a grand scale. **uera an uana:** plebeian disregard for moral distinctions (10) has infected Manlius' rhetoric. By framing the brief scene *domi* with this detail (11 ~ 13 *ueri . . . falsi*) L. concentrates attention on the truth of the *indicium*, which will become the focus of Manlius' meeting with Cossus (15–16.4; at 20.4 it is assumed to have been false); he thereby distracts us from the question of Manlius' motives. For the 'jingle' *uera ~ uana* cf. Virg. *A.* 10.630–1 with Harrison; for *uanus* of evidence see *OLD* 3a, 4. **iaceret** 'hurled' (*OLD* 7); see 11.9n. The repetition below with *iecit* (*OLD* 8) may be owing to the slight change of dependent construction (from acc. to acc. + infin.); cf. 21.5 (n.), 1.30.1, 3.2.2, 5.15.5 (Pettersson 126).   **nec . . . contentos** ~ 11.8 *non contentus*: Manlius attributes to the other patricians his own impatient nature. *contentus* + abl. gerund(ive) seems unparalleled (*TLL*); see 1.11n. **possidendis publicis agris** ~ *pecuniam . . . publicam auertant* (triple chiasmus).   **auertant** 'misappropriate', legal language (*OLD* 9).

14.12 enimuero 'naturally', emphasizing the consequence (*OLD* 1c); L. often combines it with *indignus / indignari* (W–M on 27.30.14), cf. Cic. *Ver.* 4.147 *ille enimuero . . . ait indignum facinus esse.*   **uideri:** hist. infin. (11.7n.).   **cum . . . cessisse:** his audience pick up Manlius' patricians ~ Gauls equivalence (4n.), implying that the gold should now ransom the poor from the *patres*. Antithesis brings out the unfairness of the situation: *redimendam ~ captum, ciuitatem ~ paucorum, tributo ~ praedam.*   **tributo . . . factam:** sc. *esse*: 'the payment was raised [*OLD facio* 9b] by taxation'; for *tributum* 'war tax' see Nicolet (1) 153–64. According to L., the gold came from funds *in publico* (5.50.7); for the matrons' contribution see 4.2n.   **paucorum:** political language: 'the élite' (*OLD* 5b), esp. in a negative sense (*VL* 443–6). It appears on both sides of late-republican political invective; on its roots see Seager (2) 380–1 and cf. e.g. Thuc. 4.22.2 (ὀλίγοι).   **cessisse** 'turned into' (*OLD* 17b), cf. 36.17.13, Tac. *A.* 15.45.1 *inque eam praedam etiam dii cessere* (Fletcher (2) 49). Expression and thought imitate Sall. *C.* 20.7 *res pub. in paucorum potentium ius . . . concessit*, *H.* 3.48.6 *itaque omnes concessere iam in paucorum dominationem qui . . . arcem habent ex spoliis uostris.*

14.13 exsequebantur quaerendo 'they kept on asking'. *exsequi* + participle of a verb of asking is a Livian idiom (*TLL*). **tantae rei furtum** 'a theft of so much property' (*OLD furtum* 4, *res* 1).   **differentique . . . dicenti:** abls., though used substantively

(probably to avoid *differentĕque*); see 10n.   **tempore suo:** a minor
motif in this story is that the *uir consularis* does nothing at another's
bidding (cf. 16.1, 17.3, 5).   **ceteris:** sc. *curis*.   **eo ... curae**
'everyone's concerns were directed toward that object' (i.e. getting
the gold: *OLD eo*² 1b).   **apparebatque ... fore** 'and it was
clear that no small credit would result if his information were true,
and no small offence if false'. Appeal is once again made to the
perception of the observer (∼ 2 *intuenti*), while the potential shift in
the people's mood prepares for the abrupt change in their allegiance at 20.11.   **ueri ... falsi** ∼ 11 *uera an uana*. The gens. express the source of the popularity and offence (*OLD gratia* 5; for
offensio + gen. cf. Cic. *Rep.* 2.53).   **gratiam ... offensionem:**
more political language: for *gratia* see Moussy 271–302, for *offensio*,
VL 195.

  15–16.4 Manlius and Cossus. Cossus has a chance to prove publicly
that Manlius is a fraud, but the demonstration backfires and only
the power of the state, not its moral correctness, is apparent (see
also 20.11n.). The scene echoes the confrontation between Cincinnatus and Maelius in which the latter is killed by Servilius Ahala
(4.14.1–7). In 385, however, the opposition is better organized, its
leader in no way hesitant to face his senatorial peers (Martin, *SS*
51). What begins as an exercise of dictatorial power turns into a
scene of single combat played out as a judicial *agon*, with brief
paired speeches (on their place in Latin historiography see e.g.
McGushin on Sall. *C.* 51–2, *LHA* 232–3).

  15.1 suspensis rebus refers not only to the suspense generated
by Manlius' promised *indicium* (14.13) but to the narrative, which has
been interrupted (next n.). For the form of expression cf. 38.1, Plin.
Ep. 10.31.4 *rem ... in suspenso relinqui* and see C-L 109–24 ('ablatifs
absolus de reprise').   **accitus ... in urbem** ∼ 14.1 *acciri Romam*, marking ch. 14 as a background-providing scene: the centurion's rescue presumably takes place while Cossus is fighting the
Volsci. Such resumptive ring-composition delimits a digression or
an episode that branches off from the main story but that often,
as here, also moves the story forward (e.g. W. on Vell. 75.1–76).
postero ... (2) uenit: eight separate actions are reported in this
period; the only non-continuative verb is *stipatus*, which reprises *discedere ... uetuisset* (above, p. 20). On L.'s tendency to compress intro-

ductory material into subord. clauses see Luce (2) 282.   **discedere:** technical of adjourning a meeting (*OLD* 1b, cf. 2.56.12
with O.); with *ab se* the meaning is revised to include the sense 'desert him' (*OLD* 3). The sense of *senatum* also changes from 'senate
meeting' to 'senators' (metonymy).   **stipatus:** 14.3n.   **multitudine** can mean 'gang' (Lintott 61); there is certainly a suggestion
that Cossus has a bodyguard (Lintott 83–5, 89–90). For the power
of such aristocratic throngs see David 241–59.   **sella ... posita:** the *sella curulis*, of Etruscan origin, used by holders of *imperium*
(*OCD*). *s. ponere* is officialese, cf. Cic. *Ver.* 4.56, Sall. *J.* 65.2, V. Max.
3.5.1, Suet. *Gal.* 18.3.   **in comitio:** the assembly place in front of
the *curia*; on it and the adjacent *curia* and *carcer* see Richardson 97–
8, 102–3, 71 and Millar 144–8.   **uiatorem:** an official messenger
(Powell on Cic. *Sen.* 56).

  15.2 signum ... certamen ... agmine: the confrontation is
presented as a military conflict that soon becomes a single combat
(3). For *agmen* of political groups cf. 3.11.7 *patrum a.*, 5.30.4 *principes
... a. facto in forum uenerunt*, 8.28.6 *in forum atque inde a. facto ad curiam
concurrit*; for *certamen* see 12.1n. (*dimicationem*).   **suis:** common
in military contexts (*OLD* B 6a).   **adesse certamen:** 16.6n.
tribunal: a raised wooden platform on which the magistrate sat
(O. on 3.44.9).

  15.3 intuentes ducem: 7.5n. The issue will be decided between
the commanders alone; for the same configuration in single combats
cf. 1.25.1 *in medium inter duas acies procedunt*, 7.10.6 *duo in medio armati
... destituuntur* (see 42.5n.). Of the spectators, the senators are soon
forgotten, as Cossus has all the *uis* he needs; Manlius' *turba*, on the
other hand, loses its power when its *dux* is arrested (16.3). For the
effect of single combats on Livian audiences, fictional and real, see
Feldherr 24–36, 192–234.   **constiterant:** technical of taking up
a position for fighting (*OLD* 6b); for *in acie c.* cf. *B. Afr.* 75.1, Fron. *S.*
4.1.43, Tac. *A.* 2.80.2. For the plupf. see 2.2n.

  15.4 tum dictator: Cossus' brief remarks, prefaced by a *captatio*
in which he ranges himself, the senate, and the plebs against Manlius, are chiastic in form: Manlius has generated an expectation that
the *patres* are hiding *thesauri* that could pay off the people's debt; let
him then pay the debt by forcing the *patres* to release the *thesauri* or
he will be punished for generating the expectation.   **silentio**

facto: L. often inserts a silence just before a speech (so 40.1): *LHA* 205–6.   **utinam:** Cossus has a potentially hostile crowd, so though technically addressing Manlius, he appeals in a deferential *captatio* to the people's interest (cf. *Rhet. Her.* 1.7–8). The opening gambit of a wish (only here in L.), like Cicero's favourite conditional opening (e.g. *Arch.* 1.1, *Sest.* 1.1), implies that the speaker needs the audience's help; for it cf. Cic. *Sull.* 1.1, *Phil.* 9.1, *B. Hisp.* 17.1, Sall. *H.* 1.77.1.   **ita** ∼ *quem ad modum* below.   **conueniat** ∼ *conuenturum.* The play with tenses (verbal polyptoton) is particularly effective in antitheses, cf. Sen. *Contr.* 1.5.4 *nisi quod honestius tunc maritum defenderes quam nunc raptorem defendis,* Vell. 26.2 *in qua ciuitate semper uirtutibus certatum erat, certabatur sceleribus.* Potential *consensus* becomes a rhetorical weapon with which Cossus hopes to eliminate Manlius' support (see also 12.6n.).   **de ceteris rebus** ∼ *quod ... attinet*; for *ceteris* see 1.10n.   **ad** governs both *te* and *eam rem.*   **te:** Cossus' heavy-handed use of the pronoun (4 *bis,* 5 *bis,* 6) emphasizes Manlius' solitary responsibility in this matter (∼ 7–8 *se ... se ... sibi*).   **quaesiturus:** technical of making a legal enquiry (*OLD* 10a). The periphrastic fut. conveys intention more precisely than the simple fut. (G–L §247), cf. 7.31.4 *quidquid deinde patiemur dediticii uestri passuri.*

15.5 fide incolumi 'with no damage to credit'. *incolumis* + abstract noun is Ciceronian, but *i. fides* is not attested elsewhere before the third century A.D (*TLL*).   **occultent:** sc. 'according to you' (cf. 14.11): the subjunc. is part of the *o.o.*   **creditum:** that which is already owed.   **solui posse:** 7.2n.   **cui ... adhorter** 'but I am so far from hindering this that, on the contrary, M. Manlius, I urge you'; *ut ... sim* is the subj. of *tantum abest* (*NLS* §168), *ut ... adhorter* a consecutive clause depending on it (*OLD absum* 5a).   **liberes:** Cossus challenges Manlius with the latter's own slogan, a tactic the tribunes will adopt at 19.7 (see 11.8n.). The omission of *ut* in the indir. command adds to Cossus' generally brisk and sarcastic tone (*NLS* §142).   **istos** 'the men you are accusing' (*OLD* 5b; for the ironic tone see *OLD* 2a).   **incubantes** 'brooding over', unique in this sense in L. (*incubare* is properly used of unlawful possession: *TLL* VII 1.1063.14–33). The image is of a great serpent guarding its hoard (Otto 173), cf. Mart. 12.53.3–4 *largiris nihil incubasque gazae | ut magnus draco*; for *praeda* (below) of an animal's

prey see *OLD* 2a.   **publicis thesauris** ∼ *praeda clandestina*, anti-
thetically and chiastically.   **euoluas** continues the image of patrician snakiness, cf. 26.19.7 *speciem* [sc. *anguis*] ... *euolutam*, Sil.
6.218 *serpens euoluitur antro*.

15.6 quod ... concitari: by shifting the burden of proof on to
Manlius Cossus evades the question of patrician responsibility; for
the technique see Quint. 4.1.44–5.   **nisi facis:** pres. for fut.,
idiomatic esp. in threats, solemn declarations etc.; the usual particle is *ni* (L–H–S 549, 667); cf. 24.9, 38.7, 36.28.6 *ni propere fit quod
impero, uinciri uos iam iubebo* with B.   **siue ut ... siue quia:**
12.1n.   **et ipse ... sis:** Cossus casts suspicion on Manlius' motives (cf. e.g. Sen. *Contr.* 7.4.2 with Winterbottom *s.v.* 'colours: con-
nivance and collusion'). For *in parte ... esse* 'be in on the loot', a
variation on the official *particeps praedae esse* (4.53.10 with O.), cf.
5.46.4, Grat. *Cyneg.* 247–8 *in partem praedae ueniat comes et sua norit |
praemia.*   **in uincla ... iubebo:** an official phrase, cf. 19.2, Cic.
Cat. 1.27, Sall. *J.* 33.3, Plin. *NH* 21.8, *Dig.* 1.2.2.17.   **uincla:** an
older, choicer form of *uinculum* (Adams (4) 57).   **nec ... patiar** ∼ 14.10 *ne ... patiar*. By claiming concern for plebeian welfare
Cossus hopes to steal Manlius' thunder; C. will take the same tack
at 38.6–7.   **multitudinem ... concitari:** virtually technical for
'foment revolution' (*VL* 513), a stalwart anti-*popularis* charge (Seager
(2) 378).   **fallaci spe:** proverbial (Otto 330).

15.7–13. Manlius treats the situation as if it were a judicial issue,
delivering a speech for the defence more than twice as long as the
dictator's challenge. He does not deal directly with Cossus' allegations, employing instead the evasiveness in defence recommended
by e.g. *Rhet. Her.* 2.43 (the case is analogous: *ut si quis cum accusetur
ambitu magistratum petisse, ab imperatoribus saepenumero apud exercitum donis
militaribus se dicat donatum esse*). His two chief weapons are the implicit argument, appropriate in a case where the *factum* is uncertain, that his character would prevent him from doing what he is
accused of (Lausberg §376.13), and an aggressive shifting of the burden of proof back to the patricians. He begins with an analysis of
his predicament (7–8), then treats the *crimen fauoris* chiastically (9–
10, the *turba* troubles you? save the plebs from their woes; or pay
what is left of their loans, then it will no longer trouble you), and
ends by dismissing the *crimen auri* as a patrician smokescreen (12–13).

15.7 Ad ea 'in reply'.   **nec** 'not either' (*OLD* 2a) is 'affected by L.' (O. on 3.52.9); here it indicates that Manlius knows what the other patricians know (cf. 11.9–10).   **se** is the obj. of *fefellisse*, *non ... esse* (below) its subject. Manlius claims the kind of hyper-awareness that characterizes not only a canny politician (e.g. 5.2.3, Cic. *Cat.* 1.7) but also an ideal general (Pomeroy 75 n.13), cf. 5.47.4 *anseres non fefellere*, Caes. *C.* 3.67.3, *B. Alex.* 32.2, Tac. *A.* 3.10.3 *haud fallebat Tiberium*.   **non aduersus ... nec ... sed:** the first of two anaphoric tricola. This one is foreshortened, the third element lacking a descriptive phrase; the resulting imbalance draws attention to the blunt *se ac plebem Romanam*. Manlius is much given to textbook exx. of rhetorical *figurae* (18.5–15n.); on tricola in declamation see Bonner (1) 68, and for anaphoric structures in Livian *o.o.* cf. 4.15.3–4 (*qua*), 5.21.5 (*iam*), 35.42.10–11 (*si*).   **Volscos ... expediat:** he suggests that these wars are stirred up to distract the plebs from internal affairs, a conventional anti-tyrannical accusation (e.g. Arist. *Pol.* 1313b10), cf. 27.7, 2.28.6–7, 32.1, 5.2.11.   **totiens:** attributive (14.6n.).   **falsis criminibus:** Catiline, too, complains of having been gotten at by *f. c.* (Sall. *C.* 34.2).   **in arma agant:** first here (*TLL*), cf. 30.14.10, Luc. 2.254, Tac. *H.* 3.53.1 with H.   **sed ... esse:** Livian dictators are often duplicitously appointed (cf. 2.30.3–7, 5.26.1), and L. has acknowledged this instance (11.9n.); the theme is taken up again at 16.5 (n.).   **dictatorem ... esse:** 'Basis' (4.7n.).

15.8 iam ... iam ... iam: after opposing the specious to the real, Manlius contrasts the present (*iam*) with the past (*creatum esse* above). Where the first triad (7) was built of a single sentence in which one grammatical element was repeated, each part of this tricolon is a discrete unit (for the pattern cf. Cic. *Agr.* 1.23 *sollicitam ... sustulistis*); the central member is slightly weighted. See above, p. 23 and for the anaphora see 7n.   **in se ~ aduersus ~ sibi**, three different ways of expressing disadvantage. The *uariatio* (for which see Catterall 300, 305, Sörbom 81) contrasts with the insistent initial *iam* and with the repeated *aduersus* in 7.   **profiteri patrocinium:** cf. Vell. 75.1 *professus eorum, qui perdiderant agros, patrocinium*. Cossus looks out for the money-lenders as Manlius looks out for the plebs (18.14). Patronage is one of Manlius' preoccupations, and he is the only person in Book 6 to speak in these terms (cf. 17.5n.,

18.5, 34.7n.); for clientage, a system whose 'antiquity is beyond dispute', see *FRR* 400–14.   **ex fauore:** consistently associated with 'les manifestations purement extérieures de la foule' (e.g. *clamor*: Moussy 381–3), *fauor* is rare before L.; he and Tac. favour it (*TLL*). **crimen et perniciem** 'a ruinous charge' (hendiadys).

15.9 offendit ... meo?: Manlius' offence and his *o.r.* begin simultaneously (6.8–15n.). Having redefined the *crimen* (8 *ex fauore multitudinis*) he freely admits it, then argues that he has done only what he had to do given the negligence of others (for the tactic cf. *Rhet. Her.* 1.25, *ex comparatione causa* and *ex translatione criminis causa*). He relies heavily on rhetorical questions (a variety of the figure *interrogatio*: Lausberg §§767–70, *LHA* 241) which give the user a powerful attacking stance (Canetti 284–90).   **te, A. Corneli:** 6.12n. **uos ... uestris:** Manlius answers Cossus' *tu*'s with this pronoun/ adj., which he uses liberally in the sections of his speech in which he is on the attack (9–13).   **circumfusa ... meo?:** this Pied Piper act is of the essence of *popularis* behaviour, cf. 4.13.3 *plebemque hoc munere delenitam quacumque incederet ... secum trahere* [sc. *Maelius*]. *circumfusa* is refl., 'spread around' (as a liquid: 17.6n.). It can be applied to crowds of any sort (*TLL*) but here indicates a protective surrounding; for *latus* '(vulnerable) flank' see *OLD* 3a.   **quin** 'why not?', its original sense (*NLS* §185), sparsely attested in the late republic (O. on 1.57.7). It figures prominently at Sall. *C.* 20.14 *quin igitur expergiscimini?*; for other exx. of Manlius talking like Catiline see 14.3n., 18.5n., 18.14n., 18.15n.   **uestris beneficiis:** specified by the following gerunds; on political *beneficium* see *VL* 163–9, Stevenson 425–7.   **intercedendo ... aliorum:** an asyndetic tetracolon *auctum* of gerunds in which both length and syntactical complexity increase. For other exx. see Ullmann (2) 105–6 and cf. Sall. *C.* 54.3 *Caesar dando subleuando ignoscundo, Cato nihil largiundo gloriam adeptus est.*   **intercedendo** 'by intervening'. Their failure to do so will eventually produce a crisis fuelled by tribunician *intercessio* (*interced/ss-* occurs only here in Book 6 before 35.6, then thirteen times).   **ex eo ... aliorum:** the last element, which deals specifically with economic relief, is set off by its variant word order (above, p. 22).   **opibus:** abl. of separation.   **necessitates** 'needs' (*OLD* 5).

15.10 de uestro impendatis: i.e. from their own pockets.

Having made what must have seemed a mad suggestion, Manlius now advocates a less expensive, and therefore perhaps feasible, solution analogous to that proposed in 377 (35.4: Bayet 125). For *impendere de* cf. Cic. *Ver.* 5.47; for the subjunc. without *ut* see 5n.   **sortem ... est** 'take what is left of the capital; deduct from the principal [*OLD caput* 19] what has been paid in interest'.   **pernumeratum est:** rare and perhaps technical; cf. 35.4, Pl. *Epid.* 632, Catul. 7.11, Aug. *RG* 15.1.   **turba** ~ 9 *turba* (ring composition). **quam ullius:** 'than anyone else's'. For *quam* preceding the comparative see 4.11n.   **conspectior:** cf. 4.13.3 (Maelius) *conspectus elatusque supra modum hominis priuati*; the comparative is first in L. (*TLL*). Manlius' euergetism has made him lit. conspicuous, surrounding him with a visible sign of his beneficence. He regards his own appearance as a spur to action, a very military concept (8.5n.); cf. 7.7.6 (youths placed in prominent positions *quo conspectior uirtus esset*) with Feldherr 152–70.

  15.11 at ... ago?: Manlius anticipates, and answers, a question about his own actions, another form of *interrogatio* (cf. *Rhet. Her.* 4.33–4) related to the tactic of anticipating one's opponent's arguments (= *praesumptio*, Quint. 9.2.16–17). *at enim* regularly introduces such objections (*OLD at* 4).   **solus:** 11.3n.   **ciuium curam ago:** officialese (*OLD ago* 29, *cura* 7); for *cura* as a virtue of the ideal leader, later a panegyrical motif, see Vell. 106.3 with W. *ciuium* is objective gen.   **nihilo ... seruauerim:** an inversion of the accusatory ploy whereby one proves current delinquency from past bad habits (e.g. *Rhet. Her.* 2.5).   **et ... feram:** double antithesis (*tum ... tuli* ~ *nunc ... feram, uniuersis* ~ *singulis*) of a frigid type to which Manlius is particularly addicted (18.5–15n.).   **uniuersis ... singulis:** Manlius favours this correlation, as one might expect from his 'all for one and one for all' stance.   **quam potui:** modesty is recommended when speaking of one's own advantages (= *deminutio, Rhet. Her.* 4.50).

  15.12 nam 'moreover' (*OLD* 4).   **rem ... facit:** cf. 31.39.9 *uiam suapte natura difficilem ... inexpugnabilem fecit. facilem ... facit* is an etymological play (Maltby 219), pointed by *natura* ('natural meaning' *OLD* 9c: see Fraenkel on Aesch. *Ag.* 699 and next n.).   **interrogatio** is technical both for the questioning of witnesses and for various rhetorical *figurae* (9n., 11n.); its coupling with *natura* therefore

suggests the polar expression 'nature ~ art'. Manlius exposes the artificiality of Cossus' proceedings, which changes *fac-* to *diffic-* (last
n.); but it is in fact his own *oratio* that has been artful. For the danger of *interrogatio* cf. Cic. *De orat.* 1.43 *interrogationum laqueis*, Sen. *Ben.*
4.26.1 *i. insidiosa*, Plin. *Ep.* 1.5.7 *laqueis tam insidiosae interrogationis.*
cur ... subest: Cossus' argument ('you say we have the gold:
prove it') is here thrown back at him ('why ask me to prove it: you
show us', cf. Quint. 3.10.4 on *mutua accusatione*).   **quod** =
id quod.   **in sinu** i.e. of their togas, a natural place to hide things
(*OLD* 4).   **excuti** lit. 'to be shaken out', just shying away from
the relevant technical sense 'search a person' (*OLD* 9, cf. Quint.
7.1.30 *excusserunt illi patrem et aurum in sinu eius inuenerunt*).   **ponatis:**
8.10n.   **subest** 'is lurking'.

15.13 quo ... proferatis: Manlius answers Cossus' accusation
of fraud with one of his own, his threat of force (6 *iubebo*) with a
modified one (*cogendi*). It is in no way an answer, but Manlius has
his eye on his audience, who will react against a suggestion that
they have been hoodwinked.   **argui** 'be revealed' (*OLD* 1).
'When a conjurer asks his audience to find out his trick, he is most
certain of being able to deceive them' (Stephenson).   **praestigias:** only here in L.; for the connection with rhetorical sleight of
hand cf. Cic. *Rab. post.* 35 *omnes praestigiae ... omnes fallaciae omnia
denique ... mimorum argumenta*, Quint. 4.1.77 (on Ovid).   **uestras:**
for the word order see 1.2n.   **abstuleritis ... oculos** draws
on the dual associations of *auferre* with pecuniary theft (*OLD* 5) –
hence *etiam* here – and military capture (*OLD* 4b). The plebeian
oculi – and our own – do indeed become increasingly useless (16.8–
17.6n., 20.6–9n., 20.10n.).   **obseruantibus** 'as we watched'.
ego: sc. *cogendus sum.*   **id:** internal acc. after *cogendi* (picked up by
the *ut*-clause below: G–L §333); it is retained in the passive (*NLS*
§14).   **in medium:** a demand that the patricians extend the co-
operation they once gave C. (6.18n.) to the whole state; see also
19.7n., 40.10n.

16.1 mittere ambages: cf. 34.59.1, Pl. *Cist.* 747, Hor. *S.* 2.5.9
(Gries 20–1). *ambages* are a 'verbal labyrinth' (Austin on Virg. *A.*
6.99); cf. 15.12 (n.).   **peragere ... fateri:** for the word order
see 9.6n. The position of *fateri* facilitates the elaboration of its obj.
(cf. 27.7, 38.12, 40.12).   **cogeret:** conative.   **insimulati ...**

inuidiae 'of having accused the senate with a false charge and of having inflicted [on it] the ill-will of a non-existent theft'. The gens. are epexegetical of *facinus* (*NLS* §72 (5)).   **insimulati ... crimine:** cf. Ov. *Ep.* 6.22, Vell. 77.3; Cossus picks up Manlius' *falsum crimen* (15.7).   **negantem ... se locuturum:** 14.13n. (*tempore suo*).   **inimicorum:** the power of personal enmity to motivate action and provide self-justification should not be underestimated: Caesar invaded Italy partly to defend himself *a contumeliis inimicorum* (*C.* 1.22.5), while Catiline threatened to burn Rome after being *circumuentus ... ab inimicis* (Sall. *C.* 31.9, cf. 34.2); see in general *FRR* 351–81. *inimicus* is used in this book only in ref. to Manlius; cf. Serv. on Virg. *A.* 8.652 *inimicorum oppressus factione* [sc. *Manlius*].

16.2 arreptus ... inquit: one can economically move an audience to anger and pity by the pathetic contrast of past and present (= *commutatio fortunae*: *Rhet. Her.* 2.50 with Caplan, Vell. 53.3 with W.). The historian, too, relied on inspiring *misericordia* and *indignatio*, since dramatic presentation and its accompanying emotional empathy were the surest way of teaching a moral lesson (M–W 162); for the joint participation of the audiences inside and outside the text see 14–16.4n.   **Iuppiter ... Minerua:** 4.3n. (*ante pedes*). The prayer, a form of apostrophe, is calculated to arouse indignation (Vell. 66.3 with W.). Manlius and his supporters are the only characters in the *seditio* to call on the gods, a piety that L. could, but does not, expose as false (Levene 206–8); see also 20.15n. **ceteri ... qui ... incolitis:** the inclusive formula and the specification of the god's dwelling place, often in a rel. clause, are formulaic prayer elements (Appel 83–4, 110–12).   **militem ac praesidem** 'your guardian soldier' (hendiadys): as the gods protect Rome (*OLD praeses* 1b), so Manlius protects the gods. Reminding a divinity of one's past services is a traditional means of appealing for help (Appel 151–2), cf. 18.9n.   **sinitis:** one arouses *indignatio* either by calling on the gods to prevent or avenge a disaster or by complaining that they have not or will not, cf. 18.9, 9.9.7, Cic. *Phil.* 10.5, Sen. *Contr.* 7.1.25.   **haec dextra ... erit?:** cf. 14.4. For the specific paradox of hands-that-saved-the-state-now-in-unjust-bondage cf. Sen. *Contr.* 1.7.   **in uinclis et catenis:** general + specific (see McKeown on Ov. *Am.* 1.7.1–2).

16.3 nullius nec ... nec: the copulative particles subdivide the

general negative (G–L §445).   **oculi ... aures** ∼ *attollere ... his-*
cere below. Patrician force has succeeded in stealing the people's
eyes (15.13). The stunning of eyes + ears, efficacious channels to a
person's emotions, often accompanies shock (e.g. 28.29.9, Polyb.
11.30.3) or shame (e.g. 9.7.3, Tac. *H.* 3.31.3 with H.), sometimes in
response to an event which despite – or because of – its horror has
a salutary effect (Feldherr 36–87). No lesson is learned here, however: Manlius' punishment merely results in repressed feelings (see
also 20.11n.).   **indignitatem:** 2nn.   **ferebant** 'could bear'
(G–L §233).   **sed ... fecerat** 'but the state, which was wholly
submissive to legal power, had made certain things immutable
[*OLD inuictus* 4b] for itself'.   **patientissima** ∼ *ferebant* above
(7.5n.).   **iusti:** the plebeian reaction is presented from their
point of view (cf. *indignitatem* above), creating an uncomfortable fit
between *iusti imperii* and *dictatoriam uim* below: the dictatorship was
legal – but was it just? For *iustus* 'lawful' (*OLD* 1a) used sarcastically
cf. 10.8.9 *uos solos iustum imperium et auspicium* [sc. *patres habere*]; for
iustum imperium in national propaganda see Weinstock 244.   **dicta-**
toriam uim: cf. 39.7. *uis* can refer neutrally to the power of an
office (*OLD* 11). Here, however, the context suggests violence, cf.
5.29.9 and see 1.1n.   **t. plebis ... plebs:** an ex. of the polyptoton sometimes called 'Priam and the children of Priam' (as Hom. *Il.*
1.255 Πρίαμος Πριάμοιό τε παῖδες); for the inverted word order cf.
4.33.3 *magistro equitum equitibusque*, Hor. *S.* 2.3.195 *populus Priami Pria-*
musque. The figure is said to be rare in Latin prose but there are
many exx. in L. (e.g. 38.9, 41.9, 3.15.9 *bellum ducemque belli*, 9.24.8
Romani Romanorumque ... uiri, 22.42.4 *neque seditionem neque ducem sedi-*
tionis) and some elsewhere, e.g. Cic. *Pis.* 18 *maerorem relinquis, maeroris*
aufers insignia, Caes. *C.* 1.23.1 *senatores senatorumque liberos* (Wills *s.v.*
'coordinated polyptoton').   **attollere:** first in prose at Sall. *H.*
1.126, then in L. (*TLL*).   **hiscere** 'open their mouths' in order
to speak. *non* (*audere/posse*) *hiscere* is usually associated with fear (as
9.6.12) or shame (as 9.4.7); see above (*oculi ... aures*).

    16.4 coniecto ... Manlio: adversative asyndeton.   **satis**
constat: the plebs' first step in their progress from complete submission to active hostility (cf. 5, 8, 17.6) is authorized by narrative
consensus ('all versions agree'), the same consensus e.g. that authorized the beginning of L.'s history (1.1.1). As time goes on, however,

versions differ (18.16n., 20.4n.), while plebeian authority – even over
the narrative – grows (35.10n.).   **magnam partem** ~ *multos*
m. ~ *turbam* (*uariatio* of vocabulary: 12.10n.).   **uestem ... capil-**
lum: an advocate was advised to introduce his client in as pitiful a
state as possible (M–W 163); relatives of clients also put on mourning (cf. 20.2–3), while *squalor* was regularly deployed as an act of
political protest (Lintott 16–21).   **barbam promisisse** 'let
their beards grow' (*OLD promitto* 1b), first in prose at Nep. *Dat.* 3.1,
cf. Virg. *E.* 8.34, Tac *A.* 2.39.2.   **maestam** 'in mourning' (*OLD* 2).

16.5–17 End of the year

16.5 Dictator ... ductus: the triumph notice has standard elements (*de Volscis, actum, ante currum ... ductus*: see Phillips), but they
are compromised. The plebeians, who focalize the notice, take
Cossus' triumph to epitomize the analogy *seditio* ~ *bellum* (11.1–2, cf.
15.7), an interpretation supported by the placement of the notice
immediately following Manlius' imprisonment. The parade, intended as a display of *potestas*, is read as one of *dominatio* (for the
spectator's liberty see Feldherr 11; for the calculated use of triumphal display see Marshall 123–7).   **inuidiae ... gloriae:** predicative dats. (*NLS* §68). Like Cossus' appointment, his triumph is
characterized by the substitution of the specious for the real
(11.9n.); for *inuidia* see 11.3n.   **partum** 'acquired' is regular
with *gloria, uictoria, pax* etc. (*OLD pario* 5), but *p. triumphum* is choice
(*TLL*, cf. Virg. *A.* 2.578, Ov. *Am.* 2.12.16), an instance of L. modifying a traditional expression (above, p. 20).   **de ciue non de**
hoste ~ 17.8 (frame); cf. 2.38.3, Juv. 8.107 with Mayor.   **freme-**
bant: they react while watching the parade (cf. Ov. *Ars* 1.213–28
with Hollis); for the crowd's murmur, a popular *locus* in both historiography and declamation, cf. 4.5, 17.1, 20.3, Sen. *Contr.* 1.3.2 *uoces*
indignantium descripsit and see *LHA* 206–8. Reports of collective reactions are particularly useful for introducing rumours (e.g. 1.7) or
opinions (as here) for which the historian might wish to avoid responsibility (M–W 32, cf. 12.1n.). This vocal presence, somewhat
surprising in an end-of-year notice, prepares for the outrageous intrusion of the *uoces* below (16.8–17.6n.).   **unum ... tantum** 'one
thing only was missing', a pathetic and indignant tag, cf. 23.5.5,

Virg. *A.* 12.643, Sen. *Contr.* 1.3.1, Vell. 67.3 with W., [Quint.] *Decl.* 1.15, 2.38.   **sit ductus:** defeated rulers (etc.) preceded the triumphator's chariot until it reached the ascent to the Capitoline temple, at which point they were taken off to await execution in the *carcer* – precisely where Manlius is now.

16.6 iam: 5.1n.   **haud ... erat:** cf. 15.2, 18.1, 3. These narratologically unsettling statements are part of the doubling of the *seditio*'s structure (Manlius incites the plebs (14 ∼ 18); the senate meets (15.1 ∼ 19); the two sides confront each other (15.2– 16.1 ∼ 20); Manlius appeals to the Capitoline gods (16.2–4 ∼ 20.9)); they exacerbate the widespread critical dissatisfaction with this episode (so e.g. Bayet 110, 120, Wiseman 238, 240; see 11.3n.). Yet it is L.'s habit to build tension, esp. in long episodes, by deploying such narrative 're-starts' (Burck (1) 85–6): cf. 27.6–8, the prelude to the Licinio-Sextian *seditio* (Burck (2) 324 n.3). In this case, they also add to our suspicion that the 'party line' about Manlius, that he was aiming at real revolution, is not quite right: '*now* the *seditio* was really upon them' – but the story's climax has to be engineered by the magistrates. Here, as elsewhere, L. invites such questions by obtrusively displaying the mechanics of his narrative (12.2–6n., 18.16n.).   **procul** + abl. is first in prose in L. (Riemann 272). **cuius leniendae causa:** for *seditionem lenire* cf. 5.24.4, Sen. *Contr.* 2.6.4. The technical designation was *s. sedare* (as *CIL* I^2 1 p. 20 *dictator seditionis sedandae ... causa*).   **postulante nullo ... uoluntarius:** pleonasm (Lausberg §503); cf. 6.5. *aliquo/nullo* + pres. participle (esp. *postulante, aduersante, deprecante*) is officialese (cf. 32.4, 7.11.5, 30.39.3, Cic. *Flac.* 20, *Lig.* 14, Plin. *Ep.* 5.13.1, Tac. *H.* 1.37.2, *A.* 1.2.1).   **largitor:** a popular move that the plebs rightly see as insincere (7). For *largitiones*, often including colony laws, see Seager (1) 332; for colonies as a cure for *seditio* cf. 5.24.4–5 (an attempt that also fails) and see Oakley (2) 18–22 on their economic benefits.   **coloniam** 'as a colony'; *deduci* (below) is the *uox propria* for settling colonists (*OLD* 9a).   **bina ... et semisses:** approx. 1$\frac{2}{3}$ acres apiece.   **assignati:** technical of land distribution (*OLD* 1).

16.7 et paruum et paucis: i.e. 'too little, too late'.   **mercedem** 'a bribe', cf. 2.41.9 *id* [sc. *frumentum*] ... *mercedem regni aspernata plebes*, and see 17.5n., 41.10n.   **prodendi** ∼ 17.2 *proditum*.

remedio ... seditio: cf. 3.15.7 *sedabant tumultus, sedando ... mouebant* with W–M, Tac. *H.* 1.17.2 *famam supprimentes augebant*. L.'s paradoxical language figures the civic distrust and suppressed turmoil (Plass 59 n.5); the longer the *seditio* lasts, the more disconnected its verbal expression seems from reality (cf. 17.6, 18.5–15n.). *remedium* and *irritatur* ('was aggravated' *OLD* 4) are medical metaphors often deployed in political contexts (M–W 145); for technical medical language in L. see Dutoit (1).

16.8–17.6 Voices. The speeches that spring up after the patrician authority resigns are bracketed by the annalistic details of the triumph (16.5), colony (16.6), and embassy (17.7–8), and technically form part of the 'end-of-year' material. L. liked to vary traditional material; these revolutionary *uoces* are out of place both formally (they 'should' be in a narrative section) and ideologically: their intrusion into the most traditional part of the year (above, p. 11) challenges the co-operation between the historiographical tradition and Roman power structures, just as Manlius' history challenges L.'s (11.4nn., 20.8n.). More than ever, the observer has to be aware of the potential difference between surface and reality. L. earlier stepped in to guide us (14.2, 13); now, however, the persuasive power of the opposition is only partly countered by the historiographical tradition (18–20.11n.), and it overpowers the senate, which yields to the crowd without apparent resistance (17.6).

16.8 insignis 'conspicuous' occurs in Book 6 in connection with C. (24.7, 10, 27.1) and Manlius (18.15, 20.7, 8); otherwise L. restricts it to the *dies Alliensis* (1.11 *bis*, 28.6, 8), the disaster that the two men counteracted. This is another instance of the closeness between them (11.8n.), though Manlius' conspicuousness leads him to illicit prominence, while C. is *insignis* in entirely positive ways. **sordibus et facie:** 16.4n.   **reorum:** the crowd have taken on another of their leader's characteristics (14.6n.).   **amotus ... terror** 'the removal of fear' (1.1n.). Repression through *terror* is an essential element of tyranny; for the equally conventional idea that removing the cause of fear facilitates free speech cf. Aesch. (?) *Prom.* 49–50 with Griffith, Eur. *El.* 910–11, Tac. *Ag.* 2.2–3 with Ogilvie–Richmond, Amm. 22.5.1–2.   **linguam ... liberauerat** is hard to parallel (Cic. *Diu.* 2.96 is of surgical freeing); cf. 39.40.10 *linguae*

... *liberae* and for *libertas* '(critical) free speech', see *RICH* 43, 205. For *animum liberare* cf. 24.4.4, Cic. *Brut.* 21, Sen. *Nat.* 1 *praef.* 12.

17.1 audiebantur ... uoces: these sound like Manlius, esp. in their refs. to his war deeds (4) and in their deployment of the contrast between the many and the one (5). They warm up the crowd for him as the centurion did (14.6–8). But they also unwittingly presage his death: it is here that Cassius and Maelius are first mentioned in the text as models for Manlius (henceforth adduced by both sides: 18.4, 9, 19.2, 6), here that the idea of attacking him *per ipsam plebem* (19.6) first arises, as the story shifts from a 'benefactor' to a 'tyrant' narrative (Wiseman 239).   **propalam:** rare before L. and favoured only by him. Together with the initial *audiebantur*, it strongly emphasizes the freedom Manlius' supporters enjoy. **exprobrantium:** substantive. For *exprobrare quod* cf. Cic. *Fam.* 5.15.3, Tac. *A.* 6.12.2; for the effectiveness of reproach in exhortation see 7.3n.   **quod ... destituat:** the first part of the *o.o.* consists of a claim illustrated with historical *exempla* and then restated (2). The structure is that of a *paradeigma* (M. M. Willcock, *C.Q.* 14 (1964) 142).   **in praecipitem ... tollat:** the heights to which one is led by excessive good fortune, favour, or wealth inevitably precipitate a fall (cf. 19.6, Sen. *Ag.* 57–9 with Tarrant). For *praeceps* in such formulations cf. *Praef.* 9, Sall. *J.* 31.6, [Virg.] *Cat.* 3.7, Sen. *Ep.* 8.4, Tac. *Ag.* 41.4, Amm. 22.3.12. The height imagery, which Manlius has used of himself (11.4n.), begins to take on sinister connotations (20.8n.).   **fauore:** they are quoting Manlius (15.8); the tribunes will use the *f. plebis* to destroy him (19.7). For the thought cf. Hor. *C.* 1.1.7–8 *si mobilium turba Quiritium* | *certat ... tollere honoribus* (W.).   **in ipso discrimine periculi** 'at the decisive moment of their peril', cf. 8.24.12, Gell. 3.10.14 (of disease crisis points); the gen. is possessive/partitive (*pace OLD discrimen* 5).   **destituat:** for fickle friends see 8.9n.; for the ungrateful plebs cf. *Rhet. Her.* 4.67, Sall *J.* 31.2 *quam foede quamque inulti perierint uostri defensores* (*CC* 37).

17.2 sic ... sic ... sic: like Manlius (15.7–8), the *uoces* use anaphoric tricola (also at 4).   **plebem ∼ *ciuium* ∼ *partem ciuitatis* (*uariatio*: 12.10n.).   **uocantem ... propulsantem ... extrahentem:** each champion is credited with a different area of economic relief (land, food, and debt); the physical effort required to help the plebs increases each time.   **in agros:** i.e. to take possession of them. *in aliquid uocare* has official and legal overtones (*OLD uoco* 4, 7c).   **famem:** the famine was so severe that many killed themselves rather than endure it (4.12.11); see C. Virlouvet, *Les famines et émeutes à Rome* (1985), 22–35. For *f. propulsare* cf. Cic. *Att.* 11.23.3 (*inopia*), Hor. *S.* 1.2.6 (*f. propellere*), Curt. 9.2.6, Tac. *A.* 14.24.1 with Koestermann.   **suis impensis:** cf. 4.13.2 *priuata pecunia*. In the first century B.C. senatorial fortunes were used most ominously to equip armies and secure their loyalty (e.g. Pompey, Sall. *H.* 2.98.2 *opes ... priuatas*; Crassus, Cic. *Off.* 1.25, Plin. *NH* 33.134; Caesar, Suet. *Jul.* 24.2; Octavian, Cic. *Phil.* 3.3, Aug. *RG* 1 *priuata impensa* with Gagé). See I. Shatzman, *Senatorial wealth and Roman politics* (1975).   **oppressos:** with both preceding accs. *opprimere* was almost technical of political destruction (*OLD* 5b, c), particularly of the actions of the late-republican strong-men (Vell. 61.1 with W.).   **in libertatem ac lucem:** for alliterative doublets in Livian *o.o.* see Lambert 25–8.   **extrahentem:** often used of dragging something out of the darkness, either to rescue or expose it, cf. 9.6.3 *uelut ab inferis extracti*, Cic. *Pis.* 18 *ex tenebricosa popina consul extractus*.   **inimicis:** this is Manlius' word (16.1n.).   **saginare ... iugulentur:** both can be used of sacrificial animals, but the dependence on popular favour suggests that the present metaphor is gladiatorial (*sagina* = training food; *OLD iugulo* 1b). *saginare* 'to stuff' is emphatically vulgar, used lit. of people only at 36.17.8, Sen. *Contr.* 9.2.27, Plin. *NH* 9.119; for the metaphorical use cf. Cic. *Sest.* 78 (Clodius and his 'gladiators': Fantham 129 n.27), *B. Afr.* 46.2.   **populares suos:** an unusual phrase which has been unnecessarily emended. The sense of *popularis* is close to that at e.g. Sall. *C.* 22.1 ('partner', *OLD* 1b: W–C 2), but the gladiatorial metaphor above suggests that it means 'appealing to an (audience) faction', 'favourites' (so Radice), cf. *popularis* 'admired by the *populus*' (*OLD* 6). It eventually came to designate partisans, but other arena terminology could apply both to performers and audience (e.g. *pars*): A. D. E. Cameron, *Circus factions* (1976) 40, 15. For *suos* 'its beloved' (here ironic) see *OLD* B 7.

17.3 hocine ... fuisse: 'was *this* [i.e. imprisonment] what had to be endured?' This and the following questions are rhetorical

194 COMMENTARY: 17.3–5

(*NLS* §267 (*b*)). **ad nutum dictatoris:** extremely sarcastic, cf. 38.51.4 *sub umbra Scipionis ciuitatem dominam orbis terrarum latere, nutum eius pro decretis patrum, pro populi iussis esse,* Cic. *Quinct.* 94 and see 14.13n. (*tempore suo*). **consularis:** he was consul in 392 (*MRR* 1 92). **fingerent** 'suppose that': the subjunc. is concessive (*NLS* §112 *Note* i). If necessary, rhetorical handbooks advise tentative admission of guilt, but only if absolutely necessary (*Rhet. Her.* 1.24, Sen. *Contr.* 2.5.11). This hypothetical admission is lost in the consequent *indignatio*. **mentitum:** sc. *eum esse.* **cui ... fuisse?:** the imaginary plight of someone on the opposite end of the social scale from Manlius – a kind of argument from analogy (Lausberg §394) – distracts attention from the lie.

17.4 non ... non ... non: a second anaphoric tricolon (cf. 2). Each successive element exhibits a greater degree of ellipse: *obuersatam esse memoriam ...* [sc. *obuersatam esse*] *speciem agminis ...* [sc. *obuersatam esse speciem*] *ipsius M. Manli*; cf. 7.40.6 (*si ... uestrum*), Cic. *Pis.* 1 (*pauci ... linguae*). For the phrasing here cf. Cic. *Ver.* 5.144 *numquam tibi ... species ipsa huiusce multitudinis in oculis animoque uersata est?*, S. *Rosc.* 98 (also with rhet. questions, anaphora of *non*, and *uersari*). **obuersatam ... memoriam:** first here, cf. 35.11.3, Tac. *A.* 14.63.2. At the persuasive centre of their outburst the *exprobrantes* ask the plebs to 'picture this' (= *euidentia*: 1.3n.). This is yet another spectacle, in which the reader watches the crowd watching Manlius. The progression from the real to the symbolic continues (14.11n.): here an imaginary Manlius rescues the *ciues* (see further 20.6–9n.). **noctis illius** 'that famous night' (*OLD ille* 4b), cf. Cic. *Cael.* 60. **quae ... fuerit:** cf. Curt. 10.9.3 [sc. *nox*] *quam paene supremam habuimus,* Plin. *Ep.* 6.20.15 *aeternam ... illam et nouissimam noctem mundo.* **paene ... aeterna** ~ *sudoris ac sanguinis ... paene* below. **nomini Romano** is the order Sall. and L. prefer; *R. nomen* is regular elsewhere (M–W 158). **non ... scandentis:** L. isolates the Gauls in the short central member. **speciem agminis:** the speakers invoke the *story* of the sneak attack, not the attack itself: most plebeians fled as the Gauls approached (5.40.5) and no one saw the Gauls climbing the rock (5.47.2–3; cf. B. on 35.11.3). **per Tarpeiam rupem:** the Gauls did not ascend the Tarpeian rock at 5.47.2 (Wiseman 233–8); that they do so here will enhance Manlius' final *commutatio fortunae* (20.12n.). **ipsius** ~ *ipso*

below; the implied kinship between Manlius and Jupiter is made
explicit in 5 (n.).   **plenum** 'soaked with', possibly colloquial
(W–C 2), cf. 30.7.9 *uxor ... plena lacrimarum* and (?) Virg. *G.* 4.181
crura thymo plenae [sc. *apes*].   **sudoris ac sanguinis:** 'a stock
phrase for lauding a great achievement' (O. on 2.48.2, see Otto
334).   **erepto ex hostium manibus:** of the rescue (*OLD eripio*
5) from the Gauls also at 20.16, 5.46.5, 51.3; its only other occurrence in L. (26.9.8) shows the seriousness of Hannibal's threat by
evoking the Gallic capture. There is a trace here of the tradition
according to which the Gauls tunnelled into Jupiter's temple (for
the evidence see Wiseman 233).

17.5 selibrisne farris: Manlius' reward from the Capitoline
garrison (5.47.8). L. inverts the motif of the demagogue who buys
the people with food (Seager (1) 332, 335), cf. 4.15.6 *bilibris farris sper-
asse libertatem se ... emisse*, Sall. *H.* 3.48.19 *quinis modiis libertatem omnium aestumauere.*   **seruatori patriae:** (*con*)*seruare patriam / rem pub.*
was Cicero's favourite description of his actions in 63 (e.g. *Cat.* 2.14,
3.14, 4.20, cf. his last (Livian) words at fr. 60 *moriar ... in patria saepe
seruata*). As with many Ciceronian catchwords, the related concepts
of *seruare / salus* passed into imperial self-definition (W. on Vell 49.3,
103.5). *seruator* is also an epithet of Jupiter (*OLD* 1); see below.   **et
quem ... animam?:** again the topos of the change of fortune,
combined with the ingratitude of those who should be grateful
(8.9n., 16.2n.). Manlius' *commutatio* is here explicitly formulated in
geographical terms (Capitoline ∼ *carcer*); cf. Sen. *Suas.* 1.9 with Winterbottom and see 20.12n., 41.3n.   **caelestem** 'heavenly' makes
a late appearance in Latin as an epithet of human heroism (only
here in L., cf. Cic. *Phil.* 5.28 *caelestis diuinasque legiones*, Hor. *C.*
4.2.18); Homeric δῖος became *dius* (Enn. *Ann.* 60 with Skutsch). For
caelestis in imperial panegyric, often in its lit. sense, see *OLD*
3b.   **cognomine** i.e. *Seruator* (above) as well as *Capitolinus*. Jupiter had another title which Manlius will be charged with wanting
to acquire, namely *Rex* (*OLD* 5). *inuidia* once also accused C. of
being too like Jove (5.23.6); see 11.3n.   **Capitolino:** abl. with *cognomine* or dat. with *Ioui* (=amphibole, Bell 293–303).   **in carcere, in tenebris:** concrete + abstract, cf. Cic. *Ver.* 5.21 *talis uir
in carcere, in tenebris*, Virg. *A.* 6.734, [Quint.] *Decl.* 16.9.   **carnificis arbitrio:** 14.13n.   **adeo ... esse?:** the *uoces* conclude by

sounding the key-note of Manlius' 'platform', expressed in his preferred language: antithesis strengthened by chiasmus (here triple)
combined with tense-play (*fuisse* ~ *esse*: 15.4n.). For the *epiphonema*
see 10.9n.   **auxilii:** a reciprocal duty between patron and clients
(15.8n.).

   17.6 nocte: mob violence was esp. likely at night (Lintott 8–9).
dilabebatur 'slipped away', properly used of liquid (*TLL*), to which
Livian crowds are often compared (as 15.9 *circumfusa*; Serres 263–
82). For the *uariatio* with *minabantur* below after a collective noun
see Catterall 303, Sörbom 72–3.   **remisso:** the subj. of the
abl. abs. is the following rel. clause (Roby §1250, first common in
L.).   **quod erepturi erant** 'that which they had been on the
point of snatching'. The idea was apparently proverbial, cf. Pub.
Sent. 454 M *necessitas quod poscit nisi des eripit*, [Sen.] *Oct.* 581–3.
liberatur ~ 16.8 *liberauerat*. The ring, with *non ... est* below
(~16.7), marks the intervening material as a digression.   **quo
facto:** 9.10n.   **non ... est:** the converse of the topos 'lacking a
leader' (cf. 5.46.5, 26.35.4, Cic. *Mur.* 51, and W. on Vell. 125.2). The
epiphonema is ornately patterned (11.5n.); for *seditio ... dux seditioni* see
16.3n. (*t. plebis ... plebs*); for the alliterative *dux ... datus* separated by
a single word see Kraus (3) 326 n.19.

   17.7 Per eosdem dies: a transitional formula favoured only by
L. and related to the type *dum haec geruntur* with which Caesar and
L. link theatres of action (C-L 101–5).   **Circeiensibus** ~ *a Velitris* (12.6n.). This embassy provides a break between the high points
of the *seditio* (Lipovsky 36–7).   **Volsci ... belli:** hyperbaton
emphasizing the adj. (i.e. not their *own* war: Marouzeau 1 112–
14).   **tristia ... tristiora** ~ 11.1; the device frames the year.
nefanda: cf. 14.10 *nefas*. The colonists have much in common with
Manlius, and the senate's strict response to them foreshadows their
judgment of him.   **inissent:** subjunc. of alleged reason, as if L.
were quoting the senate's response (*NLS* §242 (*b*)).

   17.8 negatum i.e. to the colonists.   **in quo** 'in a matter in
which'.   **ab** 'as regards' (*OLD* 25a). This unusual construction
with *temperare*, with which *ab* + abl. generally indicates the thing
from which one restrains oneself, is occasioned by the need to indicate both the thing avoided (*in quo*) and the person spared.   **temperauerant:** a logical change of subj. from the impersonal decree

to the senators handing it down (Pinkster 169–72).   **senatus uerbis** 'on the senate's behalf' (*OLD uerbum* 14), an abbreviated version of the formula *senatus pop. Rom. uerbis* (Paul on Sall. *J.* 21.4).   **facesserent ... ex urbe:** cf. 4.58.7 *facesserent propere ex urbe finibusque*, Sil. 11.107 *urbe facesse.* The verb is archaizing and choice (Gries 104, Tarrant on Sen. *Ag.* 300).   **ab ore atque oculis:** a traditional doublet (Otto 259 *os* (1)).   **ne ... tegeret:** cf. Cicero's justification of his treatment of the Catilinarian conspirators, e.g. *Cat.* 4.10 *qui autem rei pub. sit hostis eum ciuem esse nullo modo posse.* For *ius tegere* cf. 8.6.7, Cic. *Vat.* 22; for *ne* 'in case ... not' see *NLS* §189.   **nihil:** adv. acc.   **externo, non ciue** ~ 16.5. *externo* is substantive.   **comparatum** is technical of setting up laws etc. (*OLD* 7–8).

18–20 The year 384 B.C.

18–20.12 Internal affairs

The 'fundamental principle in the writing of annalistic pseudo-history' is that one must accept the 'facts' of the historiographical tradition (*CC* 64–5). L. is thus committed to Manlius' execution for treason. Rather than invent a plausible reason for that execution, however, he retains to the end the *color* that Manlius' aims, while highly suspicious, are not demonstrably tyrannous (on rhetorical *colores* or 'slants' in historiography see *CC* 3–8). Manlius is found guilty, but only by a last-minute trick by which the spectating plebs – now his judges (19.7, 20.11) – are made to see him in a different light (20.10–11). Yet the victory of authority is short-lived, vitiating any satisfactory resolution of the *seditio*: plebeian discontent resurfaces almost immediately (20.15–16) and continues to grow. This conforms to a pattern found elsewhere in the *AVC*: when absolute power is imposed on rebellion or dissonance, it often leaves a bad taste that L. does not remove, perhaps as a reminder that unity has its price (Solodow 260, Feldherr 73–87).

One reason that Manlius, though vanquished, retains much of his persuasiveness is that rather than suppressing his doubts about the traditional account, L. shows us where the story fails to fit (18.16, 20.4). But at the end he plays a trick on us, just as the state does on Manlius. Invoking 'what must have been' and appealing to the *consensus* of all men (20.5), he makes Manlius into a moral lesson for reader and *populus* alike. The *status quo* of the historiographical tradition, as well as that of patrician authority, is reaffirmed. Like the plebeian discontent, however, the narrative uneasiness remains (cf. 16.6n.; on plebeian voices and the narrative see 16.4n., 35.10n., 40–1n.).

18.1 Recrudescente: cf. 10.19.20 *recruduit pugna*, Cic. *Fam.* 4.6.2 *quae consanuisse uidebantur recrudescunt*, Tac. *H.* 3.10.3 *crudescere seditio* with H. The medical imagery continues in 2 (n.); for state ∼ body see 3.1n. and for the narrative 'restart' see 16.6n.   **sub exitum anni** 'just before the end of the year'; the expression seems unparalleled, but cf. Tac. *H.* 1.52.1 *sub ipsas superioris anni Kalendas* and the common *sub idem tempus* (*OLD sub* 23a).   **Camillus:** L. embeds him in the list and does not mention him again (11.3n.).

18.2 et patribus et plebi: on the expansion of this table of contents see above, p. 23 n.96.   **peropportune ... data:** cf. Sall. *C.* 16.5 *tutae tranquillaeque res omnes: sed ea prorsus opportuna Catilinae* (Valvo 41); *peropportune* is favoured only by L.   **externa pax:** *res externae* for 384 are thus summarily dismissed. For external peace ∼ internal war see above, p. 11.   **potentem:** to the plebs, Manlius' political and military power is positive (*potentia* = aristocratic influence: *VL* 240–1), but in the late republic *potentia* was code for *dominatio* (*VL* 442–3, Wirszubski 61–5). The perceived danger is shown by Augustus' careful formulation at *RG* 34.3 *potestatis ... nihilo amplius habui quam ceteri qui mihi ... collegae fuerunt* (with Gagé), and confirmed in Manlius' case by the alarming reappearance of *potens* at 15 (n.).   **ducem ... expugnandi:** the missing (external) fight is to be replaced by another (internal); for *fenoris exp.* see below.   **externo ... domesticis:** unlike the plebs, the *patres* distinguish between the two theatres.   **sanandis ... malis:** the patricians read a latent medical metaphor in *fenoris expugnandi* (*OLD expugno* 4b) and respond to it; for *sanare* of political conditions see *OLD* 2b; for *malum* 'disease' see *OLD* 7b, and see 1n.

18.3 acrior is at home in Livian battles and in descriptions of plebeian tribunes (Moore 23–6, Santoro L'hoir (1) 229).   **coorta esset** 'had sprung to the attack', first in L. in this sense (*TLL*). The narrative voice challenges the patrician self-image as doctors of the

state: both sides are at war. **propinquum ... aderat:**
16.6n. **domum:** 14.11n. **nouandarum rerum:** colometry
favours taking this with *principibus*, not *consilia*, from which it is separated by the following advs.; for *princeps* + gerundive cf. 4.48.8 *p.
agendae rei*, fr. inc. trag. 55 R *p. iuris iurandi*. The proverbially unstable
plebs typically desire *res nouae* (Otto 378). **interdiu noctuque:**
cf. 43.18.7, Sall. *J.* 38.3 *diu noctuque*, Petr. 102.5. The frozen form *noctu*
was originally a locative (L–H–S 147). **animorum irarumque**
~ 4 *iram ... spiritus* ~ 5 *inflatus exacerbatusque* (both chiastic).

18.4 accenderat ~ 5 *accensos*, another link between Manlius and
his crowd (cf. 14.6, 16.8). **ignominia ... contumeliam:** cf.
2.38.2, Cic. *Ver.* 2.139, Sen. *Const.* 19.3 and Catiline's complaint of
iniuriae contumeliaeque (Sall. *C.* 35.3: Valvo 42). **inexperto:** first
in prose in L.; the construction + *ad* seems unparalleled (*TLL*). For
the commonplace that unfamiliar wrongs make a greater impression cf. Pub. *Sent.* 234 M, Sen. *Prou.* 4.7 *magis urgent saeua inexpertos.*
quod ... potuisset: Manlius' courage, which L. analyses by
means of virtual *o.o.* (above, p. 13), derives from two sources (*quod
nec ... et*), one a historical *exemplum*, the other his own experience,
to which he accords slightly more rhetorical weight. **ausus
esset:** this and the following subjuncs. are of alleged reason (*NLS*
§240). **in se** 'in his case'. **Cincinnatus Quinctius:** reversal of the 'normal' order *nomen* + *cognomen* (4.23.1 with O., Tac. *A.*
1.8.3 with Goodyear). In historiography such reversal seems often
motivated by artistic reasons (e.g. to produce chiasmus, as 4.23.1,
Tac. *Ag.* 2.1) or (here) to single out an individual: 'even *Cincinnatus* didn't dare'. **uinculorum ... inuidiam:** 'Basis' (4.7n.).
non ... potuisset: he regards this as a military engagement,
giving himself a mini-exhortation in which he takes courage from
his enemy's inferiority (7.3n.). **abdicando:** a rare trans. use
with an office title, also at 39.1 (*TLL*); for the usual construction +
abl. cf. 1.4, 38.9 (above, p. 20).

18.5–15 Domi contionans. Manlius blends *hortatio* elements with *popularis* invective, a technique perhaps borrowed from Sallust (Keitel (2)
79) and in this instance heavily informed by Sallustian language, as
L. works closely with Catiline's two harangues (*C.* 20, 58) and those
of Licinius Macer (*H.* 3.48) and Lepidus (*H.* 1.55). The tone is not

unrelievedly *popularis*, however: there are echoes of Sallust's pro-establishment Philippus (*H.* 1.77) and of Cicero's Cicero (*Cat.* 1–4). This deployment of political rhetoric from both sides reflects Manlius' ambiguous nature (14–16.4n.; on the 'collapse of distinctions that results from the play of literary models' see Hardie 34–5). But in one important way Manlius' densely interwoven text works against him. If his nature is indeterminate, so (perhaps) are his convictions: one can read the speech as a brilliant construction with nothing inside ('empty rhetoric', in fact), an interpretation supported by the fact that at his trial he gives it *again*: it has itself become a topos (20.6–9n.).

This effect is strengthened by Manlius' style, a sustained example of what we have heard from him already, but rare in Livian oratory. The speech is constructed almost entirely of topoi (e.g. 5 'despicable enemy', 7.3n.; 8 *commutatio fortunae*, 16.2n.; 11–12 'former victories', 7.4n.; 13 the ideal general; 14–15 'name' motif, 7.5n.) elaborated through antithesis and adorned with tense-play (e.g. 8, 9, 13: 15.4n.), juxtaposition of opposites (e.g. 6–7), reasoning by questioning (11: 15.11n.). The periods are built from *incisa* (short cola, e.g. 7–8, 14) or elaborately patterned by repetition with *uariatio* (8–9, 13). Thanks to his concentrated verbal pyrotechnics, Manlius sounds more than ever like Seneca's declaimers with their clipped sentences (Bonner (1) 65) and piles of epigrams. (On the speech see also Ullmann (1) 55–6, Valvo 42–5.)

18.5 inflatus refers to Manlius' style as well as to his mood (11.6n.).   **exacerbatus:** apparently a Livian coinage (*TLL*). **iam ... accensos:** 14.9n.; on the metaphor see 14.10n. **quousque tandem:** borrowed from Cic. *Cat.* 1.1 and Sall. *C.* 20.9 at once: as an opening flourish the phrase echoes the consul, but the context fits the revolutionary. Manlius quotes them both in his dual role of *seruator patriae* and *patronus plebis* (on the phrase see D. C. Innes, *C.Q.* 27 (1977) 468).   **ignorabitis** ~ 10 *nec ... noritis?*; for the same reproachful questions in C.'s *hortatio* see 7.3–5. In each half (5–9, 10–15) Manlius begins with 'you' and moves to 'me', from the plebs' natural power (5–7, 10–12) to their potential power under his command (8–9, 13–15).   **uires ... uoluit?:** for the thought that each species has its own means of defence E. J. Kenney compares Lucr. 5.1033–40 *sentit enim uis quisque suas* etc.

(see Costa *ad loc.*); for the plebs ∼ animals cf. Sall. *H.* 3.48.6 (serving the patricians *more pecorum*) and see Otto 55, Opelt 73, 89 (*bestia/belua* in invective).   **natura** ∼ 10 *natura.*   **numerate ... habeatis:** so Macer encourages the plebs to take heart from their numerical superiority (Sall. *H.* 3.48.21); for counting the enemy cf. 12.8, 13.1, Tac. *Ag.* 15.3 *quantulum enim transisse militum si et se Britanni numerent?*   **sitis ... fuistis ... eritis:** all-encompassing; cf. Hom. *Il.* 1.70 τά τ' ἐόντα τά τ' ἐσσόμενα πρό τ' ἐόντα with Pease on Cic. *Diu.* 1.63.   **quot enim** confirms and explains the conclusion to which the plebs will have come after counting themselves.   **circa ... aduersus:** the plebeians are to move from their small crowds around individual patricians to face them as a group. For the declamatory 'antithesis of prepositions' see Bonner (1) 67.   **patronos** ∼ 14 *patronum* (15.8n.); for the word order see 1.2n.   **tot:** sc. *hostes* from *hostem* following.

   18.6 si ... essetis 'even if [*OLD si* 9] you were going to attack them one to one'. The second topic follows naturally; for 'even if' in a sequence of arguments (= the *diuisio*, see 41.4n.) cf. Sen. *Contr.* 2.1.20, 2.3.11 etc.   **acrius ... certaturos:** an old parainetic motif couched in *popularis* language, cf. 3.39.7, 7.25.6 *pro sua libertate* ∼ *pro alieno imperio*, Sall. *H.* 3.48.28 *si quidem maiore cura dominationem illi retinuerint quam uos repetiueritis libertatem*, Tac. *G.* 37.3 *regno ... acrior est ... libertas*. For the underlying idea, that one fights hardest *pro patria* (etc.), see O. p. 510.   **pro:** *certare pro* is previously in Enn. and Sall. (e.g. *C.* 58.11 *pro libertate* ∼ *pro potentia*; see H. on Tac. *H.* 3.1.1).   **dominatione:** a term of abuse in both optimate and *popularis* rhetoric, the basic idea being that anyone whose *potentia* might diminish your own is trying to enslave you (*VL* 562–3, Earl 59–60); see also 11.4n.

   18.7 ostendite ... remittent: the general summarizes the complementary actions of the two sides, with *uariatio* in the form of the protases (imper. ∼ subjunc.): cf. 7.6, 26.43.6 *apparatus belli ... simul et uos instruet et hostes nudabit.*   **ostendite ... habebitis:** good ancient military theory (J. Linderski in W. V. Harris (ed.), *The imperialism of mid-republican Rome* (1984) 133–64); for *o. bellum* cf. 7.30.17 (*auxilia*), Tac. *H.* 3.78.2 with H. One of Manlius' sources points out the converse: Sall. *H.* 1.77.17 *quanto ... auidius pacem petieritis, tanto bellum acrius erit.*   **paratos ad:** the ideal soldier, like his general, will always be prepared (cf. 6.18); for *paratus ad* in such contexts cf. 28.5.2, Caes. *G.* 1.41.2, *C.* 3.85.1, *B. Hisp.* 25.2.   **audendum ... patienda:** the shift to the impersonal prepares for the abrupt, very personal question below. Gerund(ive)s are at home in a *hortatio*; among Manlius' models cf. Sall. *H.* 1.55.7–10 *agendum atque obuiam eundum est ... seruiundum aut imperitandum, habendus metus est aut faciundus.*

18.8 Quousque: turning to his own plight, Manlius repeats the famous adverb, which occurs only once more in the extant *AVC* (33.40.1).   **circumspectabitis:** in 7 he claimed that a demonstration of war, clearly seen (*ostendite ∼ uideant*), would settle the matter. Sight here shows its impotence: his supporters have been watching, but Manlius needs the powerful action implied in *ne ... uidete* below.   **ego ... uestrum ... fortuna:** the same trio as at 12.11 (leader, troops, fortune): see n. He is quoting Cic. *Cat.* 4.18 *uobis populi R. praesidia non desunt: uos ne populo R. deesse uideamini prouidete,* cf. 3.27 *ne uobis nocere possent ego prouidi, ne mihi nocent uestrum est prouidere.*   **quidem** highlights the pronoun (*OLD* 1b).   **ipse ... depuleram:** each element within the chiastic structure (*uindex ... nullus ∼ duci ... depuleram*) is antithetical; there is heavy alliteration with *u-* throughout.   **uisum ∼ uidistis:** he again contrasts efficient 'seeing' with spectating.   **depuleram:** cf. Cic. *Cat.* 3.17 *hanc tantam molem mali a ceruicibus uestris depulissem.*

18.9 quid ... exspectem?: for the phrasing cf. Sall. *H.* 1.77.14 *quid expectatis, nisi forte pudet aut piget recte facere? an Lepidi mandata animos mouere?*   **quid sperem:** ironic; for *sperem ∼ exspectem* see 8.10n.   **inimici:** 16.1n.   **Cassi Maelique:** 17.1n.   **bene ... abominamini:** the audience takes Manlius' suggestion as an omen which they reject in the hopes of averting it (Liebeschuetz 25). The rejection can take the form of an apotropaic noise (as 4.49.16 *ingemuistis*) or a cry (next n.). *bene facitis* is colloquial (*TLL* 11 2123.56–2124.22).   **"di ... haec":** he quotes the audience's reaction to *an ... exspectem?* (40.8n.); for the cry ('originally' in the subjunc.) cf. 28.41.13 *omnes dei omen auertant,* Tac. *A.* 16.35.1 *omen ... dii prohibeant.*   **prohibebunt ∼ prohibeatis** (15.4n.); cf. 14 *prohibete.*   **sed ... descendent:** Livian characters are fond of pointing out that the gods do not actively intervene in times of crisis (e.g. 4.28.4, 5.11.16, 9.9.7). Manlius again has a Sallustian precedent, cf. Sall. *H.* 3.48.15 *quom*

uis omnis, Quirites, in uobis sit ... Iouem aut alium quem deum consultorem
exspectatis?   **uobis** ~ *mihi*: in concluding the first half he unites its
two topics (5n.) as he wishes to unite the actors in co-operation.   **sicut ... ciuibus:** again Manlius draws a parallel between his war deeds and his current activities, between the
patricians and the Gauls (14.4n.); his war service forms a transition
to the next section, in which the plebeian war record serves as foil
to their domestic passivity.   **dederunt:** sc. *mentem.* It was customary to remind the gods of their past aid when asking for more (Appel
153–4, cf. 16.2n.); claiming the gods will not intervene, Manlius
addresses that topos to his human audience.   **armato toga-**
toque ~ *hostibus ... ciuibus.* For the polar expression cf. e.g. 4.10.8
aequauit ... consul togatus armati gloriam collegae. togatus is Cicero's
word of choice to describe his consulate (O. on 4.10.8).   **ciui-**
bus: the hyperbaton (1.2n.) saves the surprise for the end: the *su-*
perbi are – citizens. Such postposition, recommended for implanting
a phrase in a listener's mind (Quint. 9.4.29–30), is a mannerism in
the declaimers, cf. Sen. *Contr.* 2.4.11 (*sed tuo*), 5.9 (*ad uirum*), 7.7.1
(*praeter patrem*).

18.10 auxilium: the tribunician right to intervene on behalf of
the plebs was a defensive power (*CAH*[2] 212–13); Manlius is looking
for offence.   **inimicos:** 16.1n.   **nisi ... sinatis:** cf. Sall. *H.*
3.48.6 *exuti omnibus quae maiores reliquere, nisi quia uobismet ipsi per suf-*
fragia, ut praesides olim, nunc dominos destinatis.   **imperari** ~ 13 *im-*
peret.   **certamen ... noritis:** cf. Sil. 14.141 *secum certamina*
norant.   **natura** lit. 'by birth', cf. Lucr. 4.834–5 *nil ... natumst in*
corpore ut uti | possemus, sed quod natumst id procreat usum.   **natura**
... usu: he tries to distinguish between two concepts which according to proverbial wisdom were virtually the same, habit (*usus* or *con-*
suetudo, cf. 11 *consuestis*) and nature (Otto 90–1, Häussler 71, 265–6).
For the old idea that no one is a slave by nature cf. Alcidamas *apud*
schol. Arist. *Rhet.* 1373b18, Philemon fr. 95 Kock.   **usu** is calculated to remind his audience of the patrician abuse of *usucapio*
('possession', *OLD* 5), cf. 5.4, 34.4.

18.11 cur ... censeatis?: the appeal to former victories is divided between military successes and political ones (12).   **tantum**
animorum ~ 10 *tam ... animus. gerere animos* 'have (proud and
visible) courage' is Livian (also at 1.25.3).   **consuestis:** 10n.

hos i.e. the patricians.   **libertatem** at the end comes as a slight
surprise (9n.): as the bone of contention between the orders, liberty
is imagined to be something the plebs periodically try to capture
(*temptare, OLD* 9) but fail to protect (*tueri, OLD* 3) once they have
it. For Manlius' military imagery see 14.4n.; for *libertatem tueri* cf.
3.45.8 (etc.), Sen. *Contr.* 5.7.

18.12 habuistis ... obtinuistis: extravagant homoioteleuton
stresses the plebeian achievement; for the decoration at the end of
a section see 11.5n.   **obtinuistis** ∼ 15 *obtinenda*.   **omnia adhuc:** e.g. the creation of *tr. pl.* (2.33.2), the right of *conubium* (4.6.3),
admission to the consular tribunate (5.12.9).

18.13 tempus ... conari: for similar transitional sentiments cf.
21.43.8–9 *satis adhuc ... uidistis; tempus est iam ... magna ... pretia me-
reri,* Sall. *J.* 89.3, Vell. 130.3 with W. For *tempus est iam* cf. Cic. *Tusc.*
1.99, Claudius at *CIL* XIII 1.1.1668.2.20.   **Experimini ... expertum:** complicated wordplay, meticulously varied throughout in
form (imper. ∼ participle, possessive adj. ∼ pers. pronoun, noun ∼
adv.). Manlius repeats C. at 5.54.6 *quae ... ratio est expertis talia alia
experiri?* For the participial resumption see 8.1n.   **modo** is idiomatic in commands (*OLD* 1b).   **felicitatem ... feliciter:** the
ideal general's skill was enhanced by *felicitas* (Vell. 106.3 with W.,
Moore 11); see further 12.11n.   **ut spero:** also in Catiline's peroration (Sall. *C.* 20.17), part of which Manlius quotes in 15.   **expertum:** 9.6n. Parainetic generals often mention their own experience
both as part of the 'former victories' topos (7.4n.) and as justification for present policy (cf. 23.9). *experientia* or *usus* ('practice') produces *scientia* and endurance, basic equipment for the ideal general
(cf. Polyb. 9.14, Cic. *Man.* 28, Diod. 15.88, Onas. 10.16, Veg. *Mil.*
3.22, 26).   **minore ... imposuistis:** isocolonic with parallel
word order; *uariatio* is supplied by tense-play with *imponere* (15.4n.)
and *imperet* ∼ *imperantibus* (32.8n.). The real motion is of the root
imper-, which the plebeian champion takes away from the *patres*. For
the wording cf. Sen. *Contr.* 2 *praef.* 1 *plus deinde laboris impendit ut simi-
litudinem eius effugeret quam impenderat ut exprimeret.*   **qui imperet:**
i.e. Manlius.   **qui resisterent:** i.e. the *tr. pl.*; for their defensive
role see 10n.

18.14 solo ... consulatusque recalls – and suggests a fitting
revenge on – the rich who have levelled the mountains in their ra-

paciousness, cf. Sall. *C.* 20.11 *quas* [sc. *divitias*] *profundant in* ... *monti-bus coaequandis.* High places were unsuitable for democracies, which were best established on the plain (Arist. *Pol.* 1330b17–20, cf. 2.9.1–3 with O.); see 19.1n.   **ut ... possit:** his insistence that drastic measures are needed to counter the imbalance in the state stands in ironic counterpoise to the even-handed *maiestas* with which C. could work (6.7, 18: Valvo 44).   **adeste** appears in calls for divine and for citizen aid, cf. 29.2, 2.55.7 with O. and Appel 115–16.   **prohibete ... dici:** Manlius refers to the economic situation for the first and last time; *ius* = 'judicial pronouncement' (*OLD* 4).   **ego ... plebis:** cf. Cic. *Cat.* 2.11 *huic ego me bello du-cem profiteor, Quirites.* For *patronus*, a title eventually adopted by the emperors and closely associated with *pater* (14.5n.), *cura* (below), and *custos* (6.15n.) see W. on Vell. 120.1; on Manlius the patron see 15.8n.   **quod ... nomen** 'a title which' ~ 15 *quo ... nomine.* **cura ... et fides:** the virtues of a patron. On *cura* see 15.11n.; on *fides* see *VL* 23–35, *FRR* 406.   **nomen induit:** cf. Cic. *Fin.* 2.73 *et torquem et cognomen induit,* Sil. 9.545–6.

18.15 uos ... utemini: he again quotes Catiline (Sall. *C.* 20.16 *uel imperatore uel milite me utimini*), a particularly sinister echo that undermines Manlius' democratic sentiments.   **insigni:** 16.8n. **imperii honorisue** 'of authority or office', virtually a hendiadys; cf. 37.11, Cic. *Sest.* 17, Sall. *J.* 4.7.   **uestrum ... ducem:** 1.2n. **eo:** the title (*Rex*) remains unspoken (see also 17.5n.). The flow of the sentence suggests that *eo*, anticipated by *si quo*, refers back to *nomine*; it may, however, pick up *ducem* (Radice), a reading sup-ported by the Sallustian *me utimini* (quoted above).   **poten-tiore** ~ 2 *potentem* ... *ducem* (n.). Manlius avoids applying the adj. to himself.

18.16 inde ... traditur: L. waits until almost the last moment to introduce the charge of *regnum* – and his doubts about it. In con-trast, Manlius' models are identified as would-be tyrants at the start (2.41.2 Cassius, 4.13.4 Maelius, Sall. *C.* 5.6 Catiline). Though his motives were a declamatory topic (Quint. 7.2.2), no other surviving narrative seems to have treated him so ambiguously: in Dio he even occupies the Capitoline (7.26.2, cf. Diod. 15.35.2, Plut. *Cam.* 36.2–3). If he is presented positively, it is exclusively in the context of the Gallic war (as Virg. *A.* 8.652–62; for traces of a pro-Manlian tradi-

tion see Wiseman 239).   **inde:** i.e. Manlius' last sentence (Lipovsky
38).   **ortum initium:** 12.10n.; for this combination cf. Caes. *G.*
5.26.1, Tac. *H.* 1.39.2 with H.   **dicitur ... traditur:** repeated
emphasis on the historiographical tradition's failure to provide a
plausible story. Diffident gestures such as *dicitur* are usually taken
to indicate that an author is unwilling to vouch for the historicity
of an event (despite their often being followed by an account of
that event, as 20.6, 40.2: J. L. Moles, *C.Q.* 41 (1991) 553). *dicitur*
appeals to the topos 'I tell the tale that I heard told' (Fehling
104, 164), with which the historian subsumes his personal authority
in the wider authority of the narrative tradition; it also gestures at
stories about Manlius that L. has chosen not to tell, introducing 'a
kind of floating narrative' (Hartog 271–2). See also 16.4n.   **cum
quibus:** since L. has ready-made conspirators (3) and could have
elaborated the *consilia* (as at 11.7–8), his use of this historiographical *praeteritio* makes Manlius act almost in a vacuum (who has lis-
tened to the speech?) while adding to the unreality of the charge
of *regnum*. The contrast with Maelius, whose plans are reported by
an informant (4.13.8–9), is instructive: L. neither has, nor has invented, a character or a source to betray Manlius.

    19.1 At ... agitat: the exhortation (18) is balanced by this coun-
cil scene (Keitel (1) 164–6), as both sides prepare for battle (cf.
18.3).   **At:** despite L.'s much-discussed liking for 'dramatic' composition, esp. peripeteia (3.4n.) and contrast (e.g. 16.2n.), he is less
fond of *at* than other historians, with *c.* 80 exx., the same number
as in the much smaller *corpora* of Sall. and Curt. (*TLL*).   **de secessione:** the possibility of secession suggested by the migrations to
Veii (4.5n.) and by the centurion (14.3–10n.) becomes a reality from
the patrician point of view. If taken to its natural extreme, Manlius'
secessio would entail plebeian occupation of the *arx*, an enemy at the
city centre pushing the *patres* out from within, and would physically
put the *patres* in the place of the Gauls, who besieged the *arx* from
their headquarters in the Forum (5.42–3, cf. 14.4n. for Manlius'
habit of comparing the patricians to the Gauls).   **in domum
priuatam:** 14.11n.   **forte ... positam:** the most important
piece of information is added, slyly, as an afterthought. Manlius'
obsession with the Capitoline (5.6n.) is an indirect clue to his tyrannical motives (Jaeger 358); see also 18.14n., 20.13n.   **imminenti**

mole: sc. *de* and cf. 7.10.9 *Gallus uelut moles superne imminens*. Manlius' house lit. overhangs the centre of *libertas*, the Forum (Duker). For the threatening high house cf. 2.7.11 *non obstabunt ... aedes libertati*, Sen. *Contr.* 2.5.1, Sen. *Thy.* 641–5 with Tarrant, Tac. *A.* 3.9.3 *domus foro imminens* (an *irritamentum inuidiae*), 15.69.1; on their size (*moles*) and prestige see T. P. Wiseman in *L'Urbs: espace urbain et histoire* (1987), 393–413.

   19.2 Seruilio Ahala 'a Servilius Ahala'; for the use of a proper name – usually plural – to indicate a type cf. 4.2.7 *Canuleios igitur Iciliosque consules fore*, Cic. *Pis.* 2 *Piso est a populo Romano factus, non iste Piso*. L. tends to name characters by *praenomen + nomen* (e.g. 6.12–14, 15.5, 38.10); *nomen + cognomen* here specifies the particular kind of Servilius needed: one derivation of the *cognomen* Axilla (later Ahala) was that C. Servilius hid the dagger with which he killed Maelius in his armpit (*ala*: Maltby 20).   **iubendo ... iactura:** 13.5n.   **irritet** ~ 16.7 *irritatur*; the *magna pars* seems to have been reading L.'s text. For characters picking up expressions from the narrative cf. 22.7 (n.), 23.9 (n.), 28.8 (n.), 5.27.3 *scelesto facinori scelestiorem sermonem addit* ~ 5.27.5 *'scelestus ipse cum scelesto munere uenisti'* and see Feldherr 158–60.   **publicum hostem:** another Catilinarian touch (Valvo 45–6), cf. e.g. Cic. *Cat.* 1.13 *exire ex urbe iubet consul hostem*, Sall. *C.* 36.2 with McGushin.   **unius ... ciuis:** cf. 2.35.3 *adeo infensa erat coorta plebs ut unius poena defungendum esset patribus*, Cic. *Cat.* 2.7 *uno ... Catilina exhausto ... recreata res pub. uidetur*. With this redefinition of *unus* Manlius changes from being *solus* in a positive sense (the 'one and only', 11.3n.) to *solus* 'abandoned' (*OLD* 2). Once *unus* for *omnes*, he will soon be *unus* against *omnes*.   **iactura:** technical of war losses (*OLD* 5). On the legal basis for tyrannicide see Lintott 54–8.

   19.3 decurritur: cf. 38.3. L. may be quoting Caes. *C.* 1.5.3 *decurritur ad illud extremum atque ultimum senatus consultum*.   **leniorem ... uim tamen:** cf. 3.40.7 *sententia asperior in speciem, uim minorem aliquanto habuit*, Tac. *A.* 2.36.4 *fauorabili in speciem oratione uim imperii tenuit*.   **sententiam:** i.e. *senatus consultum* (*OLD* 5).   **ut ... capiat:** the *senatus consultum ultimum* (Lintott 149–74). Its earliest certain use was in 121; the anachronism intensifies Manlius' ties with the late-republican politicians against whom it was passed (e.g. Catiline, Clodius, Caesar: Valvo 45).   **perniciosis:** scarce in L. (9)

and with two exceptions (4.52.3, 25.31.15) used of internecine disturbance, a connection that is entirely Ciceronian (Vell. 47.5 with W.);
on its place in anti-*popularis* invective see *VL* 532 and for *p. consilia*
cf. Cic. *Dom.* 114, Vell. 2.3.2, Sen. *Ben.* 6.8, Tac. *A.* 12.22.2.

19.4 tribunique pl.: the orders also united against Cassius
(2.41.4). The plebeians would normally meet separately (as 3.17.1,
another Catilinarian episode). Their presence here distantly heralds
the *concordia ordinum* toward which the pentad is heading (Lipovsky
85–6); more immediately, that the *tr. pl.* take the initiative (6) is a
foretaste of things to come (35–42). **quia … cernebant:**
there is room for individual *potestas* only when the whole is free; in
a *regnum* the king alone is powerful. For *cernebant* see 12.1n. **ei:**
3.7n. **et** 'also'. **patrum auctoritati:** there is 'nothing more
Ciceronian' than the image of the *concordia ordinum* dutifully subject
to the authority of the senate (Valvo 47); on that *auctoritas* see *VL*
311–12, Wirszubski 113, 119. **quid … sit** 'what they should
do'. For the archaizing and Sallustian *opus esse* + perf. pass. participle see Vretska on Sall. *C.* 1.6 and Roby §1255.

19.5 uim et caedem 'violent death' (hendiadys picked up by
eam below): the usual solution. This *seditio* is remarkable for *not* ending in violence (A. W. Lintott, *Historia* 19 (1970) 12–29). **dimicationis:** gen. of description (*NLS* §85 1 (c)). **tr. plebis:** like Licinius
and Sextius, these tribunes recommend legal methods (cf. 35.9–10);
patrician responses to domestic trouble in Book 6 are consistently
violent or excessive. For the contrast of good and bad judgment in
a council scene see Keitel (1) 165–6.

19.6–7 The *tr. pl.* propose that the people direct their seditious
violence at Manlius. His death, for which the entire community
will then be responsible, will unify the state (a version of an ancient
socio-religious pattern: in general Feldherr 49–65). Their logic is
familiar: clear sight and open demonstration (7 *uiderint … intuebuntur
… in medio*) will lead to truth. In particular, they hope that if they
can apply the 'proper' labels to the actors (Manlius = *patricius*,
plebs = *accusatores*) then words like *libertas* will be applicable to only
one side of the debate (14.5nn.).

19.6 patrum et plebis: i.e. *patrum cum plebe.* **pestiferum:**
the tribunes' adj. will be ironically fulfilled, since his death will entail plague (20.15). *pestifer* is only here in L. of a person; for the Ci-

ceronian expression cf. *Sest.* 78 *qui ab illo pestifero ac perdito ciui ... rei pub. sanguine saginantur* (also echoed at 17.2) and Opelt 138–9. **quid ... ruat?:** the tribunes' epigrammatic style is less frigid than Manlius', though using similar means to underscore a paradox: 'antithesis of prepositions' (*cum ~ per*: 18.5n.) and verbal polyptoton with *aggredi* (15.4n.). **cum plebe:** with *eum*. **suis ... ruat?:** cf. 2.44.2 *tribuniciam potestatem ... suis ipsam uiribus dissolui*, Hor. *Epod.* 16.2, *C.* 3.4.65, Luc. 1.81 *in se magna ruunt*, Tac. *H.* 4.17.3 with H. See E. Dutoit, *R.E.L.* 14 (1936) 365–73 and cf. 17.1n.

19.7 nihil ... est i.e. the word '*popularis*', derived from *populus* (= all the Romans, *OLD* 2b), is antithetical to '*rex*'. This redefinition is a Ciceronian ploy, e.g. *Har.* 42 *ut homo popularis fraudaret ... populum*, *Cat.* 4.9 *animum uere popularem saluti populi consulentem* (Seager (1) 333–6). For the form of expression cf. Cic. *Agr.* 1.23, *Lig.* 37, *Att.* 2.20.4; for the form of argument (*definitio*) see 7.3n. **simul:** 7.6n. **non:** with *secum*. **aduocatis:** non-technical ('Manlius' supporters'). **iudices:** cf. 2.35.2 *se iudicem quisque, se dominum uitae necisque inimici factum uidebat.* **accusatores ... reum:** accs.; chiasmus with *uariatio* emphasizes the adversative asyndeton. **crimen:** a third obj. of *intuebuntur*. **in medio:** 15.13n. **nulli** 'no one'. **fauebunt** 'will side with': this is a contest between Manlius and *libertas*. For *fauere* in political/legal contexts see *OLD* 3a, *VL* 177–8; for the *fauor plebis* see 17.1n.

20.1 Quod ... factum: 9.10n.

20.2 sordidatum reum uiderunt ~ 19.7 *patricium reum intuebuntur*: the plebs do not read Manlius' isolation as the *tr. pl.* intended them to. For *squalor* see 16.4n. **nec ... Manlios:** the list of those who have deserted him moves from less to more closely related; for these 'cercles de solidarité' in late-republican judicial proceedings see David 171–226. **quod** 'something which'; the following *ut*-clause is in apposition. **ad eum diem numquam:** another first, motivated by Manlius' unique action (3 *primus ... defecisset*: 11.7n.). His isolation recalls that of Catiline in the Curia (Cic. *Cat.* 1.16). **usu uenisset** 'had occurred' (*OLD usus* 8a), only here in L. **ut ... mutarent:** 16.4n. For the connection of early *squalor* with the Claudii (below) cf. 2.61.5 with O., who suggests that they may have invented the custom.

20.3 Ap. Claudio ... defecisset: the voice of the crowd

(16.5n.).   **Ap. Claudio:** the *exemplum* serves the immediate rhetorical purpose: if the Claudii could support their most infamous
member (3.58.1–6), why have the Manlii deserted their less noxious
relative (a comparison *a maiore ad minus*: Lausberg §376)? But Appius
was also the pattern of Roman tyrants (Vasaly 212–22), and possessed a domineering nature which he covered with a *popularis*
mask (3.36.1). He is an exceptionally unfortunate exemplar for Manlius. See also 40.2n., 41.10n., and for unstable *exempla* see Chaplin
118–19 on 28.43.19.   **consensu opprimi:** cf. 4.14.5 *opprimi se*
consensu patrum dicere, quod plebi benigne fecisset [sc. *Maelius*]. Focalized
by the crowd, *consensus* has an ugly tone, providing a view of authority turned to conspiracy (*OLD* 1b, *VL* 124).   **primus ... ad plebem** ~ 11.7; the ring will be closed with Manlius' obituary (12–
16 ~ 11.2).   **defecisset:** sarcastic; it would be subjunc. of alleged reason in *o.r.* Manlius' 'defection' balances the plebeian
tribunes' 'surrender' (19.4): while *defec-/defic-* is regular of Rome's
allies, only here in Book 6 is it applied to a Roman, the implication being that the plebs and *patres* inhabit separate cities, one of
which is subordinate to the other (11.7n.).

20.4–12. First the sentence, then the evidence. L.'s presentation of the
trial is curiously oblique. The accusation is perfunctory and par-
tially 'not found' (4), while the defence forms part of the moral
drawn by the narrator (5–9). It is not until 10 that the narrative
resumes. The *tr. pl.* believed that Manlius would be convicted as
soon as the plebs saw him for what he 'is', but his isolation, patrician status, and even the *crimen regni* are insufficient to turn them
against him. L. continues to play his double game, letting Manlius
speak persuasively, even emphasizing the difficulty in convicting
him, but at the same time nullifying his apology in advance by
filtering it through the lens of the *cupiditas regni* (5). At this point,
and only here, the *crimen regni* is assumed to be a true charge in
order to illustrate a higher moral point. *regnum* is unequivocally
bad in the *AVC* (e.g. 2.1.9; see in general Erskine); by presenting
Manlius as an example of its pernicious effects L. can appeal to a
new consensus – that of all men – to condemn him in advance.
Only then is Manlius allowed to speak (6–9). L.'s procedure corresponds to the magistrates': they remove Manlius' visual persuasion
(11), L. his verbal. Ostensibly offered the chance to judge the con-

flicting evidence, the *populus* and the reader are at the last presented with a *fait accompli*.

20.4 Cum dies uenit: adversative asyndeton (~1 *primo*). **praeter ... indicium:** an impressive list, comprising nearly all the standard 'proofs' of revolutionary aims (see 11.8n., 14.11n., 16.6n.). L.'s dismissal of them in this *praeteritio* is startling. See also 18.16n. **uoces** 'speeches' (*OLD* 7); cf. 15.6 *multitudinem ... concitari* (n.). **pertinentia:** technical of coming within the scope of something, esp. legally (*OLD* 7, cf. 41.4); *p. proprie* is scholarly jargon (*OLD* 3a, cf. Cels. 1.3.6, Quint. 2.10.15, Gaius *Inst.* 2.243 and the frequent use of *proprie* in scholia, e.g. Servius). **ab accusatoribus:** the prosecution presented its case first. **auctorem:** 12.2n.; for *apud* 'in (a writer)' see *OLD* 6.

20.5 nec dubito 'but I do not doubt' (*OLD nec* 5). With 4 *apud ... inuenio* this echoes the opening of L.'s first scholarly digression (12.2); in what follows, L. will deploy two of the arguments there advanced, verisimilitude and consensus (12.4–6). **haud parua:** litotes (13.8n.). **cum ... fuerit:** causal. **mora** 'obstacle'. This report of the plebeian volte-face, like the phrase *foeda ... regni* below, brings in the verdict without argument, side-stepping the trial. The plebeian action has a (motivated) parallel at Sall. *C.* 48.1 *plebs coniuratione patefacta ... mutata mente Catilinae consilia execrari*; for L.'s procedure here see 4–12n. **plebi** 'so far as the plebs were concerned'. **in causa** 'in the legal case'. **in loco:** i.e. the trial venue (10–11). **illud ... uidetur** singles out one important element, cf. Cic. *Or.* 58, Vell. 52.4, 67.2; for such impersonal statements in L. see Steele 19–20. **ut sciant homines:** an obtrusive appeal to the reader (cf. 9.26.18, 22.25.14, Sen. *Suas.* 6.1.1, Sen. *Ep.* 81.13, 95.28, [Quint.] *Decl.* 329.6, Tac. *Ag.* 42.4). For the didactic function of history see above, p. 14. **quae ... reddiderit:** cf. Vell. 72.1 *diem quae illi omnes uirtutes unius temeritate facti abstulit*. Both are versions of the theme of a noble life marred or spoiled by a shameful end (W. on Vell. 87.1). **foeda cupiditas:** cf. Curt. 5.7.1 *uini cupiditate foedauit*, Stat. *Th.* 3.370 *f. cupido*. Desire – for wealth, sex, and above all power – is the fundamental characteristic of tyranny, which 'has *eros* as its vocation' (Hartog 330, cf. *CC* 80). By identifying Manlius' motivation in these words L. can bypass all proofs: the hint of such passion damns him. *cupid-*

is restricted in Book 6 to potentially transgressive desire (6.1 plebeian *c. agri*, 35.6 *immodica c.*); for its (negative) exemplary power
see Feldherr 206–8.   **ingrata ... inuisa:** cf. Cic. *Man.* 47,
Curt. 7.1.23, Sen. *Ben.* 2.11.6. L. tells us how to interpret the spectacle we are about to witness (cf. 14.2).   **inuisa** lit. 'looked askance
at': Manlius' ambition renders the outward signs of his excellence
not only unmeaningful but actively not-to-be-watched. Yet the
moral, however easily drawn, is challenged by the subsequent demonstration of the power of visual symbols (6–9). The *decora* must
be made *inuisa* – 'invisible' – by the authorities before they can
demonstrate his guilt (10–11). For the punning connection of *inuisa*
'hateful' and sight cf. 21.63.8, Ter. *Hec.* 597 *uideo me esse inuisam*,
Austin on Virg. *A.* 2.601.

20.6–9. The defence. Manlius' show-and-tell *apologia*, the climax of
this story which has centred around display and its effects, is his
answer to the 'show me' tactics of the opposition (15.5, 19.7). The
emphasis falls not on his words but on the things he produces (6–
8), and on the way he directs his audience's point of view (9). L.
concentrates on the metonymic representations of Manlius' *facta*
(e.g. Servilius 'stands for' the battle in which Manlius saved his
life): in this speech the concept of *euidentia* is dramatized (8n.,
1.3n.). But Manlius has left it until too late. As the *seditio* narrative
has moved from *facta* to *orationes* (14.2n., 15.13n.), so Manlius' displays have become progressively less 'real': at 14.3–10 he frees a
man on the spot; at 15.9–10 he claims, in *o.r.*, to be rescuing citizens and instructs others how to do so; at 17.4 an imaginary Manlius rescues *ciues*; here he shows, in *o.o.*, symbols of his past rescues
(see also 14.11n.). Moreover, the *oratio* accompanying the display is
hardly audible (8n. (*facta ... aequando*)), while the whole is part of
the moral L. is drawing to show why Manlius was convicted (5). In
such a context it is not surprising that the tribunes can annul Manlius' content by removing his form (10–11).

20.6 homines ... prohibuisset: Manlius begins with his acts
domi; he will move backwards, ending with his Capitoline exploit.
dicitur: 18.16n.   **prope quadringentos:** this and the numbers
in 7 lend a sense of reliability to the report (the totals are traditional
and may vary, cf. Plin. *NH* 7.103); for the reassurance provided by
numerical detail see Fehling 216–17. Manlius is in effect pronoun-

cing his own eulogy (Jaeger 361, see further 7n., 12–16n.); for precise data in laudatory accounts of a career see T. P. Wiseman, *RPL* 4–7.   **produxisse:** technical of producing a witness in court (*OLD* 2b); on *testes* see David 474–87.   **quibus ... tulisset** 'to whom he had lent [*OLD fero* 24b] money without interest'.   **quorum ... quos:** for the oratorical anaphora see 40.2n.

20.7 decora ... belli: both physical (7) and metaphorical (8, the *ciues*).   **commemorasse** ~ 8 *memorasset* (n.). *commemorare* 'put on record' is the *mot juste* for recalling past services (e.g. 3.56.9, 45.44.8) or wrongs (e.g. 42.52.6) in order to compel present help or attention.   **protulisse:** technical of producing supporting evidence (*OLD* 5).   **conspicienda** 'to be looked at', like the city monuments (4.12n.); for the predicative gerundive of purpose see *NLS* §207 (3). Manlius' display resembles that of a triumphing general (for rescued citizens on parade in a triumph cf. 30.45.5 and see Weinstock 136; for crowns cf. App. *BC* 8.66), and description of triumphs was a panegyrical motif (W. on Vell 121.2): both L. and Manlius are constructing his *laudatio*, muted though it is (see also 6n.).   **spolia ... dona:** appositional to and explanatory of *decora*.   **ad** 'approximately' (*OLD* 20a).   **coronas:** the *c. muralis* (a turreted crown) was awarded for being the first to scale an enemy's walls; the *ciuica*, an oak wreath, was given *ob ciues seruatos* and in the late republic was connected with the title *parens patriae* (Weinstock 152, 163–7, 202–3; see 14.5n.). Manlius' extraordinary total of eight *c. ciuicae* makes him more than a match for the most recent recipients, Caesar and Augustus; see A. Wallace-Hadrill, *P.C.P.S.* 216 (1990) 159, 166.

20.8 ad hoc ... nominatum ~ 6 *homines*, framing the first section.   **ex hostibus ciues:** pointed juxtaposition.   **absentem:** the *mag. equit.*, who is curiously not present – because the rescue itself is not narrated in the *AVC*? – bears the same name as Maelius' assassin; L. tactfully omits his cognomen.   **pro fastigio rerum** 'in accordance with the importance of the deeds' (*rerum = r. gestarum*, cf. 1.1–2). *fastigium* in this sense is first here (*OLD* 7); it calls to mind the physical *fastigium* on which triumphal spoils were displayed (*OLD* 3a, see 7n.). The height imagery is ominous.   **fastigio ... magnifica:** a type of chiasmus (*f. rerum = summae res*) with juxtaposed opposites. Like *inflatus* (11.6n.), *magnifica*

refers both to Manlius' style (*OLD* 1d) and his manner (*OLD* 4).
facta dictis aequando: a tag that describes the difficulty of 're-
creating' events as vividly as possible, e.g. Isoc. 4.13 'it is difficult
to find words equal to the magnitude of the deeds', Plin. *Ep.*
8.4.3, Sall. *C.* 3.2, L.'s source (on writing history); on it see J. Diggle,
P.A.C.A. 17 (1983) 59–60. Manlius has already performed a literal
sub oculos subiectio by displaying his awards, and continues to use
visual aids as he points to the Capitoline. But despite the number
of 'speech' verbs in the *o.o.* (9n.), L. does not reproduce Manlius'
words before his closing prayer, which sounds eerily like his *hortatio*. If persuasion means moving an audience by drawing a word-
picture of events so convincing that they 'see it your way', then
Manlius cannot possibly persuade: the *oratio* that might have accompanied this display is several pages back. L. has effectively separated Manlius' *facta* from his *dicta* – appropriately enough, since
he is no longer speaking to an audience whom he *can* persuade (cf.
40–1n.).   **memorasset ~ 7 *commemorare*:** Manlius continues to
produce his own, alternative history (11.4n.; for *memoria* = 'history'
cf. 1.2, 17.4 and *OLD* 7–8, *memoro* 3).   **insigne ~ 7 *insignes*;** his
body bears signs of his deeds equivalent to the signs he has produced above (Serres 237–40).   **cicatricibus ... acceptis:**
14.6n.; for scars as 'evidence' at a trial see Oakley (1) 409.

    20.9 spectans: Manlius' own gaze directs the audience's toward
the hill (esp. *intuentes ... uersi* below), the culmination of his visual
display.   **deosque alios:** 16.2n.   **deuocasse** recalls his assurance that the gods would not descend on his account (18.9).
auxilium: for the various *preces iuuandi* see Appel 127–8.   **precatusque:** as he begins his peroration, the *uerba dicendi* punctuating
the speech (7–8 *commemorasset, nominatum, memorasset*) change to 'prayer'
words (cf. *orasse* below and see Lambert 56–7).   **quam ...
darent ~** 18.9. The appeal (with which cf. Dion. Hal. 14.4.6) is
couched in Manlius' typical rhetoric, with tense play (18.5–15n.),
'antithesis of prepositions' (*ad ~ in*: 18.5n.), and the *commutatio fortunae* motif (16.2n.).   **Capitolinam arcem:** in L. only otherwise at
28.39.15 (11.4n.).   **ad salutem ~ 8 *seruatos*** (17.5n.).   **dedissent ... darent:** solemn, prayer-like repetition, reinforced by the
iteration of *pop. Romanus* (for which cf. 1.24.7–8, 5.21.15).   **singulos uniuersosque:** 15.11n.   **ut ... iudicarent ~** *identidem*

... *suarum* above (*Capitolium* ∼ *Capitolium*, *intuentes* ∼ *spectans*, *ad deos* ∼ *deosque*). The parallelism makes inevitable the further correspondence *iudicarent* ∼ *auxilium*: acquittal is their only option.   **ut ... ut:** anaphora 'characteristic of a formal style' (O. on 5.21.14).

20.10 In campo ... citaretur: L. returns to the trial, whose mechanics are confused and partly anachronistic. Ancient treason trials were handled by *duumuiri*; later, the *tr. pl.* served as prosecutors and the whole ended with a vote of the *comitia centuriata*, an assembly of the *populus*, as here (Taylor 100–3). But 19.6 *per ipsam plebem* implied trial by the *concilium plebis*, an exclusively plebeian assembly (Wiseman 240, Taylor 60). L. has the *duumuiri* as a variant (12n.).   **populus:** 19.7n.   **et reus ... auertisset:** we come in on the end of Manlius' speech (∼9 *uersi*).   **manus tendens:** the quintessential supplicatory gesture (Appel 195–7); there are exx. as early as Hom. *Il.* 1.351.   **nisi ... decoris:** for a third time, the people's *oculi* are in thrall to some kind of power (cf. 15.13, 16.3). By removing the sight of the hill (below) the tribunes expect to free the people from rhetorical manipulation; one is reminded of the traitorous colonists, banished from the Romans' sight (17.8). **liberassent** represents a fut. perf. in *o.r.*; for *oculos l.* cf. Curt. 10.2.27 *liberate oculos meos*, and for the theme of freedom see 11.8n.: it is here somewhat ironically deployed.   **tanti ... decoris:** rather than refuting Manlius' glory, the prosecution sidesteps it. **memoria:** not just 'memory' but 'memorial' (*OLD* 10). On the power of *loca* cf. Cic. *Scaur.* 46–7, *Fin.* 5.2 *curiam ... solebam intuens Scipionem Catonem Laelium, nostrum uero ... auum cogitare; tanta uis admonitionis inest in locis*, Ov. *M.* 13.5–6, Sen. *Suas.* 6.21 *nulla non pars fori aliquo actionis inclutae signata uestigia erat* [sc. *Ciceronis*], Quint. 5.10.40–1, and see David 472–4 on monuments which 'enracinaient ... le souvenir de leur puissance et de leurs bienfaits dans la mémoire collective'. On Manlius' manipulation of the Capitoline see Jaeger 360–2.   **praeoccupatis** has military associations (*OLD* 1); outside L. *animos praeoc.* is at Caes. *C.* 2.34.6, *B. Alex.* 63.2.   **uero crimini:** since we are still in *o.o.* the adj. is focalized by the tribunes, not the narrator.   **locum:** in view of *praeoccupatis* above, this seems to have a military sense ('strategic position'); for *l. occupare* see *OLD locus* 8.

20.11 prodicta: technical for adjourning proceedings (*OLD*

2b).   **in ... lucum ... non esset:** on the topographical difficulties created here see Wiseman 225–43.   **concilium populi:**
10n.   **triste ... inuisum:** Manlius' near success even after L.'s
and the tribunes' trickery (18–20.11n.) casts doubt once more on the
crimen. Force, it seems, has triumphed over justice. Nor is the verdict's unpopularity mitigated by an official pronouncement on its
rightness; L. is not even sure that it was the people who con-
demned Manlius (12). See also 15n., 21n., and see Feldherr 180–3,
189.   **inuisum:** 5n.

20.12 sunt ... damnatum: the plot variant, typically, comes at
the end (12.2–6n.); for the *duumuiri* see 10n. and R. A. Bauman, *The
duumuiri in the Roman criminal law* (1969).   **damnatum:** sc. *eum
esse*.

20.12–16. End of the year

384 ends with an obituary and a plague. Ancient historians regularly wrote obituary notices for their important characters (Sen.
Suas. 6.21), a practice that can be traced back to Homer (Pomeroy
1–11). Form and content were fixed, though variations were possible. In Manlius' obituary the conventional report of a man's *gesta*
is displaced by the account of his post-mortem erasure (13–14); it is
found instead in his self-defence (6–9) which like many epitaphs details his accomplishments in peace and war, including a list of the
men he saved (cf. the fifth-century Athenian who saved three
φυλαί (Pomeroy 15–16), *CIL* VI 1527.2.11–21 (a wife saves her husband's life)).

Tribuni ... deiecerunt: for executions from the Tarpeian rock
see J.-M. David in *Du châtiment dans la cité* (1984) 131–75.   **locus
... fuit:** obituaries regularly evaluated the appropriateness of a
death, considering above all whether it matched the *fortuna* the person had enjoyed in life. Manlius' death is ironically suitable. The
sentiment is of a type particularly beloved of the declamation
schools; for place of death = place of glory cf. the nailing of Cicero's head and hands to the Rostra (e.g. fr. 60, Sen. *Suas.* 6.19)
and cf. Dio. 42.5.1–6 (day of glory = day of defeat). An additional
piquancy which L. does not mention is that the man who did *not*

alert the Capitoline garrison was similarly punished (5.47.10).
eximiae is the adj. Manlius applied to C. (11.3); it does not occur
elsewhere in the book.   **eximiae ... ultimae:** the best ∼ the
final distinction; for the word order see 9.6n. For the contrast cf.
Curt. 8.1.15, V. Max. 2.6.8 *summae dignitatis ... femina sed ultimae iam
senectutis*; for superlatives in obituaries cf. Plat. *Phaedr.* 118, Xen.
Anab. 2.6, *CIL* I² 2.9 *honc oino ploirume cosentiont R[omae]* | *duonoro
optumo fuise uiro*, Curt. 10.1.38, App. *BC* 4.132.

    20.13 notae: condemnatory marks made by the censors next
to names on the census list (*OCD*). Manlius' true nature has been
ascertained and his corpse (*mortuo*) can be stamped 'guilty'.
publica una: sc. *nota*. The would-be tyrant's house is destroyed
(Saller 354–5; on Manlius see Bayet 118–19, Wiseman 233 n.44).
Throughout the *AVC*, L. marks these spots by identifying the
places to which they correspond in contemporary Rome (cf. 2.5.2,
41.11, 4.16.1, 8.19.4). The historian thus recovers the sites for the
libera ciuitas by recording their new, safer names.   **quod ...
habitaret** is appositional to *una* (Roby §1701).   **ubi ... est:** it
is perhaps no more than coincidental that the temple eventually
built on the site of Manlius' house was attached to the mint: he
will become the guardian of the people's treasure after all. On
L.'s habit of rounding off an episode with a topographical notice
see O. pp. 77, 109; for the temple (whose site is uncertain) see A.
Ziolkowski, *C.P.* 88 (1993) 206–19.   **latum** 'a motion was proposed' (and passed: *OLD* 28a).   **ne quis ... habitaret:** 19.1n.

    20.14 gentilicia: obituaries regularly placed a man in the con-
text of his family's achievements, a topos which L. replaces with the
gentilicia nota, cf. 33.21.5, Herod. 1.30 (Tellus' children), Polyb.
36.16.6 (Masinissa's dynasty), *CIL* I² 2.12 (a Scipio whose epitaph
contains only his father's deeds), Vell. 1.11.6, Tac. *A.* 3.75.1. Manlius will serve as a positive *exemplum* for at least one of his descendants in the *AVC* (7.10.3).   **ne quis ... uocaretur:** for the ban-
ning of Manlius' *praenomen* cf. 2.2.3–11 (expelling '*Tarquinius*'), Tac.
A. 3.17.4 (Piso), Plut. *Cic.* 49.6 (Antony) and the related custom of
erasing names from the Fasti (cf. Cic. *Sest.* 33, Tac. *A.* 3.17.4) and
from inscriptions (still observed in the case of Fascist inscriptions in
Rome).   **hunc exitum habuit:** the historian's summation. For
the obituary formula *hunc exitum* cf. Plat. *Phaedr.* 118 with H. MacL.

Currie, *Latomus* 48 (1989) 344–53, Vell. 72.1 with W.   **nisi ...
esset:** if the *magis quam*-epigram facilitates a contrast between appearance and reality (10.9n.), the *nisi*-epigram embodies the essence
of point: paradox and surprise (Plass 62–4). Here the punchline
comes with the sentence-final *memorabilis* (cf. e.g. Vell. 29.3 *ciuis in
toga, nisi ubi uereretur ne quem haberet parem, modestissimus*); it is often
found in the *nisi*-clause (e.g. Tac. *H.* 1.49.4 *omnium consensu capax imperii nisi imperasset*). For *nisi*-epigrams in obituaries cf. Sen. *Suas.* 6.24
(Pollio on Cicero) *ego ne miserandi quidem exitus eum fuisse uocarem, nisi
ipse tam miseram mortem putasset*, Tac. *H.* 1.49.4 (quoted above), Dio
78.41.2–4.   **in libera ciuitate:** cf. 40.6, 4.15.3–4 *qui* [sc. *Maelius*] *natus in libero populo inter iura legesque ... spem regni conceperit.*
memorabilis: for the adjectival apodosis see Roby §1576. *memorabilis* occurs in Livian obituaries (e.g. 27.49.2, 38.53.9, fr. 61; for
the predominantly poetic adj. see Vretska on Sall. *C.* 4.4). But the
thought is far from conventional. Being memorable is the fundamental criterion for inclusion in historical narrative (M–W 170),
which in turn guarantees memory (e.g. Herod. 1.1.1); so L.'s long,
intricate narrative about Manlius makes him *memorabilis*, even to
the extent of allowing him his own bid for immortality-via-history
(8n.). This contrafactual assertion that he would have been worth
remembering seems a last (and obtrusive) attempt to sweep Manlius
and his fascination under the carpet: the historian (speaking for the
state?) claims not to remember, though the people do (15). For a
comparable dismissal of a long narrative cf. Tac. *A.* 4.32–3, *HA
Heliogab.* 18.3.

20.15 periculum ... uirtutes: the historian must balance *uitia*
and *uirtutes* in assessing a life (e.g. fr. 61, Polyb. 10.21.8 with Walbank, Sall. *J.* 95.4 with Pomeroy 130–1, Curt. 10.5.26, Dio
58.28.5). L. replaces this topos with the people's assessment, which
dismisses the *uitia* (= *periculum*) in favour of the *uirtutes*. It is the last
assessment we hear.   **recordantem:** 14n.   **desiderium:** the
great man's importance is shown by the people's grief at his passing (Pomeroy 51, 152–3), cf. 1.16.3, 7.1.9, 25.36.16, Diod. 14.112.5,
Tac. *Ag.* 43.1, *A.* 2.72.2. The people react similarly to Cassius'
execution (2.42.1).   **eius:** objective gen.   **tenuit:** *d. tenere*, an
Ennian phrase that Cicero liked, is only here in L. (cf. Enn. *Ann.*
105 with Skutsch, Cic. *Red. pop.* 1, *Fam.* 2.11.1).   **pestilentia** ~

19.6 *pestiferum* (n.).   **nullis ... causis** ∼ 19.5 *nihil cuiquam occur-
reret*. It is not unheard of, but it is unusual, to let a plague go unin-
vestigated; *pestilentiae* fall under the heading of *prodigia*, and as such
have to be expiated (Liebeschuetz *s.vv.* 'plague', 'prodigies').   **ex
Manliano ... orta:** L. neither confirms nor denies this interpretation, though the parallelism *breui* (above) ∼ *etiam breui* closely links
the *populus* and the gods. This need not mean that the plebs are
right (cf. 5.14.3–5 with Levene 177–9), but it does mean that the
final verdict on Manlius is left open.   **magnae parti** implies
that there was a dissenting opinion; L. does not elaborate.
uideri: hist. infin. (11.7n.).

20.16 uiolatum: the people's religious concern recalls Manlius'
piety (16.2n.).   **cordi** ∼ 15 *recordantem*.   **prope oculis suis:**
Manlius' death was a spectacle for the gods as well. They constitute a third audience level whose verdict on events is the most important: if they are pleased, the Romans win and their power is
increased; if not, the potential for disaster is almost limitless. This
pestilentia disrupts events for only one year; that it happens at all,
however, is telling (15n.).   **erepta ... hostium:** 17.4n.

21 The year 383 B.C.

Either a Roman victory or tranquil *res internae* would reduce doubts
about the propriety of Manlius' execution. Instead, the first half of
the book ends with indecision and delay brought about by disease.
Res externae and *internae* are not separated: the preparations for war
never come to fruition, and the enemy actions themselves take
place *domi*.

21.1 inopia ... bellum: the subjs. of the sentence enclose and
render almost invisible the notice of the change of year (*anno insequente*). For pestilence, famine, and war see Nisbet–Hubbard on
Hor. *C.* 1.21.13.   **uulgatam ... famam:** cf. Virg. *A.* 8.554,
Tac. *H.* 4.62.3 with H.   **multiplex** 'many-fronted' as an epithet
of *bellum* appears only in L., but cf. Vell. 96.3 (*m. uictoriae*), Tac. *H.*
1.3.1 (*m. casus*).

21.2 praeter ... Latium: three familiar enemies; the predict-
ability of their revolt decreases (*in aeternum* ∼ *iam diu* ∼ *suspectum*).
Volscos ... datos: 12.2n.   **uelut sorte quadam:** Roman his-

torians frequently advert to a providential force variously called *fatum, fortuna*, or *sors* that drives Rome on to her destiny, for good or for evil. Such notices can simply indicate that an event seemed inevitable (so here); more direct intervention (e.g. by the gods' anger or by an unidentified will, as 22.6, 34.5) is sometimes envisaged, though usually so vaguely as to make any precise philosophical influence unidentifiable (see Levene 30–7 and cf. Sall. *C.* 10.1, Vell. 26.2, Tac. *A.* 4.1.1, 1.2 (*deum ira*) with M–W).   **exercendo ... militi:** apart from certain frozen expressions (4n.) the gerund(ive) dat. of purpose is common only from L. on (*NLS* §207 (4) (*a*)). **Circeiosque et Velitras:** cf. 13.7–8.   **urbs:** in apposition to the Lanuvini (cf. 3.2).   **subito exorti:** cf. Cic. *Phil.* 5.43 *subito praeter spem omnium exortus*; for *exoriri* of a challenger cf. 7.16.2, Virg. *A.* 4.625, Tac. *A.* 13.7.2.

21.4 paratior: the plebs are to be prepared for war not by exhortation or training but by bribery. For *p. ad* see 18.7n.; for agrarian laws and colonies see 5.1n., 16.6n.   **diuidendo ... deducendae:** the gerund(ive) dat. of purpose in such legal expressions is old and formulaic (2n.). For the mechanics of colonization see E. T. Salmon, *Roman colonization under the republic* (1970) 13–28. **deducendae:** technical of founding a colony (*OLD* 9b).

21.5 iuberent ... iusserunt: the repetition has a legal flavour (cf. McDonald 156–7); on the repetition of *bellum* in 4–5 see 5.2n. **dissuadentibus:** a favourite tribunician tactic during the struggle of the orders was to block levies, agreeing to patrician demands only after their own were met (probably retrojected from second-century practice: *IM* 642–3; Ridley, *SS* 121–2). These *tr. pl.* have no special reason to advise against war; that they do so indicates that the issues of the *seditio* still require attention.   **tribus:** the centuriate, not the tribal assembly declared war (Taylor 100). In the mid-republic, however, the centuries were sometimes called tribes (5.18.1 with O.): L. may adopt the anachronistic designation here to point the independence of the *tribus* from the *tribuni*.

21.6 exercitus: adversative asyndeton.   **magna ... mitteretur** ∼ 8 *magna ... exirent*: a hostile expedition against Rome will replace the potential peaceful one.   **dederat ... inclinabat:** the expected apodosis of the contrafactual condition ('they would have asked for peace') is suppressed in favour of the factual state-

ment 'this delay had provided an opportunity and the majority
was inclined' (*NLS* §200).

21.7 ni: 3.8n.   **priuato ... esset:** co-operation between public and private interests in all areas was an ancient desideratum. It
was equally conventional, however, that personal gain, safety etc.
tends to be prized over public; for the present formulation cf.
34.61.8 *priuatos suo periculo peccaturos; rem pub. ... conseruandam esse*,
Cic. *Ver.* 5.77 *tu tua pericula communi periculo defendes?*, V. Max. 9.15
praef. periculi ... cum priuatim tum etiam publice late patentis.   **ut fit:**
3.5n.   **auctoresque defectionis:** 10.5n. The *-que* is epexegetical.   **ab Romanis:** with *defectionis.*   **piacula irae R.:** the
Romans have the power of gods, and must be appeased; as this
represents the ringleaders' fears it is probably sarcastic. *piaculum* of
a person is first here (*OLD*, cf. Tac. *H.* 1.58.2 with H.).

21.8 in senatu: i.e. at Lanuvium. L. often applies 'Roman' terms
to foreign institutions (a type of *interpretatio Romana*, for which see
OCD); cf. 25.7, 26.1, 31.3.   **praedatum:** supine expressing purpose, an archaizing and relatively frequent construction in L. as in
other historians (Kühnast 259, M–W 81).   **noua** ∼ 2 *noui*. The
year's unobtrusive frame includes 9 *fama* ∼ 1 *famam*, 9 *exorta* ∼ 2
exorti.   **exturbauit:** properly of sending into exile (Cic. *Mur.* 45)
or dislodging from a position (21.9.2, Veg. *Mil.* 4.15).

21.9 Praenestinorum: modern Palestrina; on its history see O.
on 2.19.2. This notice is a narrative tease: the Romans do not engage Praeneste until 380 (28–9).   **ab senatu:** in Rome.   **ut
... appareret:** their refusal to help is natural, given their inability to put an army in the field even in response to direct attacks
(6–8); but L. reports it in a way which implies that the senate is
being duplicitous; cf. 10.9.   **minus credi ... quia nollent:**
the converse of the saying, *libenter homines quod uolunt credunt* (Otto
97, Häussler 42, 54).

22.1–4 The year 382 B.C.

The third quarter opens with a short year, comprising *res externae*
only. Attention is immediately directed to Velitrae via the Papirii,
whom L. separates from the other tribunes (6.3n.); at Velitrae, the
Praenestine presence provides an almost imperceptible bridge to the

next year (4n.). With C.'s reappearance (22.6) there is an encouraging renewal of foreign wars; but domestic problems soon assume overwhelming importance (27.3).

22.1 quattuor ... relictis: abl. appendix (above, p. 21).   **ad praesidium ... et si qui:** for the *uariatio* (prep. phrase ~ condition) see Sörbom 119 and cf. 32.5.   **si** 'in case' (*OLD* 11).

22.2 secundo 'successful', esp. of military engagements (*OLD* 4b).   **propinquitas urbis:** cf. 8.16.3 *exercitus ... propinquitate urbium et ad fugam pronior et in fuga ipsa tutior fuit*. For *propinqua castra* as a place to retreat cf. 4.31.3, 27.42.5, Caes. *C.* 1.82.5, Tac. *H.* 3.18.2 *propinqua ... moenia quanto plus spei ad effugium, minorem ad resistendum animum dabant*; for preventing retreat by eliminating such *receptacula* cf. 9.23.14, Caes. *G.* 7.14.9, Fron. *S.* 1.11.21 (Fabius Maximus burns his own ships, a motif going back to Hellanicus *FGrH* 4 F 84).   **causa ... fugae** ~ *ex fuga receptaculum* (chiasmus with *uariatio*).

22.3 oppidi oppugnatione: a jingle common in military reports, cf. 10.45.10, Caes. *G.* 3.12.2, Cic. *Fam.* 5.10B.1, *B. Afr.* 5.1, Fron. *S.* 3.8.2. The similarity of sound suggests an inevitable, if not an etymological, relationship between the two.   **anceps erat** 'it could go either way' (*OLD anceps* 7a).   **nec ... censebant:** the Romans preferred to salvage as much property and personnel as possible. Captured rebels could be sold as slaves, dead ones could not; what is more, 'the dead paid no taxes' (Brunt (2) 315).   **in** 'so as to result in' (*OLD* 20), cf. 37.32.8 *ne in perniciem urbis pugnaretur*; for the interlaced alliteration (p–c–p–c) see above, p. 22.   **litterae** 'dispatches' (*OLD* 7a).   **acriores in** 'more hostile toward', cf. Sall. *H.* 4.69.20, Sen. *Marc.* 12.6, Tac. *A.* 14.31.3.

22.4 ex ... iussu: for the formal language cf. 5.51.1 *non si miliens senatus consulto populique iussu reuocaretis*, 38.45.6, Sis. fr. 119, Cic. *Vat.* 8.   **coniuncti:** technical of military alliance (*OLD* 3); the construction + dat., frequent in Caesar and L., does not seem to occur in Cicero, who instead uses *c. cum* (*TLL*).   **anno insequente:** Bayet would delete this as a (mistaken) gloss, but L. is moving toward the next magisterial appointments, which as at 6.2–3 are textually motivated by an attack on Roman interests.   **defensam:** concessive.   **foedeque in captis** ~ 3 *nec in perniciem coloniam* – a telling contrast, and one which prepares for the treatment of Tusculum (25.6–26).   **exercuere uictoriam:** a Sallustian phrase (*C.*

38.4 with Vretska), after L. found only in V. Max. before Augustine (*TLL*). For *in aliquo exercere* cf. 5.2.8 *in plebe Romana regnum exercerent*; for the treatment of defeated enemies see Pritchett V 238–42.

22.5–26 The year 381 B.C.

Affairs abroad

C.'s appearance, as in the first quarter of the book, sends Roman stock soaring. Following the pattern of 382, the present year is given over to *res externae*, two military engagements separated by a senate session (25.2–6). But the second, bloodless campaign is fought inside Tusculum (25.7–26.2) and in the Curia (26.3–8), settings which produce the feel of *res internae*.

Pursuing his exploration of the balance and effects of power, L. again gives C. an assignment *extra ordinem*, patterning this Volscian war closely on C.'s last military success (6.3–10). But instead of deferential colleagues he has a recalcitrant, even disrespectful young partner. L. Furius Medullinus resembles Manlius: a vigorous leader with a popular following, he questions C.'s excellence and the propriety of a single man's pre-eminence (23.8, see 23.1n.). In Furius, then, C. faces the rival from whom L. had separated him (11.3n.). His impeccable behaviour shows how conflict among *principes* should be handled, though his example has no effect on the increasingly difficult situation at home.

The contrast of a rash young commander with a wise old one is conventional (Keitel (1) 165–6), e.g. Nicias and Alcibiades (Thuc. 6.8–24), Fabius Maximus and Scipio (28.40–4, L.'s imitation of Thuc.: B. S. Rodgers, *T.A.P.A.* 116 (1986) 335–52); for rash youth see Eyben 44–52 and for young men in public life see Evans–Kleijwegt. This incident becomes an *exemplum* for a similar conflict (8.33.15–16, see Chaplin 52–3); the battle proper serves as a model for a skirmish before Cremona (Tac. *H.* 3.16–17).

22.5 Eam ... passi: a cliché (*OLD aegre* 2), often followed in L. by violence; it testifies to the *ira* that the colonists feared (21.7) and the Tusculans successfully avert (26.1).   **M. Furium ... Ambusto:** the modified list foregrounds C. (6.3n.).   **et ... ac ... cum ... et:** *uariatio* of connectives in a list (O. on 5.13.6, Catterall

301), a stylistic mannerism particularly associated with Tacitus (Sörbom 50–6).

22.6 M. Furio ... L. Furius ~ 25.4 *L. Furio ... M. Furium* (frame). L. usually refers to C. by his *cognomen* alone; this reminder that the two share the same *gentilicium* increases the irony of their dissimilar natures.   **extra ordinem:** as he was lit. out of order in the tribune list (5n.), so C.'s command will be figuratively 'out of order'. The technical expression contrasts C.'s direct appointment with assignment by lot (*sorte* below: O. on 3.2.2).   **adiutor** ~ 25.5 *adiutorem*; on the title see 6.12n. (*socium imperii*).   **sorte ... datur:** though this refers to the legal drawing of lots, the echo of 21.2 (n.) recalls the notion of a force guiding Rome's development; cf. also *ut ... esset* below.   **non ... petiit:** a summary table of contents with instructions about how to read the episode. C.'s public *laus* will come first (22.7–24), his private *laus* second (25.1–6). **non tam ... quam:** the initially ominous statement that C.'s personal glory took precedence over the state's good is mitigated by the fact that, as an ideal leader, C. gains private renown from public service (*et ... petiit* below).   **e re publica** 'in the republic's interest' (*OLD respublica* 2a), a solemn and senatorial phrase (Talbert 261 with n.2). For the *uariatio* prep. phrase ~ purpose clause (*ut* below) see Sörbom 114.   **materia:** 7.3n.   **ad omnem laudem** 'for every conceivable [sort of] renown' (*OLD omnis* 6a, *laus* 2), cf. Cic. *Lig.* 2 *uirum omni laude dignum*.   **publice ... priuatim** ~ *re publica ... collegae* above; the polar expression defines the (all-encompassing) parameters of *omnem* (W–M).   **rem ... restituit:** C.'s resemblance to Q. Fabius Maximus (22.5–26n.) is confirmed by this echo of Ennius' famous description of the Cunctator, *Ann.* 363 Sk *unus homo nobis cunctando restituit rem*; cf. also 23.5 *cunctatorem* (Pinsent (1) 15). In Ennius *rem = rem publicam*; here it means something like 'situation' (for *res* of battles see *OLD* 17 *fin.*).   **temeritate:** 13.1n. For the particular association of rashness with youth see Powell on Cic. *Sen.* 20.   **prolapsam** images the *res* as a fallen building (*OLD* 5b), anticipating 24.3 *Romanam inclinauit aciem* (Fantham 129–30; see next n.).   **restituit** ~ 24.8–9 *restituente ... restituitur*. The subj. is C., picked up from the dat. earlier in the sentence (see Sörbom 137–9 and 7n. *excitabant*). For *restituere* of rebuilding a structure see *OLD* 1a.   **errore ...**

gloriam ~ 24.9 *gloriam ... infamiam,* 25.6 *infamiam ... gloriam.* **eius** logically belongs both with *errore* and with *gratiam* 'goodwill'.

22.7 exactae ... restiterat: for the retired general summoned back into service the *locus classicus* is the story of Cincinnatus (4.13.12, cf. Cic. *Sen.* 56 with Powell), cf. also P. Licinius Calvus at 5.18.1–6 (replaced by his younger son).   **exactae ... aetatis:** gen. of description, 'advanced age' (*OLD exigo* 6b); on the phrase see H. on Tac. *H.* 3.33.1. It has been only five years since C.'s last vigorous performance (8.2n.) and he lives until 365 (7.1.8–10). This exaggerated emphasis on his age heightens the contrast with his *adiutor* and increases the effect of the ensuing peripeteia (Luce (2) 269–71).   **iurare ... in uerba:** 2.6n.   **parato:** sc. *Camillo.* **ualetudini:** not only is he old, he is sick as well (as at Plut. *Cam.* 37.1). For the dat. of purpose see 21.2n.; for *excusare* 'allege as a reason' see *OLD* 2a.   **consensus populi:** as in 386, C.'s appointment is urged by *consensus* (6.9n.), which with *concordia* dogs his footsteps in the military sphere even as it eludes him politically (38, 42.12n.). For *consensus* as subj. see W. on Vell. 91.1.   **uegetum ... sensibus:** alliteration reinforces the shared ancient derivation of *uiridis/uirere, uiuidus,* and *uegetum/uigere* from *uis* (Maltby *s.vv.*); for L.'s etymological play see Dutoit (2) 112. Though the equivalence of youthful energy and fresh vegetable growth is common, L.'s form of expression is as exuberant as his metaphors (next nn.).   **uegetum ... uigebat:** a flourishing spirit (*OLD uegetus* 2) in a vigorous body (*OLD pectus* 2b). For *u. ingenium* cf. 9.3.5 *uigebat uis animi consiliique,* Sall. *C.* 20.11 *uiget animus,* Sen. *Ep.* 71.25 *adulescentem ... ingenio uegetum,* Stat. *Silu.* 4.4.48 *uiget ingenium.* For *uiuido pectore* cf. Virg. *A.* 10.609–10 *u. ... dextra,* Sil. 7.64 *u. membra,* Stat. *Th.* 3.284–5 *u. rebus | pectora.*   **uirebatque:** cf. Stat. *Th.* 3.453 *mente uirebat*; for green denoting youthful vigour cf. Virg. *A.* 6.304 *uiridis senectus* with Austin, Sil. 1.405 *uirens senecta,* and J. André, *Étude sur les termes de couleur dans la langue latine* (1949) 186–7. Lucius will use the metaphor of blooming strength against C. (23.4); for other Livian characters echoing the narrative voice see 19.2n.   **integris sensibus** 'with his senses intact'; for the combination of body, mind, and senses cf. Vell. 118.2 *manu fortis, sensu celer ... promptus ingenio* with W.   **ciuiles ... res** 'politics' (*OLD ciuilis* 5).   **obeuntem**

'engaging in'; the participle is concessive. For *obire* of duties, magistracies etc. see *OLD* 5. Too late, we are given an excuse for C.'s non-participation in the *seditio* (Bayet 41 n.2: 11.3n.); his preference for war over politics reverses the behaviour expected from an old man (23.4n.).   **excitabant:** the third change of subj. in as many sentences, a syntactical jitteriness foreshadowing the to-and-fro between C. and Lucius.

22.8 scriptis ... indicto: continuative abls. (above, p. 20). **exercitu indicto** is Livian (*TLL*).   **in** 'for' (*OLD* 23a).   **profectus:** sc. *est* (1.10n.).   **Ibi ... (23.2) ostentare:** this paragraph is in strict ring form, opening and closing with the belligerent Volsci (*fidentes ... numero ... in aciem procedunt* ∼ 23.2 *explicare aciem ... fiduciam uirium*). Inside are two reports of the Roman situation, the first focalized by the Volsci (9), the second by the Romans (23.1); they too are chiastic (*dilaturi ... artes imp. unici* ∼ *unius uiri consilium ... trahendo bello*). The shifting referent of *hostis* (9 = Romans, 23.2 = Volsci) helps the shifting point of view (3.3n.).   **expugnatores** is uncommon, first at Cic. *Inu.* 1.93; cf. 23.18.7, *CIL* III 14147.3 (Gallus' grandiloquent dedication) *bis acie uictor V urbium expugnator*.   **fidentes ... numero** ∼ 9 *paucitati ... confiderent* (chiastic); for trusting in numbers see 13.1nn.

22.9 nihil ... facerent 'in no way intending to delay risking their all'. Outside L. (*nihil*) *differre quin* occurs at Suet. *Jul.* 4.2, then in the Vulgate (*TLL*); for *quin* see *NLS* §187a. For *periculum s.r.* see *OLD periculum* 1, *summa* 6b and cf. 39.1.8 *nec tamen in discrimen summae rerum pugnabatur*.   **ita ... esse:** the enemy's thoughts (above, p. 13).   **artes** 'stratagems' (*OLD* 3, Wheeler 57–8).   **unici ... solis:** sarcastic, though it will turn out to be true; the irony is pointed by the Camillan adjs. (6.17n., 11.3n.).   **confiderent:** the Volscian claim that the Romans rely solely on C.'s *artes* is closely and ironically followed by the *ardor* that makes them reject his plan.

23.1 idem: i.e. as in the enemy.   **fortunam** 'chance' (*OLD* 5), a favourite Livian usage (Levene 31).   **unius uiri:** 6.7n. The Manlian contrast of *unus* ∼ *omnes* (14–16.4n.) recurs in this episode in all its configurations: *unus* as outstanding among *omnes* (25.4); *unus* as a leader and protector of *omnes*, involved in a relationship of mutual help (24.7); and *unus* as inferior to, even a victim of, *omnes* (8, 24.9).   **consilium** refers as much to C.'s strategic skill

(Wheeler 52–6, cf. *ratio* below, *artes* above) as to his overall prudence; it is a virtue Manlius and Furius conspicuously lack (11.7n.).
imperium 'order' (*OLD* 8).   **qui ... quaerebat** 'who by putting off the war was looking for a chance of improving his strength
by strategy'.   **iuuandarum:** for *adiuuandarum*, cf. 1.15.4 *uiribus
nulla arte adiutis* with *OLD adiuuo* 4b (3.4n.). There is a latent medical metaphor in *iuuare* (*OLD* 3).   **uirium** refers to the army's
strength, but cf. Plut. *Cam.* 37.3 'he thought it best to prolong the
war ... strengthening his body (τὸ σῶμα) to fight'.   **trahendo
bello:** epexegetical of *ratione*: the delay will work to C.'s advantage
by weakening the enemy, who will become exhausted by prancing
around fully armed (cf. Fron. *S.* 2.1.1–5, 9, 15).

23.2 instare: hist. infin.   **castris ... campi ... uallo:** the
Volsci move in (3.5n.).   **explicare:** technical of deploying a line
of troops (*OLD* 4a).   **signa inferendo:** also technical ('march
forward': *OLD infero* 2a); for the modal abl. see 11.7n.   **fiduciam uirium:** cf. Vell. 112.3 *ita placebat barbaris numerus suus, ita
fiducia uirium.* For taunting the enemy, either verbally or, as here,
by display, cf. 2.45.3–5, 22.28.10, Herod. 9.20, Virg. *A.* 9.590–620,
Plut. *Alc.* 35.5 and see Miniconi 177, Pritchett II 147–55. The ultimate source is the Homeric exchange before a duel; for Homeric
influences on the form of historiography see Fornara *s.v.* 'Homer'.

23.3 aegre ... aegrius: for the polyptoton see 11.1n.   **cum
... tum** give the grounds for Furius' *ferocia* (W–C 3), cf. 1.25.1
feroces et suopte ingenio et pleni adhortantium uocibus; for the *uariatio*
causal abl. ~ participle see Catterall 304, Sörbom 89.   **multitudinis:** subjective gen. with *spe* below.   **ex incertissimo** 'from
an extremely precarious state' (*OLD* 5); the substantival superlative
occurs only here and at Sen. *Ben.* 7.26.5 (*TLL*). For the idea cf.
Tac. *H.* 3.26.3 *quippe ingrata quae tuta, ex temeritate spes* (also of soldiers); the notion that *incerta* are more attractive than *certa* may be
at the root of L.'s thought (Otto 81, Vretska on Sall. *C.* 17.6).
sumentis animos 'taking courage' is slightly mannered and first
attested in L. (Hor. *Ep.* 2.2.110 is different); see H. on Tac. *H.*
1.27.2 (Fletcher (1) 169).   **inflatus:** applied in Book 6 only to
Manlius (11.6, 18.5) and Furius, whose likeness is enhanced by the
encouragement they both take from the crowd.

23.4 insuper instigabat: 14.9n.   **eleuando ... auctorita-**

tem 'by making light of his colleague's authority with the only means he had, (C.'s) age'. Furius' own authority soon becomes trivial (24.8). For *eleuare auct.* cf. 3.21.4 with W–M and *OLD eleuo* 2b; for the gerund + dir. obj. see 4.10n.   **qua una:** sc. *re*; for the incorporated antecedent see 10.8n.   **aetate:** abl. of means. The ideal general, being neither too old for action nor too young for prudence, has an old head on young shoulders (cf. Aesch. *Sept.* 622, Onas. 1.9–10, Fron. *S.* 4.7.3).   **iuuenibus ... data:** cf. 1.22.2, Ov. *Am.* 1.9.4 with McKeown, *F.* 5.59 *Martis opus iuuenes animosaque bella gerebant*, Sil. 5.570 *frigentem in Marte senectam*; for the distinction between the respective tasks of young and old cf. Cic. *Sen.* 15, 38 with Powell.   **iuuenibus:** a choice synonym for *adulescens*, outnumbering the latter throughout the *AVC* (Adams (4) 60–1).   **dictitans:** 6.5n. (*abnuentes*).   **cum corporibus ... animos:** a commonplace (Lucr. 3.445–58 with Kenney); for the physical weakness of old age see Cic. *Sen.* 27–38; for its mental decline, Cic. *Sen.* 21–6, both with Powell.   **uigere et deflorescere:** 22.7n. Lucius speaks in antitheses (old/young, bloom/fade, delayer/fighter, storm city/waste time, add/detract); among other things, the episode makes the point that such simple oppositions are insufficient evaluative tools.

23.5 cunctatorem: 22.6n. Furius intends this as an insult (cf. 7.3), but it will be proved to connote prudence (cf. Skutsch on Enn. *Ann.* 363–5).   **bellatore:** slightly grandiose.   **qui ... rapere** ∼ point by point to *eum ... terere* below.   **adueniens** 'on his arrival' (8.5n. (*praesentia*)).   **rapere:** appropriate for a sudden attack; there is a secondary sense of 'plunder' (Tac. *H.* 1.51.4 with H.).   **residem:** not just unwarlike behaviour, but stagnation (Austin on Virg. *A.* 6.813).   **quid ... sperantem?** 'expecting what to accrue to his own forces or to disappear from the enemy's?'; cf. 25.35.4, 27.13.6. For the participial appendix see 9.3n.; for the question dependent on it see Walsh on 21.30.6.

23.6 occasionem 'timing' (Wheeler 26, 48).   **occasionem ... tempus ... locum:** objs. of *sperantem* above (*contra*, W–C 4). Furius methodically ticks off the areas C. must consider, cf. Quint. 6.4.8 *personarum instrumentorum temporum locorum habere notitiam*, [Quint.] *Decl.* 281.5 *haec occasio, hic locus, hoc tempus*. For the same items in a military checklist cf. Fron. *S.* 2.1, 2.2.   **instruendis:**

Gronovius' correction of the MSS *instruentem* is easy and plausible: there are seemingly no parallels for *ins. occasionem, locum,* or *tempus,* whereas *ins. insidias* is attested (Catul. 21.7, Apul. *M.* 7.25.3, cf. 23.35.14 *ins. fraudi*) as a variant on the slightly more usual *insidias struere* (e.g. Cic. *Clu.* 190, Tac. *H.* 1.58.2 with H.).   **frigere ... consilia:** cf. 1.41.3, Cic. *Ver.* 2.60; for *frigere* of age cf. Virg. *A.* 5.396, Stat. *Th.* 7.631, Sil. 5.570 (quoted on 4), and see Powell on Cic. *Sen.* 45 *feruor aetatis.*

23.7 sed ... uires?: in his plea to have command passed to the young, Furius appeals implicitly to the idea of a series of leaders whose *res gestae* constitute Rome's greatness (above, pp. 16–17). For the opposition single lifetime/life of the state cf. 28.28.12, Cic. *Marc.* 22 *doleoque cum res publica immortalis esse debeat, eam in unius mortalis anima consistere* and see Hardie 93; for state ∼ body see 3.1n.   **sed ... esse:** Furius says of C. what Caesar (allegedly) said of himself, cf. Cic. *Marc.* 25 *'satis diu uel naturae uixi uel gloriae'* with Ruch. *sed* is transitional (*OLD* 2a).   **corpore ... consenescere** ∼ 4 *iuuenibus ... corporibus* (frame).   **ciuitatis ... uires:** long hyperbata are 'a constant mark of highly adorned prose from the late republic onwards' (Adams (1) 13); see also 1.2n.   **quam ... deceat** 'which ought to be immortal'. For the *aeterna urbs* see Vell. 103.4 with W.; like many Augustan concepts, this has its germ in Cicero (cf. *Marc.* 22, quoted above).   **pati** depends on *attinere.*   **consenescere** 'age along with', cf. Hor. *C.* 3.5.8, Ov. *M.* 8.633.

23.8 His sermonibus: L. frequently marks the end as well as the beginning of *o.o.* (cf. 37.12, 40.1 and see Lambert 37).   **tota ... castra** = *omnes milites,* the container for the thing contained (a kind of metonymy, *OLD castra* 1d).   **posceretur pugna:** a common Livian expression found elsewhere at Tac. *H.* 4.34.3 (where see H.) and *A.* 13.36.2. Commanders were advised to withhold battle so as to excite their troops' enthusiasm (e.g. Fron. *S.* 1.11.1, 20); for soldiers forcing action on unwilling commanders see Pritchett II 155.   **sustinere ... non possumus:** Furius rhetorically ranges himself and C. against the soldiers' assault (*OLD impetus* 2a), though he has helped create the situation. For thoughtful leader ∼ impatient soldiers cf. Tac. *H.* 3.20.1–2 *militibus cupidinem pugnandi conuenire, duces prouidendo consultando, cunctatione saepius quam temeritate pro-*

desse.   **cuius ... auximus:** cf. Caes. *G.* 3.24.5 (enemy *cunctatio* makes them fearful, the Romans brave); for *animos au.* cf. 2.43.3, Pl. *Asin.* 280, Ov. *M.* 7.120.   **minime toleranda:** cf. 5.48.9 *intoleranda Romanis uox, uae uictis.*   **insultat:** the sense of 'dancing up and down' is very much present, cf. 7.10.3 *ferox praesultat hostium signis,* Lucr. 3.1032 with Kenney.   **cede** ~ 24.3 *cedentem* (the enemy ruse).   **unus omnibus:** in.   **patere ... uincas:** play with forms of *uincere* is so common as to have become, in some instances, proverbial; for conquering by being conquered see Otto 371, Häussler 226, 293. The next time the stem *ui(n)c-* appears it ironically describes the Romans just as the Volsci rout them (24.3); C. must reclaim it for Rome (24.6, see also 8.6n.).   **uinci consilio:** cf. Vell. 120.4 with W.   **maturius** 'more quickly' – but the word punningly recalls his arguments about old age (*OLD maturus* 6), which C. echoes rather sourly below (9–11 *aetatis ... aetati ... senis*).

     23.9 ad ea 'in reply'. Some of C.'s points correspond to his colleague's *o.o.* (4–7), as if he too had heard it.   **quae ... (10) impedire:** C. begins with two dicola (*quae ... praestantem; itaque ... impedire*), each of which contrasts his past with his present (*ad eam diem* ~ *nunc, consuesse* ~ *posse*). That 'now' is marked by the obtrusive presence of his *collega* (9, 10) whom he does not name (12n. (*auctor*)).   **quae ... essent:** the rel. clause is fronted for emphasis.   **suo:** reflexive words dominate C.'s speech, belying his acquiescent stance. For *unius* in apposition to the personal pron. see G–L §321 R.2.   **negare:** hist. infin.; *scire* (etc.) below are infins. in *o.o.*   **neque se neque populum:** for the negatives see 16.3n. C. makes his past successes foil to the present trial, as if in response to Furius' attempt to minimize them (4); for experience in a commander see 18.13n.; for the *conscientia bene actae uitae* as consolation in old age see Cic. *Sen.* 9 with Powell.   **consilii ... fortunae:** for C.'s *consilium* see 1n.; for the general's *fortuna* see 12.11n.   **nunc** 'but now', *OLD* 11. C. addresses Furius' first point, the disparity between his age and the young man's vigour (4).   **iure ... praestantem:** isocolonic, parallel phrases with homoioteleuton; movement is provided by the shift from 'equal' to 'superior', for which cf. 23.26.11 *uelocitate pari, robore animi uiriumque aliquantum praestanti.* For the hyperbaton with *collegam* see

2.12n.   **uigore aetatis:** C. uses the same language of Furius
that L. used of C. (22.7, see 19.2n.); for the expression cf. Tac. *H.*
2.30.2 *studia ... militum in Caecinam inclinabant ... uigore aetatis* (his
partner Valens is accused of *cunctationes*, 30.1).

   23.10 itaque properly goes with *collegae ... impedire* below ('and
so, though he had been used to command ... he could not hin-
der').   **ad exercitum** ∼ *collegae.*   **attineat:** either primary or
secondary sequence is possible after a hist. infin. (*negare* above), as
after a hist. pres.   **regere ... regi:** C. matches Furius' verbal
play (8) with his own; for the topos see Otto 295–6 and cf. 6.18n.
regere is technical of military commanding (*OLD* 11); *regimen* characterized C.'s power at 6.6 (n.), but after the Manlian episode, at the
end of which *reg-* was prominent (18.16, 19.7 *bis*, 20.4, 5), any 'innocent' use of it has been compromised.   **imperium ... impedire:** cf. *HA Opil. Macr.* 5.4 *ne ... suum impediretur imperium.*   **dis
... (11) efficiat:** in his conclusion C. chiastically explains his own
and the gods' roles in the upcoming conflict; his emphatic headings
(*dis* ∼ *aetati suae ... quae senis* ∼ *id a dis*) suggest a co-operation
among them that excludes the rash young.   **bene iuuantibus:**
for *bene iuuare* in prayers see Appel 127.   **ageret:** jussive subjunc. (*NLS* §266); its subj. is Furius.

   23.11 ueniam 'indulgence' (*OLD* 2a); the following appositive
ut-clause is epexegetical (*OLD* 39).   **munia** 'duties'.   **id ...
efficiat:** C. is given to this sort of prayer, cf. 5.21.15 and esp.
5.32.9 *precatus ab dis immortalibus si innoxio sibi ea iniuria fieret, primo
quoque tempore desiderium sui ciuitati ingratae facerent.* The latter, following a political defeat, shows an angry C. whose presence peeps out
here too (see Levene 193, 208–9).   **immortalibus** ∼ 7 *immortalem.*   **laudabile** ∼ 22.6 *laudem*; the correspondence with the narrator's predictive authority confirms the validity of C.'s plan.

   23.12 Nec ... sententia: 12.11n.   salutaris sententia ∼
piae preces below; for the expression cf. Cic. *Phil.* 2.19, V. Max. 9.10.1,
and on *salus* see 17.5n.   **auctor:** C. refuses, and the narrative is
reluctant, to use Furius' name; cf. *alieni* below, 9–10 *collegam*, 24.6
alium ducem, 24.8.   **subsidia ... firmat:** cf. 10.43.1 *subsidiaque
firma ... portis opposuit*, Tac. *H.* 3.17.2 *firmati ... densis ordinibus* (the
usual expression is *subsidiis (aciem) firmare*, as 4.37.8, Tac. *H.* 2.43.2
with H.); for the tactic of keeping troops in reserve in case the

front lines fail cf. 8.8.11, Caes. *C.* 3.64.1, Onas. 22.1–3, Fron. *S.* 2.3.21, 22.   **ipse:** 2.8n.   **spectator:** the scene is played out in a depression between two hills, the first holding the audience, the second serving as a sort of *skene* (24.2 *lenis ... cliuus*), out of which pour the enemy reserves.   **intentus in:** first in L.; he similarly innovates with *int. aduersus* (picked up by Tac. *A.* 14.3.2) and *int.* + ind. ques. (6.13), as well as construing it + dat. (25.9) and + *ad* (12.10).   **euentum ... consilii** ~ 24.11 *sensit ... euentus*; see also 8.8n., 26.2n.

24.1 simul: 7.6n.   **primo concursu** is a 'military cliché' (O. on 5.32.3).   **concrepuere arma:** cf. 24.44.8, 28.8.2; *c. armis* occurs at Sis. fr. 64 (quoted on 3.6), Caes. *G.* 7.21.1.   **dolo ... rettulit:** for the stratagem cf. 4.46.5, 31.36.2, Polyb. 5.96.3, Caes. *C.* 2.40.3, Onas. 11 (care needed in following a retreating enemy), Fron. *S.* 2.2.3, 3.14, 5.1–8 (esp. 5.2, pretended retreat to higher ground, 5.3, the ambushing force kept in camp). It tends to be employed against a numerically superior force. On ambushes see Pritchett II 177–89, Wheeler 84–6.

24.2 lenis ... erat: a 'formal pattern of descriptive technique' beginning a critical section of the narrative (O. on 1.21.3); *lenis* = 'gentle' (*OLD* 2b).   **ab** 'in the direction of' (*OLD* 23).   **quod ... suppeditabat:** the Volscian trick owes less to cleverness than to the accident of their superior mass.   **armatas instructasque:** though uncommon outside L., this looks like military jargon, cf. 24.7.4 with W–M, Hirt. 8.36.5, Curt. 3.8.22, Tac. *D.* 32.2 (an orator equipped like a soldier).   **reliquerant:** for the change to the plur. after *rettulit* (above) see 17.6n.   **quae ... erumperent:** purpose. The mood of *appropinquasset*, which would be fut. perf. indic. in *o.r.*, is due to the virtual *o.o.*: it forms an integral part of the reported command (G–L §663.1).   **inter commissum ... certamen:** for *inter* + an AUC participle (1.1n.) cf. 4.61.6 *inter eruptionem temptatam*, Sall. *C.* 43.3 with Vretska, Man. 3.117, Sen. *Contr.* 2.5.6 *inter ... tormenta saeuientia*.

24.3 Romanus: alternating subjs. in 3–4 reflect the military give-and-take (cf. 7n., 22.8n.).   **cedentem:** cf. Tac. *A.* 1.63.1 *Germanicus cedentem in auia Arminium secutus ... Arminius ... uertit repente.*   **sequendo:** 11.7n.   **pertractus** 'lured' (*OLD* 3); the verb is first in L. (Walsh on 21.28.9).   **opportunus:** the Romans are a strategically favourable spot (*OLD* 2b). For *opportunus* of a person cf. Sall. *J.* 20.2, Tac. *A.* 4.60.3; for higher ground see Fron. *S.* 2.2.2–4.12, Pritchett IV 76–85 and see IN. **uersus ... aciem:** at the turning-point, marked by the sentence-initial verb (14.7n.), *terror* takes over. **supina ualle** 'the slope of the valley' is Livian (also at 4.46.5, 7.24.5); cf. Virg. *G.* 2.276 *supinus collis* (*OLD supinus* 3). **inclinauit aciem** is choice (W. on Vell. 52.4), and picks up the collapsing-building image introduced by 22.6 *prolapsam* (n.); see *TLL* VII 1.942.49–68 for *inclinare* of buildings, largely poetic before L.

24.4 instant ... integrant: cf. Caes. *G.* 1.25.6 *rursus instare et proelium redintegrare coeperunt.* Assonance and syntactical parallelism emphasize the double Volscian threat; for *integrare*, uncommon in prose outside L., cf. Sis. fr. 89, Curt. 10.6.4. **simulata ... fuga:** the ordinary term for the manoeuvre (Wheeler 87 n.192), for which see IN.; for the hyperbaton see 1.2n. **iam ... repetebat:** cf. 28.13.9 *nihil iam ordinum memores passim ... in fugam effunduntur*; for the framing verbs see 10.2n. **recipiebat se** implies an orderly retreat; the Romans just run (*terga ... dabat* below). **miles:** collective sing. (2.12n.). **recentis** 'recent' (*OLD* 1a) ~ *recentes* 'fresh' (*OLD* 2a) above: Volscian freshness makes Roman *ferocia* a thing of the past. **ferociae:** 4.5n.; for military *ferocia* see also Moore 21 n.37 ('a temporary emotional state: confidence, boldness, or pride'). **effuso** ~ 3 *effuse*: their flight is as unthinking as their attack.

24.5 cum Camillus: a second peripeteia is effected by the aged C.'s metamorphosis from old man to vital leader (Lipovsky 93–4); for the inverted '*cum* de rupture' see 8.7n. **subiectus** 'lifted up from underneath', cf. 31.37.10, Cic. *Deiot.* 28 *cum plures in equum sustulissent, quod haerere in eo senex posset, admirari solebamus.* **ab circumstantibus:** for convenient bystanders cf. 3.5.7, 4.14.4, 37.41.11, Curt. 6.10.36, Tac. *A.* 1.22.1 *adleuatus circumstantium umeris*, Suet. *Jul.* 84.3. **oppositis:** i.e. to the fleeing soldiers; it now transpires the *subsidia* were designed as a containing wall (*opponere* is technical of opposing troops to an enemy, *OLD* 5). For the tactic cf. 10.36.6 *statione equitum ... opposita*, Onas. 32.1, Fron. *S.* 2.3.16, 8.14, Tac. *Ag.* 35.2 with Ogilvie–Richmond. **haec est ... (6) receptura sunt:** a brief *hortatio* marks the peripeteia (a Livian technique: Keitel (1) 163); for *o.r.* in the midst of battle see 8.2n. **pugna ... poposcistis?** ~ 23.8; for the rebuking question cf. 7.3. **homo ... deus:** cf. 5.43.7 *cum dis hominibusque accusandis senesceret* [sc. *Camil-*

lus], 28.7.8, Virg. *A.* 2.745 *quem non incusaui ... hominumque deorumque?*
with Austin.   **quem ... possitis?** 'for you to blame?'   **illa
... haec:** their past rashness (*OLD ille* 16a) ~ the present disaster.

24.6 secuti ... sequimini: the participle throws the disgrace
into the past; *sequimini* leads to the future where they will enjoy
their customary victory. The verb is natural in exhortations; for
this formulation cf. 7.35.12 *me modo sequimini, quem secuti estis,*
41.24.7, Caes. *C.* 2.32.6 *incerta uictoria Caesarem secuti diiudicata iam
belli fortuna uictum sequamini?*   **Camillum:** self-reference in the
third person can have something of the effect of the 'royal we'
(M–W 217); here C. relies on his name's magical power (cf. 2.9),
while Furius remains anonymous (*alium* above: 23.12n.).   **et ...
uincite:** he appeals to their past victories (7.4n.). *quod* = 'something
which'; the antecedent is *uincite* (G–L §614 R.2).   **neminem ...
receptura sunt:** for the 'conventional formula' (McDonald 169)
cf. 2.45.13 with O., 10.36.8, Caes. *C.* 3.87.5, Sen. *Contr.* 5.7.1.

24.7 Pudor ... tenuit: for *tenere* 'check' + abstract subj. see
OLD 19b and cf. 35.10.   **inde ... aciem:** the interaction between C. and the troops in 5–7, esp. the alternation of subjects in
7, replaces the physical give-and-take between Volsci and Romans
(1–4). The 'turning' words are now of facing the enemy (*circumagi
... obuerti* ~ 3 *uersus ... inclinauit*); for the scene cf. 8.2.   **praeterquam quod:** sc. *erat*, an uncommon ellipse (cf. 29.18.13 *p. quod toto
corpore laceratus* [sc. *est*], *naso quoque auribusque decisis exsanguis est relictus,*
45.7.2). For the inspirational qualities of age cf. 44.41.1 *mouebat imperii maiestas, ante omnia aetas, quod ... iuuenum munia in parte praecipua
laboris periculique capessebat,* Sen. *Contr.* 8.5 *quanta adhortatio iuuenum fui
senex fortis!*   **insignis:** a Camillan adj. (16.8n.).   **inter prima
signa** ~ 23.11 *ne ... esset. p. signa* is a Livian favourite (over 30 exx.)
found elsewhere in Curtius (3.10.3, 4.7.15 etc.).   **ubi p. labor:**
echoed at Tac. *H.* 3.17.1.   **l. periculumque:** 6.9n.   **increpare:** hist. infin. (so 8 *orare*); see 13.4n.   **adhortatio in uicem**
'their reciprocal encouragement'. *adhortatio* is first in L. (*TLL*); for
the attributive adv. see 14.6n. and for the short-hand noting of soldiers' mutual exhortations (e.g. Hom. *Il.* 17.420, Thuc. 7.70.7) see
Keitel (1) 164.   **alacri clamore:** *alacritas* is the expected result
of a *hortatio* (cf. 8.10, Tac. *Ag.* 33.1 with Ogilvie–Richmond); for
L.'s choice expression (transferring the quality from the soldiers to

their cry) cf. Tac. *H.* 5.16.3 with H.   **peruasit:** transitive in
this sense first in L. (*OLD* 2).

24.8 neque ... defuit ~ 23.11 *se non defuturum.* Furius fills C.'s
original subsidiary role. For his namelessness (*alter tr.*) see
23.12n.   **missus ... ad equites:** C. unofficially, but 'par une
sorte de nécessité fatale' (Bayet 44 n.2), apportions the traditional
commands of the dictator and *magister equitum* (cf. 6.16).   **non
castigando** ~ *ad preces uersus* below (Sörbom 112); for the modal
gerund see 11.7n.   **ad quam ... fecerat** 'a role for which his
share of the blame had left him but slight authority'. For *culpae societas* cf. Tac. *H.* 2.52.2 (Fletcher (2) 71).   **leuiorem auctorem** ~ 23.4 *eleuando ... auctoritatem*; for the expression cf. 5.15.12,
Cic. *Planc.* 57, Suet. *Claud.* 37.1. Furius' attempt to trivialize C.'s
authority has failed; C. will later lighten Furius' *infamia*
(25.6).   **ut ... eximerent** 'that they save him, though responsible for the fortune of this day, from [bearing] the charge [of it]'.
The gen. phrase interacts both with *reum* (*OLD* 4) and with *crimine.*   **fortunae eius diei:** possibly alluding to *Fortuna Huiusce
Diei,* the patron goddess of 'today's luck' to whom vows might be
made during a battle (Champeaux 263, 320).

24.9 abnuente ... sentiam: Furius' plea balances C.'s exhortation at 5–6. The transition to *o.r.* is unmarked.   **abnuente ac
prohibente:** *abnuere* is to refuse for oneself, *prohibere* to keep another from something; for the fullness of expression see 3.6n.
temeritati ~ 22.6, 24.5.   **omnium ... unius:** Lucius replaces
C.'s *alius/Camillus* antithesis (6) with his own favourite *unus/omnes*
(23.7, 8), which he turns on its head in mid-plea: *unus* (C.) was right
and *omnes* were wrong; if *omnes* lose, *unus* (Lucius) will feel the *infamia.*   **prudentiae:** 6.14n.   **in ... fortuna:** i.e. whether they
win or lose; cf. 25.4.   **ni restituitur:** 15.6n.   **quod ... est**
looks ahead (see also 3.5n.); see Goodyear on Tac. *A.* 1.39.4 and for
the form of expression see W. on Vell. 118.4.   **infamiam** ~
25.6; cf. Tac. *Ag.* 27.1 *prospera omnes sibi uindicant, aduersa uni imputan-
tur* with Ogilvie–Richmond. L. introduces the question of Furius'
fate at the point where the army's victory is all but certain.
solus: like Manlius, Furius finds that *solus* is an uncomfortable
epithet (19.2n.; see 22.5–26n.).

24.10 tradi ~ *inuadere* (*uariatio*: 12.8n.).   **equos:** for dismount-

ing in these circumstances see 2.20.10 with O., 22.49.3, Caes. *G.*
4.2.3, *B. Hisp.* 15.2.   **pugna:** abl. of manner.   **inuadere hostem:** common in Sall. and L. (*TLL*), cf. Tac. *H.* 2.15.1 with H. The
simple acc. after verbs compounded with *in-* is a 'non-classical' Livian mannerism (*LHA* 261).   **insignes ~ 7** *insignis.*   **armis
animisque:** an old doublet (Lindholm 61), cf. 29.2, 31.41.13, Pl.
Bac. 942 *armati atque animati,* Cic. *Phil.* 3.33; for the combination
with *insignis* cf. Virg. *A.* 11.291 *ambo animis, ambo insignes ... armis.*
qua premi parte: cf. Caes. *G.* 3.4.2 *ut quae pars ... premi uidebatur,
eo occurrere et auxilium ferre.* For the idiomatic incorporation of the
antedecent (G–L §616.1) cf. 24.10 and 10.8n.   **peditum copias ~ 8** *p. aciem*: the ring closes Furius' vignette as he and the
cavalry rejoin C.   **nihil ... remittitur** 'no effort was spared'
(*OLD remitto* 10b).   **apud** 'on the part of' (*OLD* 15).   **certamine
animi** 'test of courage', a favourite phrase of L.'s (B. on 37.10.2).

24.11 sensit ... opem 'thus the outcome sensed the power of
striving valour'; for *uirtus eniti* cf. Curt. 7.11.10 *nihil tam alte natura
constituit quo uirtus non possit eniti* (Drakenborch). The *euentus* for
which C. was waiting (23.12) now seems to have been waiting for
him. He has a way of dominating abstract forces (cf. 8.6 *uictoriam
secum ... trahebat*); for the personification of *euentus* cf. 9.15.3 *Papirio
... breui ad spem euentus respondit.* (*sentire* 'feel the influence of' (*OLD*
5) lends itself to such expressions.)   **Volsci ... occisi:** the battle is wrapped up quickly, the next item of interest being the Tusculans found among the captives; such efficient endings are a Livian
trademark (Luce (2) 282–3). Annalistic brevity does not entail an
absence of style: there is wordplay (next n. but one) and chiasmus
with alliteration, polyptoton, and *uariatio* (*caesi* – *capta* – *capti* – *occisi*).
simulato ... cesserant ~ 4 *simulata cesserant fuga.*   **in ... fugam effusi:** L. varies the formulaic pair *fundit fugatque* (cf. 2.31.1
with O., Vell. 112.5 with W.), sometimes by substituting forms of
effundere (also 27.1.12, 28.16.3), sometimes by varying the forms (as
4.43.2 *fuga funduntur,* 9.37.10 *fundit ... fugatosque persequitur*).   **in
fuga caesi:** a standard phrase (O. on 5.31.4, cf. 8.7n.); for
pars + plur. verb see 3.7n.

25.1 ubi ... cum 'and then when'; for connective *ubi* see *OLD*
7c.   **percontantibusque ... militasse:** 6.5n. C. will move on
to Tusculum, the captives serving as a transition from one war to the
next (14.1n.).   **percontantibus** 'in response to their questions'.

25.2–26 For *res internae* L. substitutes a military engagement that paradoxically illustrates how to avoid war. The annexation of Tusculum is presented through Roman eyes, with no hint that Roman citizenship may have been a privilege that such communities would rather not have accepted (*CAH*² 318–19). The episode is tripartite: preparations (25.2–6, a bridge passage), C. at Tusculum (25.6–26.2), the delegation to Rome (26.3–8).

In this story L. continues to consider the relationship between appearance and reality (cf. 12.1n., 14.2n.). The degree of artifice is high, on the levels of story and of discourse, as both L. and the Tusculans create a persuasive replacement for the expected picture of a town at war. The scene at Tusculum is a staged representation of peace which must be accepted as real if the city is to survive; it is also a *descriptio loci* such as historians were fond of writing (*RICH* 89 with n.78), one of the few extended descriptive passages in the *AVC* (cf. the Gallic entry into Rome, 5.41.4–10; the Caudine Forks, 9.2.6–8; the Alpine crossing, esp. 21.36–7). Wordplay (*commeatus ∼ comiter, hospitaliter ∼ hostiliter*) and L.'s focus on the paradoxical efficacy of the Tusculan 'arms' (26.1, 4) are among the devices used to demonstrate that things which resemble one another are not always alike. In the event, the specious demonstration is so persuasive that it becomes real (26.1n.).

25.2 extemplo with *ducturum* (sc. *esse*); *se* is in non-emphatic second position.   **Romam:** the two engagements are hinged by a brief interlude in the senate, as at 9.1–6; the return to the capital subordinates C.'s authority to the *auctoritas senatus* (26.2n.).   **ab societate:** Tusculum was traditionally conquered by Tarquinius Superbus, then again at the battle of Lake Regillus (*CAH*² 253, 258).   **si uideatur:** a polite gesture ('if he [i.e. Furius] approves'); for *uideri* 'seem best' (= δοκεῖ) see *OLD* 24.   **collega:** 23.12n.

25.3 documento ... praeferret: Furius has learned his lesson (see Chaplin 17 on the didactic component of *documentum*). For *dies documento esse* cf. 8.35.7 and the proverbial *discipulus est prioris posterior dies* (Otto 113).   **nec ... uidebatur** ∼ 5 *contra spem omnium*.   **placato animo** ∼ 6 *qua moderatione animi*; the abl. is one of manner.   **in ... casum:** 'to the brink of such a disaster', cf. Tac. *A.* 1.47.1 *in casum dare* with Goodyear; for *praeceps casus* cf. Enn. *Ann.* 390 Sk (death in battle), Cic. *De orat.* 3.13 (political martyrdom),

Sen. *Ag.* 71 (the shifts of fortune). *praeceps* is a Manlian word (17.1n.).

25.4 constans ... fama 'everyone said the same' (Radice) ∼ *uaria fortuna* below; for the phrase cf. Tac. *H.* 1.66.2 with H. and see 6.9n. **cum ... esset:** concessive. **uaria:** technical of mixed outcome in battle (*OLD* 5b). **in ... penes:** 2.4n. *penes* appears 'mostly in verse, elevated prose, and archaising literature' (M–W 80; see H. on Tac. *H.* 2.6.2). **secundae:** sc. *pugnae.*

25.5 persequendos has a connotation of punitive action (*OLD* 2c, 3). **adiutorem** ∼ 22.6 (n.). **unum ... contra spem omnium:** Lucius again is *unus* v. *omnes*, now singled out for distinction rather than for *infamia* (24.9n.). One *locus* of encomium is to describe a person as acting *supra spem aut expectationem, praecipue ... aliena potius causa quam sua* (Quint. 3.7.16). **permisso:** 17.6n. (*remisso*). **optaret ... optauit:** 14.11n. (*iaceret*).

25.6 moderatione: another ideal ruler's virtue, 'voluntary limitation of one's power or refusal to accept power which is offered' (Moore 72; see W. on Vell. 122.1, Wallace-Hadrill (1) 41–2); see also 6.7n. (*confusus*). C.'s treatment of Furius foreshadows the Roman treatment of Tusculum: expected punishment is replaced by magnanimity, which in turn garners greater glory than harshness (cf. 17.7n.). **leuauit infamiam** ∼ 23.4, 24.8. **tum ... peperit** ∼ 22.6, closing the Volscian narrative. Achieving vast *gloria* by modest behaviour is Catonian, cf. Sall. *C.* 54.6 *quo minus petebat gloriam, eo magis illum sequebatur* with Vretska and see 11.7n.; for *gloriam peperit* cf. Tac. *A.* 4.35.5. **Nec** 'but ... not' (*OLD* 5). **pace ... poterant:** the epigram is pointed by chiastic alliteration and the pun *arcere* ∼ *arma*, cf. Var. *L.* 5.115 *arma ab arcendo, quod his arcemus hostem* (Maltby 52). **p. constanti** 'unwavering peace' becomes a weapon to repel violence; the *constans fama* of Furius' culpability had a similarly unexpected outcome (4–5). For the unlikelihood of the Tusculan reaction cf. Cic. *Lig.* 28 *erat enim amentis, cum aciem uideres, pacem cogitare*; for *constantia* in L. see Moore 63–6. **non poterant** 'they could not have' (11.2n.).

25.7 intrantibus ... (10) fuisset: the scene is modelled on Metellus' march into Numidia (Sall. *J.* 46.5): *ipse ... in Numidiam procedit, ubi contra belli faciem tuguria plena hominum, pecora cultoresque in agris erant; ex oppidis et mapalibus praefecti regis obuii procedebant, parati frumentum dare, conmeatum portare, postremo omnia quae imperarentur facere. neque Metellus idcirco minus ... late explorare omnia, illa deditionis signa* *ostentui credere et insidiis locum temptari.* L.'s literary *aemulatio* increases the artificiality of the scene (25.2–26n.).   **itineri** 'the line of march' (*OLD* 5a).   **non ... intermissus:** agriculture is a symbol of peace, its interruption or destruction (as 31.8) a hallmark of war (Vell. 89.4 with W.); for the normal behaviour of farmers when war threatens see 6.4n.   **patentibus portis:** adversative asyndeton; see also 9n.   **togati:** the quintessential mark of peace (18.9n.); for the Roman term see 21.8n. and for the symbolic importance of dress see Marshall 121–3.   **imperatoribus:** Furius is now so cooperative that this is the only trace of him before the end of the year (27.1).   **commeatus ... comiter** punningly suggests a derivation *commeatus < comes*, cf. Apul. *M.* 2.18 *comiter amatoriae militiae breuem commeatum indulsit* (25.2–26n.).   **urbe ... agris** ~ *agrorum ... urbis* above (chiastic).

25.8 forma ... ostentaretur: since both words can denote deceptive display, inspecting the situation *intra moenia* is vital in properly evaluating this peace. A strong defence depends on an absolute separation of inside from outside; hence the instantaneous collapse of apparently impregnable cities the moment their inviolability is compromised (e.g. Sardis, Herod. 1.84). It follows, then, that if C. finds the same submission within the protecting/hiding walls, the city's guilelessness is genuine (hence *esset*, rather than *ostentaretur*, of what is inside). For C.'s cautious approach cf. Postumius at Feritrum (10.34.4–12) and the Gauls at Rome (5.39.1–3, 41.4); for the magical protection of city walls see Rykwert 65–71, 129–37, Konstan 198–201.

25.9 ubi ... uidit is the governing construction up through 10 *simile*. The scene that unfolds is a dramatization of the 'open door' topos, cf. Sen. *Ep.* 43.3–5 with Summers: *tunc autem felicem esse te iudica cum poteris uiuere in publico ... uix quemquam inuenies qui possit aperto ostio uiuere ... quid autem prodest recondere se et oculos hominum auresque uitare? ... si honesta sunt quae facis, omnes sciant* (W.). Open doors can also betoken surrender (e.g. 5.27.14).   **ianuas:** house doors.   **tabernis** 'shops' (*OLD* 3).   **proposita ... in medio:** i.e. for sale (*OLD propono* 1b), combining the ideas of *in medium* 'available' (6.18) and 'in the open' (14.3).   **intentos ... operi:** paying close attention to one's own business is characteristic of dedicated craftsmen, statesmen etc. (e.g. Cato *Agr.* 5.1, Cic. *Rep.* 1.35, Quint. 2.1.13); if all citizens do so, the state will be unified (cf. fr. 22.23–

30, V. Max. 7.2.6 *nisi concordia inest, maior aliena opera interpellandi quam sua edendi cupiditas nascitur*). The idea reflects long-standing definitions of justice: τὰ ἑαυτοῦ πράττειν 'to attend to one's own affairs', one of Hesiod's precepts (*Op.* 315–16), characterizes just behaviour at Plato *Rep.* 433a, d (in general V. Ehrenberg, *J.H.S.* 67 (1947) 46–67, Feeney 4–5). *intentus operi* is first and most frequent in L.; cf. 1.53.5, 23.35.14, Curt. 4.1.20, Sen. *Prou.* 2.9, Tac. *H.* 2.41.1 and the Greek idiom πρὸς ἔργα τρέπεσθαι (J. S. Rusten, *C.Q.* 35 (1985) 18 n. 28).   **opifices ... operi:** *figura etymologica* (Maltby 429).   **ludos ... uocibus:** ancient reading and study were done aloud (Bonner (2) 180, 220–4); for *l. litterarum* 'elementary school' (*OLD ludus* 6a) see Bonner (2) 56–7, 165–89.   **strepere** after *uidit* is an ex. of synaesthesia (Harrison on Virg. *A.* 10.895): the visual is paramount in C.'s survey. For *s. uocibus* cf. Sall. *J.* 98.6, Tac. *H.* 1.72.3, *A.* 1.25.2.   **semitas** 'sidewalks' (*OLD* 2).   **puerorum ... euntium:** dependent on *repletas* above, cf. Vitr. 10.8.5 *replet animae canales*. The rare construction + gen. (for abl.) may be a Livian innovation: *plenus* + gen. is idiomatic, and he likes modelling new expressions on old (2.14n., 12.10n., 34.4n.); moreover, that a construction occurs only once in the extant books is no guarantee that it did not recur in the lost ones, nor is a single occurrence necessarily un-Livian.   **p. et mulierum:** probably male and female slaves: the pair in this order in L. only here, suggesting a meaning different from '(citizen) women and children' (E. Wistrand, *Miscellanea Propertiana* (1977) 77–8).   **huc ... euntium:** cf. Hor. *Epod.* 4.9 *ora ... huc et huc euntium*, Sall. *H.* 3.48.26. For the picture of anonymous normality cf. Tac. *A.* 4.74.4 *Romae sueti discursus, et magnitudine urbis incertum quod quisque ad negotium pergat.*   **usuum** 'requirements' (*OLD* 13), cf. 7.39.2 *per speciem ... militarium usuum.*   **ferrent:** 8.6n. (*se intulisset*).

25.10 nihil ... simile: the neut. sums up the preceding list. For the compendious comparison (*OLD similis* 1b) see W. on Vell. 41.2 *fin.*   **ne mirantibus quidem:** one might expect a certain degree of surprise at the presence of a Roman army in their midst.   **circumspiciebat:** of military reconnoitring also at 44.5.10, Sall. *J.* 93.5 *temptans omnia et circumspiciens*, Sen. *Ep.* 74.3; cf. [Quad.] fr. 12 *circumspiciens despiciensque omnia.*   **inquirens oculis:** only here; cf. 13.1 with n.

25.11 adeo 'so true was it that' (*OLD* 5).   **amotae rei** 'that anything had been removed'.   **ad tempus** 'for the occasion' (*OLD tempus* 10c).   **uestigium:** C. not only inspects what is there but also looks for traces of what is not; for *uestigium* + perf. pass. participle cf. 31.31.15, Plin. *NH* 36.49.   **omnia ... pace:** interlocking word order juxtaposes the adjs.   **constanti ... pace** ∼ 25.6 (framing the first act).   **fama belli:** as this episode is described as a bloodless engagement (26.1n.), this result of Tusculum's submission may reflect one conventional outcome of a Roman victory, that not even a *nuntius cladis* survives (28.9n.).

26.1 uictus: the motif of the conqueror conquered (Otto 371, Häussler 226, 293). As in the Volscian battle, C. is the pivotal point of the episode (cf. 24.5–6).   **patientia** 'submissiveness', the best position for subjects of Rome, cf. *Praef.* 7, Tac. *Ag.* 16.2 (Moore 81–2).   **senatum eorum:** 21.8n.   **soli ... (2) dabit:** Tusculan submission and Roman magnanimity are interwoven: the real proof of the former is at Tusculum, of the latter at Rome, while at 4–7 the rebels verbally reprise their display, and C. here anticipates the senatorial pardon.   **soli adhuc** implies that there will be more such in the future (7n.).   **uera ... uires:** their display, which began as a sham (cf. 25.1), has become real, a suitable vehicle for the episode's central paradox, that *pax = arma* and a battle is won by losing.   **ab ira:** *tutari ab* is first in L. and outside him perhaps only at Plin. *NH* 7.2, Gell. 3.8.3.   **uestra:** neut. plur.

26.2 ite ... senatum: 'the senate was competent to confirm or reject any act of international relations carried out by a commander in the field' (Paul on Sall. *J.* 30.1; rejection happened esp. in the case of surrenders, as 9.5–12.4, the Caudine Forks, Sall. *J.* 39.3, Bestia's surrender to Jugurtha). C.'s self-restraint and respect for senatorial *auctoritas* is typical of an idealized republican (Miles (2) 202–3).   **Romam:** on the transition see 2.14n.   **ante ... nunc:** Tusculum's behaviour is designed to eliminate any such temporal distinction: they wish to prove that they have *always* been at peace (cf. 25.11 *ad tempus*). C., however, still differentiates between then (the war) and now. See also 4n.   **poenae ... ueniae:** cf. 24.45.8 *consultandum utrum prior defectio plus merita sit poenae an hic reditus ueniae*; the gens. are partitive. *uenia*, the remission of deserved punishment (Sen. *Clem.* 2.7.1), is a corner-stone of the Roman foreign policy of *misericordia/clementia* (Weinstock 237–43, Moore 83–5); see Brunt (2) 314–16.   **beneficii:** objective gen.   **euentum ... dabit** ~ 23.12 *intentus in euentum*: in both cases the characters share the reader's suspense.   **uidebitur:** sc. *dare*.

26.3 maestus: 16.4n.   **in uestibulo:** supplicants would wait in the vestibule either of a temple (M–W 261) or of the senate house (e.g. 7.31.5). *u. curiae*, a Livian phrase, is a place in which he likes to stage critical events, cf. 1.48.1 (Servius Tullius confronts Tarquin), 23.12.1 (the gold rings of Romans slain at Cannae are poured out in the Carthaginian *curia*).   **extemplo:** their immediate response contrasts with the behaviour of the typical tyrant, who is *rari aditus* (e.g. 3.36.2, Cic. *Vat.* 8, Tac. *A.* 4.74.2–3: Wallace-Hadrill (1) 34).   **iam tum** i.e. even before hearing their plea; their outward appearance has softened the *patres* as the appearance of their town softened C. For the emphatic particles see *OLD iam* 3b. **hospitaliter ... hostiliter:** a type of etymologizing *adnominatio* (Lausberg §§637–9) of which L. was fond (Dutoit (2) 111); cf. 1.58.8 with O., Virg. *A.* 4.323 with Pease, and for the effect of the pun see 25.2–26n. In Rome's early history there is easy slippage between the two, as former enemies become citizens and as *socii* repeatedly rebel (Serres 139–60, 196).

26.4 dictator Tusculanus: 3.18.2 with O.   **ita uerba fecit:** a historiographical tag, deriving ultimately from Thuc. 1.22.1 (on which see *RICH* 11–15, Moles, *LF* 104–7, Hornblower *ad loc.*) and indicating that the following speech represents what is likely to have been said under the circumstances (cf. 40.2, 4.3.1 *ita disseruit*, 21.12.8 *talis oratio*, Xen. *Hel.* 6.1.3, Sall. *C.* 20.1 *orationem huiusce modi*, *J.* 13.9, Dion. Hal. 11.36.1, Tac. *A.* 4.34.2, Dio 1.50.15). In view of their extensive historiographical background, such phrases should not be considered 'formulae [which] conceal stylistic changes of a sweeping kind' (*LHA* 237), a judgment implying that L.'s narrative source, which then comes to be regarded as the 'original', did not also contain freely composed speeches (above, p. 12).   **quibus ... (5) acceperimus:** the speech's first section is characterized by language reminiscent of legal or sacral formulae; the many pairs of closely related words joined with *-que* give an impression of abundance and precision.   **indixistis intulistisque:** cf. 1.32.13 *bellum indico facioque* (the fetial formula).   **sicut**

nunc ... ita: the Tusculans try to shift the time frame: 'then' becomes 'when C. came to Tusculum', not 'during the Volscian war' (cf. 2 *ante* (n.)); the speaker goes on to contrast the past with the future (5). **imperatoribus ... uestris:** repeated with *uariatio* in 5; the dictator verges on the obsequious in showing how well he understands Roman power.

26.5 habitus: i.e. the toga (25.7n.). **fuit eritque semper:** legalistic, cf. *CIL* 1² 2.593.29 *est erit*, 585.77 *factei createi sunt fueruntue*. **nisi si** 'unless' (*OLD nisi* 7). **a uobis proque uobis:** cf. Sall. *J.* 14.10 *pacem agitabamus, quippe quis hostis nullus erat, nisi forte quem uos iussissetis* (W–M). To have the same friends and the same enemies is the hallmark of friendship (Otto 19). **gratias ... (6) pia:** he turns to the question of peace and war, reaffirming the veracity of his town's demonstration and renouncing all *arma*, even those with which they just fought (1, 4). **ducibus ... exercitibus:** 6.11n. (*pluribus*), 30.7n. **quod ... crediderunt:** eyes are conventionally more trustworthy than ears (Otto 251); this pretty scene of reliable autopsy contrasts with the *seditio*, in which appearances *were* deceiving (14.2n., 20.10n.).

26.6 pacem ... experiemur: this submissive posture forces Rome to act magnanimously or to play the unprovoked aggressor, a role antithetical to its own military rhetoric (3.8n.). **bellum ... auertatis** is Livian (*TLL*); for the prayer to turn away evil (= *auersio*) see Nisbet–Hubbard on Hor. *C.* 1.21.13, Appel 125–6. **quid:** internal acc. (G–L §333). For the form of expression cf. Virg. *A.* 11.386–7 *possit quid uiuida uirtus | experiare licet*. **arma ... inermes** (3.8n.) ∼ *pacem ... bellum* above (chiastic). **patiendo** ∼ 1 *patientia hostium*; *pati* 'suffer punishment' is first in L. (*OLD* 2a). **di ... faciant:** a general appeal, averting any possible ill omen (Appel 171–2). **tam ... pia:** their intention is as well omened (*OLD felix* 2) as it is respectful (*OLD pius* 3d). On *pietas* in L. see Moore 56–61; one of the statesman's virtues, it was esp. promoted by Caesar and Augustus (Weinstock 228, 248–59). For *mens pia*, first here (*pace* Bömer on Ov. *M.* 8.767), cf. Sen. *Polyb.* 18.6, Plin. *Pan.* 81.1.

26.7 attinet ... nihil attinet 'is concerned ... there is no point'; for the *traductio* see 3.5n. **bellum indixistis** ∼ 4 (frame). **reuicta:** technical of rebutting a charge (*OLD* 2); the participle is

causal.   **rebus uerbis** ~ 5 *oculis ... auribus*.   **confutare:**
synonymous with *reuincere* (*OLD* 4); for the *uariatio* see 7.5n.
etiam si ... sint: an ideal protasis referring to the present,
'though they be true' – with no implication as to its fulfilment
(*NLS* §198).   **uel fateri ... censemus** 'we deem it safe for us
even [*OLD uel* 5] to acknowledge them, since we have so clearly
repented'.   **euidenter** 'for all to see' (Radice): 5n.   **peccetur ... satisfiat** 'let people sin against you, provided you are
worthy to receive satisfaction in this way'; cf. Ov. *Tr.* 2.31–2 *sed
nisi peccassem, quid tu concedere posses? | materiam ueniae sors tibi nostra
dedit*, Tac. *A.* 3.50.2. The dictator ingeniously makes this a test of
Roman *clementia* (2n.), not of Tusculan guilt, and the scene becomes
an aetiology for one kind of ideal behaviour (above, p. 15): for Tusculum as an *exemplum* of Romulus' paradigmatic policy of enlarging
the state *etiam hostibus recipiendis* cf. Cic. *Balb.* 31; for it as an illustration of Roman magnanimity and civility cf. Dion. Hal. 14.6.1–2.

26.8 tantum ... factum ~ 4 *ita ... fecit* (n.).   **ab Tusculanis:** only the dictator spoke, but by assimilating the leader to the
led L. increases the universality and legitimacy of the claim. He
further implies a desirable harmony between leader and state
(4.6n.).   **in praesentia ... post:** the temporal focus shifts
again, from past guilt/present repentance (2n.) to present pardon/
future amalgamation.   **ab Tusculo ... reductae:** a characteristically quick end (24.11n.); for the return see 4.1n.

27–9 The year 380 B.C.

27–28.4 *Internal affairs*

Domestic problems worsen, particularly the related issues of debt
and military service (both familiar from the Manlian *seditio*: 27.6–
8n.). Following the election of *tr. mil.*, the *res internae* are framed by
the appointment of censors (27.4) and of a dictator (28.3), two extraordinary offices necessitated by emergency situations. External success is still possible (witness Quinctius' triumph) but dangerously
threatened by internal strife: the censors' failure, which the *tr. pl.*
attribute to patrician corruption (27.6–8), produces civil unrest

which nearly compromises the military project (Lipovsky 39, Levene 209).

27.1 Camillus ... (2) Maluginense: the end of 381 and beginning of 380 blend into each other (1.5n.). The sentence has magnified 'wings' and a tiny centre: *C. ... insignis* (subj.) *magistratu abiit* (main clause) *creatis ... Maluginense* (appended abl. abs.: above, p. 21). **singulari:** 23.1n. **aduersus** 'with regard to' (*OLD* 11). **insignis:** qualified by a tricolon *auctum* of abls. of respect. For C.'s uirtutes see 23.1n. (*consilium*), 11.3n. (*uirtus*), 18.13n. (*felicitas*), 25.6n. (*moderatio*); for *patientia* 'forbearance' see Moore 81.

27.2 militaribus: *uariatio* for *militum* (12.10n.). **L. ... tertium:** there was a 'strongly marked tendency to group together members of the same *gens*' in such lists (Drummond (1) 93).

27.3 annus: the year is frequently personified in annalistic history (M–W 136); in L. cf. 3.15.1, 9.18.15 *in ipso conatu rerum circumegit se annus*, 27.6.17. **incertam:** i.e. that offered differing estimates of the size of the public debt (*OLD* 8b). *incerta fama* ∼ 25.4 *constans ... fama*, the latter involving military matters whose interpretation was secure. **aggrauantibus ... eleuaretur:** the reasons why the rumour was *incerta*; for abl. abs. ∼ *cum*-clause see Sörbom 115. *aggrauantibus* is a medical word (*OLD* 3a: Dutoit (1) 122). **summam:** the total of the debt (Watt 214–15), cf. 6 *summam aeris alieni*. **inuidiosius:** cf. 40.13, Vell. 45.3, Just. 12.3.9; for *inuidia* as a factor in domestic upheaval see 11.3n. **ab iis:** the money-lenders (cf. 14.3, 15.8). **quibus ... expediebat** 'in whose interest it was that the loans should appear to be in trouble because of the debtors' (lack of) reliability rather than their bad luck'. Through the figure antiphrasis (Lausberg §585) *fides* implies its opposite, cf. Luc. 2.253–4 *mundique ruinae | permiscenda fides* (i.e. *mala f.*); analogous are 27.47.9 *fessi ... somno ac uigiliis* (with which W–M cf. Hom. *Il.* 10.98, Hor. *C.* 3.4.11) and the traditional derivation *ludus quia sit longissime a lusu* (Quint. 1.6.34: Maltby 350).

27.4 creati: sc. *sunt.* **res** 'business'. **suffici** 'to be appointed in another's place' is technical (*OLD* 2); on suffect censors see O. on 5.31.6. **religio** 'taboo' ∼ 5 *religiosum* (Catterall 299); for *religio est* + infin. see *OLD* 1b.

27.5 Sulpicius ... alii ... tertios: the last element disturbs

the parallelism of case (2.2n.).   **uitio:** a ritual fault (*OLD* 6).
creati is causal.   **uelut ... accipientibus** gives the reason for
the decision, a use of *uelut* + participle first in L. (G–L §666 N,
OLD uelut 6).

27.6–8. The *tr. pl.* speak at length and without answer from the
patricians; the conflict resumes at 31.1–4, in preparation for the extended narrative of 34–42. Their allegations are familiar from the
seditio (*demersam* ∼ 14.7, 17.2; 7 *ciuium ... odio* ∼ 16.5; 8 *neruo* ∼ 11.8;
for war as a diversion from domestic problems cf. 15.7n.). But their
interpretation of the senate's motives (6) contradicts the narrative's
contention that there was a religious hindrance (4–5); similarly,
their accusation that wars are being stirred up to occupy the plebs
is at odds with L.'s presentation of those wars as retaliation for in-
juries (e.g. 21.3), and with the desperate situation that arises at 11.
Yet the *tr. pl.* have a point: the patricians, who are more interested
in power than in justice, have acted duplicitously in the past (e.g.
11.9–10, 20.10–11); moreover, *res externae* do function as a distraction
from *res internae* both within the story (e.g. 9, 21.5) and on a narrative level, as the history shifts back and forth between theatres (cf.
12–13). The ideal situation, both from the historian's and the magistrates' standpoint, is a narrative of exciting wars conducted by a
peaceful, regularly functioning state (above, p. 11 and see 1.1n.). Instead, in Book 6 domestic narrative predominates (57 per cent:43
per cent *res ext.*), and subversive voices manage by the end even to
break through the authoritative patrician voice (40–1n.). But once
the domestic tension is eased, the military machine can begin to
move: Books 7–10 increasingly subordinate *res internae* (Lipovsky 89).

27.6 uero 'but' (*OLD* 7b).   **ludificationem:** technical of
teasing tactics in warfare, such as the Cunctator's delay against
Hannibal (Wheeler 80–1): so too the patricians refuse to face the
plebs in pitched battle. *plebis* is objective gen.   **tabulas publicas** 'public records' (O. on 4.8.4), in apposition to *testes*. The census determined military and political rights and responsibilities
(Nicolet (1) 49–88).   **census cuiusque** 'of each person's property'.   **conspici:** for the claim that open display (cf. *publicas*
above) will reveal something's true nature see 12.1n., and for patricians withholding information cf. 1.10 (n.).   **quae ... sit:**
causal.   **partem a parte:** on the polyptoton see G. Landgraf,

A.L.L. 5 (1888) 180, 187; the emphatic repetition of sounds continues below with *ob- ... ob-* and *aliis ... aliis*. The theme of parts-of-the-city is developed later (37.4n.).   **obaeratam:** attested before this passage only as a masc. substantive (*TLL*).   **obiectari:** for the acc. + infin. after *cum interim* see 11.4n.; for the form of expression see Goodyear on Tac. *A.* 2.5.1 *dolo ... obiectaret.*

27.7 ab Antio ... Tusculum: 8.8n.   **intentari:** first here in prose in a metaphorical sense ('threaten', *OLD* 2), cf. 39.7, and for the frequentative see 1.11n.   **ut ... agentem:** the prohibited activities become progressively more engaged and hence more threatening. The *tr. pl.* recall their colleagues' argument at 5.2.11 *ciues eorum, non seruos militare, quos hieme saltem in domos ac tecta reduci oporteat et ... usurpare libertatem et creare magistratus.*   **respirare** 'pause for breath' (*OLD* 2), i.e. have a respite from war (cf. 32.1).   **otium:** one of the great civic blessings, along with *pax, concordia,* and *libertas* (Wirszubski 91–3); the tribunes' definition of *otium* as the chance to live politically is in pointed contrast to the Tusculans' inertial *pax* (25.6–26).   **libertatis:** objective gen.   **consistere in contione:** the third complement of *sinant,* set off by alliteration, is placed after the governing verb to accommodate the subsequent description of the *contio* (cf. 16.1).   **in contione:** L.'s plebs share the ancient crowd's fondness for listening to speeches, esp. in times of political turmoil, cf. 3.68.7 *affixi contionibus,* 4.12.7, Ar. *Kn.* 215–16, 1111–20 (the *demos* gapes after speakers), Thuc. 3.38 with Gomme, Cic. *Att.* 1.16.11 *illa contionalis ... plebecula,* Caes. *C.* 2.12.1 (soldiers), Hor. *C.* 2.13.32 with Nisbet–Hubbard, Tac. *D.* 39.4–5 with Gudeman (spectators in the Forum as in the theatre).   **ubi ... audiant:** sarcastic: 'where sometime they might hear'.   **finem** ∼ *de ... fenore* above. *agere* 'urge a course of action' (*OLD* 42) admits of both constructions, cf. 37.1.1 *nulla prius ... acta in senatu res est quam de Aetolis* and for a similar *uariatio* cf. Tac. *A.* 4.9.2 *memoriae Drusi eadem quae in Germanicum decernuntur.*

27.8 memor ... libertatis ∼ 7 *libertatis meminisse.* Memory is a powerful emotional spur that offers a chance to re-evaluate the past and consequently to change the present (20.8n., 28.8n.; above, pp. 14–15). This appeal to the 'good old days' implies that it is the people's fault that they have declined from the virtues of their fathers; for the *laudatio temporis acti* cf. e.g. 3.20.5 (the good old days were religious), Hom. *Il.* 1.260–72 (men were men), Pratinas, fr. 708 Page (there was no loud music or wild dancing on stage), Ar. *Cl.* 889–1114 with Dover (there was proper education), Sall. *J.* 41–2 with Paul (society and politics were ethical), Sen. *Contr.* 2.1.8, 18 (men were poor and virtuous), and in general Vell. 92.5 with W. On the theme of degeneracy see Feeney; on the recovery of *libertas* as a slogan see Paul on Sall. *J.* 30.3.   **inspecto ... alieno** ∼ 6 *conspici ... alieni* (frame). *inspicere* is technical of official enquiry, cf. Cic. *Balb.* 11, Trajan *apud* Plin. *Ep.* 10.48.1.   **ratione** 'a plan' (*OLD* 10a).   **sciat unus quisque:** the *tr. pl.* move from the *summa aeris alieni* (6) to each individual's status, the argument growing more pathetic as it becomes more personal. If the Tusculans' devotion each to his own business symbolized peace (25.9n.), the plebeian inability even to identify what is theirs is a very bad sign indeed. See also 36.11n.

   27.9 Merces ... excitauit: an epigrammatic transition echoing the Manlian narrative (16.7, 17.6).   **seditionis** reappears here for the first time since 18.1 (the end of a cluster: 11.1–2, 8, 14.1, 16.6, 8, 17.6 *bis*). It similarly clusters here (also at 11, 28.3, 31.1–2, 33.1); the echo should apprise us of the severity of this upheaval. **confestim:** a Livian favourite (*c.* 70 exx.) promoted otherwise by Col., Plin. *NH*, Suet., Apul. (*TLL*).   **nam et:** L. confirms part of the tribunes' statement (11.9n.).   **ad ... belli:** interlocking arrangement of a prep. phrase + qualifiers is particularly Livian (Pettersson 135); see 3.3n.   **ad** 'in response to' (*OLD* 33a). **famam belli:** the war begins as a rumour of war. L.'s narrative form mimics the actions of the Praenestini, who accelerate toward the city after a cautious and indirect approach (cf. 10 *quippe ... nuntiabatur* (parenthetical), 28.1 report of the situation at Rome, 28.2 *raptim ... protinus ... ad portam*).   **quae utraque:** sc. *res.*   **tribunicio** ∼ *plebis* (9.5n.).   **consensu:** 20.3n.

   27.10 nomina dabant: i.e. enrol for a *dilectus* (*IM* 629–30). **in praesens:** the MSS omit *in*, giving good Livian Latin (Pettersson 142 n.1) but bad sense: the distinction is not between an immediate worry and a distant one, but between which of two situations is the more drastic.   **creditae pecuniae** depends on *iuris*, which (with *dilectus* below) depends on *cura*.   **iuris exse-**

quendi 'of enforcing the statute', legal language (*TLL exsequor*). **consedisse:** technical of taking a military position (*OLD* 2). **nuntiabatur** ∼ 28.1 *nuntiatum* (a message to the enemy).

27.11 magis: with *irritauerat*; for the thought cf. 16.7, 38.9. **exstinguendam:** L. turns from the metaphor of illness (18.1n.) to the common one of fire; both image a turmoil under the surface. Cf. Sall. *C.* 31.9, 48.2 with Vretska (*incendium* was 'practically a political slogan'), Vell. 48.3 *bello ... subiecit facem* with W., Tac. *A.* 1.22.1 with Goodyear. For *seditionem exst.* cf. Cic. *Marc.* 32 (*dissensio*), Just. 11.2.4.

28.1 nullum ... uersos: anaphora of *nullum* and the placement of *esse* bring natural pairs together (army and general, *patres* and *plebs*).

28.2 occasionem rati 'thinking that this was their chance', cf. Pub. *Sent.* 680 M *seditio ciuium hostium est occasio.* **portam Collinam:** the N. E. gate, through which the Gauls came a decade earlier (5.41.4; Richardson 302). The choice of gate is not fortuitous (28.5–29n.). **intulere** ∼ 27.11 *illatum ... bellum.*

28.3 trepidatio: this and the following impers. passives convey a sense of blind reaction; with *uersi ... creauere* below the Romans exercise independent thought. **ad arma:** 'the normal call "to arms!"' (Nisbet–Hubbard on Hor. *C.* 1.35.13). **concursum:** a typical reaction to a surprise attack, cf. 5.18.11, 21.6, Caes. *C.* 3.105.4, Sall. *J.* 60.6, V. Max. 1.6.12 and see Miniconi 168. **adque:** a rare but attested collocation, cf. Sis. fr. 125, Var. *R.* 1.2.8, V. Max. 3.7.3. The paradosis *in muros atque portas* does not make much sense (they are not running into the city, as 32.18.8 *cum refugientibus in portam*), whereas *ad portas* is expected in this scene (e.g. 31.24.7 *ad portas, ad muros discurrunt*, 42.53.9 *concursu ad portas*, 44.13.3 *discurrunt armati ad portas ac moenia*).

28.4 quod ... est: the dictatorship and its attendant panoply were awe-inspiring from the first, both to the plebs (2.18.8 *magnus plebem metus incessit ut intentiores essent ad dicto parendum*) and to the enemy (2.18.9 *Sabinis ... creatus Romae dictator ... metum incussit*) – the office has a sort of magical power (see also 2.9n.). **recessere ... conuenere:** homoioteleuton. **ad** 'in obedience to' (*OLD* 34a).

28.5–29 Affairs abroad

Once again the discordant Romans unite on the battlefield (cf. 12–13). A triad of enemies (Praenestini, Volsci, Tusculani) was involved in the battle at Satricum (22.4, 25.1): L. has dealt with them in the order BCA, and now he closes the ring that opened with the Volsci (22.6–24) and of which the Tusculans formed the central panel (25–6). As the engagements grow more challenging the Romans become increasingly self-assured. In the Volscian war the conflict between tribunes nearly cost them an easy victory; Tusculum forced the militaristic Romans to adapt to an unprecedented adversarial strategy; now the Praenestini plan to win by reusing the site of Rome's greatest disaster, the Gallic victory at the Allia. The Allia's date has become part of the calendar, a *dies religiosus* to be remembered each year (1.11n.): a memory that metaphorically means that the battle 'takes place' annually as the calendrical cycle repeats. The Praenestini hope to take advantage of a similar talismanic power investing the battle-site; why, they reason, should the Allia's *locus* not be a place where history repeats itself as well (6)? But the Romans have different historical *exempla* in mind: Lake Regillus (8) and the second battle against the Gauls (9), a 'superior deployment of the past' (Chaplin 110). The paradigms represent two kinds of historical repetition: 'regressive repetition', in which an event obsessively recurs; and 'repetition-as-reversal', in which there is a chance to play things differently (Hardie 14–18). Each 18 July can be seen as inevitably ill-omened; or the original date can teach a lesson that alters each subsequent 18 July, so that its associated disaster need not recur. So too with the place 'Allia' (6n.). (On the two ways of describing time's cycle see J. De Romilly, *Time in Greek tragedy* (1968) 3–32 (the convergence of the *kairos* and the nontemporal *cosmos*); for time in historiography see A. Momigliano, *Essays in ancient and modern historiography* (1977) 179–204 and Miles (1).)

28.5 inde ... (7) suas: neatly circular, resembling a *paradeigma* (17.1n.): (1) the enemy boasted the place was *fatalis*; (2) thence would come the same fear for the Romans as in the Gallic war; (3) for (*etenim*) if they feared the day, so much more would they fear the place; (4) they would indeed see and hear the Gauls once again; (5) so the enemy relied on the *fortuna* of the place.   **fatalem:**

most recently of Rome's capture: 5.33.1 *aduentante fatali urbi clade.*
The Praenestini choose their words carefully, as if exact repetition
of epithet and site might work a kind of sympathetic magic; for
fatalis + dat. cf. Vell. 52.1 with W. **locum** ~ 7 *loci* (frame).

28.6 ac ... ac: the first *ac* = 'and', the second is with *similem*,
'the same as' (*NLS* §251). **fuerit:** for the tense see 5.3n.
contactum 'contaminated' (*OLD* 6), first in prose in L. in this
sense; cf. Lucr. 2.680 *religione animum turpi contingere* and cf. 1.11.
monumentum ... cladis: places evoke the past (cf. 20.9–10
and for battle sites see Nisbet–Hubbard on Hor. *C.* 2.1.30); among
battlegrounds, perhaps most memorable is the forest site of the
clades Variana where history nearly repeats itself within the story
(Tac. *A.* 1.61–8), while on the level of discourse it *does* repeat: the
Annales passage is textually modelled on the *Historiae* (*RICH* 168–79).
There is a similar overlap here between text and content: the enemy believe that this place will recreate the Gauls, while the Romans want to change history (8) and will set up a new *monumentum*
in the form of a narrative record of Praeneste's defeat (29.9n.).
Both are engaged in revisionist history, the Praenestini wishing literal revision, the Romans revision as change (28.5–29n.). The latter
interpretation must triumph if the city is to continue to develop: *loca*
can be named after enemies (e.g. the *lacus Curtius* at 1.13.5, the *busta
Gallica* at 5.48.3), but they must memorialize Rome's successes, not
its failures (the Sabines are incorporated into Rome and the *lacus
Curtius* later gets a second, Roman aetiology (7.6.3–5); the pyres
commemorate the Gauls' deaths, not their investment of the
city). **reformidaturos:** sc. *Romanos.* **species ... sonumque:** Gauls, stereotypically wild in appearance and loud of voice,
were particularly known for singing (Balsdon 65, 214–15, O. on
5.37.8). **in oculis ... fore:** the Praenestini go even further
than Manlius' supporters (17.4n.) in imagining the vivid recreation
of history; for eyes and ears see 16.3n.

28.7 inanium ... inanes: L.'s polyptoton exposes the enemy's
(6 *Alliensi ... Alliam*) as decoration without substance: *inanis* is the
mot juste for insubstantial reports, words, or appearances, including
those of the dead (*OLD* 10a, 11–12). **ipsas** i.e. *ipsas quoque*
(*OLD* 6). **uoluentes** of thought is choice (first at Lucr. 6.34,
then in Sall. L. Tac.; cf. 35.18.6 with B.). **fortunae loci:** Prae-

nestine reliance on *fortuna*, twice emphasized in the same words (cf. 29.1), alludes to the town's most famous feature, the temple of *Fortuna Primigenia* (Champeaux 95 n.450). **delegauerant:** properly of delegating a task or transferring a liability, ownership etc.; L.'s mannered expression suggests the degree of the enemy's trust in their goddess (last n.). **ubicumque ... hostis:** the Romans break the 'Allia argument' into pieces: first, these foes are not Gauls but Latins; second, the place does not matter (8 *locum* ∼ 5 *locum*, 7 *loci*); third (9) even if they were Gauls, the Romans could defeat them (for the *diuisio* see 18.6n.). Rome will in fact soon beat the Gauls themselves (42.4–8). **obnoxia:** the adj. is causative: the peace has made them subservient, cf. 9.10.4 *emersisse ciuitatem ex obnoxia pace,* [Quint.] *Decl.* 13.11 *obnoxia infirmitas.*

28.8 insignem ∼ 6 *insignem*; the Romans appropriate the Latins' language, cf. 29.1 *fortunae loci* (n.) and see 19.2n. **se:** obj. of *irritaturum.* **ad ... memoriam:** lit. 'to erase the record' (for *memoria* 'written record' see *OLD* 8a). The 'real' Allia stands in L.'s *memoria rerum gestarum* and the symbolic Allia in the calendar and cannot be erased; but after this engagement the site will mean both Roman defeat and Roman courage. The inevitability implied by the disaster in Book 5 is compensated for by the correction in 6 (see also 6n.). **quam ut ... faciat:** 8.10n. **ne ... suae:** in order to secure their future safety the Romans must prove that nothing can defeat them (cf. 5.6.7–8, 53.5–7). In an Augustan context, the idea that all lands are licit areas of conquest reflects the image of the city as the world, first popular in the third century but esp. so in the late republic and early empire (*urbs orbis*: W. on Vell. 85.1, Nicolet (2) 29–56). **terra ... nefasta:** cf. Stat. *Th.* 1.273–4 *delubra nefastis | imposuere locis* (Drakenborch).

28.9 ut Romae: 5.49.1–5. **ut ... ad Gabios:** sc. *pugnauerint* (5.49.6). For the repetition of *ut* see 40.2n. **ne quis hostis:** either those particular Gauls or any enemy who at any time crosses the walls. The ambiguity appropriately figures the emblematic quality of the historical action. For the defiant Roman stance cf. 1.7.2 *sic deinde, quicumque alius transiliet moenia mea* (Romulus killing Remus); on walls see 25.8n. **aduersaeque:** for the disjunctive *-que* see *OLD* 7. **nuntium ... perferret:** for the topos cf. 5.49.6 with O., adding 10.26.10, 26.2.14, 27.49.9, Fron. *S.* 2.10.2, Flor. 1.46.10, H. Melville, 'Epilogue' to *Moby Dick* and see 25.11n.

29.1 ad: used idiomatically with the names of battlefields (*OLD* 13a). *Alliam* ~ 5 *Allia*, marking the description of the preparations as mildly digressive.   **instructi intentique:** an uncommon combination (cf. 10.43.2, Sall. *J.* 53.5, Tac. *H.* 1.62.2). That it was felt to be a set phrase, however, is shown by the *uariatio* practised on it, e.g. 6.13, 36.38.2 *militem instructum tenuit intentus*, Tac. *H.* 4.69.3 *instruendo bello intentus*. It is one of three alliterative doublets (with 2 *armis animisque*; *turbatos trepidantesque*); cf. the pairs *certioris ... maiorisue* (below), 2 *uobis uiolatis nobisque ... deceptis*; *non equitem, non peditem* (Ullmann (2) 23).   **loci fortuna** ~ 28.7. Quinctius uses the Latins' own trick of repetition (28.5n.) to control their symbols; see 19.2n. and Chaplin 110.   **fretos** ~ 2 *fretus* (last n.). Each instance of human trust is followed by an appropriate divine response (*nec ... di ... dederint* ~ 2 *adeste di testes*).   **certioris:** i.e. than *fortuna*, which is by definition unreliable.   **certioris ... auxilii** 'nothing more reliably dependable or that would be of greater help'. The gens. are descriptive.   **dederint:** either a fut. perf. ('the gods will [turn out to] have given': Stephenson) or perf. subjunc. in the apodosis of a condition whose protasis is inferred from *uidesne ... constitisse*: 'even if they rely ... the gods have not given them' (W–M; see 14.4n.).

29.2 adeste ... testes: repeated sounds manifest the divine presence in advance; cf. 40.14, 41.9 (nn.).   **testes foederis:** part of the ritual declaration of war was the *testatio deorum*, calling the gods to witness that the war was just (O. p. 127); for the prayer at the making of the *foedus* cf. 21.45.8.   **Praenestini:** words beginning with *prae-* accumulate in the battle and its aftermath (up to 8 *Praeneste*), a verbal decoration enhanced by the play with forms of *primus* (3: Maltby 495) and *postquam* (3, 5). Praeneste, according to Cato (fr. 60), was so called *quia ... montibus praestet*; the Romans here show who is really on top.

29.3 praeter ... praelati: cf. 7.24.8 *praeter castra etiam sua fuga praelati ... arcem Albanam petunt*; for the topos cf. 32.9, 5.26.7, Hom. *Il.* 16.367–76, 21.608–11, Caes. *C.* 2.35.5.

29.4 ex fuga dissipata: cf. 2.59.9 *collectis ex dissipato cursu militi-*

bus, 38.27.8 *Galli ex dissipata passim fuga in unum locum congregati*. The MSS *ex f. dissipati* 'scattered fugitives' (Radice) loses the contrast between their headlong flight and subsequent regrouping, however shortlived (Madvig 134).   **quem ... communirent:** purpose. **omnibus:** neut. pl. (3.5n.).

29.5 munimentum ... moenia: in 4 they preferred their fortification (*communirent*) to the *moenia*, but the mere sight of the Romans makes them change their plan; both defensive structures are doomed to be replaced by the Roman *monumentum* (9). For the paronomasia see Maltby 388, 392, 397.   **Praeneste:** abl., as in 8; it is nom. in 3, acc. in 7.

29.6 octo ... (7) uentum: Quinctius takes his time. The eventual capitulation of Praeneste is by implication due to this methodical elimination of any possible allies, including the delinquent Velitrae (22.2).   **ad ea ... eae ... (7) id:** repeated use of a resumptive pron. is characteristic of scholarly or precise style (cf. 5.34.1–8, the Gallic ethnography) as well as evoking early prose (von Albrecht 39, Eden 80, 86–7).

29.7 ui ... per deditionem: 3.10n.

29.8 T. Quinctius ... reuertit: the language, esp. the abls. absolute, is characteristic of an official military report (3.10n.) or a dedicatory inscription (von Albrecht 60, cf. *CIL* III 14147).   **triumphans ... tulit:** 'triumph' language (4.1n.); for *ferre* see Phillips 272.   **signum ... Iouis Imperatoris:** for captured gods in triumphal parades cf. Virg. *A.* 8.726–8, Ov. *Ars* 1.223–4 (river gods), Jos. *BJ* 7.148–50 (religious objects from the Temple at Jerusalem).

29.9 cellam: 4.3n.   **monumentum r. g.:** Quinctius' *monumentum* replaces the enemy's (28.6n.).   **his ferme ... litteris:** the *tabula* has its own indeterminability, like the speeches L. 'reproduces' (26.4n.). Inscriptions and other documents lend precision (*acribeia*) to historical narratives (Fehling 133–40, 170–4), while *ferme* can be code for scholarly care (cf. 20.6n.: the adv. is generally taken to indicate that L. has abbreviated this inscription (so W–M) or is giving a traditional version of it). L. includes such 'documents' only rarely (above, p. 10 n.42); this one caps the episode, reifying the new history Quinctius has created (26.8n. and next n. but

one).　**ferme:** an archaizing equivalent of *fere* most prominent
in the third decade (Adams (4) 57).　**Iuppiter ... caperet:** like
L.'s text, the *tabula* is a historical narrative, selecting the details of
divine aid, Roman power (*dictator*), and a precise number (20.6n.)
to represent Quinctius' *res gestae*. For stories elaborated from inscriptions see T. P. Wiseman in *PP* (triumphal records were among
them: Asel. fr. 2).　**diui:** an old-fashioned form common in Livian religious *formulae* (B. on 31.7.12).　**hoc:** picked up by *ut ...
caperet*.　**dederunt** ∼ *1 nec ... dederint*, confirming Quinctius' pre-
diction that the gods would not help the enemy.
　29.10 quam 'after' (*OLD* 12b).

30 The year 379 B.C.

30.1–7 Affairs abroad

30.1 aequatus ... numerus: L. draws attention to the generic
composition of the college, whose even division heralds the imminent debate over dividing the consulship between the orders (34–
42). The year's events provide a paradigm for plebeian leadership
– patrician military command fails (6n.) and the split college produces complete peace at home (9) – but the lesson is ignored. The
structure of this year is reversed in the next (31–32.2n.).
　30.2 ex patribus creati ∼ *plebes ... dedit* (*uariatio*; cf. 7.1.2).
　30.3 genere ... gratia: a system of military promotion that
values birth and influence over prudent experience (cf. 6 *temeritate
atque inscitia*) is likely to produce disaster. The idea was esp. current
in the Marian years and after (37.11n.).　**Iulium:** the Julii,
though an old patrician *gens*, were 'obscure and undistinguished' in
the middle republic (O. on 1.30.2, Weinstock 5); the Manlii figure
prominently in L.'s narrative of these years (e.g. 11–20, 7.3.9–5,
7.9–10, 8.5.7–7).　**prouincia:** in apposition to *Volsci*.　**sine
sorte ... ordinem:** for the apportioning of provinces see 22.6n.;
comparatio, which refers to an agreement among the magistrates (O.
on 3.2.2) is otherwise unattested in this sense (*TLL*; but see *OLD
comparo*[1] 9).　**postmodo paenituit:** cf. Catul. 30.12 *quae te ut
paeniteat postmodo facto faciet tui*. Only L. (9) and Ovid (23) favour *post-*

modo; outside L. it is rare in prose (e.g. Pollio *apud* Cic. *Fam.* 10.33.1, Col. 1.8.14, Sen. *Vit.* 17.3), and in poetry outside elegy (Bömer on Ov. *M.* 12.5).

30.4 inexplorato: first in L. (Walsh on 21.25.9); on the form see 12.7n. For the necessity of sending out scouts see Pritchett II 188.   **circumuentis** 'outflanked' is part of a double dative with *praesidio* below; for its technical use see Wheeler 80, 82. This false report of a stratagem is itself a stratagem; for lying to the enemy, esp. to lure him into an ambush, see Wheeler 40, 85.   **id:** i.e. that they had been surrounded.   **asseruato** 'kept under observation'.   **pro** 'pretending to be' (*OLD* 9c). For disguise as a stratagem cf. Sall. *J.* 69.1 (Numidian cavalry mask a hostile Roman force), Fron. *S.* 2.5.10, 15 (a disguised enemy lures troops into ambush); linguistic disguise is also possible, e.g. Sall. *J.* 101.6, Plut. *Sert.* 3.2 (learning enough of a foreign language to fool the enemy). **praecipitauere:** frequent of falling into ambushes (Walsh on 21.25.9): the Roman disaster is as quick as their rush to help (*citati* above).

30.5 uirtute militum ∼ 6 *militum ... uirtus* (framing the battle).   **restantes** 'resisting' (*OLD* 2a); cf. *stabilis* below.   **caedunt caeduntturque** images the reciprocal slaughter of an infantry battle, cf. Hom. *Il.* 11.83 'destroying and being destroyed', Xen. *Cyr.* 7.1.38 'they pushed, were pushed, struck, were struck', *Hel.* 4.3.19 'they killed, they died', Dion. Hal. 9.63.6, Tac. *A.* 6.35.1 *ut conserta acies ... pellerent pellerentur*. See also 33.9n.   **iacentia:** a geographer's term: 'lying' (*OLD* 11b).

30.6 ab ducibus: for the contrast between soldierly virtue and generals' error cf. 35.6.9 (quoted below), Caes. *G.* 5.34.2 and see O. p. 510, W. on Vell. 112.5. That the soldiers can preserve their lives and their dignity without their patrician commanders foreshadows the events at the end of the book.   **temeritate ... inscitia:** cf. 8.33.17 *qui t. atque i. exercitus amisissent*; outside L. the combination is at Cic. *Prou.* 11, Tac. *A.* 13.20.3.   **quidquid ... tutata est:** cf. 35.6.9 *fortunae p. R. et militum uirtuti gratiam habendam quod res bene gesta esset* with B.   **fortunae:** partitive gen. For Rome's destiny see 21.2n. and Walsh on 21.10.6.   **stabilis uirtus:** cf. 26.41.12 *immobilis u.*, Cic. *Har.* 41 *praestabili ... uirtute*, *Phil.* 4.13 *uirtus est una altissimis defixa radicibus*, Sall. *J.* 1.1–3, V. Max. 2.2.5 *uirtutis*

... *stabilimentum.* Chaos and uncontrolled motion are among the commonest ways of describing military or political disaster (in 4–8 cf. *citati, praecipitauere, sine rectore, tumultuatum, concitatis*); for such imagery in 'civil war' language see 14.9n.

30.7 primum ... placebat: chiastic alliteration. **postquam ... afferebantur** 'once reports started to be brought in'; for *postquam* + imperf. see 10.4n. **nescire ... uti:** L. quotes Marhabal's famous criticism of Hannibal when he stopped just short of attacking Rome (22.51.4, cf. Plut. *Fab.* 17.2). Caesar is reputed to have said the same about Pompey after Dyrrachium (Suet. *Jul.* 36 with Butler–Cary); cf. Eunap. *Hist.* 265.14 Dindorf, where the accusation is hurled at a prudent commander. Not following through is one mark of inferior foreign military performance (as Sall. *J.* 38.8, the Numidians cannot 'use their victory' because they are distracted by *praeda*); see further 32.7n. **uictoria ... uti:** an expression whose Greek equivalent is more common, cf. Xen. *Hel.* 7.5.25, Caes. *C.* 3.83.4, Diod. 10.24.3, Plut. *Nic.* 16.7. **reuocati:** 4.1n. **exercitus ac duces:** in parallel constructions (as 23.1) and pairs L. prefers the order *d. + e.* (as 6.11, 26.5) by slightly more than 2:1, perhaps for the slight weight at the end.

30.7–9 *End of the year*

Otiumque inde: for the transitional markers see *OLD -que* 4, *inde* 5. **quantum a Volscis** 'as far as the Volsci were concerned' (*OLD ab* 25).

30.8 id: internal acc., expanded by *quod* 'the fact that' below. **tumultuatum:** impers. passive, found earlier at Caes. *G.* 7.61.3; the verb is regularly deponent. A *tumultus* normally led to an emergency levy (*IM* 629–31); L. simply abandons this potential story.

30.9 Setiam: acc. of end of motion (*OLD ascribo* 2b); cf. 16.6. The colony's traditional founding date is 383 (*CAH*² 280). **ipsis** i.e. the inhabitants of Setia, cf. Catul. 10.9 with Fordyce. **haud prosperis** ~ 34.1 *prosperis ... bellis.* **bello domestica:** for the usual polar expression *bellum* (in various cases)/*domi* (loc.), for which cf. 42.9 and *OLD bellum* 1b. **quies** 'peace' (*OLD* 6a), an omnipresent ideal in the middle of the first century (Weinstock 267–9, cf. esp. Caes. *C.* 3.57.4 *quietem Italiae, pacem prouinciarum, salutem imperii*). It eventually came to signify withdrawal from politics (W. on Vell. 88.2) rather than peaceful pursuit of them, as here. It is the calm before the storm (31.1).   **quam ... obtinuit** 'which the plebeian military tribunes' popularity and dignity among their followers obtained'. See 1n.   **solacium:** success in one sphere compensates for disaster in another; cf. 45.41.12, Sen. *Marc.* 3.2, 5.1–3, *Helu.* 18, Tac. *A.* 3.24.1. L.'s solace may be directed at the reader as well as the actors. Both he and Tacitus claim that 'good' history provides consolation for troubles that one must either live through or write/read about; cf. *Praef.* 4–5 (writing ancient history consoles L. for the contemporary evils toward which his readers are hurrying, i.e. the later books of the *AVC*), Tac. *H.* 1.3.1, 3.51.2 *sed haec aliaque ex uetere memoria petita, quotiens res locusque exempla recti aut solacia mali poscet, haud absurde memorabimus, A.* 6.38.1. Moreover, L. likes to exploit the interplay of story and discourse: cf. 10.47.6–7 *multis rebus laetus annus uix ad solacium unius mali, pestilentiae ... suffecit ... neque eo anno ... quicquam de ea re actum praeterquam quod ... supplicatio habita est*, where neither the 'real' *annus* – in which the consuls are busy with war – nor the narrative *annus* – which L. cuts short before he can narrate the transporting of Aesculapius – provides a *solacium* for the plague. On the overlay of the historical year and the textual year see above, pp. 11, 13; for the convention (dating back to Homer) that stories attaching to historical figures serve as consolatory *exempla* cf. the entertaining image at Vell. 19.4 *inopem ... uitam in tugurio ruinarum Carthaginiensium tolerauit, cum Marius aspiciens Carthaginem, illa intuens Marium, alter alteri possent esse solacio* (where their physical bodies encapsulate their stories, which provide the actual consolation).

31–32.2 The year 378 B.C.

New censors fail to perform their task, again precipitating revolt (31.2–4 ~ 27.4–11). The narrative of 378 responds chiastically to 379, unifying what might otherwise be disparate material: mixed college elected (30.1–2) – Roman defeat (30.3–7) – peace at home (30.8–9) ~ violence at home (31.1–2) – Roman victory (31.3–8) – patrician college elected (32.3, a bridge passage). Though brief,

378 has all its 'parts': *res internae* (1–5), *externae* (5–8), 'end of the year' (32.1–2).

31.1 Insequentis ... arsere 'the first days of the following year immediately blazed with an enormous revolt', cf. 3.33.2 *laeta enim principia magistratus eius nimis luxuriauere.* The personified year recalls 27.3 (n.); for the metaphor, continued by 2 *materia*, see 27.11n.

31.2 autem: epexegetical, with typical repetition of a word (*seditio*) from the clause it explains (*OLD autem* 4b). **et materia et causa:** hysteron proteron (Lausberg §891, Bell 271), cf. 34.4, 26.44.8 *testis spectatorque*, 26.44.9 *in uolnera ac tela ruere*, 42.60.8 *fugae terrorisque*. **impediti sunt:** this section is full of incomplete or blocked actions: the census, the levy, legal proceedings (4), the meeting with the enemy, Volscian damage to Rome (6–7). Both enemy and plebeian intransigence is eventually eliminated by the authorities (8n., 32.1–2; for the plebs ∼ foreign enemies see 4.5n.); but the plebeian tactics presage their more organized and ultimately successful action in the coming years (35.10n.).

31.3 nuntii ... fuga: cf. 3.38.4, *non nuntii solum sed per urbem agrestium fuga trepidationem iniecit*; for *trepidi nuntii*, an expression Tacitus borrows from L., cf. Tac. *H.* 1.39.2 with H.; for frightened farmers see 6.4n. **legiones:** 21.8n. **populari ... passim** ∼ *agrum attulere* below. The Roman panic implies that *passim* means 'everywhere' (*OLD* 2), but at 6–7 we learn that the Volscian raids have not been systematic, and that *passim* meant 'here and there' (*OLD* 1). It is only the Romans who can wreak wholesale destruction (8 *omnibus passim tectis ... exustis*) .

31.4 tantum afuit: 15.5n. **ciuilia ... externus:** antithesis highlighted by repeated sounds (*c ... a, c ... a, ter- ... -ter-*), chiasmus, and *uariatio* (*ciuilia ∼ externus*); for the latter opposition cf. Cic. *Balb.* 55, Aug. *RG* 3.1 *bella terra et mari ciuilia externaque ... saepe gessi*, Vell. 89.3 with W. **cohiberet:** cf. 31.48.7 *ad cohibendos ... tumultus*, Sil. 1.116 *Martem cohibentia pacta*; for the thought see above, p. 11. **contra:** adv. **eo** 'consequently': the *tr. pl.* take advantage of the *terror*. **potestas:** they are represented by their power (metonymy), cf. 16.3 *dictatoria uis*, 38.6. **impediendo dilectu:** abl. of respect with *uiolentior*, cf. 1.11n. **ne ... diceret** explains *condiciones*. **quoad debellatum esset** 'until the fighting was over', cf. 8.23.12 *ferrent ut ... pro consule rem gereret quoad debellatum ...*

esset; for *quoad* see *NLS* §223(*b*).   **tributum** ~ 32.1 *tributo* (n.).
daret ... diceret: the implied subj. of the first is a debtor, of
the second a magistrate, each to be supplied from context (Sörbom
142–6); such abrupt subj. changes can have a legalistic flavour (L–
H–S 733).

    31.5 laxamento 'respite' is legalistic (*TLL*); for *sumere* 'take (a
rest etc.)' see *OLD* 5c.   **Sp. ... Horatius:** typical asyndeton
(1.8n.), varied below with the second pair of *tr. mil.*   **dextror-**
sus ... laeua: the orientation is calculated as if one were coming from Rome (so e.g. Cis- and Transalpine Gaul): cf. Vell. 109.3
with Nicolet (2) 9 n.17, 70–3, 103; see also 7n.   **in:** Madvig's
supplement is probably right: with the paradosis, *ad* (below) has to
be understood with *oram* and *montes*, a brachylogy for which there
are prose parallels (W. on Vell. 84.1) but which is hard when the
two objs. are as far apart as they are here. *in*, which could easily
have fallen out before *m-*, is varied by *ad* (2.4n.); for *in maritimam*
oram cf. 32.29.3.   **atque Antium ... et Ecetram:** specific
terms added to general ones; the double goals match the twin commanders and divided legions. For the varied connectives see 22.5n.
Ecetram: a Volscian town included by Plin. *NH* among the lost
cities of Latium (O. on 2.25.6).

    31.6 obuius 'confronted [them]' (*OLD* 2).   **illi uagae:** sc. *po-*
pulationi, cf. Tac. *A.* 3.20.1. This is the first indication that the report
of the Volscian threat was greatly exaggerated (3n.).   **latrocinii**
more: i.e. by raiding, cf. 33.29.2 *proximum bello quod erat, in latroci-*
nium uersi with B.   **et** 'but at the same time' (*OLD* 14).   **me-**
tuens: fear has been transferred from the Romans (3 *trepidi*, 4 *tre-*
pidatione, terror) to the Volsci (cf. *per trepidationem*, 7 *timentibus*); for the
synonyms see 12.10n.   **iusto ... iusta:** the repetition matches
the Romans to their cause, though *iustus* is used in two different
senses (3.5n.): *i. exercitus* 'a fully equipped army' (*OLD iustus* 7a) ~
latrocinii more above, while *i. ira* (abl. of manner) = 'legitimate rage';
for the double meaning cf. Sen. *Contr.* 7.1.4 *mare iustis quoque nauigiis hor-*
rendum with Winterbottom.   **facta:** sc. *est*.   **grauior** i.e. the
populatio; the noun and its adj. bracket the sentence. *grauis* often describes punishment, retaliation etc. (*OLD* 11b); with it L. also alludes
to the frequent result of such raids, *grauis praeda* (e.g. 5.16.5, Tac. *A.*
3.20.1).

31.7 quippe 'indeed' (*OLD* 4a).   **timentibus** is causal.
ne ... exiret ~ *ut ... eliceret* below (the general structure is chiastic).   **ab Roma:** L. regularly uses prepositions with names
of towns (*LHA* 263); Augustus is said to have done so to avoid
obscurity (Suet. *Aug.* 86.1).   **in extrema finium** ~ *in hostico
... causa* below. The map is again oriented from the Roman
standpoint (5n.), *extrema* indicating the bits farthest from the city
(*TLL* v 2.2000.58–81: the farther from Rome, the farther from civilization). For *ext. finium* cf. 35.3.5, Plin. *NH* 3.67, Tac. *A.* 4.74.1; the
neut. + partitive gen. resembles a hendiadys (M–W 101). It is something of a mannerism in L. (Riemann 102–4); cf. 32.5, 40.11
(n.).   **etiam:** i.e. in addition to paying the Volsci back in kind
(cf. 6 *ira*).   **hostico:** sc. *agro*, originally an augural usage with a
'special, academic solemnity' (O. on 5.34.1).   **ut ... eliceret:**
10.3n.

31.8 itaque ... abacta: a tricolon framed by *omnibus* ~ *omni*,
within which Roman destruction proceeds from buildings to vegetation to animal and human life. The bipartite structure of the first
two elements is alluded to by the assonant *hominum pecudumque* of
the third.   **passim** ~ 3 (n.).   **tectis ... uicisque:** farm
buildings and villages.   **non ... relictis:** agricultural devasta-
tion is both an economic and a religious reprisal (O. on 5.24.3; for
parallels see B. on 31.30.3).   **in spem:** of the expectation of harvest or birth, cf. 1.8.4, Virg. *G.* 3.73 *in spem ... gentis* with Thomas,
Ov. *M.* 9.341 *in spem bacarum florebat*, Curt. 4.14.22, Plin. *NH*
19.39.   **hominum pecudumque:** gens. of material (cf. 21.60.8
with W–M); for booty collected on raids see Pritchett v 203–
312.   **abacta:** technical of driving off movable *praeda* (*OLD* 1). It
is picked up by 32.2–3 *coacta* (*bis*), 32.4 *adactis*, increasing the resemblance between the Roman treatment of foreigners and the patrician treatment of the plebs (2n.).   **Romam ... reducti:** 4.1n.

32.1 interuallo 'grace period'.   **quietae** 'at peace'; the *ab* is
separative (*OLD quietus* 4b).   **celebrari ... abesse:** hist. infins.;
for the choice use of *-esse* as hist. infin. see Viljamaa 17–19, and for
celebrare 'perform' see *OLD* 5.   **iuris dictio ... tributo** ~ 31.4
tributum ... ius ... diceret (frame); for the tax see 14.12n.   **spes
... fenoris:** on the word order see 3.3n. The personal construction with *tantum abesse* is rare (cf. Cic. *Marc.* 25, *B. Alex.* 22.1).

in murum ... locatum: the censors assigned contracts for public building (e.g. temples, aqueducts, walls). This is the so-called 'Servian wall' (Richardson 262–3); for *saxo quadr.* see 4.12n.   **faciundum:** the gerundive + *locare* 'contract out to' is idiomatic (*OLD loco* 5a).

32.2 cui ... plebis: the first of several echoes of the expulsion of the kings: building projects proved the last straw in plebeian tolerance of Tarquinius Superbus (1.56.1–3, 59.9). Both orders draw parallels between that crisis and the debate over plebeian consuls (34–35.9n.); allusions to it combine with reminiscences of the sack (33.5n.) to heighten the sense of urgency about the future.   **succumbere** suggests a beast of burden submitting to a load (*OLD* 2b); for the interlaced word order see 3.3n.   **quem ... impedirent** ~ 4 *nullo impediente*. For the incorporated antecedent see 24.10n.

32.3–35.9 The year 377 B.C.

32.3–33 Affairs abroad

These events are focalized primarily by non-Romans, whose psychological reactions are thereby brought to light (both techniques are characteristically Livian: 2.4n., *LHA* 168–72). The narrative follows the enemy into Antium (32.10–33.3), then to Satricum (33.4–5) and Tusculum (33.6–12; see 2.14n.). The contrast between the uncontrolled Latini and the exemplary behaviour of their former allies illustrates the self-destructive power of rage and forms an effective backdrop to the Roman *seditio* in the wings, which is conspicuous for its avoidance of extreme behaviour (for *res externae* as a foil for *internae* cf. 12–13n.).

32.3 principum opibus: 11.6n.

32.4 ad 'near' (*OLD* 13a). The preposition is thrice repeated in the course of the sentence, each time in a different sense (5: 'for' (*OLD* 44), 'to deal with' (*OLD* 32), 'towards' (*OLD* 3a)); see 3.5n.   **nullo impediente:** official language (16.6n.). Once the *patres* have gained the advantage in the election, the *tr. pl.* lose their momentum, letting this opportunity for resistance pass (cf. the Latini in 8). By exaggerating the suddenness of their capitulation L.

increases the contrast with Licinius' and Sextius' prolonged opposition (22.7n.).   **omnibus ... adactis:** formulaic language, for
which see H. on Tac. *H.* 1.55.1. The name of the oath changed to
ius iurandum in 216 (22.38.2–3).

32.5 unum ... alterum ... tertium: the first elements of this
tricolon are appositional expansions of 4 *exercitus*; the last, headed
by a deceptively parallel third acc., has its own verb (*duxere*).
ad ... qui: for the *uariatio* see Catterall 315 and cf. 22.1 (n.).
subita belli: cf. 4.27.1, Tac. *H.* 5.13.4 with H. and see 31.7n.
longe ualidissimum: both the army and the clause describing
it, which is the longest of the tricolon; see also 39.5n. *ualidissimus*,
favoured only by Tac. (18; L. comes a distant second with 7), is
habitually applied to cities, *gentes* (etc.), or military forces (but cf.
Cael. *apud* Cic. *Fam.* 8.2.1 *cum ... ualidissime fauerem ei*, Sall. *J.* 103.2
ingenia u.).

32.6 loco aequo: recommended if one lacks the advantage of a
hill: cf. 38.45.10, Caes. *C.* 1.85.2, *B. Hisp.* 25.1, Tac. *A.* 1.68.3
(Pritchett IV 78–85).   **ut ... sic** 'though ... yet' (*OLD ut* 5b).
claram: imminent brightness soon destroyed by the storm, cf.
Thuc. 7.55.1 γεγενημένης δὲ τῆς νίκης ... λαμπρᾶς (W–C 4–
5).   **prosperae spei:** descriptive gen. Paronomasia points an
etymological connection (Maltby 503), cf. Cic. *Fam.* 12.9.2 *omnia ut
spero prospere procedant.*   **imber ... diremit:** 8.7n.

32.7 aliquamdiu ... restabant: fighting like Romans is naturally best (cf. e.g. Polyb. 6.52, 18.28–32); for foreigners acquiring
such skill cf. 8.6.15, *B. Alex.* 34.4, 68.2, Vell. 109.1.   **militiam:**
for the retained acc. see 15.13n. L.'s language is imitated by Tac.
A. 4.50.2 *longo usu uim atque clementiam Romanam edoctus.*

32.8 eques immissus 'a cavalry charge' (Radice); for the participle see 1.1n., and for *eques* see 2.12n.   **turbauit; turbatis:** the
figure 'participial resumption', also called *epiploce* or *catena*, in which
a verb is resumed by a participle (often perf.), usually in a separate
clause (Wills *s.v.*). It is more common in prose than generally assumed. For Cicero see Laughton 17–19; in the historians cf. e.g.
Sis. fr. 27 *Romanos ... protelant, protelatos persecuntur*, Caes. *G.* 6.15.1
inferrent ... illatas, C. 1.28.4 *reprehendunt, reprehensas excipiunt.* It is something of a mannerism in L., e.g. (in Books 1–5) 1.10.4 *fundit ... fu-
sum*, 32.4 *temptari ... temptatam*, 2.25.5 *capitur, captum*, 4.14.6 *obtruncat*

... *obtruncati.* See also 8.1n., 12.10n.   **se inuexit** ~ *gradu demoti*;
for the latter cf. 7.8.3 *gradu mouerunt hostem,* Sen. *Const.* 19.3.   **ut
semel** 'when once' (*OLD semel* 4).   **intolerabilis ... uis** is Livian (*TLL*).

32.9 Satricum ... non castra: 29.3n.   **direptaque:** ending a sentence with -*que* or -*ue* is a Livian mannerism, otherwise
favoured only by Plin. *NH* and Tac.; it is sometimes associated
with a legalistic or communiqué style (3.10n.), as here (C. S.
Kraus, *H.S.C.P.* 94 (1992) 321–9). See also 4.10n.

32.10 agmine 'in a march' (*OLD* 6).   **uestigiis:** abl. of place
where: 'followed practically in their footsteps' (akin to abl. of the
route: Roby §1176 n.1).   **plus ... celeritatis:** the speed of fear
needs little illustration (cf. Ov. *M.* 1.539 *sic deus et uirgo est hic spe celer,
illa timore,* Mart. 1.104.14 *uelox leporum timor*); that of the angry army
is part and parcel of the *celeritas bellandi,* an important military virtue (W. on Vell. 41.1).

32.11 moenia intrauere: the motif of an army fleeing into a
city just in the nick of time goes back to Homer (*Il.* 21.526–
611).   **hostes ... Romanus:** typical Livian *uariatio* in number
(Walsh on 21.8.3).   **carpere aut morari** 'harry or failing that
[*OLD aut* 7] delay'. Both are commonplaces in military narrative;
for (*extremum*) *agmen c.* cf. 27.46.6, Caes. *C.* 1.78.4, *B. Afr.* 75.3, Sall.
J. 55.8 with Paul; for (*agmen*) *morari* cf. 28.16.4, Caes. *G.* 2.11.3,
7.40.4, *C.* 1.65.2.   **nec ... casum:** the abl. appendix explains
why they did no more than plunder (cf. 4.6n.).   **illis:** i.e. the
enemy; sc. *satis instructis ... bellico* from above.

33.1 Seditio: though dissension among the enemy is conventional (M–W 212), only here in Book 6 does L. characterize non-
Roman discord as *seditio,* inviting a comparison with events inside
Rome (32.3–33n.).   **Antiates ... (2) Latinos:** false parallelism
(nom. ~ acc.); see 32.5n., 40.14n.   **uicti ... consenuerant:**
Volscian inertia is reflected by the balanced phrases in which homoioteleuton points the awful sameness in their lives (see also next
n.). Commentators have worried about the exact length of time referred to, but the Antiates are thinking metaphorically; cf. 30.20.9
se [sc. *Hannibalem*]... *circa Casilinum Cumasque et Nolam consenuisse,*
Tac. *Ag.* 3.2 (P. Treves, *A.J.P.* 63 (1942) 131–2).

33.2 ex diutina pace noua defectio ~ *recentibus ... perseueran-*

dum in bello (chiastic). The contrastive word order distinguishes the Latins' state of mind from that of the Antiates (last n.); see also 10.2n. **pace:** cf. Vell. 110.2 *Pannonia, insolens longae pacis bonis et adulta uiribus ... arma corripuit* with W. Though long peace provides more able bodies (12.4), it tends to soften people rather than making them fierce (Balsdon 166), cf. 1.22.2, 23.18.10–16, Sall. *C.* 16.3, Sen. *Contr.* 1 *praef.* 7–8 (without competitiveness, oratory has become weak), Tac. *Ag.* 11.4 with Ogilvie–Richmond. **nihil ... perse-querentur** 'that in no way could either side keep the other from finishing [lit., could it be due to either that the others not finish] what they had started' (*OLD sto* 22); for *quo minus* see *NLS* §184, and for the absence of an impediment see 31.2n.

33.3 Latini ... Antiates: this part of the episode ends with its protagonists occurring in reverse order to their introduction (1), forming a ring. The Latini are reintroduced in 4. **ab socie-tate pacis:** for the expression cf. Plin. *NH* 14.2. **ut rebantur** looks ahead to *inhonestae* 'dishonourable' (3.5n.). **sese uindi-cauerant:** the Latini use freedom-fighter language (14.10n.). **ar-bitris ... remotis:** a conventional phrase usually indicating the removal of witnesses (e.g. 7.5.4, Cic. *Off.* 3.112, Sall. *C.* 20.1 *a. ... amotis*). Here *arbiter* must mean something like 'critic' (Radice), but the expression is odd, as if some of the Latins' hostility has leaked from the previous sentence. **salutarium consiliorum:** cf. 23.12. The gen. is objective. **urbem agrosque ... dedunt:** part of the formula for unconditional surrender (1.38.1–2 with O. pp. 153–4).

33.4 Ira et rabies 'mad anger' (hendiadys), together the subj. of *erupit* (cf. 11.4, 19.5). The Latins are entirely governed by their emotions (cf. 6). **receptaculum ... pugnae** 'their first refuge after their defeat'. The gen., here = a prep. phrase, is of the 'remoter object' (Roby §1318). **concremarent:** first in L. (*TLL*); for the pleonasm with *igni* cf. 3.53.5, 8.30.8, Sen. *Ben.* 6.22.1 (*incendio*). The lit. burning becomes metaphor in 6 (*incensos*); for the converse cf. Tac. *A.* 4.35.4 with M–W. **sacris profanisque:** a globalizing pair like *di hominesque*, cf. Tac. *H.* 3.33.2 with H. It was generally a good idea to avoid destruction of sacred property in such raids (O. on 1.29.6, Hornblower on Thuc. 3.27.3); the Latins are punished for burning these (12: Levene 208). **Matris ... templum:** Satricum was a major cult centre of this Italic fertility goddess (Scullard 150–1); on her temple see J. A. de Waele, *Med. Ned. Inst. Rom.* 43 (1981) 7–68.

33.5 uox ... amouissent: reminiscent of the divine announcement of the Gauls' approach (5.32.6–7), though the rampaging Latini heed a warning which the 'rational' Romans did not. *res externae* in these years echo parts of the Gallic struggle, events which at first remain safely outside the city, even allowing the Romans to reverse their recent humiliation (28.8n.). But the echoes continue after L. turns to internal affairs (34–35.9n.), suggesting that the city is once again in mortal danger. See also 32.2n. and for divine warning voices see Pease on Cic. *Diu.* 1.101.   **horrenda:** i.e. that causes trembling; the epithet is characteristic of sounds, esp. supernatural ones, e.g. 5.37.8 (Gauls), 21.58.5 (thunder), Virg. *A.* 9.112 (Cybele), Ov. *M.* 3.38 (Mars' serpent), Amm. 27.10.10 (barbarians). **templo ... delubris:** there may be a distinction between the sanctuary proper and the precinct (Pease on Cic. *ND* 3.94); *delubris* is 'poetic' plur. (L–H–S 16–18, Bell 72).   **tristibus minis:** also at Sen. *Phaed.* 408, *Oed.* 246, 410.   **ni ... amouissent:** the suppressed apodosis is something like 'she would punish them', cf. 38.8 (n.); for *ni* see 15.6n.   **ignes ... amouissent** reverses the technical expression *ignem admouere* (10.3n.), cf. Tib. 3.5.11 *sacrilegos templis admouimus ignis.*

33.6 rabie ... iram ~ 4; the repetition signals the second part of the Latins' rampage, which also features a threatening (though decidedly not divine) voice at its climax (11).   **impetus ... tulit** 'their momentum carried them to Tusculum'.   **concilio Lat.:** 2.3n.   **se dedissent:** subjunc. of alleged reason (*NLS* §240).

33.7 patentibus portis: Tusculum's signature posture (25.7, 9 (n.)) nearly occasions its destruction.   **improuiso:** 6.4n.   **primo clamore:** 2.14n., 4.9n.   **in arcem ... liberis:** the physical structure of ancient cities allowed an inner city to be besieged from within the outer walls. The most recent Livian parallel is that of Rome itself, which resisted the Gauls – who also entered through an open gate (5.41.4) – from the fortified *arx* (5n.).   **nuntios:** for sending messages to and from besieged positions see Fron. *S.* 3.13; again there is a recent parallel with the Gauls (~5.46.8–11: see last n.).   **certiorem ... facerent** 'inform' (*OLD certus* 12b).

The distribution of this idiom suggests that it was neither colloquial nor stylistically choice (comedy, Cic. almost exclusively *epist.*, Caes. + continuators, L.); its predominance in military narrative may reflect its status as 'ordinary' language.

33.8 haud ... duxere: the magisterial quality of this pronouncement is enhanced by the repeated *ductus ... duxere*; for Rome the rescuer see 3–4.3n.   **fide:** those surrendering to Rome, as the Tusculans had, did so *in fidem pop. Rom.*; see 3n. and Moore 43 n.10, and for Roman expansion see 2–4.3n.

33.9 Clausas portas: the besiegers' position *inside* the walls puts them in *stasis*: they cannot move any more than the Tusculani can, and the city thus becomes a self-contained set of concentric circles. The dynamic Roman advent instantly alters the configuration, enabling the Tusculans to move (10) and forcing the Latins not just to feel (*animo*) but to play their two roles simultaneously; they are eventually reduced to immobility once again (12).   **simul:** the sentence is overloaded with words reinforcing the Latins' frozen, dual status (cf. *hinc ... illinc*; *una*).   **obsidentium atque obsessorum** ∼ *hinc ... illinc* (chiasmus) ∼ *terrere ... pauere* (further chiasmus: above, p. 22). The contrast besiegers ∼ besieged is conventional (Vell. 51.2 with W.); by applying both terms to the same group L. points the paradox of their situation, a technique developed by Tacitus (Voss 124–6). For the substantive *obsidentium* see Adams (3) 130.   **uident** = 'saw' with *portas* but 'understood' (*OLD* 14) with *Latinos ... pauere* (syllepsis).   **terrere ... pauere:** cf. Tac. *A.* 1.25.2 *pauebant terrebantque* with Goodyear.

33.10 aduentus ... animos: cf. 5.19.3 *omnia repente mutauerat imperator mutatus* and see 8.5n. The plupf. 'indicates the rapidity of the change effected' (Stephenson; see Roby §1492).   **utriusque:** i.e. the Latini and Tusculani. For the proper name 'headings' (below) see 2.2n.   **arcis ... oppido:** 7n.

33.11 excipit 'answered' (*OLD* 16); for shouting see 4.9n.   **impetus** ∼ 6: the Latini have lost their momentum to the Tusculani.   **ex superiore loco:** 24.3n.   **subeuntes:** *sub-* because they have to climb the walls (*OLD* 6b); for the form of expression see H. on Tac. *H.* 2.21.1, Gries 77–8.   **obices portarum** 'the barricades (consisting of) the gates'; the gen. is appositional (*NLS* §72 (5)).

33.12 claustra portarum ∼ 9 *clausas portas.*   **anceps** 'attacking on both sides' (*OLD* 3b) is Livian, a transferral of the adj. from the contest to the contestant; it is explained by *et ... tergo* below.   **et ... et** ~ *nec ... nec* below: the champions' onslaught pinions the Latini in the centre (*in medio* below: 9n.).   **ad pugnam ... uis** 'any energy for fighting' (*OLD uis* 6).   **loci ... quicquam** 'any opening' (*OLD locus* 14).   **in medio ... omnes:** extermination of these Latins does not result in peace with the Latins; other tribes continue their raids until a truce is arranged (7.12.7). For this curt description cf. 2.50.11, 10.36.14, Caes. *C.* 2.42.5, *B. Afr.* 74.2, Curt. 4.1.33, 7.5.32.   **ad unum** 'to a man' (*OLD unus* 2b).   **reciperato ... reductus** ~ 26.8: the Romans again ride off into the sunset. See also 4.1n.

34–35.9 Internal affairs

Licinius' and Sextius' efforts to have three reform bills passed (34–42) mark the end of a process of tribunician opposition initiated in 1.6. Like the *seditio*, which this episode balances and echoes (34.7n.), this is the story of an attempt to capture Rome in which L. examines the acquisition and use of power, the manipulation of the crowd, and the issue of authority, both narrative and political. The crisis is perceived by both orders as one of extreme peril, a struggle for *libertas* and *imperium* comparable to the expulsion of the kings (34.5–11n., 37.10n., 40.10n.). In a typically Livian intertextual play, equally evocative paradigms are offered by the two main events of Book 5. The model of the Gallic sack, whose appearance is far from comforting (33.5n., 38.9n.), is given a patriotic turn in the patrician image of themselves as loyal citizens defending Rome and its *religiones* against marauders (cf. its adoption by Manlius: 19.1n.); at the end, the capture of Veii becomes the dominant narrative *exemplum* for the plebs (40–1n.). But since all of these models necessitate the replacement of one group by another, none is fully appropriate. What is wanted, and (unwittingly) offered by Appius Claudius, is a paradigm that accommodates power-sharing via (re)foundation (41.4–10n.). (On the *urbs capta* motif in historiography see 3.3n.)

Ancient sources agree that a major constitutional change occurred in 367 with the passage of these *rogationes* (legislative proposals), but there is little modern certainty about its nature. While land and debt were problems in the fourth century (2–4.3n.), the extent to which L.'s report of the two economic rogations is anachronistic is disputed. Moreover, his version of the third bill, that one consul must be plebeian, was almost certainly the purport of one of the *leges Genuciae* in 342 (*MRR* 1 134; in general R. Billows, *Phoenix* 43 (1989) 112–18). His account of this bill is further complicated by Fabia's complaint that her plebeian husband was ineligible for the consular tribunate, a statement which conflicts with L.'s own narrative (34.3n.). Momigliano suggested (most conveniently at *SSAR* 175–99) that those early holders of curule office who bear plebeian names formed part of a middle group, the *conscripti*, wealthy families who were closer to the *patres* than to the plebs; other non-patricians formed a radical group from which were elected the *tr. pl.* (these latter, however, would have been excluded from curule offices). Cornell consequently argued that in opening all magistracies even to former *tr. pl.* the rogations sanitized the revolutionary plebeian offices as well as defeating the conservative patricians – hence the opposition in L.'s narrative to the bill from both sides (Cornell 119–20). For alternative interpretations of the struggle of the orders and the rogations see *SSAR*; on the bills themselves (35.4–5) see von Fritz and *CAH*[2] 323–42.

34.1 magis qualifies *tranquilla.*   **bellis tranquilla:** an oxymoronic juxtaposition doubled by *in urbe uis* below.   **foris ... in urbe:** varying *foris ∼ domi*, cf. 1.43.2, 3.65.6 *urbano ∼ foris*, 10.6.1–2 *foris ∼ Romae.*   **uis ... miseriae:** in setting the scene L. is straightforwardly pro-plebeian. As in 385 (11.9n.), it is not the economic problems but the manner of their resolution that is in question.   **in dies** 'daily' goes with both nouns (9.6n.).   **miseriae ... plebis:** elsewhere in L. at 14.3 and 1.59.9 *addita superbia ... regis miseriaeque et labores plebis*, a double echo of Manlius and the revolt against Tarquinius Superbus.   **cum ... impediretur** 'since what hindered their ability to pay was the fact that they had to pay'. *solui* is probably impers. pass. (*OLD* 18b *fin.*), in which case *eo ... solui ∼ uis patrum* and *facultas ... impediretur ∼ miseriae plebis* above (ABAB). The paradox that something could have been done if it had not been necessary is pointed by the play with *soluere* (for similar types of incongruity see Plass 92–3). The alternative, that *solui* is personal ('by the very thing [i.e. debt] that was necessary be paid'), yields a similar paradox and may be more in keeping with the claim that the principal, augmented by cease-lessly accumulating interest, could never be paid (14.7, 15.10). **necesse:** citizens helpless before necessity appeared earlier at 3.4 (the Sutrini), and 15.9 (Manlius' crowd). But the plebeians here turn 'need' into a forceful weapon (Appius complains bitterly about the compulsion: 40.18–19, 41.3).   **impediretur:** see 31.2n.

34.2 ex re 'from their property' (*OLD res* 1).   **poenaque ... cesserat** 'and penalty had taken the place of credit', i.e. debt-bondage was automatic (*OLD cedo* 16b), with a play on *fides* 'financial credit' and 'trust' (as 27.3, 41.11; cf. Sen. *Contr.* 6.1 with Bonner (1) 69). L.'s epigrammatic expression draws on the convention that in times of civil strife 'normal' institutions etc. turn into something else (11.4n.).

34.3 obnoxios ... animos: cf. 17.5 *obnoxiam ... animam* (Man-lius), 28.7 *pace obnoxia* (the Latins) – both also subject to patrician control (4.5n.). *obnoxios* is proleptic (= *ut obnoxii fierent*: L–H–S 414).   **infimi ... principes:** this division of the plebs into classes, of which the lower have economic, the upper social woes, tallies with the modern picture of a hierarchical non-patrician so-ciety (34–35.9n.).   **tribunatum militum:** the first of several al-lusions to plebeian eligibility for the consular tribunate (cf. 37.5, 8, 39.4) which seem to contradict the premise of the Fabia story (5–11; see 34–35.9n.); but L.'s emphasis on the paralysing effects of debt makes Fabia's claim practically, if not legally, true. L. will further minimize the inconsistency by turning the focus of plebeian griev-ance to the consulate (35.5n.).

34.4 quod ... tetenderant 'which they had striven so forcefully to make permissible'.   **magistratus:** 11.7n.   **capessendos petendosque:** hysteron proteron; *-que* is slightly disjunctive (*OLD* 7). For *capessere mag.* (after *capessere rem pub.*) cf. Tac. *Ag.* 6.1, *A.* 13.29.2.   **acri:** 18.3n.   **experienti** 'enterprising' (McKeown on Ov. *Am.* 1.9.32); Manlius was *expertus* (18.13).   **animus** 'heart' (*OLD* 13b); Velleius imitates the Livian *animus ad* (119.3 with W.).   **possessionem** 'control' (*OLD* 2c) elsewhere in Book 6 refers to land (5.2–4, 39.9–10). The imagery (with next n.) suggests that the *honos* is more territory for patrician annexation, continuing the analogy between enemy and plebs (31.2n.). For military metaphors describing political strife see 15.2nn.; on the 'captured city' motif see 34–35.9n. **usurpati ... reciperasse:** both can be semi-technical of occupying or recovering land (*OLD usurpo* 1a, *recipero* 1c): last n. **honoris** 'political office', as 9. **modo** 'just now', first in 400 (1.1n.) but only infrequently, and most recently in 379 (30.2). For the tautology with *per paucos annos* below (3.4n.) cf. Cic. *Ver.* 4.6 *nuper? immo uero modo ac plane paulo ante uidimus.*

34.5–11 Fabia at home. The first, characterizing 'act' of the rogations telescopes into one the opening scenes of the Manlian *seditio.* Fabia's domestic *inuidia* ~ Manlius' jealousy of C. (ch. 11), while the use of a single person's predicament to introduce, inspire, and generally set the tone of the following narrative complements his rescue of the centurion (ch. 14). Like Lucretia, of whose story hers is a romanticized reflection, Fabia is a private catalyst of political change, an explicit echo of the founding of the republic (Kraus (2)). But, unlike Lucretia, Fabia is neither oppressed nor tragic; unlike Manlius, in her world there is no unbridgeable gap between the orders. The trivial injury causing this *res ingens* reflects the post-sack world of realism (1.2–3) and semi-honourable motivations (36.10n.), while Fabia's marriage, which exemplifies socio-political transgression and co-operation, foreshadows and facilitates the eventual political compromise. The incident is told, for the most part, in simple and repetitive language, a domesticated style complementing the private content and contrasting with the oratorical scenes ahead (cf. O. on 1.11.5–9, Tarpeia). Both thematically and stylistically Fabia is a 'small cause' for a great event.

34.5 Ne ... esset: cf. 7.27.1 *ne nimis laetae res essent* (21.2n.). **laetum ... rem ingentem** ~ 1 *prosperis ... crescebant*, signalling a new phase in the narrative; *laetum* recurs at 35.9 to frame the year. **parti:** 37.4n. **parua:** L. marks this episode's phases as he did the *seditio*'s (11.1n.), cf. 36.7 *maiore*, 38.3 *ultima* (Lipovsky 42–7). For the topos of the 'small cause' see Kraus (2) 322 n.33, adding E. Dutoit, *Lettres d'humanité* 5 (1946) 186–205. **ut ... solet:** 3.5n. (*ut fit*). **interuenit:** cf. 3.4n.; this is the only other occurrence of the verb in the book, and marks an intervention as decisive as C.'s at Sutrium. **M. Fabi:** the Fabii had a 'sort of vocation' for making diverse alliances, both political and matrimonial (Bayet

127, 130); in the first decade they play a conciliatory role in Livian
politics (e.g. 2.42–51.3 with O.). For the connections of the Licinii
with patrician families cf. 39.4 with O. on 5.12.9.   **uiri:** 11.2n.
corporis 'class' (*OLD* 15d) implies a natural unity (Tac. *H.* 4.64.1
with H.). Here it recalls C.'s designation as *caput rei Romanae* (3.1),
ironically alluding to the wholeness of the state just as the narrative
enters into its most divisive phase (on the state-body correspondence
see 3.1n., 37.4n.).   **ad plebem** 'in plebeian eyes' (*OLD ad* 17b).
potentis ... ad echoes 18.15, implying a kinship between Fabius and
Manlius – but the former uses his power responsibly (see also
37.7n.).   **haudquaquam:** a Livian favourite with an 'archaic
flavour' (McGushin on Sall. *C.* 3.2), uncommon elsewhere (*TLL*).
inter id genus ~ *inter sui corporis homines* above; for *genus* 'social
class' see *OLD* 7c.   **contemptor:** rare before L. (cf. Sall. *J.* 64.1
with Koestermann; the fem. is at Pl. *Bac.* 531). Historians liked these
vivid verbal nouns in *-tor* (Syme (2) 721, 723).   **eius:** objective
gen.   **filiae duae:** the wife-competition in the Lucretia story
(1.57.6 with O.) is reflected by this sisterly rivalry.   **maior, minor
... erat:** after introducing the Fabiae together, L. considers each
separately (distributive apposition: G–L §323); with *erat* sc. *nupta*.
illustri ... plebeio: cf. Vell. 117.2 *inlustri magis quam nobili ...
familia.*   **quidem** emphasizes a contrasting term (*OLD* 3a).
affinitas ... spreta: causal. By allying himself with Licinius, Fabius added a new set of relations to his *familia*; on *affinitas* and the
ideal of co-operation between father- and son-in-law see Treggiari
107–9.   **ad uulgum** ~ *ad plebem* above; for the rare masc. form
(e.g. Sis. fr. 48, Sall. *J.* 69.2) see Austin on Virg. *A.* 2.99.   **quaesierat** 'had earned' (*OLD* 7a).

   34.6 forte: 9.10n.   **in ... domo** 'in the (physical) house'
(Saller 343). *domus* and related words (*forem* below, 10 *apud*) are
thrice repeated at either end of the scene, a repetition that helps
domesticate these 'historiographical' words (e.g. 1.1 *domi* ~ *foris*)
and thus anchors the story in a private, ordinary setting. The *domus*
is here upset by an unexpected, unfamiliar noise; things will get far
worse (36.8n.).   **ut fit** ~ *ut mos est* (below); it signals the normality of the scene (cf. 3.5n. and see Steele 41). For women talking cf.
Pl. *Stich.* 1–47, Juv. 6.398–412 with Courtney; for such a quiet scene
as the prelude to action cf. 1.57.5, 7.26.1 (before Corvus' duel). That

the Fabiae are not engaged in a worthy occupation (like Lucretia's wool-making, 1.57.9) fits the less serious tone of this episode: cf. Pl. *Trin.* 796 *diem sermone terere segnities mera est.* **sermonibus** 'conversation', often 'gossip' (*OLD* 4). **lictor:** an official attendant carrying the *fasces* (*OCD s.vv.*). The role of the tyrant in this modern Lucretia story is shared among the patrician characters, nearly all of whom abuse the plebs (Kraus (2) 320–1). But lictors are part of the tyrant's entourage (*CC s.v.* 'lictors'), a convention obliquely reflected by this attendant who – in Fabia's eyes, at least – encapsulates patrician dominance. **is:** i.e. Sulpicius. **ut mos est:** a phrase at home in ethnographical descriptions (L. will also use it of Roman habits, as 9.38.14): M–W on Tac. *A.* 4.49.3, adding 5.39.1, Sall. *J.* 6.1. It suggests that what is customary to other Romans is foreign to Fabia, partly because of her youth, partly because of her plebeian connection (continuing the 'second city' motif: 11.7n.). Adding to the effect is *insuetus* (below), which often describes unfamiliarity with foreign customs (e.g. 28.18.6, 38.17.5, Caes. *C.* 1.44.3, Justin 1.8.6, Amm. 20.4.16). **uirga:** elsewhere in L. (and in prose before him: *OLD* 2a) the lictor's rod is an instrument of punishment, an association which increases its threat here (next n.). **percuteret:** the normal comic verb for knocking on doors (*OLD* 4a), but its only such use in L., who reserves it overwhelmingly for state executions (10.5n.). Given his subject matter, one should not expect otherwise; we might jump a little, however, at this harmless use of a dangerous word. **ad id ... insueta** ∼ *ignorare id* below, a chiastic arrangement centred on the sisters' reactions. With *ad id* 'in response to this' cf. 15.7, 23.9. **moris eius:** with *insueta*, cf. *Rhet. Her.* 4.6, Sall. *H.* 1.29. **expauisset:** comic characters regularly react to the sound of a door (e.g. Pl. *Bac.* 234 with Barsby); for such unease as a mark of inner disturbance cf. Sen. *Clem.* 1.7.3 *inter trementes et ad repentinum sonitum expauescentes, Ira* 3.35.3 *miser expauescis ... ad ... ianuae impulsum.* **risui:** predicative dat., cf. 4.35.10 *risui patribus fuisse* [sc. *plebeios*], *HA Opil. Macr.* 11.7. **sorori ... miranti:** 2.12n.

34.7 ceterum 'but' (*OLD* 5c). **is:** heavy-handed use of resumptive pronouns throughout the scene lowers the stylistic level (5–11n.). **stimulos,** previously at 11.8 (of debt), is one of a complex of words that occur only in the *seditio* and the rogations. Some are pointed repetitions (1n., 5n., 15.9n., 35.2n., 36.12n., 38.1n., 38.5n., 38.6n., 40.6n., 40.11n., 42.10n.); others, like this one, create formal links between the episodes. Cf. 2 *in ... cesserat* ~ 14.12; 7 *arbitrio* ~ 16.1; 35.1 *rerum nouandarum* ~ 18.3, *uim aeris alieni* ~ 11.9; 35.4 *pernumeratum esset* ~ 15.10; 35.6 *mortales* (subst.) ~ 11.5; 35.7 *stipati* ~ 15.1; 35.8 colloquial *bene* ~ 18.9, *isto* ~ 15.5; 35.10 *solitudo* ~ 12.5; 36.6 *memorabile* ~ 20.14; 36.10 *productos* ~ 20.6, *interrogando* ~ 15.12; 36.11 *postulare* ~ 16.6; 37.1 *indigna* ~ 14.12; 37.4 *in parte ... fore* ~ 15.6; 37.11 *excellant* ~ 11.6, *imp. atque hon.* ~ 18.15; 38.4 *aduersariorum* ~ 18.5; 38.8 *peragerent* ~ 16.1; 38.13 *fastigium* ~ 20.8; 39.10 *inter* + gerundive ~ 11.5; 40.1 *silentium* ~ 15.4; 40.5 *incolenti* ~ 16.2; 41.9 *nefas* ~ 14.10.   **paruis ... muliebri:** a commonplace (Otto 231), cf. 1.58.3 (Lucretia). *muliebris* is mildly pejorative (Santoro L'hoir (2) 80–3); for the word order see 3.3n. Fabia's exaggerated response to a small thing is a microcosm of her story's effect in the narrative.   **subdidit:** conventional with spurs, goads, etc. (*OLD* 1c). Fabia's relationship to her sister is expressed in race imagery (W.), cf. *stimulus* above and *anteiri* below (as Ov. *Ars* 2.726, Tac. *A.* 3.66.4 *festinatio exstimulabat dum ... antire parat*), 8 *morsu* (cf. *mordere* of a bit at Sil. 7.68), 9 *iuncta* (*OLD* 1), *impari* (as Virg. *G.* 3.533, cf. Grat. 263 *iunge pares*), *honos* ('prize', *OLD* 2c, cf. Ov. *Pont.* 2.11.21). **frequentia:** the crowd of Sulpicius' *clientes*. The picture (cf. Cic. *Mur.* 70, *Mil.* 1) is probably somewhat anachronistic; for the abl. with *fortunatum* (below) cf. Cic. *Sen.* 29 *comitatu nobilium iuuenum fortunati uidebantur*, Sall. *C.* 25.2 with Vretska.   **prosequentium:** an escort, cf. 2.31.11, Suet. *Jul.* 71.   **num quid uellet:** a leave-taking formula (*OLD uolo* 3b).   **credo:** L. intervenes (9.3n.) to identify a second reason for Fabia's strong reaction; the reiterated *causam doloris* (8–9) underscores the importance of getting at the truth. The historian's preoccupation with *causae*, which can be traced back to Hom. *Il.* 1.8, traditionally involves distinguishing an immediate reason from an underlying one, as here (Thuc. 1.23.6 with Hornblower, Fornara 76–90); see also 11.7n. (*primus*), 12.1n.   **fortunatum:** for *fortunatum m.* cf. Pl. *Aul.* 387 *f. nuptiae*, Ov. *M.* 2.803–4 (*coniugium*). The respects in which a person can be *fortunatus* ~ the different senses of *fortuna*; Fabia envies her sister's position (*OLD fortuna* 11b), cf. Cic. *Off.* 2.69 *fortunati et potentis*. **suique:** sc. *matrimonii*; the gen. is with *paenituisse*.   **malo arbitrio**

'owing to the misguided judgment'; *quo* (below) is causal.   **quo
... uult:** cf. Tac. *H.* 4.70.2 *ut ferme acerrime proximorum odia sunt.*
This sisterly *inuidia* palely reflects the upcoming social conflict: 'fra-
ternal enmity is a microcosm of civil war' (M–W 230). But the igno-
bility of Fabia's motivation does not compromise the success of the
enterprise she initiates.

34.8 confusam ... (9) posset: a historiographical period
(above, p. 21) interweaving Fabia's and her father's reciprocal
actions.   **ex ... morsu animi:** *morsus* of a mental pain, only
here in L., is hyperbolic, and in this context slightly humorous; the
medical language (*OLD* 6) also colours 10 *bonum animum* (n.). *ex* = 'in
consequence of' (*OLD* 18a).   **pater forte:** Fabius' appearance is
unmotivated except by L.'s favourite 'by chance' (9.10n.): the family
relationships with which the ch. is riddled (*soror* e.g. occurs six
times) are all-important (6n.).   **satin salue?:** an old-fashioned,
colloquial greeting (1.58.7 and O.) and a significant echo of the
Lucretia story.   **auertentem** 'trying to get rid of' so that her
father would not discover it, an extension of the normal use of *auer-
tere* (cf. *OLD* 4); it is the dir. obj. of *elicuit* below. Fabia knows she is
behaving like a bad wife (see below).   **piam ... honorificam:**
pius, though eventually 'spoiled by politics' (Syme (2) 712), is appropriate of familial relations (*OLD* 3). On the other hand, *honorificus* is
a very public word, used primarily of political behaviour (*TLL*): not
even a Fabia can bring her plebeian husband *honor* (cf. 9).   **aduersus ... in:** *uariatio* (2.4n.); the prepositions form the central terms
of a chiasmus (cf. 37.4).   **admodum** 'altogether' (*OLD* 2b).
uirum 'husband' (*OLD* 2a), a domestication of the word (cf. 5 *uiro*
'a (real) man'). Fabia shares her jealousy, the domestic complement
of *immodica cupido* (35.6n.), with other aristocratic wives (O. on
1.46.8, cf. Otto 13–14). Good wives were ambitious for their hus-
bands but not critical of them (Treggiari 183–228).

34.9 comiter 'with relaxed encouragement' (Hollis on Ov. *Ars*
1.710), the way to deal with young people (e.g. Cic. *Cael.* 13), and
'an important element in the acquisition and preservation of friendship, civil concord, and alliance between states' (Moore 98; see also
Wallace-Hadrill (1) 42).   **ut fateretur** depends on *elicuit*, a rare
construction (*TLL*) but by easy analogy with *efficere ut.* See above,
p. 20.   **causam doloris:** 7n. (*credo*).   **iuncta ... esset:** cf.

1.46.7 (Tullia encourages Tarquin to depose Servius Tullius) *se rec-tius uiduam … quam cum impari iungi*, a sinister parallel for Fabia also suggested by 10 (n.). *impar* of birth is first in Sall. *J.* 11.3; for the motifs of the marriage yoke and unequal unions see Nisbet–Hubbard on Hor. *C.* 1.33.7–11, 2.5.1 and Treggiari 83–100.   **quam … posset:** the *domus* has taken on a figurative sense of an (absent) 'symbol of high birth and family renown' (Saller 348–55); on the historical problems raised by Fabia's claim see 34–35.9n. **intrare:** for its abstract subj. cf. Cic. *Har.* 37, Sen. *Ag.* 285 with Tarrant.

34.10 consolans: cf. 1.58.9 *consolantur aegram animi* (Lucretia). The verb's only other occurrences in Books 1–10 are at *Praef.* 3 and 9.6.8 (failed consolation after the Caudine surrender). Its re-stricted distribution suggests the intense privacy of consolation in a text such as the *AVC*, where even grief is turned to state purposes (e.g. Verginius at 3.50.2–51.6), and elevates Fabia – however incon-gruously – to the level of Lucretia and the defeated soldiers, whose calamities earn a moment of private response before the public re-venge.   **bonum … habere:** a 'formula of reassurance' (O. on 1.41.5, *OLD animus* 13b) enlivened by 8 *morsu animi*, which implies a more precise sense of *bonum* ('healthy': *OLD* 14a).   **eosdem … uideat:** cf. 1.46.8 *si sibi eum quo digna esset di dedissent uirum, domi se propediem uisuram regnum fuisse quod apud patrem uideat.* Fabius' quota-tion of the patricidal Tullia threatens this calm narrative. The con-comitant parallels with Lucretia point to Fabia's role as facilitator of a new *libertas*; but the allusion to Tullia's ambition (9n.) reminds us that any kind of fierce desire can turn into tyrannical lust (20.5n.).   **uisuram:** sc. *eam esse.*

34.11 genero: 8nn.   **adhibito:** continuative: 'and they brought in …' (4.5n. (*qui … contulerant*)). Sextius will be the first plebeian consul (42.9); the liberator Brutus is similarly introduced as an ap-parent afterthought (1.58.6).   **strenuo … deesset ~ 5 *illustri … plebeio*:** Sextius' status, like Licinius', belies his worth.   **strenuo adulescente:** L. associates *strenuus* primarily with plebeians (Moore 18). *adulescens*, which can apply to men in their 40s, de-scribes someone who is not old enough or has not risen far enough on the *cursus honorum* to qualify for an office (Evans–Kleijwegt 186–7).   **cuius … deesset ~** *strenuo* above, a type of *uariatio* attested early but not developed until the first century B.C.; the rel. clause regularly takes a characterizing subjunc. (L–H–S 561). **spei** 'prospects' (*OLD* 3). **praeter ... patricium:** despite the allure and power of noble birth, the topos of humble worth was a favourite (Sen. *Contr.* 1.6.3–4 with Winterbottom, Vell. 128.1–3 with W.). *praeter* is frequent in such quick character sketches, where it can have the same bite as *nisi* (20.14n.), cf. Vell. 80.3 *nihil praeter nomen trahens*, 117.3 with W., Tac. *A.* 13.45.2. **genus** ∼ *genero* above (Maltby 255). **deesset:** 16.5n.

35.1 occasio ... nouandarum 'there seemed to be a chance for revolution'. After the private anecdote L. returns to the economic situation that makes Fabius' initiative possible (1 ∼ 34.1–2), but soon concentrates again on the question of *honor* (2 ∼ 34.3–4); for the 'alliance of temporary convenience' between the non-patrician groups see Brunt (1) 55–6. **ingentem uim:** cf. Sall. *C.* 16.4 *quod aes alienum ... ingens erat* (Valvo 22 n.69). **cuius ... speraret** 'a trouble from which the plebs could expect no relief if they did not place their own in the highest office'. This is the beginning of their self-exhortation (2nn.); for *in imperio (vel sim.) locare* cf. Cic. *Mur.* 30 *locare homines in amplissimo gradu dignitatis*, Virg. *A.* 4.374. **leuamen:** poetic except for Cic. *Att.* 12.16 *quod si esset aliquod leuamen, id esset in te uno*, Tac. *H.* 5.3.2 (with H.); for *l. mali* cf. Ov. *Ep.* 12.79, Tac. *A.* 4.8.3 with M–W. **nisi ... locatis:** 1.4n. **speraret:** for 'the only hope' in exhortations see Keitel (2) 81 n.22. **accingendum ... esse:** sc. *sibi*. L. is first with *accingere ad* and *in* (*TLL*). **cogitationem** 'plan' (*OLD* 7).

35.2 conando agendoque: *-que* introduces an immediate consequence (*OLD* 5b). For the combination cf. Cic. I *Ver.* 5 *audax est ad conandum ... obscurus in agendo*. **eo ... fecisse** 'have progressed to a point' correlates with the consecutive *unde ... posset* below (*OLD eo*² 2); for the language cf. Quint. 3.6.8 *ad ea quae sunt potentiora gradum ... fecisse*. Images of a road (3: see Fantham 117) and climbing combine here and at 37.6–10; the height metaphors recall Manlius (11.4n., 17.1n.). **plebeios** ∼ 3 *sibimet ipsi*: the planners turn from the general to the specific (37.10n.). **adnitantur:** perhaps borrowed from Sall. *J.* 85.47 *adnitimini mecum et capessite rem pub.*, the only earlier absolute use (*TLL*). **ad summa:** cf. Vell. 61.1 *summa consecutus* with W., Quint. 10.1.4 *peruentri ad summa nisi ex* *principiis non potest*; for *peruenire* of completing a journey see *OLD* 2a, of climbing cf. Sall. *J.* 93.4 *in ... planitiem peruenit* (cf. *aequari* below). **aequari:** Manlius wanted to raze the high offices (18.14); these ambitious plebeians will raise themselves to them.

35.3 fieri placuit 'they decided to become' ∼ 34.11 *consilia inire*. The *tr. pl.* entered office in mid-December, regardless of when the magistrate year began (above, p. 29); it may be owing to confusion between the two official years that L. or his source has omitted the *tr. mil.* of 376 (*MRR* 1 108–9; Bayet 127–30). **uiam ... aperirent:** the choice expression recalls C.'s military success (2.11n.); for the metaphor see 2n.

35.4 C. Licinius et L. Sextius: L. generally refers to them together, joined either with *et* (as a hendiadys? *OLD* 8b) or with *-que*, as if they were synonymous (*OLD* 1c); Appius' imaginary plebeian addresses them as *tu* (40.12). That they are in fact two people, however, lets them avoid the danger posed by Manlius *solus*: they cannot be reduced to a symbol, either of heroism or of tyranny (14–16.4n.). This is not a story about *unus uir*. Instead, the paired tribunes are fitting representatives for the *uulgus*, which is by definition plural, and they function as a sort of narrative omen for the political doubling that fills the final sections (42.11n.). **promulgauere:** technical of publicizing a proposed legislation (*OLD* 1a). **leges:** they were in fact plebiscites, but the terms are interchangeable in our sources (*CAH*[2] 341); for ancient refs. to these see *MRR* 1 108–9 and in general 34–35.9n. **omnes** 'every one' (*OLD* 4a). After describing the bills separately (*unam ... crearetur* below) L. resumes them with 5 *cuncta ... possent*, a long apposition to *leges*. The accumulation of superlatives (*omnes, cuncta, maximo*, 6 *omnium*) marks this as a crisis point. **commodis:** a 'traditional portmanteau word' of *popularis* language (Seager (1) 336) and a theme of the rogations (36.9, 39.8, 10, 40.3, 5, 12). **unam:** cf. Manlius' proposal (15.10). **triennio** 'over a period of three years'. **portionibus:** *pensionibus* (Cuiacius) 'instalments' is attractive, cf. 7.27.3, *B. Afr.* 90. 3.

35.5 alteram: debate over the distribution of the *ager publicus*, to which this probably refers (Cornell 116), began in Book 6 at 5.1–5. **modo** 'amount' (*OLD* 1a). **tertiam:** the consulate has intermittently been anathema to plebeian rhetoric (cf. 3.9.4 *quippe duos* *pro uno* [sc. *rege*] *dominos acceptos,* 5.29.2 *inuisus plebi magistratus*). This demand for its reinstatement, necessitated by the story's logic (only this office remains closed to plebeians), shifts the focus from the consular tribunate (34.3n.) while reinforcing these plebeian leaders' affinity with the *patres*: others are not keen to elect consuls (cf. 39.2). **consulumque ... crearetur:** on the bill see 34–35.9n. Admitting plebeians to the consulate was first proposed at 4.1–6, a debate that is recalled more than once here (40.4n., 40.18, 41.10n.). **utique** 'without fail' (*OLD* 1b). **ingentia et quae:** 34.11n.

35.6 simul qualifies *proposito* (below). **quarum ... est:** L. serves up traditional ethics in Sallustian language: the Catonian *cupido*, which L. uses for effect, is overwhelmingly preferred to *cupiditas* by Sall. and Tac. (Gries 28–9); for *mortales* see 11.5n. Sall. was prominent in blaming Rome's civil wars on *cupido*, cf. *C.* 33.4 (perhaps recalled here) *non imperium neque diuitias petimus, quarum rerum causa bella ... inter mortalis sunt,* Lucr. 3.59–89 with Kenney and see Du-Quesnay 34–5. **immodica c.:** cf. Vell. 25.1 *immodica cupiditas.* The desirability of *modus* is proverbial (Otto 216, 226), as are the dangers inherent in desire (20.5n.). **honorum:** desire for *honor* in every sense was, of course, Rome's driving force (Wiseman, *RPL* 3–19); but the need to regulate even this had long been recognized (DuQuesnay 47–8, *FRR* 442). **conterriti:** proper and common of the fear induced by military attack (e.g. Cic. *Prou.* 33 *ceteras* [sc. *nationes*] *conterruit compulit domuit*), though it can be used hyperbolically ('scared to death', as Cic. *De orat.* 1.214, Col. 1 *praef.* 28). **cum ... consiliis** 'after scurrying about, frightened, in public and private meetings' (*OLD trepido* 2a). **nullo ... inuento:** 'Chinese box' word order, cf. 14.9n. (L–H–S 734). **praeter ... intercessionem** ~ 19.5 *praeter uim et caedem.* On that occasion the *tr. pl.* voluntarily suggested a solution; now the *patres* manipulate some of them into vetoing the bills. Their lack of independence means their resistance will not last long (36.8). **multis:** not as often as the patrician rhetoric claims (Ridley, *SS* 109); for the veto see O. on 4.6.6. **comparauerunt** 'procured' (in the worse sense). Splitting tribunician colleges is a Claudian tactic (*CC* 91 n.111) which may here anticipate Appius' climactic appearance (chh. 40–1).

35.7 tribus ... citari: the assembly is the *concilium plebis*

(20.10n.); *suffragium inire* = 'begin to vote' (*OLD suffragium* 2).   **sti-pati praesidiis:** the somewhat anomalous picture – the men at the centre of such a bodyguard should be patrician (14.3n.) – fig-ures this unequal co-operation: the *tr. pl.* are both protected and en-gulfed by their patrician 'helpers'.   **nec recitari ... passi sunt:** for contemporary parallels (including one *tr. pl.* who put his hand over the reciter's mouth) see Lintott 70–1. Though exercise of such a veto could easily involve or lead to violence (Lintott 209–16), L. restricts the possibility of *uis* to C.'s dictatorship (38.6–8.).   **sollemne** 'customary' with *ad* + gerund, by analogy with other adjs. that may be construed either thus or + dat. of purpose (e.g. *idoneus, opportunus*), cf. 3.36.2 *idus tum Maiae sollemnes ineundis ma-gistratibus erant.*   **ad sciscendum plebi:** 'so that the plebs could vote'. *plebi* is a loose dat. with the gerund; cf. the (easier) Cic. *Mur.* 66 *ad imitandum uero tam mihi propositum exemplar illud est quam tibi* ('as much for you to imitate as for me').   **passi sunt** ∼ 10 *passi sunt*: patrician intransigence will be more than matched by the *tr. pl.*

35.8 concilio: sc. *plebis* (7n.).   **pro** 'as good as' (*OLD* 9b). *anti-quare* is technical for rejecting a bill (Taylor 35).   **bene habet** 'fine' is colloquial (*TLL* II 2123.39–55).   **inquit Sextius:** the trib-unes' only *o.r.*, and the only time they do not speak in unison. It is common, though by no means invariable (cf. 3.45.6–11, 4.3–5), for Livian plebeians during the struggle of the orders to use *o.o.*, a tendency esp. noticeable in situations where tribunician *o.o.* ∼ patrician *o.r.* (e.g. 5.2–7). Patrician authority, in effect, extends to the narrative, in which they control presence in one of its most ba-sic forms. The opponents in this debate fight for control of speech: Licinius and Sextius crowd the text with their *o.o.* (36.7–37n.), while the patricians annex even the tribunician word *ueto* (9, 36.8), suc-cessfully appropriating *o.r.* almost to the end – until Appius lets the plebeians speak out loud (40.8n.).   **quando ... plebem:** Sex-tius is indignantly alliterative.   **telo:** a throwing weapon, hence often figuratively applied to words (Fantham 157); it is associated with tribunician action at 3.55.3, 5.29.9, Sall. *H.* 3.48.12.   **tuta-bimur:** cf. 38.6. Ideal leaders protect their people; for *tutela*, a popular imperial concept with late-republican roots, cf. Vell. 105.3 with W.

35.9 comitia ... creandis: 4.7n.   **faxo:** an archaic subjunc. of *facere* which L. restricts to *o.r.*; the 1st pers. sing. can = simple

fut., as here (Roby §1486). The only other ex. in the first decade is
at 41.12 (cf. 34.4.21 with B.). **uox** 'word' (*OLD* 10a). See 8n.
qua: abl. of (musical) instrument (cf. Tac. *H.* 5.5.5 *tibia tympanisque
concinebant* with H.). **concinentes:** sarcastic. For the metaphor
see Pease on Cic. *ND* 1.16; for 'chanting' lessons cf. 40.8.10 *meorum
... praeceptorum quae uereor ne uana surdis auribus cecinerim.*

35.10 haud ... minae: Sextius' words have the instantaneous
efficacy of a divinity's (cf. 1.10.7, Ov. *M.* 7.217–19 and see
McKeown on *Am.* 1.1.21). For the proleptic *irritae* cf. 2.31.5 *irritaque
... promissa eius caderent*; for *c. minae* cf. Sen. *Thy.* 573. **comitia
... habita:** 'end-of-year' material; only plebeian officers are
elected. **aedilium:** 4.6n.

The years 375–371 B.C. Licinius' and Sextius' veto puts a new twist
on the time-honoured practice of vetoing levies (21.5n.). Suspension
of the annual round of elections has two consequences: (1) those responsible are liable to the charge of *regnum* (11.4n.), since *libertas*
is inseparable from the rotation of magistracies (cf. 2.1.7, 5.1.3 *Veientes
... taedio annuae ambitionis ... regem creauere*, Tac. *A.* 1.1.1 with Goodyear). Nor will the *patres* miss the opportunity to accuse Licinius and
Sextius of regal aspiration (40.7, 10, 41.10). (2) On another level, this
figurative seizure of power is very real. The absence of curule
magistrates means that there are no officials by whom to date a
year. But L. is writing *annales*, a kind of history based on the annual
magistrate lists (above, pp. 9–10), and without them there can be no historiographical narrative from 375 to 371. By eliminating the authorities by whom time is measured the tribunes effectively take control
of narrative authority as well, while the state and its record simply
stop – a splendid illustration of Croce's *dictum*, 'where there is no
narrative, there is no history' (cf. Canetti 397–9). This veto marks
the culmination of the plebeian use of the thematics of delay first
concentrated in chh. 31–2 (31.2n.); later, patrician forces adopt the
obstructionist tactics, while Licinius and Sextius try other tacks
(37.12n., 39.5–41n., 40–1n.).
refecti distantly echoes the city's rebuilding, occurring here for
the first time since 1.6 (see n.). On re-election of *tr. pl.* see O. on
3.64–5, Ridley, *SS* 108; on iteration in general – severely curtailed
later in the century – see *CAH*[2] 341–7. **solitudo m.** 'absence
of magistrates', a calque on ἀναρχία, lit. 'lack of an archon', for
which cf. *Ath. Pol.* 13.1 with Rhodes *ad loc.* and on 35.1, Plut. *Cam.*

39.2.   **reficiente ... tollentibus:** internal *plebeian* action continues, but consists only of complementary acts of creation and destruction, perfectly maintaining this *stasis* (see above).   **per quinquennium:** the number of years without curule magistrates varies in the tradition (above, p. 29 n.125). L. accepts the longest *solitudo*, making his rogations last ten years, an epic length commensurate with the sieges of Troy and of Veii; epic, too, is his concentration on the last part of this long period: the major part of the narrative (36.6–41) covers only 369–368.   **tenuit** 'kept in check' (*OLD* 17–19); the city cannot move forward because its time has stopped (see above).

36.1–6 The year 370 B.C.

36.1 Alia bella: 1.10n.   **gestientes otio:** cf. Catul. 51.14 *otio exsultas nimiumque gestis*; the verb indicates 'physical restlessness [and] riotous emotion' (Fordyce *ad loc.*). This *otium* ironically picks up *quieuere* above: it is not 'rest' but 'spare time' (*OLD* 1a).   **esset:** subjunc. of alleged reason (*NLS* §240).

36.3 remittentibus 'relaxing (their policy/attitude)': *OLD* 11b.   **per interregem:** 1.5n.   **in ... in** 'in the case of' (*OLD* 42).   **habuere** 'found' (*OLD* 26).

36.4 ingentique: the *-que*, which connects the whole sentence, is slightly adversative (*OLD* 8). As at 31.5–8, once the legions are conscripted the military operation goes smoothly, though it will lack closure (6n.).   **summouere:** military jargon (*OLD* 3): 'dislodged'.

36.5 Nec ... potuere: an obligatory change of generals, the converse of the political situation, where the *tr. pl.* are entrenched. The first attested prorogation of a military command is in 326 (8.23.11–12).

36.6–37 The year 369 B.C.

36.6 Affairs abroad

36.6 ante 'before that' (*OLD* 3a). The army remains in place, serving as a counter in the patrician arguments (9, 37.12) and as

backdrop to the *res internae* (38.1); the end of the campaign is barely
noticed (42.4). L.'s treatment of these *res externae* palely reflects the
situation *domi*: nothing seems to change (38.1n.) and the end is anticlimactic.   **nihil ... factum:** cf. 5.14.6 *his tribunis ad Veios nihil
admodum memorabile actum est*. Since only memorable things are included in a history (20.14n.), and judgments as to what was worth
remembering varied (cf. Cato fr. 77, Asel. fr. 2), such statements as-
sure of us L.'s critical selectivity: he could have described the siege
rather than the *res internae*. This selectivity is related to the historian's rejection of other narratives as not credible (12.2–6n.): both
establish his superior credentials as observant judge of the material
through which he is guiding us (Hartog 283–94).

36.7–37 Internal affairs

The section is the first of a series of concentric brackets, as follows:
patrician arguments (36.8–9 ~ chh. 40–1) surround tribunician *o.o.*
(36.10–37 ~ 39.5–12) which encloses dictatorial appointments (38.3–
4 ~ 39.3–4) framing the confrontation between C. and the *tr. pl.*
(38.5–13). Though decisive progress there, as elsewhere, is interrupted (38.9), this is the episode's only 'action' scene. Otherwise,
the rogations are full of oratory, including allusions to speeches
not reported in the narrative: L.'s description of the *tr. pl.* as *artifices iam tot annorum usu tractandi animos plebis* (36.10) implies that
what 'really' happened during the missing years 375–371 was more
of the same. The use of speeches to replace action – a development
of their role in crystallizing arguments, analysing policies and character, etc. (above, p. 12) – is not rare in the ancient historians. Diod.
20.1–2 criticizes those who let long speeches interrupt the narrative,
while the Augustan Trogus apparently thought no *o.r.* should be included (Justin 38.3.11). To judge from comparison with parallel accounts, in reworking a narrative tradition L. often condenses several
speeches into one or omits them altogether (Burck (1) *passim*; see
42.4n.). The present abundance of oratory is consonant with the
subject matter: such issues were fought out in words.

36.7 In maiore ... domi: the second stage (34.5n.), cf. 14.1
maior domi exorta moles.   **nam ... (9) ferret:** three main verbs
joined by *et* (*ferebat, erant, praetendebant*) form a frame on which the

descriptive background for the scene is arranged. **octauum:**
adv. acc., epigraphical except for here and August. *Ep.* 53.4 (*TLL*),
cf. 40.8 (n.). From this point until the end of the book L. heads
years by plebeian as well as consular tribunes' elections (cf. 39.6,
42.1): the double dating suggests that plebeian control of the narrative year continues (35.10n.), while their 'second city' has become a
reality (11.7n.). **tribunus ... socer:** now that formal debate has
begun, L. identifies Fabius by both his public and private roles
(34.8n. (*pater*)). **auctor ... suasorem:** cf. Cic. *Deiot.* 29, Tac.
H. 3.2.4, *A.* 3.28.1 (parodic) *suarumque legum auctor idem ac subuersor.*
auctor 'an influential person behind a legal proposal' (Powell on
Cic. *Sen.* 10). The *seditio*'s second act similarly singled out an *auctor*
(14.1). Acting alone, Manlius lost his *auctoritas* to the *auct. patrum*
(19.4); in co-operation with plebeian leaders, Fabius' patrician
authority and support (*OLD suasor* 1b) anticipate the senate's final
approval (42.14 *auctores*), despite Appius' claim that the *auct. patrum*
is at risk (41.10). See also 38.9–13n. and for the advantages of co-
operation see 35.4n.

  36.8 ferme 'as a rule' (*OLD* 3). **desciscunt:** properly of formal defection (*TLL*); L. reserves it almost exclusively for the actions
of allies (e.g. 25.2). The co-opted *tr. pl.* have figuratively gone over
to the enemy (cf. *capti* below and 20.3 *defecisset*, where the same technique is used of Manlius). **capti et stupentes:** *amplificatio* enhances the strong language (Ullmann (2) 23). For accusations of
madness and treachery in political invective see W. on Vell. 83.1;
for *capti ... animi* 'mentally paralysed' cf. Tac. *H.* 3.73.1 with H.
animi is gen. (11.3n.). **stupentes** ~ 40.1 *stupor*, anchoring the
correspondence between this and chh. 40–1 (36.7–37n., see also
next n.), though Appius' diatribe will throw the whole structure
out of balance. **uocibus alienis** 'in others' words', an image
literalized by Appius' *sermocinatio* (40.8n.); for the theme see 35.8n.
domi 'privately', as 34.2.9 *mos ... in publicum ... uiros alienos appel-
landi? illud ... domi rogare non potuistis?* 'Home' is no longer either a
familial or a dynastic setting (34.6n., 34.9n.) but a locus of conspiracy; by 11–12 the patrician *domus* has become a prison while the
plebs has no home at all. **praetendebant** 'offered as a pre-
text' (*OLD* 4a); the internal obj. *id* is explained by the *o.o.* in 9.
The *tr. pl.* were literally screened by patricians at 35.7 (*stipati*).

36.9 in exercitu: i.e. in service, cf. Cic. *Balb.* 49 *in bello, in acie, in exercitu … in defendenda re publica.* Citizens had to be in Rome to vote, though legislative and voting schedules might be arranged to take account of who would be in the city (Taylor 68, cf. 3.29.8). **differre debere** ~ *suffragium ferret* below: the borrowed words have a sing-song quality (cf. 40.9n.). For *comitia diff.* cf. 9.34.25, Cic. *Att.* 2.20.6; outside L. and Cic. *differre* is far more regular of postponing judicial proceedings.   **de suis … ferret:** they appeal to *popularis* slogans: for *commoda* see 35.4n., for *suffragium* see 40.7n.

36.10–37. Licinius and Sextius outline their position in a single speech, broken at 37.1 by an outburst from the listening *corona.* They begin with an *interrogatio* covering the first two bills (36.11–12), then address the crowd directly about the plebeian consul. The body of their *oratio* is tripartite and circular: *propositio* (37.2–4: liberty is possible only through sharing power), two arguments, each divided into claim + historical evidence (37.4–7: eligibility for the consulate is not enough – look at what happened with the consular tribunate; 37.8–9: they cannot say we are inferior – look at Licinius Calvus and the plebeian quaestors), and a *conclusio* (37.10–11: only the consulate will give us liberty and equality).

36.10 artifices … plebis: cf. Quint. 11.1.85 *summus ille tractandorum animorum artifex* [sc. *Cicero*], discussing a particularly skilful (and misleading) argument. Licinius and Sextius can manipulate others' minds while their colleagues lack control even over their own (8). Strictly speaking, L.'s phrase indicates that they are good orators (*TLL* II 699.1–15), since all oratory aims to 'manage' its listeners' minds so as to persuade (cf. Quint. 12.10.59 *docere delectare mouere,* Lausberg §257). But persuasion is dangerous, and *artifex* can suggest chicanery (e.g. Cic. *Ver.* 5.183, Prop. 1.2.8 with Fedeli, Virg. *A.* 2.125, Tac. *H.* 2.86.2), strengthening the impression that the *tr. pl.* are most interested in their own *commoda* (cf. 35.2–3, 39.5–12). **primores:** this synonym for *principes,* used by L. in the first decade and favoured by Tac., 'had a recherché flavour' (Adams (4) 56). Licinius and Sextius bypass the tribunician collaborators and go directly to the source.   **productos:** as witnesses (20.6n.); for the 'press conference technique' see Taylor 18–19. The speeches will have been delivered in the Comitium (15.1n.); on the topography see 12n.   **fatigabant:** cf. 36.11.1 *cum patrem … rogando fatigasset,*

Tac. *H.* 4.41.3 *cuius interrogationibus fatigabatur* with H.

36.11 auderentne: ind. ques. depending on *interrogando* above (*NLS* §268 (*a*)).   **bina ... agri:** the second rogation (35.5). **iugera ... iugera** ~ *possiderent agros ... pateret ager* below; the *tr. pl.* meticulously differentiate between the orders. For the polyptotic repetition of *ager* see 5.2n.   **ipsis** is emphatic, *sibi* being understood (*NLS* §37 (iii)).   **ciuium** (possessive gen.) qualifies *agros* below. **ad** '(enough) for' (*OLD* 42b).   **tectum necessarium:** the bare minimum to keep out the rain, cf. Sall. *C.* 20.11 *quis ... tolerare potest illis diuitias superare ... nobis rem familiarem etiam ad necessaria deesse ... larem familiarem nusquam ullum esse?*, Sen. *Helu.* 11.1, Tac. *D.* 22.4. **suus ... ager:** 1.2n.   **locum sepulturae:** a traditional motif (Soph. *OC* 789–90 with Jebb, Ar. *Ecc.* 592 with Ussher) to which L. lends characteristic vividness with the precision of his vocabulary (next n.).   **pateret** 'extend', technical of measuring space (*OLD* 7a). Exact plot dimensions are ubiquitous on sepulchral inscriptions (*CIL* I² 2 *s.v.* 'ager'; for *patere* cf. *CIL* I² 2.2137); for anxiety about owning a place for burial see J. M. C. Toynbee, *Death and burial in the Roman world* (1971) 74–91 and for paupers' group graves cf. Hor. *S.* 1.8.8–10 (a *commune sepulchrum* for the *misera plebs*) with Toynbee 48–9.

36.12 fenore: the first rogation (35.4).   **soluat:** for the tense see 5.3n.   **sortem** 'the principal'.   **neruum ac supplicia:** concrete + abstract.   **gregatim:** historians had a marked fondness for adverbs in *-im* (e.g. 38.8 *contemptim*, Coel. fr. 30 *dubitatim*, Sis. fr. 65 *festinatim*); they had an old-fashioned flavour (Kenney on Apul. *M.* 6.1.5). This one, though not rare elsewhere, is only here in L., and recalls the animal imagery at 32.2. For a list of these advs. in L. see Kühnast 348; for *grex* used pejoratively see *OLD* 2c. **dare ... duci:** 12.8n.   **repleri ... esse?:** a chiastic structure (*uinctis ... domus* ~ *habitet ... carcerem*) of which the second part rephrases the first. On the metamorphosis of the *domus* in chh. 34–6 see 8n.; on the great patrician houses see 19.1n.   **nobiles:** i.e. *nobilium* (*OLD* 5d), a transferred epithet (Lausberg §685, Bell 315–29); the juxtaposition with *uinctis* is deliberately insulting.   **carcerem:** the state prison figured prominently in the *seditio* (16.4, 17.5–6). The *tr. pl.* replace it with these private prisons which they map onto an imaginary plan of Rome, whose *forum* is occupied by usurers (39.9) and whose *arx*, the consulate, is barricaded by patricians (37.6, 10), while there is scarcely room for a plebeian house (37.11). Apart from this imaginary plan, after Sulpicius' trip *de foro* to his home (34.6), the rogations lack virtually any place indicators, a topographical imprecision that would normally be unremarkable (14.3n.); when set in contrast to the *seditio*, however (cf. 14.3, 15.1–2, 19.1, 20.10–11), and to the tribunes' map, this vagueness makes the latter stand out (cf. 40.17n.). Their metaphor helps to legitimize the plebeian attack on the patrician 'usurpers'; as Appius will say, the plebs behave as if they inhabited a different city (40.5 (n.)).

37.1 Haec ... (2) fecissent 'After complaining loudly about these scandalous things, deplorable to hear, to an audience who feared for themselves and whose indignation was greater than that of the speakers, they asserted that, all the same, the only limit there would ever be either to patrician land-annexation or to their butchering the plebs with usury would be if they [i.e. the plebs] made one of the consuls plebeian, as a guardian of *their* freedom'. The difficulties in this sentence are caused primarily by the need to imagine the scene's dynamics: *indignatione* represents a noise made by the crowd (cf. 18.9n.), to which *atqui* (which qualifies *fore*) responds (i.e. 'even though you indicate your disgust, there will be no end unless you elect a consul').   **indigna ... auditu** ~ *audientium indignatione* below. The repetitions figure the tribunes' rhetorical success: what they say has the exact effect intended, not least because they themselves appear to feel the emotion they wish to inspire (the audience just feels *more*; cf. e.g. Cic. *Planc.* 104, *De orat.* 2.189–96).   **miseranda:** for the rare following supine cf. Heges. 2.18 *passio acerba uisu et auditu miseranda* (fourth century A.D.).   **apud** 'in front of' (*OLD* 8a).   **timentes ... ipsos:** because of the threat of imprisonment. The existence of this larger audience was implied by the questioning at 36.10.   **sibimet ipsos:** Cic. habitually puts the pers. pronoun + *-met* in the same case as an accompanying form of *ipse*; Sall. habitually does not. L. has exx. of each (Riemann 153–5).   **audientium:** substantive (= *auditorum*): Adams (3) 120, 124.   **indignatione:** 16.2n. An orator wanted his listeners to react in support (see above), though too much enthusiasm could become a riot; for their emotional reaction cf. Cic. *Q. fr.* 2.5.1, *Or.* 131, Catul. 53; for heckling cf. Cic. *Fam.* 1.56.1, *Rab. perd.* 18.

37.2 atqui: 1n.   **modum ... alium** 'any limit other than' anticipates the following *nisi*-clause. Postposition of *alius* emphasizes its noun (Marouzeau 1 183); the distribution of noun + adj. in separate clauses is a poetic trick (as Hor. *S.* 1.5.72, Luc. 1.350: see Housman on Man. 1.269–70).   **alium:** they also refuse to accept substitutes for their demands at 4 *nec ... putet*, 8 *nec ... dici*; as if in answer, Appius will repeatedly substitute his version of statements for theirs (40.8n.).   **occupandi:** regular of taking possession (*OLD* 3, cf. 4.5), but here with a suggestion of military occupation (34.4n.).   **fenore ... plebem:** cf. Cic. *Cael.* 42 *ne fenore trucidetur* with Austin. *trucidandi* implies indiscriminate slaughter of unresisting victims (cf. 36.12 *gregatim*); see Vell. 119.2 with W.   **patribus:** dat. of the possessor.   **nisi ... fecissent:** the protasis of a fut. logical condition (*NLS* §280.8).   **custodem:** 6.15n.   **suae libertatis** ~ 10 *libertatem suam* (frame); the adj. implies that plebeian and patrician liberties are separate (Bruno (2) 114–19).

37.3 contemni: the first of several sentence-initial verbs (with 4 *non posse ... nec esse*); the same emphatic word order closes the first argument and begins the second at 7–8.   **potestas** 'magistracy' (*OLD* 3a).   **suam ... frangat:** for the motif, esp. fitting in a context of internecine strife (*RICH* 131–2), cf. 19.6n.   **intercedendo** 'by using the veto'.

37.4 aequo iure 'with equal rights' ~ *in parte pari* below. *aequum ius* is synonymous with *aequa libertas*, 'equality before the law, equality of personal rights, and equality of the fundamental political rights ... it does not preclude differentiation beyond this sphere' (Wirszubski 11, 15).   **imperium ... auxilium:** for the word order cf. 34.8; for *auxilium* see 18.10n.   **nisi ... communicato:** 1.4n.   **in parte ... fore** 'would have an equal share in the government'; on the form of expression see 15.6n. Opposed to the communal ideal in which citizens bring things *in medium* (6.18n.) – an ideal which seems conveniently limited to patricians – is the division of the state, a reality reflected by the attempts to share the *ager publicus* (5.4, 36.11) and important offices (12, 42.2), and by the complaint that one group is oppressing the other (27.6, 40.18). The plebeians, who argue that only composite unity will solve the domestic crisis, propose a sort of pie model to replace the existing division in which the patrician *pars* submerges the plebeian *pars*. To the *patres* such division threatens uncontrolled fragmentation of something which ideally functions as a corporeal unity (3.1n.), a civil *sparagmos* tantamount to the physical destruction of the city (cf. 2.28.3 *nunc in mille curias contionesque dispersam et dissipatam esse rem pub.* and see Serres 89–117). The claim that equality comes only with shared power is 'proved' by the play *imperio* – *parte* – *pari* (Maltby 452, Serres 99; for related puns see Ahl 106–13). **nec esse ... putet** 'nor is there cause [*OLD sum* 6d] for anyone to consider it enough', the first of two anticipated objections (*praesumptio*: 15.11n.). **si plebeiorum ratio ... habeatur** 'if plebeians are taken into account' (i.e. made eligible: *OLD ratio* 8c). The substantive *si*-clause is in apposition to *satis* above (*OLD satis* 3); *comitiis* is dat. **alterum consulem:** 34–35.9n.

37.5 an 'or can it really be that', expecting a negative answer (*OLD* 1). **memoria exisse:** they back up their assertion with history (cf. 17.1–2). For the expression cf. Sen. *Ben.* 3.38.2 *opus ... nequiquam memoria hominum exiturum.* **idcirco** correlates with the following *ut*; for the admission of plebeians see 1.1n. **pateret ... honos** ~ 36.11 *pateret ager*, an echo which neatly points the two plebeian groups' respective preoccupations (cf. 34.3n., 39.9–10). **quattuor ... annis:** 34.4n. (*modo*). The temporal abl. conveys duration, a sense common from L. on (*NLS* §54 *Note* 1).

37.6 qui ... habuerint?: the argument from precedent (5) is followed by one from character: if the patricians were unwilling to share eight places, will they share two? The *tr. mil.* were paired with the decemvirs at 1.1 (n.); this claim that the former have monopolized their office suggests a tyrannous logic behind that pairing. **impertituros:** Appius will have the same complaint about plebeian unwillingness to share (40.18); on *pars* in the rogations see 4n. **octona** 'eight at a time' (*OLD* 2), the largest number attested, though erroneously (*CAH*[2] 193 n.58); cf. 5.2.9 *non fuisse ne in octo quidem tribunis militum locum ulli plebeio ... nunc iam octoiuges ad imperia obtinenda ire.* The adj. is commonest in technical lit. (e.g. Plin. *NH*, Col.), though it also occurs in poetry (Ov. *M.* 13.753, Stat. *Silu.* 3.3.146). **loca ... creandis:** *locus* + dat. suggests 'strategic position' (*OLD* 8), cf. 5.54.4 *urbi condendae locum*; for the gerundive of purpose see 21.2n.   **uiam ... saeptum:** 35.2n.

37.7 lege ... per gratiam: they conclude their first argument by restating its premise (4). For the antithesis cf. Cic. *Caec.* 74 *si ... ius ciuile ... publica lege contra alicuius gratiam teneri non potest*; for abl. ∼ prep. see 3.10n.   **relictus:** sc. *consulatus*; the participle is conditional.   **potentioris:** Might is Right (see Vretska on Sall. *C.* 2.2), and patricians are by definition *potentes* (34.5n.). That the *tr. pl.* are correct is proved by the lapse to patrician colleges soon after these rogations are passed (7.17.13).

37.8 nec iam posse ∼ 4 *nec esse*: a second objection is anticipated and countered, again with an argument from history. **soliti sint:** Appius will deploy precisely this argument, though concentrating on religious/ritual fitness (40.19, 41.4–10).   **idoneos** 'suitable', like *dignus* (40.19n.) but without the latter's implication of a necessary connection between the fitness and the reward to which it is entitled (*VL* 392–3).   **numqui** (adv.) like *num* expects the answer 'no'; for its place in rhet. questions see *OLD num* 3a. **socordius aut segnius:** a jingle of near synonyms expressing the opposite of *industria*, perhaps the most valued leadership quality (Vell. 88.2 with W. p. 241). *socordius* is Sallustian and very rare (Tac. *H.* 2.15.1 with H., Syme (2) 728); there is a similar adverbial combination of familiar + choice at 1.3.   **rem ... posse** 'is it possible to run the state', i.e. the first plebeian tribunate did not alter things so as to make good government intrinsically impossible. This virtually impersonal *potest* + active infin. is a Livian idiom (O. on 3.23.4).   **post ... tribunatum:** sc. *gestum*; for the brachylogic *post* see M–W 196.   **primus:** 11.7n.   **gesta sit** ∼ *administrare* above (7.5n.).

37.9 patricios ... damnatos: most recently Sergius and Verginius in 401 (5.12.1) and Fabius in 389 (1.6–7, indicted but not tried); Ridley, *SS* 123–6. This claim must be read ironically against the knowledge that Licinius will be convicted for violating his own agrarian law (7.16.9).   **quaestores:** financial officers, first including plebeians in 409 (Syme (2) 704–5, *CAH*[2] 239).   **populum R.:** their argument broadens to include the whole state in preparation for the peroration.

37.10 superesse 'remains' (*OLD* 6); given the height imagery that surrounds this office (*arcem* below, 5 *summus*, 11 *excellant*), the lit. meaning 'to be higher than' (*OLD* 1a) is also felt (35.2n.). While the *tr. pl.* speak in general terms (*plebeiis*) they are probably thinking primarily of themselves (cf. 35.2–3, 36.10n.).   **eam ... id:** 9.1n. **arcem ... columen:** the bulwark and support (Fantham 124, 45– 6), cf. 3.45.8 *tribunicium auxilium et prouocationem ... duas arces libertatis tuendae*; the metaphorical use of 'column' is esp. old (Nisbet– Hubbard on Hor. *C.* 1.35.14). For the topography see 36.12n.   **eo peruentum:** cf. 35.2 *peruenire ad summa*. The peroration begins with images of arrival.   **exactos ... reges:** the logical culmination of an argument which locates the patricians *in arce*, like tyrants (19.1n.). The *tr. pl.* appeal to two of Rome's most emotionally charged images of self-identification, the regal expulsion (34– 35.9n.) and the founding act that creates a tradition to be pre- served for posterity (11: 41.4–10n.).   **stabilem:** 30.6n.   **liber- tatem suam** ~ 2 *suae libertatis* (frame).

37.11 ex illa die: what the plebs do now will have a permanent effect both on their *libertas* (10) and on their *liberi* (below) – a neat joint appeal to patriotism and self-interest. Since it is impossible to bequeath such things as *gloria belli*, the tribunes must refer to the possibility of honours and glory which a noble name facilitates (Sal- ler 348 n.40): they thus encourage the plebeians to emulate their enemies in one of the areas they most dislike, patrician use of *genus* to gain influence and power (6.13n., 30.3n.; cf. Cornell 118–19). **excellant:** 35.2n.   **imperium ... relinquenda:** a rhetorically elaborate expansion of *omnia*: a pair joined by *atque* + an asyndetic tricolon + an asyndetic rhyming pair heightened by the shift from *magna* to *maiora* (11.1n.). The formal devices and ref. to posterity pro- vide strong closure (11.5n., Smith 130–1).   **gloriam belli:** the *sine qua non* of the Roman system of honours (Harris 10–41), em- bodied in Books 5 and 6 by C.   **genus nobilitatem:** a virtual hendiadys. The claim that these derive from one's achievements, not vice versa, is esp. typical of the later republic (e.g. *CIL* 1^2 2.15 (after 139 B.C.) *stirpem nobilitauit honor*; *Rhet. Her.* 3.10, *res externae* to a person include *genus, potestates, gloriae*): see Paul on Sall. *J.* 85, W. on Vell. 128.1.   **nobilitatem** has its semi-technical sense: descen- dants of patricians or of plebeians who had held curule office (P. A. Brunt, *J.R.S* 72 (1982) 1–17; see also *VL* 224–33).   **fruenda**

... relinquenda: for the rhyme + increasing colon length cf. Cic. *Mil.* 98 *gratiis agendis et gratulationibus habendis.*   **liberis:** the converse of the exhortation not to degenerate from one's parents (27.8n.) is to leave something for posterity. Such formulations tend to subordinate the present to the future (e.g. Cic. *Sest.* 143 *praesentis fructus neglegamus, posteritatis gloriae seruiamus*), since the future looks backward for its models (what is 'left' is an ideal to measure up to: e.g. Tac. *Ag.* 46 with Ogilvie–Richmond). But the *tr. pl.* need to inspire energy now if there is to be any plebeian legacy.

   37.12 Huius generis orationes: 26.4n.; for marking the end of *o.o.* see 23.8n. This section comprises the end-of-year material for 369.   **nouam rogationem:** this proposal will prove to be a sort of diversionary tactic paving the way for the rest of the legislation (42.2); for other stratagems see 35.10n.   **duumuiris:** 5.8n. **pars** 'half' (cf. Tac. *A.* 2.48.1 with Goodyear).   **omniumque ... obsidebat** ∼ 36.9; the co-opted *tr. pl.* carry the day.

   38.1 prius ... reducerentur: it is uncertain whether this means 'before the legions were brought back' i.e. they did return at the beginning of 368 (Bayet, cf. 32.11n.) or 'before they could be brought back' (Radice, implying that they were not); 42.4 suggests that the siege does not end until 367 and is in keeping with this expedition's general indeterminacy (36.6n.; but cf. 39.8n.).

38–42.3 The year 368 B.C.

Internal affairs

This year's two scenes are separated by the dictatorial appointment and accompanying annalistic material at 39.1–4. There are no *res externae.*

   38 Camillus to the rescue? The confrontation between C. and the tribunes, though constituting the formal centre of the rogations, raises more questions about C.'s authority than it answers. L.'s narrative structure tends to deflate and deflect C.'s presence. His politically motivated appointment comes late, a last resort (3) that cannot stop the plebeian momentum; during his tenure he is stereotypically patrician, verging on the violent (6n., 8n.). L. magnifies the importance of his resignation by digressing at length on the reasons for it, once again raising issues of authority when his authoritative characters are in trouble (9–13n., cf. 12.2–6n.). He then removes C. from the political scene: the major debate occurs in the interval between his dictatorships (39.5–41), while after the Gallic invasion the rogations trickle to an end, with little help from C. (42.9n., 42.12n.). C. can work admirably within the traditional senatorial framework (ch. 6) – but he is as out of place in the new political climate as Manlius was (Kraus (2) 323–5).

38.1 suspensa ... res ~ 15.1 *Ita suspensis rebus*, the first of several echoes of Manlius and Cossus (4 *causam ... armant* ~ 15.2; 5 *stipatus ... consedisset* ~ 15.1 *stipatus ... sella, certamine* ~ 15.2; 7 *non patiar* ~ 15.6). Both dictators try to persuade the people that their champion is working against them (6–7 ~ 15.4–6) but, stymied by the obstinate response of the plebeian leader(s), turn to force, with limited success. The final, patrician move toward conciliation works only to plebeian advantage (39.3–4 ~ 17.6). The present crowds, however, are neither simply spectators nor followers of a charismatic leader: their potential to exert democratic control means that their momentum, as encapsulated by the stubborn *tr. pl.*, is unstoppable (Millar 141–2). Different, too, from Cossus' scene, and contributing to the absence of definition and due process, is the lack of topographical precision: L. does not tell us where the confrontation takes place (36.12n.). **plebis tr.:** inverted order stresses the gen., in antithesis with *tribunos mil.* above (Adams (5) 75, 78). **reficiebat** 'was still re-electing' (1.6n.).

38.3 principio ... anni: L. is fond of placing *statim* between *principio* (*et sim.*) and a dependent noun, cf. 4.47.2 *primo statim proelio*, 21.4.1; neither Caes. nor Cic. has the mannerism, but cf. Fron. *S.* 1.8.9, Tac. *Ag.* 3.1, *H.* 2.69.1 (etc.; none in *D.* or *A.*), Suet. *Vesp.* 2.3. **ad ultimam dimicationem:** the final stage (34.5n.); for *dimicationem* see 12.1n. The slight oxymoron *principio ... ultimam* refers to both the narrative content and form (*ultimam* = 'extreme' and 'last': cf. 20.12); for the textual year see 1.5n. and for the playful language cf. 1.2.6 *secundum* ['favourable'] *inde proelium Latinis, Aeneae etiam ultimum operum mortalium fuit.* **uocarentur:** inceptive: 'as they were preparing to be summoned' (G–L §233). **nec ... obstaret:** *obstare* 'impede' is legal language (*TLL*), cf. 40.9.8, Sen. *Contr.* 1.2.13. **trepidi ... decurrunt:** cf. 19.3, 35.6. The *patres*

counter extremism with extremism, though because *tr. pl.* were
sacrosanct (Lintott 24, 52) they cannot handle this situation as
roughly as Cossus did Manlius. L. translates the impossibility of
touching them physically into a narrative impasse (cf. 9n. (*neutro*)).   **ad duo ... ad ciuem:** the pattern prep./- - -/prep.,
where the last two elements are appositional to the first, seems to
be a Livian idiom (Pettersson 110 n.2), cf. 2.52.3, 42.10.13 (where
edd. emend); it is similar to the brachylogy discussed on 31.5.
duo ultima auxilia ∼ *tribunos ... duos ... ultimam* above.   **auxilia:** a tribunician word (used technically below) which the patricians
try to appropriate as they did '*ueto*' (35.8n.).   **summum** ∼ *decurrunt* (oxymoron); for the imagery see 35.2n.

38.4 cooptat: while *creare* 'elect, appoint' can = *cooptare* 'make a
member of a group' (Vell. 43.1 with W.), the reverse equivalence
does not seem to obtain (*TLL*). Elsewhere L. uses *cooptare* of priestly
colleges (40.42.12) and of patricians inserted into the plebeian tribunate (e.g. 5.10.10). There may then be an implication of subornment
here; or L. may simply be experimenting (the regular verb of appointing a *mag. equit.* is *dicere*: 2.5n.).   **quoque ... et ipsi:**
marking respectively the action and actors (cf. 3.21.3 with W–M).
aduersus ... aduersariorum: cf. 4.49.14 *aduersus tam crudeles
superbosque aduersarios*, Enn. *scen.* 255 J *aduersum aduersarios*.   **apparatum:** 'war equipment' (*OLD* 4c), with a suggestion of 'show'
(*OLD* 2), the patrician pomp that will fail to stand up to plebeian
pluck (*ingentibus animis* below).   **causam ... armant:** cf. Cic.
Mur. 46 (*lex* arms the *accusatio*), Apul. *M.* 5.11 *animis armatae*.
concilio ... indicto: 20.10n.

38.5 Cum ... dicerent: four paratactic verbs set the scene,
each with a different subj.; cf. 15.1–2, 36.7–8 (n.).   **stipatus:**
14.3n.   **irae minarumque** ∼ 8 *ira ... minas*. The last time we
saw C. he was behaving with exemplary moderation in war (25.6,
27.1). His typically aristocratic reaction here, which recalls his
wrath against the plebs at 5.29.8–10, tends to support Manlius'
claims about him (11.4); and though from a conservative patrician
point of view he is right to support traditional legality, he has badly
misjudged the people's mood.   **consedisset:** properly of judges
(*OLD* 1b), with an element of the military sense, 'take up a position
in readiness' (*OLD* 2a).   **ferentium ... intercedentiumque:**

bracketing word order emphasizes the stalemate: proposal and veto are happening at the same time to the same thing. The participles are picked up chiastically by *quanto ... tantum* below.   **quanto ... tantum:** concessive: 'though the veto was by law more powerful, still it was conquered by' (E. Mikkola, *Die Konzessivität bei Livius* (1957) 81 n.4).   **tantum:** adv. acc., used for *tanto* when a verb with comparative force replaces a proper comparative (G–L §403 N.2).   **iure ~ *fauore*** below; cf. 37.7 *lege ... per gratiam.*   **uinceretur:** sc. *intercessio.*   **fauore:** more negatively charged than *gratia*, implying unregulated partisanship (15.8n.), while *gratia* is the accepted currency of political influence; for disregard of a veto due to *fauor* cf. 10.37.11–12, 25.2.6–7.   **'uti rogas':** the formula for voting 'yes' (Taylor 35). *dicere* introduces *o.r.* under special circumstances; here it fills in for the unattested impf. subjunc. of *inquit* (*NLS* §264).   **tum C.:** once again C. breaks in at the last moment (3.4n.), this time to stop the decisive action that is at last on the point of happening.

38.6 Quirites: an appellation of the Romans, traditionally derived either from Quirinus or from a Sabine town-name at the time of the amalgamation of the two tribes (Maltby 517). It conveys respect and not a little flattery, and tends to cluster: in Cic. *Cat.* 3 e.g. nearly half of the twenty-five instances come in the last three pp. In Book 6 it is otherwise used by Manlius (14.10) and Appius (40.3, 5, 13, 15).   **libido ... potestas:** L. has taken one member from each of two natural antitheses (*libido/licentia ~ libertas*, e.g. Wirszubski 7–9, *VL* 558–9; *potestas ~ dominatio*, 18.2n.), a kind of *antallage* (Bell 340–1). Each element implies its opposite: the *tr. pl.* reign with greedy passion, not the *libertas* that takes account of others' rights, and hence exercise *dominatio*, not legitimate *potestas*. Cf. Tac. *A.* 6.42.2 *nam populi imperium iuxta libertatem, paucorum dominatio regiae libidini propior est*; for *tribunicia libido* cf. Cic. *Dom.* 106. **regit** is appropriate with *libido* (20.5n., 23.10n.).   **intercessionem secessione:** a certain linguistic *libido* pervades C.'s speech in this section. Aside from this jingle with -*cessio*-, the transformatory potential of uncivil discourse (11.4n.) is suggested by the *uariatio rei pub. ~ uestra*, the polyptoton with *parere* (15.4n.), and the near-anagram *euersum ~ uestrum* (flagged by *euertere* 'overturn', cf. 15.12n.). Similarly self-conscious anagrammatic play is common, see Ahl *s.v.*

'anagrams'; for *uert-/uort-* see Friedländer 31–2, and on paronomasia in general see *Rhet. Her.* 4.29–32.   **uobis:** dat. with both *partam* and *irritam*.   **eadem ... peperistis:** the converse of the topos that one exercises power with the same methods with which one acquires it (Vell. 57.1 with W.).   **ui:** the first *secessio* was in fact completely peaceful, and before it the *patres*, as here, were the more extremist of the two groups (Ridley, *SS* 127–30). But C. is right that the plebeians' seditious behaviour is like *secessio*: both tactics involve creating an impasse by withdrawing from ordinary procedures (both *seditio* and *secessio* = 'going apart' (Maltby 556); on these 'prohibition crowds' see Canetti 55–8).   **irritam:** technical for making an act, decree etc. null and void (*OLD* 1a).   **dictator ... adero:** C.'s action is as paradoxical as the *tr. pl.* lending their veto to the patrician cause, as he admits by referring to himself by title.   **auxilium imperio:** this tantalizing proximity of the disparate powers of plebeians and patricians will not lead to the partnership Licinius and Sextius have in mind (37.4n.), but to increased patrician dominance: *tutela*, after all (next n.), is the protection of the weak by the strong.   **tutabor:** 35.8n.

38.7 itaque ... non patiar: C. shifts the blame to the *tr. pl.*: he is merely protecting those who cannot protect themselves (15.6n.).   **intercessioni ... cedunt:** *figura etymologica*; for the tense of *cedunt* see 15.6n.   **nihil:** adv.   **patricium magistratum:** C.'s mock-polite refusal wantonly to contaminate the plebeian assembly anticipates Appius' imagery of mixed categories (40.12).   **inseram:** inserted into the centre of an antithetical, chiastic pair; for the sense cf. 33.47.4 *factionibus Carthaginiensium inserere publicam auctoritatem. inserere* (*OLD*2) has a technical sense, of administering medication or poison (*TLL* VII 1.1870.55–72), which again anticipates Appius' simile (40.12).   **tamquam captae ciuitati:** tyrants were conventionally accused of treating their own cities as enemy territory (E. Keitel, *A.J.P.* 105 (1984) 309–11); in the struggle of the orders cf. e.g. 40.5, 3.19.4–6, Dion. Hal. 11.2.2. C.'s apotropaic comparison is designed to diffuse the tribunician influence by arousing indignation. But the *tr. pl.*, who are indeed trying to capture this city (34–35.9n.), clearly have the people behind them.   **leges** 'terms' (*OLD* 13); *l. imponere* is officialese (*OLD impono* 11a).   **ten-**

dent 'strive'; the dependent infin. is predominantly poetic (*OLD* 13b).
uim ... dissolui: cf. 2.44.2 (quoted on 19.6), 4.48.6 *uiam unam dissoluendae tribuniciae potestatis per collegarum intercessionem*. If the tribunician force, like an unregulated growth, is self-destructive (19.6n.), then the patricians, who protect the state as a whole, have to protect the people's rights. C.'s argument is clearly specious: it is the *patres* who have weakened the tribunician power by suborning some of the *tr. pl.* As Licinius and Sextius have already pointed out (37.3), if the plebs are to win, they must do so not by further division, but unifying against the patricians (37.4n., 39.2n.).

38.8 aduersus ... educturum: while the immediate contest is between C. and the *tr. pl.*, the plebs is the real prize, since without its support the laws will not pass. C. wants to convert the civic crowd into an army which can be easily governed (Canetti 311–13, Serres 201, 235); even his verbs are pushy: *emou-*, *adact-*, *educt-*. But he is unable to dissipate the indocile, ubiquitous plebeians, who, unlike Manlius' crowds, cannot be neutralized by removing their leaders, whom they simply keep re-electing.   **contemptim:** 36.12n.
peragerent ~*percitus* below; both sides are equally stubborn. On laws passed illegally (*per uim*) see Lintott 132–48.   **percitus** denotes 'irrational emotion' (Walsh on 21.53.7) and is often found with *ira*; cf. 7.5.4, Pl. *Cas.* 628, Cic. *Mil.* 63, *B. Afr.* 46.1.   **lictores:** 34.6n.   **emouerent:** outside L., who introduced it into prose (*TLL*), this choice compound takes a personal obj. at Hor. *Ep.* 2.2.46 (Brink). The usual verb in this context is *summouere* (Nisbet–Hubbard on Hor. *C.* 2.16.9).   **minas:** explained by *si ...
educturum* (as 37.43.3, cf. 33.5).   **adacturum:** sc. *se.*   **exercitumque ... educturum:** a remarkable assonant accumulation.

38.9 incusserat: the *mot juste* for striking fear into someone (*OLD* 3a); for the plupf. see 33.10n.   **plebi: ducibus plebis:** adversative asyndeton; for the polyptoton see 16.3n. The contrast between the plebs and their leaders reflects a conventional view of the crowd as a shapeless mass that can be swayed by persuasion but is itself essentially without initiative (Otto 378).   **accendit ...
minuit:** having one's back to the wall should inspire acts of courage, and the tribunes' response is like that of a brave soldier; for the topos of necessity see Keitel (1) 156–7. The phrase is highlighted by

sound play (-*min-*/-*nim-*/*min-*); for the paronomasia *magis* ∼ *minuit* cf. 6.7n. (*nec ... concessissent*).   **certamine** 'fighting spirit' (Stephenson; see *OLD* 1a), abl. of cause (G–L §408).

38.9–13. The second of three scholarly digressions (cf. 12.2–6, 42.5–6), this discussion of C.'s abdication suspends the narrative at a point of tension. It takes the form of an expanding catalogue: beginning with two possible grounds for C.'s abdication, that he was *uitio creatus* or resigned under threat of a fine, L. rejects the second reason on the grounds of character, utility, possibility, and historical precedent (nn.). The digression's unusual length in proportion to the scene on which it comments (they are approx. equivalent) enhances its importance. Since that scene (5–9) contains the rogations' only physical action, this exaggeratedly unverisimilar interruption reduces the mimetic effectiveness of C.'s authoritative display: the text is forced back to the level of text. Moreover, C. as a character finds his authority reduced even further: not only has he abdicated, but he has done so under mysterious circumstances that L. exacerbates by protesting too much. Story and discourse reflect each other on a subtler level as well. L. has a sure hand in resolving this technical problem (in contrast to the first digression: 12.2–6n.); but in identifying these particular possible reasons for C.'s abdication, he duplicates the narrative concerns in his 'own' voice, viz. a conflict between plebeian power and the arcana of a patrician élite who control events by ritual fiat. Though L. absolves C. from cowardice and impotence, the surrounding narrative shows the combined powers of plebs and *tr. pl.* to be irresistible; moreover, as D. S. Levene points out, in bowing to the demands of patrician-controlled ritual C. is hoist with his own legalistic petard.

re ... inclinata: military jargon (8.7n.).   **neutro:** if the *seditio* seemed never to get under way (16.6n.), the rogations show every sign of never finishing. Here the political stalemate interferes with the historian's voice, which like the story is suspended by C.'s abdication, caught in a balanced construction of alternatives (*seu ... seu* below). But L. eventually inclines – because of the weight of the evidence – to one side of this source debate, a move that distantly prefigures the narrative resolution.   **seu ... seu:** 12.1n.   **uitio:** this ritual fault may indicate that the gods are displeased at the patrician behaviour (Levene 210); it would be in L.'s manner to record the *uitium* and let his readers draw their own conclusions (cf. 5.13–17.4 with Levene 177–9). **ut ... quidam:** for refs. to other narratives and for L.'s sources see 12.2nn.; for *quidam* see Steele 26–7. **tribuni ... sciuit:** formal language. This plebiscite is assumed at Plut. *Cam.* 39.4, whose C. yields to the *tr. pl.* partly because he fears a second exile. His first (2.12n.) was accompanied by a large fine (5.32.8–9) and immediately followed by the Gallic invasion. Though L. does not mention the first exile here, his C.'s departure from office, under analogous circumstances to those in Book 5 and at a comparable stage in the narrative, is potentially ominous (33.5n.); his return to the narrative – also in response to a Gallic threat – is decidedly anticlimactic (42.4n.). **pro** 'in his capacity as' (*OLD* 8).

38.10 sed ... deterritum 'but that he was put off more by the [bad] auspices than by a precedent-setting bill'. **noui exempli:** gen. of description (cf. Vell. 66.1 with W.); for *exemplum* 'precedent' see *OLD* 5 and in general Chaplin 11–17; for punishing a magistrate for doing his job cf. 5.29.7 (W–M). Influenced perhaps by the pressure to say things in innovative ways (cf. Sen. *Contr.* 9.6.16), descriptions of legal manoeuvres (as Tac. *A.* 4.34.1 with M–W), crimes (as 5.27.8), tortures or death (as Sen. *Contr.* 2.5.6) as 'new types' became popular in declamatory and imperial literature (Plass 98, 102); but such shock tactics were not new (e.g. Cic. I *Ver.* 13 *nouo nefarioque instituto*). **ingenium** 'temperament' (*OLD* 1a). **extemplo:** the four reasons are organized in two pairs, each comparing 'now' to 'later', the first precise ('immediately' ~ 11 'the next year'), the second less so (12 'at the time' ~ 13 'up to our day'). The move away from specifics is signalled by the absence of proper names in 12–13. **quem ... attinebat** 'and what would have been the point of appointing *him* for a fight in which M. Furius had been beaten?' An argument from utility based on a comparison *a maiore ad minus* (Lausberg §396): if C. were beaten, P. Manlius must be. The tenses are those of an unreal condition, with a conditional rel. protasis and an indic. apodosis containing a verb of potentiality (*NLS* §200 (i)). **certamen** ~ 13 *certatum*; the inner *quod*-clauses are connected by 11 *fractum ... in se imperium* ~ 12 *se ... cogi*.

38.11 et quod: L. considers what C.'s character would make

him do (cf. 10 *ingenium* and see 15.7–13n.); for the humiliation entailed by a political loss see 40.17n.   **dictatorem** 'as dictator'.
annus habuit: 27.3n.   **fractum ... imperium:** cf. 37.3, Hor.
C. 1.35.16 (the seditious populace smashes *imperium*).   **in se** 'in
his case'.   **repetiturum** 'likely to take steps to recover' (*OLD*
5b) fits better with running for office after a defeat (e.g. 39.32.6);
for *imperium rep.* cf. 28.31.4 and for fut. participle = descriptive rel.
clause (first in L.) see *NLS* §98 (*a*).

38.12 simul introduces a further argument (*OLD* 5b), which
considers whether something is possible (Lausberg §231): either C.
could have blocked both the original bills and the fine, or none of
them. Since he did block the former, his abdication cannot have
been motivated by the fine.   **qua ... uidebat** 'by which he
saw himself being forced back into line', a military metaphor first
in L. (*TLL*), and before this only of Appius and the decemvirs
(3.35.6, 51.13), a fitting background for C.'s arrogant behaviour.
obsistere ~ *impedire* below (7.5n.).

38.13 et quod ... fuit: this argument from history addresses
the nature of the dictatorship itself: the character of the office
makes the fine improbable, as does C.'s *ingenium* (10). But L.'s assertion fits uncomfortably with a narrative in which dictators *domi* have
limited and invidious success (16.1–4), help the plebs (39.3–4), or
lose to them (42.9).   **usque ad memoriam nostram:** 'up to
our time' (*OLD memoria* 6a), a Ciceronian phrase (*Man.* 54 *bis*, *Phil.*
9.4, *Leg.* 2.56) with a solemn air (as 2.41.3, the first agrarian law
and its consequences, Sall. *J.* 114.2, the mock-heroic conclusion).   **tribuniciis ... est:** *uiribus certare* is first in L. (Tac. *H.*
2.31.2 with H.); for the word order see 3.3n.   **dicta-turae:** adversative asyndeton.   **altius:** 35.2n.

39.1–4. A paragraph of annalistic details, including an 'as if' interregnum (1), provides a transition between dictators. The formal
devices give the impression of a change of year (above, p. 11),
though no such change occurs. P. Manlius plays no part in events
except to appoint the first plebeian *mag. equit.*, which Licinius and
Sextius take as an omen for the plebeian consulate (39.8); on these
dictatorships see Momigliano 114–15.

39.1 Inter ... initam: L. adverts to P. Manlius' appointment
twice (also at 38.10) before reporting it (3), a preparation which en-

hances the real shock of the new dictatorship and which L. does *not* anticipate: its plebeian *mag. equit.* For *inter* + AUC participle see 24.2n.; for the omission of *dictaturam* in the second colon cf. 1.1 (n.). **ab tribunis ... habito:** on the dictator's abdication the consular tribunes resumed their authority, but the *tr. pl.* ignore them; for the interregnum see 1.5n. **plebi ... latoribus:** this split may reflect a fight between the moderate and radical wings of the plebeian leadership, the latter having been willing to help the patricians in the interest of maintaining the revolutionary character of the plebeian tribunate (34–35.9n.). The sudden plebeian reluctance to follow its leaders prepares for the exhortation below (Lipovsky 45 n.1).

39.2 iubebant ... antiquabant 'they were on the point of' (inceptive imperfs.: 38.3n.), not 'they did' (*pace* von Fritz 11). *iubere* = 'decree' (*OLD* 5a). **tribuni:** i.e. Licinius and Sextius. **in omnia ... consulere:** perhaps modelled on *in commune cons.* 'take common counsel' (*OLD consulo* 3b). The proposed separation of the bills threatens to perpetuate the socio-political divisions that Licinius and Sextius are trying to eliminate, and they take a hard line – though they are more conciliatory once concessions are made to them (42.3). The theme of all-or-nothing, a social reflection of the Manlian/Camillan 'one and only' (23.1n.), is developed by Appius (40.11, 18). **consulere** plays on *consule* above (Maltby 152): the *tr. pl.* are doing what consuls do.

39.3 C. Licinio ... dicto 'by appointing C. Licinius' (cf. 8 *dicendo*). Plut. *Cam.* 39.5 makes Stolo the *mag. equit.*, but L.'s *qui ... fuerat* specifies another Licinius (*MRR* I 112). **qui ... fuerat:** the story's major inconsistency is again paraded (34.3n.). For the descriptive clause differentiating this Licinius from his lower-ranking relative see M–W 167.

39.4 accipio: the footnote is in place in this archival section (1–4n.); for refs. to L.'s sources see 12.2nn. **propinqua cognatione:** slightly pleonastic, cf. Cic. *Lig.* 8, Nep. *Praef.* 7; for the Licinii see 34.5n. (*M. Fabi*). As private strife occasioned by intermarriage began the rogations (34.5–11), so this political appointment, also brought about by intermarriage, tips the balance decisively in favour of the plebs.

39.5–41 Vrbs capta. C. is replaced as patrician spokesman in the

second part of the year, in which oratory again replaces action as
Licinius and Sextius face off against Appius Claudius Crassus (36.7–
37n.). The inequality of power between the two sides is figured in
the speeches' imbalance, the patrician having the advantage in
form (*o.r.*), length, and position (second). L. can use such inequality
to suggest ethical or practical superiority (e.g. 4.2 ∼ 4.3–5, patricians v. Canuleius; 5.2 ∼ 5.3–6, *tr. pl.* v. Crassus; in both cases the
second, direct speech wins). Here, however, the more vivid speech
loses. Nor are the tribunes' arguments persuasive enough to explain their victory, which is due in large part to Appius himself
(40–1n.; for paired speeches see 15–16.4n.).

Because they are arguing for their own advancement, Licinius
and Sextius (39.5–12) are less direct than the *uoces exprobrantium*
(17.1–5), but they use some of the same topoi, esp. the ungrateful
crowd and the unrewarded servant of the state (10: see 17.1n.,
17.5n.). Their approach belongs to the genre of *insinuatio* (5n.), ad-
visable when an audience has been won over by the opposition or
is tired of listening to speeches; instead of making his point directly, the orator should proceed *occulte, per dissimulationem* (*Rhet.
Her.* 1.9–11; Lausberg §265, §281). So the *tr. pl.* feign retreat (cf.
37.12n.), asking only for gratitude in return for *commoda*; but their
cupido honoris is nakedly apparent (and shocks the decorous *patres*:
40.1). As with Fabia, however, the vulgar motivation does not compromise their success. The speech, essentially a *hortatio*, is simply
structured: a frame (5 *continuari honorem* ∼ 12 *continuatione honoris*) encloses castigation (6–10) and exhortation (11–12).

39.5 tribunorum ... comitia: 4.7n.   **negando ... plebem:** a typically irrational crowd response, cf. Thuc. 4.28.3 'but,
as a crowd is wont, the more Cleon tried to escape the expedition ...
the more they ... shouted to him to sail'.   **sibi:** dat. of advantage
with *continuari*.   **continuari:** regular since Cic. *Rep.* 1.68 and Sall.
J. 37.2 of extending the tenure of a magistracy.   **acerrime accenderent** ∼ *petebant plebem*: by postponing the obj. of *accenderent* L.
brackets the sentence with alliteration.   **dissimulando:** L. labels
this speech as one of *insinuatio* (39.5–41n.), telling us how to read it
as well as suggesting with *accenderent ... plebem* what its outcome will
be. The artificiality is fitting in a context where speech is action; for
other self-referential passages cf. 3.6n., 25.2–26n., 32.5n., 40.2n.

39.6 nonum ... annum 'for the ninth year'; for the dating by tribunician years see 36.7n.   **uelut in acie:** 15.3n.   **optimates:** a late-republican political catchword which L. uses sparingly (14) and here sarcastically; it denotes in general the (self-styled) 'maintainers of conservatism and tradition' (Seager (1) 328–9, *VL* 500–5).   **periculo ... emolumento:** more late-republican language, cf. 4.35.7 with O., Cic. *De orat.* 2.346 (*uiri fortes* who take risks without reward); on the tribunes' self-interest see 36.10n.   **stare** 'stood up for combat' (*OLD* 2).   **consenuisse** ∼ 10 *senes*; for the metaphor see 33.1n.

39.7 primo ... deinde ... postremo: L. marks the stages as he does those of a battle (10.3n.), a clarity in contrast with the relative formlessness of the past years, but which in turn imposes a retrospective shape on them as the *tr. pl.* recapitulate the narrative. **in leges suas** ∼ *in se* below. Licinius and Sextius use a tricolon similar to Manlius' at 15.8 (n.).   **ablegatione:** a rare noun (*TLL* quotes Plin. *NH* 7.149, Symm. *Ep.* 8.19.2), possibly a Livian coinage from *ablegare*, which he favours.   **dictatorium:** the echo of 16.3 (n.) recalls Cossus' invidious treatment of Manlius. **fulmen:** cf. 45.41.1, L.'s only other fig. use of the word (elsewhere he applies it to real thunderbolts, usually as prodigies: *OLD* 1b): the *tr. pl.* imply that the dictator acted like Jupiter (McKeown on Ov. *Am.* 1.6.16). For its application to anger cf. Pub. *Sent.* 214 M *fulmen est ubi cum potestate habitat iracundia*, and for its use of oratory – are they referring to C.'s angry speech at 38.6–7? – see W. on Vell. 64.3.   **in ... intentatum:** first in L. (Tac. *H.* 1.69 with H.); cf. 27.7 (+ dat.).

39.8 iam ... obstare: like Manlius (cf. 15.8), they turn to the present with initial *iam*, dismissing the previous obstacles in the order of their introduction above.   **nec bellum** implies that the siege of Velitrae is over (but see 38.1n.).   **omen** + dat. is choice, cf. 5.18.3 (*pace* O.), Sall. *H.* 1.109, Luc. 6.397, *Pan. Lat.* 11.10.3. Licinius and Sextius follow the portent of the *fulmen* (7n.) with a good omen; cf. 5.18.3, where the election of a plebeian consular tribune is an *omen concordiae*. Their religious sensitivity, however rhetorical, pre-empts Appius' claim that a mixed consular college will pollute all ritual (41.4–9); see also 16.2n.   **plebeio** ∼ *ex plebe* (9.5n.), the outer terms of a chiasmus.   **se ... sua:** framing reflexives bring home the point, for which cf. 37.3, 38.7.   **plebem:** subj. of *morari*; on delay see 31.2n., 35.10n., 38.9n.

39.9 liberam ... posse: after touching on their primary goal, the consulate (8), the *tr. pl.* dwell on the other bills in an appeal to their audience's self-interest; for the theme of *libertas* see 11.8n. **liberam ... creditoribus** ∼ *liberos ... possessoribus*. The dir. objs., decorated by anaphora and homoioteleuton, are almost exactly parallel, though the acc. is elaborated in the first member, the abl. in the second.   **urbem ac forum:** general + specific, expressing one notion (*OLD atque* 10a); for the urban topography see 36.12n. **uelit:** sc. *plebs*. The last sections of the speech are sprinkled with forms of *uelle*, recalling the remark that started the whole thing (34.7 *num quid uellet*); cf. 11n.

39.10 quae: connective and adversative.   **munera** implies that the *tr. pl.* are *munifici*, i.e. that they have distributed *largitiones* designed to win *gratia*, esp. in elections (*VL* 219 n.12). But the ideal benefactor is not motivated by thoughts of reward, just as the ideal recipient automatically reciprocates (Stevenson 426, cf. 14.7n.): so the *tr. pl.* try to mask their unseemly wish for *emolumentum* by appealing to their listeners' better nature (see below).   **aestimaturos:** sc. *esse*, in acc. + infin. as a disguised statement ('you will never be grateful enough for these gifts if you cut short the expectation ...'), cf. 3.62.1 *quando autem se, si tum non sint, pares hostibus fore?* (*NLS* §269 (*b*)). Like Manlius, the tribunes worry about the correct evaluation of heroic deeds (cf. 11.4 *aestimare*), though Appius will claim they are unwilling to be judged (41.2).   **inter accipiendas ... rogationes:** 11.5n.   **spem ... incidant:** a metaphorical expression that was 'quite a fad' of L. (Lyne on *Ciris* 276, its only non-Livian attestation). *incidere* is properly used of horticultural and surgical incisions (*OLD* 1a-b); for *spes* of growth cf. 31.8n.   **modestiae:** gen. of characteristic. This is 'the restraint of those under the control of others' (Moore 75), cf. 25.6n. The tribunes recall the audience to their 'real' selves, thereby combining frank speech (= the figure *licentia*) with *laus*, as recommended by e.g. *Rhet. Her.* 4.49. **iniuria** 'unlawfully', legal language (*OLD* 1b).   **inducatur** 'be brought in', more legal vocabulary (*TLL* VII 1.1237.41–57).   **per quos:** in adversative antithesis to *ipse* above.   **senes** ∼ 6 *conse-*

nuisse. For *tribunicius* 'ex-tribune' see *OLD* 3; the *tr. pl.* would like to grow old as *consulares.*   **honore ... spe honoris:** 16.3n.

39.11 primum ... deinde: they end as methodically as they began (7n.).   **statuerent ... declararent** = imperatives in *o.r.* (*NLS* §266); for *statuere* + ind. ques. see *NLS* §144 (3).   **apud animos** 'in their minds' (*OLD apud* 8d), infrequently attested before L. (Cic. *Fam.* 2.3.1, Sulp. *apud* Cic. *Fam.* 4.5.5, Sall. *J.* 110.3), but common after him (*TLL*). The phrase ∼ *in comitiis* below.   **uellent ... uoluntatem:** 6.5n. The best way to move an audience is to use arguments *ad explendas cupiditates* (Cic. *Part.* 96): hence the repeated stress on what this audience wants. The figure used is a variant of *permissio*, recommended for inspiring pity; see 41.7n. **coniuncte:** cf. 40.9 *coniunctim*, each a Livian *hapax*, though regular elsewhere.   **ab se:** i.e. by the tribunes (*NLS* §36 (iii)).   **esse quod** 'there was reason' (*OLD sum* 6d).   **perlaturos:** sc. *tribunos.*   **promulgauerint:** they switch back to primary sequence (cf. 8–10): 5.3n.

39.12 sin ... honoris: the audience is meant to follow the *tr. pl.* in subordinating private considerations to the public good (e.g. 6 *nullo publice emolumento*; cf. 21.7n.). But the finale is a threat: give us what we want or you will have nothing (the last word is *habituros*). On the conflict between rhetoric and reality in the speech see also 8n., 10n.   **quod ... sit** 'what each one privately required', resumed by *id* below (*OLD opus* 13b). The Tusculan policy of non-interference (25.9n.) is now seen as detrimental to the interests of the state, since justice demands that the whole take precedence over the part.   **priuatim** ∼ 11 *coniuncte.*   **accipi** ∼ 10 *accipiendas*, both technically of agreeing to a *lex* or *rogatio* (*OLD* 16a), a sense found primarily in L. (*TLL*). See also 40.8n.   **opus esse nihil** 'there was no need for' (*OLD opus* 12a). The repetition from the preceding clause points the potential difference between the plebs and the *tr. pl.*, whose needs may be diametrically opposed.   **inuidiosa:** the Manlian theme of envy attaching to success (11.3n.).   **continuatione:** only L. and *HA Alex.* 1.4 have this of office, but cf. 5 *continuari* (n.), Vell. 99.2 *c. laborum.*

40–1. The patrician answer. Appius Claudius' *oratio* structurally balances two earlier speeches against tribunician proposals, his own advice (5.3–6) to persevere in the Veian siege and C.'s plea (5.51–4) that the Romans not abandon their sacked city for Veii. Those *orationes* are in counterpoise to each other (O. p. 626); this one, in which Claudius recalls his own arguments about civic duties and C.'s about the religious rightness of the *status quo*, makes Books 5–6 into a unit in which foreign campaigns (Veii and the Gauls) are mirrored and metaphorically replayed by domestic ones (Manlius and the rogations: see below). The structure also creates formal expectations that Appius will reunify the strife-torn city and enable it to resume its progress. Instead, he not only fails to move his audience, but actively contributes to the patrician defeat.

Appius relies on the rhetorical devices *sermocinatio* (40.8n.) and *permissio* (41.7n.), each of which allows him to caricature, and then temporarily to concede, the plebeian position in order to counter it. There is a danger inherent in these rhetorical devices that the conceded position will seem more valid than the speaker's own (so *Rhet. Her.* 4.37 on the related device *praeteritio*), a danger increased by the hostile crowd (cf. 39.5, 40.2), which deprives his speech of the authorization it would receive from an audience that accepted his fundamental premises (cf. 20.8n.). Appius is careful, therefore, to make his opposition voices as unpleasant as possible in order to gain sympathy for his own counter-arguments. Within the story, his strategy results in a stalemate: the audience is not convinced, but the vote is postponed (42.1). On the level of discourse, however, Appius loses the battle for the *patres*. The *uoces alienae* (36.8n.) in which he speaks are all plebeian, and they fragment his argument as strife fragments the city. Manlius saw his political fight as a second Gallic sack, resonances of which continue into the rogations (34–35.9n.). But the decisive act in the plebeian capture of Rome is troped on the other major episode in Book 5. Like the rogations, the capture of Veii took ten years (5.22.8), relied on plebeian manpower (esp. 5.20–21.7; during the Gallic war, on the other hand, the plebs left the city, 5.40.5), and ended only when the Romans tunnelled into the Veian citadel, where they clinched their victory by snatching the sacrificial *exta* (5.21.8–10). Appius' speech in defence of the patrician *arx*, the consulate (37.10), figuratively re-enacts this scene: like the Veian walls, it is honeycombed with enemies and at its climax it parades the auspices and priesthoods and

dares the plebs to snatch them away (41.9n.) – which they promptly
do, by forcing the election of plebeian *decemuiri sacris faciundis* (42.2).

Together with the paradigms of the sack and the regal expulsion
(33.5n.), the Veian model offers a third way of understanding this
part of the struggle of the orders. Patricians and plebeians appear
in different guises – as long-time enemies and sometime allies
(Etruscans), as wild barbarians (Gauls), or as savage tyrants (kings) –
but are always at variance with one another; the city they inhabit
is physically, socially, and economically double, a reality underscored by the persistent threat of secession, which evokes the proposed migration to Veii (42.10n.). Civil conflict continues until the
two cities are apparently reconciled in 300 (10.7–9, when the priesthoods are opened to plebeians; see Levene 233); but in fact it takes
a last *secessio plebis* (*per.* 11) to bring the orders into parity.

40.1 Aduersus 'in response to' (*OLD* 13b).   **prae ... rerum**
'in the face of the outrageousness of the things they said';
res = 'content' of their speech (Lausberg §45, §§255–7).   **stupor
silentiumque:** the patricians have two conventional reactions to
this shocking behaviour: most are silent (cf. *Rhet. Her.* 4.12 *nequeo
uerbis consequi, iudices, indignitatem rei* and see Lausberg §§887–9 on
the figure *reticentia*), but Appius' indignation is unsuppressible
(6n.). For L.'s preparatory silences see 15.4n.   **ceteros:** 1.10n.
patrum: appositional gen. (technically partitive: Riemann 268).

40.2 Ap. Claudius: *tr. mil.* 403; he is not the focus of a coherent
episode, but appears as needed in Books 4–6 to oppose the *tr. pl.*
(Vasaly 222–5). The historiographical tradition knew two types of
Claudii, the wise patrician and the arrogant tyrant (*CC* 57–103);
Crassus has elements of both (nn.).   **nepos decemuiri:** L.
twice introduces Crassus thus. The first time (4.48.5) the man immediately repositions himself as the descendant of Ap. Claudius Sabinus
(4.48.6 *proauum*), claiming wider kinship with the family than simply
with the tyrannical Decemvir (20.3n.); later he is described only as
imbutum iam ab iuuenta certaminibus plebeiis (5.2.13). The present return
to the tag *nepos decemuiri* makes most sense in the light of the Fabia–
Lucretia parallel (34.5–11n.). The Decemvir's tyranny over the plebs
was epitomized by his seizure of Verginia (a second Lucretia-story:
3.44.1); Crassus shares the diffused role of the tyrant in this episode
(34.6n.), blocking plebeian *libertas*.   **dicitur** appeals to the

historiographical tradition (18.16n.), while *in hanc fere sententiam* (below) signals the historian's artifice (26.4n.). This double-edged reminder of the narrator's presence undercuts Appius' direct, almost impulsive speech that is supposedly a product of uncontrolled emotion (*odio ... iraque*).   **odio ... iraque:** L. sabotages Appius' professed fairness in advance (cf. Ov. *M.* 13.3, the losing Ajax is *impatiens irae* as he begins to speak; see Vasaly 224 n.49: *contra, CC* 84); for Claudian *ira* and *odium* cf. 2.29.9, 58.6, 61.3.   **ad dissuadendum** 'to argue against them', a technical expression that labels the *oratio* as a deliberative speech opposing a disadvantageous proposition (*inutile*: Lausberg §60.2b). The gerund depends on *processisse* below (proper of coming forward to speak: *OLD* 4a).   **sententiam:** an opinion given in an assembly (*OLD* 4a). Crassus maintains that the speciously popular rogations in reality threaten plebeian *commoda*. After an elaborate *principium a nostra persona* (3–5) he argues this *propositio* (6–7) under the rubrics of the 'advantageous' (8–14), the 'secure' (15–18), the 'right' (19–41.3), and the 'religious' (41.4–10). Each of the first three topics begins with a quotation and ends with an *epiphonema* (10.9n.). (Ullmann (1) 66–7 has a different division.) His sharp tone is intensified by the short, choppy cola produced by his favourite doublets and antitheses (3nn.). He tends to couch these in anaphoric structures (7n.) characteristic of oratory, in which a single element may be multiplied, causing the sentence to puddle out around a given phrase rather than moving forward in the manner of narrative periods (cf. 4.5.5 eight *si*'s, 5.54.4 five appositional phrases, Cic. *Sull.* 19 eleven *cum*'s) and increasing the periodic suspension which further distinguishes *oratio* from *narratio* (above, p. 21).

40.3 neque ... (5) posse: the meticulously structured opening politely posits a hypothetical, two-pronged attack on himself (*praesumptio*: 15.11n.), then refutes it point by point. The measured tone befits an *exordium* (cf. *Rhet. Her.* 3.22 *utile est ad firmitudinem sedata uox in principio. quid insuauius quam clamor in exordio causae?*).   **neque ... sit:** the apodosis comes before its protasis *si ... audiam* (word order rarer in Livian oratory than narrative: Dangel 41), the construction of which is incomplete before the following infin. clauses. This periodic suspension increases in 5 (n.).   **nouum ... inopinatum:** novelty and surprise are recommended for catching an audience's attention (Lausberg §270); Appius turns the topos on its head by denying that he will be surprised. The doublet is a 'rhetorical cliché' (O. on 3.26.5); for other pairs (most of increasing length: above, p. 22) cf. 4 *nego* ~ *infitias eo* (synonyms), 5 *priuatos* ~ *in magistratibus*, 9 *placent* ~ *displicent*, *utiles* ~ *inutiles* (polar expressions), 41.10 *leges* ~ *magistratus*, *centuriatis* ~ *curiatis comitiis* (complementary pairs) and see below.   **Quirites:** 38.6n.   **quod unum** 'the one thing which', quickly divided into its component parts (*alterum ... alterum* below).   **familiae ... ego quoque:** Appius situates himself as part of a larger whole, partly as a matter of family pride, partly to address immediately the worst aspect about him, his *nomen* (13); see also 6n. *familia* here approximates to *gens* (below): Saller 341–2.   **seditiosis:** 11.8n.   **antiquius** 'more important' (*OLD* 10a), lit. '(more) before', cf. Vell. 52.4 *neque prius neque antiquius quicquam habuit* and Bettini 117–19. The adj., uncommon in L. (5), fits this tradition-minded Claudius (*CC* 70, 85).   **patrum ... plebis:** antitheses are as much to Appius' taste as doublets: both devices make manifest the controlled abundance of his anger and hatred (2). Cf. 5 *utilitatem* ~ *uoluntatem*, 6 *Claudiae familiae* ~ *unus Quiritium*, 8 *petunt* ~ *fastidimus*, 12 *uitale* ~ *mortiferum*, 14 *res* ~ *auctores*, *secundis* ~ *aduersis*, 18 *partem* ~ *totum*, 19 *uoluntate* ~ *necessitatem*, 20 *lege* ~ *suffragio*, 41.1 (n.) *extorqueant* ~ *petant*, *occasionibus* ~ *uirtute*, 41.2 *serua* ~ *liberis*, 41.3 *uolueritis* ~ *nolueritis*, 41.6 *priuatim* ~ *in magistratibus* and see Ullmann (2) 88–90.   **maiestate ... commodis** ~ 4 *maiestas*, 5 *incommodum*; see further 6.7n., 35.4n.   **aduersatos:** sc. *eos*, agreeing with the implied masc. plur. in *gentis* above. For *adu. commodis* cf. Tac. *A.* 1.27.2.

40.4 quorum ... (5) posse: the longest period in the speech, full of *politesse* and constructing an identity between the Claudii and the plebs so strong that in 6 Appius can speak in their voice as well as his own.   **alterum:** dir. obj. of *nego* (etc.), explained by *nos ... posset* ('the first I do not deny, viz. ...').   **infitias eo** has an old-fashioned tone (E. W. Fay, *A.J.P.* 20 (1899) 149–68); for the doublet with *nego* see 3n.   **ex quo:** sc. *tempore* (*OLD qui*[1] 15c).   **adsciti sumus:** being a circumlocution for a noun ('adoption'), the indic. is retained in *o.o.* (*NLS* §287). The Claudii traced their descent from the Sabine Attus Clausus (2.16.4–5); their renowned *superbia* (Vasaly 206) and exclusivity thus have a fundamental contradiction

at heart, since like all Romans the Claudii were originally immigrants (as Canuleius points out: 4.3.10–17); see 4.4n., Balsdon 82–
96.   **in ciuitatem et patres:** general + specific, in the logical
order (Lindholm 4; cf. 1.28.7, 4.3.14); *simul* is a not so subtle reminder that the Claudii went directly to the top.   **aucta** depends on
dici ... posset below ('might truly be said to have been increased').
Claudius plays on the derivation of *maiestas* (also with *imminuta*, 5
maioribus); see 6.7n. and cf. 41.8.   **inter quas ... uoluistis:**
the retained indic. reports a fact (*NLS* §287); for *inter* 'in the class
of' see *OLD* 3. Appius, like the *tr. pl.* (39.11), appeals to the people's wish (cf. 15–18), though he admits a distinction between what
is good for them and what they want (5).   **dici ... posset** ~ 5
uere ... posse.

     40.5 illud alterum: a second objection, more elaborated than
the first. *alterum ... contendere* is completed by *nihil ... fecisse nec ...
posse* below (3n.).   **pro ... meis:** the pronominal incarnation of
the 'Priam' figure (16.3n.), like it quite common in L. (e.g. 41.3,
Praef. 10 *tibi tuaeque rei publicae*, 5.27.12 *a uobis et imperatore uestro*,
24.8.11, 29.18.7) and found in other prose (e.g. Herod. 5.24 ἐμοί
τε καὶ τοῖσι ἐμοῖσι πρήγμασι, Cic. *Planc.* 59 *nos et nostros liberos*,
Caes. *C.* 2.32.2 *uos enim uestrumque factum*). Its frequent appearance
in prayers suggests a solemn or old-fashioned nuance (e.g. 3.17.6,
Cato *Agr.* 134.2, Cic. *Dom.* 145, *CIL* III 1933.9–10, Curt. 9.2.28,
Macr. *Sat.* 3.9.7, 10).   **nisi ... quis putet** 'unless someone
thinks that things done on behalf of the whole state are detrimental
to the plebs, as if they lived in another city'. The thought is structured by antithetical chiasmus (*pro uniu. re pub.* ~ *plebi ... aduersa*)
and couched in a form that pre-empts possible objection: there
could be no such person (cf. 41.4n.).   **tamquam ... urbem:**
like C. (38.7) Appius introduces the dangerous point in a simile;
see 11.7n., and for the hyperbaton *aliam ... urbem* see 1.2n.   **priuatos** ~ *in magistratibus* (3n.); for the *uariatio* see 9.5n.   **scientes**
'consciously' (*OLD* 2).   **factum dictumue:** 3n.   **utilitatem
... uoluntatem:** cf. Cic. *Sul.* 25 *nisi forte regium tibi uidetur ... populi utilitati magis consulere quam uoluntati*, *Rep.* 5.8 fr. 2, Sen. *Ben.*
2.14.1.   **referri** 'be adduced in reply' (*OLD* 12d).

     40.6 An ... (7) esse?: he states his thesis in a hypothesis. The
argument is based on an underlying comparison *a minore ad maius*

(Lausberg §397): if the average man cannot keep silent, how can a Claudius? This is the first of several substitutions distracting attention from his own status, which was elaborated in the *exordium* but is now a foil for the 'ordinary Roman'. **hoc:** obj. of *reticere* below and expanded by 7 *L. illum ... esse?* **si ... sciam:** Appius' restrained organization continues in an isosyllabic triad (*si ... sim, nec ... ortus, sed ... quilibet*), the last element of which is expanded by the chiastic rel. clause (also isosyllabic). **Claudiae ... patricio** ∼ 13 *patricius ... Claudius*, ending the first topic (2n.). **familiae ... ortus** ∼ *Quiritium ... ortum* below, a parallelism which implies that the Quirites are a family too (cf. *ingenuis*), with the same obligations of loyalty to and respect for *maiores* as the Claudii. *familiae* is a possessive gen. used predicatively (G–L §366). **ex ... sanguine** ∼ *ingenuis* below (9.5n.). **unus ... quilibet:** a purely hypothetical creation at this point, the 'average man' will speak out loud at 10. By recalling the Manlian/Camillan heroism of the *unus uir* (23.1n.), Appius' *unus ciuis* suggests an equivalence between the high and low ends of the social scale in this one area: you need not be larger than life to act *pro patria* (cf. 25.9n.). Appius transforms this *unus* as he goes along: at 20 he singles out the proposed consul (*unus ... plebeius*) as one who extorts honours (i.e. a tyrant); at 41.3 the rogations will make the lowest Roman (*quis est ... tam humilis*) more eligible for the consulate than an aristocrat; at 41.9 *quilibet* becoming a flamen shows the corruption of all ritual. Unfortunately, however, this anonymous plebeian takes on a life of his own (8n., 10n.). **in libera ciuitate** ∼ 12 *libera ... ciuitas*; the phrase is echoed from 20.14. For the Claudian preoccupation with *libertas populi* see *CC* 79, 85. **reticere possim:** the *indignatio* that kept the other *patres* silent (2) forces Claudius to speak, cf. Cic. *Phil.* 1.29 *sed per deos immortalis! ... non possum de utriusque uestrum errore reticere.* Like C. (38.7) and Cossus (15.5–6), Appius represents his own actions as having been forced on him by the anti-popular behaviour of the plebeian champions.

40.7 L. illum Sextium: Appius is the only Livian orator to separate *praenomen* from *nomen* with a form of *ille* or *hic* (cf. 17 and see Douglas on Cic. *Brut.* 10, Marouzeau III 160). The resulting disjunction can specify an individual (e.g. Cic. *Cael.* 34 *Quinta illa Claudia*), or (as here) 'introduce' a character: Sextius is the dominant one (cf.

35.10), and will become consul (42.9).   **si ... placet:** an excla-
mation that L. 'keeps for special effect', often to heighten indignation (4.3.9 with O.; Fraenkel II 63–4).   **licentiae:** the bad side of
libertas (38.6n.), which will pre-empt plebeian freedom (for *(non) licet*
cf. 10–11, 15, 18–19).   **regnant** 'have been reigning'; *nouem annis*
(above) is used by analogy with *olim, dudum* etc. to give the pres. the
sense of a progressive perf. (G–L §230). For the conventional charge
of *regnum* see 11.4n., 41.10n.   **negent ... non ... non:** 16.3n.
potestatem liberam suffragii: a late-republican *popularis* slogan
encompassing freedom both in voting (i.e. by secret ballot) and in
nominating candidates; the latter was always limited by *dignitas*,
and those urging *liberum suffragium* 'strove to break the exclusiveness
of the nobility, not its pre-eminence' (Wirszubski 54). For the ap-
propriation of *popularis* arguments and the attempt to show that
their deployers are working against the people see 19.7n.   **non
... non:** for Appius' doublets see 3n.; he uses anaphora also at 11,
13, 17, 18, 41.4, 41.8, 41.10 (2n.).

   40.8 "sub ... tribunos": Appius favours the figure *sermocinatio*
(Lausberg §§820–5), a device which brings an adversary or a sup-
porter 'to life' by conjuring them up inside one's own discourse
(esp. the dead, e.g. Cic. *Cael.* 33–4, or abstract entities, e.g. Cic.
Cat. 1.18). It is common in Cicero and in Seneca's declaimers; in
L. cf. 5.3.7 (also Appius, a characterizing device: *CC* 85 n.76) and
see Ullmann (2) 67–70. With it, Claudius sets up a dialogue between the *tr. pl.* and their supporters. The effect this rhetorical tactic has on the audience is not specified. Narratively, however, it is
counter-productive, as it gives the plebs a direct voice – indeed, a
multiplicity of voices – for the first time since 35.8, ending patrician monopoly on *o.r.* and making Appius into his own heckler.
See further 40–1n.   **"sub condicione":** cf. 21.12.4 *sub condicionibus*, a legalism (*OLD condicio* 4c); otherwise L. has the abl. of means
(42.10) or manner (as 30.16.13). The 'terms' are that all three bills
must pass together (39.11–12).   **inquit:** an idiomatic use of the
sing. to introduce a remark made by more than one person (*TLL*),
cf. *nos* below and 10 *uestra*; in 12 the crowd sharpens its attack by
addressing Licinius and Sextius as *tu* (on them as a unit see
35.4n.).   **decimum:** adv., only here and 42.1 (*TLL*), cf. 36.7
(n.).   **quid est aliud** 'is a formula of everyday speech, expres-

sing indignation' (Nisbet on Cic. *Pis.* 47): 'what is this if not to
say'. The figure *definitio* (7.3n.), used also at 16, 19, 41.7, allows Appius to present the same idea in different *colores*, rhetorical slippiness
expected from one who has been described as *par ... in contionibus
... tribunis plebis* (5.7.1). Like his introduction of other speakers,
however, this play of substitution helps decentralize Appius' own
authority.   **mercede:** a cynical translation of the tribunes' *emolumentum* (39.6) and *honos* (39.10).   **"accipiamus":** Appius parrots
this tribunician verb (39.10, 12) half a dozen times in 8–15; see also
13n.

40.9 tandem underlines the irony, which is characteristic of
Appius' speeches (cf. 41.5, 9, 5.4.12, 6.17 and see Ullmann (2) 46–
9).   **qua:** abl. of price.   **"ut ... accipiatis":** appositional
to *merces* above (as Pl. *Amph.* 646, V. Max. 5.3.2f).   **seu ...
sunt:** he reduces his opponents' platform to a jingle of antithetic
pairs (3n.).   **utiles:** the economic rogations are patently advantageous to the plebs (*OLD utilis* 2), but Appius deflects that point
by mentioning them first in this attack on the inseparability of the
bills, where he affirms their utility within the safe confines of the
tribunician restrictions (the consular bill being impossible, the economic ones are in no danger of passing).   **coniunctim:** cf. 39.11;
for adverbs in *-im* see 36.12n.   **"accipiatis":** 8n.

40.10 obsecro: paratactic with *putate* below (*OLD* 3).   **Tarquinii:** Tarquinius Superbus was the worst and last of the kings and
the father of Lucretia's rapist; after the foundation of the republic
even the name 'Tarquinius' had to be eliminated (2.2.3–11). It is a
good insult for a would-be tyrant (Opelt 150; cf. 3.11.13, 39.3 (the
decemvirs) and for other 'expulsion' imagery see 32.2n.). But in
equating the *tr. pl.* to members of the ruling class it opens the way
for them to be like patricians in other respects (L. nowhere else applies it to plebeians). The next kings to whom Crassus compares the
tr. pl. are even more problematic (41.10n.).   **putate** 'imagine'
(*OLD* 9).   **ex media contione:** the notion of 'middle' recurs.
As at 14.3 and 25.9, we are in a public space, but rather than being
the centre of attention (e.g. 19.7 *regni crimen in medio*) the 'middle' is
now the *corona*, a dense group of citizens who incarnate the *res publica*, while the *tr. pl.* are on an oligarchic pedestal (next n. but one).
unum ciuem ∼ *omnes coniunctim* (above). Appius becomes an indivi-

dual making a selection, a Claudius reduced to his basic element (*me* = *ciuem*). He adopts the role of the anonymous *ciuis* to show that every element of the state should oppose these bills, but he also thereby collapses the distinction between the orders: if he = *unus Quiritium quilibet* (6), why should that citizen not = a Claudius? See also 6n., 8n.   **succlamare:** the prefix emphasizes the difference in height between the *tr. pl.* on their platform and the man in the street (cf. 28.26.12 *ferociter in forum ad tribunal imperatoris ut ultro territuri succlamationibus concurrunt* and see T. P. Wiseman, *Cinna the poet* (1974) 17–18). Tyrants, too, live on high (19.1n., cf. 35.2n.); for shouts from the *corona* see 37.1n.   **"bona ... alias":** for *succlamare* + *o.r.* cf. Phaedr. 5.1.4, Vell. 32.1, Fro. *M. Caes.* 1.6.1 Van den Hout.   **uenia:** the deferential *ciuis* anticipates causing offence (*OLD* 3a, b).   **liceat** 'may we'.   **salubres** introduces a medical metaphor (*OLD* 1) developed below (12). If citizens treat their own problems, it implies indifference or worse at the helm (e.g. Cic. *S. Rosc.* 91); conversely, however, bad leadership forces people to take matters into their own hands. For self-healing cf. Sulp. *apud* Cic. *Fam.* 4.5.5 with Otto 307 *sapere* (2); for *salus* and the state see 17.5n., and Seager (1) 333 on its links with the *commoda plebis*.

40.11 "non ... uideas": the *tr. pl.* answer. The connection between what the citizen wants (*tu ... iubeas*, the economic bills) and the undesired result (*hoc ... fiat*, the consular bill) is inescapable. The second half of the sentence (*et hoc ... uideas*), is focalized by Appius, who cannot stay out of his own *sermocinatio* (so Gronovius *ad loc.*).   **licebit** governs the following subjuncs. (*OLD* 1c).   **hoc portenti** 'this portent', which the plebs try to reject (see below), recalls the tribunes' claim that they had a good omen for the consulate (39.8). *portentum* 'monster' is common in political invective (Opelt *s.v.*); for the partitive gen. see G–L §369 and cf. 31.7n.   **uti ... uideas** explains the nature of the portent.   **quod ... quod:** 7n.   **abominaris:** cf. 18.9; in each case it describes a futile apotropaic gesture. See 34.7n.   **accipe:** 8n.   **"fero":** on the present see 15.6n.

40.12 ut ... admisceat: this claim that the tribunes will produce not unity but contamination is further developed in the section *de religionibus* (41.9, cf. 38.7). 'Mixing' is a metaphor for civil war (14.9n.), but Appius' simile depends on the conception of the state as a body (3.1n.). For plebeian and patrician notions of political division see 37.4n.; for medical imagery (which Appius uses also at 5.3.6, 5.12) in discussions of the state's well-being see 16.7n. **ut si** 'as if' + following subjunc. (*OLD ut* 8d).   **uenenum ... cum cibo:** cf. Dio 7.29.6, where Licinius tells the plebs not to accept only some of the rogations since 'they should not drink unless they would eat'. The image of food mixed with poison or inedibles is widespread, applied to demagogic rhetoric at e.g. Ar. *Kn.* 1399, imaging moral upset at Sen. *Ep.* 95.26–9, deadly deceit at Ov. *Am.* 1.8.104 (with McKeown). The irony here is that the plebs know the poison is there and are still forced to eat it. On 'composite food' see E. Gowers, *The loaded table* (1992) 109–26.   **ponat** 'were to serve' (*OLD* 5).   **abstinere ... admisceat:** both depend on *iubeat*, as 33.31.11 *decretum est ... redderetur ... retineri*, 36.1.9 (Catterall 315, Sörbom 113). For the word order cf. 16.1, 27.7, 38.12; for *iubere* + subjunc. see *OLD* 3b.   **si ... succlamassent:** mixed unreal condition: 'if the state were (now) free would a crowd not (already) have shouted up at you'. Appius moves from impersonating one citizen (10) to taking on the voice of the crowd; boldness and a certain (compromised) freedom come with numbers. For *liber* 'free to criticize' see 16.8n. (proper 'freedom of speech' in assemblies was limited by *dignitas*: Wirsubski 18, 21).   **tibi:** 8n. (*inquit*). **frequentes** summons up both positive and negative sides of the crowd: a growth mechanism (4.6) and the *uulgus* in the Forum (5.1, 6.1, cf. Nisbet–Hubbard on Hor. *C.* 1.35.14).   **"abi hinc cum":** 'archaically colloquial' (1.26.4 with O.); for the *o.r.* see 8n.   **quid?** expresses surprise at an imagined objection (*OLD quis*[1] 10). Livy characterizes Appius with this Ciceronian interjection (15, 5.5.4, 5.8).   **si ... ferat?:** for the indignant ques. see 15.9n.   **commodum ... accipere** 'beneficial for the people to accept'. He deliberately refers not to the plebs but to the *populus* (19.7n.); for *accipere* see 8n.

40.13 illud anticipates the *o.r.* below.   **si quis ... si quis:** 7n. Claudius reinstates the difference between his patrician self and the plebs in preparation for his next arguments, based on security and rightness (15–41.3); at the same time he moves out of the sing. and into the plur. (*accipite ... uestrum ... uos* below), in part to refer more precisely to the crowd whose voice he has just simulated (12), in part to put more distance between himself and his listeners. **patricius** ~ *inuidiosius* and *Claudius*, cf. 14 *res* ... *auctores* (n.). **diceret:** 8n.; for *dicere* + *o.r.* see 38.5n.   **"fero"** ~ *ferret* (below), the sense changing from 'propose' to 'endure' (3.5n.); so 14 *accipietis* 'listen' ~ 13 *accipite* 'accept' (8n.). The *traductio* invites the audience to think carefully about what they are doing: can they bear what the *tr. pl.* propose, and is the passive act of listening to *popularis* talk tantamount to active approval of these bills? (see also Plass 41–2).

40.14 numquamne ... spectabitis 'will you never consider the facts rather than their advocates?' The antithesis, iconically represented by the *res* hidden inside *auctores*, rests on the opposition between the 'thing' (= reality) and its usually deceptive representative, human or verbal (Otto 297, *OLD res* 5). See 11.4n. and Lausberg §374 (*res* and *persona* the two main topics in legal argument).   **quae ... dicet** ~ *quae ... dicentur* below, with *uariatio* of case (acc. ~ nom., cf. 33.1n.) and voice.   **magistratus:** 11.7n.; for the metonymy cf. 31.4, 38.6.   **secundis ... aduersis:** 3n.   **ab nostrum quo:** cf. *CIL* I² 2.585.17 *ab eorum quo. quo* is indefinite; the gen. is fronted in antithesis with *magistratus ille* (13.4n.).

40.15 The main point of Appius' second topic (15–18) is the military implication of plebeian consuls (= *tutum*, *Rhet. Her.* 3.3): it is too dangerous to let them take command (17).   **"At hercule":** 'direct, personal, and rhetorical' (Syme (2) 708); it introduces a plebeian interjection (*OLD at* 11d).   **sermo** probably refers to the tribunician remarks above (so edd.), as the plebs wake up to reality; but Appius may be conjuring up an objection to his *own* remarks, which he then counters with *quid ... simillima* ('what? well, my language is no worse than their bill'): that would fit the increasing distance he is putting between himself and the plebs (13n.).   **"ciuilis":** befitting a *ciuis*, a prescriptive concept new in Sall. and L.: 'only after the fabric of the *societas ciuilis* had been destroyed by the triumphs of dynasts could *ciuilis* begin to refer to an ideal ... [I]t was the behaviour of the civil Augustus that provided the impulse for [its] development' (Wallace-Hadrill (1) 43). For the reasoning by question and answer see 15.11n.   **rogatio qualis est:** he wants his audience to believe that the proposed reforms will destroy the *ciuitas*. They *do* go to the heart of the traditional citizen roles in a renewed attempt to redraw the limits of what it means to be a *ciuis Romanus*: the traditional plebeian contention (40.4n.), and one implicit in Claudius' argument, is that, just as the division between *ciuis* and non-*ciuis* has always been flexible, so should that between privileged and non-privileged *ciuis*.   **rogatio** ~ *sermoni* plays on the conventional idea, going back to Homer, that an unpleasant question is answered in kind (Pearson on Soph. fr. 929.4 has copious exx.).   **"consules":** obj. of *facere*; it is fronted for emphasis, being the leitmotif of the next sections (16, 17 *bis*, 18). This time Appius leads with his 'translation' of the tribunician demands; *an ... permittit* (16) completes the *definitio* (8n.).

40.16 rogat ~ *iubet* below: the 'request', on which Claudius has dwelt (*rogatio ... rogo* above) is really an order.   **qui ... permittit?:** for the indignant questions in 16–19 see 15.9n.; on the probable provisions of the bill see 34–35.9n.

40.17 si ... dimicare?: a mixed protasis (ideal, *sint* + unreal, *peteret*) + unreal apodosis (*possetisne*). The only action whose possibility he thereby affirms is the advent of war; he flatteringly assumes the plebs would be unable to tolerate the logical outcome of the rogation.   **quale ... quale:** 2n.   **Etruscum ... Gallicum:** Rome's two closest brushes with disaster: there were versions of both sieges according to which the city was captured (O. p. 255, Enn. *Ann.* 228 with Skutsch; *contra* T. J. Cornell, *J.R.S* 76 (1986) 248). Porsenna was allied with the Tarquins in their attempt to recapture *regnum* in Rome; for the Gauls in the rogations see 34–35.9n.   **haec** is deictic: Appius gestures to the surrounding Forum. He attempts to construct a topography that is both patriotic (here) and invidious (41.3, 10) to rival the tribunes' map (36.12n.); but despite the persuasive Camillan precedent (5.52, 54 *passim*, see 5.6n. and Jaeger 355–6), at 41.9 he ignores the opportunity to draw a sacral map, instead listing priesthoods etc. with no ref. to their place in the city.   **hostium:** possessive.   **consulatum ... peteret:** the point is weakened by the fact that if a serious war broke out a dictator would inevitably be appointed (cf. 42.4). Moreover, by introducing C. (*hoc* implies that he is present) Appius reminds us that C. has been defeated already by the *tr. pl.* (38.9); in setting him up as a potential rival to Sextius he also recalls C.'s curious non-rivalry with Manlius (11.3n.).   **ille:** 7n.

Sextium ... dimicare?: isocolonic, picking up the persons of the protasis in reverse order.   **haud pro dubio** 'without doubt' (*OLD pro* 9d).   **Camillum:** given his other Catonian attributes (2.12n., 11.7n., 25.6n.), this connection of C. with *repulsa* may further the analogy between the two (next n.).   **de repulsa:** election defeats were a fact of life and though they need not have a lasting effect (*FRR* 369–71), they were rhetorically useful (cf. Hor. *C.* 3.2.17–18, Cato an *exemplum* of *uirtus* rising above defeat) and could inspire open warfare (cf. Caes. *C.* 1.4.1 *Catonem ueteres inimicitiae Caesaris incitant et dolor repulsae* and V. Max. 7.5 *praef.* on the blow to *dignitas* they cause); on 'aggressive individualism' see J. Paterson, *RPL* 21–43.

40.18 in commune ... uocare 'to bring public offices into joint possession' (*OLD commune* 1b, *uoco* 8a); the infin. clause is predicated of *hocine* (above) and further explained by the following four substantive clauses. He charges the *tr. pl.* with reverse discrimination; for turning an accusation against the accuser see 15.6n. and for the argument from fairness see Lausberg §123, §202.2.   **duos plebeios ... liceat:** the following clause is identically framed (anaphora + homoioteleuton), while the next two sentences are isocolonic: the symmetry enhances Appius' apparent rationality. **necesse sit:** 34.1n.   **praeterire** 'pass over', esp. in an election (*OLD* 6).   **societas ... consortio:** near synonyms, coupled in the only other Livian uses of *consortio/-um*: 4.5.5 *si in consortio, si in societate rei pub. esse*, 40.8.12, cf. Cic. *Brut.* 2, Hor. *C.* 3.24.60, [Quint.] *Decl.* 376.2, Plin. *Pan.* 60.5.   **parum ... traxeris?** 'is it not enough that you become legally entitled to [*OLD uenio* 10] part of something of which you never yet had a share, unless in seeking part you carry off the whole?' The thrice repeated *pars* – ironically anticipated by *parum* – sounds like Appius mimicking yet another tribunician 'slogan' (8n.); for division in the rogations see 37.4n. and for the image here cf. 34.3.3 *extemplo simul pares esse coeperint, superiores erunt*, Luc. 1.290–1 (to Caesar) *partiri non potes orbem, | solus habere potes.*   **parum est:** 'a regular rhetorical form of beginning an attack on an opponent for presumption or encroachment' (Stephenson). For the hyperbolic progression *parum ... pars ... totum* see Lausberg §910 and cf. 41.8.   **si ... uenis:** subj. of *est* above (*OLD si* 12a).   **tua:** 8n. (*inquit*).   **traxeris:** often of plunder (*OLD* 5). It is the *patres* who want all or nothing when they once again elect a patrician college (7.18.4 *aut toto cedendum ... aut totum possidendum*).

40.19 The third topic (through 41.3) considers what is right (*iustum*), e.g. electing men with *dignitas*, upholding traditional standards etc. (*Rhet. Her.* 3.3–4).   **"Timeo ... plebeium":** cf. 37.4–7 and for the quotation see 8n.   **quid est dicere aliud:** 8n.   **indignos:** specifically those who do not have enough *dignitas* ('position', 'political standing': *VL* 388–415) to become consuls. In anticipating this argument the *tr. pl.* had used *idoneus*, which lacks a political connotation (37.8n.).   **uoluntate ... necessitatem:** he counters the tribunes' claim that they care about the people's wish (39.11n.); for *necessitas* see 34.1n. and for the antithesis see 40.3n.   **creaturi non estis** 'you have no intention of electing'.

40.20 quid ... dicat?: if the system of *beneficia* (15.9n.) breaks down then the political system as a whole is at risk. This argument appeals to the audience's *commoda* (35.4n.).   **sequitur** 'is the logical consequence' (*OLD* 7).   **nisi ut** 'other than' introduces a substantive clause (*OLD nisi* 6c).   **debeat:** the subj. is *unus ... plebeius* below.   **populo:** 19.7n.   **unus** has become once again a privileged figure (6n.), but in an invidious sense, while the patricians come in pairs (*duobus* above), as republican magistrates should (e.g. 2.7.6).   **lege ... non suffragio:** cf. 37.7 *lege ... per gratiam*. The tribunes' *lex* was a protection; Appius paints it as a constraint. He also replaces *gratia*, which works to the advantage of its possessor, with *suffragium*, the people's power (38.1n.; see Serres 118–36). For 'free suffrage' see 7n.

41.1 'What I tell you three times is true.' Appius draws out the implications of the failure of *beneficia*, each time using a different antithetical structure (X *non* Y [the figure *correctio*: Lausberg §§784–6]; *ita* X ... *ut nihil* Y; X *potius quam* Y). For the repetition of *petere honores* see above, p. 24.   **extorqueant ... petant:** antithesis demonstrates the falsity of a position by equating it to its opposite (e.g. 'not truth but lies'); it is related to *definitio* (40.8n.), and like it relies on the self-conscious deceitfulness of rhetoric to argue paradoxically for the speaker's honesty ('they say ... but I say, and my version is more "real" than theirs'; see Plass 26–55). In exposing the tribunes' 'true' aims Appius also exposes the falsity of their lan-

guage; see 10.9n., 11.4n., and for these verbs cf. Quint. 10.1.110 (on
Cicero's eloquence) *ut ipsa illa quae extorquet impetrare eum credas.*   **et
... debeant** 'and they intend to gain the most important things
in such a way that they incur no debt, not even such as would be
owing for the least important'. Antithetical superlatives show the
tribunes' duplicity (last n.). The virtues of hard work and deserved
reward figured prominently in Claudian political speeches (*CC* 65–
6, 85); for *maxima* of office, rank etc. see *OLD magnus* 12c and cf.
7.5, 35.2.   **occasionibus ... uirtute:** as appropriate in a military as a political context: for *occasio* see 23.6n.; for the opposition
with *uirtus* cf. 7.12.4, Tac. *Ag.* 27.2, and for military language in a
political sphere cf. 34.4n. Opportunity *has* helped the plebeians
(35.1, 36.1); for the idea that it is *uirtus*, not chance factors, that en-
noble a man – an anti-aristocratic ideal that Appius is subversively
deploying – see 37.11n.   **potius quam:** 10.9n. (*magis ... quam*).

41.2 In a tetracolon of rel. clauses of characteristic, Appius
imagines the sort of person who would welcome this bill: *aliquis*
shuns public scrutiny in the first and third colon and overturns the
existing system in the second and fourth. The second pair repeats
and intensifies the first; a move from reflexives to 2nd pers. adjs.
encourages the audience's indignation to rise.   **aliquis:** a Gre-
cism, 'many a' (*TLL* I 1615.44–54, cf. LSJ τίς A.II 1).   **inspici
aestimari:** an appeal to the ideal world in which plain sight produces fair valuation (an ethical 'open door', 25.9n.): inspection and
assessment go together in a neat inevitability unthreatened by
messy, deceptive rhetoric (cf. 12.1n.). For the asyndeton *bimembre*
see 4.10n.   **certos:** predicative.   **uni:** 40.20n.   **necessaria:** predicative; for compulsion see 34.1n.   **pro** 'instead of'
(*OLD* 6).   **serua:** accusations of threatened *seruitium* flew freely
on all sides in late-republican politics but esp. in *popularis* rhetoric
(*VL* 559). The argument – filtered through the aristocratic association of democracy with tyranny – that if the consulate were opened
to the plebs they would lose their liberty is a masterpiece of perver-
sity; for parallels see Seager (1) 338, and for 'free suffrage' see 40.7n.

41.3 omitto ... fiat?: Appius does not need to go to the top:
even the humblest plebeian will do for an illustration (*in Capitolio ~ humilis*), cf. Cic. *Pis.* 24 *qui latrones igitur, siquidem uos consules ...
nominabuntur?* with Nisbet and see 17.5n. For the *praeteritio* see 7.4n.;

for the metamorphosis of the *unus uir* see 40.6n.   **annos** 'years
of office' (*OLD* 4).   **tamquam regum:** probably referring ana-
chronistically to the kings' statues on the Capitoline (W–M, cf.
Suet. *Jul.* 76.1).   **quis ... humilis:** the hyperbole should catch
the audience up in the speaker's emotion, an effect that has been
carefully prepared by the preceding portrait of the disdainful would-
be consul; Appius is beginning in earnest the process of dismantling
his 'worthy plebeian' interlocutor and reconstructing the deserving
patrician whose position is being challenged. For the mixing of
high and low, 'the conventional complaint of Roman constitutional-
ists against radical innovators', see Nisbet–Hubbard on Hor. *C.*
1.34.12.   **uia ... facilior** 'easier access' (*OLD uia* 5c); for the
metaphor see 35.2n.   **occasionem** ~ 1 *occasionibus.*   **nobis
... nostris:** 40.5n.   **siquidem** 'seeing that' (*OLD* 3). The concluding *epiphonema* (10.9n.) is decorated with antithesis, wordplay,
and homoioteleuton.   **necesse sit:** 34.1n.

41.4–10. Appius finally turns from men to gods, a topic 'entirely
consistent with the god-fearing Claudii of the favourable tradition'
(*CC* 85) and one which would have afforded an inspiring peroration
(10n.). Like C. before him (5.51–4) Appius argues against a proposal
to change Rome by pressing the claims of ritual and tradition; but
unlike C., he is not rallying the citizen body against the destruction
caused by a foreign foe, but has to persuade one part of the *ciuitas*
to remain divided from the other. He does his best to gain plebeian
sympathy by shifting the focus: not plebs v. *patres* but 'traditionally
worthy/correct' v. 'wrong' (4). He grounds his argument in rituals
associated with foundation, as did C. (4n., 9n.); but instead of reaffirming the city's original founding he unwittingly offers a model for
a new start, in which plebeians and patricians share power (10n.).
See further 40–1n.; for Livian foundations see above, pp. 25–6.

41.4 De indignitate refers primarily to the last section (40.19–
41.3), though *indignitas* has been a theme throughout (e.g. 40.11), and
recalls the emotion that stupefied the patricians (40.1).   **satis
dictum est:** an orator will make his *diuisio* clear, summarizing
what he has said and announcing the next topic (*transitio*: Lausberg
§§849–50), though it is not always a good idea to be too specific
about one's argumentation (Lausberg §275 β and Rawson 334–6).
Appius' obtrusive transition and organized categories (*pertinet* ...

proprie below) distract attention from the increasing formlessness of
his content (next n.).   **quid ... loquar?** 'what shall I say?', the
figure *dubitatio* (Lausberg §§776–8). Appius continues to draw attention to himself as speaker (cf. 40.6, 10, 13). Though his uncertainty
here sits ill with his organized presentation (last n.), it prepares for
his emotional and aporetic stance in 9–10 (nn.).   **religionibus
... auspiciis:** taken up chiastically below, as Appius tries a combination of appeal to tradition and scare tactics; for manipulation of
religio cf. 1.10 (n.).   **quae ... est** 'contempt of and injury to
which particularly concern the immortal gods'; *quae* = *quorum* (objective gen.). *propria* continues the classificatory theme (*OLD* 7, see
20.4n.).   **contemptio:** 'impiety was a typical tyrant's crime' (*CC*
81): Appius again turns the tables on the *tr. pl.* by suggesting that
they are out-patricianing the patricians.   **auspiciis ... geri:**
C. similarly stressed the importance of the auspices (4–10n., cf.
5.52.2, 9, 15, 16). For Appius' anaphora see 40.7n.; for *auspicia* see
2.5n.   **bello ac pace** ∼ *domi militiaeque* (chiastic with *uariatio* of
connectives).   **quis est qui ignoret?:** a particularly effective
appeal to the authority of consensus: anyone who admits to not
knowing is an outsider or a fool (cf. 40.5).   **penes quos ...
(5) patres:** Appius answers his own question (15.11n.). It was
this argument about *auspicia* that so incensed the plebs in 445 that
the patricians were forced to cede the right of *conubium* to avoid
plebeian consuls (4.6.1–4). Its repetition here is in keeping with
Appius' traditional outlook (40.3n.), but bodes ill for the success of
his cause.   **igitur:** for the conjunction in an indignant question
see *OLD* 1b; placement of postpositives after a prep. phrase is regular (*OLD autem* Intro.).

41.5 penes patres: patrician 'ownership' of the auspices was
maintained even after plebeians became consuls: they could use,
but not possess, the *auspicia* (Linderski, *SS* 40–7).   **nam ...
creatur:** true at the end of the republic as well (Linderski, *SS*
40–1). Appius justifies his assertion of patrician superiority with an
elaborately balanced proof: *nam ... creatur* ∼ 6 *quae ... habent*, in-
corporating a chiastic opposition of the orders (*plebeius ... nobis* ∼
nos ... isti) organized by a series of antitheses and repetitions
(*non solum ... sed ... quoque, creat* ∼ *creet, quos pop. creat* ∼ *sine suffra-*

gio pop., *priuatim* ∼ *in magistratibus*, *habeamus* ∼ *habent*).   **quidem:**
34.5n. (the contrast is with 6 *nobis*).

41.6 propria ∼ 4 *proprie*. Appius' argument is based on possession (cf. 5 *penes*, 6 *habeamus*, 7 *habere*); to make sure his audience understands, he uses *auspic-* ten times in 4–7 (it is *his* word).   **quos
... creat:** the rel. clause precedes its antecedent (*patricios magistratus*).   **interregem:** 1.5n.   **priuatim** i.e. even as senators not
currently holding a magistracy (Linderski, *SS* 35–7). For *priuatim* ∼ *in magistratibus* below see Catterall 308, Sörbom 95.

41.7 quid igitur aliud: sc. *facit*; a final *definitio* (40.8n.) closes
this section of the last topic.   **tollit ... auspicia:** if the city was
founded on auspices (4), destroying them is tantamount to undoing
the foundation. The final sections (8–11) investigate the consequences of such an unfounding (nn.); it, too, ends with destruction
(11 *tollitur*).   **aufert:** sc. *auspicia*; for the *uariatio* of vocabulary
with *tollit* above see 7.5n.   **eludant nunc licet religiones:** cf.
26.22.14 *eludant nunc antiqua mirantis*, Curt. 5.11.10 *eludant me licet*.
This is the figure *permissio* (Lausberg §857), which recurs in 9–10.
Like the *dubitatio* in 4, it ironically cedes control to the opposition,
who are imagined to be so powerful as to have taken away the
speaker's words or will: it is a kind of *praesumptio* (15.11n.), conced-
ing a position in order to refute it in advance. Yet, as with *sermocinatio* (40.8n.), its danger lies in its being literalized, which is what
happens: the rules *do* change, though Appius' worst-case scenario
does not come to pass.   **religiones** 'rituals' (*OLD* 8b).

41.8 "quid enim est" 'for what does it matter?' (*OLD quis*[1] 8d),
completed by the following *si*-clauses.   **si ... si ... si:** 40.7n.
pulli: Appius begins with auspicatory ritual, then generalizes the
topic (9–10). Chickens were used for divination before military actions: if they did not eat, or emerge quickly enough from their
cages, the omens were bad. The Claudii were closely connected
with these chickens: Claudius Pulcher (cos. 249) famously ordered
them drowned when they did not eat (*per.* 19, *CC* 90–2), while a
later Claudius Pulcher (cos. 54) wrote a treatise on augury which
may have concentrated on bird divination (*CC* 130–1; see Scullard
Pl. 6).   **pascentur:** middle (*OLD* 6a), prob. technical augural
language; for it and the cage (*cauea*) below see Pease on Cic. *Diu.*

2.72.   **tardius** 'too slowly' (G–L §297.2).   **occecinerit auis?:**
ill-omened cries of augural birds (*oscines*) are meant; see Cic. *Diu.*
1.12, 1.120 with Pease. *occinere* is very rare (also at 10.40.14, Apul.
Fl. 13 of bird omens; of trumpets at Sall. *H.* 1.135, Tac. *A.*
2.81.2).   **parua:** as in Fabia's case, *parua* lead to *maxima* (below);
the reappearance of the topos (34.5n.) signals the end of the rogation narrative. Fabia's *res ingens* and Appius' *maxima res* are one and
the same: the new Rome.   **non contemnendo:** both Appius
and C. argue that Roman success and failure are linked to the presence or absence of religious morality as epitomized by, among other
things, correct ritual practice (Levene 200–2; on ritual as a 'public
cognitive system' see S. R. F. Price, *Rituals and power* (1984) 7–
11).   **maiores uestri:** the appropriate middle term between the
small beginnings and the great modern state (for an analogous progression cf. 40.18).   **maximam ... fecerunt:** cf. Cic. *Cael.* 39
Camillos Fabricios Curios omnesque eos qui haec ex minimis tanta fecerunt,
Sall. *C.* 51.42, Suet. *Aug.* 31.5.

41.9 nunc ... polluimus: criticism of the present (*insectatio tem-*
poris praesentis), the obverse of the *laus temporis acti* (27.8n.), cf. Sen.
Contr. 2.7.3 with Winterbottom *s.v.* 'Commonplaces: on the age'.
pace deorum: 1.12n.   **omnes ... polluimus:** he echoes C. at
5.53.1 *at enim apparet quidem pollui omnia* (by the Gallic desecration);
for the contamination of the divine by plebeian rights cf. 4.2.5–7
colluuionem gentium, perturbationem auspiciorum ... omnia diuina humanaque
turbentur, and cf. Sall. *C.* 23.6 (the consulate polluted by *noui ho-*
mines) with Vretska.   **uulgo ergo:** ugly sounds for an ugly idea;
there is a similarly barbarous collocation at 5.46.3 *neglegens gens* (the
Gauls). Appius concludes with the figure *percursio* (Lausberg §881),
running quickly through a number of items; the catalogue gives
the impression of abundant evidence at his disposal.   **ponti-**
fices ... nefas est: his list begins with a tricolon whose outer
members themselves contain asyndetic tricola (Ullmann (2) 104–5);
permissio (7n.) is deployed throughout. The priesthoods are not currently at risk (with the exception of the decemvirate, which Appius
does not mention), but are the natural end-point of his argument.
Again following C.'s lead (5.52.7, 13), he singles out *religiones* that
with one exception (next n.) are associated with Numa, who re-
founded Rome *iure ... legibusque ac moribus* (1.19.1; on C. see Levene

201). But it is possible to invert his list of pollution and destruction and thereby to discover a covert programme for the building of the new Rome (40–1n.), from *auspicia* (4–7) to priesthoods, laws etc. (9–10) to territorial expansion and alliance (11 *in agris ... societas*).   **pontifices ... reges:** the *pontifices* and *flamines* (below) were introduced by Numa, the augural priesthood sollemnized on his accession (1.20.1–2, 5, 18.6); the *rex sacr.* was created at the founding of the republic (2.2.1).   **cuilibet:** 40.6n.   **apicem:** the cap worn by the Flamen Dialis, the priest of Jupiter; the *apex* proper was an olive twig fixed to the top (J. H. Vangaard, *The Flamen* (1988) 24–5, 40–5; Scullard Pl. 4).   **dummodo homo sit** 'provided he is human'. *homo* is the lowest form of social designation, even when not modified by a pejorative adj.; it is regular in Cic. and L. of foreigners, slaves, and plebeians (Santoro L'hoir (2) 16–28, 69–76).   **ancilia:** the shields of Mars used by the Salii (Scullard 85–6, Pl. 19). With the Vestal Virgins (below) they were instituted by Numa (1.20.3–4).   **penetralia:** *sacra*, including the *penates* brought from Troy, kept in the *penus* of the *aedes Vestae* (Scullard 149).   **deos deorumque curam:** he sums up with an archaic repetition (16.3n.); the pair forms a unit capping its tricolon, as does *sacrificuli reges* above.   **quibus:** i.e. *iis quibus*.

41.10 The second part of the catalogue is a triad expanding both in length and in social importance (magistrates ... senate ... kings); each element contains one of Appius' preferred anaphoric dicola (40.3n.).   **non** for *ne* in prohibitions is idiomatic when the negation is concentrated on a single word (*auspicato*: G–L §270 R.1).   **nec ... fiant:** he imagines the final act of urban destruction to be the loss of patrician authority to ratify decisions (whatever that may have been: *CAH*[2] 185). But they have effectively lost it already, partly through Fabius' defection (36.7n.), partly through C.'s failure as dictator (38.9–13n.). For the assemblies see 20.10n., Taylor 3–5.   **et ... ac:** 22.5n.   **Romulus ac Tatius:** in Appius' topsy-turvy new state Licinius and Sextius are the first tyrants. It was conventional to compare *popularis* leaders to Romulus (Opelt *s.v.*, Miles (2) 203); in Appius' schema these kings are appropriate models because each gained power illicitly: Tatius thanks to Tarpeia's treachery (1.11.5–9), Romulus by the murder of his brother (1.7.1–3); in one version Romulus even ended like Caesar (1.16.4

with O.). But in the refoundation that Appius unknowingly facilitates (9n.), they are equally good models for the co-operation between the orders: Romulus, a king by birth, and Tatius, a foreigner who captures the city, joined political forces as a result of intermarriage and doubled the size of Rome (Canuleius draws the parallel between national and political synoecism at 4.3; on the Sabine marriage as a microcosm of political alliance see G. B. Miles, 'The first Roman marriage' in *Innovations of antiquity*, edd. R. Hexter and D. Seldon (1992) 168–9, 179). See also 40.4n., and on unstable *exempla* see 20.3n.   **in urbe ... regnent:** cf. the oath sworn at the beginning of the republic: 2.1.9 *iure iurando adegit neminem Romae passuros regnare.*   **quia ... dant:** in conclusion Claudius returns briefly to the economic rogations, which he paints as bribes for *regnum* (cf. 40.9 and 16.7n.). This new material detracts from his lofty conclusion but allows him to dismiss the other bills as *inutiles* since they have pernicious consequences.

41.11 dulcedo 'charm', restricted to the first decade, of the seductiveness of *commoda* (2.42.1), power (3.52.9), anger (9.14.13), words (4.12.7), and *libertas* (1.17.3).   **ex alienis:** one mark of a Catilinarian wastrel, cf. Sall. *C.* 5.4 *alieni appetens* with Vretska. **praedandi:** cf. 10.2.8, Tac. *H.* 2.7.2 *dulcedo praedarum* with H.; for Claudian resistance to agrarian legislation see *CC* 73–4.   **solitudines uastas:** the expression (before L. only at Cic. *Rep.* 6.20) also describes Rome before its foundation (1.4.6) and during the first *secessio plebis* (3.52.5), echoes which suggest that Appius again has it backwards: it is removal of the plebs, not the *patres*, that will unfound Rome (9n.). The purpose of the agrarian bill is of course not to leave the fields desolate but to put plebeian farmers in place of the *nobiles*, whose occupation of the *ager publicus* (5.4n.) eventually produced the *solitudo Italiae* to which L. alludes at 12.5 (n.).   **dominos:** properly of property owners (*OLD* 1a), but with unfortunate political resonances (18.6n.).   **fidem:** Claudian rhetoric was preoccupied with *fides* (*CC* 70, 79, 83), which here combines its economic and social senses, as at 34.2 (n.).   **cum ... tollitur:** though it was proverbial that if *fides* were lost, all was lost (e.g. Pub. *Sent.* 196 M, 209 M), to allow the plebeians to pay off their debts would probably not result in the end of civilization as the patricians know it; it certainly would not abolish economic *fides*, which has suffered because of the debt (27.3). **societas:** 9n.

41.12 censeo: Ciceronian evidence suggests that this Curial formula was not used in speeches before a *contio* (34.4.21 with B.). In that case its appearance here may flatter the predominantly plebeian audience; but it also suggests that his listeners constitute a kind of senate – the last thing Appius wants (cf. 39.2n., 40.10n.). **quod ... fortunare:** cf. 34.4.21; this is a simplified version of the prayer *quod bonum faustum felix fortunatumque sit* (Pease on Cic. *Diu.* 1.102). For *faxitis* see 35.9n., and for Claudian signing-off prayers see *CC* 85 n.77.

42.1–3 End of the year

42.1 Oratio ... proferretur: 'in the first pentad an Appian speech is usually followed by plebeian unrest and the ultimate failure of the argument advanced' (Vasaly 224). Crassus was unexpectedly successful at 5.3–6, owing to a combination of his speech and a subsequent symbolic action, the volunteering of private horse (5.7.5–12). The result of C.'s speech, too, is uncertain until an omen caps his argument (5.55.1–2; see Chaplin 102–4). This pattern of *oratio* followed and ratified by sign does not recur here. Instead, Appius' argument is countered by two 'omens', one preceding his speech (the plebeian *mag. equit.*, 39.8) the other following (the decemviral election (2), which the plebs take as predictive of plebeian consuls). **Appi:** L. often refers to Appii Claudii by their 'rare and aristocratic *praenomen*', perhaps reflecting first-century usage (J. N. Adams, *C.Q.* 28 (1978) 153).

42.2 decimum: 36.7n. (*octauum*).   **ex parte** 'partly' (*OLD pars* 3c), in fact half (37.12n.).   **iam uia facta ... uidebatur:** that the election is marked by no divine displeasure (unlike C.'s dictatorial appointment: 38.9n.) significantly counters Appius' forebodings about plebeian priests (Levene 210); for the road metaphor see 35.2n. and for the 'omen' see 1n.

42.3 uictoria: for *uictoria contentus* cf. 10.17.5, 32.13.12, Cic. *Prou.* 32, Vell. 46.1.   **cessit ... ut:** an unusual construction with a legal flavour (*TLL* III 728.51–7), cf. Flor. 1.36.2, Tac. *A.* 12.41.1.

42.4–14 The year 367 B.C.

42.4–8 Affairs abroad

42.4 obsidionem: the siege, in which L. has not shown much interest (36.6n.), becomes a narrative foil for the Gallic attack. **tardi ... dubii:** cf. Sil. 1.554 *tardaque paulatim et dubio uestigia nisu*; the gens. are descriptive.   **rem ... res:** repetition of *res* is something of a Livian mannerism (Pettersson 105–7).   **fama repens belli:** Appius' worst-case scenario (40.17) is suddenly at hand, but there is no hesitation in appointing a dictator.   **M. Furius:** Book 6 opens and closes under Camillan auspices (Bayet 93), though L. seems uneasy about C.'s part in the events of 367 (Momigliano 114–15). This Gallic war (which probably did not exist, and is therefore perhaps less important historically: Polyb. 2.18.6 with Walbank) lent itself to a full-blown battle description together with speeches (e.g. Dion. Hal. 14.8–10) and offered an opportunity to digress on the invention of new kinds of defensive armour (Plut. *Cam.* 40.3–4). But L. treats the war curiously (next n.) and meagrely; and rather than letting his victory reinvest C. with an authority with which he could then settle the conflict at home (as Plut. *Cam.* 40–2), L. hardly adverts to him in the last, domestic scene (9n.). See also 38n.

42.5–6. Digression. The last and shortest of the scholarly discussions in Book 6 (cf. 12.2–6, 38.9–13), framed by *cum Gallis eo anno* ∼ *hoc autem anno ... cum Gallis*. The problem is caused by T. Quinctius Poenus, who is *mag. equit.* here but was dictator when Manlius had his duel (7.9.3: *MRR* I 114 n.1, 119 n.2); as is his habit with discrepancies in names, L. places the variant before its episode (Luce (1) 216). Brief though the discussion is, it takes as much space as C.'s battle (5–6 ∼ 7–8), pre-empting the latter's importance; moreover, it contains a summary description of Manlius Torquatus' duel, almost as an advertisement for Book 7 (5n.). A similarly brief account of the *bellum Pannonicum* at Vell. 96.2–3, also ending with a triumph and containing a digressive advertisement, provides a useful contrast. Velleius' 'other story' is about the places, peoples, and victorious wars encountered by his hero (see W.'s nn.); it replaces the expected account of the war with rich and tantalizing material for Tiberius' praise, thereby enhancing the status of the untold war as well.

42.5 bellatum ... pugnatam: for the framing verbs cf. 10.2n. **circa** 'near' (*OLD* 3a). **auctor est Claudius** ~ 6 *pluribus auctoribus*. Q. Claudius Quadrigarius' account of this duel (fr. 10b) is one of the extended extant passages of L.'s precursors for Books 6–10 (cf. also [Quad.] fr. 12, Calp. fr. 27); for L's version see 7.9.3–10 and von Albrecht 86–101; for Claudius see above, pp. 10, 25. **inclitam ... pugnam:** with L.'s précis cf. Cic. *Off.* 3.112 *T. Manlius ... ad Anienem Galli quem ab eo prouocatus occiderat torque detracto cognomen inuenit*, singling out the same essentials (name, site, challenge, death, necklace). **pugnam ... pugnatam:** the cognate acc. is a *figura etymologica* (L–H–S 38–9). **prouocatus** 'after being challenged' to a duel (*OLD* 3a), an essential feature in Roman accounts of single combat (Oakley (1) 407–8). **conseruit ... spoliauit:** retained indics. reporting facts (*NLS* §287). **in conspectu ... exercituum:** cf. 4.32.4 (an enemy king killed), 10.44.3 (victorious soldiers praised). This is the sort of edifying spectacle one expects in scenes of single combat (Oakley (1) 400, 407); on Torquatus see Feldherr 210–19 and cf. 14–16.4n. **torque:** abl.; for *spoliare* 'strip' of a defeated enemy see *OLD* 2 and for the custom see Oakley (1) 409 n.143, Pritchett III 277–93. **tum:** L. answers two chronological questions: when did they fight the Gauls at the Anio (= *eo anno* above) and when was Manlius' duel (= *tum*, i.e. in that *bellum*)?

42.6 pluribus auctoribus: 12.2n. (*auctores*). The historians are regarded as instruments (standing for their books? G–L §401 R.1), cf. 3.57.8, 4.45.3. **adducor:** 9.3n. **decem ... annos** 'at least ten years later' (G–L §403 N.4 (a)). In L.'s own narrative the fight in fact happens six years later; for the approximation see 20.6n. and Fehling 226–9 on the number 10. **autem:** strongly adversative. **signa collata** 'that battle was joined' (*OLD confero* 15b).

42.7 nec ... fuit: cf. 9.40.18 *nec dubia nec difficili uictoria*. The Roman victory fulfils the promise of 28.9. **quamquam ... attulerant:** the sack is relegated to the background, subordinated in syntax and tense; the easy Roman victory is partly guaranteed by their previous transcendence of the evil omen of the Allia (28.8n.). **multa milia:** the only even vaguely precise casualty figure in Book 6, though L. can be very precise; for these (imaginary) numbers see *IM* 694–7, Fehling 230, 232, 238.

42.8 fuga … longinqua: flight into far-off places, cf. 30.29.10 (*aquationis*), Cic. *ND* 1.24 (*solis abscessu*), Tac. *A.* 3.24.4 (*peregrinatione*).   **se** or *sese* (below) should be retained, but not both (*pace* Pettersson 101–2); the idiomatic position of *se* (Wackernagel's law) tips the balance slightly in its favour.   **fuga … quod:** for the *uariatio* (abl. ~ *quod*-clause) inside a *cum* … *tum* construction see 1.2n.   **pauor errorque:** Harant's text makes sense with *distulerant* below, but the MSS *p. terrorque* is a formulaic combination (12.10n.) and may be right (Pettersson 101 n.1).   **consensu:** a unity consonant with C.'s military successes (6.9n.) but vitiated by the *seditio* (9). The lapidary closing sentence is marked by alliteration of *d* and *p* (cf. W. on Vell. 48.5).   **decretus:** sc. *est* (1.10n.).

42.9–11 Internal affairs

The delays to which we have become accustomed in the rogations (31.2n.) mysteriously disappear, and the episode concludes with unseemly haste even for L., who likes quick endings (24.11n.). Part of the reason is that the outcome has already been decided within Appius' speech (40–1n.). But L.'s report of violent struggles (9 *atrocior … seditio, ingentia certamina,* 10 *prope secessionem, terribiles … minas*) seems gratuitous if he will not give us a satisfying finale. Elsewhere in this last section, L. sidesteps famous stories in an almost Hellenistic narrative fashion, leaving clues to what has been omitted (4n., 12n.); T. P. Wiseman convincingly suggests that here too L. is playing narrative games, alluding to but refusing to elaborate what must have been a heroic set-piece treatment of the plebeian triumph, in Licinius Macer's pro-plebeian *Annales* which will have been too partisan for L.'s history (not only was Macer himself a *popularis*, but he may have given Licinius Stolo too big a role: cf. 7.9.5 on his familial bias). By ostentatiously eliminating any climax, and by depicting the bills' passing neither as a triumph nor a defeat, L. maintains his balance between the orders; he also signals that the end to the struggle has not yet come.

42.9 eum: i.e. Camillus.   **atrocior … seditio:** cf. 28.25.14, 32.3.2; *bellum atrox*, implied here, is first at Sall. *J.* 5.1, though it is

L. who promotes it, as he extends the range of *atrox* in general
(*TLL*). The language hints at stories of cruelty and disaster, standard elements in ancient historiography (Paul on Sall. *J.* 5.1,
RICH 28–32, 165–7, 189–90).   **excepit** 'confronted' (Vell. 55.2
with W.).   **ingentia certamina:** a Livian expression imitated
by Curt. Sen. Tac. (Fletcher (2) 63; add Stat. *Silu.* 5.1.7–8).   **dictator:** L. often refers to officials by their titles and will leave out
names to streamline a story (O. on 5.15.3); but this avoidance of
C.'s name in favour of his title (also in 8, 11, 13; cf. ch. 38, where
the name predominates) is of a piece with his unwillingness to fore-
ground his former hero (Kraus (2) 325).   **consulum:** 4.7n.
aduersa nobilitate 'in spite of the aristocracy' (*OLD aduersus*[1]
9a).   **quibus ... factus:** for his consulship see 7.1.1–6; Licinius
is cos. 364 (7.2.1–3.2: *MRR* I 116).   **primus:** 11.7n.

    42.10 auctores: 41.10n.   **prope** 'near (in condition)' (*OLD*
11), first in L.; cf. Tac. *H.* 3.21.1 *prope seditionem* with H.   **prope
secessionem plebis:** at Ov. *F.* 1.643–4 there is an actual *secessio*,
settled by C.'s vow of the temple of Concord (12n.). L.'s threatened
secession is the last of several nagging reminders of the real possibility that the plebs might leave Rome, first in the recall of Veian
settlers (4.5n.), then in Manlius' rescue of the centurion (14.3–10n.)
and in the meetings at his house *in arce* (19.1n.), lastly in C.'s allusion to the first *secessio* (38.6, cf. 18.13); these threats are reinforced
by the complex of refs. to the plebeian city (11.7n., 36.7n., 40–
1n.).   **res:** nom. sing.   **terribiles ... minas:** governed by
prope above; for the combination cf. Enn. *scen.* 18 J *terribilem minetur
... cruciatum*, [Quint.] *Decl.* 2.23, 15.1 *terribilis et minax*, Val. Fl.
1.722–3 *iraque minaci | terribilis*.

    42.11 per dictatorem: 9n. L. gives C. the credit but no more;
for the flattering possibilities of a Camillan intervention at this point
cf. Plut. *Cam.* 42.3–4.   **condicionibus ... concessumque:** cf.
2.33.1 *concessumque in condiciones ut plebi sui magistratus essent* (the settlement of the first Secession).   **ab nobilitate ... ex patribus:**
mutual concessions expressed in balanced phrases. The present doubling of the governing class, reinforced by the other sets of doubles
(decemuiri, aediles) and the return to consuls, recalls the foundation
of the republic, where the royal power was multiplied by two (2.1.7–
8).   **plebeio** ~ *ex patribus* below (9.5n.).   **de praetore:** he

took over the consuls' judicial functions, leaving them free for military matters (*CAH*² 194).   **creando:** with both *consule* and *praetore* above.

42.12–14 *End of the year*

42.12 ita ... (13) facturos: 'And so from longstanding anger the orders were finally brought back into concord; the senate deemed the situation was a worthy one and that it should deservedly happen [then] (if ever at any other time) that the Ludi Maximi be celebrated and a day be added to the three; when the plebeian aediles refused this duty the patrician youths clamoured that they would willingly perform it with due respect for [*OLD causa* 17c] the immortal gods.' The language is very awkward, and the text has been disturbed by the intrusion of *causa ... facturos* from 13. Edd. (e.g. W–M) have taken *dignam ... ut* as a unit ('worthy of having the games celebrated'), but the colometry is against this; for the continuative cola see above, p. 20.   **in concordiam redactis:** for the expression cf. 3.52.3 (the second Secession), Pl. *Am.* 475. This is perhaps an allusion to the Camillan temple of Concord, a structure which may never have existed (Richardson 98–9; *contra*, A. M. Ferroni in E. M. Steinby, ed., *Lexicon topographicum urbis Romae* (1993) I 317), but which was traditionally attributed to C. and would have admirably crowned his conciliatory activities here as it does at Ov. *F.* 1.641–4 and Plut. *Cam.* 42.4. L.'s sidelong nod at a well-known tradition is in keeping with the tone of this conclusion (9–11n.); for other untold stories incorporated by allusion cf. Quinta Claudia and the Magna Mater's ship (29.14.12, cf. Ov. *F.* 4.305–47; see *CC* 97, Levene 69–72) and the Dioscuri at Lake Regillus (2.20.12; see Levene 153). On the cult of Concordia see Pease on Cic. *ND* 2.61, Scullard 167–8.   **merito:** *deum immortalium* (below) is probably a dittography from 13 (though *m. deum imm.* occurs at 28.9.8); for *merito* alone in dedicatory contexts cf. 37.59.1, *CIL* I² 2.9, 1827, 2247.8 (*et saep.*).   **id** is explained by the following *ut*-clause; for *censere* 'decree' + acc. and infin. see *OLD* 5a.   **si ... alias:** the pleonasm is in L.'s manner, cf. 22.58.2 *numquam alias antea*, 32.5.8 *si quando umquam ante alias*.   **ludi maximi:** i.e. the *ludi Romani*, from this point celebrated yearly (Scullard 183–6) and bal-

anced by the *ludi plebeii*. The regularity of games, as of other
festivals, gave a sacral and familiar structure to the Roman year,
while their celebration ideally brought the populace together in literal and spiritual unity (M. Clavel-Lévêque, *A.N.R.W.* II 16.3 (1986)
1413–14, 1487–96).

42.13 recusantibus: this curious refusal results in a further balanced college being created as a pendant to the decemviri (2; see
Bayet 132) and pictures the *patres* serving the state as they have
claimed to do all along. That the *iuuenes* volunteer heightens the
sense of accomplishment, since early-republican patrician youth
tend to be depicted as violently anti-plebeian (Eyben 52–6); on the
aediles see 4.6n.   **conclamatum ... iuuenibus:** for the interlaced word order see Adams (1) 13 and cf. 3.3n.   **honoris** depends on *causa* (below).

42.14 The book closes with little fanfare but with sufficient sense
of an ending. The new offices and the announcement of elections
look forward to 7.1.2, where the officials are named; further linking
is obtained by C.'s death (7.1.8–10), which L. does not use to round
off Book 6, choosing instead to begin Book 7 with the first year of
plebeian consuls (Pomeroy 168). Balancing these connective elements are an accumulation of closural words (*uniuersis, factum, auctores, omnibus*), coupled with state celebrations (12n.) and the return
of constitutional normality (27.6–8n.). The concord does not last
long (40–1n.).

REFERENCES AND ABBREVIATIONS

(1) In the Commentary C. = Camillus, L. = Livy. All dates are B.C. unless otherwise stated. References to Book 6 are given without book number; within the same chapter they are given without chapter number.

(2) Livian fragments are cited from W–M; fragments of Sallust's *Historiae* from Reynolds' OCT where possible, otherwise from Maurenbrecher's edn (Leipzig 1891–3). Fragments of the historians are numbered as in H. Peter, ed., *Historicorum romanorum reliquiae* (Leipzig 1906–14). Notes of older commentators are collected in A. Drakenborch, ed., *T. Livii Patavini historiarum ab urbe condita libri quae supersunt omnes* (Amsterdam 1738).

(3) Abbreviations of periodicals generally follow *L'Année philologique*. Other works referred to by short title may be found in the following list.

Adams (1)	Adams, J. N. (1971). 'A type of hyperbaton in Latin prose', *P.C.P.S.* 17: 1–16
Adams (2)	(1972). 'The language of the later books of Tacitus' *Annals*', *C.Q.* 22: 350–73
Adams (3)	(1973). 'The substantival present participle in Latin', *Glotta* 51: 116–36
Adams (4)	(1974). 'The vocabulary of the later decades of Livy', *Antichthon* 8: 54–62
Adams (5)	(1976). 'A typological approach to Latin word order', *I.F.* 81: 70–99
Ahl	Ahl, F. (1985). *Metaformations*. Ithaca
von Albrecht	Albrecht, M. von. (1979, 1989). *Masters of Roman prose*. Trans. N. Adkin. Leeds
Appel	Appel, G. (1909). *De Romanorum precationibus*. Giessen
B.	Briscoe, J. (1989[2], 1981). *A commentary on Livy books XXXI–XXXIII* and *XXXIV–XXXVII*. Oxford
Badian	Badian, E. (1966). 'The early historians', in Dorey, T. A., ed., *Latin historians*. London. 1–38

Balsdon	Balsdon, J. P. V. D. (1979). *Romans and aliens.* London
Bayet	Bayet, J. (1989²). *Tite-Live: Histoire romaine. Tome VI. Livre VI.* Paris
Bell	Bell, A. J. (1923). *The Latin dual and poetic diction.* Oxford
Béranger	Béranger, J. (1953). *Recherches sur l'aspect idéologique du principat.* Basel
Bettini	Bettini, M. (1988, 1991). *Anthropology and Roman culture.* Trans. J. van Sickle. Baltimore
Bonner (1)	Bonner, S. F. (1949). *Roman declamation.* Liverpool
Bonner (2)	(1977). *Education in ancient Rome.* London
Booth	Booth, W. C. (1983²). *The rhetoric of fiction.* Chicago
BRE	Raaflaub, K. A. and Toher, M., edd. (1990). *Between republic and empire: interpretations of Augustus and his principate.* Berkeley
Bruno (1)	Bruno, L. (1966). '"Crimen regni" e "superbia" in Tito Livio', *G.I.F.* 19: 236–59
Bruno (2)	(1966). '"Libertas plebis" in Tito Livio', *G.I.F.* 19: 107–30
Brunt (1)	Brunt, P. A. (1971). *Social conflicts in the Roman republic.* London
Brunt (2)	(1990). *Roman imperial themes.* Oxford
Burck (1)	Burck, E. (1964²). *Die Erzählungskunst des T. Livius.* Berlin/Zurich
Burck (2)	(1966). *Vom Menschenbild in der römischen Literatur.* Heidelberg
CAH²	Walbank, F. W., Astin, A. E., Frederiksen, M. W., and Ogilvie, R. M., edd. (1989). *The Cambridge ancient history.* 2nd edn Vol. VII. Part 2. *The rise of Rome to 220 B.C.* Cambridge
Cairns	Cairns, F. (1972). *Generic composition in Greek and Roman poetry.* Edinburgh
Canetti	Canetti, E. (1960, 1963). *Crowds and power.* Trans. C. Stewart. New York
Catin	Catin, L. (1944). *En lisant Tite-Live.* Paris

Catterall	Catterall, J. L. (1938). 'Variety and inconcinnity of language in the first decade of Livy', *T.A.P.A.* 49: 292–318
CC	Wiseman, T. P. (1979). *Clio's cosmetics.* Leicester
Champeaux	Champeaux, J. (1982). *Fortuna.* Vol. 1. Rome
Chaplin	Chaplin, J. D. (1993). *Livy's use of exempla and the lessons of the past.* Diss. Princeton
CIL	*Corpus inscriptionum latinorum* (1863–). Berlin
C-L	Chausserie-Laprée, J.-P. (1969). *L'Expression narrative chez les historiens latins.* Paris
Cornell	Cornell, T. J. (1983). 'The failure of the plebs', in Gabba, E. ed., *Tria corda: scritti in onore di Arnaldo Momigliano.* Como. 101–20
Dangel	Dangel, J. (1982). *La phrase oratoire chez Tite-Live.* Paris
David	David, J.-M. (1992). *Le patronat judiciaire au dernier siècle de la république romaine.* Rome
Develin	Develin, R. (1983). 'Tacitus and techniques of insidious suggestion', *Antichthon* 17: 64–95
Drummond (1)	Drummond, A. (1978). 'Some observations on the order of consuls' names', *Athenaeum* 56: 80–108
Drummond (2)	(1989). 'Early Roman clientes', in Wallace-Hadrill, A., ed., *Patronage in ancient society.* London. 89–115
DuQuesnay	DuQuesnay, I. M. Le M. (1984). 'Horace and Maecenas', in Woodman, T. and West, D., edd., *Poetry and politics in the age of Augustus.* Cambridge. 19–58
Dutoit (1)	Dutoit, E. (1948). 'Tite-Live s'est-il intéressé à la médecine?', *M.H.* 5: 116–23
Dutoit (2)	(1956). 'Le souci étymologique chez Tite-Live', in *Hommages à M. Niedermann.* Brussels. 108–114
Earl	Earl, D. (1967). *The moral and political tradition of Rome.* London
Eden	Eden. P. T. (1962). 'Caesar's style: inheritance versus intelligence', *Glotta* 40: 74–117

Erskine	Erskine, A. (1991). 'Hellenistic monarchy and Roman political invective', *C.Q.* 41: 106–20
Evans–Kleijwegt	Evans, R. J. and Kleijwegt, M. (1992). 'Did the Romans like young men?', *Z.P.E.* 92: 181–95
Eyben	Eyben. E. (1992). *Restless youth in ancient Rome.* Trans. P. Daly. London
Fantham	Fantham, E. (1972). *Comparative studies in republican Latin imagery.* Toronto
Feeney	Feeney, D.C. (1986). 'History and revelation in Vergil's underworld', *P.C.P.S.* 32: 1–24
Fehling	Fehling, D. (1971, 1989). *Herodotus and his 'sources'.* Trans. J. G. Howie. Leeds
Feldherr	Feldherr, A. M. (1991). *Spectacle and society in Livy's History.* Diss. Berkeley
Fletcher (1)	Fletcher, G. B. A. (1931). 'More Livy not in the *lexica*', *C.Q.* 25: 165–71
Fletcher (2)	(1964). *Annotations on Tacitus.* Brussels
Fornara	Fornara, C. W. (1983). *The nature of history in ancient Greece and Rome.* Berkeley
Fraenkel	Fraenkel, E. (1964). *Kleine Beiträge zur klassischen Philologie.* 2 vols. Rome
Friedländer	Friedländer, P. (1941). 'Pattern of sound and atomistic theory in Lucretius', *A.J.P.* 62: 16–34
von Fritz	Fritz, K. von. (1950). 'The reorganisation of the Roman government in 366 B.C. and the so-called Licinio-Sextian laws', *Historia* 1: 1–44
FRR	Brunt, P. A. (1988). *The fall of the Roman republic and related essays.* Oxford
Gabba	Gabba, E. (1981). 'True history and false history in classical antiquity', *J.R.S.* 71: 50–62
Ginsburg	Ginsburg, J. (1981). *Tradition and theme in the Annals of Tacitus.* New York
G–L	Gildersleeve, B. L. and Lodge, G. (1895³). *Latin grammar.* London

Gries	Gries, K. (1949). *Constancy in Livy's latinity*. New York
H.	Heubner, H. (1963–82). *P. Cornelius Tacitus: Die Historien*. 5 vols. Heidelberg
Hansen	Hansen, M. H. (1993). 'The battle exhortation in ancient historiography. Fact or fiction?', *Historia* 42: 161–80
Hardie	Hardie, P. (1993). *The epic successors of Virgil*. Cambridge
Harris	Harris, W. V. (1979). *War and imperialism in republican Rome 327–70 B.C.* Oxford
Hartog	Hartog, F. (1980, 1988). *The mirror of Herodotus*. Trans. J. Lloyd. Berkeley
Häussler	Häussler, R. (1968). *Nachträge zu A. Otto: Die Sprichwörter und sprichwörtlichen Redensarten der Römer*. Hildesheim
Hellegouarc'h	Hellegouarc'h, J. (1970). 'Le principat de Camille', *R.E.L* 48: 112–32.
Henderson	Henderson, J. (1989). 'Livy and the invention of history', in Cameron, A., ed., *History as text*. London. 66–85
IM	Brunt, P. A. (1971). *Italian manpower 225 B.C.–A.D. 14*. Oxford
Jaeger	Jaeger, M. K. (1993). '*Custodia fidelis memoriae*: Livy's story of M. Manlius Capitolinus', *Latomus* 52: 350–63
Keitel (1)	Keitel, E. (1987). 'Homeric antecedents to the *cohortatio* in the ancient historians', *C.W.* 80: 153–72
Keitel (2)	(1987). 'Otho's exhortations in Tacitus' *Histories*', *G.&R.* 34: 73–82
Konstan	Konstan, D. (1986). 'Narrative and ideology in Livy: Book I', *C.A.* 5: 199–215
Kraus (1)	Kraus, C. S. (1989). 'Liviana Minima', *H.S.C.P.* 92: 215–21
Kraus (2)	(1991). '*Initium turbandi omnia a femina ortum est*: Fabia Minor and the Election of 367 B.C.', *Phoenix* 45: 314–25

Kühnast	Kühnast, L. (1872). *Die Hauptpunkte der livianischen Syntax.* Berlin
Lambert	Lambert, A. (1946). *Die indirekte Rede als künstlerisches Stilmittel des Livius.* Diss. Zürich
Laughton	Laughton, E. (1964). *The participle in Cicero.* Oxford
Lausberg	Lausberg, H. (1960, 1975). *Manual de retórica literaria.* Sp. trans. J. P. Riesco. 3 vols. Madrid
LCH	Luce, T. J. (1977). *Livy, the composition of his history.* Princeton
Levene	Levene, D. S. (1993). *Religion in Livy.* Leiden
LF	Gill, C. and Wiseman, T. P., edd. (1993). *Lies and fiction in the ancient world.* Exeter
LHA	Walsh, P. G. (1961). *Livy, his historical aims and methods.* Cambridge
L–H–S	Leumann, M., Hofmann, J. B., and Szantyr, A. (1965). *Lateinische Grammatik.* Teil 2. *Lateinische Syntax und Stilistik.* Munich
Liebeschuetz	Liebeschuetz, J. H. W. G. (1979). *Continuity and change in Roman religion.* Oxford
Lindholm	Lindholm, E. (1931). *Stilistische Studien.* Lund
Lintott	Lintott, A. W. (1968). *Violence in republican Rome.* Oxford
Lipovsky	Lipovsky, J. (1981). *A historiographical study of Livy books VI–X.* Salem, N. H.
Luce (1)	Luce, T. J. (1965). 'The dating of Livy's first decade', *T.A.P.A.* 96: 209–40
Luce (2)	(1971). 'Design and structure in Livy: 5.32–55', *T.A.P.A.* 102: 265–302
Madvig	Madvig, J. N. (1860). *Emendationes livianae.* Hauniae
Maltby	Maltby, R. (1991). *A lexicon of ancient Latin etymologies.* Leeds
Marouzeau	Marouzeau, J. (1922–53). *L'Ordre des mots dans la phrase latine.* 4 vols. Paris
Marshall	Marshall, A. J. (1984). 'Symbols and showmanship in Roman public life: the fasces', *Phoenix* 38: 120–41

McDonald	McDonald, A. H. (1957). 'The style of Livy', *J.R.S.* 47: 155–72
Miles (1)	Miles, G. (1986). 'The cycle of Roman history in Livy's first pentad', *A.J.P.* 107: 1–33
Miles (2)	(1988). '*Maiores, conditores*, and Livy's perspective on the past', *T.A.P.A.* 118: 185–208.
Millar	Millar, F. (1989). 'Political power in mid-republican Rome: Curia or Comitium?', *J.R.S.* 79: 138–50
Miniconi	Miniconi, P.-J. (1951). *Etude des thèmes 'guerriers' de la poésie épique gréco-romaine.* Paris
Moles	Moles, J. L. (1993). 'Livy's preface', *P.C.P.S.* 39: 141–68
Momigliano	Momigliano, A. (1942). 'Camillus and concord', *C.Q.* 36: 111–20
Moore	Moore, T. J. (1989). *Artistry and ideology: Livy's vocabulary of virtue.* Frankfurt
Moussy	Moussy, C. (1966). *Gratia et sa famille.* Paris
MRR	Broughton, T. R. S. (1951–86). *The magistrates of the Roman republic.* 3 vols. New York
M–W	Martin, R. H. and Woodman, A. J. (1989). *Tacitus: Annals book IV.* Cambridge
Nicolet (1)	Nicolet, C. (1976, 1980). *The world of the citizen in republican Rome.* Trans. P. S. Falla. London
Nicolet (2)	(1988, 1991). *Space, geography, and politics in the early Roman empire.* Trans. H. Leclerc. Ann Arbor
NLS	Woodcock, E. C. (1959). *A new Latin syntax.* London
O.	Ogilvie, R. M. (1970²). *A commentary on Livy books 1–5.* Oxford
Oakley (1)	Oakley, S. P. (1985). 'Single combat in the Roman republic', *C.Q.* 35: 392–410
Oakley (2)	(1993). 'The Roman conquest of Italy', in Rich, J. and Shipley, G., edd., *War and society in the Roman world.* London. 9–37
OCD	Hammond, N. G. L. and Scullard, H. H., edd. (1970). *The Oxford classical dictionary.* 2nd edn Oxford

OLD   Glare, P. G. W., ed. (1968–82). *Oxford Latin dictionary*. Oxford

Opelt   Opelt, I. (1965). *Die lateinischen Schimpfwörter und verwandte sprachliche Erscheinungen*. Heidelberg

Otto   Otto, A. (1890). *Die Sprichwörter und sprichwörtlichen Redensarten der Römer*. Leipzig

Pettersson   Pettersson, O. (1930). *Commentationes livianae*. Uppsala

Phillips   Phillips, J. E. (1974). 'Form and language in Livy's triumph notices', *C.P.* 69: 265–73

Pinkster   Pinkster, H. (1992). 'The Latin impersonal passive', *Mnemosyne* 45: 159–77

Pinsent (1)   Pinsent, J. (1977). 'Livy 6.3.1 (*caput rei Romanae*): some Ennian echoes in Livy', *L.C.M.* 2: 13–18

Pinsent (2)   (1988). 'Notes on Livy 6 (1.1)', *L.C.M.* 13: 2–6

Plass   Plass, P. (1988). *Wit and the writing of history*. Madison

Pomeroy   Pomeroy, A. J. (1991). *The appropriate comment*. Frankfurt am Main

PP   Moxon, I. S., Smart, J. D., and Woodman, A. J., edd. (1986). *Past perspectives: studies in Greek and Roman historical writing*. Cambridge

Pritchett   Pritchett, W. K. (1974–). *The Greek state at war*. 5 vols. Berkeley

Radice   Radice, B. R., trans. (1982). *Livy: Rome and Italy*. Harmondsworth

Rawson   Rawson, E. (1991). *Roman culture and society. Collected papers*. Oxford

RE   (1893–). *Paulys Real-Encyclopädie der classischen Altertumswissenschaft*. Stuttgart

RICH   Woodman, A. J. (1988). *Rhetoric in classical historiography*. London

Richardson   Richardson, L., Jr. (1992). *A new topographical dictionary of ancient Rome*. Baltimore

Riemann   Riemann, O. (1885[2]). *Etudes sur la langue et la grammaire de Tite-Live*. Paris

Roby	Roby, H. J. (1879). *A grammar of the Latin language.* 2 vols. London
RPL	Wiseman, T. P., ed. (1985). *Roman political life 90 B.C.–A.D. 69.* Exeter
Rykwert	Rykwert, J. (1976). *The idea of a town.* Princeton
Saller	Saller, R. P. (1984). '*Familia, domus,* and the Roman conception of the family', *Phoenix* 38: 336–55
Santoro L'hoir (1)	Santoro L'hoir, F. (1990). 'Heroic epithets and recurrent themes in *Ab urbe condita*', *T.A.P.A.* 120: 221–41
Santoro L'hoir (2)	(1992). *The rhetoric of gender terms.* Leiden
Schlicher	Schlicher, J. J. (1933). 'Non-assertive elements in the language of the Roman historians', *C.P.* 28: 289–300
Scullard	Scullard, H. H. (1981) *Festivals and ceremonies of the Roman republic.* London
Seager (1)	Seager, R. (1972). 'Cicero and the word *popularis*', *C.Q.* 22: 328–38
Seager (2)	(1977). '"Populares" in Livy and the Livian tradition', *C.Q.* 27: 377–90
Serres	Serres, M. (1983, 1991). *Rome: the book of foundations.* Trans. F. McCarren. Stanford
Smith	Smith, B. H. (1968). *Poetic closure.* Chicago
Solodow	Solodow, J. B. (1979). 'Livy and the story of Horatius, 1.24–26', *T.A.P.A.* 109: 251–68
Sörbom	Sörbom, G. (1935). *Variatio sermonis Tacitei aliaeque apud eundem quaestiones selectae.* Uppsala
Spilman	Spilman, M. (1932). 'Cumulative sentence building in Latin historical narrative', *U.C.P.C.P.* 11: 153–247
SS	Eder, W., ed. (1990). *Staat und Staatlichkeit in der frühen römischen Republik.* Stuttgart
SSAR	Raaflaub, K. A., ed. (1986). *Social struggles in archaic Rome.* Berkeley
Stadter	Stadter, P. A. (1972). 'The structure of Livy's history', *Historia* 21: 287–307
Steele	Steele, R. B. (1904). 'The historical attitude of Livy', *A.J.P.* 25: 15–44

Stephenson	Stephenson, H. M. (1892). *Livy book VI.* Cambridge
Stevenson	Stevenson, T. R. (1992). 'The ideal benefactor and the father analogy in Greek and Roman thought', *C.Q.* 42: 421–36
Syme (1)	Syme, R. (1939). *The Roman revolution.* Oxford
Syme (2)	(1958). *Tacitus.* 2 vols. Oxford
Syme (3)	(1959). 'Livy and Augustus', *H.S.C.P.* 64: 27–87 = Badian, E., ed., *Roman papers* (Oxford 1979). I 401–54
Talbert	Talbert, R. J. A. (1984). *The senate of imperial Rome.* Princeton
Taylor	Taylor, L. R. (1966). *Roman voting assemblies.* Ann Arbor
TLL	*Thesaurus linguae latinae* (1900–). Leipzig
Treggiari	Treggiari, S. (1991). *Roman marriage.* Oxford
Ullmann (1)	Ullmann, R. (1927). *La technique des discours dans Salluste, Tite Live et Tacite.* Oslo
Ullmann (2)	(1929). *Etude sur le style des discours de Tite Live.* Oslo
Valvo	Valvo, A. (1983). *La sedizione di Manlio Capitolino in Tito Livio.* Inst. Lombardo. Acc. di Scien. e Lett., Classe di Lett., Sc. Mor. e Stor. 38.1. Milan
Vasaly	Vasaly, A. (1987). 'Personality and power: Livy's depiction of the Appii Claudii in the first pentad', *T.A.P.A.* 117: 203–26
Viljamaa	Viljamaa, T. (1983). *Infinitive of narration in Livy.* Turku
VL	Hellegouarc'h, J. (1963). *Le vocabulaire latin des relations et des partis politiques sous la république.* Paris
Voss	Voss, B.-R. (1963). *Der pointierte Stil des Tacitus.* Münster
W.	Woodman, A. J. (1977–83). *Velleius Paterculus: The Tiberian narrative* and *The Caesarian and Augustan narrative.* Cambridge ('W.' unaccompanied by a ref. to Velleius indicates notes privately communicated.)

Wallace-Hadrill (1) Wallace-Hadrill, A. (1982). '*Civilis princeps*: be-
                     tween citizen and king', *J.R.S.* 72: 32–48
Wallace-Hadrill (2) (1987). 'Time for Augustus', in Whitby, M.,
                     Hardie, P., and Whitby, M. edd., *Homo
                     viator: classical essays for John Bramble*. Bris-
                     tol. 221–30
Walsh   Walsh, P. G. (1974). *Livy. Greece & Rome* New
                     Surveys in the Classics no. 8. Oxford
Watt   Watt, W. S. (1991). 'Notes on Livy 6–10', *Clas-
                     sica et Mediaevalia* 42: 213–20
W–C   Walters, W. C. F. and Conway, R. S. (1918).
                     'Restorations and emendations in Livy
                     VI.–X.', *C.Q.* 12: 1–14
Weinstock   Weinstock, S. (1971). *Divus Julius*. Oxford
Wheeler   Wheeler, E. L. (1988). *Stratagem and the vocabu-
                     lary of military trickery*. Leiden
White (1)   White, H. (1978). *Tropics of discourse*. Baltimore
White (2)   (1987). *The content of the form*. Baltimore
Wilkinson   Wilkinson, L. P. (1963). *Golden Latin artistry*.
                     Cambridge
Wills   Wills, J. E. *Repetition in Latin poetry*. Oxford,
                     forthcoming
Wirszubski   Wirszubski, C. (1950). *Libertas as a political idea
                     at Rome during the late republic and early prin-
                     cipate*. Cambridge
Wiseman   Wiseman, T. P. (1987). *Roman studies*. Liverpool
W–M   Weissenborn, W. and Müller, H. J. (1880–
                     1911). *Titi Liui ab urbe condita libri*. Berlin
Woodman   Woodman, T. (1992). 'Nero's alien capital', in
                     Woodman, T. and Powell, J., edd. *Author
                     and audience in Latin literature*. Cambridge.
                     173–88

INDEXES

1 GENERAL

ablative: ~ dative, 195; of duration of time, 289; with adjs., 94, 171
  abl. abs.: in speeches, 164; linking, 179; one word, 163; rel. clause as subj., 196
adverbs: 98, 272, 286, 290, 305; attributive, 174; comparative ~ superlative, 100
accusative, retained, 186, 263
agrarian legislation, 95, 115, 154, 269, 278, 326
'all or nothing', see 'one and only'
Allia, 93–4, 117, 191, 250–5, 329
alliteration and assonance, 22, 24, 84, 99, 104, 196, 225, 238, 253, 259, 297, 302, 316, 324
allusion and cross-reference, 25, 332; as didactic tool, 14–15; link episodes, 90, 166, 248, 274–5, 300, 322, 324; see also repetition
analogy and comparison, argument from, 194, 210, 299, 310–11
anaphora, 95, 134, 164, 166, 183, 192, 213, 215, 249, 304, 312
ancestors, 16–17, 126, 247, 255, 324
antithesis, 110, 178, 185, 200, 228, 319; ~ antallage, 295; ~ correctio, 319; of prepositions, 201; word order strengthens, 168, 293, 316
appearance ~ reality, 18, 121, 149–50, 154, 156–7, 166, 170–1, 189, 191, 237–44, 305, 316, 319–20
assemblies, 115, 215, 220, 325
asyndeton: adversative, 114, 188, 209, 220, 239; bimembre, 113; in lists, 91, 118, 127, 175, 324
attraction of antecedent, 145, 236, 262; of demonstrative, 138, 291
audience, see reader; sight and spectacle

Augustus: ~ Camillus, 108, 120–2; experimentalism, 8; and Livy, 2–3, 6–9; ~ Manlius, 177, 213; a popularis, 153; uses republican concepts, 8, 124–5, 229, 243
auspices, augural language, 97, 117, 163, 322–5
authority: and history, 6, 206; narrative, 12–13, 139, 146–7, 158–63, 188–91; of Senate, 208, 241, 284, 306, 325; of state, 11–12, 157, 170, 191, 197, 246, 280, 292–3, 298–300

beginnings of sentences, 114–15, 125, 140, 192, 233, 303, 317
booty, 100, 114, 261, 329
building, expensive, 116, 155; new Rome, 89–90, 111–12, 324–5
bystanders, 233

Caesar (Julius), 105, 124, 139, 142, 144, 196, 229, 243, 293, 318, 325
Camillus, M. Furius, 25–6, 88–9, 94–5, 101, 128, 223, 245, 291–300, 325, 328–33; is angry, 231, 303; ~ Augustus, 108, 120–2; ~ Caesar, 229; ~ Cato, 154; death postponed, 333; dominates nature, 236; exile, 299; ~ Q. Fabius Maximus, 224, 228; ~ Jupiter, 303; ~ Manlius, 104, 117–18, 148–51, 163, 191, 195, 198, 223, 226, 293, 317; modesty challenged, 122, 149, 294; virtues, 245
capital punishment, 144, 216
Cassius, Sp., 96, 146, 192, 208
Cato, M. Porcius, 17, 113, 170, 279
Cato, M. Porcius Uticensis, 154
character, basis for argument, 182, 185, 289, 299–300

2 LATIN WORDS

religio, 93
renouo, 117
repente, 119
res redit ad, 118; *r. restituo*, 224

sagino, 193
salus, 314
seditio ∼ *secessio*, 296
segniter, 130
senecta, 135
sequor in exhortations, 234
seruator, 195
si dis placet, 312
simul = simul ac, 134
siue ... siue, 157
socius imperii, 126
socordius, 290
solacium, 258
solitudo, 326
spes (of birth), 261; *s. incido*, 304
statim + principio (etc.), 293
subolis, 130
succlamo, 314
sumo animos, 227

superstitiosus, 117

tantum for *tanto*, 295
Tarquinius, 313
tempero, 196
terribilis, 136
traho, 104, 129, 136, 318–19
tristitia, 132

uado, 135
ualidus ∼ *firmus*, 139; *ualidissimus*, 263
uegetus, 225
uehemens, 152
uelut + participle, 246
uestibulum curiae, 242
uis = βίη, 140
uiuidus, 225
uindico in libertatem, 162, 177, 265
unicus, 128
uniuersi ∼ *singuli*, 111
uoluo, 251
usque ad memoriam, 300
ut fit, 105; *ut mos est*, 273
uulgus (masc.), 272